Decadent Verse

An Anthology of Late Victorian Poetry, 1872–1900

Caroline Blyth teaches English at Royal Holloway, University of London and is a Visiting Fellow of St Edmund's College, Cambridge. She was previously Fellow and Director of Studies at St Edmund's College, Cambridge, and held a Newton Trust Fellowship and a British Academy Postdoctoral Fellowship in the Faculty of English.

John Lane's Bookshop

Decadent Verse

*An Anthology of Late Victorian Poetry,
1872–1900*

Edited and with an Introduction by
Caroline Blyth

ANTHEM PRESS
LONDON · NEW YORK · DELHI

Anthem Press
An imprint of Wimbledon Publishing Company
www.anthempress.com

This edition first published in UK and USA 2011
by ANTHEM PRESS
75-76 Blackfriars Road, London SE1 8HA, UK
or PO Box 9779, London SW19 7ZG, UK
and
244 Madison Ave. #116, New York, NY 10016, USA

Introduction, editorial matter and selection © 2011 Caroline Blyth

The moral right of the authors has been asserted.

The illustration on the cover is 'The Mirror' (1900), by Sir William Orpen, reproduced by permission of the Tate. The illustration on page 35 is 'Queen Victoria' (1899), by Benjamin Constant, reproduced by permission of The Royal Collection © 2008 Her Majesty Queen Elizabeth II.

All rights reserved. Without limiting the rights under copyright reserved above,
no part of this publication may be reproduced, stored or introduced into
a retrieval system, or transmitted, in any form or by any means
(electronic, mechanical, photocopying, recording or otherwise),
without the prior written permission of both the copyright
owner and the above publisher of this book.

The publishers have made every attempt to respect due copyrights for the work
within this collection. Should there be any issues regarding this matter,
please contact Anthem Press at the address above.

British Library Cataloguing in Publication Data
A catalogue record for this book is available from the British Library.

Library of Congress Cataloging in Publication Data
A catalogue record for this book has been requested.

ISBN-13: 978 0 85728 403 7 (Pbk)
ISBN-10: 0 85728 403 7 (Pbk)

This title is also available as an eBook.

In memoriam
PAT

The feeling of strangeness that overcomes the actor before the camera is basically of the same kind of estrangement felt before one's own image in the mirror.

Walter Benjamin,
The Work of Art in the Age of Mechanical Reproduction

It is in a way like St Paul's 'groanings which cannot be uttered' [. . .] It is what I have always felt even from a boy, and what as a boy I called 'the passion of the past'. And it is so always with me now; it is the distance that charms me in the landscape, the picture and the past, and not the immediate today in which I move.

Tennyson at Aldworth,
quoted by Sir James Knowles

The old pre-industrial community and culture are gone, and cannot be brought back. Nor is it desirable that they should be. They were too unjust, too squalid, and too custom-bound. Virtues which were once nursed unconsciously by the forces of nature must now be recovered and fostered by a deliberate effort of the will and the intelligence. In the future, societies will not grow of themselves. They will either be made consciously or decay.

W. H. Auden,
The Oxford Book of Light Verse

> Though the great song return no more
> There's keen delight in what we have:
> The rattle of pebbles on the shore
> Under the receding wave.

W. B. Yeats,
'The Nineteenth Century and After'

Contents

Preface	xxxv
Acknowledgements	xli
Decadent Art 1872–1900	xliii

Introduction   1

  (I)   The Politics of Poetry   1
  (II)   Versifications   12
  (III)   Fictions of Empire and the City   23
  (IV)   1900: Turn off the Century   32

Comparative Prose 1872–1900   49

Proem: The Way We Live Now   53

  (i)   John Addington Symonds (1840–1893)   53
          The Camera Obscura
  (ii)   Joseph Skipsey (1832–1903)   53
          'Get Up!'
  (iii)   Alice Meynell (1847–1922)   54
          Song of the Night at Daybreak
  (iv)   Robert Louis Stevenson (1850–1894)   54
          'The morning drum-call on my eager ear'
  (v)   Louisa S. Guggenberger (formerly Bevington) (1845–1895)   54
          Afternoon
  (vi)   Robert Bridges (1844–1930)   55
          'The evening darkens over'
  (vii)   Thomas Hardy (1840–1928)   56
          I Look Into My Glass
  (viii) Rosamund Marriott Watson (1860–1911)   56
          Aubade
  (ix)   A. Mary F. Robinson (1857–1944)   57
          Twilight
  (x)   Mathilde Blind (1841–1896)   58
          The Red Sunsets, 1883
  (xi)   William Renton (*fl.* 1852–post 1905)   59
          After Nightfall
  (xii)   Gerard Manley Hopkins (1836–1904)   59
          Moonrise

William Frederick Stevenson (*fl.* 1883)   59

  1.   *Life and Impellance*   59
  2.   *A Planet of Descendance*   60

R. (Rowland) E. (Eyles) Egerton-Warburton (1804–1891)   60

3. Modern Chivalry   60
4. French Clocks, 1876   61
5. A Mystery   61
6. Argument of a Dissenter   62

Frederick Tennyson (1807–1898)   62

7. The Prospect of Evil Days   62

Charles (Tennyson) Turner (1808–1879)   63

8. The Hydraulic Ram; or, the Influence of Sound on Mood   63

    from *Anacreon*
9. The Muses, Eros, and Beauty   63
10. Eros and the Bee   63
11. Letty's Globe   64

Alfred Lord Tennyson (1809–1892)   64

    from *Public Poems*
12. England and America in 1782   64
13. To the Queen   66
14. Ode on the Opening of the Colonial and Indian Exhibition by the Queen, Written at the Request of the Prince of Wales   68
15. Carmen Sæculare: A Jubilee Ode   70

    from *Ballads and Other Poems* (1880)
16. Rizpah   72
17. Prefatory Sonnet to the 'Nineteenth Century'   76

    from *Idylls of the King* (1859–1885)
18. Balin and Balan   77

    from *Tiresias, and Other Poems* (1885)
19. To E. FitzGerald   84
20. Despair   88
21. Locksley Hall Sixty Years After   93
22. The Dead Prophet   106
23. 'Frater Ave atque Vale'   111
24. Poets and their Bibliographies   111

    from *Demeter, and Other Poems* (1889)
25. To the Marquis of Dufferin and Ava   112
26. Vastness   115
27. To Ulysses   118
28. Merlin and the Gleam   121

29.	By an Evolutionist	127
30.	Far – Far – Away	128
31.	Beautiful City	129
32.	On One Who Affected an Effeminate Manner	130
33.	The Oak	130

from *The Death of Oenone, Akhbar's Dream, and Other Poems* (1892, post.)

34.	The Church-Warden and the Curate, with glossary	131
35.	June Bracken and Heather	134
36.	The Dawn	134
37.	The Making of Man	136
38.	Mechanophilus	136
39.	Poets and Critics	139

from *Dream*

40.	The Silent Voices	139
41.	God and the Universe	140
42.	Crossing the Bar	141

Mary Cowden-Clarke (neé Novello) (1809–1898)   142

43.	Body and Soul	142

Alfred Domett (1811–1887)   143

44.	Fireworks	143
45.	Invisible Sights	146

William Bell Scott (1811–1890)   146

46.	Music	146

Edward Lear (1812–1888)   147

47.	'"How pleasant to know Mr Lear!"'	147
48.	The Quangle Wangle's Hat	148
49.	The Dong with a Luminous Nose	150
50.	The Jumblies	152
51.	'There was an Old Man at a Station'	154
52.	'There was an Old Man of Thames Ditton'	155
53.	'There was an Old Person of Skye'	155
54.	'There was a Young Person of Ayr'	155

Robert Browning (1812–1889)   155

from *Pacchiarotto and How He Worked in Distemper* (1876)

55.	House	155
56.	Shop	157

xii Contents

     from *Dramatic Idyls: Second Series* (1880)
57.   Clive   161

     from *Jocsoseria* (1883)
58.   'Wanting is – what?'   167

     from *Asolando: Fancies and Facts* (1889)
59.   Speculative   168
60.   Bad Dreams I   168
61.   Bad Dreams II   169
62.   Bad Dreams III   171
63.   Bad Dreams IV   172
64.   Inapprehensiveness   174
65.   The Lady and the Painter   174

     from *Uncollected Poems*
66.   Lines for the Jubilee Window   175
67.   To Edward FitzGerald   176
68.   Why I am a Liberal   176
69.   Suggestion for a Telegraphic Birthday Greeting   177
70.   Conclusion of a Sonnet on 'Keely's Discovery'   177

Shirley Brooks (1816–1874)   177

71.   Waggawocky   177

George Eliot (1819–1880)   178

72.   The Death of Moses   178

John Ruskin (1819–1900)   181

73.   Trust Thou Thy Love   181

Jean Ingelow (1820–1897)   182

74.   Letters on Life and the Morning   182
75.   Perdita   185
76.   An Ancient Chess King   187
77.   The Long White Seam   188

Frederick Locker-Lampson (formerly Locker) (1821–1895)   189

78.   My Song   189

Matthew Arnold (1822–1888)   190

79.   Geist's Grave   190

William Cory (formerly Johnson) (1823–1892) — 192

80.	*Nuremberg Cemetery*	192
81.	*Sappho's Cursing*	193

Coventry Patmore (1823–1896) — 194

82.	*The Girl of All Periods: An Idyll*	194

from *The Angel in the House*

83.	Canto IX. *The Friends:* Preludes: *II. The Foreign Land*	195
84.	*A London Fête*	195
85.	*The Scorched Fly*	196
86.	*The Year*	197

Sydney Thompson Dobell (1824–1874) — 197

87.	*Perhaps*	197

William Allingham (1824–1889) — 198

88.	*Writing*	198
89.	*'I will not be a critic where I love.'*	199
90.	*Æolian Harp*	199
91.	*A Poet's Epitaph*	200

(Sir) Francis Turner Palgrave (1824–1897) — 200

92.	*Eutopia*	200
93.	*Père La Chaise*	201

George MacDonald (1824–1905) — 202

94.	*No End of No-Story*	202
95.	*The Shortest and Sweetest of Songs*	207

John Askham (ca. 1825–1894) — 207

96.	*A Dream: July 22nd, 1881*	207

Mortimer Collins (1827–1876) — 208

97.	*The Positivists*	208
98.	*Couplets*	209

Emily Pfeiffer (1827–1890) — 209

99.	*'Peace to the odalisque, whose morning glory'*	209
100.	*Any Husband to Many a Wife*	210

101.	Six Studies in Exotic Forms of Verse: Triolet	210
102.	To Nature	210
103.	Past and Future	212
104.	To a Moth that Drinketh of the Ripe October	212
105.	A Chrysalis	213

George Meredith (1828–1909) — 214

106.	The Nuptials of Attila	214
107.	Lucifer in Starlight	228
108.	Society	228
109.	A Ballad of Past Meridian	229
110.	King Harald's Trance	229
111.	England Before the Storm	232

Dante Gabriel Rossetti (1828–1882) — 233

from *the House of Life*

112.	XLV. Secret Parting	233
113.	XLVIII. Death-in-Love	234
114.	LIX. Love's Last Gift	234
115.	LXXXI. Memorial Thresholds	234
116.	LXXXVIII. Hero's Lamp	235
117.	Astarte Syrica (For a Picture)	235
118.	Proserpina (Per un Quadro)	236
119.	Proserpina (For a Picture)	236
120.	Dawn on the Night-journey	237
121.	The Orchard-pit	237

Gerald Massey (1828–1907) — 238

122.	Only a Dream	238
123.	True Poets	238
124.	A Peculiar Person	239
125.	A Greek Reply	240
126.	Womankind	240
127.	An Angel in the House	240

Elizabeth ('Lizzie') Siddal (later Rossetti) (1829–1862) — 240

128.	The Lust of the Eyes	240
129.	Dead Love	241

Christina Rossetti (1830–1894) — 242

130.	In an Artist's Studio	242
131.	A Coast-Nightmare	242
132.	Two Thoughts of Death	243

133.	Cor Mio	244
134.	Yet a Little While ('I dreamed and did not seek…')	245
135.	Yet a Little While ('Heaven is not far, tho' far the sky…')	245
136.	Love Lies Bleeding	245
137.	A Ballad of Boding	246
138.	Advent	251
139.	A Christmas Carol	251
140.	Autumn Violets	253
141.	'A city plum is not a plum'	253
142.	'How many seconds in a minute?'	253
143.	'I planted a hand'	254
144.	'Stroke a flint, and there is nothing to admire'	254
145.	'Hollow-Sounding and Mysterious.'	254
146.	Touching 'Never'	255
147.	Passing and Glassing	256
148.	'Earth has clear call of daily bells'	256
149.	'Endure hardness'	257
150.	'Sooner or later: yet at last'	257
151.	'Balm in Gilead'	258
152.	Until the Day Break	259
153.	An 'Immurata' Sister	259
154.	Monna Innominata No. 3	260

T. (Thomas) E. (Edward) Brown (1830–1897) — 261

155.	Opifex	261
156.	Ibant Obscuræ	262
157.	'High overhead'	262
158.	I Bended unto Me	263
159.	A Sermon at Clevedon: Good Friday	263

from *Roman Women*

160.	XII. 'Why does she stare at you like that? The glow'	265
161.	XIII. 'O Englishwoman on the Pincian'	265
162.	Dartmoor: Sunset at Chagford	267

Sebastian Evans (1830–1909) — 272

163.	The Enigma Solved	272

James Clerk Maxwell (1831–1879) — 273

164.	To the Chief Musician upon Nabla: A Tyndallic Ode	273

C. (Charles) S. (Stuart) Calverley (1831–1884) — 275

165.	'Forever'	275

Isa (Craig) Knox (1831–1903) — 276

166. *The Box* — 276
167. *The Building of the City* — 277

(Edward) Robert Bulwer Lytton (Earl of Lytton, Owen Meredith) (1831–1891) — 279

168. *Sorrento Revisited* — 279

'Lewis Carroll' (Charles Lutwidge Dodgson) (1832–1898) — 279

169. *Poeta Fit, Non Nascitur* — 279
170. 'In winter, when the fields are white' — 282
171. *The Hunting of the Snark* — 284
172. *Jabberwocky* — 301

Joseph Skipsey (1832–1908) — 302

173. *The Darling* — 302
174. *A Golden Lot* — 302

Richard Watson Dixon (1833–1900) — 302

175. *The Mystery of the Body* — 302

James Thomson (B.V.) (1834–1882) — 303

176. *The City of Dreadful Night* — 303
177. *In the Room* — 334

Roden (Berkeley Wriothesley) Noel (1834–1894) — 340

178. *At Court* — 340
179. *A Vision of the Desert* — 342

William Morris (1834–1896) — 348

180. Tr. *The Odyssey of Homer (Book I)* — 348
181. Tr. *The Aeneids of Virgil (Books I and VI)* — 350
182. *The Story of Sigurd the Volsung* — 356
183. *Atalanta's Race* — 358

Chants for Socialists: — 377

184. (i) *The Voice of Toil* — 377
185. (ii) *All for the Cause* — 378
186. (iii) *The March of the Workers* — 379
187. *A Garden by the Sea* — 381
188. *Tapestry Trees* — 382
189. *The Flowering Orchard* — 383

190.	*The Forest*	383
191.	*Pomona*	383
192.	*For the Briar Rose*	384
193.	*Drawing near the Light*	384
194.	*Verses for Pictures*	385
195.	*The Roots of the Mountains*	386
196.	*Love Fulfilled*	388
197.	*Love's Gleaning-Tide*	389
198.	*Mine and Thine (from a Flemish poem of the fourteenth century)*	390

John (Byrne) Leicester Warren, Lord de Tabley (1835–1895) (G. F. Preston, W. P. Lancaster) — 391

199.	*The Pilgrim Cranes*	391
200.	*A Song of Faith Forsworn*	391
201.	*Circe*	393

Sir Alfred Comyns Lyall (1835–1911) — 394

from *Studies at Delhi* (1876)
| 202. | I. *The Hindu Ascetic* | 394 |
| 203. | II. *Badminton* | 395 |

Alfred Austin (1835–1913) — 395

| 204. | *At the Gate of the Convent* | 395 |
| 205. | *Love's Blindness* | 404 |

F. (Frances) Ridley Havergal (1836–1879) — 405

206.	*An Indian Flag*	405
207.	*A Worker's Prayer*	406
208.	*Consecration Hymn*	407

Thomas Ashe (1836–1889) — 408

209.	*Pall-Bearing*	408
210.	*To Two Bereaved*	410
211.	*To the Maids, Who Will Marry*	410

(Jane) Ellice Hopkins (1836–1904) — 410

| 212. | *Life in Death* | 410 |
| 213. | *A Vision of Womanhood* | 412 |

W. (William) S. (Schwenk) Gilbert (1836–1911) — 413

| 214. | 'If you're anxious for to shine in the high aesthetic line' (Bunthorne's Recital and Song from *Patience*) | 413 |

H. (Henry) Cholmondeley Pennell (1836–?) — 415

215. 'Faite À Peindre' — 415

Algernon Charles Swinburne (1837–1909) — 415

216. Fragment on Death — 415
217. Ballad of the Lords of Old Time — 416
218. Nephelidia — 417
219. The Higher Pantheism in a Nutshell — 418
220. Sonnet: Hope and Fear — 419
221. A Midsummer Holiday — 420

from *A Century of Roundels*
222. I. *To Catullus* — 421
223. II. *In Guernsey* — 421
224. A Sequence of Sonnets on the Death of Robert Browning — 422

(Julia) Augusta Webster (1837–1894) — 424

225. The Flowing Tide — 424
226. The Lovers — 425
227. We Two — 425
228. Where Home Was — 426
229. The Flood of Is in Brittany — 427
230. Mother and Daughter: An Uncompleted Sonnet-Sequence (I, IX, X, XI) — 429

Sarah ('Sadie') Williams (1837/8–1868) — 431

from *Nature Apostate*
231. The Life of a Leaf — 431
232. President Lincoln — 432

Charlotte Elliot ('Florenz') (1839–1880) — 433

233. The Pythoness — 433

Walter Pater (1839–1894) — 435

234. Style — 435

John Todhunter (1839–1916) — 436

235. Snake-Charm — 436

John Addington Symonds (1840–1893) — 437

236. Personality — 437
237. The Will — 438

238.	A Dream of Burial in Mid Ocean	439
239.	An Invitation to the Sledge	439
240.	Love in Dreams	440

(William) Cosmo Monkhouse (1840–1901) — 441

241.	Her Face	441
242.	Under the Oak	444
243.	The Christ upon the Hill: A Ballad	445
244.	Any Soul to Any Body	452

(Henry) Austin Dobson (1840–1921) — 453

245.	The Ballad of Prose and Rhyme	453
246.	The Poet and the Critics	454
247.	On the Hurry of this Time	455
248.	In After Days	456
249.	A Garden Song	456

Harriet Eleanor Hamilton King (1840–1920) — 457

| 250. | A Mid May Mystery | 457 |
| 251. | Working-Girls in London | 459 |

W. (Wilfrid) S. (Scawen) Blunt (1840–1922) — 461

252.	He is Not a Poet	461
253.	On the Shortness of Time	462
254.	Chanclebury Ring	462

from *The Love Lyrics of Proteus*
| 255. | Song (Love Me a Little) | 463 |
| 256. | At a Funeral | 464 |

from *The Idler's Calendar*
| 257. | I. October: Gambling at Monaco | 466 |
| 258. | II. November: Across Country | 467 |

from *From the Arabic*
| 259. | I. The Camel-Rider | 467 |

Mathilde Blind (1841–1896) — 470

| 260. | Green Leaves and Sere | 470 |
| 261. | The Forest Pool | 471 |

from *Love in Exile*
| 262. | VI. 'Many will love you; you were made for love' | 471 |
| 263. | X. 'On Life's long round by chance I found' | 472 |

264.	XIII. 'We met as strangers on life's lonely way'	472
265.	*Manchester by Night*	473
266.	*Haunted Streets*	473
267.	*Scarabæus Sisyphus*	474
268.	*A Fantasy*	474
269.	*The Message*	476
270.	*Autumn Tints*	483
271.	*A Winter Landscape*	484
272.	*Mourning Women*	484

from *The Ascent of Man*

273.	I. 'Struck out of dim fluctuant forces and shock of electrical vapour'	485
274.	II. *Motherhood*	485

Robert Buchanan (T. Maitland) (1841–1901) — 486

275.	*The Cities*	486

Rosa Mulholland (Lady Gilbert) (1841–1921) — 486

276.	*Poverty*	486

Margaret Veley (1843–1887) — 487

277.	*A Game of Piquet*	487
278.	*A Japanese Fan*	489
279.	*A Town Garden*	494

Edward Dowden (1843–1893) — 496

280.	*Burdens*	496
	Sonnets:	
281.	*A Disciple (The Inner Life)*	496
282.	*Seeking God (The Inner Life)*	497

Mary Montgomerie Lamb ('Violet Fane', Mrs Sinclair) (1843–1905) — 497

283.	*Victoria*	497
284.	*At Christie's*	498
285.	*The Siren*	499

Arthur O'Shaughnessy (1844–1881) — 501

286.	*Ode*	501

Gerard Manley Hopkins (1844–1889) — 503

287.	*A Trio of Triolets*	503
288.	*The Wreck of the Deutschland*	504

289.	The Silver Jubilee	513
290.	'Hope holds to Christ the mind's own mirror out'	514
291.	The Starlight Night	514
292.	The Lantern Out of Doors	515
293.	In the Valley of the Elwy	515
294.	The Caged Skylark	516
295.	Hurrahing in Harvest	516
296.	Harry Ploughman	517
297.	Tom's Garland: on the Unemployed	517
298.	Epithalamion	518
299.	'What shall I do for the land that bred me'	520
300.	'The shepherd's brow, fronting forked lightning, owns'	520
301.	Felix Randal	521
302.	Spelt from Sibyl's Leaves	521
303.	'Thee, God, I come from, to thee go'	522
304.	'Repeat that, repeat'	523
305.	To his Watch	523
306.	Spring	523
307.	To R.B.	524

Andrew Lang (1844–1912) ... 524

308.	Ballade of Blue China	524
309.	The Haunted Homes of England	525
310.	The Last Chance	526
311.	Good-bye	526

Caroline (née Fitzroy), Lady Lindsay (1844–1912) ... 527

312.	To My Own Face	527
313.	Of a Bird-Cage	528

Samuel Waddington (1844–1923) ... 528

314.	Soul and Body	528

Edward Carpenter (1844–1929) ... 529

315.	In a Manufacturing Town	529

Robert Bridges (1844–1930) ... 530

316.	Eros	530
317.	London Snow	531

Lucy Knox (1845–1884) ... 532

318.	Sonnet: A Cry to Men	532

L.(Louisa) S. Bevington (Mrs Guggenberger) (1845–1895) — 532

319.	Three	532
320.	'Egoisme À Deux'	535
321.	Stanza	535
322.	Revolution	536
323.	Am I to Lose You?	536
324.	Love and Language	537
325.	Twilight	537

Eugene Lee-Hamilton (1845–1907) — 538

326.	Introduction to *Imaginary Sonnets*	538
327.	What the Sonnet Is	539
328.	Lethe	539
329.	On Leonardo's Head of Medusa	540
330.	To My Wheeled Bed	540
331.	Henry I to the Sea	541
332.	Ipsissimus	541

Alexander Anderson ('Surfaceman') (1845–1909) — 544

333.	Reading the Book	544
334.	The San' Man	545
335.	Move Upward	547
336.	Song of the Engine	549
337.	The Violet	552

Emily H. (Henrietta) Hickey (1845–1924) — 554

338.	Her Dream	554
339.	A Sea Story	556

William Canton (1845–1926) — 557

340.	Sea-Pictures I	557

Alexander MacGregor Rose (1846–1898) — 557

341.	Tour Abroad of Wilfrid the Great	557
342.	'Kaiser and Co. or, Hoch der Kaiser'	561

'Michael Field' (Katherine Harris Bradley, 1846–1914, and Edith Emma Cooper, 1862–1913) — 563

343.	Cyclamens	563
344.	Irises	563
345.	La Gioconda	563
346.	A Portrait	564

347.	'Thanatos, thy praise I sing'	565
348.	'A girl'	566
349.	Renewal	567
350.	Constancy	567
351.	Tiresias: but that I know by experience	568

James Logie Robertson (1846–1922) — 570

352.	The White Winter – Hughie Snawed Up	570
353.	The Discovery of America	572

Alice Meynell (née Thompson) (1847–1922) — 573

354.	A Song of Derivations	573
355.	Builders of Ruins	574
356.	Renouncement	576
357.	'I Am the Way'	576
358.	The Lady Poverty	577
359.	Cradle-Song at Twilight	577
360.	After a Parting	578

George R. (Robert) Sims (1847–1922) — 578

361.	A Garden Song	578

L. (Laura) Ormiston Chant (1848–1923) — 579

362.	Hope's Song	579

W. (William) E. (Ernest) Henley (1849–1903) — 581

from *In Hospital*

363.	I. *Enter Patient*	581
364.	II. *Waiting*	582
365.	XXIII. *Music*	582
366.	XXIV. *Suicide*	583
367.	XXVIII. *Discharged*	584
368.	'On the way to Kew'	584

Henry Bellyse Baildon (1849–1907) — 585

369.	Alone in London	585

W. (William) H. (Hurrell) Mallock (1849–1923) — 588

370.	Every Man His Own Poet: or, The Inspired Singer's Recipe Book	588
371.	Christmas Thoughts, by a Modern Thinker	593

Edmund Gosse (1849–1928) — 595

372. *Lying in the Grass* — 595

Philip Bourke Marston (1850–1887) — 597

Sonnets:
373. *No Death* — 597
374. *Flower Fairies* — 598
375. *Grief's Aspects* — 599

Robert Louis (formerly Lewis) Balfour Stevenson (1850–1894) — 600

376. 'The tropics vanish, and meseems that I' — 600
377. *Fragment* — 600
378. *The Light-Keeper* — 601
379. 'My house, I say. But hark to the sunny doves' — 603
380. *Browning* — 603
381. 'So live, so love, so use that fragile hour' — 604

from *A Child's Garden of Verses*
382. VI. *Block City* — 604
383. XVII. *The Land of Nod* — 605
384. XVIII. *My Shadow* — 605

Elizabeth Rachel Chapman (1850–? [post 1897]) — 606

385. *A Woman's Strength* — 606

(The Revd. Canon) Hardwick Drummond Rawnsley (1851–1920) — 607

386. *The Jet Worker* — 607

Francis William Bourdillon (1852–1921) — 607

387. *The Night has a Thousand Eyes* — 607

F. (Francis) B. (Burdett) Money-Coutts (1852–1923) — 608

388. *The Inquest* — 608

William Renton (*fl.* 1852–post 1905) — 608

389. *Cloud Groupings* — 608
390. *Moon and Candle-light* — 609
391. *The Fork of the Road* — 610

Herbert Edwin Clarke (1852–?) — 610

392. *Age* — 610

393.	A City Rhyme	611

Annie Matheson (1853–1924) — 612

394.	A Song for Women	612

Oscar (Fingal O'Flahertie Wills) Wilde (1854–1900) — 614

395.	Poems in Prose: The Artist	614
396.	On the Sale by Auction of Keats' Love Letters	614
397.	Symphony in Yellow	615

from *Fantaisies décoratives*

398.	II. Les Ballons	615
399.	The Harlot's House	616
400.	The Ballad of Reading Gaol	617
401.	Requiescat	635

Fiona MacLeod (William Sharp) (1855–1905) — 635

402.	Lullaby	635
403.	Prayer of Women	636

(Juliana Mary Louisa) May Probyn (1856–1909) — 637

404.	Changes	637

Margaret L. (Louisa) (Bradley) Woods (1856–1945) — 638

from *Aeromancy*

405.	VI. 'I hear the incantation of the bells'	638

Eliza Keary (1857–1882) — 639

406.	Doctor Emily	639
407.	Old Age	642

John Davidson (1857–1909) — 643

408.	London	643
409.	Piper, Play!	643
410.	Serenade	645
411.	A Ballad of Euthanasia	646
412.	Insomnia	649
413.	A Ballad of an Artist's Wife	650
414.	Holiday at Hampton Court	654
415.	Matinées I & II	655
416.	The Last Ballad	656
417.	The Last Rose	666

Jane Barlow (1857–1917) — 667

418. Expectation — 667

A. Mary F. Robinson (Mme Darmesteter, Mme Duclaux) (1857–1944) — 668

419. To my Muse — 668
420. Sonnet: 'God sent a poet to reform His earth' — 668
421. The Idea — 669
422. Personality — 669
423. A Pastoral of Parnassus — 671
424. The Bookworm — 672
425. Rispetti — 673

Constance (Caroline Woodhill) Naden (1858–1889) — 673

from *Evolutional Erotics*
426. Solomon Redivivus — 673
427. Poet and Botanist — 675
428. The Nebular Theory — 676
429. Speech and Silence — 676
430. Love's Mirror — 676
431. The Lady Doctor — 677
432. Moonlight and Gas — 679
433. The Two Artists — 680
434. The Pantheist's Song of Immortality — 681

Dollie (Caroline) (Mrs Ernest) Radford (née Maitland) (1858–1920) — 682

435. Two Songs — 682
436. From the Suburbs — 683

Edith Nesbit (Mrs Bland, Mrs Tucker) (1858–1924) — 685

437. Under Convoy — 685
438. Inspiration — 686
439. Among His Books — 687
440. The Forest Pool — 689

(Sir) William Watson (1858–1935) — 689

441. Imaginary Inscription (on a rock resembling colossal human features) — 689
442. The Metropolitan Underground Railway — 690

Elizabeth ('Bessie') Craigmyle (*fl.* 1886) — 690

443. Catullian Hendecasyllabics — 690
444. Beginning Work — 690

445.	*My Bookcase*	691
446.	*Heaven and Earth*	693
447.	*Clasped Hands*	694
448.	*Love's Resurrection*	695
449.	*A Woman's 'Yes'*	695
450.	*Dream of the Pine*	696
451.	*The End of the Story*	696

J. (James) K. (Kenneth) Stephen (1859–1892) — 697

452.	*A Parodist's Apology*	697
453.	*Steam-launches on the Thames*	698
454.	*The Philosopher and the Philanthropist*	699

A. (Alfred) E. (Edward) Housman (1859–1936) — 699

455.	'Oh who is that young sinner with handcuffs on his wrists?'	699
456.	'The laws of God, the laws of man'	700
457.	'Yonder see the morning blink'	701

from *A Shropshire Lad*

458.	II. 'Loveliest of trees, the cherry now'	701
459.	XVI. 'It nods and curtseys and recovers'	701
460.	XXXIX. 'My dreams are of a field afar'	702
461.	XL. 'Into my heart an air that kills'	702

Francis Thompson (1859–1907) — 702

462.	*The Hound of Heaven*	702
463.	*Memorat Memoria*	707
464.	*A Dead Astronomer*	707
465.	*To the Dead Cardinal of Westminster*	708
466.	*The End of It*	713
467.	*The Singer Saith of his Song*	713
468.	*Poems on Children: Daisy*	714

Arthur I. (Ignatius) Conan Doyle (1859–1930) — 715

469.	*The Frontier Line*	715

Ernest Rhys (1859–1946) — 717

470.	*At the Rhymers' Club*	717
471.	*The Night Ride*	718
472.	*An Autobiography*	718

Rosamund Marriott Watson (Graham R. Tomson) (1860–1911) — 719

473.	*Vespertilia*	719

474.	A Ballad of the Were-Wolf	721
475.	Of the Earth, Earthy	722
476.	In the Rain	723
477.	Old Pauline	724
478.	The Moor Girl's Well	724
479.	Hic Jacet	726

Amy Levy (1861–1889) — 727

480.	Magdalen	727
481.	London Poets	729
482.	To Death	730
483.	Borderland	730
484.	The Birch-Tree at Loschwitz	730
485.	Captivity	731
486.	Run to Death (A True Incident of Pre-Revolutionary French History)	732

from *Moods and Thoughts*

487.	The Old House	734
488.	To Vernon Lee	735
489.	Oh, is it Love?	735
490.	Ballade of an Omnibus	735
491.	A Ballad of Religion and Marriage	736

from *Two Translations of Jehudah Halevi from the German of Abraham Geiger*

492.	Jerusalem	737
493.	Epitaph	738

Mary E. (Elizabeth) Coleridge (1861–1907) — 738

494.	Winged Words	738
495.	The Other Side of a Mirror	738
496.	Master and Guest	739
497.	Doubt	740
498.	Marriage	741
499.	L'Oiseau Bleu	741
500.	A Moment	741
501.	Gone	742
502.	Eyes	742
503.	'True to myself am I, and false to all'	743
504.	On a Bas-Relief of Pelops and Hippodameia	743

Katharine Tynan (Hinkson) (1861–1931) — 744

505.	Only in August	744
506.	To Inishkea	744
507.	Fra Angelico at Fiesole	745

508.	The Children of Lir	746

Mary Byron (M. Clarissa Gillington) (1861–1936)   748

509.	The Tryst of the Night	748

Owen Seaman (1861–1936)   749

510.	Lilith Libifera	749

May Kendall (1861–1943)   749

511.	Lay of the Trilobite	749
512.	A Pure Hypothesis	751
513.	Ballad of the Ichthyosaurus	753
514.	Woman's Future	755
515.	The Philanthropist and the Jelly-Fish	756
516.	Church Echoes	757
517.	The Sandblast Girl and the Acid Man	758
518.	Underground	760
519.	The Ballad of the Flag Painter	761
	from *Songs from Dreamland*	
520.	I. A Warning to New Worlds	763
521.	II. Ether Insatiable	764
522.	The Conscientious Ghost	765

A. (Arthur) C. (Christopher) Benson (1862–1925)   766

523.	Courage	766
524.	Self	767

Victor Plarr (1863–1929)   767

525.	Shadows	767
526.	Epitaphium Citharistriæ	768
527.	Of Change of Opinions	768
528.	Ad Cinerarium	769
529.	The Imperial Prayers	770
530.	Twilight-Piece	770

Stephen Phillips (1864–1915)   771

531.	The Apparition	771
532.	'O thou art put to many uses, sweet!'	773

Herbert Percy Horne (1864–1916)   774

533.	Corona Corinnae	774

534.	*Paradise Walk*	777
535.	*'Bella immagine d'un fior'*	777
536.	*Cease, Cease Reproachful Eyes!*	778

W. (William) B. (Butler) Yeats (1865–1939) — 778

from *Crossways* (1889)

537.	*Down by the Salley Gardens*	778
538.	*The Ballad of Father O'Hart*	779

from *The Rose* (1893)

539.	*The Lake Isle of Innisfree*	780
540.	*The Sorrow of Love*	780
541.	*A Dream of Death*	781
542.	*To Ireland in the Coming Times*	781

from *The Wind Among the Reeds* (1899)

543.	*The Lover Mourns for the Loss of Love*	783
544.	*The Poet Pleads with the Elemental Powers*	783
545.	*He Wishes for the Cloths of Heaven*	783

Rudyard Kipling (1865–1936) — 784

546.	*Mandalay*	784
547.	*Danny Deever*	785

Arthur Symons (1865–1945) — 786

from *Amoris Victima*

548.	II. *Why?*	786
549.	XIII. *'And yet, there was a hunger in your eyes'*	787
550.	*The Street-Singer*	787
551.	*During Music*	788
552.	*Morbidezza*	788
553.	*The Absinthe-Drinker*	788
554.	*La Mélinite: Moulin Rouge*	789
555.	*Palm Sunday: Naples*	790

from *Days and Nights*

556.	*Translations: Posthumous Coquetry*	790
557.	*Maquillage*	791

Dora Sigerson (later Shorter) (1866–1918) — 792

558.	*Unknown Ideal*	792
559.	*With a Rose*	793
560.	*A Vagrant Heart*	793
561.	*The Wind on the Hills*	794

John Gray (1866–1934)		795
562.	Sensation	795
563.	The Vines	796
564.	'Lord, if thou are not present, where shall I'	796
565.	A Crucifix	797
566.	Spleen	798
567.	Crocuses in Grass	798
568.	Poem	799
569.	Battledore	799
570.	The Forge	802
571.	The Barber	804
572.	Mishka	805
573.	Summer Past	806
Richard Le Gallienne (1866–1947)		806
574.	The World is Wide	806
575.	A Ballad of London	807
576.	A Library in a Garden	808
Ernest Dowson (1867–1900)		809
577.	Vitae Summa Brevis Spem Nos Vetat Incohare Longam	809
578.	Non Sum Qualis Eram Bonae Sub Regno Cynarae	809
579.	Flos Lunae	810
580.	Spleen	810
581.	'You would have understood me, had you waited'	811
582.	Terre Promise	812
583.	To William Theodore Peters on his Renaissance Cloak	812
584.	Nuns of the Perpetual Adoration	813
585.	To One in Bedlam	814
Lionel Johnson (1867–1902)		814
586.	A Decadent's Lyric	814
587.	A Stranger	815
588.	Love's Ways	816
589.	The Dark Angel	816
590.	By the Statue of King Charles at Charing Cross	818
591.	Lambeth Lyric	819
George William Russell ('A.E.') (1867–1935)		820
592.	Sacrifice	820
593.	The Mid-World	821

(Robert) Laurence Binyon (1869–1943) — 821

from *London Visions*
594. I. *Whitechapel High Road* — 821
595. *The Evening Takes Me From Your Side* — 823

Hubert Crackanthorpe (1870–1896) — 823

from *Vignettes*
596. *Rêverie* — 823
597. *In St. James's Park* — 823
598. *In the Strand* — 824

Hilaire Belloc (1870–1953) — 824

599. *The Poor of London* — 824
600. *The Harbour* — 825
601. *The Modern Traveller* — 826
602. *The Marmozet* — 827
603. *The Big Baboon* — 827

Nora Hopper (Mrs Chesson) (1871–1906) — 829

604. *Finvarragh* — 829
605. *Two Women* — 830
606. *Marsh Marigolds* — 830

Theodore Wratislaw (1871–1933) — 831

607. *The Music-Hall* — 831

from *Etching*
608. III. *At the Empire* — 831
609. *Orchids* — 832
610. Ἔρος δ'αὖτε... — 833
611. *Odour* — 833

Aubrey Beardsley (1872–1898) — 834

612. *The Three Musicians* — 834

(Lady) Olive Eleanor Custance (Mrs Lord Alfred Douglas) (1874–1944) — 835

613. *Glamour of Gold* — 835

Cicely Fox Smith (1882–1954) — 836

614. *The Colonists* — 836

Evelyn Pyne (*fl.* 1875–1890)		837
615.	A Witness	837
Sarah Robertson Matheson (*fl.* 1894)		840
616.	A Kiss of the King's Hand	840
Jane Leck (*fl.* 1895)		841
617.	My Gourd	841
618.	Disappointment	841
619.	Woman's Rights	842
Ada (Bartrick) Baker (*fl.* 1900)		844
620.	House-Hunting	844
621.	'Queen's Night'	847
622.	In Hospital	847
Thomas Hardy (1840–1928)		848
623.	The Young Glass-Stainer	848
624.	The Temporary the All	848
625.	Nature's Questioning	849
626.	Unknowing	850
627.	Rome (The Vatican: Sala delle Muse)	851
628.	A Wife in London	852
629.	The Slow Nature	852
630.	An August Midnight	853
631.	Her Immortality	854
632.	Thoughts of Phena	856
633.	Friends Beyond	856
634.	Drummer Hodge	858
635.	Retrospect	858
636.	De Profundis III	860
637.	The Darkling Thrush	860
638.	V.R. 1819–1901: A Rêverie	861
Sources and Notes		863
Index of Titles		873
Index of First Lines		881
Index of Poets		893

Preface

This book presents a selection of poetry from 1872–1900, with Queen Victoria's Golden Jubilee year of 1887 serving as a 'mid-point'. Most of the poems have been published before or in 1900, with two exceptions: Gerard Manley Hopkins, whose main body of work was published in 1918, and A. E. Housman's verse written after the trial of Oscar Wilde: composed in 1895; yet not published until 1937. A feature of these years is the quality and quantity of verse produced by less well-known writers alongside the established 'major authors' Tennyson, Browning, Gerard Manley Hopkins, 'early' Hardy and 'early' Yeats, and the traditional poets of the *fin-de-siècle*. Where possible, the poetry is contextualised in terms of the significant intellectual and historical forces informing the later phases of Victoria's Empire. In a poem discussed in the introduction, for example, Constance Naden speaks of Darwin as a 'Seer, savant, merchant, poet'.

As is common with the agonies of selection in an undertaking such as this, it simply has not been possible to include every one and every thing. Though there are many poets here, the main criteria has been 'quality rather than quantity', as well as a conviction that, however modish the expectation, one can err by 'overinclusion'. A favourite Venetian saying of Robert Browning's was '*Tutti ga i so gusti e mi go i mii*' ('Everyone follows his taste, and I follow mine'). Yet I hope that, among the hundred and fifty voices represented here, a characteristic and representative flavour of the intelligence of this period can be found. (I mean intelligence probably most in the Paterian sense of a quickness of mental apprehension, tempered by a perception of the more medieval inference, which reverberates throughout this period, of intelligence as sagacity.) On this note the reader may like to bear in mind that it is often, unsettlingly, at those impressive, decadent moments when verse seems at its least 'characteristic' that it is at its most 'representative'. This is a time when past and future selves co-exist; as many of the poems of this period suggest, there is no time like the present.

'The old pre-industrial community and culture are gone,' W. H. Auden reflected in his landmark anthology, *The Oxford Book of Light Verse* (1938), 'and cannot be brought back'.

> Nor is it desirable that they should be. They were too unjust,
> too squalid, and too custom-bound. Virtues which were once nursed
> unconsciously by the forces of nature must now be recovered and
> fostered by a deliberate effort of the will and the intelligence.
> In the future, societies will not grow of themselves. They will either
> be made consciously or decay.[1]

Not all modernists would have read 'change' like this; the sorcerer/fatalist in Hardy would slant 'change' towards 'chancefulness', and the mystic in W. B. Yeats towards 'flux'. But the change to which Auden gestures, a change on a scale that no previous century experienced, was one so obvious it is often overlooked: a radical shift throughout the period in the numbers of people who could read. Literacy had increased dramatically from 51.1 percent (women) and 67.3 percent (men) in 1841, to 92.7 percent (women) and 93.6 percent (men) by 1891. Forster's Education Act of 1870 influenced this development, although changes in

---

1 W. H. Auden, ed., *The Oxford Book of Light Verse* (Oxford: Clarendon Press, 1938), p. xix.

lifestyle, working hours, and the provision throughout Britain of free libraries, played their part. The following poems, whether 'bad' or 'good', 'weak' or 'strong' are testimony to this important cultural development. In the words of Richard Le Gallienne, 'here was not so much the ending of a century as the beginning of a new one.'[2]

Although the majority of the poets represented here are male, fifty of them are female (some of whom, like George Eliot, adopted masculine identities). Vital acknowledgement has been made of contemporary scholarship in this area, which, in recent years, has either discovered or recovered poets previously stymied in nineteenth-century verse anthologies. The growing appreciation for the work of Mary Robinson, May Kendall, Amy Levy, Constance Naden, Emily Pfeiffer, among others, can therefore be appreciated not only alongside their male contemporaries, but in contrast and comparison with Christina Rossetti, whom Ford Madox Ford regarded as 'the most valuable poet that the Victorian age produced'. The majority of the 'late Christina Rossetti' selection here may also be new to some readers as much of the poet's popular anthologised work tends to come from the mid-nineteenth century, rather than the latter years, and this can also be true of Robert Browning and Tennyson.

The emphasis I have placed in this selection then is on the experimentalism of versification in this late-nineteenth-century period—there are, for example, prose poems included, subtly indicative of the pressures exerted upon nineteenth-century poetry by the Novel. Victorian verse in the transitional, late-nineteenth-century phase of becoming 'modern'—even to the extent of moving into the realms of 'free verse', as in the examples below—is one of the distinctive interests of this period. The powerful tension between fixed verse forms on the one hand and fluidity, refinement and dissolution on the other, is one of the paradoxes I wanted especially to address in this selection. Victorian poetry can be as audacious as some of the achievements of the Romantics, or the more ebullient work of the Elizabethans. Would the line,

Sail the blue peacefully. Green flame the hedgerows.

strike you as Victorian? Or, these extraordinary verses of Henley's, which were written in 1873–1875:

> These are the streets [. . .]
> Each is an avenue leading
> Whither I will!
> Free [. . .]![3]

Even Ezra Pound, famously allergic to the Victorians, could not but admire the pure 'Imagism' of Lionel Johnson's poem 'April' (1895): 'Clear lie the fields, and fade into blue air.'[4] That these lines, 'the new poetry' of its day, were published alongside more conventional nineteenth-century verse is part of the period's enigma. Working on this book has confirmed to me how, still, the poetic imagination of the Victorians can be undervalued. The sequence of twelve poems simulating a 'nineteenth-century day' at the beginning of this anthology

---

2 Derek Stanford, ed., *Writing of the 'Nineties: From Wilde to Beerbohm* (London: Dent [Everyman], 1971), p. xvii.

3 W. E. Henley's *In Hospital* sequence of poems was first published in the *Cornhill* in 1875, as examples of some of the early free verse of the late-Victorian period. The first line cited here comes from 'Pastoral', No. XXII in *In Hospital*. The second example is from 'Discharged', No. XXVIII.

4 R. K. R. Thornton, *Poetry of the 'Nineties* (Penguin, 1970), p. 186.

('The Way We Live Now') distils this quality. It is typical of a decadence which is ostensibly conventional yet at unforeseen moments breaks strikingly unexpected ground in theme or form—such as the late-Victorian vogue for sonnets, triolets, ballades and the rondel, all types of verse which can propose a deceptive levity masking social and political concerns, especially the ballade. I am also rather interested in why the first quatrain of many Victorian sonnets does not set the scene. Some of the poetry here is thus revolutionary as well as evolutionary.

Some readers may feel it provocative not to have included more Swinburne (or some of his narrative verse, such as *Tristram of Lyonesse*), but my reasonable grounds are that he is more associated with the 1860s, rather than the later nineteenth-century period; although deliberate attention is paid to his influence on prosody (the study of meter), especially on rhyme and verse form. Likewise, space accorded to the multi-lingual Augusta Webster (who also wrote under the name 'Cecil Home') is comparatively confined; my rationale for this is, again, that Webster's most significant work (by her own admission) was published in and before 1870, not after. It includes, for enquiring readers, Greek translations of the drama of Aeschylus (1866) and Euripides (1868), as well as verse (1866, 1867 and 1870), much of which adapts the conventions of dramatic monologue for *female* personae. Less well-known 'lesser poets' such as Digby Mackworth Dolben and William Brighty Rands who are represented in the brilliant Ricks and Karlin anthologies of Victorian poetry, are also excluded as being out of time. One of a rash of Old Etonian poets of the late-Victorian period, some of whom are represented here, Dolben was nineteen when he drowned swimming in a Northamptonshire lake in 1867; and other than the strange 'Doll Poems', the children's verse of journalist Brighty Rands again appears mainly throughout the 1860s. Charles Weekes and Hall Caine, the latter known principally for his fiction, were very nearly selected, as was Theodore Watts. The Irish poet Fanny (Frances Isabelle) Parnell, sister of Charles, whose *Land League Songs* (1882) achieved huge sales, was excluded after some debate on the principle that her most successful protest work was first published in nineteenth-century America. By contrast, 'Florenz', the pen-name for Charlotte Elliot, is here even though most of her verse was written earlier, as continual craving for 'The Pythoness', the main poem for which its author is (perhaps justly) remembered, could only be satisfied by a melodramatic reprinting in 1878.

Marginally less Swinburne and Webster, then, but more of those poets which many readers may never have encountered, such as Elizabeth 'Bessie' Craigmyle, or Jane (Ellice) Hopkins, and a fresh look at those who have been met on other occasions. William Morris's late-Victorian verse, which has tended to be less anthologised than his prose of the same period, is given comparatively generous attention in all its metrical variety; this includes his translations of Virgil's *Aeneid* and Homer's *Odyssey* 'done into English verse', in 1876 and 1887 respectively, as well as his 'Chants for Socialists' and love lyrics. *The Earthly Paradise* and *The Life and Death of Jason* fall outside my editorial boundaries, but some of Morris's other longer poems are excerpted here, such as 'The Story of Sigurd the Volsung', which, in common with his rendering of Homer, is written in the crafty anapestic couplet Morris made peculiarly his own. Other late-Victorian writers who again are more celebrated for their prose include Robert Louis Stevenson, an unexpectedly fine poet, as well as George Eliot, and John Ruskin, who regarded his efforts at verse as 'a disgrace'. For readers who want to sample some of the classic longer poems of the period, there is Hopkins' *The Wreck of the Deutschland*, and Tennyson's 'Arthurian' *Idyls of the King*. Alongside the 'English' writers,

I have respected the Celtic Revival, whether Irish, Welsh or Scottish, as a crucial dimension of this twilight age.

Certainly, late-Victorian poetry is haunted by rapidly declining light, and 'faint horizons'; the obscurity of evening and darkness, of twilight, of half-light, of gas-light, of doors left slightly ajar, of existing through loss and shadow; mourning, with the Queen's loss of her beloved husband, and the deaths of Browning, in 1889, and Tennyson, in 1892, the passing not just of the century, but of an era. (Laments for loss, from the onerous to the rarified, recur again and again.) Pound reserved a special word in his lexicon of dynastic contempt for this unforgivably anti-objectivist Victorian nonsense: 'crepuscular' (which is in fact a seventeenth-century word).[5] Pound's term is infuriating: he adored Whistler, the most crepuscular artist of them all. What he was driving at, though, was that 'the crepuscular spirit' was redundant morally, too mawkishly vague and uncritically sentimental to mean anything concrete as art. 'Go in fear of abstractions' was Pound's order to young Imagists. Indeed, one of the original figurative connotations of 'crepuscular' is 'imperfectly enlightened'. The tone of much of the verse in this anthology suggests how the literary climate 1872–1900—for prose as well as for poetry—is as shadowy, heterogeneous, complex, experimental and volatile as the country that produced (and consumed) it. Victorian poetry has been seen fruitfully as light and dark; but with Daniel Karlin I hope I would resist an interpretation that this intricate relationship was in any sense black and white.

As Christopher Ricks observes, 'Things changed and counterchanged; even the Queen often proved a surprise, though it may be thought that she was a surprise like a Browning character, by being even more herself than one would ever have anticipated.'[6] Late-nineteenth-century English poetry as anthologised here proves and, I hope, preserves those secret surprises: the most unexpected secret of all (although Virginia Woolf's Mrs Swithin would never have us believe it) that there could be, indeed, such people—or such poetries. The richness of literary possibility throughout these sybilline, valedictory times is suggested by a remark of the most intrinsically Victorian poet of all, Tennyson, when reacting to contemporary reviews of his *Idylls of the King*: 'I hate to be tied down to say, "This means that", because the thought within the image is much more than any one interpretation.' But it is also acutely felt by a poem of Tennyson's, 'Frater Ave Atque Vale' (1883) ['Brother, hail and farewell'], which alludes to the death of his brother Charles. (The verse of Tennyson's other brother, Frederick, is also included in this book.) 'Frater Ave Atque Vale' is monorhyme, although, by virtue of being written in octameters (an eight-foot line)—rare for any age—as well as in trochaic meter, it is formidably difficult to hear and say:

> Row us out from Desenzano, to your Sirmione row!
> So they rowed, and there we landed—'O venusta Sirmio!'

The poem as a whole is a characteristically Victorian 'take' on a classical theme, a second wave of Catullus; it rows 'us' into (as well as out from) a wafting sea of sound—row/Sirmio/glow/grow/woe/ago/fro/below/Sirmio—out eight-foot deep. The rhyme is mono-tonous

---

5 Ezra Pound, 'Revolt Against the Crepuscular Spirit in Modern Poetry'. In the first edition of *Personae* (1909).
6 Christopher Ricks, ed., *The New Oxford Book of Victorian Verse* (Oxford: Oxford University Press, 1987), p. xxx.

without being monotonous, just about right for a poem in which Tennyson mingles the shifting moods of sadness and joy he appreciated in the Latin sources.[7] Farewells in Tennyson are never static, even if they seem to sound so: in this 'olive-silvery' tone-poem the 'rhyme' decadently blends and blurs as its moves, in an accumulation and return of sound-waves that are intensified by the 'Row [. . .] row/So [. . .] Sirmio' double-bind of the first two lines. As if to an era as well as an individual, the poem is literally, artfully, waving goodbye. A prayer for a safe crossing of a ship (sometimes carrying a poet or a hero) is an ancient idea, conventional in Horace; Tennyson, in his most desolate hour, had sought consolation in it before, in section IX of the earlier 'In Memoriam A.H.H' (1850) and would do so again in 'Crossing the Bar' (1889), the famous poem composed when Tennyson and his wife, Emily, had settled at Aldworth, his woodland retreat in Surrey, which was built in 1868 to coincide with the opening of the new railway line at Haslemere. Many of Tennyson's poems included here date from this time, a period as exacting as it is elusive.

An anthology is literally a gathering of flowers, a drawing together of a posy from scattered places or sources—a form of content. Yet the flower, often regarded as the most conspicuous part of a plant, is also its most reticent; the site of a complex agency of 'sexuality', the 'female' pistils and/or 'male' stamens contained within protective sepals, or calyx (from the Greek *kalupto*, hide) 'crowned' by a corolla of petals. The intrinsic and enigmatic relationship between the visible and the unseen lies, as it does in flowers, at the heart of late-Victorian verse, symbolising the contradictions and displacements of its writers' inner, and outer, worlds. 'Seer, savant, merchant, poet': each image is refracted through the looking glass of these profoundly stylish, sensational years. The same, but not the same.

Caroline Blyth
Cambridge, 2008

---

[7] For further commentary on the poem see either p. 70 of the Ricks edition of *The Poems of Tennyson*, previously cited, or Ricks, ed., *Tennyson: A Selected Edition* (Longman, 1989), p. 627.

Acknowledgements

Any scholar of this period owes an inestimable debt to the late great anthologiser of Victorian poetry A. H. Miles; but I cannot thank adequately his successors, the editors of two exemplary, learned and inspiring English anthologies, Christopher Ricks, editor of *The New Oxford Book of Victorian Verse*, and Danny Karlin, editor of *The Penguin Book of Victorian Verse*, whose scrupulous enthusiasm for and resilient engagement with my task has been the greatest source of encouragement. They have both been very patient with me. The groundbreaking writing and research of Isobel Armstrong and Angela Leighton has also been influential, and I am especially grateful to Angela Leighton for also reading drafts of the manuscript. I have learned from Valentine Cunningham's awesome *Anthology of Victorian Poetry and Poetics*, which revives a welcome interest in poetics. Auden has been a mainstay throughout. In addition, to Christopher Ricks's *The Poems of Tennyson* I have suffered for years from a chronic addiction for which there is no known cure. With regard to the religious, social and cultural pressures of the period I have learned from Marek Kohn, Jonathon Dollimore, Regenia Gagnier, A. N. Wilson and Stefan Collini. Many colleagues offered invaluable comment and criticism at various stages, as did the Cambridge Nineteenth-Century Research Seminar, where a version of this work was first given an outing. I have benefited from the endless questions asked by students I have supervised on all manner of Victorian poets over the years, some of which are addressed in the following pages (least of all, what is decadence) and it is my hope that this book will be of some modest use to them and others discovering for the first time the binding spell of the late-Victorian period, whether on undergraduate or postgraduate courses. There are individual colleagues to whom I owe a gratitude for more specialist dialogue, especially John Beer, Stephen Gill, Catherine Phillips, John Harvey, Rod Edmond, Clive Wilmer and Myra Stokes. Jeremy Prynne helped me reflect upon how to be instructive about poetry without being didactic, and I have profited much from his wisdom over the years. Henry Woudhuysen read parts of the manuscript and made pertinent suggestions as to emphasis, as did John Kerrigan. Frank Kermode also absorbed early drafts and helped refine a point about John Gray. I would like to thank particularly Rod Mengham, Paul Luzio, Michael Robson, and Marjorie Wynne, as well as Robert Douglas-Fairhurst, advisory editor, and all at Anthem for overseeing the final stages. Thanks too are owed to Anthony Ramsden—both express and implied. Day after day, the staff of the Rare Books Room at Cambridge University Library have been unfailingly helpful both to me and to my research assistant Dr Brendan Cooper, who lessened the load in the very last few months. My parents have been supportive in countless ways. I am also grateful to the Faculty of English, University of Cambridge, and to the Master and Fellows of St Edmund's College, Cambridge for electing me to Fellowships which enabled this work to be completed.

Decadent Art 1872–1900

The following provides an outline of some significant paintings and decadence-related events of the late-Victorian period, many influenced by developments in France, which readers of this book may like to pursue in relation to the poetry and the prose. Although it falls outside the period it would be important to note Simeon Solomon's classic painting, *Dawn* (1871), which ushers in the vogue for decadent art in England in the following decades.

1873	Walter Pater, *Studies in the History of the Renaissance*
1877	Ruskin accuses Whistler of 'flinging a pot of paint into the public's face'; Whistler sues him and wins
1880	Arnold Böcklin, *The Island of the Dead*.
1881	Paul Bourget publishes an essay on Baudelaire in *La Nouvelle Revue*, entitling part of it, 'Théorie de la décadence'.
1882	Burne-Jones, *The Mill* completed and exhibited (composed 1870–1882)
1884	J. K. Huysmans, *A Rebours* ('Against the Grain')
	Gustave Moreau, *Sappho*
1885	Jean Moréas launches Symbolism in a series of manifestos George Frederick Watts, *Hope*
1886	Anatole Bajou founds *Le Décadent*
1888	Pater's 'Conclusion' to *The Renaissance*
	Paul Gauguin, *The Vision After the Sermon*
1890	Symbolist reviews established: *La Plume*, *'L'Ermitage*, *Mercure de France*
1891	Oscar Wilde, *The Picture of Dorian Gray*
1893	Munich 'Secession'
1894	Henri Fantin-Latour, *Dawn and Night*
1896	Ferdinand Khnopff, *The Caress* and *Medusa Asleep*
1897	Klimt is first President of the Vienna Secession
1898	Aubrey Beardsley dies, aged 26
1900	World Fair in Paris; Sir William Orpen exhibits *The Mirror*, Giacomo Balla, *The World's Fair At Night (Luna Park)* and Benjamin Constant, *Queen Victoria*

Introduction

I. The Politics of Poetry

'The Victorians,' Mrs Swithin mused. 'I don't believe,' she said with her odd little smile, 'that there ever were such people. Only you and me and William dressed differently.'
'You don't believe in history,' said William.

Virginia Woolf, *Between the Acts*

The starting point for this book is 1872, where, in the middle of the first of four Liberal administrations under Prime Minister William Gladstone, Victorian poetry can be said to enter its 'late' phase.[1] It is a peculiar time, because it is in these final decades of the age, partly mediated through the loss of Dickens in 1870, John Stuart Mill in 1873, and, subsequently, the deaths of Browning in 1889, Tennyson in 1892, and Ruskin, Wilde, and Nietzsche in 1900 that the idea of what it is to be 'Victorian' begins to take shape. Interpretations of the period are complicated further by the 'apocalyptic paradigm' of the *fin-de-siècle*: suggesting patterns of disclosure, of revelation.[2] Yet as the century turned, many of these patterns remain, in the Kermodian sense, 'disconfirmed'. In 1900 alone Freud published *The Interpretation of Dreams*, Thomas Mann *Buddenbrooks*, Henry James abandoned the novel he would never finish in order to start work on *The Ambassadors*, and Conrad's *Lord Jim* appeared. Husserl published his *Logic*, and Russell, *Critical Exposition of the Philosophy of Leibniz*. The same year, the decadent poet Richard Le Gallienne repudiated Catholicism in a pamphlet entitled 'The Beautiful Life of Rome'—a gesture less radical than ritualistic, as many late-Victorian moments are—symbolising decades of nineteenth-century religious crisis still unresolved. 1900 may be the terminus for this anthology, but it figures an ending less finished than burnished.

The most experimental poet of the period to embrace this questioning spirit is Gerard Manley Hopkins. Hopkins composed a fragment of a sonnet form addressed 'To his Watch' (included in this selection, as are all the poems noted in this preface and introduction). Like the mirror, the image on the cover of this book to which I will return in the concluding pages of this introduction, the watch symbolises the visible and the unseen: an apprehension measured in the emotionally unpredictable spring-ticking of the poem. It was intended to be a sonnet; yet, as scholars have noted, it 'is one syllable longer than a curtal sonnet but lacks the proportions of that form'.[3] It is a sonnet in which the first quatrain, untraditionally,

---

[1] Disraeli and the Conservatives came to power in 1874. Gladstone was Prime Minister four times, from 1868–1874; 1880–1885; 1886; 1892–1894.
[2] See Frank Kermode, *The Sense of an Ending: Studies in the Theory of Fiction* (Oxford University Press, 1966) p. 99.
[3] See Catherine Phillips, 'The Effects of Incompleteness in Three Hopkins Poems.' *Renascence* 42, 1–2 (Fall 1989/Winter 1990), pp. 21–33, especially pp. 26–29. This quotation is taken from p. 29. The sonnet was written circa 1885–1886. The article notes controversy over line 3, whether 'force' was in fact 'forge'. On p. 27 Phillips comments, 'If one takes the word as 'force', the revision changes the emphasis

does not set the scene. Instead, the voice and movement of the poetry insist on a contemporary, urgent prescience of the 'mortality' of time at cross-purposes with the convention of Time's immortality. And, although the developing situation fulfils expectations in the second quatrain, by the 'end' of the poem, such as it is in its incomplete form of eleven lines, there is no Comfort of the Resurrection: things, in a peculiarly late-nineteenth-century way, just get 'worse'. Morning never comes. It is not just his watch that's in bits—'ruins of, rifled'—but his world. Why should Hopkins finish it? His sonnet represents the terrible waste of time:

> Mortal my mate, bearing my rock-a-heart
> Warm beat with cold beat company, shall I
> Earlier or you fail at our force and lie
> The ruins of, rifled, once a world of art?
> The telling of time our task is; time's some part,
> Not all, but we were framed to fail and die —
> One spell and well that one. There, ah thereby
> Is comfort's carol of all or woe's worst smart.
>
> Field-flown, the departed day no morning brings
> Saying 'This was yours' with her, but new one, worse,
> And then that last and shortest [. . .]

Time and causality are particularly late-Victorian concerns, and they trouble Hopkins, and many writers of this period.[4] By 'time' (never easy to define satisfactorily in any age), I do not particularly mean chronicity, a continuum of existence, although indeed that is a concept to which the late-Victorians might have responded. I am interpreting 'time' as *kairos*, a season—the 'point in time filled with significance, charged with a meaning derived from its relation to the end'—*kairos* in the Augustinian sense of 'critical time'.[5] 1872–1900 is such a special season, where time becomes subjected to the hazardous pressure of 'ce vertige du Temps écrasé'—that which Barthes, for whom the concept of *kairos* was also suggestive, terms the *punctum*.[6] The late-nineteenth century is a time shot through with unexpected crisis;

---

from what watch and poet create to the spring of their being—in the case of the watch, the spring that initiates its entire operation, and in the case of the poet, physical life. It was used by Shakespeare in a related way of the body's strength in sonnet 91—'Some glory [. . .] in their body's force.' I am grateful to Dr Phillips for further discussion about this fragment, including its probable date of composition. For text, see *The Poems of Gerard Manley Hopkins*, 4th edn., ed. W. H. Gardner and N. H. MacKenzie (Oxford: Oxford University Press, 1967, rpt., 1970), p. 193 (No. 153). For further discussion of the curtal sonnet see the 'Victorian Poetries' section of this introduction.

4 In the above article Catherine Phillips comments on Hopkins's lines 'The times are nightfall and the light grows less', also written in either 1885 or 1886. She also reminds us more generally of 'the idling, wasting of time for which Hopkins admonished himself even as an undergraduate' and notes Hopkins's concern with 'the larger time-scale' of Revelation 8:12.

5 Frank Kermode, *The Sense of an Ending* (Oxford University Press, 1966), particularly pp. 46–50.

6 Roland Barthes, *La chambre claire: Notes sur la photographie* (Paris: Cahiers du Cinéma, Gallimard, Seuil, 1980), p. 151. For Barthes, writing both through Proust and through the death of his mother, the *punctum* is 'cette zébrure inattendue qui venait parfois traverser ce champ' (p. 148). For Barthes' revised thinking about the concept of the 'punctum' in contrast to the 'studium' see, particularly, p. 49 and pp. 148–151. Barthes, too, writes of 'le kaïros du désir'. (p. 95). Also see the discussion of G. W. Wilson's 1863 photograph of Queen Victoria, which is pertinent to the late-Victorian period, pp. 91–93.

a crisis of the imagination, the most unimaginable crisis of all.[7] By 'causality' the mid-seventeenth-century sense of the word is recalled as this, philosophically, hovers over the Victorian period, refusing to go away entirely: the operation or relation of cause and effect.[8]

With mechanisation, the *tempo* of the language during this time increases. In 1895 this mechanical dimension to the language is fully wound on; according to the OED, the verb to 'time' something comes to mean, 'to adjust the parts of [a mechanism] so that a succession of movements or operations takes place at the required intervals and in the desired sequence'. Victorian literature 1872–1900, and its concern with 'the visible and the unseen', is excited by this late-nineteenth-century European context; in which the French philosopher Louis Bergson argued in *Time and Free Will* (1890) and *Matter and Memory* (1896) that the Western concept of time was inadequate, insofar as it had been regarded by the positivists and notably the British philosopher Herbert Spencer. Real time (or *durée*), Bergson argued, is unpredictable, and unquantifiable. Is it any coincidence that the word 'Time-limit' dates from 1880, and 'time-keeper' from 1884? Dobson's poem 'On the Hurry of the Time' (1882) ups the rate.

Not surprisingly, these questions worry many nineteenth-century English poets. Hardy especially was exercised by 'Time', not least because a notion of time, whether it is wasted or not, questions further the relations between habit and 'the will'.[9] (This is also caught spatially in the painting on the cover of this anthology, in the different 'time-zones' explored in the foreground and the mirror.) Yet the question of time was not confined to the traditional poets. Here is the opening part of Mathilde Blind's poem, 'Chaunts of Life'. Characteristic of this late-Victorian period, in form and content the poem is both typical and atypical. The 'dim' force of the opening line will have become realised as blazing 'light' at the close of the verse. In the terms in which Gillian Beer has described Darwin's language, the emphasis, the teleological drive, is on 'process, rather than stable origins'.[10] Time now, about to run into the 1890s, is 'limitless', as the poem hurtles forward with post-pentametric 'measureless speed':

> Struck out of dim fluctuant forces and shock of electrical vapour,
> Repelled and attracted the atoms flashed mingling in union primeval,
> And over the face of the waters far heaving in limitless twilight
> Auroral pulsations thrilled faintly, and, striking the blank heaving surface,
> The measureless speed of their motion now leaped into light on the waters.

---

7 The word 'Time' was a continual preoccupation to the late-Victorian imagination, and, like 'subjectivity', it attracted various accretions of meaning, from the expression 'doing time', which dates from 1865, to the idea of 'fast time', one who completes a race in fast time, which dates from 1891.
8 However, in 1874 'causality' takes on another shade of meaning derived from the context of phrenology (the scientific study of the mental faculties, put forward earlier in the nineteenth century by the theories of Gall and Spurzheim): from 1874 'causality' also means the faculty of tracing effects to causes. Domett's poem 'Fireworks', composed the same year in 1874, and discussed in the 'Victorian Poetries' section of this introduction, could be read as a 'verse essay' in the new Victorian meaning attributed to causality.
9 For further discussion of this important topic see 'The Idea of Character: Private Habits and Public Virtues' in Stefan Collini, *Public Moralists: Political Thought and Intellectual Life in Britain 1850–1930* (Oxford: Clarendon, 1991), pp. 91–104.
10 Gillian Beer, ed., Charles Darwin, *The Origin of Species* (Oxford World's Classics, 1996, rpt., 1998), p. xix.

The startling juxtaposition of realism and phantasmagoria, of contemporary scientific discourse with the traditional language of creation ('the face of the waters') is signal of the fusion of scientific culture with religion in the period, itself part of the expanding verbal empire of systematic philology. Blind's poetry draws on the Bible; as her contemporary Constance Naden's verse does, in its analogue of Darwin as Solomon. For Hopkins, 'The telling of time our task is [. . .]'. As readers of this 'time', then, where do we start? Whose time do we tell?

The introduction to *The Penguin Book of Victorian Verse* (1997) delineated Victorian poetry in terms of a 'two-party system'—in *voice*, speech and song; in *tone*, light and dark. Leaving aside the question of two-party politics for a moment, to these critical principles of 'voice' and 'tone' let us add *movement*; for, however inert and corrosive Yeats and Eliot would influentially see it to be, nineteenth-century poetry—and prose—does move, with different structural and thematic emphases, at different times. This movement could be traced as a gradual shift between subject-object relations throughout the literary consciousness of the nineteenth century; most simply explained, in terms of poets, as the move from Wordsworth to Hardy.[11] Victorian 'movement' in the late phase of the age—like its 'religion', 'politics', or 'sexuality'—is powerful, not least because the energies simultaneously put in motion would have repercussions for the way that poetry would develop in the twentieth century (in Britain and, more radically, in America).[12] 'Change has come suddenly,' wrote Yeats in 1936, 'the despair of my friends in the 'nineties part of its preparation.'[13]

The movements of the 1872–1900 period can be traced in three of late-Victorian England's most dynamic and diverse collections of poetry. In the 1870s, Matthew Arnold published his *Poems of Wordsworth* (1879). In 1887, Victoria's Golden Jubilee year, Mrs Elizabeth A. Sharp edited *Women's Voices*, a beautifully produced volume with a specially engraved cover, dedicated to her mother and 'to women everywhere'. Three years later this was revised in 'pocket book' format as *Women Poets of the Victorian Era*—with a dedication to Mona Caird, one of the leading feminist polemicists of the day. The 1890s are well known for *The Yellow Book: An Anthology* (1894–1897), edited by Fraser Harrison.[14] Each of these three books summarises a development in the literary culture and imagination of the final years of the nineteenth century: changing perceptions of the poet, the self and the reader; the emergence of the 'New Woman'; and, taking inspiration from France, Symbolism and Decadence (from *de-cadere*, to fall)—out of which, in the early twentieth century, the phoenix of Modernism would arise and fall. The respective deaths of Dickens, Browning and Tennyson also mark each of the last three decades of the nineteenth century.

---

11 For further treatment of this subject see the introduction in Daniel Karlin, ed., *The Penguin Book of Victorian Verse* (London: Penguin, 1997), pp. lxx–lxxv.
12 Isobel Armstrong and Joseph Bristow, eds., *Nineteenth-Century Women Poets* (Oxford: Clarendon Press, 1996), p. xxix.
13 W. B. Yeats, ed., 'Introduction' to *The Oxford Book of Modern Verse* (Oxford: Clarendon Press, 1936), p. xxviii.
14 It should be noted that there are other collections of poetry, for example, William Davenport's *The Comic Poets of the Nineteenth Century: Poems of Wit and Humour by Living Writers* (1876), an anthology dedicated to light verse.

However diverse, these late-Victorian 'anthologies' have in common the uncommon: lyric and narrative eclecticism, a linguistic and metrical heterogeneity, a range not just of 'voice' but of voices: representing a range of cadence and register, and a depth of apprehension and critical resilience, wholly peculiar to this late-Victorian period, and at times surprising. That which may appear in a poem as insufferably mannered, punishingly 'monotonous', pedestrian or prosaic, questions one's Romantic assumptions of 'voice', or diction, or rhythm, or rhyme (a signal nineteenth-century critical concern); the same goes for novels which can seem, thematically, repetitive. Commenting that 'Life, we know too well, is not a Comedy, but something strangely mixed', Meredith's *An Essay on Comedy and the Uses of the Comic Spirit* (1877), which began life as a lecture, introduces into the latter years of the century a paradoxical critical idiom, a dilemma he pursued in the title *The Tragic Comedians*, the novel that followed the year after *The Egoist* (1879).[15] Robert Browning's poem 'Aristophanes' Apology' (1875), a 'verse-essay', also sets the ambivalent tone, prophetic of the 'tragi-comic' verse of the future.[16] The 1872–1900 period is invigorated, then, less by a visible movement as such—although a robust sense of one exists in places—than by a subtle series of changes and movements, of poetries and poems.

Matthew Arnold's and Mrs Elizabeth Sharp's editions of verse may be less well-known today than *The Yellow Book* but they are nevertheless signal, and *Poems of Wordsworth* (1879) has been reprinted more than forty times in 110 years.[17] As a critic Arnold is best known for *Culture and Anarchy* (1864). His Wordsworth is more anarchic than cultural. The philosophically reductive model of Wordsworth Arnold championed here makes readers question not only how the late Victorians were being encouraged to think about

---

15 From the text of the lecture reprinted in George Meredith, *The Egoist*, ed. Robert M. Adams (Norton Critical Edition, 1979), p. 434. The lecture was originally printed in the *New Quarterly Magazine* in April 1877, but first separately published in 1897, when it was reviewed by George Bernard Shaw in the *Saturday Review*. See also Gillian Beer's essay reprinted in the same Norton edition of *The Egoist*, 'The Two Masks and the Idea of Comedy', which observes that Meredith 'sees further that since the flouting of reason is the root of comedy, comedy may have a tragic issue in the lives of human beings', and that '*The Egoist* becomes an exploration of the boundaries beyond which comedy cannot venture', p. 489. [Reprinted from ch. 4 of *Meredith: A Change of Masks* (London, 1970), pp. 114–139].

16 The poem was described as 'an essay in verse' in a review in *The Athenaeum*, 17 April 1875. The full title of the poem is 'Aristophanes' Apology Including a Transcript of Euripides Being the Last Adventure of Balaustion'. The poem is 'paired' with 'Balaustion's Adventure' (1871), the first poem Browning wrote after *The Ring and the Book* (1868). A focus for Browning's concern in 'Aristophanes' Apology' was the critical hostility accorded to Euripides (his favourite dramatist) by Browning's immediate interpretative predecessors and contemporaries (e. g. A. W. von Schlegel's *Lectures on Dramatic Art and Literature*, which had been published in 1871, a lot longer after they were given). Schlegel's 'negative' commentary came in the wake of what Browning had perceived to be an unappreciative introduction to T. A. Buckley's 1868 translation of Euripides' *Tragedies*. The decade of the 1870s, as the subject of Meredith's *Lecture* suggests, tended to see more theoretical interest accorded to Comedy. For further commentary on the poem see W. C. DeVane, *A Browning Handbook* (New York: Appleton-Century-Crofts, 1955), pp. 375–384.

17 For discussion of the conception of Wordsworth consciously promoted by Arnold through the publication and marketing of this book see Stephen Gill, *Wordsworth and the Victorians* (Oxford: Oxford University Press, 1998), pp. 107–109. See also Stefan Collini, *Matthew Arnold: A Critical Portrait*, pp. 28–30.

Wordsworth (chiefly as a truncated lyric poet), but how 'Arnold's Wordsworth' could also be seen as contributing to the broader change in how Romanticism was perceived by their inheritors. It is significant too that Arnold's selection appeared just before the decade in which a gradual yet noticeable shift in the role of the reader emerges.[18] The increased awareness by artists, whether poets or prose writers, of the role of the reader is a particular feature of late-Victorian literature, itself part of a broader literary transition between subject-object relations. Arnold's *Poems of Wordsworth* represents, then, a text raising major critical questions. It is pertinent, not only to the construction of the Victorian Wordsworth, but also to the movement away from Romantic 'subjectivity', and the questioning of the poet as a source of authority.

Mrs Elizabeth Sharp's 1887 anthology of female poets made a timely mark on all this restlessness. The inspiration came readily enough, from a moving cultural apparatus that was ceaselessly producing, 'agglomerating', printing magazines such as Emily Faithfull's *Victoria Magazine*, which ran from 1863 until 1880, Lydia Backer's *Women's Suffrage Journal* and Louisa M. Hubbard's *Work and Leisure*—popular literature that built on the proto-suffragist mode of the mid-century *English Woman's Journal*.[19] A movement was happening contemporaneously in nineteenth-century America, with the re-appearance in 1871 of *Pearls from the American Female Poets*—a re-issuing of the pioneering volume *The American Female Poets* (1848), edited by Caroline May. The novel as a genre was quick to latch on to the 'New Woman' culture of the 1880s, as can be seen in Meredith's comparatively radical treatment of his female characters in *The Egoist* (1879), and *Diana of the Crossways* (1885), as well as in Gissing. The pages of *The Westminster Review*, increasingly one of the most influential political and philosophical journals of the later nineteenth century—it is possibly notable that it became a 'monthly' as opposed to a quarterly in the year of the Golden Jubilee—were also becoming more supportive of the 'New Woman' movement. Although George Eliot's association with the journal had long ceased, her connection had been a powerful one.[20] The journal regularly began including laudatory reviews of female poets as well as articles by some of the leading polemicists of the day. Mona Caird's *Westminster* essay on 'The Morality of Marriage' provoked, allegedly, thousands of indignant responses in the letters column of the *Daily Telegraph* when it was first published in 1888. Caird's rebellion continued into the 'Nineties in her 'feminist-mythological' novel, *The Daughters of Danaeus* (1894), a story whose title alludes to the myth of the King of Argus. He had fifty daughters, all promised in marriage to their cousins. This is a ghastly transmogrification of the Victoria-Albert union, although presumably not intended as such.[21] Many of the contributors to the *Westminster* were also notable poets, such as Mathilde Blind and L. (Louisa) S. Bevington ('Mrs Guggenberger'). But the *Westminster* continued to set a

---

18 For further discussion of this large subject see David Trotter, *The Making of the Reader: Language and Subjectivity in Modern American, English and Irish Poetry* (London: Macmillan, 1984). On p. 3 Trotter cites Malcolm Bradbury's suggestion that 'From about 1880 [. . .] English culture failed to provide the homogeneity which would have nurtured Common Readers.'
19 For further discussion of this subject, see the first introduction in Angela Leighton and Margaret Reynolds, eds., *Victorian Women Poets: An Anthology* (Oxford: Blackwell, 1995), pp. xxiv–xxxiv.
20 Eliot became assistant editor in 1851.
21 See Andrea Broomfield and Sally Mitchell, eds., *Prose by Victorian Women: An Anthology* (New York and London: Garland, 1996), p. 625.

tone for the age that was anti-didactic in register, challenging of 'double standards', a spirit reflected in much of its verse.[22]

With political unease came religious and scientific complexity and confusion. Not only was there now, in part through the work of Darwin, greater anxiety about sexual difference than ever before. Darwin's 'dense, enthusiastic writing gave scope to others to press out counter-meanings'.[23] In Constance Naden's and Mathilde Blind's verses, myths of creation are more subject to scrutiny than ever before, more even than in the 1830s. Naden, who also wrote a sonnet on 'Poet and Botanist' (1887), takes as a comic subject the Darwinian thesis of 'Natural Selection'—and, from *The Descent of Man*, 'Sexual Selection'. The fusing of art and science is a distinctive feature of the late-Victorian period. Evolutionary theory, botany, physics and zoology become the new poetry to the late-Victorians, as geology and meteorology were to the writers of the 1820s and 1830s. Blind composed a long dialogic poem 'The Ascent of Man' (1889) explicitly to engage with *The Descent of Man* (1871, second, revised edition 1874)—which, with the *Origin of Species* (1859), cast a long shadow over late-Victorian social philosophy and religious and political thinking. 'Man still bears in his bodily frame the indelible stamp of his lowly origin' were the concluding words of *The Descent of Man*. *The Descent of Man* had been publicly denounced. The part of the book dealing candidly with that which Darwin called 'sexual selection' among mammals, birds and insects was regarded by many as especially offensive. Based on the tracing back of all forms of life to a primordial protoplasm, Darwin claimed that there was no evidence that belief in God was instinctive; belief could be acquired, but was not an innate human quality. To many Victorians this was the stuff of blasphemy—at least as blasphemous as the Pope, who declared his infallibility the year that Darwin's volume appeared. So in 1874 Darwin revised *The Descent of Man*, taking account of some of the criticisms he had received in the early 1870s.

The late period of the nineteenth century is also characterised by profound, if not obsessive, denominational differences about the nature of public worship, which brought to the surface (again) the long, residual English problem of the degree of interference between Church and State. In 1874 Prime Minister Disraeli had introduced the Public Worship Regulation Act. This meant, among other things, that it became illegal to perform certain ritual acts in Anglican churches, such as the mixing of water into wine, and the wearing of Eucharistic vestments. Those cynical of politicians would claim that Disraeli was mainly investing energy in this affair to win over the Queen, whose disdain for the 'Ritualists' was well-known—when at Balmoral she made a point of worshipping with the Presbyterians. To many Protestant believers, such 'rituals' seemed treachery of the highest order, and were little other than covert adoption of Romanist practices. (One notes the broader anti-Catholic sentiment stabilising in other European countries during the 1870s, notably by the German Chancellor Bismarck; see the poem by Hopkins called 'The Wreck of

---

22 For further discussion of the political implications of female verse during this time see Isobel Armstrong and Virginia Blain, eds., *Women's Poetry: Late Romantic to Late Victorian: Gender and Genre 1830–1900* (Houndmills: Macmillan, 1999, especially the essay by Armstrong entitled 'Msrepresentations: Codes of Affect and Politics in Nineteenth-Century Women's Poetry', 3–32).

23 Gillian Beer, ed., Charles Darwin, *The Origin of Species* (Oxford World's Classics, 1996, rpt., 1998), p. xxvi.

the Deutschland' which narrates a story about the fate of Catholic nuns expelled under the Falck Laws.) The Queen, whose manner was to write always in the third person, declared:

> She thinks a *complete Reformation* is what we want.
> But if *that* is *impossible*, the archbishop should have the *power* given him, by *Parliament*, to *stop* all these ritualistic practices, dressings, bowings, etc. and everything of that kind, and *above all, all* attempts at *confession*.[24]

Five English clergymen were imprisoned for failing to obey the Public Worship Act. The furore this business caused in 1874 sits uncomfortably alongside another classic of late-Victorian double standards: the Contagious Diseases Acts. Gladstone claimed to have prostitutes' interests at heart, but it took him longer than one might have expected to make English law back these claims. Until they were somewhat paradoxically repealed by Gladstone in 1886 under pressure from the feminist reformer Josephine Butler, the Contagious Diseases Acts defined any woman detained by the police in garrison towns, or a certain radius therein, as a common prostitute.[25] Women, especially poor women, were apprehended and arrested; *habeas corpus* was suspended completely. Of course in another terrible sense—*habeas corpus* translates as 'you may have the body'—having the body was, on the contrary, literally what happened, as women who refused to comply with the horrors of a Victorian medical examination (to prove their inherent 'contamination') faced long-term prison sentences. No attempt was made to punish men or regulate the spread of venereal diseases by men—particularly syphilis. An implication of the Contagious Diseases Act was that men, British soldiers and sailors particularly, needed prostitutes as a 'natural' indulgence, while the woman who provided these services was wicked. The Contagious Diseases Act goes a long way to explaining how, during the late nineteenth century, woman in literature is presented as a source of moral, as well as sexual, contamination, combining with a tradition of personification of woman as Error that goes back much further.[26] But the 'women's voices' of the late-Victorian period could now query these assumptions; challenging, when Constance Naden died (from the after-effects of an operation to remove ovarian cysts), Herbert Spencer's public expression of the view that the cause of the poet's death was 'the inevitable outcome of over-taxing with mental tasks "the feminine organisation" '.[27]

The *Yellow Book* attempted to transform the painful dissent that had been intensifying over two decades into the pleasure of satire. Oscar Wilde was the spiritual mentor, although Zola and Maupassant were influential; and the 'Book' was rivalled only by other yellowish

---

24 This letter from Victoria to Dean Stanley is reproduced in Owen Chadwick's *The Victorian Church*, 2 vols. 1966 and 1970 (1966, p. 321). Cited in A.N. Wilson, *The Victorians* (London: Hutchinson, 2002), p. 368. Wilson makes the point that it was Church ritual to which the monarch objected; 'she still expected "bowings etc." to herself by her subjects.' See also Wilson's sequel volume.
25 The Contagious Diseases Act was first passed in 1864. Subsequent amendments were made in 1866, 1868 and 1869. The Acts were repealed in 1886.
26 The background to these Acts is discussed in A. N. Wilson, *The Victorians* (London: Hutchinson, 2002), pp. 308, 369, 473–474. See also, Lucy Bland, *Banishing the Beast: English Feminism and Sexual Morality 1885–1914*, rpt. (London: IB Taurus, 2001).
27 This quotation is from Virginia Blain, ed., *Victorian Women Poets: A New Annotated Anthology* (London: Longmans, 2001) p. 246 and p. 236. See also her notes to 'Solomon Redivivus'.

anthologies of the decade, *The Book of the Rhymer's Club* (1892) and *The Second Book of the Rhymer's Club* (1894), to which John Gray, Victor Plarr, Lionel Johnson and Arthur Symons all contributed.[28] These 'Nineties poets are later recalled by Yeats in his poem 'The Grey Rock' (1914) as 'Poets with whom I learned my trade,/Companions of the Cheshire Cheese'. Artists jostled amongst the writers in *The Yellow Book*, reflecting the competition within the late-Victorian economy, and, during the 'Nineties especially, between literature and the visual arts (now including photography), as well as competition between different kinds of literature. There were portraits by Philip Wilson Steer, Walter Sickert and Will Rothenstein. The illustrations for which *The Yellow Book* is most celebrated, however, were those of its art editor, Aubrey Beardsley. (see Fig. 1) Beardsley held this position until he was dismissed in the fallout of the Wilde trial in 1895, with the result that, according to E. F. Benson, (author of *Dodo*), *The Yellow Book* 'turned grey overnight'.

As we have seen, however, *The Yellow Book* is not the only voice to speak for these decadent years, nor for the late period as a whole. It was never intended to; it was far too intimate an affair for that. By contrast, its writers opted deliberately for the conversational, the modish, the exclusive, the corrupting; in satire of all that tiresomely mid-Victorian rhetoric of the grandiloquent and socially-conscientious public sage. The anthology was supported by fashionable 'Nineties publisher John Lane, and gave collective *éclat* to many writers of the *belle époque* who might not have been noticed as individuals.[29] Notable contributors were John Davidson and Ernest Dowson, as well as Rosamund Marriott Watson (who wrote as Graham R. Tomson) and William Watson. Experimental prose flourished, especially through the genre of the short story; Hubert Crackanthorpe, George Gissing (Crackanthorpe's tutor), Arnold Bennett and Henry James were all contributors, as well as other short-story writers Ella D'arcy, George Egerton (the pen-name of Mary Chevelita Dunne), Ada Leverson (Wilde's Sphinx), Lena Milman, and Netta Syrett.[30] Another short-story writer was Charlotte Mew: 'Passed' (1894) first appeared in *The Yellow Book*, although Mew's poetry falls for the most part outside the 1872–1900 period. Fraser Harrison's Anthology also featured the essay, notably those of Max Beerbohm; his essay '1880' offers an aesthetic barometer of the age.[31]

One other late-Victorian 'anthology' should be mentioned. It was not published between 1872–1900, but it was much reprinted during this time.[32] Hardy, a figure to whom I will

---

28 For a comprehensive account, see Norman Alford, *The Rhymer's club: Poets of the Tragic Generation* (Houndmills: Macmillan, 1994) and also Linda Hughes, 'Women Poets and Contested Spaces in the Yellow Book', in *Studies in English Literature* 44 (2004): 849–872. Talia Schaffer's book on T*he Forgotten Female Aesthetes; Literary Culture in Late Victorian England* (Charlottesville: Virginia UP, 2000 is also useful, as is Karen Alkalay-Gut's essay on 'Aesthetic and Decadent Poetry' in Joseph Bristow, ed. *The Cambridge Companion to Victorian Poetry* (Cambridge: Cambridge University Press, 2000).
29 A frontispiece depicting John Lane's bookshop is reproduced at the start of this anthology.
30 The short story is not a late-Victorian invention, however: it flourished in the early-Victorian period and English developments in the genre were influenced by American writers, notably Edgar Allen Poe.
31 For further discussion of the aesthetic tensions of this period, especially in relation to Dollie Radford's publication in *The Yellow Book*, see Ruth Livesey, 'Dollie Radford and the Ethical Aesthetics of Fin-de-Siecle Poetry' in *Victorian Literature and Culture* (2006): pp. 34, 495–517.
32 The second series dates from 1897.

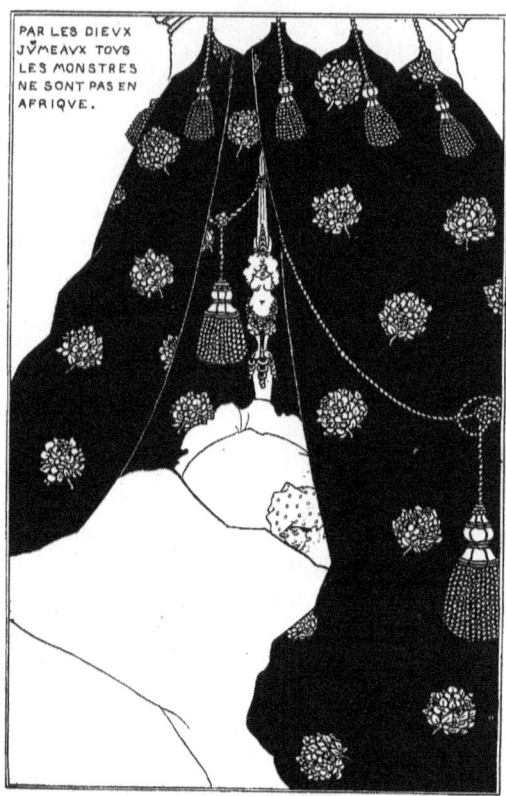

Fig. 1 Aubrey Beardsley, 'Portrait of Himself' from *The Yellow Book* (1894)

return, knew it better than most. That book was Francis Turner Palgrave's influential anthology, *The Golden Treasury of Best Songs and Lyrical Poems in the English language* (1861). *The Golden Treasury* was promoted not while Palgrave was Professor of Poetry at Oxford, but during his former thirty-year career as an official in the education department from 1855–1884—a pedagogical legacy of high Victorian poetic imperialism that would persist up until the Second World War, and after, as for the twentieth century Palgrave became the standard text for generations of schoolchildren. Tennyson had a close hand, and a closer ear, in the selection of the golden treasures. The anthology consisted entirely of dead English poets, with the deliberate omission of Donne and another resistant poet, William Blake, ever dubious to the Victorians apart from Yeats, Dante Gabriel Rossetti and Robert Browning; although Palgrave did include Marvell, a favourite of Tennyson's. The absence of Donne was a lacuna which Grierson's pioneering annotated *Donne* of 1912, and his *Metaphysical Lyrics and Poems of the Seventeenth Century* anthology of 1921 (swiftly followed by Eliot's exemplary revisionist essay-commentary on Grierson) canonically rectified.[33]

---

33 T. S. Eliot, 'The Metaphysical Poets'. First published in *The Times Literary Supplement*, 20 October 1921. In *Selected Prose of T S Eliot*, ed. Frank Kermode. (London: Faber, 1975), pp. 59–67.

Arnold's Wordsworth, *Women's Voices*, the *Yellow Book* and the mass dissemination of Palgrave's *Golden Treasury*, symbolise, as Christopher Ricks has appreciated, the changes, and counter-changes that characterise the late-Victorian period. It is an awareness of changeability heard above all in the dramatic monologue, a form diagnostic of the dissonances of the late period, but also of the true sound of the age as a whole.[34] The late-Victorian dramatic monologue not only engages with Matthew Arnold's 'dialogue of the mind with itself';[35] it subjects to critical scrutiny a myth of that which Stefan Collini has described as the 'moral harmony posited in the dominant culture [...] as a universal ethical condition'.[36] This is partly because the dramatic monologue 'allowed the unsayable [...] to be said and heard with impunity'—the cruelty of husbands to wives, the shameful prejudice and corruption at the heart of many trials.[37] Command of the mode is demonstrated admirably in the work of Browning, a poet formidably alert to the shifting culture of the author-reader relationship, and the poetic containment of the objectification (or drama) of psychological experience through ventriloquism and *personae*—which is why he would provide such an irresistible creative model for modernist writers, particularly for Ezra Pound. But the mode of the dramatic monologue is also appreciative, that is to say understanding of Victorian literature's formal ambivalences, and vocal and tonal complexities, releasing the subject from interiority and Romantic inversion.

Verse of the late part of the Victorian age is animated by that which Christina Rossetti describes as 'marvellous modern' movement: a protean fluidity of poetries, rather than a fixed sense of 'poetry'—or, indeed a fixed sense of 'the Novel'. As Valentine Cunningham observes:

> The keynote of Victorian culture and society is numerosity —
> bigness, density, multiplicity, mass-ness. This was
> 'the age of great cities', of massive agglomerations of people,
> huge productivity of things, vast fortunes and gigantic outputs
> of printed words—newspapers, books, novels, poems. There
> were more writers making their mark than ever before in Britain.[38]

---

34 Dramatic monologues were not confined to the late-Victorian period nor were they an innovation at this time of literary history; they were written throughout the whole of the Victorian era. This is a large subject beyond the scope of this introduction; however there are some exceptions and discriminations to be made; for example, some of Browning's dramatic monologues rhyme, and Eugene Lee-Hamilton writes dramatic monologues in sonnet form.
35 From Arnold's Preface to the First Edition of *Poems* (1853) in *The Complete Prose Works of Matthew Arnold*, ed. R. H. Super, eleven volumes (Ann Arbor: The University of Michigan Press, 1960–1977), i. 1. (*On the Classical Tradition*) Arnold writes of how 'the dialogue of the mind with itself has commenced; modern problems have presented themselves [...]'.
36 Stefan Collini, *Public Moralists: Political Thought and Intellectual Life in Britain 1850–1930* (Oxford: Clarendon, 1991), p. 90.
37 Andrew St George, *The Descent of Manners: Etiquette, Rules and the Victorians* (London: Chatto and Windus, 1993), p. 256.
38 Valentine Cunningham, *The Victorians: An Anthology of Poetry and Poetics* (Oxford: Blackwell, 2000), p. xxxv. For a comprehensive analysis of the period see Regenia Gagnier, *The Insatiability of Human Wants: Economics and Aesthetics in Market Society*. (Chicago: Chicago University Press, 2000).

This is not just a period of 'productivity' (in the quantitative sense of literature being produced); or even, in the Darwinian sense of the term, 'hyperproductivity'.[39] It is, for the first time in English literary history, a culture characterised now by re-productivity; an age where technological evolution allowed, among other things, the human voice to be recorded and mechanically heard again. 'The voice is inseparable from the person to whom it belongs,' writes Christina Rossetti in 1885.

> The voice which charms one generation is inaccessible to the next. Words cannot describe it, notes cannot register it; it remains a tradition, it lingers only as a regret; or, if by marvellous modern appliances stored up and re-uttered, we listen not to any imitative sound, but to a reproduction of the original voice.[40]

II. Versifications

> Come
> Home.
>
> George MacDonald
> ('The Shortest and Sweetest of Songs')

Many of the poetic modes of the late nineteenth century are themselves 'descendents' of earlier metrical forms—such as the *villanelle*, or the *rondeau*, or the *ballade*, all of which have their feet, as it were, in the past.[41] They carry the imprint, or 'indelible stamp', of these earlier poetries, but have evolved and adapted fresh patterns for a new age—and for the late Victorians, 'new' carried with it an additional connotation of 'artificial'.

> What am I? Ah, you know it,
> I am the modern Sage,
> Seer, savant, merchant, poet —
> I am, in brief, the Age.

---

39 For 'hyperproductivity' see the introduction to Gillian Beer, ed., Charles Darwin, *The Origin of Species* (Oxford World's Classics, 1996, rpt., 1998), p. xx.
40 Christina Rossetti, *Time Flies: A Reading Diary* (SPCK, 1885), p. 30. For further discussion of the trope of 'voice' with particular reference to later Rossetti see Alison Chapman, *The Afterlife of Christina Rossetti* (London: Macmillan, 2000), pp. 28–45.
41 Yopie Prins considers this question in 'Victorian meters' in Joseph Bristow, ed., *The Cambridge Companion to Victorian Poetry. (*Cambridge: Cambridge University Press, 2000). She comments how the 'publication of historical surveys and theoretical treatises on meter rose dramatically throughout the Victorian period, ranging from Edwin Guest's *A History of English Rhythms* (1838, revised 1882) to George Saintsbury's *History of English Prosody*' (1906–1910). Warwick Slinn's 'Experimental form in Victorian Poetry' in the same volume is more useful for earlier phases of nineteenth-century poetry as it focuses *inter alia* on the 'larger formal purpose' of Elizabeth Barrett Browning's work from the 1840s.

This could be about Victoria—or about Ruskin, Tennyson, Browning, Hardy, William Morris, Wilde or Yeats. Or, for that matter, Freud, Nietzsche or Comte.[42] Yet the 'modern Sage' here refers to Charles Darwin. These lines, as I mentioned in the preface, come from a poem called 'Solomon Redivivus' (1886) by Constance Naden, and play with the idea (caught in the mock-classical title) of kingship being brought back to life. 'Solomon Redivivus' is the final poem in Naden's sequence called 'Evolutional Erotics', the title given to a quartet of verses 'based loosely on an exploration of the impact of evolutionary theories on human courtship rituals'.[43] The poem teases Darwin through the convention of wisdom: the Solomon of Kings I and II, often accompanied by peacocks and apes, listed among his treasures, was also famed as a solver of riddles, through which his 'proverbial wisdom' was expressed.

Both Naden's and MacDonald's verses invite the reader to appreciate one of the most intriguing poetic riddles of this period: why, and how, does so much Victorian poetry rhyme? By now the heroic couplet, the spinal chord of eighteenth-century verse-anatomy, had fallen into decline, although William Morris, ever keen to recover lost English skills, made use of it in his earlier poetry (not, though, after 1860). Hardy too, in the 1890s, played around with the dactylic hexameter or 'heroic' line.[44] In his essay 'In Defence of Cosmetics', Beerbohm spoke of the 1890s as 'the elaborate era'. It is one of the many paradoxes of the period that a time of such fluidity, of things dissolving at the edges, is so taken with fixed verse forms.[45] Was it the sense of a ritual, more than the sense of an ending, these *fin-de-siècle* writers craved?[46]

However, more innovation and experimentation with rhyme characterises this late period than is recognised. The experimentalism with that which the poet Gerard Manley Hopkins called 'new words', and the coinage of 'old' words in new and unexpected contexts—religion/science, art *qua* craftsmanship/art *qua* technology—is characteristic of late-nineteenth-century language. Yet these are years not just of new words, and new poems, but of new languages—'new', again, with a peculiar connotation of 'artificial'. Esperanto, from the Spanish *esperanaza*, 'hope', was launched officially by L. L. Zamenhof in 1887. Volapük, Esperanto's short-lived predecessor, was proposed by J. M. Schleyer in 1879. More interestingly, however, it is the more intricate and dainty poetic forms that seem to have aroused a special fascination to the 'new' versifiers of this artifice-obsessed culture, such as

---

42 Comte's influence on the late-nineteenth-century mind was considerable. The first volume of *System of Positive Polity* was published in translation by John Henry Bridges in 1875. The first volume describes Comte's biological account of human emotion, the theory of the cerebral functions, which are analysed in terms of a progressive scale from egoism to altruism. Comte categorizes the egoistic functions in three stages, moving progressively towards the individual's awareness of and involvement in society. These ideas were influential on many literary figures of the period, especially Frederic Harrison, who was president from 1880–1905 of the English Positivist Committee, on the philosophy of Herbert Spencer and on George Eliot and Meredith.
43 Virginia Blain, *Victorian Women Poets: A New Annotated Anthology* (London: Longmans, 2001), p. 246.
44 See, for example, the poem 'In Tenebris III'. For further discussion see Dennis Taylor, *Hardy's Metres and Victorian Prosody* (Oxford: Clarendon Press, 1988), p. 262.
45 I am grateful to Daniel Karlin for provoking further thinking about this question.
46 Frank Kermode writes in *The Sense of an Ending* of the 'fin de siècle, where all the elements of the apocalyptic paradigm clearly co-exist.' Cited in R. K. R. Thornton, ed., *Poetry of the 'Nineties*. (Penguin, 1970), p. 226. For a broader account of verse in this period, see Joseph Bristow, ed., *The Fin-de-Siècle Poem: English Literary Culture and the 1890s*. (Athens, Ohio: Ohio University Press, 2005.)

the the triolet, the *rondeau* and the villanelle—rhyme as a form of dress (or fancy-dress). It was only natural for Beerbohm to dress up as Baudelaire as he claimed, 'Artifice is the strength of the world.'

The innovative impulse of late-Victorian poetry lies mainly, as it does in the art of the period, in revival. Revival, in theme, of classical subjects, like Tennyson's poem about his brother. Revival, in form, of the medieval world: old French fixed forms like the rondel, the *rondeau*, the triolet, the ballade, all common in the Middle Ages; and, in the 'Nineties especially, the villanelle (the origins of which are found in the Renaissance). There are other treasures from France that can be found in unexpected places, like *vireli,* an ancient Provençal verse form discovered by Dobson, but these are the principal forms. The stylistic innovation in rhymed poetry of the period, as distinct from adaptions and reworkings of existing forms, is the curtal sonnet (created by Hopkins in the 1870s); although the roundel, developed by Swinburne in the 1880s, has an inventive quality.

Much Victorian verse, including Swinburne's, celebrates the fun of rhyme, its versatility as a game; a feature of many other forms of poetry and related arts throughout the period. The popular success of W. S. Gilbert's libretti (of Gilbert and Sullivan) depends a good deal on his ear for absurd internal rhyme. The comic operetta *Patience* (1881) was conceived as a parody of the Aesthetic Movement, in which the lead characters are based on Wilde and Swinburne.

> If you're anxious for to shine in the high aesthetic line as a man of culture rare,
> You must get up all the germs of the transcendental terms, and plant them everywhere.
> You must lie upon the daisies and discourse in novel phrases of your complicated state of mind
> The meaning doesn't matter if it's only idle chatter of a transcendental kind.
>   And everyone will say,
>   As you walk your mystic way,
> 'If this young man expresses himself in terms too deep for *me,*
> Why what a very singularly deep young man this deep young man must be!'

Nursery rhyme, such as Robert Louis Stevenson's *A Child's Garden of Verses* (1885) and *vers de société* (occasional verse, often for light-hearted recital in public) make rhyme without making it utilitarian. The clerihew (invented by Edmund Clerihew Bentley in a boring Victorian chemistry lesson) and the limerick are other features of light verse of the age; part of the broad nineteenth-century reaction against didacticism in the late-Victorian period, although it would be misleading to suggest that there is no frivolity in the poetry of the 1840s and 1850s. Nonsense verse, such as Lewis Carroll's, questions 'sense', as do other classic 'laughable lyrics' created by Edward Lear; such as the 'Dong With a Luminous Nose' (1877); or 'The Jumblies', who, with admirable confidence, 'went to sea in a Sieve'—which—luckily for them—rhymes with 'live'.[47] Rhyme even erupts in the 'Thamuris marching' section of Browning's long poem 'Aristophanes' Apology' (1875), otherwise composed in blank verse. (The whole question of blank verse—unrhymed five-stress lines, properly in iambic pentameters—remains intriguing for the period.) This part of the poem reworks material from Browning's earlier 'Childe Roland to the Tower Came' from *Men and Women* (1855). Browning, whose faculty for rhyme impressed Tennyson greatly, said that he could make a rhyme for every word in the English

---

47 I am referring to the 6th edition of 1888.

language. So at a dinner Browning was given 'rhinoceros'.[48] The swiftest of 'Replies to Challenges in Rhyme' ensued:

> If you ever meet a rhinoceros
> And a tree be in sight
> Climb quick! for his might
> Is a match for the gods: he could toss Eros!

Yet another dimension to rhyme is its suitability for political purpose, its ease for mass appropriation, especially in the 'chant'. 'The March of the Workers' from William Morris's 'Chants for Socialists' (1885) depends on rhyme's simplicity and repetition for effect, combining Christian symbolism (the host) with a 'dance' that is military in form (the march). Morris instructed the following rhyme, with its refrain, to be sung to the tune of 'John Brown's Body':

> Hark the rolling of the thunder!
> Lo the sun! and lo there under
> Riseth wrath, and hope, and wonder,
>   And the host comes marching on.

A Victorian way of looking at rhyme could be in terms of an evolutionary relationship between cause and effect. The Camberwell poet Alfred Domett's verse, 'Fireworks', was published in 1877 (although composed in March 1874). An experimental chain of forty-five bony couplets, the poem engages with the hypothesis of the 'Missing Link'—those creatures assumed to be the evolutionary link between man and ape. Yet Domett puts a spin on it. The poem as a whole revolves as well as evolves, whirling its lines out like a Catherine-wheel. (The poem refers to 'flame-petals' in line 21.) The rush of such images—a dreaming speaker, a great crowd, the Missing Links, the Cambodian Temple, odious shapes, flat skulls—gives the verse a phantasmagoric as well as pyrotechnical element of surprise, and a troublesome note of imperialist propaganda. The image of the 'ruined Fane'—a 'Fane' is a temple—adds a squib of Gothic, at odds with the rest of the language. It is just one in a vast masquerade of images and ideas 'set before' the reader. The 'great crowd' is an emotive concept for this period of Empire:

> I dreamt. There was a great crowd gazing
> At fireworks set before them blazing.
>
> The crowd were 'Missing Links'; Cambodia's
> Great Temple shows no shapes more odious!;
>
> Flat skulls, flat brows, yet convex noses,
> Such as her ruined Fane discloses [. . .]

Late-nineteenth-century English religious verse, both Catholic and Anglican, worshipped at the altar of the rhyme revival. Palgrave's *Golden Treasury* was published the same year as the classic tome of Anglican hymnody, *Hymns Ancient and Modern* (1861) to which Palgrave himself contributed. These late-Victorian enthusiasms can make the twenty-first century reader forget how the singing of hymns at all, and to certain extent Church music in general, not so long ago had often been perceived as doctrinally dangerous; and also how

---

48 Robert Browning, *The Poems*, Vol. II. ed. Pettigrew, p. 1154.

the growth of hymn-singing and the writing and production of hymns by the Anglicans during the Victorian period masks the Nonconformist, dissenting roots of congregational hymn singing. The commercialisation and 'colonisation' of rhyme and hymn in the time of High Imperialism (for example, Dr Bridges's *Yattendon Hymnal* of 1899) is another intrinsically late-Victorian question. Other forms of religious lyric, notably the work of the Catholic poet Alice Meynell, Coventry Patmore and Francis Thompson illustrate degrees in the potential for stylistic movement within rhyme doxology. The poetic possibilities of the canticle, the antiphon and the prayer were to various degrees metrically exploited by Hopkins. The carol, in the wider European sense of a festive religious song (originally an Italian form—*carola*—later combining elements of the sixteenth-century French *noël* and the German *Weihnachtslied*) was, like the hymn, (from the Greek 'song in praise of a god or hero'), a poetic re-presentation in its own right throughout the nineteenth century, reviving a form which had dwindled since the Reformation. Christina Rossetti's 'In the Bleak Mid-Winter' is the most memorable carol of the period.

It is also paradoxical that at a time when English poetry is most visibly obsessed with fixity, with structures, *vers libre* comes into existence—a development with its origins in France. The metrical seeds of *vers libre* were sown during the 1872–1900 phase (Henley's *In Hospital* sequence is an example) and flower, eventually, post-1900, in the free verse of modernist poetry. *Vers libre* is 'free verse', or, more accurately, 'freed verse'. Taking its impetus chiefly from Verlaine in the 1880s—although Rimbaud, in *Marine* and *Mouvement* (1872–1873) could be said to have written some of the earliest French poems in free verse—the intention, originally to liberate French versification from Classical conventions, had growing influence throughout the later years of the nineteenth century on English poetic development, especially upon the decadents. (Jules Laforgue is a man to mention here.) The literary influence of France was pervasive in this period, extending beyond *vers libre*, and affecting English 'decadence' in several respects. Writing of Ernest Dowson, Arthur Symons, author of *The Symbolist Movement in Literature* (1899), commented that his 'care over English prose was like that of a Frenchman writing his own language with the respect that Frenchmen pay to French. Even English things had to come to him from France [. . .]'.[49] There are affinities here with the emergence of a genre during this time that was neither, strictly speaking, prose nor poem: the prose-poem, exemplified by Pater's debt, again, to Baudelaire.

The French fixed form with which Victorian poetry is most associated, especially in the 'Nineties and the *fin-de siècle*, is the villanelle (from *villano*, peasant, indicative of the rustic theme traditionally taken by this verse form.) Dowson's 'Villanelle of His Lady's Treasures', Wilde's 'Theocritus', or John Gray's 'Les Demoiselles de Sauve' are all supremely decadent moments, Dowson's combed below:

> Villanelle of His Lady's Treasures
>
> I took her dainty eyes, as well
> As silken tendrils of her hair:
> And so I made a Villanelle!

---

49 Arthur Symons, 'Ernest Dowson'. In Derek Stanford, *Writing of the Nineties: from Wilde to Beerbohm* (London: Dent [Everyman], 1971), p. 36.

This is setting itself up to be parodied, and both the villanelle's frivolity of form and subject as penned by male 'Decadent' poets are mocked by James Joyce in Stephen's lazy pseudo-'Nineties villanelle in chapter five of *A Portrait of the Artist as a Young Man* (1916):

> Are you not weary of ardent ways,
> Lure of the fallen seraphim?
> Tell no more of enchanted days.

However, late-Victorian poets danced beyond the villanelle. The rondel, with the *rondeau*, was one of Christina Rossetti's most effective modes, an enthusiasm shared by her contemporaries. Swinburne, Dobson, Robert Louis Stevenson, Henley, and Edmund Gosse all attempted one or other of them as well as Christina Rossetti.

> A Roundel is wrought as a ring or a starbright sphere,
> With craft of delight and with cunning of sound unsought,
> That the heart of the hearer may smile it to pleasure his ear
> A roundel is wrought.

That's a roundel, as writ, or, rather, as wrought by Swinburne, in his *A Century of Roundels* (1883). Technically distinct from the rondel and *rondeau*, although related to them, the roundel Swinburne developed consists of an eleven-line poem in three stanzas, the twice repeated refrain consisting of the opening lines of the poem. In this Swinburne was influenced by old French precedents; Charles d'Orléans wrote in roundels. Roundels, the rondel, and *rondeau*, are all circular forms, a poetic manifestation of the late-nineteenth-century preoccupation with the idea of eternal return and the broader concern with the relationship between originality and tradition.

The triolet, or 'little three' (a delightful French fixed form, originally consisting of eight lines and two rhymes, the first line repeated as the fourth, and the seventh, and the second as the eighth), attracted Henley and Dobson, and also Robert Bridges, notably, as this form is rare in English verse. (In French poetry of the nineteenth century, writers of triolets include Daudet and Théodore de Banville.) Female poets also experimented with the form, such as this beautifully controlled example from Emily Pfeiffer (who also wrote a long poem entitled 'A Rhyme for the Time'). 'Triolet' (1873) is the first from her sequence of 'Six Studies in Exotic Forms of Verse':

Triolet

> Warm from the wall she chose a peach
> She took the wasps for councillors;
> She said: 'such little things can teach:'
> Warm from the wall she chose a peach;
> She waved the fruit within my reach,
> Then passed it to a friend of hers: —
> Warm from the wall she chose a peach,
> She took the wasps for councillors.[50]

---

50 The text here is from the 2nd edn. of her collection *Gerard's Monument and Other Poems* (1878).

Late Victorian poets also excelled, more than in any other period of English literary history, in re-inventing another ancient and intricate form, the ballade. (A ballade differs structurally from the looser form of the ballad, as I will indicate.) Again, the ballade was a popular mediaeval form in France, perfected by Villon in the fifteenth century, ridiculed by Molière in the seventeenth, with an extremely complicated rhyme-scheme—difficult to produce in the English language under any circumstances given its inherent paucity of 'easy' rhymes. Nevertheless, several late-Victorian poets, including Henley, Swinburne and Amy Levy attempted the ballade, often for the ostensible purposes of 'light' verse. (As we recall, light verse is often used to mask darker concerns.) Titles can be deceptive: Levy's bold poem 'A Ballad of Religion and Marriage' is technically a ballade, as is 'The Ballad of Prose and Rhyme' (1878) by Dobson. Dobson at least gestures the reader to the more accurate subtitle of *Ballade à Double Refrain*. His verses follow the typical ballade schema of three eight-line stanzas (rhymed ababbcbc) followed by a four-line *envoi*. In each stanza the last line is repeated, so that it becomes a refrain.

Envoy

In the work-a-day world,—for its needs and woes,
There is place and enough for the pains of prose;
But whenever the May-bells clash and chime,
Then hey!—for the ripple of laughing rhyme!

Amy Levy's 'Ballade of an Omnibus' (1889) also follows the conventional ballade form. She adapts the rhyme scheme of her envoi, however, so that in her poem the envoi rhymes acac. (Usually the envoi of a ballade echoes the rhyme scheme bcbc, as in the Dobson poem.) In Levy's poem the refrain is the mock-solemn 'An omnibus suffices me'—a reference to the four-wheeled horse-drawn passenger bus which appeared in 1829 and which was still in use on London streets in the latter years of the nineteenth century. (The repetition mimics the fixed route of the bus.) Although not reproduced below, the poem has an epigraph ('To see my love suffices me') from Andrew Lang's *Ballades in Blue China* (1880, 1881).

Ballade of an Omnibus

Some men to carriages aspire;
On some the costly hansoms wait;
Some seek a fly, on job or hire;
Some mount the trotting steed, elate.
I envy not the rich and great,
A wandering minstrel, poor and free,
I am contented with my fate—
An omnibus suffices me.

In common with other poets, female and male, Levy used the deceptive levity of the ballade form to present serious social concerns: 'Ballade of an Omnibus' has a sardonic touch, in its treatment of how travel is determined by class and social status. 'Some men to carriages aspire', while the poor poet can only afford the bus. May Kendall's 'Woman's Future' (1887), gaining confidence from the 'New Woman' movement, similarly confronts political issues. This poem is a mutant variant of ballade—with four stanzas rather than three. After the final prophetic stanza its feminist 'Envoy' shoots from the hip:

> On Fashion's vagaries your energies strewing,
>   Devoting your days to a rug or a screen,
> Oh, rouse to a lifework—do something worth doing!
>   Invent a new planet, a flying-machine.
> Mere charms superficial, mere feminine graces,
>   That fade or that flourish, no more you may prize;
> But the knowledge of Newton will beam from your faces,
>   The soul of a Spencer will shine in your eyes.

Envoy

> Though jealous exclusion may tremble to own us,
>   Oh, wait for the time when our brains shall expand!
> When once we're enthroned, you shall never dethrone us—
>   The poets, the sages, the seers of the land!

How does this differ from the ballad (another poetic form of great antiquity)? The ballad remains popular in its two main forms in the late-Victorian period: both the anonymous folk ballad (urbanised in this industrial age into the 'street ballad'), belonging to an oral tradition, and the literary ballad—which is written down—such as Wilde's 'Ballad of Reading Gaol By C.3.3' (written 1897–1898), one of the most notorious of the age, or Kipling's 'Danny Deever' (1890). Wilde's title alludes to his cell number.

    Characteristic of the experimental nature of the period, the ballad (from the Italian ballare, to dance) also varies its steps. Traditionally the ballad consists of a quatrain, or four-line stanza, containing alternating four-stress and three-stress lines (rhyming abcb or abab) often with a refrain. The decadent poet Richard Le Gallienne's 'Ballad of London' follows the traditional form. The verses suggest a view of the metropolis which contrasts sharply with the sordid London of Dickens, Besant and Gissing in fiction and the hellish London depicted in many poems of the time, such as those by Coventry Patmore and Henry Bellyse Baildon. The aesthetic life must have got the better of Le Gallienne when he wrote:

> Ah, London! London! our delight,
> Great flower that opens but at night,
> Great City of the Midnight Sun
> Whose day begins when day is done.

Reverting to the cold realist light of day, and to some of the uglier crimes of the capital, Kipling's characteristically soldierly poem 'Danny Deever' adapts this format:

> 'What are the bugles blowin' for?' said Files-on-Parade.
> 'To turn you out, to turn you out,' the Colour Sergeant said.
> 'What makes you look so white, so white?' said Files-on-Parade.
> 'I'm dreadin' what I've got to watch,' the Colour-Sergeant said.

> For they're hangin' Danny Deever, you can hear the Dead March play,
> The regiment's in 'ollow square—they're hangin' him to-day;
> They've taken of his buttons off an' cut his stripes away,
> An' they're hangin' Danny Deever in the mornin'.

Dedicated to the memory of a wife-murderer, Charles Thomas Wooldridge, 'The Ballad of Reading Gaol' is even more harrowing, with its details of Victorian prison executions. The 'quicklime' on the boots of the prison warders recalls how corpses of inmates were covered in the substance (calcium oxide) to hasten the decomposition process. Again, the question of 'Time' figures throughout this poem. The 'prison-clock' in lines 379–384 tolls death, but it also compounds the sense of previous stanzas, suggesting the bell of St Lawrence Church, Reading, which started tolling at 7.45 a.m. and continued until after 8 a.m., the time designated for executions ('For the stroke of eight is the stroke of Fate').[51] No wonder Wilde's ballad is stuck on the depressing treadmill of a six-line stanza. To 'do time' is to 're-do' it, for eternity. The following are not consecutive stanzas; there is another smote between them:

> We waited for the stroke of eight:
>   Each tongue was thick with thirst:
> For the stroke of eight is the stroke of Fate
>   That makes a man accursed,
> And Fate will use a running noose
>   For the best man and the worst.
>
> With sudden shock the prison-clock
>   Smote on the shivering air,
> And from all the gaol rose up a wail
>   Of impotent despair,
> Like the sound that frightened marshes hear
>   From some leper in his lair.

Probably the last thing on the minds of inmates was the question of poetic innovation of the period (as distinct from renovation). In keeping with the late-Victorian attraction to elaborately rhyming forms, a claim to originality is the curtal sonnet of Gerard Manley Hopkins. I glanced earlier at Hopkins's 'Watch': and the observation of how, among several unusual features, the first quatrain of this sonnet does not set the scene, a departure from the conventional Shakespearean and Petrarchan sonnet. The experimental possibilities afforded by the sonnet had been revived throughout the post-Romantic period, and 1872–1900 is rich in this respect, with poets writing heterogeneous sonnets that are neither wholly Shakespearean ('the English sonnet'), nor Petrarchan ('the Italian sonnet'). In keeping with a culture which liked not just things, but lots of things, a feature of this time is the sonnet *sequence*. The major example of the period is Christina Rossetti's 'Monna Innominata' although she also wrote a sequence of three sonnets called 'The Thread of Life' (1881) and another exercise, 'Later Life: A Double Sonnet of Sonnets'. George Eliot's 'Brother and Sister' sonnets (1874) and Robert Bridges's *The Growth of Love* (1876), Dante Gabriel Rossetti's Petrarchan *Sonnets from the House of Life* (1881) and Augusta Webster's unfinished 'Mother and Daughter' sequence, published posthumously in 1895, are all examples of the genre.

---

51 Valentine Cunningham, *The Victorians*, p. 954.

(Augusta Webster also wrote *rispetti*, showing again the variety of rhyme patterns creatively explored throughout the age, by female poets as well as male poets.)[52]

'Spelt from Sibyl's Leaves' is another of Hopkins's sonnets: an experiment of brilliant eccentricity, combining the inherent durability of the alexandrine, the longest line in 'normal' use in the French language, with the syncopations of 'Sprung-Rhythm'. ('Spelt from Sibyl's Leaves' was written in 1885, at around the same time as 'To his Watch', although not published, like the majority of Hopkins poems, until 1918.) In the summer of 1877, however, Hopkins claimed to have invented an original form, the 'Curtal sonnet', exemplified in his poem 'Pied Beauty' which begins 'Glory be to God for dappled things —'. As W. H. Mackenzie points out, the 'curtal sonnet' is 'compressed, not simply cut short':[53] it consists, as in the case of 'Pied Beauty', of a reduction of the normal octave (that is, two quatrains) into two tercets rhyming abcabc (things/cow/swim; wings/plough/trim). Hopkins wrote 'Pied Beauty' in 'sprung paeonic rhythm'—a rhythm (until Hopkins) rare in English verse. A term deriving from Classical prosody, the 'paeon' is a foot of one stressed and three unstressed syllables. (Hopkins's poem 'The Windhover', a version of experiment with the sonnet form, is paeonic.)

There are sonnets in the late-Victorian period that follow convention more closely than Hopkins's poetry. Yet even with sonnets that at first sight seem to be traditional in form, and in some respects are, there are often subtle resistances to conforming entirely, in content as well as in form. L. S. Bevington's sonnet 'Am I To Lose You?' (1882) is faintly 'Shakespearean', with a closing couplet that technically rounds off the propositions in the three preceding quatrains. Emotionally, though, the sonnet, like its title, leaves the 'argument' of the poem unresolved:

> What is your answer? Mine must ever be,
> 'I greatly need your friendship: leave it me.'

It is typical of the period for some sonnets to fuse elements of different conventions. For example, a final 'Shakespearean' rhyming couplet in a sonnet form that is more akin to the French sonnet *renversé* (or 'upside-down sonnet'), with the sestet (the last six lines) on top of the octave. The Hertfordshire poet Gerald Massey's 'Only a Dream' (1889), a poem about the nightmare of marriage for many Victorian women under English law, turns away from the traditional place of sonnets as *amoretti*. Love poem as 'legal lust' poem: Massey's rhyme scheme proposes abaaab ccddeeff, and a dismally unseductive resolution at the poem's vicious end:

> She must show black and blue, or no divorce
> Is granted by the Law of Physical Force.

The 'Petrarchan' sonnet appears to be the form with which most poets of the period experimented artistically, presumably for its versatility.[54] Eugene Lee-Hamilton was the

---

52 See notes to Augusta Webster's poem 'Marjory: English Stornelli' in Valentine Cunningham, ed., *The Victorians: An Anthology of Poetry and Poetics* (Oxford: Blackwell, 2000), p. 769. *Rispetti* are '8-line stanzas, as here, lines 1–4 rhyming alternately, lines 5–8 rhyming in pairs'.

53 W. H. Mackenzie, *A Reader's Guide to Gerard Manley Hopkins* (London: Thames and Hudson, 1981), p. 228.

54 I have not come across any Spenserian sonnets in the late-Victorian period, although the nine-line Spenserian stanza was evidently influential as a narrative form upon Keats, Byron and Shelley. Yeats writes in *ottava rima*, a stanzaic form related to Spenser's innovation – 'Sailing to Byzantium' and 'Among School Children' are in *ottava rima*—but not in his early poetry.

most productive. Although bedridden for twenty years after a physical and mental breakdown (hence, alas, 'wingless'), he sonneteered, tirelessly: like the perfectly Petrarchan 'What the Sonnet Is' (1894) from his collection *Sonnets of the Wingless Hours* (1894):

> Fourteen small broidered berries on the hem
>   Of Circe's mantle, each of magic gold;
>   Fourteen of lone Calypso's tears that roll'd
> Into the sea, for pearls to come of them;
>
> Fourteen clear signs of omen in the gem
>   With which Medea human fate foretold;
>   Fourteen small drops, which Faustus, growing old,
> Craved of the Fiend, to water Life's dry stem.
>
> It is the pure white diamond Dante brought
>   To Beatrice; the sapphire Laura wore
> When Petrarch cut it sparkling out of thought;
>
> The ruby Shakespeare hewed from his heart's core;
>   The dark deep emerald that Rossetti wrought
> For his own soul, to wear for evermore.

Charles Tennyson Turner's lovely 'Letty's Globe' (1880) is Petrarchan, but experiments with the rhyme-scheme of the sestet (bliss/eye/cry/there/kiss/hair). Robert Browning's 'Why I am A Liberal' (1885) is brazenly Petrarchan, and, unusually, rhymes the opening word of the octave with the closing word of the sestet (attractively for Browning, this word happens to be 'Why?'). And although the question posed by the start of the sonnet is answered decisively at the end ('That is why'), there is more politics than poetry at stake. 'THAT LITTLE IS ACHIEVED THROUGH LIBERTY' (the capitalized second line of Browning's sestet) is antithetical to the eye as well as to the ear, although that was how this is meant to be, since this sonnet was first published as the 'lead' statement in a book entitled *Why I am A Liberal, Being Definitions by the Best Minds of the Liberal Party* edited by Andrew Reid. (Browning's sonnet-advertisement appeared immediately before Gladstone's contribution.) Mathilde Blind's 'Manchester by Night' (1893) is also Petrarchan, although in this case the sestet is separated from the octave rather than forming one solid block of poem. Yet, even with Blind's sonnet, one could argue that while the form is conventional, the presentation of the subject is not. Traditionally the first eight lines of a Petrarchan sonnet present the thesis of the poem and the sestet resolves it. (Say, Sir Thomas Wyatt's 'The pillar perisht is whereto I leant', which is also a translation of Petrarch.) Blind's poem, by contrast, leaves the reader with an overwhelming feeling, so true throughout this time, of the impossibility of harmony: the structural problem of Manchester remains at the end of the poem, as the structural problem of England remains at the end of the age. All that division of labour had produced was division of souls.

So full circle: one of the conventions of rhyme is a structure of expectation through proposal and answer, a structure of expectation which had become progressively shattered as nineteenth-century determinism took its dissonant, modernizing course. As the century turned, so did the verse. Playing with the politics and aesthetics of rhyme is one of the ways that English poetry of the late-Victorian period comes to terms with its own voicing;

and to an extent, its sub-vocality, which will emerge on a towering scale with *The Waste Land*. The dissonance is registered in the shortest poem of the period—one of the best short poems in the English language, George MacDonald's 'The Shortest and Sweetest of Songs' (1892):

> Come
> Home.

Desire/death, this poem beckons towards speech, while falling short of its own storytelling, relying on slant-rhyme to propose only to unanswerability. If there is one last line to remember about the Victorians, it is a song that has been much rehearsed but is worth hearing again, however faint the echo, the degree to which these physical and metaphysical uncertainties touched the apprehension (and apprehensiveness) of daily nineteenth-century living, dying, dreaming, writing, and thinking; in ways that the post-secular culture of the twenty-first century at times can barely hope to grasp. The 'sunless gulfs of doubt' that wracked Tennyson and his contemporaries—the word 'agnostic' was coined by T. H. Huxley in 1869—sound and re-sound; each 're-sounding' widening or closing the 'gulfs' of recognition between how fiction and poetry wanted things to be and how in fact things were. It may be overstating the case to say that during these valedictory, evanescent years the writer's moral relation to language actually changed, but, in Yeatsian eyes, it could be transformed:

> I see, indeed, in the arts of every country those faint lights
> and faint colours and faint outlines and faint energies which
> many call 'the decadence', and which I, because I believe that
> the arts lie dreaming of things to come, prefer to call the
> autumn of the body.

Yet by 1903 Yeats had lost patience with his theory of the autumn of the body: even those keener than most to glimpse Byzantium come home to how precarious in the modern world that relation will be.

III. Fictions of Empire and the City

> It has been alleged that Africa labours under a natural incapacity for civilization [...]
>
> William Pitt the Younger (1792), quoted by Henry Stanley in 1890

The fiction of this period as well as the poetry shows how not just moral but political complications had arisen for Victoria's writers, not only in terms of England but in terms of Empire. High Imperialism, Bloody Sunday, the intricacies of Irish nationalism, the Turkish Question, Anglo-Indian political relations, the Boer War: the last thirty years of the nineteenth century was a turbulent time for an England that could no longer be perceived as insular, whether in terms of foreign or domestic policy. 'With empire came war,' write Isobel Armstrong and Joseph Bristow, and 'with war came many writings engaging with the unseen psychological terrors and visible legacies of military conflict, by women and by men.'⁵⁵ Many Victorians would have disliked this remark, because there was no official European 'war' between 1815 and 1914 and no doubt Queen Victoria would have seen her role as 'head of the family' as the significant contributory factor in keeping the fiction of 'peace'. Yet as Edward Said notes in *Culture and Imperialism* (1993), the concept of the 'little war' (as opposed to the notion of 'major war') arose in accordance with the rise of empire: 'little' wars were fought throughout the nineteenth century and in the post-1872 period there were conflicts, often arising from unresolved wars of the previous years.⁵⁶ A common feature of Victorian High imperialist discourse is the Roman invasion of Britain, setting a moral precedent for English colonial policy—an irony being that when the Romans arrived in 54 BCE their legions would have included soldiers from North Africa, and the Angles and the Saxons would not arrive for several more centuries.⁵⁷ This is a significant feature of Conrad's *Heart of Darkness*. *The Times* of 4 October 1892 reported the following speech by Henry M. Stanley, the man who had 'found' the celebrated missionary David Livingstone on Lake Tanganyika in 1871, and author of the book *In Darkest Africa* (1890); Stanley's voice in turn approvingly quotes a speech made by the British Prime Minister William Pitt the Younger in 1792:

> It has been alleged that Africa labours under a natural incapacity for civilisation [. . .] Allow of this principle as applied to Africa, and I should be glad to know why it might not also have been applied to ancient and uncivilised Britain. Why might not some Roman Senator have predicted with equal boldness—'There is a people destined never to be free, a people depressed by the hand of nature below the level of the human species, and created to form a supply of slaves for the rest of the world'? Sir, we were once as obscure among the nations of the earth, as debased by our morals, as savage in our manners, as degraded in our understandings as these unhappy Africans at present.⁵⁸

By the turn of the century, the British Empire had expanded hugely, having colonised Burma, the Pacific, Egypt, and southern Africa. British control of the Suez Canal was secured in 1875—not by Gladstone, but by the Tory Disraeli, who had won a resounding victory for the Conservatives the previous year. In 1900, the six colonies of Australia became a Commonwealth; Canada had become a Dominion in 1867 (New Zealand had been part of the British Empire since 1840). The title 'Queen-Empress of India' had been bestowed

---

55 Isobel Armstrong and Joseph Bristow, eds., *Nineteenth-Century Women Poets* (Oxford: Blackwell, 1996), p. xxviii.
56 See Edward Said, *Culture and Imperialism* (London: Chatto, 1993), p. 126. Two British overseas campaigns towards the later part of the century besides the Boer War were in West Africa in 1874 and in Egypt in 1882; there were also the two Afghan wars.
57 The connotations of 'Roman' in the Victorian period are also significant for Arnold, in terms of his views of the state; see Stefan Collini, *Matthew Arnold: A Critical Portrait* (Oxford: Clarendon Press, 1988; 1994), p. 91.
58 Cited by Cedric Watts in his 1990 Oxford World's Classics Edition of *Heart of Darkness*, and reprinted by Robert Hampson in his 1995 Penguin edition of the novel (rpt. 2000), p. 128.

upon Victoria (again by Disraeli) in 1876: the Queen celebrated this personally by acquiring her own Indian servant after the 1877 Jubilee celebrations when Indian royalty was in attendance. In addition to these territorial affiliations, by the end of her reign Victoria had been related either by marriage or directly to the royal houses of Germany, Russia, Greece, Romania, Sweden, Denmark, Norway and Belgium. The imperial rhetoric of King Leopold II of Belgium in particular, symbolising white supremacy over the non-white population, is again ironised in Conrad's fiction.[59] In his capacity as laureate Tennyson wrote several verses on Empire, especially during the years of High Imperialism. 'Hands All Round' (1882) was composed for Victoria's birthday, and set to music by Tennyson's wife Emily, and a poem written in 1886 to celebrate the 'Opening of the Indian and Colonial Exhibition' by the Queen bore the refrain, 'Britons, hold your own!' and the command 'Sons be welded each and all,/Into one imperial whole'. The subtle resistance of a perfect rhyme ('all'/'whole') though, leaves a lingering timbre of unease.

It is pertinent to mention one novel by an author who is also a poet. W. H. Mallock's *The New Republic* (1876) was written at the age of twenty-eight, and set the scene for his later *Critical Examination of Socialism* (1909), an attack on Marx, whose *Capital* had been published in 1867.[60] The interest of Mallock's work for literary criticism has persisted well into the twentieth century, notably in the writing of Raymond Williams, who viewed the 'fragile brilliance' of *The New Republic* as 'as good a starting point for this period as could be found'.[61] This novel/*roman à clef* brings together a group of key figures from the period's intellectual history, Arnold (Mr Luke), Pater (Mr Rose), Ruskin (Mr Herbert), Jowett (Dr Jenkinson), as well as figures representing Herbert Spencer and Violet Fane, all of whom attend a weekend house-party where they discuss their different versions of an ideal republic. It is not a detective novel—but it could be, as the reader is implicated here as in a murder-mystery weekend, guessing who or what killed the body politic. The second chapter of the third book is the one Williams found most useful for understanding not just the scepticism but the 'valedictory' (Williams's word) mood of the age. Valediction: the act, and art, of bidding farewell. In the second half of the nineteenth century, a culture of loss, a second wave of the bereavement experienced by the earlier Victorian poets at Romanticism's sudden death, still prevails. But arguably now the grief is harder: in this period it was not farewell to others; as England underwent changes unprecedented in any other era, it became farewell to the self. Jonathan Dollimore writes that 'there is residual

---

59 In September 1876 King Leopold II began his geographical conference on Central Africa with the words: 'To open to civilisation the only part of our globe where it has yet to penetrate, to pierce the darkness which envelopes whole populations, it is, I dare to say, a crusade worthy of this century of progress.' In Thomas Pakenham, *The Scramble for Africa* (Weidenfeld and Nicolson, 1991; Abacus, 1992), p. 21. Cited in Robert Hampson's Penguin edition of Conrad's *Heart of Darkness*, p. 132.

60 Marx and Engels are not represented in this anthology of 'English' literature, but, as with Comte, Nietzsche, Bergson and Freud, their significant works should be consulted by anyone open to the forces shaping the intellectual history, the theory and the practice of the late-Victorian 'darkling' age or the culture out of which poems and prose such as those included or excluded here emerged.

61 Raymond Williams, *Culture and Society 1780–1950*, (London: Chatto, 1958, rpt., Penguin, 1961, 1982), p. 166.

terror in the seductive encounter with non-being'.[62] No part of the nineteenth century was to be more dis-orientated by this encounter than late-Victorian England.

As so often in this period, public disquiet was mirrored in the Queen's personal unrest. In 1861, Prince Albert of Saxe-Coburg, Queen Victoria's husband, had died of typhoid. Loss of spouse precipitated the monarch into a legendary grief and psychological stasis that would paralyse the late phase of her reign. She withdrew from public events for a quarter of a century, until the Jubilee Celebrations of 1887. With bereavement came a festering of resentment towards her eldest son. Edward's liaison with an Irish actress had plagued Albert on his deathbed. It was one of several high-profile affairs, which, to the Queen's mortification, surrounded the royal name with scandal for the rest of the century. (Would she have been aware of her son's public nickname 'Edward the Caresser'?) Edward was never forgiven. After his father's death he was, stubbornly, refused any share in government, continuing a Hanoverian tradition of suspicion towards the heir-apparent. This in turn is an enactment of a repetition, a phenomenon that would in due course interest Freud, of that which Victoria herself had faced in 1837, when the spectacle of a woman taking the throne unsettled the cultural prejudices of Hanoverian Salic Law (which decreed that no woman could inherit the throne).[63] When William IV died in 1837, it was assumed that Victoria would be incapable. Revenge was re-enacted upon her eldest child after his father's death, as well as in many ways to do with Empire. In *Beyond the Pleasure Principle*, Freud had to look no further than to the English Royal Family during the nineteenth century for classic instances of repetitive child's play.

It is one of the many unsettling nuances in this literature how the word for leaving, 'departure', a word Hopkins chooses in the poem 'To his Watch', coincides with a discreet Victorian euphemism for death. The grief-stricken Victoria departed London for Windsor, or retired to the estate she had had built in the Scottish Highlands beside Loch Muick in the late 1860s. (She despaired even of Balmoral, and, on the Isle of Wight, Osborne, retreats she had purchased early on in her reign.) The unprecedented growth of the railway and branch lines enabled her to journey as no monarch before her; several of the poems and novels included here are about travel, 'time-travel' especially. Buckingham Palace, which after Albert's death became redundant and abandoned for nearly forty years, became referred to by Edward as 'the Sepulchre'.[64] Its pale sepulchral shadow—the empty rooms, a sense of being suddenly out of scale, an unbearable vacancy—falls over the poetry, the novels and the art. The stark silhouette of the handful of 'chiselled white' flowers in the poem 'Cyclamens' (1893) by Katherine Harris Bradley and Edith Emma Cooper—who collaborated under the masculine pen-name 'Michael Field'—is an image that cuts into this sombre, tomb-like

---

62 Jonathan Dollimore, *Death, Desire and Loss in Western Culture* (London: Penguin, 1998), p. 150.
63 The Queen's accession finally separated England from Germany, reflected symbolically in the removal of the German coat of arms from the English—as remains the case today.
64 See Matthew 23: 27–8 'Woe unto you, scribes and Pharisees, hypocrites! For ye are like unto whited sepulchres, which indeed appear beautiful outward, but are within full of dead men's bones, and of all uncleanness.' The Biblical passage is reverberative for Conrad, with Marlow's description of 'a city that always makes me think of a whited sepulchre'. In Robert Hampson's Penguin edition of *Heart of Darkness*, p. 24.

atmosphere. If Queen Victoria were at home these are just the kind of flowers one would expect to find:

Cyclamens

> They are terribly white:
> There is snow on the ground,
> And a moon on the snow at night;
> The sky is cut by the winter light;
> Yet I, who have all these things in ken,
> Am struck to the heart by the chiselled white
> Of this handful of cyclamen.

There are many sleepless poems in these years, where, as the Queen found, the house is too big, or too small, or too like a prison, a hospital or an asylum (psychic as well as physical constructions for the Victorians). Or too burdened with memories as to become uninhabitable: poems that shy away from the widowed present to the wedded securities of the past.[65] Two ancient forces, *Eros* and *Thanatos*, intransigent but symbiotic, structure this literature. Death, or dying, abound as subjects in poems across the entire period, from Alice Meynell's 'Parted' (1876) to Tennyson's 'Crossing the Bar' (1889). Many poems take winter or autumn as their theme, painting, like Whistler, 'nocturnes'. The Scots poet William Renton writes the following poem 'After Nightfall' (1876)—although it could well have been called 'After Goethe', since the German poet's 'Uber allen Gipfeln/Ist Ruh' looms behind it. Perhaps this is why Renton chooses to not make things rhyme at the end of the line, and instead sets up unpredictable patterns of assonance and dissonance within the body of the poem (peaks/within the peaks [. . .] air/hour/clear [. . .] self/self-surrender/selfless self-approval). The conflict between Self and Nature is figured through the language of Empire ('mountain thrones'), and its shifting vocabulary of power and control (abnegation, obeisance, surrender, approval).

> Ample the air above the western peaks;
> Within the peaks a silence uncompelled.
> It is the hour of abnegation's self,
> In clear obeisance of the mountain thrones,
> And cloudless self-surrender of the skies:
> The very retrospect of skiey calm,
> And selfless self-approval of the hills.

Victoria's disaffection with London grew. The late period of the nineteenth century shows the displacement of London, the shift in metropolitan topography *away* from London. To Manchester, most obviously, but also, pre-figuring Eliot's 'Unreal City' of the Modernist *Waste Land*, towards the disturbingly unspecified, ungeneric location of Edward Carpenter's 'Manufacturing Town'—which could now be anywhere—or the urban nightmare figured in Thomson's 'City of Dreadful Night'. When novels and poems deal with London in the

---

[65] Not all Victorian poetry shares this view of Victoria. Kipling's Barrack-Room Ballad, 'The Widow at Windsor', sees the widow as powerful and energetic.

late-nineteenth-century period, it is often to emphasise the loneliness, cruelty, estrangement and Tennysonian vastness of the city, its capacity for human exploitation, the absence of community and fracturing of personal identity which unregulated and sordid urban development had brought about—rather than the glittering, progressive London of the 1851 Great Exhibition celebrated in mid-Victorian literature, unified under one roof before the world. Coventry Patmore's unhappy cameo about a dismal city hanging bears this out (dismal, like *The Waste Land's* sex in the city, in its routine violence), as does Henry Bellyse Baildon's poem 'Alone in London' (1877) about a destitute woman:

> By her fault or by ill-fate,
> Left in great London, desolate
> Of helpers and comforters,
> Without one heart to beat with hers, —
> Without one hand in tenderness
> And sympathy her hand to press, —
> A lone soul, left dispassionate,
> Without one link of love or hate.

Metropolitan unease is felt in Belloc's guilty 'verse-philanthropy' on London poverty, 'The Poor of London' (1896), and in Arthur Symons; even in Victor Plarr's *fin-de-siècle* piece about gleaming Greenwich—literally a safe haven. Here, 'Far out' (the first words of the poem), the speaker watches a ship glide in darkness on the Thames, not into London, a city of 'grim formless features [...]/big with life *and doom*' (my italics), but *away* from it, out to the North Sea. It could be out of Africa; London had become its own dark continent. The binding spell of 'Far-Far-Away' (1889), a Tennysonian preoccupation, is felt throughout the period. Katharine Tynan's 'The Foggy Dew' (1901) sees London but longs for Ireland. Yeats's homesickness for 'The Lake Isle of Innisfree' from his early collection *The Rose* (1893), is triggered by Fleet Street, shamelessly.[66]

Fear of London, the emergence of a late-Victorian mistrust of the commercialised world-empire, is felt in Richard Jeffries's novel tellingly entitled *After London* or in Walter Besant's 'slum school fiction', *All Sorts and Conditions of Men: An Impossible Story* (1882), set in the East End, a curious twist on the mid-Victorian 'condition-of-England'/social-problem novel.[67] An impossible story: even by 1882 this is what London and Victoria's Empire had become. Gissing shows the misery of struggling London authors in *New Grub Street* (1891). In *The Nether World* (1889) the novelist is far more drawn to the subject's potential for phantasmagoria than to realism. Nominally, like Besant's, *The Nether World* explores the East End, but Gissing's eschatology transforms the recognisably Dickensian landscape of nineteenth-century London into the nether world of Dante's Hell (conceived always in Dante as a doleful *city*, a 'città dolente'), the 'layers' of London like the circles of an *Inferno*,

---

66 For the importance of London to some of the minor poets of the period, especially James Thomson, see Paul Turner, ed., *Victorian Poetry, Drama, and Miscellaneous Prose 1832–1890*. Vol. XIV of *The Oxford History of English Literature* (Oxford: Oxford University Press, 1989, rpt., 1990), p. 177.
67 For a survey of these and other minor late-Victorian novelists see Michael Wheeler, *English Fiction of the Victorian Period 1830–1890* (London: Longmans, 1985, rev. ed. 1994).

its *topos* a 'city of the damned, such as thought never conceived before this age of ours'.[68] This will remain a controlling Victorian metaphor up to Eliot; the epigraph to *The Love Song of J. Alfred Prufrock* (1917) from *Inferno* 27, addressed to Dante by one of the damned souls (in the form of a flame, a human inferno), effectively warns the reader that walking through this poem/city will be like walking through an inescapable hell. ('If I thought you'd go back and tell the world what it's like here,' the damned soul tells Dante, 'I wouldn't tell you anything, but because no one ever leaves hell, I don't mind answering you; I know you'll never return to let on what you've seen.')[69] James Thomson's 'The City of Dreadful Night' takes its Italian epigraph from Dante: 'This way forward for the sorrowful city'—the inscription at the entrance of Hell from *Inferno*, Canto III. i.

On an historically unprecedented scale, fear of Hell, dread of the city, masked fear of 'the poor'. The subjection of the individual to the economy of the mass is a development of the period. Not the 'rural poor', those quiescent individuals left outside the cities, who were pitied and patronised as industrial progress left them behind (an undercurrent of *Middlemarch*), but the urban 'poor', an entirely new and frightening English phenomenon. Fear of mass movement, of the underclass now teeming in the metropolis—suspicion of democracy and the supremacy of the liberal subject only years before espoused by Mill—spread like Indian cholera among the white 'middle classes'.[70] The city began to be equated with another kind of defilement, with miasmic spiritual sickness; a promiscuous, blasphemous, morally degenerate abyss made up of a lying, slovenly, lazy 'working class'. In 1889 the social reformer Charles Booth compiled a new map, 'The Descriptive Map of London Poverty'. Each area of London was 'colour-coded' and graded street by street: gold, pink and red for the affluent areas; dark blue and black for the slums. Here, Booth believed, was the real heart of the Inferno, the 'vicious' class of casual workers, some of them 'foreigners'—Jews, blacks, the Chinese—who were not only poor, but degenerate. To the north of the Edgware Road lay one of the darkest shadings; an area, like much of London today, situated eerily next to rose-coloured respectability. By the 1870s Paddington was reaping the benefits of a canal that had been built at the turn of the nineteenth century, and now at the end of it, a spectacular new railway terminus. On Praed Street St Mary's Hospital occupied a comparatively salubrious site, yet quivered on the border of one of the most

---

68 Stephen Gill has drawn attention to the points of contact and departure between Dickens and Gissing in his World's Classics introduction to Gissing's *The Nether World* (Oxford: Oxford University Press, 1992) pp. xx–xxi.
69 Dante, *Inferno* 27, pp. 61–67. For an offical translation see *The Divine Comedy* [Parallel Text translated by John D. Sinclair] (Oxford: Oxford University Press, 1939, rpt. 1961). The idea of the corrupt city (or, in fact, cities) is central to Canto 27 (in turn situated within the broader Dantesque concept of the city as a site of deception and exile) and to *The Divine Comedy*: Guido da Montefeltro (c. 1220–1298), the damned soul with whom Dante holds his conversation, was captain general of the Ghibellines in the Romagna part of Italy before he was exiled; the cities of the Romagna were in constant turmoil during the thirteeenth century. This canto recalls their struggle for power and the corrupt and evil practices that held sway while they were all at loggerheads.
70 The word 'middle-class', denoting the class of society between the 'upper' and the 'lower' class, dates from 1812. By 1893, the term had acquired a depreciative connotation.

deprived areas of London. Here in 1874, C. R. Alder Wright, a chemistry lecturer at St Mary's, came up with a new configuration of opium alkaloid: boiling morphine with acetic anhydride to create diacetylmorphine: heroin, the 'Hamlet of cough mixtures', was born.

'Heroin' (it was not given its tragic name until 1898) was not 'just' a dangerous drug which was widely available. It was an element in a constellation of addictive ideas. One of them was that 'the poor' took drugs or opium-based preparations, not for medicinal purposes, but, rather, in order to be deviant and, more unacceptably, for pleasure. Heroin's pervasiveness from 1872–1900, its relation to late-Victorian constructions of 'degeneracy', 'race', 'poverty' and 'Empire', as well as medical discourse, is a part of the cultural history of the late-nineteenth-century. Like electricity, heroin was both visible and yet unseen: an elusive ethos which defines the period, yet a ubiquitous presence. (Gladstone, it was reputed, took laudanum in his coffee every morning before he could face addressing the House of Commons.) I mentioned how Queen Victoria's bereavement pervades the period, as well as the deaths of Dickens, Browning and Tennyson within a few years of each other.[71] Contained in and through this narcotic language of stillness and death, sleep and dream, are all the other unrecorded opium deaths of the period at the other end of the social scale: the countless, often illegitimate, working-class infants, drugged and 'lost' since birth. How skilled the Victorians had become in making their art, like their children, into objects that don't make a sound.[72]

Heroin is a powder. Mythologised with disarming rapidity, it became a fluid, a flood, a foreign tide engulfing an insecure island colonial power. Metaphors of drowning dominate the novel in the mid-nineteenth century, which often ends in death by water, such as George Eliot's *The Mill on the Floss* or Charlotte Brontë's *Villette*. The fear of drowning found in the novel persists in later Victorian narrative poetry; in occasional verse, like Hopkins's 'The Wreck of the Deutschland' (1876). In the late-Victorian novel the idea of maritime death becomes modified into death by drowning not in water, but in the city—drug-fuelled and impoverished, the Orient Within. Dickens's unfinished novel, *The Mystery of Edwin Drood* (1872) gives the flip-side to rural Middlemarch, and to the age. Its opening pushes the reader off the streets, and unexpectedly into an opium den, one of the Chinese dwellings in the London slums around Limehouse, Poplar and Stepney. This represents an ideal concentration for Dickens's descriptive genius, but also a perfect general introduction to the smoking, racist, hallucinatory forces of the imperialist period: telling the tale, as so much of Dickens does, like Dante, from the inside of the inferno. For although the opium dens represented a tiny community (there were only 665 Chinese people living in Britain in 1881), these became the source of a wildly disproportionate xenophobic

---

[71] For further discussion of Victorian attitudes to death see Samantha Matthews, *Poetical Remains: Poets' Graves, Bodies and Books in the Nineteenth Century*, (Oxford: Oxford University Press, 2004.)

[72] Heroin was used in the wilful drugging of babies and children. 'Mrs Winslow's Soothing Syrup', 'Godfrey's Cordial', 'Atkinson's Infants Preservatives' and the chilling-sounding 'Street's Infant Quietness' were all laudanum preparations, or substitute stupefying preparations, some of which had been on the market since the 1840s. These were administered by mothers or, for those women who could afford them, by 'child-minders', in a belief that opium was good for children because it helped them grow—quietly. See Marek Kohn, *Narcomania: On Heroin* (London: Faber, 1987), p. 54.

dread of inner evil.⁷³ The attendant who leads Dr Watson into an opium den in the Sherlock Holmes story 'The Man With the Twisted Lip' is described as 'a sallow Malay'. It is in this den, to the good doctor's surprise and the reader's pleasure (because Holmes is the fulfilment of a wish) that Watson discovers the detective, lazing and gazing into the fire, like Jasper in *Drood*. It is the Malay who supplies the drug. Imperialist attitudes to these, very literally, 'foreign bodies' are implicated in the vocabulary of late-Victorian discoveries into bacteriological research into tuberculosis and cholera, and other diseases often associated with urban poverty, or immigrant communities.⁷⁴ As Laura Otis has written in her study of *Membranes: Metaphors of Invasion in Nineteenth-Century Literature, Science and Politics* (1999), 'Smallness itself became menacing':

> In the 1880s, because of their minuscule size and deadly effects, bacteria became a metaphor through which one could articulate fears about all invisible enemies, military, political, or economic.⁷⁵

For Conan Doyle, these connections were not arbitrary. He was a novelist and he also wrote verse; but he also served as a doctor in the Boer War (for which he was knighted), witnessing five thousand British troops in the hospital he commanded dying of enteric fever. Later in the period Wilde's *The Picture of Dorian Gray* (1891) revisits this other inner hell of London: 'opium dens, where one could buy oblivion, dens of horror where the memory of old sins could be destroyed by the madness of sins that were new.'⁷⁶ As Marek Kohn has suggested, 'Dickens's unfinished story could be said to inaugurate a period in which a new seriousness entered what had hitherto been only a marginal source of anxiety.'⁷⁷

In *Gissing in Context* (1975), Adrian Poole noted the 'unprecedented *intransigence* in the terms of the opposition between the inner, personal and subjective, and the outer, public and objective [...] the taking of sides in a world of decreasing options and manoeuvrability' as the key to 'a specific historical consciousness' of the late-Victorian world.⁷⁸ Negotiating a path through such intransigence creates that which has been observed, in the context of late-Victorian detective fiction, as an equation with the reader as sleuth.⁷⁹ This persona of 'the reader', a by-product itself of the detective fiction of the 1860s, is left by the author at the scene of crime, to pick a way through the tragedy, find and identify the body, following the crisis and dismemberment of belief that characterised English religious thought from the

---

73 The Anglo-Oriental Society for the Suppression of the Opium Trade was founded in 1874.
74 Conan Doyle, *The War in South Africa: Its Cause and Conduct* (1902). Cited in Laura Otis, *Membranes: Metaphors of Invasion in Nineteenth-Century Literature, Science and Politics* (The Johns Hopkins University Press, 1999), p. 94. Related corporeal anxieties are also explored in Kirstie Blair's *Victorian Poetry and the Culture of the Heart* (Oxford: Oxford University Press, 2006), which examines the significance of the physical heart to the Victorians, as well as the heart's more traditional symbolism.
75 Laura Otis, *Membranes*, p. 92.
76 Jonathan Dollimore draws attention to the pernicious influence of Max Nordau's *Degeneration* and degeneration theory on the Wilde trial—the 1895 translation came out a few months before Wilde was accused of sodomy. See *Death, Desire and Loss in Western Culture*, p. 128.
77 Marek Kohn, *Narcomania: On Heroin* (Faber, 1987), p. 10.
78 Adrian Poole, *Gissing in Context* (London: Macmillan, 1975), p. 8.
79 John Kerrigan, 'Sophocles in Baker Street'. In *Revenge Tragedy: Aeschylus to Armageddon* (Oxford: Oxford University Press, 1996), p. 65.

early 1870s. The creator of Sherlock Holmes had been brought up a Roman Catholic, during 'the years when Huxley, Tyndall, Darwin, Herbert Spencer and John Stuart Mill were our chief philosophers, and [...] even the man in the street felt the strong sweeping current of their thought', and Catholicism had failed him, as it disillusioned many of Conan Doyle's contemporaries throughout the century.[80] Sherlock Holmes, the period's most elusive drug addict, images these concerns. Holmes and his hypodermic, figuring the ritual puncturing of the spirit of late-nineteenth-century religious England—Holmes's forearm and wrist are 'all dotted and scarred with innumerable puncture-marks'—repeat a narrative pattern of euphoria lapsing into chronic depression—the narcotic and 'tragic', cadence of the age.[81] How will the story end?

IV. 1900: Turn off the Century

> I will not pretend that I have completely uncovered the
> meaning of this dream or that its interpretation is without gap.
> I could spend much more time over it, derive further information
> from it and discuss fresh problems raised by it.
>
> Sigmund Freud, *The Interpretation of Dreams* (1900)

The displacement in subjectivities which make the 1872–1900 period so intriguing is felt in the changing of the terms of literary representation itself, a less easily delineated and less obdurate symbolic and semantic relationship between the visible and the unseen. This idea is as crucial to an understanding of the gradualism of late-nineteenth-century English politics as it is to the prose and the poetry. This emphasis on 'unseen' experience (manifested, for example, in the fad for Spiritualism), on the 'Unconscious', on dreaming and on fear, contrasts with the extreme self-consciousness of the period, manifested in the visible, public worlds of 'Family', Empire, Commerce, Science and Technology.

That which is *not* seen—electricity, subjectivity, time, and, for a good deal of her reign, Queen Victoria, who hid herself away after her husband's death in 1861 until the Golden Jubilee Celebrations of 1887 coaxed her out again to public view—is another dimension to

---

80 Arthur Conan Doyle, *Memories and Adventures*, 2nd edn. (London, 1930), pp. 39–40. Cited in John Kerrigan, *Revenge Tragedy: Aeschylus to Armageddon*, p. 60.

81 Conan Doyle's story 'The Sign of Four' starts with a striking description of Holmes injecting himself; not with heroin but with cocaine, yet Watson's question 'Which is it to-day, morphine or cocaine?' suggests that it could be either. In Sir Arthur Conan Doyle, *The Penguin Complete Sherlock Holmes* (Penguin, 1981), pp. 87–158. By the end of the nineteenth century, heroin was given as a relief for everything from rheumatism to respiratory illnesses and nervous diseases, especially in its popular and more affordable alcoholic preparation, laudanum, so Holmes's addiction would not be surprising. Many conditions were treated the same way, a legacy throughout the period of the 1868 Pharmacy Act, where heroin notoriously escaped classification as a Part One drug. Its sale as a poison was also unregulated, although the Act called for chemists to have a licence to sell it. See Marek Kohn, *Narcomania: On Heroin* (London: Faber, 1987), p. 45; 51.

late-Victorian literature. Another recurrent image in these years, beside the mirror, is the 'mask'.[82] 'Insufficiency of sight in the eye looking outward has deprived them of the eye that should look inward,' writes Meredith of those who resist 'the comic idea', and his riddle diffuses many of the tensions exercised through the period.[83] The precariously-named *Jekyll-and-Hyde* of Robert Louis Stevenson's story figures the empirical and emotional uncertainties, the disguises, secrets, resistances and hypocrisies, a quality of moral embarrassment, at the heart of questions of Victorian identity and self-realisation. Alexander Welsh writes how Victorian novels, with their concern with the 'secrets of the past', provide a paradigm for twentieth-century psychoanalysis, with its interest in the 'effects of concealment of guilty thoughts'.[84] (In fact one of the novels he has in mind here is *Middlemarch*, which, like *Daniel Deronda*, Freud knew well.) Freud's writing of *The Interpretation of Dreams* (1900)—with, as Welsh emphasises, its focus on concealment, on invisible worlds—is the fulfilment of a wish: Freud dreams himself as the author he wants to be. It works because the reader wants to share these wishes. Dickens's *Great Expectations* works in the same way. The psychoanalytic difference of this novel with, say, George Gissing's *The Nether World*—and this is an instance where the mid- and the late-Victorian novel part company—is that the reader doesn't want to do this any longer.

What has been hitherto described as the 'intransigence' of late-Victorian literature is extended to the pushing of the conscious boundaries of realism, the mid-nineteenth-century question which, like Romanticism for Victorian poetry, had created more problems than it could solve for its ambivalent prose inheritors. Towards the latter years of the century realism now converges with phantasmagoria, with writers feeling more at home in the unworldliness of the latter than in the worldly verisimilitude of the former. Part of this is because, as Tennyson put it, Nature's 'bonds/Crack'd'.[85] The post-Darwinian close of the century is characterised by a growing unease with Nature, a sense of its phantasmagoric weirdness, its 'unnaturalness' as an agency rather than its consoling spiritual power. A collision of styles between phantasmagoria and realism is one of the most essential features of art at this time. It is figured in the decadent visions of John Davidson's poetry, in Gissing's London, in the shifting, uneasy ambience of a Burne-Jones painting, torn between solidity and dream, in what Tennyson calls 'this roaring moon of daffodil/And crocus';[86] and in the unearthly prose of late Ruskin, agonising between the materialist foundations of nineteenth-century art and culture and the invisible, disembodied promise of modernity. The concern with thresholds, both the idea of being on the edge of an imaginary and amazing world, and the drive towards an illimitable art that transcends mortal constraints, is distinctive of this period.

82 See the second introduction in Angela Leighton and Margaret Reynolds, eds., *Victorian Women Poets: An Anthology* (Oxford: Blackwell, 1995), p. xxxvi.
83 Meredith, *An Essay on Comedy and the Uses of the Comic Spirit*, cited in the Adams edition of *The Egoist*, p. 448.
84 Alexander Welsh, *Freud's Wishful Dream Book* (Princeton University Press, 1994), p. 39. See also p. 47.
85 Tennyson, 'Lucretius' (1868). First published in *Macmillan's Magazine*. This and all subsequent references to Tennyson's poetry are taken from Christopher Ricks, ed., *The Poems of Tennyson*, 2nd edn., 3 vols (London: Longman, 1987).
86 Tennyson, 'Prefatory Sonnet to the Nineteenth Century', first published, without a title, in the first number of the *Nineteenth Century*, March 1877.

One of the most definitive statements of turn-of-the-century phantasmagoria was the *Exposition Universelle* in Paris, where Sir William Orpen (the painter of the image on the cover of this anthology) and others, exhibited paintings in 1900. The chromo-kinetic Paris Exhibition proposed to the world a madly entertaining aesthetic combination of art, sex and dream-technology, way ahead of the now embarrassingly old-fashioned English 'Great Exhibition' of 1851. The French emphasis on the 'universal' calibre of their exhibition further diminished the scale of the 'great' one. Sophisticated inventions in Paris made even the technological talking points of the 1889 Paris Fair (the *Galerie des Machines*, and the *Tour Eiffel*) look anachronistic: signs of how rapidly a modern world was lurching forwards, how no-one could really expect to keep up. The biggest turn-of-the-century spectacle of all at the Paris Fair was electricity, the regenerative goddess of modern life, that had now, at the touch of a switch, made light the miraculous reality that the gas-lit Victorian world had been dreaming of since the invention of the electric bulb in 1879. It was phantasmagoria for real: electricity transformed travel to the Fair, with a two-mile-long *trottoir roulant*, or moving pavement, allowing visitors to see each display in transit, while an electric train could 'magically' encompass the whole site (277 acres) in just twenty minutes.[87] (For France it was *La Fée électricité*, the electricity *fairy*.)[88] Every evening at the foot of the Champ-de-Mars, 5,700 coloured bulbs would illuminate the 'Electrical Palace', the startling showpiece of the Exhibition, presided over by the 'electricity fairy'.

Giacomo Balla caught the moment in *The World's Fair At Night (Luna Park)*. Here the Electrical Palace sparkles away, its 'fairy-lights' beckoning towards a brightly-lit, magical world where the clanking and the crepuscular could be banished forever. The painting serves as a complementary irony to the gloomy aura of Benjamin Constant's painting of *Queen Victoria* (Fig. 2), a picture with which it nevertheless shares structural similarities. Both these paintings were exhibited alongside Orpen's *Mirror*. Each shows the Janus Face of 1900, and the contradictory complexion of the late-Victorian period as a whole: one looking to the 'future', the other back to the 'past'. It is tempting to look at these paintings in the way that the French writer Roland Barthes looks at his snapshots. 'I read two things at once: it will be and it has been'—it is a feature of this period that both states co-exist.[89] The contrast is cruel: between the Italian futurist's radiant Electrical Palace, lighting up the Paris skies, enchanting in its iridescence, and Benjamin Constant's depressingly dark symbol of Buckingham Palace, fading away in its fusty interior. The erotically-charged force celebrated in *The World's Fair at Night (Luna Park)* is *branché* (switched on), invisible, powerful, disembodied, free: it conjures up a fairytale possibility of 'modernity', although this would risk a 'modernism' couched in masculinist terms. Contrast this with Constant's depiction of

---

87 Robert Rosenblum, 'Art in 1900: Twilight or Dawn?' in *1900: Art at the Crossroads*, Royal Academy Exhibition Catalogue (Harry N. Abrams Publishing, New York, 2000), pp. 30–31. There is a separate essay by Maryanne Stevens, 'The *Exposition Universelle*: 'This vast competition of effort, realisation and victories' in the same catalogue, pp. 55–71.
88 The idea was illustrated by Louis-Ernest Barrias's '*L'Electricité*' (1889), a sculpture originally exhibited at the 1889 Paris World Fair, but deemed to be so successful that it was re-exhibited in 1900.
89 'Je lis en même temps: cela sera et cela a été.' Roland Barthes, *La chambre claire: Notes sur la photographie* (Paris: Cahiers du Cinéma, Gallimard, Seuil, 1980), p. 150.

Fig. 2 Benjamin Constant, *Queen Victoria* (1899)

Fig. 3 Photograph of Queen Victoria and members of the royal family (1872)

the old lady tethered to the throne. Balla's vision (of Europe) is *fin-de-siècle*; Constant's (of Victorian England) is *fin-de-globe*.⁹⁰

In 'The Darkling Thrush', arguably the last poem to be written in the Victorian period, the nineteenth century is figured by Hardy as a ghastly (male) 'corpse': 'His crypt the cloudy canopy,/The wind his death-lament.' Verse as shroud—or (worse) verse as hearse: it is the poetic equivalent of Constant's 1899 portrait, displayed, cruelly, in the French section of the *Exposition Universelle*—the same place where Orpen's *The Mirror* went on show. The jaded monarch is depicted half as ghost, half as anachronistic relic, aged, stricken, alone, remote from her subjects: the painting, seen from a French perspective, is a mocking analogue of the fear of defenestration, of loss of power and control. Compare this with the following photograph from 1872 of the Queen surrounded by her family: six children who would in turn produce forty grandchildren and nearly as many great-grandchildren (Fig. 3). In Constant's representation, Victoria's hands rest gingerly on the throne as if it is an electric chair; used for the first time in 1890, a sorry application of the new technology of electricity. The small Imperial crown is not on her head but seems to dance above her, out of reach: a marked contrast with a famous photograph of Empress Victoria taken on her sixtieth birthday in 1879, on the verge of a decade of High Imperialism, where the crown is unquestionably, territorially,

---

90 The phrases occur in Oscar Wilde, *The Picture of Dorian Gray*. The first version of the novel was published in *Lippincott's Monthly Magazine* (June 1890); the expanded version by Ward Lock in April 1891.

Fig. 4 Photograph of Queen Victoria wearing the Imperial Crown on her 60th birthday (1879)

made part of her (Fig. 4).⁹¹ In Constant's painting the Queen's hair flows long and loose, traditionally, in terms of the iconography of Christian art, the symbol of a penitential woman, as well as one in mourning. The hair is so entwined in the fragile lace of the head-dress that it looks white, a whiteness that enfolds the Queen like a Miss Havisham ever unable to relinquish her bridal dress. The spectral quality of the Queen's demeanour that Constant was so keen to portray contrasts with the solidity of the surroundings: the heavy golden-brown pillars flanking each side of the painting, the darkness that occupies most of the canvas, and the asymmetric simmer of crimson on the floor, like a burning fire just under the throne, one of the many Dantesque images that smoulder through the entire period. Constant's Victoria is a final image of decrepitude and degeneracy.⁹² Woman as depravity

91 For this and further images of late-nineteenth century Victoria see Eric R. Delderfield, *Kings and Queens of England and Great Britain*, (David Charles, 1990, rpt., 1998), p. 129.
92 The term is given most theoretical credence in Max Nordau's *Degeneration* (1892) which was very influential in the 1890s, not just in England (it was translated in 1895) but in Europe. For ways in which degeneration theory influences the fiction of the time see David Trotter, *The English Novel in History 1895–1920* (London: Routledge, 1993), especially pp. 111–127. Trotter defines 'degeneration' as 'a falling-off from original purity, a reversion to less complex forms of structure'. (p. 111). See also Daniel Pick, *Faces of Degeneration: A European Disorder, c. 1848–c.1918* (Cambridge: Cambridge Univerity Press, 1989; rev. ed., 1993.)

is a cult object in turn-of-the-century French art, and this is subtly reflected in the picture. It is as if Constant trains the harshness of a brand new spare bulb on the face of England's Queen for one ruthless stroboscopic moment, showing her literally in a bad light. She's caught, *in camera*, if not on camera, at her most artificial.

Let us finally return to the vexed domestic question of 'two-party' politics—what Tennyson calls in 1885 'Raving politics, never at rest'.[93] By 1900, the recognition and inspiration of what in England politically would come to be called Pluralism, exemplified in F. W. Maitland's translation of the German Otto von Gierke's *Political Theories of the Middle Age*, had become an unavoidable part of the late-Victorian scene, and the modern European imagination. *The Principles of Political Obligation* (1885) by T. H. Green and Bernard Bosanquet's *Philosophical Theory of the State* (1899), both influenced by Hegelian Idealism, are other indications of this development of a sceptical consciousness that formed and informed the intellectual culture of the time, independent of 'two-party' politics. So, while the notion of a 'two-party system' is a benchmark to bear in mind for the Victorian period 'as a whole', it needs to be refined in any discussion of the *late*-nineteenth century, as opposed to the middle years of Queen Victoria's reign, or the earlier part of it. For in contrast with other decades, these late years of the nineteenth century saw the emergence of a more complicated political consciousness than the old Whig/Tory polarisation could reasonably accommodate. With the death of Henry Sidgwick, in 1900, Britain saw the departure of the last major figure of the radical Utilitarian tradition derived from Bentham (itself a different shade of democratic liberalism from that preached by John Stuart Mill). In the same year Leslie Stephen published his three-volume study *The English Utilitarians*, eleven years after J. A. Hobson's discourse on the free market economy, *The Physiology of Industry* (1889). But it was in 1900, too, that the British Labour Party could be said to have come into existence, at least in name, thus demarcating territory neither crudely Tory nor Whig, taking its origins from the moment when William Morris's Socialist League (which had been founded in 1884, as a splinter group from Hyndman's Social Democratic Federation) amalgamated with Keir Hardie's militant Independent Labour Party. Added to this political crucible in 1900 were still the conservative traditionalists, the old-style Tories critical of liberal doctrine and 'democracy'—particularly Mill's version of democracy.[94] Both 'Conservative' and 'Liberal' administrations introduced significant legislation throughout the late-Victorian period. Gladstone introduced the Ballot Act of 1872, and was actively in favour of Home Rule in Ireland in the 1880s, the latter leading to his resignation from office in the summer of 1886. Disraeli brought in the Public Health Act of 1875, and introduced a series of Factory Acts (1874, 1878).

Writers of the late-Victorian period were inevitably affected by these political and social ideas and absorbed them in their work. Hardy's comparatively under-rated second novel *Under The Greenwood Tree* (1872) is indebted to his reading of the mid-nineteenth-century utilitarian doctrines of Mill on liberty, for example, and the best-selling novelist Mrs Humphry Ward's *Robert Ellsmere* (1888) intensely explores the consequences of the anglicised Idealist social thinking of T. H. Green.[95] There are both 'communist' and 'conservative' aspects

---

93 Tennyson, 'Vastness', second stanza.
94 These ranged across the entire late-Victorian period, from Fitzjames Stephens's *Liberty, Equality and Fraternity* (1873), at the one end, to W. E. H. Lecky's *Democracy and Liberty* (1896) at the other.
95 See the prose chronology at p. 49.

to late Ruskin, seen in his *Fors Clavigera*; and traditional dimensions to the revolutionary 'socialist' thought of William Morris; there was a 'liberal' side to the Fabians. Other prominent literary figures grouped themselves around Fabian ideals towards the end of the century, notably the 'Utopian' work of H. G. Wells. Drama is not our focus but one should mention briefly George Bernard Shaw, a prime mover in The Fabian Society, and affected by late-nineteenth-century socialist works such as the American Henry George's *Progress and Poverty* (1879) (and in a broader sense, the legacy of Hegel). Contrary to popular belief the art critic John Ruskin was not a socialist in the partisan sense, although his work and ideals had a significant part to play in the formation and advancement of socialist thinking upon writers and artists in late-Victorian England—especially upon William Morris and, of course, Shaw himself. Ruskin was also influential upon 'Guild Socialism', which was popularised in the Edwardian era by A. R. Orage's weekly paper *The New Age*, started in 1907. Ruskin's social and economic criticism *Unto This Last* (1860) pre-dates the period with which this anthology is concerned, though, and his writing from the 1870s and 1880s is of a different creative order entirely. Both Benjamin Kidd's *Social Evolution* (1894) and C. H. Pearson's *National Life and Character* (1893) added to an emerging genre of late-Victorian 'scientific' political writing, established by, for example, Walter Bagehot's *Physics and Politics* (1869), and discuss the social application of Darwinian evolutionary principles to the contemporary *polis* (often, it has to be said, in idiosyncratic ways). This type of writing itself would contribute to the notable growth in England, in the first decade of the twentieth century, of literature dealing with questions of social psychology, continuing yet departing from a much more established British empirical tradition.[96]

Hardy's work demonstrates the consequences of this gradual change in literary consciousness—a change picked up in the 1870s by the radar of Browning and Meredith, and by *Middlemarch*—not just for the reader but for language. Hardy's (a)tonal and often inhospitable ironies are predicated around a proto-modernist poetics of 'divergence/Fused', symptomatic of the aesthetic crisis that Pound found so regrettable in late-nineteenth-century English poetry. A novelist and a poet, Hardy is evocative when considering the mobile, plural imaginative character of the 1872–1900 period. He is not a 'decadent', in its local sense, although he absorbed decadent qualities and tendencies in his late-Victorian work, the novels especially. He is not a 'feminist', although his fiction shows that at times he took great pleasure in behaving as one; and he has, to various degrees, a poetic kinship not only with Wordsworth, but with Browning, Tennyson, Swinburne, Meredith, and other voices of the age. Albeit mentally in a far less strenuous way—Hardy is too romantic to be 'Romantic'—Hardy explores many of the issues and anxieties which Wordsworth's poetics generate. Naden's quip 'I am the modern Sage [. . .]/I am, in brief, the Age', written for Darwin, is not impossible for Hardy. The paradox of Hardy could be summed up by saying that he is a characteristic writer because he is so uncharacteristic: of his age, of late-Victorian and decadent poetry. And yet he is so representative: of his age, of late-Victorian and decadent poetry.

These anxieties and contradictions are exceptionally present in, and prescient in, Hardy's poem 'The Darkling Thrush'—the fleshly precursor to Yeats's 'golden bird' in 'Sailing to Byzantium' (1928). 'The Darkling Thrush' is at once elusive and allusive; although, with

---

96 For example, William McDougall, *Introduction to Social Psychology* (1908) and Fabian Graham Wallis, *Human Nature in Politics* (1908).

Dennis Taylor, I suspect that 'Hardy resists the urbanity of allusiveness which confirms a high culture of the best that is thought and wrote'.[97] The thrush's song laments the decline of Art as self-expression, yet cannot quite sing out the modern quest of Art as the search for impersonal beauty. Hardy's poem weaves these subject–object relations, through the uneasy and unstable movement between the 'visible' and the 'unseen'. The poet is doing more here than ruffling a few feathers. Hardy's thrush calls into question the primary association of a poet as one who creates an unfettered lyric identity, as poets did in earlier years of the nineteenth century—the Romantic poet identifying both himself and his artistic practice through birdsong, like Keats's nightingale, or Shelley's skylark.

The idea of poetic decline, and especially of decline in the perceived cultural status of poetry, is mediated through the starkly silhouetted landscape drawn in the first stanza, in which 'The tangled bine-stems scored the sky/Like strings of broken lyres.' This idea had a power for Hardy beyond this poem. Through Palgrave's *Golden Treasury*, the classic anthology of poetry published the same year that Albert, Queen Victoria's husband, died, Hardy knew Gray's 'The Progress of Poesy' with its opening words 'Awake, Aeolian lyre'.[98] Hardy's quivering thrush has been subjected to intolerable aesthetic pressure by the age, as after Romanticism's death Victorian poets were. Is it any wonder, too, that Hopkins writes of the menacing windhover, or kestrel, which hangs in the air before unpredictably descending on its prey—poetical worlds away from the frolicsome flight of the Romantic skylark, soaring upwards while singing; or that Yeats writes in 1916 of the 'Yellow-eyed hawk of the mind'? Hardy, like his other dialect-poet kinsmen, was passionate about the English language and what was happening to it—what, in fact, in the Victorian age, *had* happened to it. The last poem of the nineteenth century, or the first poem of the twentieth, depending on where you are coming from, and whom you are with, signals an appalling recollection: of subjectivity. Romanticism's final 'fling' (l. 23) is ironised in the thrush. The poem shows not just the shift from subjective and privately-sourced knowledge and authenticity ('he [the bird] knew') to collective, universal objective ignorance (the 'I' of the poem 'was unaware' of the meaning of the bird's song) but what such a change has meant.

'The Darkling Thrush' is a favourite threshold piece for anthologists; its author, now, far from a 'threshold' poet (which was not always the case).[99] Written on 31 December 1900, calendrically on the very turn of the century, half in, half out, 'The Darkling Thrush' sums up much of the mood of the late-Victorian age as whole. The poem can be read in several directions, signalling the dawn of the twentieth century as well as the twilight of the nineteenth: as William Morris writes in one of his loveliest poems, in these final tenuous years 'Night treadeth on day', and the frail voice of the thrush and the tone of its darkling are emblematic of the wider discrepancies of this turn-of-the-century dilemma.[100]

---

97 Dennis Taylor, 'Hardy's Minute Way of Looking' in his *Hardy's Literary Language and Victorian Philology* (Oxford: Clarendon Press, 1993), p. 293.
98 See Dennis Taylor, *Hardy's Metres and Victorian Prosody* (Oxford University Press, 1998), p. 150. Taylor reminds us of Gray's rebuke to a reviewer that an Aeolian lyre was not the same as an Aeolian harp.
99 'T. S. Eliot's and Yeats's reactions to Hardy are recounted in the introduction to Christopher Ricks, ed., *The New Oxford Book of Victorian Verse* (Oxford: Oxford University Press, 1987), p. xxx.
100 From William Morris, 'Lines written for an embroidered hanging', designed and worked by his daughter May Morris, for his bed at Kelmscott, 1891.

Hardy's thrush, like Yeat's gyre, Darwin's bank, Orpen's mirror, and Hopkins's watch, is 'a figure for the co-existence of the past and future at a time of transition.'[101]

Edna Longley opens her collection of *The Bloodaxe Book of Twentieth-Century Poetry* (2000) with 'The Darkling Thrush'. She adds the observation, 'If his [Hardy's] poetry does not alter, this is because alteration is structural.'[102] This comment is as signal to the late-Victorian age as it is to the century that would follow. 'The Darkling Thrush' is again the first choice, 'representing' the year 1900, in the Faber anthology *News that Stays News: The 20th Century in Poems*, edited by Simon Rae (1999). Yet the same poem concludes C. J. Dixon's selection of *fin-de-siècle* poetry *1860–1900*. The persuasiveness of the poem to both centuries at the same time is felt in the title; but there are other histories. 'Darkling' is Shakespeare's (from *King Lear*), and both Keats and Arnold let its magic work on them before Hardy: Keats in the 'Ode to a Nightingale', and Arnold in 'Dover Beach'. The impossibility of knowing what 'Darkling' means contributes to the 'ancient pulse' of the poem's imaginations.[103] Is Hardy, who wrote for the ear as well as the eye, nearer here to Keats's sense of the word than he is to Arnold's or to Shakespeare's? In this poem Hardy's mysterious phrasing of 'darkling' works, I think, through a slow and complex kinship with all of them, as well as, more broadly, a trajectory of English poetry from Wordsworth, and before him, Gray, to Yeats.

Constant's painting of Queen Victoria is about, to play with one of Hardy's strongest words in the poem, the 'weakening' of subject-object relations. The country the Queen had inherited from her uncle in 1837—which in the 1830s alone had seen the first Reform Bill (1832), the abolition of slavery in the British colonies (1833), the first reform of the Poor Law since the seventeenth century and, as if in *katharsis*, the burning down of the Houses of Parliament the same year (1834)—had undergone a gradual series of devastating changes. By 1900 what was left was only a residue, or unpleasant sediment, the 'dregs' (Hardy's word) of a landscape once known, as opposed to the sublime confidence of Romantic conception in place. It is witnessed by the traumatised 'speaker' objectified in the poem. For the Romantics it was location, location, location: for the Victorians it was dis-location, if, that is, you had ever had any sense of where you had been at all. The disturbing economy expressed by the catchphrase 'the very dregs of the population', for example, comes into the language in 1876—this continuing to be a time of much philological change—reviving a much older linguistic and figurative sense of 'the dregs' as the 'refuse', but transferring it from rubbish to people.[104] (A reading of this poem in terms of Marx's theory of commodification could suggest that, rather than the other way round, subjects have become objects.) Hardy's 'dregs' of winter also exude, with the abstract and universal connotation of feculence, a nastier, specifically late-nineteenth-century hermeneutic whiff of *miasma*.[105] Miasma ('defilement'),

---

101 Frank Kermode, *The Sense of an Ending* (Oxford University Press, 1966), p. 100.
102 Edna Longley, ed., *The Bloodaxe Book of Twentieth-Century Verse* (Newcastle: Bloodaxe, 2001), p. 25.
103 For more extensive discussion of Hardy's literary language see Dennis Taylor, *Hardy's Literary Language and Victorian Philology*, Oxford: Clarendon Press, 1993. This contains an appendix, 'Hardy's Notable Standard Words in the *OED*'.
104 For further related discussion about the signal importance of the concept of mess to the age as a whole, see David Trotter, *Cooking with Mud: The Idea of Mess in Nineteenth-Century Art and Fiction* (Oxford: Oxford University Press, 2000).
105 See Robert Parker, *Miasma: Pollution and Purification in Early Greek Religion*, (Oxford, 1983) and John Kerrigan, *Revenge Tragedy*, esp. pp. 42–44.

an idea discussed more readily in the context of Greek Tragedy but in several ways applicable to, and explicable of, the Paterian flux of the late-nineteenth-century imagination, signals an order of corruption that belongs to the moral; and thus to the tragic, and one is never so far from tragedy in Hardy. These are years that bear the pressure of a tragic consciousness. It is a tragedy that will conspire to overdetermine the thrush.

The idea of suspense is, delicately, central to the literary poise of this turn-of-the-century poem. The first line figures as the top bar of the gate of the poem upon which the speaker leans, watching and waiting—suspended between history and tragedy, the present and the future, the rural and the urban, the I and the me, the then and the now—all displacements in this late-Victorian period. And with him, also watching and waiting, the invisible, silent presence of the reader, a mere shadow cast on the page in the act of reading, but a shadow that looms larger as the poem gets longer, eventually darkling the thrush. My sense of the reader in 'The Darkling Thrush' suggested here is a more hermetic figuring out of the way he or she is constructed by the poem than in Karlin's account, although I think we are ultimately talking about the same thing. One of his most penetrating critical reflections upon the poem is that it is the (late-Victorian/early modernist) *reader* who will become the visible presence in and for the poem in contrast with the diminished importance of the (Romantic) bird: 'The reader is addressed, precisely because the thrush is not.'[106] *Why* this should be is beyond the scope of this introduction; it is nevertheless another question raised by late-Victorian poetics. Hardy's poetry shows us *how*.

It is crucial to the eschatological suspension of the poem, as well as its suspense, that the 'speaker' never actually sees the bird. Leaning, the speaker thinks but remains in fact speechless and ultimately 'unaware'. Like an inverted Victorian child, the thrush is to be heard but not seen. It's pretty dark anyway by the third stanza of the poem—and night always falls too quickly in Hardy. So, alone in this most 'desolate' terrestrial 'gloom' while others remain indoors, the ethereal encroachment upon him, of the *sound* of the old 'blast-beruffled' thrush's 'evensong' becomes more powerful through visual reticence. In the same way, there is more (and less) to the thrush itself, for example, than the fanciful doff at Anglo-Saxon gentility that 'beruffled' in the third stanza alone would have suggested. Another of the poem's key tri-syllabics (like 'canopy'), the effortless compound adjective 'blast-beruffled', insofar as it is capable of transitive action, doubles up at once at the crushingly Tennysonian *blast* of the age, harks back to Blake's primal terror of verbal curse (the harrowing 'Blasts [. . .]' of 'London'), and in turn sets a concealed microphone for Pound and the aggrandised BLAST of the Vorticist manifesto. Clear through them all, though, is the Wordsworthian speaker's address to the bird in 'Hark! 'tis the Thrush' sonnet of 1838—the year after Queen Victoria came to the throne (a poem of which Karlin reminds us). The speaker of that poem plucked up the courage, accompanied by the thrush, to 'front the blast'. Hardy's thesaurus of lament for the passing age charts these movements, tones and voices.

Movement in Hardy is always violently local, to history and to the word. The tri-syllabic 'Canopy', thrown over the end of line three of the second stanza of this poem, for instance, has strikingly fatalistic connotations. Originally deriving both from the Greek for 'a bed with mosquito curtains' and from the word for gnat, this word carries residual miasmic power. This, too, is typical of Hardy's fascination with the theatre of insects, such as the not unrelated

---

106 Daniel Karlin, ed., *The Penguin Book of Victorian Verse* (London: Penguin, 1997), p. lxx.

poem 'An August Midnight', dated 1899, with its cast of 'winged, horned, and spined' creepy-crawlies and the image of the 'sleepy fly that rubs its hands [. . .]' on the writer's page. There are many words to do with gnats that bite into the bloodstream of the English language in the 1880s; as, incidentally, throughout this decade, the language of invasion, both bacteriological and imperial, shows as an instance of the 'extreme porosity' of Victorian language.[107] A sense of foreboding is suggested by the dismal fate of the Victorian coppice, only grown in order to be felled; while the architectural meaning of 'canopy' as a 'roof-like projection over a tomb' could hardly have escaped the author of *Jude the Obscure* (1894–1895). This example (a canopy is figurative of both suspension and suspense) is in turn part of a simple yet elaborate architectonics of 'longer' Hardyesque words left hanging throughout the poem: 'desolate', 'weakening', 'fervourless', 'ecstatic'. These give the reader of the poem, like the speaker catching the thrush, pause; for a moment longer than is metrically usual.

Hardy often contrasted Tennyson's 'storied past' with the 'impossible story' of the English present. 'The citizen's *Then* is the rustic's *Now*' is an emblem of *Far From the Madding Crowd* (1874), and nags away in the prose published twenty years after this as well as in Hardy's early poetry. No wonder Hardy's thrush wanted to flee; and, by 1928, Yeats felt that the only possible poetic course of action was to turn him, and by implication the figure of the poet, into an immortalised metal bird, in a mythical land where superego would forever vanquish the *id*.

Hardy focuses attention to this in a poem called 'The Temporary the All'. By the end of the nineteenth century, 'The Temporary' is 'All' there is; a recognition intensified by the first word of the poem, 'change':

> Change and chancefulness in my flowering youthtime,
> Set me sun by sun near one unchosen;
> Wrought us fellowlike, and despite divergence
>   Fused us in friendship.

'The Temporary the All', the first lyric in *Wessex Poems* (1898), is a poem about many things, including the language of vision ('Truth and Light outshow') and the question of 'Time'. It is also an instance of the revival of and experimentation with antique and ancient poetic forms which is so characteristic of this late-Victorian period. Hardy was a modern who began his poetic career in this very nineteenth-century way; not as an originator, but as an imitator.

The poem is composed in '(Sapphics)', the classical metre associated with the ancient poet Sappho (seventh-century BCE). Hardy added the parenthetical subtitle in 1916, showing his debt to Swinburne.[108] Sapphic verse consists of a quatrain stanza with a particularly complex 'irregular' rhythmical scheme of unstressed and stressed syllables repeated thrice, and a shorter, hymn-like, fourth line. The fourth line consists of two feet (called an 'adonic'). The challenge presented by this particular metre was not confined to Hardy. Tennyson and Swinburne both explored the Sapphic ode; as would Pound, even if

---

107 Valentine Cunningham, *The Victorians: An Anthology of Poetry and Poetics* (Oxford: Blackwell, 2000), p. xxxv. Also note the 'murmur of gnats' in stanza XVIII of Tennyson's poem 'Vastness' (1885). On the question of Hardy's language, see Dennis Taylor's *Hardy's Literary Language and Victorian Philology* (Oxford: Clarendon Press, 1993).
108 For further discussion of this poem and Hardy's metrical range in general, see Dennis Taylor, *Hardy's Metres and Victorian Prosody* (Oxford: Clarendon Press, 1988), p. 258.

only to show the strain of using dactyls and trochees as the basic feet in English verse. The poem, which at one level seems disablingly wordy, turns around a recognition of classic reticence contained in (and by) the last line of the penultimate stanza of the poem, 'Thus I [. . .] But lo, me!' The ellipsis signals the estrangement between subjective and objective but also the movement of the estrangement: the interiorized and autonomous subjective self (the 'I') has become displaced and objectified ('me'). This prepares the framework (or, rather, 'earthtrack') for the final stanza of the poem, where representations of others diffuse the intensive remembrance of self, and where one's 'achievement' on earth is ritually externalised, or formalised, through the modest drama of marks of 'showance'. Life, says Hardy's laconic adonics, and this could be signal of the late-Victorian period as a whole, is pretty bad to look at, but really has got to be seen to be believed.

In a famous letter to Fliess on 12 June 1900 Freud describes a later visit to Bellevue, the house in which he spent the summer of 1895, situated near the Kahlenberg hill just outside Vienna. Disturbed by the events of a summer day, he had one of his most remarkable dreams (and interpretations) here, concluding that the dream 'was a particular state of affairs as I should have wished it to be'. 'Do you suppose,' he wrote, 'that someday a marble tablet will be placed on the house, inscribed with these words?'

> In this House, on July 24th, 1895,
> the Secret of Dreams was Revealed
> to Dr Sigm. Freud

'At the moment,' Freud concludes, 'there seems little prospect for it.'[109] The conscientious objection of the age to providing easy interpretations to its secrets and dreams similarly subjects the interpretation of Victorian poetry to the pressures of the contradiction between dream-life and waking life; the imaginative and clinical thresholds of late-nineteenth-century consciousness that Freud was daring to cross at the end of his century, thresholds that Dickens, Conrad and Conan Doyle allowed their protagonists to cross, are, in so many respects, similar thresholds today's reader of Victorian poetry continually encounters.[110]

I conclude this introduction as I began, with an enigma: the picture by the Irish painter Sir William Orpen, which is shown on the cover of this anthology. Entitled *The Mirror*, it was displayed at the Paris Exhibition of 1900. Unsettlingly reminiscent of a Vermeer interior, an artist at his easel and a female figure are depicted in a mirror, while the gaze of the girl in the foreground looks away. It is a study in the art of watching. The mirror both contains and reflects a world of its own; a world of its own time, depicting a silent drama at once intimate yet remote from the viewer. The main figure in the picture is dis-orientated, off-centre; rather than a monolithic representation dominating the whole of the canvas, as in much eighteenth-century portraiture. The young woman does not smile. Her face is partially cast under shadow, like so many faces in art at this time, especially the faces of women; part of a late-nineteenth-century Western European genre of paintings of female figures seated amongst interior emptinesses. Compare, for example, the Symbolist work of Whistler, or the paintings

---

109 'The Interpretation of Dreams' (1900). In *The Standard Edition of the Complete Psychological Works of Sigmund Freud* Vol. IV. (London: Hogarth Press, 1953), p. 121.
110 For further account of Freud's interest to this period see Jonathan Dollimore, *Death, Desire and Loss in Western Culture* (Penguin, 1998) pp. 180–197.

of Albert Rutherston, or Vilhelm Hammershoi, or Sir William Rothenstein (Orpen's future brother-in-law), all of whom deal with similar subject matter at this time. This girl is something of a cult figure.

Recent readings of Victorian poetry have drawn attention to the frequency of mirrors as symbols, more in the second half of the nineteenth century than in the first.[111] 'The mirror functions to bring the divided subject and object together,' writes Angela Leighton,

> in a meeting which may be either a reassertion of identity or a traumatic mis-match [...] the mirror gives back a story which is both true and untrue, both fixed and arbitrary, both public and private.[112]

Towards the end of the nineteenth century, however, the mirror image comes to depict a threat. It acts as a warning, representing the return of the ultimate spectre of the self—an embodiment of 'subjectivity'—and that's what many Victorians were trying to resist. Orpen calling his painting 'The Mirror' in 1900 is a provocation, both to the era he is leaving and to the epoch that will follow.

So how do readers of the twenty-first century chart this resistant and exotic period, an age in which conviction in the moral superiority of Art (and, by the turn of the century, of Artifice) replaces that of Nature? Orpen's art describes a displacement in late-Victorian poetry and prose: mirror and girl are at odds, and the viewer/reader/spectator does not quite know where to look. This contributes to an atmosphere of unease, despite the fact that in the painting the figure is seated. (Unease with domestic location is a concern of both late-Victorian fiction and poetry, whether in Charles Dickens's unfinished *The Mystery of Edwin Drood*, written in 1872, which opens in an opium den, in Thomas Hardy's *Under The Greenwood Tree* (1872), or George Eliot's finest novel, with Dorothea wondering how on earth people are going to live in Middlemarch.)[113] Orpen's young woman is leaning forward awkwardly and tensely: she is watching and waiting. The painter—and the century—waits with her. The viewer watches the waiting. Still Life? Realism, or Modernism? Viewer or Camera? 'How does the cameraman compare with the painter?' asks the German critic Walter Benjamin in his classic essay, 'The Work of Art in the Age of Mechanical Reproduction'.[114] It is a question that could be asked of no other century than the nineteenth, and of no other part of that century than the last five years, when cinema came to life, came to art.[115] Like the picture in Oscar Wilde's *The Picture of Dorian Gray*, *The Mirror* becomes a visual, and yet in many psychoanalytically resistant ways, anti-visual, representation of the voyeuristic crisis in turn-of-the-century self-consciousness.

---

111 The transitive sense of the verb 'to mirror', 'to reflect in the manner of a mirror', dates from 1820.
112 Angela Leighton and Margaret Reynolds, eds., *Victorian Women Poets: An Anthology* (Oxford: Blackwell, 1995), p. xxxvii.
113 Publication of *Middlemarch* commenced in 1871; although this extended to 1872.
114 This question is posed on p. 233 of Benjamin's essay. In Hannah Arendt, ed., Walter Benjamin, 'The Work of Art in the Age of Mechanical Reproduction', in *Illuminations: Essays and Reflections*, tr. Harry Zohn. (New York: Harcourt, Brace and World [Shocken Books], 1968). The introductory Benjamin quotation is from p. 230. See also p. 220.
115 For further discussion, especially with relation to the significance of cinema as a late-nineteenth-century machine, see Stephen Heath, *Questions of Cinema* (Bloomington: Indiana University Press, 1981).

One significant reason for this, as I have shown, is the rupture wrought upon the late-Victorian period by Darwin. Looking at a bank at the end of *The Origin of Species* (1859) Darwin reflected on 'these elaborately constructed forms, so different from each other, and dependent on each other in so complex a manner'.[116] The same could be said of the burgeoning empire of late-Victorian poetry, evolving in canonical accordance with the Darwinian laws of Natural Selection: Growth with Reproduction; Inheritance; and Variability, 'entailing Divergence of Character and the Extinction of less-improved forms'. Like the famous overgrown bank of the *Origin*, late-Victorian verse is characterised by its uncharacteristic nature, through its refusal of standardised patterns of growth and form. One of Tennyson's late, great poems is called 'Vastness' (from *vastus*, void), and this unnerving signal of Gargantuan shapelessness, an immense image at once unimaginably immense, is indicative of all that Queen Victoria's sprawling 'Empire' had become.

The Darwinian idea of 'descent with modification', like the daring concept of an origin of species, is intimate not just to patterns in natural science, but to the wider artistic concerns of the late-Victorian period as a whole. While some of Darwin's assumptions—such as the notion of European superiority over the 'savages', with their 'low morality'—remained acceptable to his Victorian audience in ways which today would seem abhorrent, the publication of *The Descent of Man, And Selection on Relation to Sex* in 1871 continued a climate of provocation generated by *The Origin of Species*. Darwin's significance became of such dimension that, by 1889, Alfred Russell Wallace, in *Darwinism: an Exposition of the Theory of Natural Selection with some of its Applications*, announced that the phenomenon of 'Darwinism' 'is now universally accepted as the order of nature in the organic world'.

Above all, however, the verse of Darwin's age recalls how versions of subjectivity were unsettled. During the late Romantic period the word meant, variously, 'consciousness of one's perceived states' (1821); 'the quality or condition of viewing things exclusively through the medium of one's own mind or individuality' (1827); 'that quality of art which depends on the expression of the personality or individuality of the artist; the individuality of the artist expressed in his work' (1830). Two years after Queen Victoria ascended the throne in 1837, the term 'subjectivism' developed, sometimes used as a synonym for subjectivity. Subjectivism in turn sharpened its philosophical meaning, becoming the theory according to which all claims to knowledge are subjective and relative.[117] By the final quarter of the century, the period that concerns me here, subjectivity also had come to mean 'the quality or condition of resting upon subjective facts or mental representation; the character of existing in the mind only' (1877). Subjectivism now proposed an ethical sense: the aim of a morality based upon the attainment of states of feeling (1897).

---

116 Gillian Beer, ed., Charles Darwin, *The Origin of Species* (Oxford: World's Classics, 1996, rpt., 1998), p. 396. The full title of Darwin's work is 'On the Origin of Species By Means of Natural Selection, or the Preservation of Favoured Races in the Struggle for Life'. For further discussion of Darwin's significance to the Victorian period, especially in fiction, see Gillian Beer, *Darwin's Plots: Evolutionary Narrative in Darwin, George Eliot and Nineteenth-Century Fiction* (London: Routledge and Kegan Paul, 1983; rpt., 1985) and her 'Darwin and the Growth of Language Theory' in John Christie and Sally Shuttleworth, eds., *Nature Transfigured: Science and Literature* (Manchester University Press, 1989).

117 The Victorian philosophical concept of the 'subjective method' refined this position further. The subjective method is the method of analysis and argument based upon *a priori* assumptions.

The Mirror is about the absence of the original—and the aesthetic consequences of this predicament—and thus the removal from the scene of what Benjamin determined in his essay as 'the prerequisite to the concept of authenticity'. As a visual text, *The Mirror* represents the tension between 'cult value' (the hidden or ritual meaning accorded to objects) and 'exhibition value' (the painting being on public view, in this case literally in Paris at the Fair). A question here, of concern to writers in this late period, from Christina Rossetti to Oscar Wilde, is a late-nineteenth-century complex of relations increasingly at stake in the technology of artistic reproduction. The painting is a reminder that the function of art—like the function of criticism at the present time, as it was in the 1860s to Matthew Arnold, and the function of society in the future, as it was in the 1890s to Thomas Hardy—would change for ever as the century finally came to an end. Turn-off-the-century: the Victorians couldn't bear to look at themselves any longer. By the turn of the century the poetic face reflected in the mirror of the nineteenth century was no longer Wordsworth's, but Wilde's.

Comparative Prose 1872–1900

Two pieces of prose fiction selected here represent each year from 1872–1900, in order for the reader to situate the following poems in a broader *fin–de–siècle* context. The first piece is an extract from a novel or a short story. The second is, usually, 'non-fictive prose'—an essay, article, autobiography, or other literary tract of the period not always easily accessible to readers, which illuminates some of the wider concerns of the age as whole. Important sensations of the period are also mentioned, such as the Ruskin-Whistler case. Twenty novelists have been selected. Half of these are established Victorian literary figures: Eliot, Hardy, Conrad, Stevenson, Trollope, Meredith, Wilde, Pater, Gissing, and Wells. Hardy and Conrad appear three times, as writers of short stories as well as novels. Robert Louis Stevenson is represented as a poet, as well as in his more familiar capacity as the author of *Treasure Island* (1883) and *Dr Jekyll and Mr Hyde* (1886). The other ten novelists are less well-known, but are selected on the basis of writing fiction that exemplifies late–nineteenth century imaginative concerns, especially the apocalyptic vision of a utopia or ideal society. This is epitomised in W. H. Mallock's novel, *The New Republic*.

All the writers are British, with the notable exception of Henry James, whose short story, 'Daisy Miller' (1878) was published in England before it appeared in America. The popularity of the short story as a genre at this time is a feature of the late–Victorian period; while the novel held sway throughout the century, the exploration of other late–nineteenth century literary forms is important to appreciate, especially forms signal for Modernism.

The polemical writing of Clementina Black, Mona Caird, Sarah Grand, 'Vernon Lee', and Edith Simcox, will give the reader the chance to sample some of the non–fictive prose by women in the period, and short stories by Charlotte Mew and Christina Rossetti are also listed. This may explain, then, why only five women novelists are represented: George Eliot (*Daniel Deronda*), Anne Isabella Thackeray Ritchie (*Old Kensington*), Sabine Baring-Gould (*Mehalah*) Mary (Mrs Humphry) Ward (*Robert Ellesmere*), and Marie Corelli (*The Sorrows of Satan*). Anne Isabella Thackeray Ritchie's novel was influential on Virgina Woolf in her *Night and Day*; *Mehalah* was compared by Swinburne to *Wuthering Heights*; *The Sorrows of Satan* proved to be the best–seller of the nineteenth century. During these years women writers experimented with other genres beside the novel—the short story and the essay, as well as verse. Signalling these other art forms as well as the novel compensates, I hope, those who feel more female novelists could have been represented; my criteria has been quality rather than quantity.

The role of book production and serial publication is another important feature of the late-nineteenth–century period, and it is hoped that in the following list seeing a text in the year in which it originally appeared to its late-Victorian audience will further enhance the reader's critical appreciation of the bibliographic complexities of textual transmission at this time. Thus Conrad's *Heart of Darkness*, for example, which first appeared in *Blackwoods* in 1889, but was not published as a book until 1902, appears in the year in which Victorian readers first encountered it.

1872   Charles Dickens, *The Mystery of Edwin Drood*
John Stuart Mill, *Autobiography*
W. J. Courthorpe, 'The Latest Development in Literary Poetry', *Quarterly Review*, January 1872, 63

1873	Anne Isabella Thackeray Ritchie, *Old Kensington* Pater, *Studies in the History of the Renaissance* Matthew Arnold, *Literature and Dogma* R. H. Hutton, obituary for John Stuart Mill, *Spectator*, 17 May
1874	Charles Darwin, Conclusion to *The Descent of Man*, 2nd. edition. Christina Rossetti, 'Speaking Likenesses' Henry Mayhew, *London Children*
1875	Anthony Trollope, *The Way We Live Now* G. H. Lewes, *Problems of Life and Mind*
1876	George Eliot, *Daniel Deronda* Gladstone, 'Bulgarian Horrors and the Question of the East'
1877	W. H. Mallock, *The New Republic* George Meredith, 'On the Idea of Comedy'
1878	Henry James, 'Daisy Miller'
1879	George Meredith, *The Egoist* Henry George, *Progress and Poverty*
1880	Sabine Baring Gould, *Mehalah* Edwin Ray Lankester, *Degeneration: A Chapter in Darwinism* Max Beerbohm, '1880'
1881	Thomas Hardy, *A Laodicean* Froude's *Reminiscences of Carlyle*
1882	Walter Besant, *All Sorts and Conditions of Men*
1883	Robert Louis Stevenson, *Treasure Island* Thomas Hardy, 'The Dorsetshire Labourer'
1884	Robert Louis Stevenson, *The Strange Case of Dr Jekyll and Mr Hyde* Herbert Spencer, *Man versus the State* John Ruskin, 'The Storm Cloud of the Nineteenth Century'
1885	Richard Jefferies, *After London* Walter Pater, *Marius the Epicurean* John Ruskin, *Praeterita*
1886	Rider Haggard, *She* Frederic William Henry Myers, *Phantasms of the Living*
1887	Thomas Hardy, *The Woodlanders* Conan Doyle, 'A Study in Scarlet' Pater, *Imaginary Portraits* Edith Simcox, 'Women's Work and Women's Wages' (*Westminster Review*) and 'The Capacity of Women' (*The Nineteenth Century*) William Morris, 'Facing the Worst' (from *The Commonweal*)

1888	Mrs Humphry Ward, *Robert Ellesmere* Matthew Arnold, *Essays in Criticism*, second series
1889	George Gissing, *The Nether World* Pater, *Appreciations*/'Essay on Style'
1890	Arthur Conan Doyle, 'The Sign of Four' William Morris, *News from Nowhere*/ 'Story of the Glittering Plain' Mona Caird, 'The Morality of Marriage' (*Fortnightly Review*)
1891	Oscar Wilde, *The Picture of Dorian Gray* Oscar Wilde, 'The Critic as Artist' from *Intentions*
1892	Ford Madox (Hueffer) Ford, 'The Brown Owl' Walter Crane, *The Claims of Decorative Art* William Morris, Preface to the Kelmscott Press edition of Ruskin's 'The Nature of Gothic'
1893	Edward Frederic Benson, *Dodo* Clementina Black, 'The Dislike to Domestic Service' (*Nineteenth Century*) and 'What is a Fair Wage?' (*New Review*) C. H. Pearson, *National Life and Character*
1894	Charlotte Mew, 'Passed' William Morris, 'The Wood Beyond the World' Arthur Machen, *Great God Pan*
1895	Marie Corelli, *The Sorrows of Satan* H. G. Wells, *The Time Machine*
1896	Pater, 'Modernity' from *Gaston de Latour* Vernon Lee, 'Art and Life' I; III (*Contemporary Review*)
1897	Hubert Crackanthorpe, 'The Turn of the Wheel' Hallam, *Life of Tennyson*
1898	Joseph Conrad, 'An Outpost of Progress' W. B. Yeats, 'The Autumn of the Body' Sarah Grand, 'The New Woman and the Old' (*Lady's Realm*)
1899	Joseph Conrad, *Heart of Darkness* H. G. Wells, *When the Sleeper Wakes* Arthur Symons, *The Symbolist Movement in Literature*
1900	Joseph Conrad, *Lord Jim* Rudyard Kipling, 'The Way That He Took'

Proem: The Way We Live Now

John Addington Symonds (1840–1893)

i.
The Camera Obscura

Inside the skull the wakeful brain,
Attuned at birth to joy and pain,
Dwells for a lifetime; even as one
Who in a closed tower sees the sun
Cast faint-hued shadows, dim or clear, 5
Upon the darkened disc: now near,
Now far, they flit; while he, within,
Surveys the world he may not win:
Whate'er he sees, he notes; for nought
Escapes the net of living thought; 10
And what he notes, he tells again
To last and build the brains of men.
Shades are we; and of shades we weave
A trifling pleasant make-believe;
Then pass into the shadowy night, 15
Where formless shades blindfold the light.

(1880)

Joseph Skipsey (1832–1903)

ii.
'Get Up!'

'Get up!' the caller calls, 'Get up!'
   And in the dead of night,
To win the bairns their bite and sup,
   I rise a weary wight.

My flannel dudden donn'd, thrice o'er 5
   My birds are kiss'd, and then
I with a whistle shut the door,
   I may not ope again.

(1881)

Alice Meynell (1847–1922)

iii.   *Song of the Night at Daybreak*

    All my stars forsake me,
    And the dawn-winds shake me.
    Where shall I betake me?

    Whither shall I run
    Till the set of sun,   5
    Till the day be done?

Robert Louis Stevenson (1850–1894)

iv.   'The morning drum-call on my eager ear'

    The morning drum-call on my eager ear
    Thrills unforgotten yet; the morning dew
    Lies yet undried along my field of noon.

    But now I pause at whiles in what I do,
    And count the bell, and tremble lest I hear   5
    (My work untrimmed) the sunset gun too soon.

    (1895)

Louisa S. Guggenberger (formerly Bevington) (1845–1895)

v.   *Afternoon*

    Purple headland over yonder,
        Fleecy, sun-extinguished moon,
    I am here alone, and ponder
        On the theme of Afternoon.

    Past has made a groove for Present,   5
        And what fits it *is*: no more.
    Waves before the wind are weighty;
        Strongest sea-beats shape the shore.

Just what is is just what can be,
    And the Possible is free;   10
'Tis by being, not by effort,
    That the firm cliff juts to sea.

With an uncontentious calmness
    Drifts the Fact before the 'Law';
So we name the ordered sequence   15
    We, remembering, foresaw.

And a law is mere procession
    Of the forcible and fit;
Calm of uncontested Being,
    And our thought that comes of it.   20

In the mellow shining daylight
    Lies the Afternoon at ease,
Little willing ripples answer
    To a drift of casual breeze.

Purple headland to the westward!   25
    Ebbing tide, and fleecy moon!
In the 'line of least resistance',
    Flows the life of Afternoon.

(1876)

Robert Bridges (1844–1930)

vi. 'The evening darkens over'

The evening darkens over.
After a day so bright
The windcapt waves discover
That wild will be the night.
There's sound of distant thunder.   5

The latest sea-birds hover
Along the cliff's sheer height;
As in the memory wander
Last flutterings of delight,
White wings lost on the white.   10

There's not a ship in sight;
And as the sun goes under
Thick clouds conspire to cover
The moon that should rise yonder.
Thou art alone, fond lover.   15

(1890)

Thomas Hardy (1840–1928)

vii. *I Look Into My Glass*

I look into my glass,
And view my wasting skin,
And say, 'Would God it came to pass
My heart had shrunk as thin!'

For then, I, undistrest   5
By hearts grown cold to me,
Could lonely wait my endless rest
With equanimity.

But Time, to make me grieve,
Part steals, lets part abide;   10
And shakes this fragile frame at eve
With throbbings of noontide.

Rosamund Marriott Watson (1860–1911)

viii. *Aubade*

The lights are out in the street, and a cool wind swings
Loose poplar plumes on the sky;
Deep in the gloom of the garden the first bird sings:
Curt, hurried steps go by
Loud in the hush of the dawn past the linden screen,   5
Lost in a jar and a rattle of wheels unseen
Beyond on the wide highway:–
Night lingers dusky and dim in the pear-tree boughs,
Hangs in the hollows of leaves, though the thrushes rouse,
And the glimmering lawn grows grey.   10
Yours, my heart knoweth, yours only, the jewelled gloom,
Splendours of opal and amber, the scent, the bloom,

Yours all, and your own demesne—
Scent of the dark, of the dawning, of leaves and dew;
Nothing that was but hath changed—'tis a world made new—   15
A lost world risen again.

The lamps are out in the street, and the air grows bright—
Come—lest the miracle fade in the broad, bare light,
The new world wither away:
Clear is your voice in my heart, and you call me—whence?   20
Come—for I listen, I wait,—bid me rise, go hence,
Or ever the dawn turn day.

A. Mary F. Robinson (1857–1944)

Twilight

When I was young the twilight seemed too long.

How often on the western window seat
   I leaned my book against the misty pane
     And spelled the last enchanting lines again,
The while my mother hummed an ancient song,   5
Or sighed a little and said: 'The hour is sweet!'
When I, rebellious, clamoured for the light.

But now I love the soft approach of night,
   And now with folded hands I sit and dream
     While all too fleet the hours of twilight seem;   10
And thus I know that I am growing old.

O granaries of Age! O manifold
And royal harvest of the common years!
There are in all thy treasure-house no ways
But lead by soft descent and gradual slope   15
To memories more exquisite than Hope.
Thine is the Iris born of olden tears,
And thrice more happy are the happy days
That live divinely in thy lingering rays.

So autumn roses bear a lovelier flower;   20
So in the emerald after-sunset hour
The orchard wall and trembling aspen trees
Appear an infinite Hesperides.

Ay, as at dusk we sit with folded hands,
Who knows, who cares in what enchanted lands   25
We wander while the undying memories throng?

When I was young the twilight seemed too long.

Mathilde Blind (1841–1896)

x.
The Red Sunsets, 1883

The boding sky was charactered with cloud,
    The scripture of the storm—but high in air,
    Where the unfathomed zenith still was bare,
A pure expanse of rose-flushed violet glowed
And, kindling into crimsom light, o'erflowed   5
    The hurrying wrack with such a blood-red glare.
    That heaven, igniting, wildly seemed to flare
On the dazed eyes of many an awe-struck crowd.

And in far lands folk presaged with blanched lips
Disastrous wars, earthquakes, and foundering ships,   10
    Such whelming floods as never dykes could stem,
Or some proud empire's ruin and eclipse:
    Lo, such a sky, they cried, as burned o'er them
    Once lit the sacking of Jerusalem!

The Red Sunsets, 1883

The twilight heavens are flushed with gathering light,
    And o'er wet roofs and huddling streets below
    Hang with a strange Apocalyptic glow
On the black fringes of the wintry night.
Such bursts of glory may have rapt the sight   5
    Of him to whom on Patmos long ago
    The visionary angel came to show
That heavenly city built of chrysolite.

And lo, three factory hands begrimed with soot,
    Aflame with the red splendour, marvelling stand,   10
And gaze with lifted faces awed and mute.
    Starved of earth's beauty by Man's grudging hand,
O toilers, robbed of labour's golden fruit,
    Ye, too, may feast in Nature's fairyland.

William Renton (*fl.* 1852–post 1905)

xi.
After Nightfall

Ample the air above the western peaks;
Within the peaks a silence uncompelled.
It is the hour of abnegation's self,
In clear obeisance of the mountain thrones,
And cloudless self-surrender of the skies: 5
The very retrospect of skiey calm,
And selfless self-approval of the hills.

(1876)

Gerard Manley Hopkins (1836–1904)

xii.
Moonrise

I awoke in the Midsummer not-to-call night, in the white and the walk of the morning:
The moon, dwindled and thinned to the fringe of a fingernail held to the candle,
Or paring of paradisaïcal fruit, lovely in waning but lustreless,
Stepped from the stool, drew back from the barrow, of dark Maenefa the mountain;
A cusp still clasped him, a fluke yet fanged him, entangled him, not quit utterly.   5
This was the prized, the desirable sight, unsought, presented so easily,
Parted me leaf and leaf, divided me, eyelid and eyelid of slumber.

William Frederick Stevenson (*fl.* 1883)

I.
Life and Impellance

There went most passionately to Life, Impellance,
And thrilled it with the high perception of divines;
And through a blight of gloom its request fought for
Heaven, its hospice, light, investure ante-natal,
And hope, impact of fathom, lucid suavity.   5

2.   *A Planet of Descendance*

>A planet of descendance rent,
>   A scatter of an effluence;
>Before the princes of content,
>   Angels of deliverance.
>
>See, methought, the silent hills,   5
>   And the valleys, and the sea;
>There is propent death of skills,
>   And invalid's puissancy.

R. (Rowland) E. (Eyles) Egerton-Warburton (1804–1891)

3.   *Modern Chivalry*

>   I.
>
>Time was, with sword and battle-axe,
>   All clad in armour bright,
>When cleaving skulls Asunder
>   Was the business of a knight.
>
>   II.
>
>Now chivalry means surgery,   5
>   And spurs are won by him
>Who can mend a skull when broken,
>   Or piece a fractured limb.
>
>   III.
>
>Our knights of old couch'd lances,
>   Drew long swords from the sheath,   10
>Now knighthood couches eye-balls,
>   And chivalry draws teeth.
>
>   IV.
>
>See! rescued from confinement,
>   To charm our ravish'd fight,
>Fair ladies are deliver'd   15
>   By the arm of a true knight.

V.

Behold! the knight chirurgeon
   To deeds of blood advance,
A bandage for a banner!
   And a lancet for a lance!   20

VI.

To heroes of the hospital
   The "bloody hand" is due,
But ye heralds bend the fingers,
   Or the fee may tumble through.

French Clocks, 1876

Electric clocks in Paris now on trial,
   So prompt are Frenchmen to adopt improvement;
We truſt the hands may not be on the dial
   Symbols of revolutionary movement.

Working by pendulum, like old French clock   5
   Ne'er yet have Frenchmen gone two days alike;
Bleſt would they be, could one electric ſhock
   Compel them all in uniſon to ſtrike.

A Mystery

Thus a young wife, alighting from the train,
Rebuk'd her huſband in the gentleſt ſtrain,
"When we in darkneſs through a tunnel glide,
You ſhould not kiſs me, deareſt, though your bride."
"Kiſs you! Not I! I kiſſed you not." The pair   5
In mute amazement at each other stare.

6.   *Argument of a Dissenter*

          IN FAVOUR OF THE BURIAL BILL

          I never to the church will give
          My foul's fubmiffion while I live;
          But why fhould fhe exclude when dead
          My body from a churchyard-bed?
          Becaufe when fhe haf feen it laid   5
          In fafety by her fexton's fpade
          She furely cannot feel diftrefs
          That there is one Diffenter lefs.

Frederick Tennyson (1807–1898)

7.   *The Prospect of Evil Days*

          'Tis not a time for triumph and delight,
          For dance and song, for jocund thoughts and ease;
          Like cloud on cloud before a stormy night
          Sorrows I see, and doleful deeds increase:
          Destruction, like the Uragan, shall come,   5
          And change, like mighty winds, whose lowering moan
          Swells to a shout that makes the thunder dumb;
          And bloody Anarchs call the earth their own.
          But when this time of terror and despair
          Is past, tho' I be weary and o'erworn,   10
          Still let me live to breathe the freshened air,
          And hail the glory of that happy morn,
          When the new day shall o'er the mountains roll,
          And love again pour down his sunny soul!

Charles (Tennyson) Turner (1808–1879)

8.
The Hydraulic Ram;
or, the Influence of Sound on Mood

In the hall grounds, by evening-glooms conceal'd,
He heard the solitary water-ram
Beat sadly in the little wood-girt field,
So dear to both! "Ah! wretched that I am!"
He said, "and traitor to my love and hers! 5
Why did I vent those words of wrath and spleen,
That chang'd her cheek, and flush'd her gentle mien?
When will they yield her back, those jealous firs,
Into whose shelter two days since she fled
From my capricious anger, phantom-fed? 10
When will her sire his interdict unsay?
Or must I learn a lonely lot to bear,
As this imprison'd engine, night and day,
Plies its dull pulses in the darkness there?"

from *Anacreon*

9.
The Muses, Eros, and Beauty

Eros, bound, in flowery bands,
The Muses placed in Beauty's hands;
In vain does Cytherea sue
To win him back by ransom due;
Little recks he of such demands, 5
Nor whence they come; but stays with Beauty;
He hath learn'd a bondman's duty.

10.
Eros and the Bee

A bee, within a rosebud lying,
'Scap'd the infant Love's espying;
With finger stung and sobbing cry,
To his fond mother did he fly.

"Mother," he said, "I faint, I die,
This wound a little wingèd snake,
Which rustics call a bee, did make."

But she answer'd, "If the sting
Of bees be such a painful thing,
What think'st thou of their bitter smart,
The hapless victims of thy dart?"

11. *Letty's Globe*

When Letty had scarce pass'd her third glad year,
And her young, artless words began to flow,
One day we gave the child a colour'd sphere
Of the wide earth, that she might mark and know,
By tint and outline, all its sea and land.
She patted all the world; old empires peep'd
Between her baby fingers; her soft hand
Was welcome at all frontiers. How she leap'd,
And laugh'd, and prattled in her world-wide bliss;
But when we turned her sweet unlearned eye
On our own isle, she raised a joyous cry,
'Oh! yes, I see it, Letty's home is there!'
And, while she hid all England with a kiss,
Bright over Europe fell her golden hair.

(1880)

Alfred Lord Tennyson (1809–1892)

from *Public Poems*

12. *England and America in 1782*

Published *New York Ledger*, 6 Jan. 1872; then 1874, Cabinet Edition. T. 'had been offered £1000 by the *New York Ledger* for any poem of 3 stanzas' (*Mat.* iii 177). This version was sent 10 Nov. 1871 (*Mem.* ii 110), but T. was adapting a poem originally written in 1832–4. The early version is at *Harvard* (*MS Eng. 952.6*), along with *I loving Freedom* (II 43) and *O mother Britain* (II 46); there it has no title.

All variants from this MS are below. *H.Lpr 50* is entitled *Thoughts of a liberal Englishman anno 17–*; see ll. 10ˬ 11*n*. T. had thought of incorporating ll. 16–20 in *Ode on Wellington* (1852), *T.Nbk 25. 1782*: the end of the War of Independence. Cp. the appeal to America for aid, in *Hands All Round!* [1852] (II 475).

I.

O thou, that sendest out the man
    To rule by land and sea,
Strong mother of a Lion-line,
Be proud of those strong sons of thine
    Who wrench'd their rights from thee!   5

II.

What wonder, if in noble heat
    Those sons thine arms withstood,
Retaught the lesson thou hadst taught,
And in thy spirit with thee fought–
    Who sprang from English blood!   10

III.

But Thou rejoice with liberal joy,
    Lift up thy rocky face,
And shatter, when the storms are black,
In many a streaming torrent back,
    The seas that shock thy base!   15

¶12. ENGLAND AND AMERICA IN 1782 (1872)

1–5]   O! thou, the centre of the world,
        That sendest out the ships,
    Give welcome when they come from far,
    The freemen of the western star–
        Be friendly with thy lips. *H.MS Eng.*

7. Those] These *MS.Eng.*
10] For they were British blood ? *MS.Eng.*
10 ˬ*11*]   Their speech is thine, their vigour thine,
        Another Thou begun.
    Behold, were Europe lost in night,
    The stars of freedom, there a light
        Beyond our darkened sun. *H.Lpr 50*

IV.

Whatever harmonies of law
   The growing world assume,
Thy work is thine—The single note
From that deep chord which Hampden smote
   Will vibrate to the doom.   20

(1872)

13.   *To the Queen*

Published *1873*, Imperial Library Edition. T. had sent it to Knowles prior to 18 Dec. 1872 (*Letters* iii); T. is described as having 'just written' it, 25 Dec. 1872 (*Mem.* ii 119). Cp. *To the Queen* (II 462). Knowles hoped to be allowed to publish it in the *Contemporary Review*, New Year 1873. 'After considering the idea of letting it appear first in the *Contemporary*, T. wrote to Knowles from Farringford just before Christmas that there would then be no time for the Queen to see it first, and that he preferred to let it find its own way "silently among the people"' (P. Metcalf, *James Knowles*, 1980, p. 259; *Letters* iii).

    O loyal to the royal in thyself,
    And loyal to thy land, as this to thee—
    Bear witness, that rememberable day,
    When, pale as yet, and fever-worn, the Prince
    Who scarce had plucked his flickering life again   5
    From halfway down the shadow of the grave,
    Past with thee through thy people and their love,
    And London rolled one tide of joy through all
    Her trebled millions, and loud leagues of man
    And welcome! witness, too, the silent cry,   10
    The prayer of many a race and creed, and clime—
    Thunderless lightnings striking under sea
    From sunset and sunrise of all thy realm,

16–20. See headnote.
17. growing] future *MS.Eng.*
18. single] warning *MS.Eng.*
19] The single [On that strong *1st reading*] chord that Hampden smote *MS Eng.* John Hampden refused to pay ship-money to Charles I; cp. *Hail Briton* 57–60: 'Not such was Hampden when he broke/Indignant from a silent life,/A single voice before the strife/That, as it were a people, spoke.'
¶**13. TO THE QUEEN (1873)**
3. 'When the Queen and the Prince of Wales went to the thanks-giving at St Paul's (after the Prince's dangerous illness) in Feb. 1872' (T.).

And that true North, whereof we lately heard
A strain to shame us 'keep you to yourselves; 15
So loyal is too costly! friends—your love
Is but a burthen: loose the bond, and go.'
Is this the tone of empire? here the faith
That made us rulers? this, indeed, her voice
And meaning, whom the roar of Hougoumont 20
Left mightiest of all peoples under heaven?
What shock has fooled her since, that she should speak
So feebly? wealthier—wealthier—hour by hour!
The voice of Britain, or a sinking land,
Some third-rate isle half-lost among her seas? 25
There rang her voice, when the full city pealed
Thee and thy Prince! The loyal to their crown
Are loyal to their own far sons, who love
Our ocean-empire with her boundless homes
For ever-broadening England, and her throne 30
In our vast Orient, and one isle, one isle,
That knows not her own greatness: if she knows
And dreads it we are fallen.—But thou, my Queen,
Not for itself, but through thy living love
For one to whom I made it o'er his grave 35
Sacred, accept this old imperfect tale,
New-old, and shadowing Sense at war with Soul,
Ideal manhood closed in real man,
Rather than that gray king, whose name, a ghost,
Streams like a cloud, man-shaped, from mountain peak, 40
And cleaves to cairn and cromlech still; or him
Of Geoffrey's book, or him of Malleor's, one
Touched by the adulterous finger of a time
That hovered between war and wantonness,

14–17. 'Canada. A leading London journal had written advocating that Canada should sever her connection with Great Britain, as she was "too costly": hence these lines' (T.). Referring to *The Times*. T. wrote to E.T., 8 Nov. 1872: 'Lady F[ranklin] has sent me that Canadian bit of the *Times*. Villa[i]nous!' (*Letters* iii); see also T.'s letter to William Kirby, 18 March 1873 (*Letters* iii).
20. Hougoumont: 'Waterloo' (T.).
35. See the *Dedication* to the Prince Consort (III 263).
38] *1899; not 1873–98.* See III 259.
39. 'The legendary Arthur from whom many mountains, hills, and cairns throughout Great Britain are named' (H.T.).
42. 'Geoffrey of Monmouth's', and 'Malory's name is given as Maleorye, Maleore, and Malleor' (T.).
43. Kathleen Tillotson points out that F. J. Furnivall in 1864 had drawn attention to Arthur's incest: 'It was perhaps because of such reference to the incest episode that Tennyson made the disclaimer' (*Mid-VictorianStudies*, 1965, p. 98).

And crownings and dethronements: take withal 45
Thy poet's blessing, and his trust that Heaven
Will blow the tempest in the distance back
From thine and ours: for some are scared, who mark,
Or wisely or unwisely, signs of storm,
Waverings of every vane with every wind, 50
And wordy trucklings to the transient hour,
And fierce or careless looseners of the faith,
And Softness breeding scorn of simple life,
Or Cowardice, the child of lust for gold,
Or Labour, with a groan and not a voice, 55
Or Art with poisonous honey stolen from France,
And that which knows, but careful for itself,
And that which knows not, ruling that which knows
To its own harm: the goal of this great world
Lies beyond sight: yet—if our slowly-grown 60
And crowned Republic's crowning common-sense,
That saved her many times, not fail—their fears
Are morning shadows huger than the shapes
That cast them, not those gloomier which forego
The darkness of that battle in the West, 65
Where all of high and holy dies away.

(1873)

14. *Ode on the Opening of the Colonial and Indian Exhibition by the Queen, Written at the Request of the Prince of Wales*

I

Welcome, welcome with one voice!
In your welfare we rejoice,
Sons and brothers, that have sent,
From isle and cape and continent,
Produce of your field and flood, 5
Mount, and mine, and primal wood,
Works of subtle brain and hand,
And splendours of the Morning Land,
Gifts from every British zone!
        Britons, hold your own! 10

II

May we find, as ages run,
The mother featured in the son,
And may yours for ever be
That old strength and constancy,
Which has made your Fathers great,   15
In our ancient island-state!
And,—where'er her flag may fly
Glorying between sea and sky—
Makes the might of Britain known!
           Britons, hold your own!   20

III

Britain fought her sons of yore,
Britain fail'd; and never more,
Careless of our growing kin,
Shall we sin our fathers' sin,
Men that in a narrower day—   25
Unprophetic rulers they—
Drove from out the Mother's nest
That young eagle of the West,
To forage for herself alone!
           Britons, hold your own!   30

IV

Sharers of our glorious past,
Brothers, must we part at last?
Shall not we thro' good and ill
Cleave to one another still?
Britain's myriad voices call   35
"Sons, be welded, each and all,
Into one Imperial whole,
One with Britain heart and soul!
One life, one flag, one fleet, one Throne!"
           Britons, hold your own!   40
               And God guard all!

(1886)

15.   *Carmen Sæculare: A Jubilee Ode*

I.

Fifty times the rose has flower'd and faded,
Fifty times the golden harvest fallen,
Since our Queen assumed the globe, the sceptre.

II.

She beloved for a kindliness
Rare in Fable or History,   5
Queen, and Empress of India,
Crown'd so long with a diadem
Never worn by a worthier,
Now with prosperous auguries
Comes at last to the bounteous   10
Crowning year of her Jubilee.

III.

Nothing of the lawless, of the Despot,
Nothing of the vulgar, or vainglorious,
All is gracious, gentle, great and Queenly.

IV.

You then joyfully, all of you,   15
Set the mountain aflame to-night,
Shoot your stars to the firmament,
Deck your houses, illuminate
All your towns for a festival,
And in each let a multitude   20
Loyal, each, to the heart of it,
One full voice of allegiance,
Hail the fair Ceremonial
Of this year of her Jubilee.

V.

Queen, as true to womanhood as Queenhood,   25
Glorying in the glories of her people,
Sorrowing with the sorrows of the lowest!

VI.

You, that wanton in affluence,
Spare not now to be bountiful,
Call your poor to regale with you,   30
All the lowly, the destitute,
Make their neighbourhood healthfuller,
Give your gold to the Hospital,
Let the weary be comforted,
Let the needy be banqueted,   35
Let the maim'd in his heart rejoice
At this glad Ceremonial,
And this year of her Jubilee.

VII.

Henry's fifty years are all in shadow,
Gray with distance Edward's fifty summers,   40
Ev'n her Grandsire's fifty half forgotten.

VIII.

You, the Patriot Architect,
You that shape for Eternity,
Raise a stately memorial,
Make it really gorgeous,   45
Some Imperial Institute,
Rich in symbol, in ornament,
Which may speak to the centuries,
All the centuries after us,
Of this great Ceremonial,   50
And this year of her Jubilee.

IX.

Fifty years of ever-broadening Commerce!
Fifty years of ever-brightening Science!
Fifty years of ever-widening Empire!

X.

You, the Mighty, the Fortunate,   55
You, the Lord-territorial,
You, the Lord-manufacturer,
You, the hardy, laborious,
Patient children of Albion,
You, Canadian, Indian,   60

Australasian, African,
All your hearts be in harmony,
All your voices in unison,
Singing "Hail to the glorious
Golden year of her Jubilee!" 65

XI.

Are there thunders moaning in the distance?
Are there spectres moving in the darkness?
Trust the Hand of Light will lead her people,
Till the thunders pass, the spectres vanish,
And the Light is Victor, and the darkness 70
Dawns into the Jubilee of the Ages.

(1887)

from *Ballads and Other Poems* (1880)

16. *Rizpah*

Published *1880*. Written 1878; it was recited, as *Bones*, 5 June 1879 (Mary Drew, née Gladstone, *Diaries*, 1930, p. 158). It is based on the story of a man executed in 1793; Mary Brotherton (*Mem.* ii 249) says:

'I told him the story one day at Farringford, knowing it would touch him, and he came up to see my husband and me next day, and asked me to tell it him again: on which I gave him the little penny magazine I found it in. It was an unpretentious account of "Old Brighton." Many months after he took me up to his library, after a walk, and read me what he called *Bones*. That was before it was called *Rizpah* and published.'

T. comments: 'founded on a fact which I read related in two or three lines in some *Leisure Hour*' (*Eversley draft, British Museum*). The issue is that of 8 Dec. 1877. The relevant paragraph, describing the mother's gathering and interring the bones, is quoted *Mem.* ii 250–1; it ends 'What a sad story of a Brighton Rizpah!' (*Mem.* ii 249 mistakenly says that the name of the magazine–not of the article–was *Old Brighton*.) For the story of Rizpah, see *2 Samuel* xxi 8–10: 'But the king took the two sons of Rizpah.... And he delivered them into the hands of the Gibeonites, and they hanged them in the hill before the Lord.... And Rizpah the daughter of Aiah took sackcloth, and spread it for her upon the rock, from the beginning of harvest until water dropped upon them [the bones] out of heaven, and suffered neither the birds of the air to rest on them by day, nor the beasts of the field by night.' In a trial edition of *1880* (Lincoln), the title *The Mother* was added, preceding *Rizpah*, together with an introductory note on the story which ended: 'She is here represented on her deathbed with a lady visitor.'

I

Wailing, wailing, wailing, the wind over land and sea–
And Willy's voice in the wind, 'O mother, come out to me.'
Why should he call me tonight, when he knows that I cannot go?
For the downs are as bright as day, and the full moon stares at the snow.

II

We should be seen, my dear; they would spy us out of the town. 5
The loud black nights for us, and the storm rushing over the down,
When I cannot see my own hand, but am led by the creak of the chain,
And grovel and grope for my son till I find myself drenched with the rain.

III

Anything fallen again? nay–what was there left to fall?
I have taken them home, I have numbered the bones, I have hidden them all. 10
What am I saying? and what are *you?* do you come as a spy?
Falls? what falls? who knows? As the tree falls so must it lie.

IV

Who let her in? how long has she been? You–what have you heard?
Why did you sit so quiet? you never have spoken a word.
O–to pray with me–yes–a lady–none of their spies– 15
But the night has crept into my heart, and begun to darken my eyes.

V

Ah–you, that have lived so soft, what should *you* know of the night,
The blast and the burning shame and the bitter frost and the fright?
I have done it, while you were asleep–you were only made for the day.
I have gathered my baby together–and now you may go your way. 20

VI

Nay–for it's kind of you, Madam, to sit by an old dying wife.
But say nothing hard of my boy, I have only an hour of life.
I kissed my boy in the prison, before he went out to die.
'They dared me to do it,' he said, and he never has told me a lie.

¶16. RIZPAH

12. *Ecclesiastes* xi 3: 'In the place where the tree falleth, there it shall be.' J. Adler notes that the chapter as a whole combines a great many elements of the poem: the wind, the clouds, the darkness; and xi 5: 'As thou knowest not what is the way of the spirit, nor how the bones do grow in the womb of her that is with child: even so thou knowest not the works of God who maketh all' (*VP* xii, 1974, 367–8).

I whipt him for robbing an orchard once when he was but a child— 25
'The farmer dared me to do it,' he said; he was always so wild—
And idle—and couldn't be idle—my Willy—he never could rest.
The King should have made him a soldier, he would have been one of his best.

VII

But he lived with a lot of wild mates, and they never would let him be good;
They swore that he dare not rob the mail, and he swore that he would; 30
And he took no life, but he took one purse, and when all was done
He flung it among his fellows—I'll none of it, said my son.

VIII

I came into court to the Judge and the lawyers. I told them my tale,
God's own truth—but they killed him, they killed him for robbing the mail.
They hanged him in chains for a show—we had always borne a good name— 35
To be, hanged for a thief—and then put away—isn't that enough shame?
Dust to dust—low down—let us hide! but they set him so high
That all the ships of the world could stare at him, passing by.
God 'ill pardon the hell—black raven and horrible fowls of the air,
But not the black heart of the lawyer who killed him and hanged him there. 40

IX

And the jailer forced me away. I had bid him my last goodbye;
They had fastened the door of his cell. 'O mother!' I heard him cry.
I couldn't get back though I tried, he had something further to say,
And now I never shall know it. The jailer forced me away.

X

Then since I couldn't but hear that cry of my boy that was dead, 45
They seized me and shut me up: they fastened me down on my bed.
'Mother, O mother!'—he called in the dark to me year after year—
They beat me for that, they beat me—you know that I couldn't but hear;
And then at the last they found I had grown so stupid and still
They let me abroad again—but the creatures had worked their will. 50

XI

Flesh of my flesh was gone, but bone of my bone was left—
I stole them all from the lawyers—and you, will you call it a theft?—
My baby, the bones that had sucked me, the bones that had laughed and had cried—
Theirs? O no! they are mine—not theirs—they had moved in my side.

---

51. *Genesis* ii 23: 'And Adam said, This is now bone of my bones, and flesh of my flesh.'

XII

Do you think I was scared by the bones? I kissed 'em, I buried 'em all– 55
I can't dig deep, I am old–in the night by the churchyard wall.
My Willy 'ill rise up whole when the trumpet of judgment 'ill sound,
But I charge you never to say that I laid him in holy ground.

XIII

They would scratch him up–they would hang him again on the cursèd tree.
Sin? O yes–we are sinners, I know–let all that be, 60
And read me a Bible verse of the Lord's good will toward men–
'Full of compassion and mercy, the Lord'–let me hear it again;
'Full of compassion and mercy–long-suffering.' Yes, O yes!
For the lawyer is born but to murder–the Saviour lives but to bless.
He'll never put on the black cap except for the worst of the worst, 65
And the first may be last–I have heard it in church–and the last may be first.
Suffering–O long-suffering–yes, as the Lord must know,
Year after year in the mist and the wind and the shower and the snow.

XIV

Heard, have you? what? they have told you he never repented his sin.
How do they know it? are *they* his mother? are *you* of his kin? 70
Heard! have you ever heard, when the storm on the downs began,
The wind that 'ill wail like a child and the sea that 'ill moan like a man?

XV

Election, Election and Reprobation–it's all very well.
But I go tonight to my boy, and I shall not find him in Hell.
For I cared so much for my boy that the Lord has looked into my care, 75
And He means me I'm sure to be happy with Willy, I know not where.

---

59. *Deuteronomy* xxi 22–3: 'And if a man have committed a sin worthy of death, and he be to be put to death, and thou hang him on a tree: His body shall not remain all night upon the tree, but thou shalt in any wise bury him that day; (for he that is hanged is accursed of God)'; noted by Adler, who adds (remarking l. 73)
Galatians iii 11–13: 'The just shall live by faith ... Christ hath redeemed us from the curse of the law, being made a curse for us: for it is written, Cursed is every one that hangeth on a tree.'
63. *Psalm* lxxxvi 15: 'But thou, O Lord, art a God full of compassion, and gracious: long-suffering, and plenteous in mercy and truth.'
66. *Mark* x 31: 'But many that are first shall be last; and the last first' (Adler).
73. *Election and Reprobation*: the antitheses in the Calvinistic doctrine of predestination.

XVI

And if *he* be lost–but to save *my* soul that is all your desire:
Do you think that I care for *my* soul if my boy be gone to the fire?
I have been with God in the dark–go, go, you may leave me alone–
You never have borne a child–you are just as hard as a stone.   80

XVII

Madam, I beg your pardon! I think that you mean to be kind,
But I cannot hear what you say for my Willy's voice in the wind–
The snow and the sky so bright–he used but to call in the dark,
And he calls to me now from the church and not from the gibbet–for hark!
Nay–you can hear it yourself–it is coming–shaking the walls–   85
Willy–the moon's in a cloud–Good-night. I am going. He calls.

17.   *Prefatory Sonnet to the*
                         'Nineteenth Century'

Published, without a title, in the first number of the *Nineteenth Century*, March 1877; then *1880*. James Knowles had been the editor of the *Contemporary Review*, 1870–77 (I. 3); he requested T. to write something, 6 Jan. and 20 Jan. 1877, and acknowledged T.'s promise on 23 Jan. (*Lincoln*). See P. Metcalf, *James Knowles* (1980), pp. 276–9. Knowles, with T., was a founder of the Metaphysical Society (II. 9–14; *Mem.* ii 166). T. has unconsciously recalled the prefatory sonnet to John Moultrie's *Poems* (1838, *Lincoln*); cp. T.'s I. 8 with Moultrie's 'And braves once more the doubtful sea and sky'. T. and Moultrie share the same extended metaphor, and the rhymes: *past/fast/mast*. T. read Moultrie in Nov. 1850, and wrote to him on 18 Sept. 1852 (*Letters* i 343, ii 44).

> Those that of late had fleeted far and fast
> To touch all shores, now leaving to the skill
> Of others their old craft seaworthy still,
> Have chartered this; where, mindful of the past,
> Our true co-mates regather round the mast;   5
> Of diverse tongue, but with a common will
> Here, in this roaring moon of daffodil
> And crocus, to put forth and brave the blast;
> For some, descending from the sacred peak

¶17. **PREFATORY SONNET TO THE 'NINETEENTH CENTURY'**
3. *seaworthy still*: Knowles was hurt by this reference to the *Contemporary Review*, with which he had broken. 'A long agonized letter on 13 February implored a change to "adventuring still", as less complimentary, but no change was made' (Metcalf, *Knowles*, p. 279).

Of hoar high-templed Faith, have leagued again 10
Their lot with ours to rove the world about;
And some are wilder comrades, sworn to seek
If any golden harbour be for men
In seas of Death and sunless gulfs of Doubt.

from *Idylls of the King* (1859–1885)

18. *Balin and Balan*

Published *1885*. H.T. comments: 'Partly founded on Book II of Malory, written mostly at Aldworth, soon after *Gareth and Lynette* [completed 1872] ... The story of the poem is largely original. "Loyal natures are wrought to anger and madness against the world".' Written 1872–4 (according to *CT*, pp. 402, 484). Apart from the final fight between Balin and Balan, T. takes very little from Malory; the theme of Guinevere's guilt and the appearance by Vivien are additions. The poem was to lead into *Merlin and Vivien*; in *H.MS*, T. incorporated an account by Vivien at court (*Cornhill* cliii (1936) 552–3):

'I bring thee here a message from the dead'.
And therewithal shewing Sir Balan's hair,
'Know ye not this? not so, belike; but this
A most strange red, is easier known'. The Queen
Took the dead hair and slightly shuddering asked 5
'Sir Balin's? is he slain?' 'Yea, noble Queen,
Likewise his brother, Balan: for they fought,
Not knowing—some misprision of their shields—
I know not what. I found them side by side
And wounded to the death, unlaced their helms, 10
And gave them air and water, held their heads,
Wept with them; and thy Balin joyed my heart
Calling thee stainless wife and perfect Queen,
Heaven's white earth-angel; then they bade me clip
One tress from either head and bring it thee, 15

Proof that my message is not feigned; and prayed
King Arthur would despatch some holy man,
As these had lain together in one womb,
To give them burial in a single grave—
Sent their last blessings to their King and thee, 20
And therewithal their dying word, that thou,
For that good service I had done thy knights,

14. *sunless gulfs*: incorporated from *This Earth is wondrous* 21.

Wouldst yield me shelter for mine innocency'.
To whom the Queen made answer, 'We must hear
Thy story further; thou shalt bide the while.   25
I know no more of thee than that thy tale
Hath chilled me to the heart. Ghastly mischance,
Enough to make all childless motherhood
Fain so to bide for ever. Where do they lie?'
And Vivien's voice was broken answering her.   30
'Dead in a nameless corner of the woods,
Each locked in either's arms. I know the place,
But scarce can word it plain for thee to know'.
'And therefore damsel shalt thou ride at once
With Arthur's knights and guide them through the woods.   35
Thy wish, and these dead men's, if such were theirs,
Must bide mine answer till we meet again.'
After, when Vivien on returning came
To Guinevere and spake 'I saw the twain
Buried, and wept above their woodland grave.   40
But grant me now my wish and theirs', ...

For T.'s prose draft of the story of Pellam (H.Nbk 37), see D. Staines, *Harvard Library Bulletin* xxii (1974) 306–7. Staines is persuasive that T.'s prose account of the poem, 'The "Dolorous Stroke"' (*Eversley* v 425–32; *Mem.* ii 134–41), is not a prose draft but a recollection of the synopsis of the plot. See J. M. Gray, 'Tennyson's Doppelgänger: *Balin and Balan*' (1971); also Gray (pp. 37–42). D. F. Goslee has traced 'The Stages in Tennyson's Composition of *Balin and Balan*', thirteen stages through the MSS (*Huntington Library Quarterly* xxxviii, 1975, 247–68).

Pellam the King, who held and lost with Lot
In that first war, and had his realm restored
But rendered tributary, failed of late
To send his tribute; wherefore Arthur called
His treasurer, one of many years, and spake,   5
'Go thou with him and him and bring it to us,
Lest we should set one truer on his throne.
Man's word is God in man.'
                              His Baron said
'We go but harken: there be two strange knights
Who sit near Camelot at a fountain-side,   10
A mile beneath the forest, challenging
And overthrowing every knight who comes.
Wilt thou I undertake them as we pass,
And send them to thee?'
                         Arthur laughed upon him.
'Old friend, too old to be so young, depart,   15

Delay not thou for aught, but let them sit,
Until they find a lustier than themselves.'

So these departed. Early, one fair dawn,
The light-winged spirit of his youth returned
On Arthur's heart; he armed himself and went, 20
So coming to the fountain-side beheld
Balin and Balan sitting statuelike,
Brethren, to right and left the spring, that down,
From underneath a plume of lady-fern,
Sang, and the sand danced at the bottom of it. 25
And on the right of Balin Balin's horse
Was fast beside an alder, on the left
Of Balan Balan's near a poplartree.
'Fair Sirs,' said Arthur, 'wherefore sit ye here?'
Balin and Balan answered 'For the sake 30
Of glory; we be mightier men than all
In Arthur's court; that also have we proved;
For whatsoever knight against us came
Or I or he have easily overthrown.'
'I too,' said Arthur, 'am of Arthur's hall, 35
But rather proven in his Paynim wars
Than famous jousts; but see, or proven or not,
Whether me likewise ye can overthrow.'
And Arthur lightly smote the brethren down,
And lightly so returned, and no man knew. 40

Then Balin rose, and Balan, and beside
The carolling water set themselves again,
And spake no word until the shadow turned;
When from the fringe of coppice round them burst
A spangled pursuivant, and crying.'Sirs, 45
Rise, follow! ye be sent for by the King,'
They followed; whom when Arthur seeing asked
'Tell me your names; why sat ye by the well?'
Balin the stillness of a minute broke
Saying 'An unmelodious name to thee, 50
Balin, "the Savage"–that addition thine–

¶18. BALIN AND BALAN (WR. 1872–4)
16. *aught*] ought *Eversky, 1885*. Emended here for consistency with T.'s 'aught' in *Merlin and Vivien* 387.
23–5. Cp. Robert Bloomfield's *Rosy Hannah* (*Rural Tales*, 1801, *Lincoln*), which begins:'A spring, o'erhung with many a flower,/The grey sand dancing in its bed.' Also Coleridge, *Inscription for a Fountain*:'Nor ever cease/Yon tiny cone of sand its soundless dance,/Which at the bottom ... dances still.' 'Suggested by a spring which rises near the house at Aldworth' (H.T.).

My brother and my better, this man here,
Balan. I smote upon the naked skull
A thrall of thine in open hall, my hand
Was gauntleted, half slew him; for I heard 55
He had spoken evil of me; thy just wrath
Sent me a three-years' exile from thine eyes.
I have not lived my life delightsomely:
For I that did that violence to thy thrall,
Had often wrought some fury on myself, 60
Saving for Balan: those three kingless years
Have past—were wormwood-bitter to me. King,
Methought that if we sat beside the well,
And hurled to ground what knight soever spurred
Against us, thou would'st take me gladlier back, 65
And make, as ten-times worthier to be thine
Than twenty Balins, Balan knight. I have said.
Not so—not all. A man of thine today
Abashed us both, and brake my boast. Thy will?'
Said Arthur 'Thou hast ever spoken truth; 70
Thy too fierce manhood would not let thee lie.
Rise, my true knight. As children learn, be thou
Wiser for falling! walk with me, and move
To music with thine Order and the King.
Thy chair, a grief to all the brethren, stands 75
Vacant, but thou retake it, mine again!'

   Thereafter, when Sir Balin entered hall,
The Lost one Found was greeted as in Heaven
With joy that blazed itself in woodland wealth
Of leaf, and gayest garlandage of flowers, 80
Along the walls and down the board; they sat,
And cup clashed cup; they drank and some one sang,
Sweet-voiced, a song of welcome, whereupon
Their common shout in chorus, mounting, made
Those banners of twelve battles overhead 85
Stir, as they stirred of old, when Arthur's host
Proclaimed him Victor, and the day was won.

   Then Balan added to their Order lived
A wealthier life than heretofore with these
And Balin, till their embassage returned. 90

   'Sir King' they brought report 'we hardly found,
So bushed about it is with gloom, the hall
Of him to whom ye sent us, Pellam, once

A Christless foe of thine as ever dashed
Horse against horse; but seeing that thy realm   95
Hath prospered in the name of Christ, the King
Took, as in rival heat, to holy things;
And finds himself descended from the Saint
Arimathæan Joseph; him who first
Brought the great faith to Britain over seas;   100
He boasts his life as purer than thine own;
Eats scarce enow to keep his pulse abeat;
Hath pushed aside his faithful wife, nor lets
Or dame or damsel enter at his gates
Lest he should be polluted. This gray King   105
Showed us a shrine wherein were wonders—yea —
Rich arks with priceless bones of martyrdom,
Thorns of the crown and shivers of the cross,
And therewithal (for thus he told us) brought
By holy Joseph hither, that same spear   110
Wherewith the Roman pierced the side of Christ.
He much amazed us; after, when we sought
The tribute, answered "I have quite foregone
All matters of this world: Garlon, mine heir,
Of him demand it," which this Garlon gave   115
With much ado, railing at thine and thee.

  'But when we left, in those deep woods we found
A knight of thine spear-stricken from behind,
Dead, whom we buried; more than one of us
Cried out on Garlon, but a woodman there   120
Reported of some demon in the woods
Was once a man, who driven by evil tongues
From all his fellows, lived alone, and came
To learn black magic, and to hate his kind
With such a hate, that when he died, his soul   125
Became a Fiend, which, as the man in life
Was wounded by blind tongues he saw not whence,
Strikes from behind. This woodman showed the cave
From which he sallies, and wherein he dwelt.
We saw the hoof-print of a horse, no more.'   130
    Then Arthur, 'Let who goes before me, see
He do not fall behind me: foully slain
And villainously! who will hunt for me
This demon of the woods?' Said Balan, 'I'!
So claimed the quest and rode away, but first,   135

126–8. 'Symbolic of slander' (H.T.).

Embracing Balin, 'Good my brother, hear!
Let not thy moods prevail, when I am gone
Who used to lay them! hold them outer fiends,
Who leap at thee to tear thee; shake them aside,
Dreams ruling when wit sleeps! yea, but to dream   140
That any of these would wrong thee, wrongs thyself.
Witness their flowery welcome. Bound are they
To speak no evil. Truly save for fears,
My fears for thee, so rich a fellowship
Would make me wholly blest: thou one of them,   145
Be one indeed: consider them, and all
Their bearing in their common bond of love,
No more of hatred than in Heaven itself,
No more of jealousy than in Paradise.'

So Balan warned, and went; Balin remained: 150
Who–for but three brief moons had glanced away
From being knighted till he smote the thrall,
And faded from the presence into years
Of exile–now would strictlier set himself
To learn what Arthur meant by courtesy,   155
Manhood, and knighthood; wherefore hovered round
Lancelot, but when he marked his high sweet smile
In passing, and a transitory word
Make knight or churl or child or damsel seem
From being smiled at happier in themselves–   160
Sighed, as a boy lame-born beneath a height,
That glooms his valley, sighs to see the peak
Sun-flushed, or touch at night the northern star;
For one from out his village lately climbed
And brought report of azure lands and fair,   165
Far seen to left and right; and he himself
Hath hardly scaled with help a hundred feet
Up from the base: so Balin marvelling oft
How far beyond him Lancelot seemed to move,
Groaned, and at times would mutter, 'These be gifts,   170
Born with the blood, not learnable, divine,
Beyond *my* reach. Well had I foughten–well–
In those fierce wars, struck hard–and had I crowned
With my slain self the heaps of whom I slew–
So – better! – But this worship of the Queen,   175
That honour too wherein she holds him–this,
This was the sunshine that hath given the man
A growth, a name that branches o'er the rest,
And strength against all odds, and what the King

So prizes—overprizes—gentleness. 180
Her likewise would I worship an I might.
I never can be close with her, as he
That brought her hither. Shall I pray the King
To let me bear some token of his Queen
Whereon to gaze, remembering her—forget 185
My heats and violences? live afresh?
What, if the Queen disdained to grant it! nay
Being so stately-gentle, would she make
My darkness blackness? and with how sweet grace
She greeted my return! Bold will I be— 190
Some goodly cognizance of Guinevere,
In lieu of this rough beast upon my shield,
Langued gules, and toothed with grinning savagery.'

   And Arthur, when Sir Balin sought him, said
'What wilt thou bear?' Balin was bold, and asked 195
To bear her own crown-royal upon shield,
Whereat she smiled and turned her to the King,
Who answered 'Thou shalt put the crown to use.
The crown is but the shadow of the King,
And this a shadow's shadow, let him have it, 200
So this will help him of his violences!'
   'No shadow' said Sir Balin 'O my Queen,
But light to me! no shadow, O my King,
But golden earnest of a gentler life!'

So Balin bare the crown, and all the knights 205
Approved him, and the Queen, and all the world
Made music, and he felt his being move
In music with his Order, and the King.

(wr. 1872–4)

---

193. Langued gules: 'red-tongued – language of heraldry' (H.T.).

from *Tiresias, and Other Poems* (1885)

19.   *To E. FitzGerald*

Published *1885*, introducing *Tiresias* (I 622). Written June 1883; Edward FitzGerald died 14 June, and T. wrote to Frederick Pollock: 'I had written a poem to him within the last week–a dedication–which he will never see' (17 June 1883; *Letters* iii). T. therefore concluded *Tiresias* by returning to FitzGerald and mourning his death (below). The poem recalls the last visit by T. and H.T. to FitzGerald in Sept. 1876, as H.T. points out. For T.'s change of conception, see ll. 50–6n (H.Nbk 46).

  Old Fitz, who from your suburb grange,
   Where once I tarried for a while,
  Glance at the wheeling Orb of change,
   And greet it with a kindly smile;
  Whom yet I see as there you sit   5
   Beneath your sheltering garden-tree,
  And while your doves about you flit,
   And plant on shoulder, hand and knee,
  Or on your head their rosy feet,
  As if they knew your diet spares   10
  Whatever moved in that full sheet
   Let down to Peter at his prayers;
  Who live on milk and meal and grass;
   And once for ten long weeks I tried
  Your table of Pythagoras,   15
   And seemed at first 'a thing enskied'
  (As Shakespeare has it) airy-light
   To float above the ways of men,
  Then fell from that half-spiritual height
  Chilled, till I tasted flesh again   20
  One night when earth was winter-black,
   And all the heavens flashed in frost;

¶19. TO E. FITZGERALD
1. *grange*: FitzGerald's home, Little Grange, Woodbridge, Suffolk. 3. *the wheeling Orb*: as in *On golden evenings* (*1827*), by T.'s brother Charles.
11–12. *Acts* x 11–13: 'And a certain vessel descending unto him, as it had been a great sheet knit at the four corners, and let down to the earth: Wherein were all manner of four-footed beasts of the earth, and wild beasts, and creeping things, and fowls of the air. And there came a voice to him, Rise, Peter: kill, and eat.'
15. Pythagoras's vegetarianism is connected with the belief that the transmigration of souls included animals.
16. *Measure for Measure* I iv 34–5: 'I hold you as a thing enskied and sainted/By your renouncement–an immortal spirit.' 'Renouncement' (Isabella's nunhood) calls out the allusion, which leads into ll. 18–19.

And on me, half-asleep, came back
    That wholesome heat the blood had lost,
And set me climbing icy capes   25
    And glaciers, over which there rolled
To meet me long-armed vines with grapes
    Of Eshcol hugeness; for the cold
Without, and warmth within me, wrought
    To mould the dream; but none can say   30
That Lenten fare makes Lenten thought,
    Who reads your golden Eastern lay,
Than which I know no version done
    In English more divinely well;
A planet equal to the sun   35
    Which cast it, that large infidel
Your Omar; and your Omar drew
    Full-handed plaudits from our best
In modern letters, and from two,
    Old friends outvaluing all the rest,   40
Two voices heard on earth no more;
    But we old friends are still alive,
And I am nearing seventy-four,
    While you have touched at seventy-five,
And so I send a birthday line   45

23–8. 'One of the most wonderful experiences I ever had was this. I had gone without meat for six weeks, living only on vegetables; and at the end of the time, when I came to eat a mutton-chop, I-shall never forget the sensation. I never felt such joy in my blood. When I went to sleep, I dreamt that I saw the vines of the South, with huge Eschol branches, trailing over the glaciers of the North' (*Mem*. ii 317).
28. Numbers xiii 23: 'And they came unto the brook of Eshcol, and cut down from thence a branch with one cluster of grapes, and they bare it between two upon a staff' (Eshcol, meaning 'a cluster of grapes').
32. The Rubáiyát of Omar Khayyám, published 1859 and subsequently revised.
41. James Spedding, died 1881; and W. H. Brookfield, died 1874.
43–5. A Horatian touch; cp. *Epistles* I xx 27: *me quater undenos sciat implevisse Decembris* ('let him know that I completed my forty-fourth December in ...'). T. would be 74 on 6 Aug. 1883; since FitzGerald was born 31 March 1809 and died 14 June 1883, he never 'touched at seventy-five', nor are these two ages compatible. T. thought that FitzGerald was 75 in March 1883, and his 'birthday greeting' was going to be a month or two late. T. made the mistake because of misreading the end of FitzGerald's letter of 19 April 1883, as 'Yours and all yours as ever at 75' (*Mem*. ii 275–6); the letter, pinned into Mat. (*Lincoln*), ends 'as ever–æt: 75'; *anno ætatis suae*: in his 75th year. (C. Ricks, *The Library* 5th ser. xxv, 1970, 156.) A. M. and A. B. Terhune retain the error in their edition of FitzGerald's *Letters*, and then say that FitzGerald calculated eccentrically. T.'s lines resemble Peacock's *Letter to Lord Broughton*, a copy of which is among T.'s papers (*Lincoln*): 'Old friend, whose rhymes so kindly mix/Thoughts grave and gay with seventy–six,/I hope it may to you be given/To do the same at seventy–seven;/Whence your still living friends may date/A new good wish for seventy–eight;/And thence again extend the line,/Until it passes seventy–nine.'
45–6]   At seventy-five! I asked a friend
                What I should send you on the day

      Of greeting; and my son, who dipt
    In some forgotten book of mine
        With sallow scraps of manuscript,
    And dating many a year ago,
        Has hit on this, which you will take   50
    My Fitz, and welcome, as I know
        Less for its own than for the sake
    Of one recalling gracious times,
        When, in our younger London days,
    You found some merit in my rhymes,   55
        And I more pleasure in your praise.

      When you were born. He answered, 'Send
        Bound in the sumptuousest way
      Your books'–'He knows them line by line'–
        'Well then, send this', for he had dipt

                                          H.Nbk 46 1st draft

49. many a] forty MS 1st reading.
50. this: Tiresias.
50–6] *There are many fragmentary drafts in MS:*
(i)   And found these lines, which you will take,
                      Old Fitz, and value, as I know,
                        Less for their own than for my sake,
                    Who love you,
                              Yours
(ii)   includes as ll. 53–4:
                  Of me remembering gracious times,
                      Who keep the love of older days,
(iii)   Has hit on this, which you will take,
                      My Fitz, and welcome, as I know,
                        Less for its own, than for my sake,
                  Who love you always.
                              Ah if I
                  Should play Tiresias to the times,
                I fear I might but prophesy
                  Of faded faiths, and civic crimes,
              And fierce Transition's blood-red morn,
                  And years with lawless voices loud,
              Old vessels from their moorings torn,
                  And cataclysm and thundercloud,
              And one lean hope, that at the last
                  Perchance-if this small world endures-
              Our heirs may find the stormy Past
                  Has left their Present purer.
                                Yours

'One height and one far-shining fire'
   And while I fancied that my friend
For this brief idyll would require
   A less diffuse and opulent end,   60
And would defend his judgment well,
   If I should deem it over nice—
The tolling of his funeral bell
   Broke on my Pagan Paradise,
And mixt the dreams of classic times,   65
   And all the phantoms of the dream,
With present grief, and made the rhymes,
   That missed his living welcome, seem
Like would-be guests an hour too late,
Who down the highway moving on   70
With easy laughter find the gate
   Is bolted, and the master gone.
Gone into darkness, that full light
   Of friendship! past, in sleep, away
By night, into the deeper night!   75
   The deeper night? A clearer day
Than our poor twilight dawn on earth—
   If night, what barren toil to be!

An earlier draft of the last four lines reads:
   And yet if our poor earth should last,
      And evolution still endures,
   Our heirs may find that stormy Past
      True mother of their Present.
                     Yours

T. and FitzGerald had been friends since about 1835. Cp. FitzGerald's letter of 1862: 'You can't remember this: in old Charlotte Street, ages ago' (*Tennyson and His Friends*, p. 130). The passage of political prophecy in (iii) links the dedication and *Tiresias* itself (cp. *Tiresias* 71–5), but T. must have decided that its fierceness and lack of connection with FitzGerald would obtrude. Cp. ll. 54–6 with Byron, *Don Juan* XVI lxxxii 1: 'I knew him in his livelier London days', rhyming with 'earned its praise' (in a stanza which rhymes on 'Lincoln' and so is the more likely to have lodged with T.). 57. From the closing line of *Tiresias* (I 630), which followed l. 56 in *1885*.

64∧5]
   And drove the shadows far apart
      With echoes of our College hall—
   Old voices. Hushed the loyal heart,
      The wit, truth, delicate humour, all. *MS, deleted*

This MS also has a deleted passage that continues from l. 80:
   Who, sorrowing, send you, to be laid
      Upon your coffin, flowers, a sign
   You flower in me and will not fade
      While my few years on earth are mine.

>   What life, so maimed by night, were worth
>   Our living out? Not mine to me 80
>   Remembering all the golden hours
>   Now silent, and so many dead,
>   And him the last; and laying flowers,
>   This wreath, above his honoured head,
>   And praying that, when I from hence 85
>   Shall fade with him into the unknown,
>   My close of earth's experience
>   May prove as peaceful as his own.

                                    (1885)

[1883. *Prologue* and *Epilogue* to *The Charge of the Heavy Brigade*—see III 91–2]

20.   *Despair*

Published *Nineteenth Century*, Nov. 1881, with subtitle. *A Dramatic Monologue*; then *1885*. It is dated 9 June 1881 in *H.Lpr 48*. A letter from T. to Knowles, editor of the *Nineteenth Century*, in 1882, replied to his protest at the publication of *The Charge of the Heavy Brigade in Macmillan's*: 'You distinctly refused it and accepted *Despair* which at that time I scarcely wished to publish without its pendent poem of *Hope or Faith*. However you prevailed upon me to let you have it' (mid-Jan.; *Letters* iii). In *1892*, T. published *Faith* (III 250). The subject was suggested by Mary Gladstone; her paragraph was expanded to provide the headnote (*Mem.* ii 264). T.'s early headnote (*H.Nbk 48*) had said that 'the subject of this poem was taken from a newspaper', and had elaborated: 'A man and his wife the Other day flung themselves into a river with the intention of committing suicide. The man was rescued, the woman drowned. I have substituted the sea for the river and hypothesized the feelings of a would-be-suicide in this latter half of our nineteenth century.' Horror at a Godless universe and at a belief in eternal torment were lifelong preoccupations of T. Possibly he was influenced by James Thomson's *The City of Dreadful Night* (1870–4; in volume form, 1880); it tells of those 'whose faith and hope are dead, and who would die': 'when the tide/Swept up to her there kneeling by my side,/She clasped that corpse-like me, and they were borne/Away.' On 'Victorian attitudes towards suicide', in relation to the poem and its reception, see B. Gates, *TRB* iii (1979) 101–110.

>   A man and his wife having lost faith in a God, and hope of a life to come,
>   and being utterly miserable in this, resolve to end themselves by drowning.
>   The woman is drowned, but the man rescued by a minister of the sect he had
>   abandoned.

                                    I

> Is it you, that preached in the chapel there looking over the sand?
> Followed us too that night, and dogged us, and drew me to land?

II

What did I feel that night? You are curious. How should I tell?
Does it matter so much what I felt? You rescued me—yet—was it well
That you came unwished for, uncalled, between me and the deep and my doom, 5
Three days since, three more dark days of the Godless gloom
Of a life without sun, without health, without hope, without any delight
In anything here upon earth? but ah God, that night, that night
When the rolling eyes of the lighthouse there on the fatal neck
Of land running out into rock—they had saved many hundreds from wreck— 10
Glared on our way toward death, I remember I thought, as we past,
Does it matter how many they saved? we are all of us wrecked at last—
'Do you fear?' and there came through the roar of the breaker a whisper, a breath,
'Fear? am I not with you? I am frighted at life not death.'

III

And the suns of the limitless Universe Sparkled and shone in the sky, 15
Flashing with fires as of God, but we knew that their light was a lie—
Bright as with deathless hope—but, however they sparkled and shone,
The dark little worlds running round them were worlds of woe like our own—
No soul in the heaven above, no soul on the earth below,
A fiery scroll written over with lamentation and woe. 20

IV

See, we were nursed in the drear night-fold of your fatalist creed,
And we turned to the growing dawn, we had hoped for a dawn indeed,
When the light of a Sun that was coming would scatter the ghosts of the Past,
And the cramping creeds that had maddened the peoples would vanish at last,
And we broke away from the Christ, our human brother and friend, 25
For He spoke, or it seemed that He spoke, of a Hell without help, without end.

V

Hoped for a dawn and it came, but the promise had faded away;
We had past from a cheerless night to the glare of a drearier day;
He is only a cloud and a smoke who was once a pillar of fire,

---

¶20. DESPAIR
13. *fear?*] 1894/fear, Eversley, 1881–5.
20. *Ezekiel* ii 9–10: 'A roll of a book ... and there was written therein lamentations, and mourning, and woe.'
21. *drear*] 1885; dark 1881.
29. *Exodus* xiii 21.

The guess of a worm in the dust and the shadow of its desire— 30
Of a worm as it writhes in a world of the weak trodden down by the strong,
Of a dying worm in a world, all massacre, murder, and wrong.

VI

O we poor orphans of nothing—alone on that lonely shore—
Born of the brainless Nature who knew not that which she bore!
Trusting no longer that earthly flower would be heavenly fruit— 35
Come from the brute, poor souls—no souls—and to die with the brute—

VII

Nay, but I am not claiming your pity: I know you of old—
Small pity for those that have ranged from the narrow warmth of your fold,
Where you bawled the dark side of your faith and a God of eternal rage,
Till you flung us back on ourselves, and the human heart, and the Age. 40

VIII

But pity—the Pagan held it a vice—was in her and in me,
Helpless, taking the place of the pitying God that should be!
Pity for all that aches in the grasp of an idiot power,
And pity for our own selves on an earth that bore not a flower;
Pity for all that suffers on land or in air or the deep, 45
And pity for our own selves till we longed for eternal sleep.

IX

'Lightly step over the sands! the waters—you hear them call!
Life with its anguish and horrors, and errors—away with it all!'
And she laid her hand in my own—she was always loyal and sweet—
Till the points of the foam in the dusk came playing about our feet. 50
There was a strong sea-current would sweep us out to the main.
'Ah God' though I felt as I spoke I was taking the name in vain—
'Ah God' and we turned to each other, we kissed, we embraced, she and I,
Knowing the Love we were used to believe everlasting would die:
We had read their know-nothing books and we leaned to the darker side— 55
Ah God, should we find Him, perhaps, perhaps, if we died, if we died;
We never had found Him on earth, this earth is a fatherless Hell—

30–32. Cp. *Job* xxv 6: 'How much less man, that is a worm: and the son of man, which is a worm.'
35. Cp. the hope of *In Memoriam: Epilogue* 132–6: 'Nature like an open book'; 'all we thought ... is but seed/Of what in them is flower and fruit' (II 458).
55. know-nothing: 'agnostic' was a topical word apparently put in circulation by Huxley in 1869; cp. I. 94.

'Dear Love, for ever and ever, for ever and ever farewell,'
Never a cry so desolate, not since the world began,
Never a kiss so sad, no, not since the coming of man!   60

X

But the blind wave cast me ashore, and you saved me, a valueless life.
Not a grain of gratitude mine! You have parted the man from the wife.
I am left alone on the land, she is all alone in the sea;
If a curse meant aught, I would curse you for not having let me be.

XI

Visions of youth—for my brain was drunk with the water, it seems;   65
I had past into perfect quiet at length out of pleasant dreams,
And the transient trouble of drowning—what was it when matched with the pains
Of the hellish heat of a wretched life rushing back through the veins?

XII

Why should I live? one son had forged on his father and fled,
And if I believed in a God, I would thank him, the other is dead,   70
And there was a baby-girl, that had never looked on the light:
Happiest she of us all, for she past from the night to the night.

XIII

But the crime, if a crime, of her eldest-born, her glory, her boast,
Struck hard at the tender heart of the mother, and broke it almost;
Though, glory and shame dying out for ever in endless time,   75
Does it matter so much whether crowned for a virtue, or hanged for a crime?

XIV

And ruined by *him*, by *him*, I stood there, naked, amazed
In a world of arrogant opulence, feared myself turning crazed,
And I would not be mocked in a madhouse! and she, the delicate wife,
With a grief that could only be cured, if cured, by the surgeon's knife,–   80

XV

Why should we bear with an hour of torture, a moment of pain,
If every man die for ever, if all his griefs are in vain,
And the homeless planet at length will be wheeled through the silence of space,

---

61. *blind wave*: Merlin and Vivien 230.
75. *glory and shame*] 1885; *name and fame* 1881.
77–9. All the details here suggest *Maud*, as do ll. 30–2.

Motherless evermore of an ever-vanishing race,
When the worm shall have writhed its last, and its last brother-worm will have fled   85
From the dead fossil skull that is left in the rocks of an earth that is dead?

XVI

Have I crazed myself over their horrible infidel writings? O yes,
For these are the new dark ages, you see, of the popular press,
When the bat comes out of his cave, and the owls are whooping at noon,
And Doubt is the lord of this dunghill and crows to the sun and the moon,   90
Till the Sun and the Moon of our science are both of them turned into blood,
And Hope will have broken her heart, running after a shadow of good;
For their knowing and know-nothing books are scattered from hand to hand–
We have knelt in your know-all chapel too looking over the sand.

XVII

What! I should call on that Infinite Love that has served us so well?   95
Infinite cruelty rather that made everlasting Hell,
Made us, foreknew us, foredoomed us, and does what he will with his own;
Better our dead brute mother who never has heard us groan!

XVIII

Hell? if the souls of men were immortal, as men have been told,
The lecher would cleave to his lusts, and the miser would yearn for his gold,   100
And so there were Hell for ever! but were there a God as you say,
His Love would have power over Hell till it utterly vanished away.

XIX

Ah yet–I have had some glimmer, at times, in my gloomiest woe,
Of a God behind all–after all–the great God for aught that I know;
But the God of Love and of Hell together–they cannot be thought,   105
If there be such a God, may the Great God curse him and bring him to nought!

---

86. ˄XVI] No glib craniologist then with his babble of type and of shape And how we had mellowed at last into man from the manlike ape. *H.Nbk 49*.
88–9. Adapted from 'Wherefore, in these dark ages of the Press/(As that old Teuton christened them)' (II 153). Cp. *Locksley Hall Sixty* 137: 'Bring the old dark ages back without the faith, without the hope'.
91. *Joel* ii 31, 'The sun shall be turned into darkness, and the moon into blood, before the great and the terrible day of the Lord come.'
96. cruelty] 1885; wickedness 1881.
97. Combining *Romans* viii 29: 'For whom he did foreknow, he also did predestinate'; and. *Matthew* xx 15: 'Is it not lawful for me to do what I will with mine own?'

XX

Blasphemy! whose is the fault? is it mine? for why would you save
A madman to vex you with wretched words, who is best in his grave?
Blasphemy! ay, why not, being damned beyond hope of grace?
O would I were yonder with her, and away from your faith and your face! 110
Blasphemy! true! I have scared you pale with my scandalous talk,
But the blasphemy to *my* mind lies all in the way that you walk.

XXI

Hence! she is gone! can I stay? can I breathe divorced from the Past?
You needs must have good lynx-eyes if I do not escape you at last.
Our orthodox coroner doubtless will find it a felo-de-se, 115
And the stake and the cross-road, fool, if you will, does it matter to me?

21.   *Locksley Hall Sixty Years After*

Published *1886*. Written 1886, recited 27 Oct. (*Mem.* ii 324, 506). The title in the trial edition of *1886* (*British Library*) is *Locksley Hall 1886*. See *Locksley Hall* and headnote (Il 118). H.Nbks *51, 53* (1885–6) and Lpr *128* contain many drafts; some of the more important variants are given below, but without distinguishing in general between first and final readings. J. H. Buckley (p. 234) points out that T. 'strove through heavy revision of several early drafts to control the invective...late in the composition of the poem he added several lines' [151–4] of retreat, as he did in *Maud*. 'The nucleus of the poem' (T.) was Il.13–15, which had been dropped from *Locksley Hall*. The idea of a sequel probably owed something to a comment by A. H. Japp in 1865 (*Three Great Teachers*, p. 132):

'The poet has here carried the poem to the strict limit of his experience at the time it was written. It closes, but does not cease. It abounds with suggestions as to a higher result in prospect. It points to a region of lofty possibility. In one respect, however, it was unsafe for the poet to leave his hero here; that is, when viewed simply from the formally moral stand-point, which requires that a direct lesson be drawn from everything. If, however, the poet ever again wrote on a kindred theme, it would test at once his insight and fuller experience,—whether he would conduct his hero to a more worthy goal.'

Possibly T. was again influenced by the Moâllakát, the acknowledged source of *Locksley Hall*; Amriolkais says, 'O how oft have I rejected the admonitions of a morose adviser, vehement in censuring my passion for thee; nor have I been moved by his reproaches!' For an important reply to T.'s onslaught on the age, see W. E. Gladstone, *Nineteenth Century*, Jan. 1887. On the biographical level, Rader (p. 58) suggests that T. was reappraising Rosa Baring and her husband (Il. 239–40). 'Edith' is T.'s wife Emily ('very woman of very woman,' l. 51, is applied to her, *Mem.* i 331), to whom the volume was dedicated. Sir Charles Tennyson (p. 493) stresses the reconciliation with the other branch of T.'s family at Bayons (e.g. Il. 43–4). For the death of T.'s son Lionel, see l. 55n. T. said that it was 'a dramatic poem, and the Dramatis Personae are imaginary'. 'My father said that the old man in the second *Locksley Hall* had a stronger faith in God and in human goodness than he had had in his youth; but he had also endeavoured to give the moods of despondency which are caused by the decreased energy

115–6. The suicide was traditionally buried at the crossroads with a stake in his heart.

of life.' T. said: 'There is not one touch of biography in it from beginning to end' (*Mem.* ii 329–31). T. wrote to C. Esmarch, 18 April 1888: 'I must object and strongly to the statement in your preface that *I* am the hero in either poem. I never had a cousin Amy. Locksley Hall is an entirely imaginative edifice. My grandsons are little boys. I am not even white-haired, I never had a gray hair in my head. The whole thing is a dramatic impersonation, but I find in almost all modern criticism this absurd tendency to personalities. Some of my thought *may* come out in the poem but am I therefore the hero? *There is not one* touch of *autobiography in it from end to end*' (*Letters* iii).

Late, my grandson! half the morning have I paced these sandy tracts,
Watched again the hollow ridges roaring into cataracts,

Wandered back to living boyhood while I heard the curlews call,
I myself so close on death, and death itself in Locksley Hall.

So—your happy suit was blasted—she the faultless, the divine;　　　　5
And you liken—boyish babble—this boy-love of yours with mine.

I myself have often babbled doubtless of a foolish past;
Babble, babble; our old England may go down in babble at last.

'Curse him!' curse your fellow-victim? call him dotard in your rage?
Eyes that lured a doting boyhood well might fool a dotard's age.　　　10

Jilted for a wealthier! wealthier? yet perhaps she was not wise;
I remember how you kissed the miniature with those sweet eyes.

In the hall there hangs a painting—Amy's arms about my neck—
Happy children in a sunbeam sitting on the ribs of wreck.

In my life there was a picture, she that clasped my neck had flown;　　15
I was left within the shadow sitting on the wreck alone.

Yours has been a slighter ailment, will you sicken for her sake?
You, not you! your modern amourist is of easier, earthlier make.

Amy loved me, Amy failed me, Amy was a timid child;
But your Judith—but your worldling—*she* had never driven me wild.　　20

¶21. **LOCKSLEY HALL SIXTY YEARS AFTER**

9–10]　　　Curse the old goat, you say? poor goat, that through the desert bears the curse.
　　　　　　Should be yours! the would-be widow thinks he bears the longer purse. *H.MS*

13–16. The nucleus of the poem, deleted in proof from *Locksley Hall*. Cp. the painting in *The Lover's Tale* ii 165ff.

She that holds the diamond necklace dearer than the golden ring,
She that finds a winter sunset fairer than a morn of Spring.

She that in her heart is brooding on his briefer lease of life,
While she vows 'till death shall part us,' she the would-be-widow wife.

She the worldling born of worldlings—father, mother—be content,   25
Even the homely farm can teach us, there is something in descent.

Yonder in that chapel, slowly sinking now into the ground,
Lies the warrior, my forefather, with his feet upon the hound.

Crossed! for once he sailed the sea to crush the Moslem in his pride;
Dead the warrior, dead his glory, dead the cause in which he died.   30

Yet how often I and Amy in the mouldering aisle have stood,
Gazing for one pensive moment on that founder of our blood.

There again I stood today, and where of old we knelt in prayer,
Close beneath the casement crimson with the shield of Locksley—there,

All in white Italian marble, looking still as if she smiled,   35
Lies my Amy dead in child-birth, dead the mother, dead the child.

Dead—and sixty years ago, and dead her agèd husband now—
I this old white-headed dreamer stoopt and kissed her marble brow.

Gone the fires of youth, the follies, furies, curses, passionate tears,
Gone like fires and floods and earthquakes of the planet's dawning years.   40

Fires that shook me once, but now to silent ashes fallen away.
Cold upon the dead volcano sleeps the gleam of dying day.

Gone the tyrant of my youth, and mute below the chancel stones,
All his virtues—I forgive them—black in white above his bones.

Gone the comrades of my bivouac, some in fight against the foe,   45
Some through age and slow diseases, gone as all on earth will go.

---

42. Cp. *Mariana in the South* 89–96n, *1832* text: 'gleamed, volcano-like'. Here influenced by T.'s memories of 'the still more magnificent view of the dead volcanoes' in 1861 (*Mem.* i 476). 'My father always quoted this line as the most imaginative in the poem' (H.T.).

43–4. Martin (pp. 212–13) adduces the tablet to the memory of T.'s grandfather, 'the Old Man of the Wolds', erected by T.'s uncle Charles Tennyson d'Eyncourt and slighting the Somersby Tennysons.

Gone with whom for forty years my life in golden sequence ran,
She with all the charm of woman, she with all the breadth of man,

Strong in will and rich in wisdom, Edith, yet so lowly-sweet,
Woman to her inmost heart, and woman to her tender feet, 50

Very woman of very woman, nurse of ailing body and mind,
She that linked again the broken chain that bound me to my kind.

Here today was Amy with me, while I wandered down the coast,
Near us Edith's holy shadow, smiling at the slighter ghost.

Gone our sailor son thy father, Leonard early lost at sea; 55
Thou alone, my boy, of Amy's kin and mine art left to me.

Gone thy tender-natured mother, wearying to be left alone,
Pining for the stronger heart that once had beat beside her own.

Truth, for Truth is Truth, he worshipt, being true as he was brave;
Good, for Good is Good, he followed, yet he looked beyond the grave, 60

Wiser there, than you, that crowning barren Death as lord of all,
Deem this over-tragic drama's closing curtain is the pall!

Beautiful was death in him, who saw the death, but kept the deck,
Saving women and their babes, and sinking with the sinking wreck,

Gone for ever! Ever? no—for since our dying race began, 65
Ever, ever, and for ever was the leading light of man.

48] As our greatest is man-woman, so was she the woman-man. MS. 'What he called "the man-woman" in Christ, the union of tenderness and strength' (*Mem.* i 326). A recurring aspiration of T.'s; cp. *The Princess*, and contrast *On One Who Affected an Effeminate Manner* (III 217).
49. yet so lowly-sweet] *1888;* loyal, lowly, sweet *1886.*
50. Woman…woman] *1888;* Feminine … feminine *1886.*
55. Suggested by the death of T.'s son Lionel (a name cognate with Leonard) at sea, on his return from India in April 1886; ll. 59–60, 71–2, 'were written immediately after the death of my brother, and described his chief characteristics' (*Mem.* ii 329).
59–60] She in him was wise and truthful, she in him was good and brave.
    Love your father. She had taught him not to shudder at the grave. MS
61–2. Cp. *The Play* (III 217).
66 ⁁ 7] Prove that all the race will perish wholly, worst and best,
    Give me chloroform, set me free of it—without pain—and let me rest. MS
Mem. ii 35 tells of a man chloroforming himself: '"That's what I should do," my father said, "if I thought there was no future life".'

Those that in barbarian burials killed the slave, and slew the wife,
Felt within themselves the sacred passion of the second life.

Indian warriors dream of ampler hunting grounds beyond the night;
Even the black Australian dying hopes he shall return, a white. 70

Truth for truth, and good for good! The Good, the True, the Pure, the Just—
Take the charm 'For ever' from them, and they crumble into dust.

Gone the cry of 'Forward, Forward,' lost within a growing gloom;
Lost, or only heard in silence from the silence of a tomb.

Half the marvels of my morning, triumphs over time and space, 75
Staled by frequence, shrunk by usage into commonest commonplace!

'Forward' rang the voices then, and of the many mine was one.
Let us hush this cry of 'Forward' till ten thousand years have gone.

Far among the vanished races, old Assyrian kings would flay
Captives whom they caught in battle—iron-hearted victors they. 80

Ages after, while in Asia, he that led the wild Moguls,
Timur built his ghastly tower of eighty thousand human skulls,

Then, and here in Edward's time, an age of noblest English names,
Christian conquerors took and flung the conquered Christian into flames.

Love your enemy, bless your haters, said the Greatest of the great; 85
Christian love among the Churches looked the twin of heathen hate.

From the golden alms of Blessing man had coined himself a curse:
Rome of Cæsar, Rome of Peter, which was crueler? Which was worse?

France had shown a light to all men, preached a Gospel, all men's good;
Celtic Demos rose a Demon, shrieked and slaked the light with blood. 90

Hope was ever on her mountain, watching till the day begun—
Crowned with sunlight—over darkness—from the still unrisen sun.

---

70. 'Some Negros, who believe the Resurrection, think that they shall rise white', Thomas Browne's *Christian Morls* ii 6 (where it derives from the traveler Mandelslo).
72 ∧ 3] So at least it seems to me, that man can never wholly die *MS*.
74–5] *Transposed in the earlier MS.*

Have we grown at last beyond the passions of the primal clan?
'Kill your enemy, for you hate him,' still, 'your enemy' was a man.

Have we sunk below them? peasants maim the helpless horse, and drive   95
Innocent cattle under thatch, and burn the kindlier brutes alive.

Brutes, the brutes are not your wrongers—burnt at midnight, found at morn,
Twisted hard in mortal agony with their offspring, born-unborn,

Clinging to the silent mother! Are we devils? are we men?
Sweet St Francis of Assisi, would that he were here again,   100

He that in his Catholic wholeness used to call the very flowers
Sisters, brothers—and the beasts—whose pains are hardly less than ours!

Chaos, Cosmos! Cosmos, Chaos! who can tell how all will end?
Read the wide world's annals, you, and take their wisdom for your friend.

Hope the best, but hold the Present fatal daughter of the Past,   105
Shape your heart to front the hour, but dream not that the hour will last.

Ay, if dynamite and revolver leave you courage to be wise:
When was age so crammed with menace? madness? written, spoken lies?

Envy wears the mask of Love, and, laughing sober fact to scorn,
Cries to Weakest as to Strongest, 'Ye are equals, equal-born.'   110

Equal-born? O yes, if yonder hill be level with the flat.
Charm us, Orator, till the Lion look no larger than the Cat,

Till the Cat through that mirage of overheated language loom
Larger than the Lion,—Demos end in working its own doom.

Russia bursts our Indian barrier, shall we fight her? shall we yield?   115
Pause! before you sound the trumpet, hear the voices from the field.

95–8. 'The modern Irish cruelties' (T.); he had deplored them in 1883 (*Mem.* ii 457).
97. *wrongers*] landlord *MS*.
99] Falling from their roasted bowels ...; Jutting from the silent mother ... *MSS*.
110 ∧ 1] Nature, Caesar, and Napoleon give your equal men the lie. *MS*.
115. *Indian*] Afghan *MS*. Russia attacked Penjdeh, 30 March 1885, and for some weeks war seemed imminent.
116. *Pause ... trumpet*] What is Afghan? wars are taxes *MS*.

Those three hundred millions under one Imperial sceptre now,
Shall we hold them? shall we loose them? take the suffrage of the plow.

Nay, but these would feel and follow Truth if only you and you,
Rivals of realm-ruining party, when you speak were wholly true.   120

Plowmen, Shepherds, have I found, and more than once, and still could find,
Sons of God, and kings of men in utter nobleness of mind,

Truthful, trustful, looking upward to the practised hustings-liar;
So the Higher wields the Lower, while the Lower is the Higher.

Here and there a cotter's babe is royal-born by right divine;   125
Here and there my lord is lower than his oxen or his swine.

Chaos, Cosmos! Cosmos, Chaos! once again the sickening game;
Freedom, free to slay herself, and dying while they shout her name.

Step by step we gained a freedom known to Europe, known to all;
Step by step we rose to greatness,–through the tonguesters we may fall.   130

You that woo the Voices—tell them 'old experience is a fool,'
Teach your flattered kings that only those who cannot read can rule.

Pluck the mighty from their seat, but set no meek ones in their place;
Pillory Wisdom in your markets, pelt your offal at her face.

Tumble Nature heel o'er head, and, yelling with the yelling street,   135
Set the feet above the brain and swear the brain is in the feet.

Bring the old dark ages back without the faith, without the hope,
Break the State, the Church, the Throne, and roll their ruins down the slope.

118] Subject to the voice of one who sees one yard beyond his plow. *MS.*
122. Cp. *John* i 12–13: 'But as many as received him, to them gave he power to become the sons of God, even to them that believe on his Name: Which were born, not of blood, nor of the will of the flesh, nor of the will of man, but of God'.
130. See *Freedom* 21–4*n* (III 130).
131. Suggesting (with l. 134) *Coriolanus* II iii, where Coriolanus solicits votes.
133. *Luke* i 52.
134] Pillory the dead face …; Pillory the dumb corpse … *MSS.* These suggest that T. is remembering the indignities inflicted by the mob in the French Revolution; he had written about such in *Come hither* (I. 165). Cp. *The Dead Prophet* (III 111). Cp. T.'s letter: 'Burlesque, the true enemy of humour, the thin bastard sister of poetical caricature who I verily believe from her utter want of human feeling would in a revolution be the first to dabble her hands in blood' (*Letters* iii, mid-Nov. 1882; *Mem.* ii 423).
137. Cp. *Despair* 88: 'For these are the new dark ages'.

Authors—essayist, atheist, novelist, realist, rhymester, play your part,
Paint the mortal shame of nature with the living hues of Art. 140

Rip your brothers' vices open, strip your own foul passions bare;
Down with Reticence, down with Reverence—forward—naked—let them stare.

Feed the budding rose of boyhood with the drainage of your sewer;
Send the drain into the fountain, lest the stream should issue pure.

Set the maiden fancies wallowing in the troughs of Zolaism,— 145
Forward, forward, ay and backward, downward too into the abysm.

Do your best to charm the worst, to lower the rising race of men;
Have we risen from out the beast, then back into the beast again?

Only 'dust to dust' for me that sicken at your lawless din,
Dust in wholesome old-world dust before the newer world begin. 150

Heated am I? you—you wonder—well, it scarce becomes mine age—
Patience! let the dying actor mouth his last upon the stage.

Cries of unprogressive dotage ere the dotard fall asleep?
Noises of a current narrowing, not the music of a deep?

Ay, for doubtless I am old, and think gray thoughts, for I am gray: 155
After all the stormy changes shall we find a changeless May?

---

139. essayist, atheist] *1888; transposed 1886.*
139–40] Wild young Poet, glancing forward, drag us backward,
  play your part,
 Crown the dying filths of Nature with the living flowers of Art.

 Dying are they ? No, nor will, and would that I myself were dead
 Ere the living body of Britain die beneath her dying head. *MS.*
140. Cp. *Art for Art's sake* (III 12). *living hues*: as in Shelley, *West Wind* 12.
145] Till the delicate lady wallow in the sewer of Zolaism, *MS.*
148. Cp. *Passing of Arthur* 25–6: 'All my realm/Reels back into the beast'.
149–50] Only this worldweary being, sick of senseless rage and sin
 Fain would lie below the surface ere this newer world begin. *MS.*
152ʌ 3] Who'd have thought of so much blood–to quote our Lady of
  Macbeth–
 'So much blood in the old man' yet, who stumbles down the steps of death. *MS.*
153–4] *Added later to MS.*
156] Earth may come to iceless winters, Earth may find a deathless May. *MS.*

After madness, after massacre, Jacobinism and Jacquerie,
Some diviner force to guide us through the days I shall not see?

When the schemes and all the systems, Kingdoms and Republics fall,
Something kindlier, higher, holier–all for each and each for all?   160

All the full-brain, half-brain races, led by Justice, Love, and Truth;
All the millions one at length with all the visions of my youth?

All diseases quenched by Science, no man halt, or deaf or blind;
Stronger ever born of weaker, lustier body, larger mind?

Earth at last a warless world, a single race, a single tongue–   165
I have seen her far away–for is not Earth as yet so young?–

Every tiger madness muzzled, every serpent passion killed,
Every grim ravine a garden, every blazing desert tilled,

Robed in universal harvest up to either pole she smiles,
Universal ocean softly washing all her warless Isles.   170

Warless? when her tens are thousands, and her thousands millions, then–
All her harvest all too narrow–who can fancy warless men?

Warless? war will die out late then. Will it ever? late or soon?
Can it, till this outworn earth be dead as yon dead world the moon?

Dead the new astronomy calls her.... On this day and at this hour,   175
In this gap between the sandhills, whence you see the Locksley tower,

Here we met, our latest meeting–Amy–sixty years ago–
She and I–the moon was falling greenish through a rosy glow,

---

157. Jacquerie: 'Originally a revolt in 1358 against the Picardy nobles; and afterwards applied to insurrections of the mob' (T.).
159] Light on some new form of Power, after Europe's rulers fall, *MS*.
165. Cp. *Isaiah* ii 4: 'Neither shall they learn war any more'.
165–6. T. adapts an unadopted stanza of *Freedom*:
        On Earth so old, but yet so young,
          Of equal day from pole to pole,
            A warless world, a single tongue ...
166 ∧ 7] When the great elastick name will flash through all from end to
        end,
        Make, as in the simple body, every member friend with friend. *MS*.
178. The tints at twilight were due to the eruption of Krakatoa in Aug. 1883; cp. the opening of *St Telemachus* (III 224).

Just above the gateway tower, and even where you see her now—
Here we stood and claspt each other, swore the seeming-deathless vow.... 180

Dead, but how her living glory lights the hall, the dune, the grass!
Yet the moonlight is the sunlight, and the sun himself will pass.

Venus near her! smiling downward at this earthlier earth of ours,
Closer on the Sun, perhaps a world of never fading flowers.

Hesper, whom the poet called the Bringer home of all good things. 185
All good things may move in Hesper, perfect peoples, perfect kings.

Hesper—Venus—were we native to that splendour or in Mars,
We should see the Globe we groan in, fairest of their evening stars.

Could we dream of wars and carnage, craft and madness, lust and spite,
Roaring London, raving Paris, in that point of peaceful light? 190

Might we not in glancing heavenward on a star so silver-fair,
Yearn, and clasp the hands and murmur, 'Would to God that we were there'?

Forward, backward, backward, forward, in the immeasurable sea,
Swayed by vaster ebbs and flows than can be known to you or me.

All the suns—are these but symbols of innumerable man, 195
Man or Mind that sees a shadow of the planner or the plan?

Is there evil but on earth? or pain in every peopled sphere?
Well be grateful for the sounding watchword, 'Evolution' here,

Evolution ever climbing after some ideal good,
And Reversion ever dragging Evolution in the mud. 200

185–6. T. compares Sappho (as in *Leonine Elegiacs* 13): Ϝέσπερε, πάντα φέρεις, ὅσα φαίνολις 'ἐσκέδασ' αὔως, φέρεις ὄϊν, φέρεις αἶγα, φέρεις ματέρι παῖδα. ('Evening Star that bringest back all that lightsome Dawn hath scattered afar, thou bringest the sheep, thou bringest the goat, thou bringest her child home to the mother'.)

187–92. Cp. T.'s words to Emily Sellwood (?c. 1 Oct. 1839): 'To me often the far-off world seems nearer than the present, for in the present is always something unreal and indistinct, but the other seems a good solid planet, rolling round its green hills and paradises to the harmony of more steadfast laws. There steam up from about me mists of weakness, or sin, or despondency, and roll between me and the far planet, but it is there still' (*Letters* i 174).

193. the immeasurable sea: Shelley, *Daemon of the World* i 190.

What are men that He should heed us? cried the king of sacred song;
Insects of an hour, that hourly work their brother insect wrong,

While the silent Heavens roll, and Suns along their fiery way,
All their planets whirling round them, flash a million miles a day.

Many an Æon moulded earth before her highest, man, was born, 205
Many an Æon too may pass when earth is manless and forlorn,

Earth so huge, and yet so bounded—pools of salt, and plots of land—
Shallow skin of green and azure—chains of mountain, grains of sand!

Only That which made us, meant us to be mightier by and by,
Set the sphere of all the boundless Heavens within the human eye, 210

Sent the shadow of Himself, the boundless, through the human soul;
Boundless inward, in the atom, boundless outward, in the Whole.

★ ★ ★ ★

Here is Locksley Hall, my grandson, here the lion-guarded gate.
Not tonight in Locksley Hall—tomorrow—you, you come so late.

Wrecked—your train—or all but wrecked? a shattered wheel? a vicious boy! 215
Good, this forward, you that preach it, is it well to wish you joy?

Is it well that while we range with Science, glorying in the Time,
City children soak and blacken soul and sense in city slime?

There among the glooming alleys Progress halts on palsied feet,
Crime and hunger cast our maidens by the thousand on the street. 220

There the Master scrimps his haggard sempstress of her daily bread,
There a single sordid attic holds the living and the dead.

There the smouldering fire of fever creeps across the rotted floor,
And the crowded couch of incest in the warrens of the poor.

201. *Psalm* viii 4.
204. Cp. *The Window: Marriage Morning*: 'Flash for a million miles'.
217–24] *Added later on separate sheet of MS.*
217] Well that while we range with Science glorying through the field of Time, MS.
219. glooming] squalid MS.
222] There among his living orphans lies the still-unburied dead. MS.

Nay, your pardon, cry your 'forward,' yours are hope and youth, but I– 225
Eighty winters leave the dog too lame to follow with the cry,

Lame and old, and past his time, and passing now into the night;
Yet I would the rising race were half as eager for the light.

Light the fading gleam of Even? light the glimmer of the dawn?
Agèd eyes may take the growing glimmer for the gleam withdrawn. 230

Far away beyond her myriad coming changes earth will be
Something other than the wildest modern guess of you and me.

Earth may reach her earthly-worst, or if she gain her earthly-best,
Would she find her human offspring this ideal man at rest?

Forward then, but still remember how the course of Time will swerve, 235
Crook and turn upon itself in many a backward streaming curve.

Not the Hall tonight, my grandson! Death and Silence hold their own
Leave the Master in the first dark hour of his last sleep alone.

Worthier soul was he than I am, sound and honest, rustic Squire,
Kindly landlord, boon companion–youthful jealousy is a liar. 240

Cast the poison from your bosom, oust the madness from your brain.
Let the trampled serpent show you that you have not lived in vain.

Youthful! youth and age are scholars yet but in the lower school,
Nor is he the wisest man who never proved himself a fool.

Yonder lies our young sea-village–Art and Grace are less and less: 245
Science grows and Beauty dwindles–roofs of slated hideousness!

There is one old Hostel left us where they swing the Locksley shield,
Till the peasant cow shall butt the 'Lion passant' from his field.

Poor old Heraldry, poor old History, poor old Poetry, passing hence,
In the common deluge drowning old political common-sense! 250

Poor old voice of eighty crying after voices that have fled!
All I loved are vanished voices, all my steps are on the dead.

236 ∧ 7] Like our earthly streams that lapse into the level from the steep, Time is not a still canal that moves still forward to the deep. *MS.*
250. Cp. *Far shines that land* 21 (III 633): 'to drown in deluge all the Old.'

All the world is ghost to me, and as the phantom disappears,
Forward far and far from here is all the hope of eighty years.

★ ★ ★ ★

In this Hostel—I remember—I repent it o'er his grave— 255
Like a clown—by chance he met me—I refused the hand he gave.

From that casement where the trailer mantles all the mouldering bricks—
I was then in early boyhood, Edith but a child of six—

While I sheltered in this archway from a day of driving showers—
Peept the winsome face of Edith like a flower among the flowers. 260

Here tonight! the Hall tomorrow, when they toll the Chapel bell!
Shall I hear in one dark room a wailing, 'I have loved thee well.'

Then a peal that shakes the portal—one has come to claim his bride,
Her that shrank, and put me from her, shrieked, and started from my side—

Silent echoes! You, my Leonard, use and not abuse your day, 265
Move among your people, know them, follow him who led the way,

Strove for sixty widowed years to help his homelier brother men,
Served the poor, and built the cottage, raised the school, and drained the fen.

Hears he now the Voice that wronged him? who shall swear it cannot be?
Earth would never touch her worst, were one in fifty such as he. 270

Ere she gain her Heavenly-best, a God must mingle with the game:
Nay, there may be those about us whom we neither see nor name,

Felt within us as ourselves, the Powers of Good, the Powers of Ill,
Strowing balm, or shedding poison in the fountains of the Will.

Follow you the Star that lights a desert pathway, yours or mine. 275
Forward, till you see the highest Human Nature is divine.

Follow Light, and do the Right—for man can half-control his doom—
Till you find the deathless Angel seated in the vacant tomb.

267–8] I that never turned away the truthful pauper from my door,
    I that being poor myself have ever striven to raise the poor! *MS.*
269–76, 279–80] *Added later on separate sheet of MS.*

Forward, let the stormy moment fly and mingle with the Past.
I that loathed, have come to love him. Love will conquer at the last. 280

Gone at eighty, mine own age, and I and you will bear the pall;
Then I leave thee Lord and Master, latest Lord of Locksley Hall.

22.   *The Dead Prophet*

Published *1885*. Written 1882–4, judging from MSS in H.*Nbks 52* and *68* and from its probably being occasioned by J. A. Froude's frank revelations about Carlyle's private life (1882–4). In a letter to Watts, 10 Dec. 1885, H.T. said that it was one of 'the old ones' that he had made T. touch up, and that it was 'written ten or twelve years ago' (*Letters* iii); but this is unlikely and may be protective. T. said it was 'about no particular prophet', but H.T.'s note goes on: 'At this time he said of Mr and Mrs Carlyle: "I am sure that Froude is wrong. I saw a great deal of them. They were always 'chaffing' one another, and they could not have done that if they had got on so 'badly together' as Froude thinks."' Froude's Preface (1882) had spoken of Carlyle as a 'teacher and a prophet in the Jewish sense of the word', and in 1884 his introductory note described Carlyle as 'a man who could thus take on himself the character of a prophet'. Cp. the beldam's argument in ll. 44–56 with Froude:

'When a man has exercised a large influence on the minds of his contemporaries, the world requires to know whether his own actions have corresponded with his teaching, and whether his moral and personal character entitles him to confidence. This is not idle curiosity; it is a legitimate demand. In proportion to a man's greatness is the scrutiny to which his conduct is submitted.'

Froude's introductory note spoke too of vague biographies as leaving great men 'a prey to be torn in pieces'. Moreover M. D. Conway (who himself had preceded Froude with a study of Carlyle) wrote of this controversy: 'Tennyson's main trouble seemed to be that the bones of Carlyle should be flung about' (*Autobiography*, 1904, ii 192)—note the metaphor. Froude protested, 20 March 1882, at T.'s having said Froude 'had sold [his] Master for thirty pieces of silver'; H.T. placated him, denying the rumour since T. had said no more than that 'it would have been better if you had omitted 3 or 4 pages' (*Lincoln*).
The poem does not appear in No. 1 of the *British Museum* trial editions of *1885*. No. 2 followed the poem with *By a Darwinian* (III 10), entitled *Reversion*, which is on the same subject. The fact that *Reversion* was, in this trial edition, on the same page is probably due to the printer; in the earlier trial edition *(Lincoln), Reversion* is in MS on the Verso of the last page of the MS of *The Dead Prophet*. No. 3 added the note: 'It may be as well to state that this allegory is not in any way personal. The speaker in it is as imaginary as the prophet'. The false date '182–' does not appear in the *BM* trial editions; when T. first added a date to a *Lincoln* trial edition, he put '17—'. (Like *Aylmer's Field*, '1793', this suggests the French Revolution.) Cp. the veiling of *To—, After Reading a Life and Letters* (II 297), which is on the same theme of the intrusive biography, and which includes the germ of *The Dead Prophet*: 'For whom the carrion vulture waits/To tear his heart before the crowd!' Since this was about Keats, '182–' may have been suggested by Keats's death (1821). Cp. also T.'s poem of *1827, Come hither* (I 165), on the mocked corpse of Henri IV: 'There came a woman from the crowd and smote/The corpse upon the cheek.' (See l. 25*n*.) Since *Come hither* is about the French Revolution, by 1882 it might have come to suggest Carlyle. T.'s source for *Come hither* (*Quarterly Review* xxi (1819) 376) included: 'When the King is dead, his body was placed upon a carriage in such a position that the head hung down to the ground and the hair dragged upon the ground; a woman followed and with a besom threw dust upon the head of the corpse. At the same time, a cryer proclaimed, with a loud voice, O men! behold

your King! he was your master yesterday, but the empire which he possessed is passed away.' Cp. also the MS versions of *Locksley Hall Sixty* 134: 'Pillory the dead face ...', 'Pillory the dumb corpse ...' A *Lincoln* trial edition added as epigraph (slightly misquoted) *Henry V* IV i 229–31: 'O hard condition,/ Twin-born with greatness, subject to the breath/Of every fool.'

I

Dead!
   And the Muses cried with a stormy cry
'Send them no more, for evermore.
   Let the people die.'

II

Dead!   5
   'Is it *he* then brought so low?'
And a careless people flocked from the fields
   With a purse to pay for the show.

III

Dead, who had served his time,
Was one of the people's kings,   10
Had laboured in lifting them out of slime,
   And showing them, souls have wings!

IV

Dumb on the winter heath he lay.
   His friends had stript him bare,
And rolled his nakedness everyway   15
   That all the crowd might stare.

V

A storm-worn signpost not to be read,
   And a tree with a mouldered nest
On its barkless bones, stood stark by the dead;
   And behind him, low in the West,   20

¶22. THE DEAD PROPHET
1] There lay a prophet [dead man *1st reading*] on the heath, H.*Nbk 68*.
5–12] A prophet dead upon the heath *MS*.
14. *friends had*] best friend *MS*. The MS points to Froude.
15] Tore all the decent coverings off *MS*.
17–24] Not *MS*.

VI

With shifting ladders of shadow and light,
    And blurred in colour and form,
The sun hung over the gates of Night,
    And glared at a coming storm.

VII

Then glided a vulturous Beldam forth,   25
    That on dumb death had thriven;
They called her 'Reverence' here upon earth,
    And 'The Curse of the Prophet' in Heaven.

VIII

She knelt–'We worship him'–all but wept–
'So great so noble was he!'   30
She cleared her sight, she arose, she swept
    The dust of earth from her knee.

IX

'Great! for he spoke and the people heard,
    And his eloquence caught like a flame
From zone to zone of the world, till his Word   35
    Had won him a noble name.

X

Noble! he sung, and the sweet sound ran
    Through palace and cottage door,
For he touched on the whole sad planet of man,
    The kings and the rich and the poor;   40

XI

And he sung not alone of an old sun set,
    But a sun coming up in his youth!
Great and noble–O yes–but yet–
    For man is a lover of Truth,

25] There came a beldam from the crowd *MS*. Cp. 'There came a woman from the crowd', *Come hither*
21. See headnote.
26. *dumb death*] dead flesh *MS*.
27 *here*] *Not MS*.
29–68] *Not MS*.

XII

And bound to follow, wherever she go 45
    Stark-naked, and up or down,
Through her high hill-passes of stainless snow.
    Or the foulest sewer of the town—

XIII

Noble arid great—O ay—but then,
    Though a prophet should have his due, 50
Was he noblier-fashioned than other men?
    Shall we see to it, I and you?

XIV

For since he would sit on a Prophet's seat,
    As a lord of the Human soul,
We needs must scan him from head to feet 55
    Were it but for a wart or a mole?'

XV

His wife and his child stood by him in tears,
    But she—she pushed them aside.
'Though a name may last for a thousand years,
    Yet a truth is a truth,' she cried. 60

XVI

And she that had haunted his pathway still,
    Had often truckled and cowered
When he rose in his wrath, and had yielded her will
    To the master, as overpowered,

54] And preached of a deathless soul *H.Nbk 52 1st reading*. This MS has pages missing, and consists only of ll. 49–56, plus two stanzas on different pages:
    He found his truth in an old shadow-land,
        In a ghost-tale told us afresh.
    We prize a truth that is closer at hand,
        The Truth, my friends, in the flesh.'
    And one of the People arose with a frown,
        'Will you help the People to be
    By pulling the People's leaders down
        To the People's level?' but she,

XVII

She tumbled his helpless corpse about.   65
   'Small blemish upon the skin!
But I think we know what is fair without
   Is often as foul within.'

XVIII

She crouched, she tore him part from part,
And out of his body she drew   70
The red 'Blood-eagle' of liver and heart;
   She held them up to the view;

XIX

She gabbled, as she groped in the dead,
   And all the people were pleased;
'See, what a little heart,' she said,   75
   'And the liver is half-diseased!'

XX

She tore the Prophet after death,
   And the people paid her well.
Lightnings flickered along the heath;
One shrieked 'The fires of Hell!'   80

(1885)

69] She tore the Prophet's hidden part *Nbk 68*.
71. *Blood-eagle: 1885* note: 'Old Viking term for lungs, liver, etc., when torn by the conqueror out of the body of the conquered.'
73] Her talons raked into the dead *MS*.
76 ∧ 7]   'The People! the People!' a thin ghost-cry
        Fled over the blasted tree,
    Far away to be lost in a stormy sky,
       'I had lifted them up:' but she, *BM trial edition 2*
80] They were the fires of Hell. *MS*. Perhaps suggested by Froude's introductory note: 'The fire in his soul burnt red to the end, and sparks flew from it which fell hot on those about him.'

23.   *'Frater Ave atque Vale'*

Published *Nineteenth Century*, March 1883; then 1885. Written on a visit to Sirmio, June 1880 (*Mem.* ii 247). It alludes to T.'s brother Charles, who had died in 1879 (cp. *Prefatory Poem to My Brother's Sonnets*, III 45). The beauty of Sirmio is the subject of Catullus's *Poem* xxxi, which begins *Paene insularum, Sirmio, insularumque/ocelle* (T.'s 'all-but-island'); exclaims *o venusta Sirmio* (T.'s l. 2); and ends *o Lydiae lacus undae:/ridete, quicquid est domi cachinnorum* (T.'s l. 8). T. characteristically combines this poem of joy (*o quid solutis est beatius curis*) with the sadness of Catullus's *Poem* ci, an elegy for his dead brother, beginning *Multas per gentes et multa per aequora vectus* (apt to T.'s travels), and ending *atque in perpetuum, frater, ave atque vale*. The mingling of the two moods resembles *Tears, idle tears*: '. . . gather to the eyes,/In looking on the happy Autumn-fields'.
    T. wrote to Gladstone, 3 Nov. 1880 (*Letters* iii; *Mem.* ii 239): 'I am glad too that you are touched by my little prefatory poem [*Prefatory Poem to My Brother's Sonnets*], so far as to honour it by a comparison with those lovely lines "Multas per terras [*for* gentes] et multa per aequora vectus", of which as you truly say neither I "nor any other can surpass the beauty"–no, nor can any modern elegy, so long as men retain the least hope in the afterlife of those whom they loved, equal in pathos the desolation of that everlasting farewell, "Atque in perpetuum frater Ave atque Vale"' On the importance of Catullus' poem to T., see J. Ferguson, *English Studies in Africa* xii (1969) 54–7.

> Row us out from Desenzano, to your Sirmione row!
> So they rowed, and there we landed–'O venusta Sirmio!'
> There to me through all the groves of olive in the summer glow,
> There beneath the Roman ruin where the purple flowers grow,
> Came that 'Ave atque Vale' of the Poet's hopeless woe,   5
> Tenderest of Roman poets nineteen-hundred years ago,
> 'Frater Ave atque Vale'–as we wandered to and fro
> Gazing at the Lydian laughter of the Garda Lake below
> Sweet Catullus's all-but-island, olive-silvery Sirmio!

                                                                (1883)

24.   *Poets and their Bibliographies*

Published *1885*. The title was added in 1888. T. ran through many titles: *Book-making* (*Lincoln* trial edition of *1885*); *Old Poets*; *On publishing every discarded scrap of a Poet*; *Poets and Bibliophils* (another *Lincoln* trial edition). A matter that often irritated T., but he may have thought in particular of R. H. Shepherd, who tried to reprint T.'s early poems, and whose *Tennysoniana* (2nd edn, 1879) caused

¶23. 'FRATER AVE ATQUE VALE'
3. *through all*] among H.Nbk 47 1st reading.
6. T. had apparently called Catullus 'tenderest of Roman poets' in 1846–7 (*Mem.* i 266).
8. *laughter*] laughters *MS*. D. Bush, *Major British Writers* (1959) ii 463, observes that the ancient Etruscans of this region were said to be descended from the Lydians of Asia Minor.

T. reluctantly to print, in 1884, *Lines on Cambridge*. The present poem immediately precedes those *Lines* in *H.Nbk 47*, apparently dating from *c.* 1883 at this point. William Allingham: 'Put last now (it was first) is a Sonnet against raking together and publishing the fragments of a deceased Poet'.(*Diary*, 1907, p. 344; 6 Nov. 1885). The poem is the first in the *British Library* trial edition. It cost T. some difficulty, as is clear from the MS, from this trial edition, and from one at *Lincoln*. Theodore Watts recorded, in a presentation copy of *1885* from the poet, 'This sonnet alludes to Southey's foolish remark that mere quantity of production is important in estimating a poet' (W. Baker, *TRB* iii, 1979, 123).

> Old poets fostered under friendlier skies,
> > Old Virgil who would write ten lines, they say,
> > At dawn, and lavish all the golden day
> To make them wealthier in his readers' eyes;
> And you, old popular Horace, you the wise   5
> > Adviser of the nine-years-pondered lay,
> > And you, that wear a wreath of sweeter bay,
> Catullus, whose dead songster never dies;
> If, glancing downward on the kindly sphere
> > That once had rolled you round and round the Sun,   10
> > You see your Art still shrined in human shelves,
> You should be jubilant that you flourished here
> > Before the Love of Letters, overdone,
> Had swampt the sacred poets with themselves.

from *Demeter, and Other Poems* (1889)

25.   *To the Marquis of Dufferin and Ava*

Published *1889*. It is not in the *Virginia* trial edition of *1889*. Its subject is the death in April 1886 of T.'s son Lionel (born 1854) in the Red Sea when returning from India where he had caught fever. His host had been Lord Dufferin (1826–1902), the Governor-General of India (1884–8) and an old friend of T.'s. Dufferin took care of Lionel for the months of his illness before the fatal journey. Since the poem acts as the introduction to *1889* (see 11. 15–16), it was probably written in that year or in 1888 (supported by its placing in *H.Nbk 55*). T. would have had it in mind since 1886. He uses the *In Memoriam* stanza. Martin (pp. 558–9) compares *In Memoriam* vi 13–16(II 323).

¶24. **POETS AND THEIR BIBLIOGRAPHIES**
5–6. Ars Poetica 386–90.
8. Catullus iii, on Lesbia's sparrow.

I

At times our Britain cannot rest,
   At times her steps are swift and rash;
  She moving, at her girdle clash
The golden keys of East and West.

II

  Not swift or rash, when late she lent   5
The sceptres of her West, her East,
To one, that ruling has increased
Her greatness and her self-content.

III

Your rule has made the people love
   Their ruler. Your viceregal days   10
  Have added fulness to the phrase
Of 'Gauntlet in the velvet glove.'

IV

But since your name will grow with Time,
  Not all, as honouring your fair fame
    Of Statesman, have I made the name   15
A golden portal to my rhyme:

V

But more, that you and yours may know
  From me and mine, how dear a debt
  We owed you, and are owing yet
    To you and yours, and still would owe.   20

¶25. TO THE MARQUIS OF DUFFERIN AND AVA

1–4. Sir Charles Tennyson (*1931*, p. 74) points out that these lines had been *Hail Briton!* 21–4: 'For Britain had an hour of rest;/But now her steps' etc., *verbatim* (I 521).

2. At ... steps] Her steps at times *T.Nbk 27, trial edition or proofs, corrected then.*

6. Dufferin had been Governor-General of Canada, 1872–8.

7–8. Cp. *Ode on Wellington* 170 ∧ 71: 'Perchance our greatness will increase'.

10–12. Dufferin's rule in India was characterized by a strengthening of the army and by many military operations.

19. owed you, and] feel that we *trial edn, corrected then.*

VI

For he—your India was his Fate,
   And drew him over sea to you—
   He fain had ranged her through and through,
To serve her myriads and the State,—

VII

A soul that, watched from earliest youth,   25
   And on through many a brightening year,
   Had never swerved for craft or fear,
By one side-path, from simple truth;

VIII

Who might have chased and claspt Renown
   And caught her chaplet here—and there   30
   In haunts of jungle-poisoned air
The flame of life went wavering down;

IX

But ere he left your fatal shore,
   And lay on that funereal boat,
   Dying, 'Unspeakable' he wrote   35
'Their kindness,' and he wrote no more;

X

And sacred is the latest word;
   And now the Was, the Might-have-been,
   And those lone rites I have not seen,
And one drear sound I have not heard,   40

21–4. Lionel's work in the India Office, including a Blue Book, had been very successful (*Mem*, ii 322–3). Jowett wrote to the Tennysons, 12 Dec, 1858 (*Mem*. i 434) suggesting a subject for T.: 'The subject I mean is "In Memoriam" for the dead in India. It might be done so as to include some scenes of Cawnpore and Lucknow; or quite simply and slightly, "Relatives in India", the Schemings and hopings and imaginings about them, and the fatal missive suddenly announcing their death. They leave us in the fairness and innocence of youth, with nothing but the vision of their childhood and boyhood to look back upon, and return no more. Perhaps you know what sets my thoughts upon this, the death of my dear brother, the second who had died in India.'

25–8. Cp. the similar praise of the dead Lionel in *Locksley Hall Sixty Years After 59–60* (III 151).

39. lone] last *trial edn, corrected* then.

XI

Are dreams that scarce will let me be,
　Not there to bid my boy farewell,
　When That within the coffin fell,
Fell—and flashed into the Red Sea,

XII

Beneath a hard Arabian moon　　　　　　　　　　　　　　45
　And alien stars. To question, why
　The sons before the fathers die,
Not mine! and I may meet him soon;

XIII

But while my life's late eve endures,
　Nor settles into hueless gray,　　　　　　　　　　　　　50
　My memories of his briefer day
Will mix with love for you and yours.

(1889)

26.　　　　　　　　　　　*Vastness*

Published *Macmillan's Magazine*, Nov. 1885; then *1889*. J. H. Buckley (pp. 231–2) discusses the draft in *H.Nbk 52* (with poems of *1885*), noting that the poem originally consisted of stanzas i–iii, xviii. It is on one of T.'s recurring themes; cp. *Despair* (III 86). 'His MS note is, "What matters anything in this world without full faith in the Immortality of the Soul and of Love?" ' (*Mem.* ii 343).

41–2] But sounds, shapes, shadows, trouble me,
　　　Black decks, sea-whirl, muffled bell, *H.Nbk 55 1st reading*.
42–6. F. T. Palgrave, in an article set up in type but not published (*Lincoln*), juxtaposed these lines with an extract from 'the *Melbourne Argus* of the 24th of July [1886], written by a fellow-passenger on board the vessel; as the short personal description gave a sad pleasure to the bereaved father: "No mistaking the likeness [to Lord Tennyson] in the massive head, the flowing beard and hair, as he lay, pale and wan, on a couch on deck. Six hours afterwards, at nine o'clock, the crew is mustered by the tolling of a muffled bell ... A reverend clergyman and missionary reads the beautiful Burial Service of the Church of England, which seems more impressive here than on shore. There are many wet eyes at the words 'We therefore commit' ... Then the coffin slides with a solemn splash into the dark water, a bubble of phosphorescent light is seen for a moment, the waves close over it, and broken voices repeat *Our Father*" ...' (*TRB* ii, 1972, 20). T.'s 'flashed' is illuminated by the phosphorescence; and cp. also 11. 34, 47.
48. *Not mine*] Vain, vain *H.MS*.

I

Many a hearth upon our dark globe sighs after many a vanished face,
Many a planet by many a sun may roll with the dust of a vanished race.

II

Raving politics, never at rest—as this poor earth's pale history runs,—
What is it all but a trouble of ants in the gleam of a million million of suns?

III

Lies upon this side, lies upon that side, truthless violence mourned by the Wise, 5
Thousands of voices drowning his own in a popular torrent of lies upon lies;

IV

Stately purposes, valour in battle, glorious annals of army and fleet,
Death for the right cause, death for the wrong cause, trumpets of victory,
    groans of defeat;

V

Innocence seethed in her mother's milk, and Charity setting the martyr aflame;
Thraldom who walks with the banner of Freedom, and recks not to ruin a realm
    in her name. 10

VI

Faith at her zenith, or all but lost in the gloom of doubts that darken the schools;
Craft with a bunch of all-heal in her hand, followed up by her vassal legion of fools;

VII

Trade flying over a thousand seas with her spice and her vintage, her silk and her corn;
Desolate offing, sailorless harbours, famishing populace, wharves forlorn;

VIII

Star of the morning, Hope in the sunrise; gloom of the evening, Life at a close; 15
Pleasure who flaunts on her wide down-way with her flying robe and her
    poisoned rose;

¶26. VASTNESS
9. *Exodus* xxxiv 26: 'Thou shalt not seethe a kid in his mother's milk.'
13–16] *1889; not 1885.* A draft of 11. 15–16 was inserted by T. between 1. 6 and 1. 7 in the offprint of *1885* he sent to Gladstone (*British Library*).
14. *offing*: the sea seen from the shore.

IX

Pain, that has crawled from the corpse of Pleasure, a worm which writhes all day, and at night
Stirs up again in the heart of the sleeper, and stings him back to the curse of the light;

X

Wealth with his wines and his wedded harlots; honest Poverty, bare to the bone;
Opulent Avarice, lean as Poverty; Flattery gilding the rift in a throne;   20

XI

Fame blowing out from her golden trumpet a jubilant challenge to Time and to Fate;
Slander, her shadow, sowing the nettle on all the laurelled graves of the Great;

XII

Love for the maiden, crowned with marriage, no regrets for aught that has been,
Household happinesss, gracious children, debtless competence, golden mean;

XIII

National hatreds of whole generations, and pigmy spites of the village spire;   25
Vows that will last to the last death-ruckle, and vows that are snapt in a moment of fire;

XIV

He that has lived for the lust of the minute, and died in the doing it, flesh without mind;
He that has nailed all flesh to the Cross, till Self died out in the love of his kind;

---

19. Cp. *By an Evolutionist* 8: 'Youth and Health, and birth and wealth, and choice of women and of wines'.
19–20] 1889; *the second half of the lines transposed with each other in* 1885.
20. in] 1889; of 1885.
21–2] 1889; *not* 1885.
24]   Comely consort, rosy Children,
               homely service sober and clean, *H.Nbk* 52;
          Debtless competence, comely children,
               happy household, sober and clean *W. Ward*.
Ward records T.'s reading the poem before publishing it in 1885: 'His hearers smiled very visibly at the last words. Tennyson looked up. "Why are you laughing?" he asked. "If we laughed perhaps others might laugh," was ventured. "True," he said, and closed his book. Next day he called us, and read as follows' (as published); *Tennyson: Interviews and Recollections*, ed. N. Page (1983), p. 103.
25. *spites … spire*] hates of the litterateur *H.MS*.

XV

Spring and Summer and Autumn and Winter, and all these old revolutions of earth;
All new-old revolutions of Empire—change of the tide—what is all of it worth? 30

XVI

What the philosophies, all the sciences, poesy, varying voices of prayer?
All that is noblest, all that is basest, all that is filthy with all that is fair?

XVII

What is it all, if we all of us end but in being our own corpse-coffins at last,
Swallowed in Vastness, lost in Silence, drowned in the deeps of a meaningless Past?

XVIII

What but a murmur of gnats in the gloom, or a moment's anger of bees in their hive?— 35

* * * *

Peace, let it be! for I loved him, and love him for ever: the dead are not dead but alive.

27.   *To Ulysses*

Published *1889*. Written early 1888 (11. 6–8), and read to F.T. Palgrave in Nov. (*Mem.* ii 507). T. comments that *Ulysses* was 'the title of a number of essays by W. G. Palgrave. He died at Monte Video before seeing my poem'. Palgrave was the brother of F.T. Palgrave (friend of T., and editor of *The Golden Treasury*); T. had met him many times since 1860. His *Ulysses* was published in Nov. 1887, and T. was presented with a copy; he died 30 Sept. 1888 (*Mem.* ii 507). T. uses the *In Memoriam* stanza to praise the book, as in *To E.L.* (II 465). On Palgrave and his book, *Ulysses: or, Scenes and Studies in Many Lands*, see W. N. Rogers, *VP* xix (1981) 351–66.

33. Cp. *Pierced through* 17: 'A carcase in the coffin of this flesh'.
36]   Save for a hope that we shall not be lost in the Vastness,
            a dream that the dead are alive ? *MS 1st reading*
        Peace, for I hold that I shall not be lost in the darkness,
            the dead are not dead but alive. *MS 2nd reading*
        Nay, for I knew thee, O brother, and loved thee,
            and I hold thee as one not dead but alive. *MS 3rd reading.*
The end is usually taken as referring to Arthur Hallam, but J. H. Buckley suggests that T. may have been thinking of his brother Charles, who died in 1879. But Hallam seems more likely; for the word 'brother', cp. *In Memoriam* ix 16, 20: 'My friend, the brother of my love …/More than my brothers are to me.' Also ciii 14–15: 'him I loved, and love/For ever'. Wilfrid Ward wrote of T. and this poem: it 'had, as he first read it to me, two distinct voices – the last line being placed in the mouth of a separate speaker who answers the rest of the poem' (*New Review* xv (1896) 84).

I

Ulysses, much-experienced man,
    Whose eyes have known this globe of ours,
    Her tribes of men, and trees, and flowers,
From Corrientes to Japan,

II

To you that bask below the Line,   5
    I soaking here in winter wet—
    The century's three strong eights have met
To drag me down to seventy-nine

III

In summer if I reach my day—
    To you, yet young, who breathe the balm   10
    Of summer-winters by the palm
And orange grove of Paraguay,

IV

I tolerant of the colder time,
    Who love the winter woods, to trace
    On paler heavens the branching grace   15
Of leafless elm, or naked lime,

V

And see my cedar green, and there
    My giant ilex keeping leaf
    When frost is keen and days are brief—
Or marvel how in English air   20

¶27. TO ULYSSES

1–3. Palgrave's epigraph (in explanation of his title) had been *Qui multorum hominum mores et vidit et urbes*, i.e. Horace's *Epistles* I ii 19–20: *qui ... multorum providus urbes/et mores hominum inspexit*, from *Odyssey* i 3. Cp. *Ulysses* 13: 'Much have I seen and known; cities of men...'.

4. *Corrientes*: in Argentina.

10–11. Cp. *The Brook* 196: 'breathes in April–autumns'.

11. *summer-winters*] sunnier summers H.Nbk 55.

14. *the winter woods,*] with careful [patient *1st reading*] eye MS.

17. *And*] Who MS.

20. *Or ... how*] While yonder out MS *1st reading*.

VI

My yucca, which no winter quells,
    Although the months have scarce begun,
    Has pushed toward our faintest sun
A spike of half-accomplished bells–

VII

Or watch the waving pine which here   25
    The warrior of Caprera set,
    A name that earth will not forget
Till earth has rolled her latest year–

VIII

I, once half-crazed for larger light
    On broader zones beyond the foam,   30
    But chaining fancy now at home
Among the quarried downs of Wight,

IX

Not less would yield full thanks to you
    For your rich gift, your tale of lands
    I know not, your Arabian sands;   35
Your cane, your palm, tree-fern, bamboo,

---

21. *My*] One *MS 1st reading*.
23. *our faintest*] the hazy *MS 1st reading*; our feeblest *MS 2nd reading*.
25. *Or*] Who *MS 1st reading*. *waving pine*] slim pine waye *MS 1st reading*.
26. *1889* note: 'Garibaldi said to me, alluding to his barren island, "I wish I had your trees."' 'T. noted that Garibaldi planted a Wellingtonia at Farringford, April 1864. *Caprera*: Garibaldi's home, an island off Sardinia.
29. *once half-crazed*] yearning once *MS 1st reading*; once half-mad *MS 2nd reading*. Cp. *You ask me, why* 26–8: 'I seek a warmer sky,/And I will see before I die/The palms and temples of the South.' Recalled perhaps because it uses the *In Memoriam stanza*.
31. *chaining fancy now*] now with fancy chained *MS 1st reading*.
33. *Not less*] I yet *MS 1st reading*.
34. *1889* note: 'The tale of Nejd' (in Arabia).

X

The wealth of tropic bower and brake;
   Your Oriental Eden-isles,
   Where man, nor only Nature smiles;
Your wonder of the boiling lake;   40

XI

Phra-Chai, the Shadow of the Best,
   Phra-bat the step; your Pontic coast;
   Crag-cloister; Anatolian Ghost;
Hong-Kong, Karnac, and all the rest;

XII

Through which I followed line by line   45
   Your leading hand, and came, my friend,
   To prize your various book, and send
A gift of slenderer value, mine.

28.   *Merlin and the Gleam*

Published *1889*, written Aug. (*Mem.* ii 366). It is not in the *Virginia* and *Trinity* trial editions of *1889*, but is added by hand to a *Lincoln* trial edition, with many corrections and variants. T. says: 'In the story of *Merlin and Nimuë* I have read that Nimuë means the "Gleam", which signifies in my poem the higher poetic imagination.' The Vivien (in the equating of Nimuë and Vivien) is not the Vivien of the *Idylls*; G. S. Haight, *SP* xliv (1947) 559, shows that T.'s source was W. F. Skene's *The Four Ancient Books of Wales* (1868, *Lincoln*)—'which my father often quoted' (H.T.). J. Kill-ham (*Notes and Queries*, Dec. 1958) endorses M. W. MacCallum's point that T. was influenced by John Veitch, who had recently identified Merlin's early love with 'The Gleam', in his poem *Merlin* (April 1889). T. was possibly also influenced by Robert Buchanan's *Book of Orm* (1870), which is metrically comparable; it tells of a

38. 1889 note: 'The Philippines'. Cp. *Locksley Hall* 164: 'summer isles of Eden'. Palgrave may have been thinking of this (he was certainly thinking of *The Lotos-Eaters*) when he called the Philippines 'isles of Eden, lotus-lands' (p. 113). T., as it were, returns the compliment.
40. *wonder*] marvel *MS 1st reading*. 1889 note: 'In Dominica' (West Indies).
40–44. The listing of the natural wonders suggests *On Sublimity* 81–100 (I 131).
41. 1889 note: 'The Shadow of the Lord. Certain obscure markings on a rock in Siam, which express the image of Buddha to the Buddhist more or less distinctly according to his faith and his moral worth.'
42. *Phra-bat*: 1889 note: 'The footstep of the Lord on another rock.'
43. 1889 notes: 'The monastery of Sumelas', and 'Anatolian Spectre stories'.
44. *Hong-Kong*: 1889 note: 'The Three Cities' (the title of Palgrave's chapter on Hong-Kong). *Karnac*: 1889 note: 'Travels in Egypt'. *rest*.] rest. 1889, 1894, *Eversley*. Rogers (see headnote) puts the case against the full stop; to his argument should be added that *H.MS* has no punctuation here.

quest to see 'the Face', and refers to 'the Master'. T.'s metre has the rhythms of Old Welsh poetry, and is also intended to give something of the effect of Anglo–Saxon verse; cp. *Battle of Brunanburh* (III 18), which is likewise mainly trochaics and dactylics in 2-stress lines. T. had used the pseudonym 'Merlin' when publishing *The Third of February* (1852). As Haight observes, Wordsworth had juxtaposed 'gleam' with poetic imagination in a poem that was one of T.'s favourites (*Mem.* i I5l), *Elegiac Stanzas suggested by a Picture of Peele Castle* 14–16: 'add the gleam,/The light that never was, on sea or land,/The consecration, and the Poet's dream.' T. had long used it for the idealist's vision: 'Gleams that untravelled world, whose margin fades' (*Ulysses* 20); 'For one fair Vision ever fled...now she gleamed' (*The Voyage* 57, 65); 'O follower of the Vision, still/In motion to the distant gleam' (*Freedom* 13–14).

Biographical allegory. 'For those who cared to know about his literary history he wrote *Merlin and the Gleam*' (H.T.). But it presents difficulties. H.T. gives 'the reading of the poet's riddle as he gave it to me'. Section i, 'From his boyhood he had felt the magic of Merlin–that spirit of poetry'. ii, the poetry of T.'s youth. iii, 'the harsh voice of those who were unsympathetic' iv, renewed inspiration from romantic fancy and nature, or 'the early imagination' (T.). v, Eclogues and English Idyls, or 'the Pastorals' (T.). vi, 'human love and human heroism', and he 'began what he had already devised, his Epic of king Arthur'. vii, the death of Arthur Hallam 'made him almost fail in this purpose'. viii, finding 'a stronger faith his own'. ix, 'Up to the end he faced death with the same earnest and unfailing courage that he had always shown, but with an added sense of the awe and the mystery of the Infinite'. But is the poem meant to be chronological, and if so should not Hallam's death come much earlier ? Unless iii refers, not to the reviewers of *1832*, but, as Sir Charles Tennyson suggests (p. 517), to the family troubles which followed Dr Tennyson's death in 1831, and the attempts made by T.'s grandfather to divert him from poetry. In which case iii–vi would be the development during T.'s friendship with Hallam. Yet H.T. took iii as the reviewers: 'the "Raven croaked" ominously in the shape of the *Quarterly*. This Review and the death of Arthur Hallam almost "deadened the melody" '(*Mat.* i 141). These sentences were dropped for *Mem.*, but there is no telling whether simply as one of many cuts or because H.T. thought them mistaken. Haight argues that the poem is not a systematic account of the published volumes, but of the various inspirations, so that iv becomes 'early imagination' and the supernatural; v, common life spurred on by Wordsworth; vi, Arthurian matter beginning with *The Lady of Shalott*. A summary conclusion might be that T. did not mind its being enigmatic, a 'riddle' (H.T.), but that it was meant to be chronological; what thwarted this was the gap of seventeen years between Hallam's death and the publication of *In Memoriam*. T. had to present these events in consecutive stanzas, since otherwise the poem might seem casual about both Hallam's death and the 'stronger faith', but in doing so T. was forced to obscure the chronology. On the lifelong diverse importance of Merlin to T., se C. B. Stevenson, *VN* No. 57 (1980) 14–23.

I

O young Mariner,
You from the haven
Under the sea-cliff,
You that are watching
The gray Magician   5
With eyes of wonder,
I am Merlin,
And *I* am dying,
I am Merlin
Who follow The Gleam.   10

II

Mighty the Wizard
Who found me at sunrise
Sleeping, and woke me
And learned me Magic!
Great the Master,   15
And sweet the Magic,
When over the valley,
In early summers,
Over the mountain,
On human faces,   20
And all around me,
Moving to melody,
Floated The Gleam.

III

Once at the croak of a Raven
    who crost it,
A barbarous people,   25
Blind to the magic,
And deaf to the melody,
Snarled at and cursed me.
A demon vext me,
The light retreated,   30
The landskip darkened,

¶28. MERLIN AND THE GLEAM

11] A mighty Master *Lincoln trial edition 1st reading;* Mighty the Master *trial edition.* Haight suggests a reference to the Wizard of the North, Walter Scott, who was a major influence on the young T. (*Mem.* i 12). *24–34.* Reviewers or family or both? See headnote. Haight, like T. O. Mabbott (*Notes and Queries,* 10 Jan. 1948), takes 'croak' as suggesting J. W. Croker, who reviewed *1832* in QR; and H.T. might seem to support this. But Veitch's *Merlin* had spoken of 'the croak of the raven brood', and T. used the word elsewhere of ravens. J. H. Buckley (p. 287) prefers Christopher North, whose journalist's familiar was a raven, 'since the raven was associated with North and since [T.] believed that North had not only attacked in his own review but had also instigated Croker's'. Cp. Byron on the reviewers of *Hours of Idleness, Edinburgh Review* (1808): 'I was bent on falsifying their raven predictions, and determined to show them, croak as they would, that it was not the last time they should hear from me' (*Works,* 1832–3, vii 223). Mabbott notes that the transition from 'raven' to 'barbarous' suggests the Danes and their standard (apt to the Anglo-Saxon tone of the poem); he compares *Guinevere* 132–4: 'The Raven, flying high, / Croaked ... / For now the Heathen of the Northern Sea ...'.
24] *Added in trial edition.*
26] Who hated Magic, *trial edition 1st reading.*
27] *Added in trial edition.*
28. Snarled] Railed *trial edition.*

             The melody deadened,
             The Master whispered
             'Follow The Gleam.'

                    IV

             Then to the melody,   35
             Over a wilderness
             Gliding, and glancing at
             Elf of the woodland,
             Gnome of the cavern,
             Griffin and Giant,   40
             And dancing of Fáiries
             In desolate hollows,
             And wraiths of the mountain,
             And rolling of dragons
             By warble of water,   45
             Or cataract music
             Of falling torrents,
             Flitted The Gleam.

                     V

             Down from the mountain
             And over the level,   50
             And streaming and shining on
             Silent river,
             Silvery willow,
             Pasture and plowland,
             Innocent maidens,   55
             Garrulous children,
             Homestead and harvest,
             Reaper and gleaner,
             And rough-ruddy faces
             Of lowly labour,   60
             Slided The Gleam—

                    VI

             Then, with a melody
             Stronger and statelier,
             Led me at length
             To the city and palace   65

32] *Added in trial edition.*
33] I heard a whisper *trial edition 1st reading.*
54 ∧ 5] Horses and oxen, *1889.*

Of Arthur the king;
Touched at the golden
Cross of the churches,
Flashed on the Tournament,
Flickered and bickered   70
From helmet to helmet,
And last on the forehead
Of Arthur the blameless
Rested The Gleam.

VII

Clouds and darkness   75
Closed upon Camelot;
Arthur had vanished
I knew not whither,
The king who loved me,
And cannot die;   80
For out of the darkness
Silent and slowly
The Gleam, that had waned
    to a wintry glimmer
On icy fallow
And faded forest,   85
Drew to the valley
Named of the shadow,
And slowly brightening
Out of the glimmer,
And slowly moving again to a
    melody   90
Yearningly tender,
Fell on the shadow,
No longer a shadow,
But clothed with The Gleam.

72–4. C.Y. Lang notes Blanche Warre Cornish: 'He explained that he meant Arthur Hallam' (*London Mercury* v, 1921, 153).
75–80. Cp. *Morte d'Arthur* (II 3).
79] *Trial edition has more explicit drafts*:
    (a) The friend who loved me,
          And heard my counsel,
    (b) He that I leaned on,
          Arthur, who loved me,
          The king who prized me,
          And heard my counsel,

VIII

And broader and brighter   95
The Gleam flying onward,
Wed to the melody,
Sang through the world;
And slower and fainter,
Old and weary,   100
But eager to follow,
I saw, whenever
In passing it glanced upon
Hamlet or city,
That under the Crosses   105
The dead man's garden,
The mortal hillock,
Would break into blossom;
And so to the land's
Last limit I came—   110
And can no longer,
But die rejoicing,
For through the Magic
Of Him the Mighty,
Who taught me in childhood,   115
There on the border
Of boundless Ocean,
And all but in Heaven
Hovers The Gleam.

IX

Not of the sunlight,   120
Not of the moonlight,
Not of the starlight!
O young Mariner,
Down to the haven,
Call your companions,   125
Launch your vessel,
And crowd your canvas,
And, ere it vanishes
Over the margin,
After it, follow it,   130
Follow The Gleam.

(1889)

29.   *By an Evolutionist*

Published *1889*. Written Feb. 1889 (*Mem.* ii 353), between attacks of a severe illness. T. created it from separate epigrams. W. Boyd Carpenter said T. quoted the poem in July 1887 (*Some Pages*, 1911, p. 257), but this will probably have been ll. 1–4, which appear as an epigram in *H.Nbk* 55. In the enlarged poem, l. 11 is very likely to be precise. The poem is not in the *Virginia* trial edition of *1889*; in a *Lincoln* trial edition, it consists of ll. 1–8, 13–16 only. In another *Lincoln* trial edition, ll. 9–12 are added by hand, apparently as a separate epigram, 'Old Man' to 'Old Age'. It will be these lines to which *Mem.* ii 348 refers: 'At the crisis of his illness [end of 1888] he made an epigram about himself, and on the pain killing the devil that was born in him eighty years back.'

> The Lord let the house of a brute to the soul of a man,
>   And the man said 'Am I your debtor?'
> And the Lord– 'Not yet: but make it as clean as you can,
>   And then I will let you a better.'

I

> If my body come from brutes, my soul uncertain, or a fable,   5
>   Why not bask amid the senses while the sun of morning shines,
> I, the finer brute rejoicing in my hounds, and in my stable,
>   Youth and Health, and birth and wealth, and choice of women and of wines?

II

> What hast thou done for me, grim Old Age, save breaking my bones on the rack?
>   Would I had past in the morning that looks so bright from afar!   10

OLD AGE

> Done for thee? starved the wild beast that was linkt with thee eighty years back.
>   Less weight now for the ladder-of-heaven that hangs on a star.

I

> If my body come from brutes, though somewhat finer than their own,
>   I am heir, and this my kingdom. Shall the royal voice be mute?
> No, but if the rebel subject seek to drag me from the throne,   15
>   Hold the sceptrè, Human Soul, and rule thy Province of the brute.

¶29. **BY AN EVOLUTIONIST**
1. Cp. *Happy* 32: 'This house with all its hateful needs no cleaner than the beast'.
8. Cp. *Vastness* 19: 'Wealth with his wines and his wedded harlots'.

II

  I have climbed to the snows of Age, and I gaze at a field in the Past,
    Where I sank with the body at times in the sloughs of a low desire,
  But I hear no yelp of the beast, and the Man is quiet at last
    As he stands on the heights of his life with a glimpse of
      a height that is higher.   20

(1889)

30.   *Far – Far – Away*

         (For Music)

Published *1889*. Recited Aug. 1888 (*Mem.* ii 346), though H.T. also says that it was written after T.'s severe illness, which began Sept. 1888. T. presumably revised it. 'The words "far, far away" had always a strange charm for me' (T. on his early childhood). He made many changes to the drafts in *H.Nbks 54* and *87* (*A* and *B* below), including the change from 'I' to 'he' throughout. He altered the sequence of lines and stanzas, and the poem cost him great difficulty. Stanzas that found no place in *1889* are given below, 1.18*n*. A trial edition of *1889* (*Virginia*) has only four stanzas. T. rewrote the poem in the *Trinity* trial edition or proofs (*T.Nbk 27*).

    What sight so lured him through the fields he knew
    As where earth's green stole into heaven's own hue,
      Far – far – away?

    What sound was dearest in his native dells?
    The mellow lin-lan-lone of evening bells   5
      Far – far – away.

    What vague world-whisper, mystic pain or joy,
    Through those three words would haunt him when a boy,
      Far – far – away?

    A whisper from his dawn of life? a breath   10
    From some fair dawn beyond the doors of death
      Far – far – away?

¶30. FAR – FAR – AWAY

1] What field so witched him in the land he knew *Harvard B 1st reading*.
2. *hue*] blue *Harvard B 1st reading*.
5. Sir Charles Tennyson (*1931*, p. 78) compares 'lin, lan, lone', *New Year's Eve*, from *c.* 1837.
7–8]   That strange world-whisper came to me, a boy,
     A haunting notice, neither grief, nor joy, *Harvard A*

> Far, far, how far? from o'er the gates of Birth,
> The faint horizons, all the bounds of earth,
>   Far — far — away?   15
>
> What charm in words, a charm no words could give?
> O dying words, can Music make you live
>   Far — far — away?

31.   *Beautiful City*

Published *1889*. 'Paris' (T.). On the French Revolution, cp. *Aylmer's Field* 763–8, and *In Memoriam* cxxvii 8. T. is thinking too of the revolution of 1848 and the Paris Commune of 1871. It was written in T.'s eightieth year (H.T., note with MS, *Nat. Lib. of Australia*), presumably 1884. It is not in the *Virginia* and *Trinity College* trial editions of *1884*; there are two drafts by hand in a *Lincoln* trial edition. T. may well have sympathized with Boulanger, who in April 1889 fled to England and was arraigned in France. A late notebook of T. (*Lincoln*) has the jotting: 'Revolution–to speak epigrammatically–is against Evolution.' In 1884 (apparently), he said that 'evolution has often come through revolution' (*Mem*. ii 303).

> Beautiful city, the centre and crater of European confusion,
> O you with your passionate shriek for the rights of an equal humanity,
> How often your Re-volution has proven but E-volution
> Rolled again back on itself in the tides of a civic insanity!
>
>   (1889)

14] And all the faint horizons of the earth, *Harvard A*; Beyond the faint horizons of his earth, *Harvard B 1st reading*.
17. dying] poor dead *Harvard B 1st reading*.
18] *The following stanzas appear in the MSS (the sequences of which are quite different from 1889)*:
        (i) That weird soul-phrase of something half-divine,
            In earliest youth, in latest age is mine,
                    Far — far — away. *Harvard A*
       (ii) Ghost, do the men that walk this planet seem
          [Ghost, can you see us, hear us? do we seem *1 st reading*]
            Far, far away, a truth and yet a dream,
                    Far — far — away? *Harvard B*
      (iii) What whisper? Whence? From summers long gone by
            And twilight times when I was growing I,
                    Far — far — away? *T.MS*

32. On One Who Affected an Effeminate Manner

Published *1889*. It is not in the *Virginia* trial edition; it is added by hand to a *Lincoln* trial edition, with the title *To one who affected effeminacy*. The *Trinity* trial edition or proofs (*T.Nbk 27*) has it added by pen, at first as:

> Though none is born, or made, on earth, complete,
> In earth's best man, the men and women meet.
> He types Creation's male and female plan,
> But, friend, man-woman is not woman-man.

Then revised to *1889* (at first with 'half-complete').

Cp. T.'s praise of 'manhood fused with female grace', *In Memoriam* cix 17; also 'She with all the charm of woman, she with all the breadth of man', *Locksley Hall Sixty Years After* 48, which was even stronger in MS: 'As our greatest is man-woman, so was she the woman-man', alluding to Christ (*Mem.* i 326). Cp. *The Princess*. A late notebook of T. (*Lincoln*) has the jotting, 'Men should be androgynous and women gynandrous, but men should not be gynandrous nor women androgynous.'

> While man and woman still are incomplete,
> I prize that soul where man and woman meet,
> Which types all Nature's male and female plan,
> But, friend, man-woman is not woman-man.

33. The Oak

Published *1889*. Probably written 1889 (it is in *H.Nbk 54*). 'My father called this poem "clean-cut like a Greek epigram." The allusion is to the gold of the young oak leaves in spring, and to the autumnal gold of the fading leaves (at Aldworth)' (H.T.).

> Live thy Life,
>   Young and old,
> Like yon oak,
> Bright in spring,
>   Living gold;   5
>
> Summer-rich
>   Then; and then
> Autumn-changed,
> Soberer-hued
>   Gold again.   10

¶33. THE OAK
1] Be your life, *H.MS*.
4] All your Spring *MS*.
6] Summer-green *MS*.
8–9] Transposed *MS*.

>   All his leaves
>   Fallen at length,
>   Look, he stands,
>   Trunk and bough,
>   Naked strength.   15

                              (1889)

From *The Death of Oenone, Akhbar's Dream, and Other Poems* (1892, post.)

34.   *The Church-Warden and the Curate, with glossary*

Published *1892*. Written 1890 (H.T.), 'founded on two sayings which Canon Rawnsley told him [May 1890]. One of a "Lincolnshire Church-warden" [ll. 49–50]. The other, that of a Lincolnshire farmer [ll. 15–16]'. The latter is told of a farmer's wife, not specifically in Lincolnshire, in *A Memoir of C. M. Young* by J. C. Young (1871, ii 265); she says of Baptists to the clergyman, 'I aint no idea of their coming and leaving all their nasty sins behind them in my water.' *1892* note: 'This is written in the dialect which was current in my youth at Spilsby and in the country about it.' All notes below are T.'s. T. wrote a note (*T.Nbk 37*) of which the revised draft runs: 'This like many of my smaller poems is purely dramatic, and if anyone believes or conjectures that I myself am carping at Baptists or Churchwardens or tradesmen or glancing at some particular Bishop from under the mask of my Dramatis Persona, I must beg to remind him (Parvis componere magna) that Aeschylus did not murder Agamemnon, nor Shakespeare King Duncan.

I

Eh? good daäy! good daäy! thaw it beän't not mooch of a daäy,
Nasty, casselty weather! an' mea haäfe down wi' my haäy!

II

How be the farm gittin on? noäways. Gittin on i'deeäd!
Why, tonups was haäfe on 'em fingers an' toäs, an' the mare brokken-kneeäd,
An' pigs didn't sell at fall, an' wa lost wer Haldeny cow,   5
An' it beäts ma to knaw wot she died on, but wool's looking oop ony how.

13] There he stands, *MS*; Stand, like him, *MS alternative.*
¶**34. THE CHURCH-WARDEN AND THE CURATE, WITH GLOSSARY**
2. *casselty*: 'casualty, chance weather.' *haäfe down wi' my haäy*: 'while my grass is only half-mown.'
4. *fingers an' toäs*: 'a disease in turnips.'
5. *fall*: 'autumn.'

III

An' soä they've maäde tha a parson, an' thou'll git along, niver fear,
Fur I beän chuch-warden mysen i' the parish fur fifteen year.
Well—sin ther beä chuch-wardens, ther mun be parsons an' all,
An' ift'ōne stick alongside t'uther the chuch weänt happen a fall. 10

IV

Fur I wur a Baptis wonst, an' ageän the toithe an' the raäte,
Till I fun that it warn't not the gaäinist waäy to the narra Gaäte.
An' I can't abeär 'em, I can't, fur a lot on 'em coomed ta-year—
I wur down wi' the rheumatis then—to *my* pond to wesh thessens theere
Sa I sticks like the ivin as long as I lives to the owd chuch now. 15
Fur they weshed their sins i' *my* pond, an' I doubts they poisoned the cow.

V

Ay, an' ya seed the Bishop. They says 'at he coomed fra nowt—
Burn i' traäde. Sa I warrants 'e niver said haafe wot 'e thowt,
But 'e creeäpt an' 'e crawled along, till 'e feeäld 'e could howd 'is oan,
Then 'e married a greät Yerl's darter, an' sits o' the Bishop's throän. 20

VI

Now I'll gie tha a bit o' my mind an' tha weant be taakin' offence,
Fur thou be a big scholard now wi' a hoonderd haäcre o' sense—
But sich an obstropulous lad—naay, naay—fur I minds tha sa well,
Tha'd niver not hopple thy tongue, an' the tongue's sit afire o' Hell,
As I says to my missis todaay, when she hurled a plaäte at the cat 25
An' anoother ageän my noäse. Ya was niver sa bad as that.

VII

But I minds when i' Howlaby beck won daäy ya was ticklin' o' trout,
An' keeäper 'e seed ya an rooned, an' 'e bealed to ya 'Lad coom hout'
An' ya stood oop naäkt i' the beck, an' ya telled 'im to knaw his awn plaäce
An' ya called 'im a clown, ya did, an' ya thrawed the fish i' 'is faäce, 30
An' 'e torned as red as a stag-tuckey's wattles, but theer an' then
I coämbed 'im down, fur I promised ya'd niver not do it ageän.

---

10. *if' t'ōne stick alongside t'uther:* 'if the one hold by the other. "Ōne" is pronounced like "own".'
12. *fun:* 'found.' *gaäinist:* 'nearest.'
13. *ta-year:* 'this year.'
15. *ipin:* 'ivy.'
23. *obstropulous:* 'obstreperous—here the Curate makes a sign of deprecation.'
24. *hopple:* 'or "hobble", to tie the legs of a skittish cow when she is being milked.'
28. *bealed:* 'bellowed.'
31. *torned:* 'in such words as "torned" (turned), "hurled", the r is hardly audible.' *stag-tuckey:* 'turkey-cock.'

VIII

An' I cotched tha wonst i' my garden, when thou was a height-year-howd,
An' I fun thy pockets as full o' my pippins as iver they'd 'owd,
An' thou was as peärky as owt, an' tha maäde me as mad as mad,   35
But I says to tha 'keeap 'em, an' welcome' fur thou was the Parson's lad.

IX

An' Parson 'e 'ears on it all, an' then taäkes kindly to me.
An' then I wur chose chuch-warden an' coomed to the top o' the tree,
Fur Quoloty's hall my friends, an' they maäkes ma a help to the poor,
When I gits the plaäte fuller o' Soondays nor ony chuch-warden afoor,   40
Fur if iver thy feyther 'ed riled me I kep' mysen meeäk as a lamb,
An' saw by the Graäce o' the Lord, Mr Harry, I ham wot I ham.

X

But Parson 'e *will* speäk out, saw, now 'e be sixty-seven,
He'll niver swap Owlby an' Scratby fur owt but the Kingdom o' Heaven;
An' thou'll be 'is Curate 'ere, but, if iver tha meäns to git 'igher,   45
Tha mun tackle the sins o' the Wo'ld, an' not the faults o' the Squire.
An' I reckons tha'll light of a livin' somewheers i' the Wowd or the Fen,
If tha cottons down to thy betters, an' keeäps thysen to thysen.
But niver not speäk plaain out, if tha wants to git forrards a bit,
But creeäp along the hedge-bottoms, an' thou'll be a Bishop yit.   50

---

33. *height-year-howd*: 'eight-year-old.'
34. *'owd*: 'hold.'
35. *peärky*: 'pert.'
46. *Wo'ld*: 'the world. Short *o*.'
47. *Wowd*: 'wold.'

GLOSSARY

'Casselty,' casualty, chance weather.

'Haäfe down wi' my haäy,' while my grass is only half-mown.

'Fingers and toes,' a disease in turnips.

'Fall,' autumn.

'If t'ōne stick alongside t'uther,' if the one hold by the other. One is pronounced like 'own.'

'Fun,' found.

'Gaäinist,' nearest.

'Ta-year,' this year.

'Ivin,' ivy.

'Obstropulous,' obstreperous—here the Curate makes a sign of deprecation.

'Hopple' or 'hobble,' to tie the legs of a skittish cow when she is being milked.

'Beal'd,' bellowed.

XI

Naäy, but tha *mun* speäk hout to the Baptises here i' the town,
Fur moäst on 'em talks ageän tithe, an' I'd like tha to preäch 'em down,
Fur *they*'ve bin a-preächin' *mea* down, they have, an' I haätes 'em now,
Fur they leäved their nasty sins i' *my* pond, an' it poisoned the cow.

35.   *June Bracken and Heather*

To –

Published *1892*. A dedication to T.'s wife Emily (as was *A Dedication*, II 683), it was written June 1891. The date is deduced from 1.6 (Emily was born 9 July 1813), and confirmed by *T.Nbk.37*. Martin (p. 576) notes that it is a wedding-anniversary tribute (June 1850).

> There on the top of the down,
> The wild heather round me and over me June's high blue,
> When I looked at the bracken so bright and the heather so brown,
> I thought to myself I would offer this book to you,
> This, and my love together,   5
> To you that are seventy-seven,
> With a faith as clear as the heights of the June-blue heaven,
> And a fancy as summer-new
> As the green of the bracken amid the gloom of the heather.

(1892)

36.   *The Dawn*

Published *1892*, 'written at the end of his life' (H.T.). It is in *H.Nbk 56* with other poems of *1892*.
   Epigraph: T. applies to his purposes Plato's *Tinaeus* 22: 'Whereupon one of the priests, a prodigiously old man, said, "O Solon, Solon, you Greeks are always children: there is not such a thing as an old Greek." And on hearing this he asked, "What mean you by this saying?" And the priest replied, "You are young in soul, every one of you. For therein you possess not a single belief that is ancient and

> In such words as 'torned' (turned), 'hurled,' the *r* is
> hardly audible.
>   'Stag-tuckey,' turkey-cock.
>   'Height-year-howd,' eight-year-old.
>   ''Owd,' hold.
>   'Pearky,' pert.
>   'Wo'ld,' the world. Short *o*.
>   'Wowd,' wold.

derived from old tradition, nor yet one science that is hoary with age. And this is the cause thereof:
There have been and there will be many and divers destructions of mankind, of which the greatest are
by fire and water, and lesser ones by countless other means".'

You are but children.

EGYPTIAN PRIEST TO SOLON

I

Red of the Dawn!
Screams of a babe in the red-hot palms of a Moloch of Tyre,
    Man with his brotherless dinner on man in the tropical wood,
    Priests in the name of the Lord passing souls through fire to the fire,
Head-hunters and boats of Dahomey that float upon human blood!   5

II

Red of the Dawn!
Godless fury of peoples, and Christless frolic of kings,
    And the bolt of war dashing down upon cities and blazing farms,
    For Babylon was a child new-born, and Rome was a babe in arms,
And London and Paris and all the rest are as yet but in leading-strings.   10

III

Dawn not Day,
While scandal is mouthing a bloodless name at *her* cannibal feast,
And rake-ruined bodies and souls go down in a common wreck,
    And the press of a thousand cities is prized for it smells of the beast,
Or easily violates virgin Truth for a coin or a cheque.   15

IV

Dawn not Day!
Is it Shame, so few should have climbed from the dens in the level below,
    Men, with a heart and a soul, no slaves of a four-footed will?
    But if twenty million of summers are stored in the sunlight still,
We are far from the noon of man, there is time for the race to grow.   20

¶36. THE DAWN

5. T. said in conversation, c. 1869–70: 'On the accession of a king in Dahomey [W. Africa] enough women victims are killed to float a small canoe (with their blood)' (Sir Charles Tennyson, *Twentieth Century* clxv (1959) 37). T. owned a copy (Lincoln) of Sir Richard Burton's *A Mission to Gelele, King of Dahome* (1864), which discusses sceptically the 'report that the king floated a canoe and paddled himself in a tank full of human blood' (i 344).

19. As estimated by scientists like William Thomson.

V

    Red of the Dawn!
Is it turning a fainter red? so be it, but when shall we lay
  The Ghost of the Brute that is walking and haunting us yet, and be free?
  In a hundred, a thousand winters ? Ah, what will *our* children be,
The men of a hundred thousand, a million summers away?   25

            (1892)

37.   *The Making of Man*

Published *1892*, 'written at the end of his life' (H.T.). It is not in the first trial edition of *1892* (Lincoln); in the later one, the title is *It is Finished*. *T.Nbk 34*. Cp. *Maud* i 136: 'So many a million of ages have gone to the making of man'.

  Where is one that, born of woman, altogether can escape
  From the lower world within him, moods of tiger, or of ape?
    Man as yet is being made, and ere the crowning Age of ages,
  Shall not æon after æon pass and touch him into shape?

  All about him shadow still, but, while the races flower and fade, 5
  Prophet-eyes may catch a glory slowly gaining on the shade,
    Till the peoples all are one, and all their voices blend in choric
  Hallelujah to the Maker 'It is finished. Man is made.'

38.   *Mechanophilus*

    (In the Time of the First Railways)

Published *1892*. Written *c.* 1833, as is clear from *H.Nbk 17* and *T.Nbk 17*. It is one of T.'s many political poems of this date. *H.MS* (all variants are below, as *MS*) is entitled *Æonophilus*, the lover of the age, and has four extra stanzas; *T.Nbk 17* differs only slightly from *H.MS*, except that at some points it ordered the stanzas differently. *T.Nbk 20* has revisions. The poem is not in the first trial edition of *1892* (Lincoln).

    Now first we stand and understand,
     And sunder false from true,
    And handle boldly with the hand,
     And see and shape and do.

¶37. **THE MAKING OF MAN**
1. *Job* xiv 1: 'Man that is born of a woman is of few days, and full of trouble.'
8. *John* xix 30: 'It is finished.'
¶38. **MECHANOPHILUS**
4. *see*] act *H.MS*.

Dash back that ocean with a pier, 5
    Strow yonder mountain flat,
A railway there, a tunnel here,
    Mix me this Zone with that!

Bring me my horse—my horse? my wings
    That I may soar the sky, 10
For Thought into the outward springs,
    I find her with the eye.

O will she, moonlike, sway the main,
    And bring or chase the storm,
Who was a shadow in the brain, 15
    And is a living form?

4 ∧ 5]
    Away with shadows! render all
        Plain, palpable and bold,
    Then give the crude material
        That we may carve and mould.

    All other times were but the shade—
        The preface unto this.
    Now knowledge comes, a mortal maid,
        Whom we may clasp and kiss: *MS*
(*T.Nbk 20* 1st reading: Now Truth comes like a mortal . . .)
5–8] *MS has these lines following l. 16.*
5. *that ocean*] those breakers *MS.*
7. *railway*] railroad *MS.*
8] Knit me this town to that! *T.Nbk 20.*
8. *Zone*] realm *MS.*
9] Bring me my horse–bring me my wings *MS.*
12. *find*] see *MS.*
13–14]
    Soon moonlike will she rule the main
        And puff the cloud and storm. *MS*
15. *Who*] She *MS.*
16. *And*] She *MS.*
16 ∧ 17] *MS here (i.e. ll. 8 ∧ 17) inserts in the margin three stanzas:*
[i]   *ll. 33–6, in the order 35–6, 33–4* (Yet what. . .)
[ii]
    Till thick grass clothe the craggy way,
        Thick corn the barest glen,
    And by his hearth the cotter weigh
        The thoughts of mighty men.
[iii]
    Till in his office none be mute,
        But equal to the hour,
    To add, to prune, to substitute
        By gradual scales of power.

Far as the Future vaults her skies,
    From this my vantage ground
To those still-working energies
    I spy nor term nor bound.   20

As we surpass our father's skill,
    Our sons will shame our own;
A thousand things are hidden still
    And not a hundred known.

And had some prophet spoken true   25
    Of all we shall achieve,
The wonders were so wildly new,
    That no man would believe.

Meanwhile, my brothers, work, and
        wield
The forces of today,   30
And plow the Present like a field,
    And garner all you may!

You, what the cultured surface grows,
    Dispense with careful hands:
Deep under deep for ever goes,   35
    Heaven over heaven expands.

---

18. my] high *MS*.
20] I see no term or bound. *MS*.
21–4. T. signed and inscribed these lines (1. 24: *Scarce a* ...), 25 June 1884, in a volume given to Sir Henry Parkes, prime minister of Australia for most of the 1870s and 1880s (*Mitchell Library, Sydney*).
25–8]   But if what will be once achieved
                              Had prophets speaking true,
                        The wonder would not be believed,
                            It were so strange and new. *MS*
29] Meantime, push forward, work and wield. *MS*; Heap fact on fact nor faint nor yield. *T.Nbk* 20; Quick with strong engines crush and wield *T.Nbk*
20. added in margin.
30] Let man be really man *MS*
31. And] To *MS*.
32. you may!] he can. *MS, which had at first ended here, but see ll. 16 ˄ 17n.*

39.   *Poets and Critics*

Published *1892*. Written 1833–4, referring to the reviews of *1832*. All variants from *H.Nbk 17*, of this early date, are given below.

        This thing, that thing is the rage,
        Helter-skelter runs the age;
        Minds on this round earth of ours
        Vary like the leaves and flowers,
        Fashioned after certain laws;   5
        Sing thou low or loud or sweet,
        All at all points thou canst not meet,
           Some will pass and some will pause.

        What is true at last will tell:
        Few at first will place thee well;   10
        Some too low would have thee shine,
        Some too high –no fault of thine–
           Hold thine own, and work thy will!
        Year will graze the heel of year,
        But seldom comes the poet here,   15
           And the Critic's rarer still.

                    (1892)

from *Dream*

40.   *The Silent Voices*

Published *1892*. 'Written at the end of his life' (H.T.). It is in *H.Nbk 56* with Other Poems of *1892*. Cp. H.T.'s observation that in 1880, 'after my uncle Charles' death my father was very unwell, suffering from a liver attack, and hearing perpetual ghostly voices' (*Mem*. ii 244).

        When the dumb Hour, clothed in black,
        Brings the Dreams about my bed,

¶**39. POETS AND CRITICS**
10. *place*] weigh *H.MS*.
13. *Hold thine own*] Strike thy harp *MS*.
14. *Will*] doth *MS*.
15. *But*] And *MS*.
16. *And*] But *MS*.

¶**40. THE SILENT VOICES**
1–2] Not *T.Nbk 37*, earlier draft.

Call me not so often back,
Silent Voices of the dead,
Toward the lowland ways behind me,
And the sunlight that is gone!   5
Call me rather, silent voices,
Forward to the starry track
Glimmering up the heights beyond me
On, and always on!   10

(1892)

41.   *God and the Universe*

Written and published *1892* (*Mem*. ii 398). The title in a trial edition of *1892* (*Lincoln*) had been *God and the World*.

I

Will my tiny spark of being wholly vanish in your deeps and heights?
Must my day be dark by reason, O ye Heavens, of your boundless nights,
Rush of Suns, and roll of systems, and your fiery clash of meteorites?

II

'Spirit, nearing yon dark portal at the limit of thy human state,
Fear not thou the hidden purpose of that Power which alone is great,   5
Nor the myriad world, His shadow, nor the silent Opener of the Gate.'

4. *dead*] Vanish'd *T.MS*.
5] Toward the long-forsaken track *T.MS*.
6. *sunlight*] moment *T.MS*.
7. *rather*] forward *T.MS*.
8] Not *T.MS*.
9] Up the mountain height before me *T.MS*.
10] Ever on and on. *T.MS*.

¶41. GOD AND THE UNIVERSE
3. Cp. *In Memoriam: Epilogue* 122: 'star and system rolling past'; and *Author and Critics* 5: 'The clash of so many a meteorite', deriving from J. N. Lockyer's *The Meteoritic Hypothesis* (1890).
6. Cp. the open gates in *Faith* 6–7.

42.   *Crossing the Bar*

Published *1889*. It is not in the *Virginia* trial edition of *1889*. Written Oct.1889 while crossing the Solent: 'When he repeated it to me in the evening, I said, "That is the crown of your life's work." He answered, "It came in a moment" ' (H.T.). P. L. Elliott notes that in *MS Mat.* (Lincoln) H.T.'s words had been: 'That is one of the most beautiful poems ever written' (*The Making of the Memoir*, 1978, p. 14). T. said to W. F. Rawnsley that he 'began and finished it in twenty minutes' (*Nineteenth Century* xcvii (1925) 195). It had been in T.'s mind since April or May 1889, when his nurse suggested he write a hymn after his recovery from a serious illness (J. Tennyson, *The Times*, 5 Nov. 1936). For the image, cp. *De Profundis* (III 67), and *The Passing of Arthur* 445: 'From the great deep to the great deep he goes.' The 'bar' is the sandbank across the harbour-mouth. All variants from *H.Nbk* 54 are below. D. Sonstroem argues that the poem is a reconciliation of a great many of T.'s earlier poems (*VP* viii, 1970, 55–60). The poem is here printed out of sequence because of T.'s wish: 'Mind you put my *Crossing the Bar* at the end of all editions of my poems.'

    Sunset and evening star,
        And one clear call for me!
    And may there be no moaning of the bar,
        When I put out to sea,

    But such a tide as moving seems asleep,   5
        Too full for sound and foam,
    When that which drew from out the boundless deep
        Turns again home.

    Twilight and evening bell,
    And after that the dark!   10
    And may there be no sadness of farewell,
        When I embark;

¶42. CROSSING THE BAR

2. And] But *H.MS*. The 'call' is a marine term, a summons to duty, here suggesting that of God; but it is ominous too. Cp. the death of Enoch Arden, when 'There came so loud a calling of the sea' (II 649 and *n*).

3. Cp. Charles Kingsley's *The Three Fishers*, a poem on death: 'And the harbour bar be moaning'. T. had a copy (Lincoln) of *Andromeda and Other Poems* (*1858*), in which this poem appeared. He read some of Kingsley's poems to E.T. in 1858 (her Journal). P. Hope-Wallace suggests that Kingsley referred to the common estuary in Barnstaple Bay, where the joining of two rivers' waters and the incoming sea can produce a loud moaning sound above the sand-bar at the mouth of the inlet (*Tennyson*, ed. K. Amis, 1973, p. 218). *7. drew*] came *MS*. 'The boundless deep' recurs often in T., with something of the same mood and theme in *The Ancient Sage* 189–94; and cp. *Sea Dreams* 85–6: 'such a tide', 'from out the boundless outer deep'. Cp. *In Memoriam: Epilogue* 123–4: 'A soul shall draw from out the vast/And strike his being into bounds.'

10. after that] then *MS 1st reading.*
11. And] But *MS*.

> For though from out our bourne of Time and Place
>   The flood may bear me far,
> I hope to see my Pilot face to face 15
>   When I have crost the bar.

Mary Cowden-Clarke (neé Novello) (1809–1898)

43.   *Body and Soul*

> The roses on thy grave are now breast high:
> Keen as their thorns the thought that thou dost lie
> Beneath, instead of in mine arms—and yet—
> Thy spirit, like the fragrance of the rose,
> Within my heart doth evermore repose. 5

---

13. For ... our] Alone from out the *MS*. *bourne*: suggested by Hamlet on death, 'from whose bourn/No traveller returns', III i 79–80.

13–16. J. H. Buckley (p. 287) compares H. F. Lyte's famous hymn: 'Praise, my soul, the King of Heaven .../Ye behold him face to face .../Dwellers all in time and space.' Also *1 Corinthians* xiii 12: 'For now we see through a glass, darkly; but then face to face.' As so often, T.'s mind may have gone back to Arthur Hallam, to *In Memoriatn* cxxxi: 'And come to look on those we loved/And that which made us, face to face' *H.MS*.

Hallam's poem *To Two Sisters* (Mary and at this point Emily T.) had said: 'Till our souls see each other face to face' (Motter, p. 90).

14] Alone I sail, and far, *MS*.

15. 1] But *MS*. 'The pilot has been on board all the while, but in the dark I have not seen him' (T.). 'He explained the Pilot as "that Divine and Unseen Who is always guiding us" ' (H.T.). T. J. Assad discusses the objections to the image, *Tulane Studies in English* viii (1958) 153–63. P. L. Elliott notes that H.T., at an earlier stage of *Mem.*, deleted: 'They [T. and Herbert Warren in 1892] spoke together of *Crossing the Bar* and of the absurdity of the "Pilot" being Arthur Hallam or my brother Lionel' (*The Making of the Memoir*, p. 27).

Alfred Domett (1811–1887)

44. *Fireworks*

I dreamt. There was a great crowd gazing
At fireworks set before them blazing.

The crowd were 'Missing Links'; Cambodia's
Great Temple shows no shapes more odious!;

Flat skulls, flat brows, yet convex noses, 5
Such as her ruined Fane discloses,

Men's heads in conflict fierce off-twisting,
Spite of tame elephants assisting;—

Such gibbering folk as grinned in ages
Long ere men lived o'er Lakes on stages; 10

Left shells on midden—flints in barrow,
Or split hyena-bones for marrow.

The Pyrotechnist was a creature
Of noblest presence—Greek in feature.

He sent a single cracker bouncing — 15
The Links' delight there's no pronouncing:

A single squib he showed them fizzing—
Their rapture drowned the small tube's whizzing:

One Roman candle fireball-shotted—
Down on their hams from fear they squatted: 20

One Catherine-wheel's flame-petals playing—
Their gibbering hushed seemed almost praying:

A rocket skyward rushed up solely—
They shrieked him God—a Fetish wholly;

So wondrous fine his working—scheming; 25
He, too, so like themselves in seeming!

Then the good Pyrotechnist lastly
Brought one great work to please them vastly;

So grand, he felt in its ignition
The climax of his Exhibition.

He fixed it–lighted–set it whirling;
Squibs fizzed in streams from its unfurling:

It whirled away; in its progression,
Up flew fireballs in bright succession!

Still on it whirled; such gems emitting,
Such gold-thorns branching, fire-flowers flitting,

Such rings of flame, concentric, linking,
Such panting discs, expanding, shrinking;

The very Saint from whom they named it,
If such *her* wheel, could scarce have blamed it!

Still on it whirled–such rockets dashed up,
As if to heaven's keystone they flashed up;

Then split in melting stars and fine tails,
Long-stealing jewelled cats-o'-nine-tails;

You would have thought the Man-Ape nation
Must have gone mad with admiration!

But who can hit Men-Monkeys' notions?
Who guess a Missing-Link's emotions?

For up jumped one–lank, sly and shifty–
(His 'facial angle' well-nigh fifty)

Cries out, 'Pray stop your mopping, mowing;
He no more made the things he's showing–

'The toys by Time and Chance provided–
Made them no more than you or I did!

'Until a squib that one could pocket,
Grows of itself into a rocket!'

This sudden light, first notions scattering,
Makes that swart tribe one sea of chattering;

Their flow of veneration staunches—
They can but blink and scratch their haunches: 60

Still more so when up danced a second,
(*His* brow some forty-five was reckoned)

Who mouthed at, mocked the placid showman:
'That Thing's a Phantom, friends, and *no* man!

'O Monkey-Men, 'tis clear; for seeing 65
The firework-making proved his Being,

'That myth of firework-making banished –
Argal, his Being too has vanished:

'Your senses cheat you, in conclusion: –
Anthropo-Simian brain-illusion!' 70

His lofty scorn, his eyebrows twitching
High-raised, his logic so bewitching,

His lips protruded, red eyes leering,
Set all the mob the Showman jeering:

'Off with you, spectre! bogle flimsy, 75
Dissolving ghost, exploded whimsy!

You once packed off, that explanation
Leaves "LINK" the Lord of all Creation!' –

The Showman seemed at this reviling
To fade into the background, smiling: 80

Bedimmed by dust-clouds light-defying
Their antics kept about them flying:

Some Ape-Men who (quite mad reputed)
Still thought they saw him, were so hooted,

I woke – with admiration glowing 85
To find the Missing-Links so knowing.

(1874)

45.   *Invisible Sights*

    'So far away so long–and now
       Returned to England?–Come with me!
    Some of our great "celebrities"
       You will be glad to see!'

                ....

    Carlyle–the Laureate–Browning–*these*!   5
       These walking bipeds–Nay, you joke! –
    Each wondrous power for thirty years
       O'er us head-downward folk

    Wrapt skylike, at the Antipodes, –
       Those common limbs – that common trunk!   10
    'Tis the Arab–Jinn who reached the clouds,
       Into his bottle shrunk.

    The flashing Mind – the boundless Soul
       We felt ubiquitous, that mash
    Medullary or cortical –   15
       That six inch brain-cube! – Trash!

William Bell Scott (1811–1890)

46.   *Music*

    Listless the silent ladies sit
    About the room so gaily lit;
    Madame Ions likes the cups or ray,
    But thinks it scarce enough to say:
    Mistress Cox is gone astray   5
    To the night-light in her own nursery,
    Wonders if little Maude was led
    Without long coaxing into bed:
    Miss Jemima Applewhite,
    On a low stool by the fire,   10
    Concentrates her confused desire, –
    Perhaps will do so all the night,
    On an unused rhyme for 'scan,'
    And can but find the stiff word *man*:

Miss Temple pets the little hound, 15
That has a tendency to whine,
To-night its cushion can't be found;
And wonders when they'll leave the wine
Few take, but which men still combine
To linger over when they dine. 20

Indeed a frightful interval!
Madame Ions wants her game,
Or she must have her usual wink;
But now satiric Bertha Stahl
Jumps upon the music-stool, 25
And breaks into a sportive flame;
But what of all things do you think
She plays, that laughter-loving fool?
The funeral march, Dead March of Saul!
Oh, Lord of Hosts! their mailéd tread, 30
Bearing along the mailéd dead,
Makes me bow my stubborn head.
Never underneath the sun
With this heart-fathoming march be done;
Still, Lord of Hosts! to Thee we cry, 35
When our great ones, loved ones, die,
Still some grand lament we crave,
When we descend into the grave.

I turn, afraid that I may weep, –
Jemima's pestered wits still ran 40
After the unused rhyme for 'scan,'
Dear old Ions was asleep.

(1882)

Edward Lear (1812–1888)

47. ' "How pleasant to know Mr Lear!" '

'How pleasant to know Mr Lear!'
  Who has written such volumes of stuff!
Some think him ill-tempered and queer,
  But a few think him pleasant enough.

His mind is concrete and fastidious; –
    His nose is remarkably big; –
His visage is more or less hideous; –
    His beard it resembles a wig.

He has ears, and two eyes, and ten fingers, –
    (Leastways if you reckon two thumbs;)
Long ago he was one of the singers,
    But now he is one of the dumms.

He sits in a beautiful parlour,
    With hundreds of books on the wall;
He drinks a great deal of Marsala,
    But never gets tipsy at all.

He has many friends, laymen and clerical;
    Old Foss is the name of his cat;
His body is perfectly spherical; –
    He weareth a runcible hat.

When he walks in a waterproof white
    The children run after him so!
Calling out, – 'He's come out in his night-
    gown, that crazy old Englishman, – O!'

He weeps by the side of the ocean,
    He weeps on the top of the hill;
He purchases pancakes and lotion,
    And chocolate shrimps from the mill.

He reads, but he cannot speak, Spanish;
    He cannot abide ginger-beer.–
Ere the days of his pilgrimage vanish, –
    'How pleasant to know Mr Lear!'

48.   *The Quangle Wangle's Hat*

On the top of the Crumpetty Tree
    The Quangle Wangle sat,
But his face you could not see,
    On account of his Beaver Hat.
For his Hat was a hundred and two feet wide,

With ribbons and bibbons on every side,
And bells, and buttons, and loops, and lace,
So that nobody ever could see the face
    Of the Quangle Wangle Quee.

The Quangle Wangle said
    To himself on the Crumpetty Tree, –
'Jam; and jelly; and bread;
    Are the best of food for me!
But the longer I live on this Crumpetty Tree,
The plainer than ever it seems to me
That very few people come this way
And that life on the whole is far from gay!'
    Said the Quangle Wangle Quee.

But there came to the Crumpetty Tree,
    Mr and Mrs Canary;
And they said, – 'Did ever you see
    Any spot so charmingly airy?
May we build a nest on your lovely Hat?
Mr Quangle Wangle, grant us that!
O please let us come and build a nest
Of whatever material suits you best,
    Mr Quangle Wangle Quee!'

And besides, to the Crumpetty Tree
    Came the Stork, the Duck, and the Owl;
The Snail, and the Bumble-Bee,
    The Frog, and the Fimble Fowl;
(The Fimble Fowl, with a Corkscrew leg;)
And all of them said, – 'We humbly beg,
We may build our homes on your lovely Hat, –
Mr Quangle Wangle, grant us that!
    Mr Quangle Wangle Quee!'

And the Golden Grouse came there,
    And the Pobble who has no toes, –
And the small Olympian bear, –
    And the Dong with a luminous nose.
And the Blue Baboon, who played the flute, –
And the Orient Calf from the Land of Tute, –
And the Attery Squash, and the Bisky Bat, –
All came and built on the lovely Hat
    Of the Quangle Wangle Quee.

And the Quangle Wangle said
   To himself on the Crumpetty Tree, –
'When all these creatures move
   What a wonderful noise there'll be!'
And at night by the light of the Mulberry moon 50
They danced to the Flute of the Blue Baboon,
On the broad green leaves of the Crumpetty Tree,
And all were as happy as happy could be,
   With the Quangle Wangle Quee.

49.   *The Dong with a Luminous Nose*

When awful darkness and silence reign
   Over the great Gromboolian plain,
      Through the long, long wintry nights; –
When the angry breakers roar
   As they beat on the rocky shore; – 5
      When Storm-clouds brood on the towering heights
Of the Hills of the Chankly Bore: –

Then, through the vast and gloomy dark,
There moves what seems a fiery spark,
   A lonely spark with silvery rays 10
   Piercing the coal-black night, –
   A Meteor strange and bright: –
Hither and thither the vision strays,
   A single lurid light.

Slowly it wanders, – pauses, – creeps, – 15
Anon it sparkles, – flashes and leaps;
And ever as onward it gleaming goes
A light on the Bong-tree stems it throws.
And those who watch at that midnight hour
From Hall or Terrace, or lofty Tower, 20

Cry, as the wild light passes along, –
      'The Dong! – the Dong!
   The wandering Dong through the forest goes!
      The Dong! the Dong!
   The Dong with a luminous Nose!' 25

        Long years ago
     The Dong was happy and gay,
Till he fell in love with a Jumbly Girl
     Who came to those shores one day.
For the Jumblies came in a sieve, they did, –
Landing at eve near the Zemmery Fidd
     Where the Oblong Oysters grow,
     And the rocks are smooth and gray.
And all the woods and the valleys rang
With the Chorus they daily and nightly sang, –
    'Far and few, far and few,
    Are the lands where the Jumblies live;
    Their heads are green, and their hands are blue,
    And they went to sea in a sieve.'

Happily, happily passed those days!
     While the cheerful Jumblies staid;
    They danced in circlets all night long,
    To the plaintive pipe of the lively Dong,
     In moonlight, shine, or shade.
For day and night he was always there
By the side of the Jumbly Girl so fair,
With her sky-blue hands, and her sea-green hair.
Till the morning came of that hateful day
When the Jumblies sailed in their sieve away,
And the Dong was left on the cruel shore
Gazing – gazing for evermore, –
Ever keeping his weary eyes on
That pea-green sail on the far horizon, –
Singing the Jumbly Chorus still
As he sate all day on the grassy hill, –
    'Far and few, far and few,
    Are the lands where the Jumblies live;
    Their heads are green, and their hands are blue,
    And they went to sea in a sieve.'

But when the sun was low in the West,
     The Dong arose and said; –
    – 'What little sense I once possessed
     Has quite gone out of my head!' –
And since that day he wanders still
By lake and forest, marsh and hill,
Singing – 'O somewhere, in valley or plain
Might I find my Jumbly Girl again!
For ever I'll seek by lake and shore
Till I find my Jumbly Girl once more!'

    Playing a pipe with silvery squeaks,   70
    Since then his Jumbly Girl he seeks,
    And because by night he could not see,
    He gathered the bark of the Twangum Tree
     On the flowery plain that grows.
     And he wove him a wondrous Nose, –   75
    A Nose as strange as a Nose could be!
Of vast proportions and painted red,
And tied with cords to the back of his head.
    – In a hollow rounded space it ended
    With a luminous Lamp within suspended,   80
     All fenced about
     With a bandage stout
      To prevent the wind from blowing it out; –
    And with holes all round to send the light,
    In gleaming rays on the dismal light.   85

And now each night, and all night long,
Over those plains still roams the Dong;
And above the wail of the Chimp and Snipe
You may hear the squeak of his plaintive pipe
While ever he seeks, but seeks in vain   90
To meet with his Jumbly Girl again;
Lonely and wild – all night he goes, –
The Dong with a luminous Nose!
And all who watch at 'the midnight hour,
From Hall or Terrace, or lofty Tower,   95
Cry, as they trace the Meteor bright,
Moving along through the dreary night, –
   'This is the hour when forth he goes,
   The Dong with a luminous Nose!
   Yonder - over the plain he goes;   100
    He goes!
    He goes;
   The Dong with a luminous Nose!'

50.   *The Jumblies*

  They went to sea in a Sieve, they did,
   In a Sieve they went to sea:
  In spite of all their friends could say,
  On a winter's morn, on a stormy day,
   In a Sieve they went to sea!   5
  And when the Sieve turned round and round,

And every one cried, 'You'll all be drowned!'
They called aloud, 'Our Sieve ain't big,
But we don't care a button! we don't care a fig!
   In a Sieve we'll go to sea!'   10
     Far and few, far and few,
        Are the lands where the Jumblies live;
      Their heads are green, and their hands are blue,
        And they went to sea in a Sieve.

They sailed away in a Sieve, they did,   15
   In a Sieve they sailed so fast,
With only a beautiful pea-green veil
Tied with a riband by way of a sail,
   To a small tobacco-pipe mast;
And every one said, who saw them go,   20
'O won't they be soon upset, you know!
For the sky is dark, and the voyage is long,
And happen what may, it's extremely wrong
   In a Sieve to sail so fast!'
     Far and few, far and few,   25
        Are the lands where the Jumblies live;
      Their heads are green, and their hands are blue,
        And they went to sea in a Sieve.

The water it soon came in, it did,
   The water it soon came in;   30
So to keep them dry, they wrapped their feet
In a pinky paper all folded neat,
   And they fastened it down with a pin.
And they passed the night in a crockery-jar,
And each of them said, 'How wise we are!   35
Though the sky be dark, and the voyage be long,
Yet we never can think we were rash or wrong,
   While round in our Sieve we spin!'
     Far and few, far and few,
        Are the lands where the Jumblies live;   40
      Their heads are green, and their hands are blue,
        And they went to sea in a Sieve.

And all night long they sailed away;
   And when the sun went down,
They whistled and warbled a moony song   45
To the echoing sound of a coppery gong,
   In the shade of the mountains brown.
'O Timballo! How happy we are,
When we live in a sieve and a crockery-jar,

And all night long in the moonlight pale,
We sail away with a pea-green sail,
   In the shade of the mountains brown!'
      Far and few, far and few,
         Are the lands where the Jumblies live;
            Their heads are green, and their hands are blue,
               And they went to sea in a Sieve.

They sailed to the Western Sea, they did,
   To a land all covered with trees,
And they bought an Owl, and a useful Cart,
And a pound of Rice, and a Cranberry Tart,
   And a hive of silvery Bees.
And they bought a Pig, and some green Jack-daws,
And a lovely Monkey with lollipop paws,
And forty bottles of Ring-Bo-Ree,
   And no end of Stilton Cheese.
      Far and few, far and few,
         Are the lands where the Jumblies live;
            Their heads are green, and their hands are blue,
               And they went to sea in a Sieve.

And in twenty years they all came back,
   In twenty years or more,
And every one said, 'How tall they've grown!
For they've been to the Lakes, and the Torrible Zone,
   And the hills of the Chankly Bore!'
And they drank their health, and gave them a feast
Of dumplings made of beautiful yeast;
And every one said, 'If we only live,
We too will go to sea in a Sieve,–
   To the hills of the Chankly Bore!'
      Far and few, far and few,
         Are the lands where the Jumblies live;
            Their heads are green, and their hands are blue,
               And they went to sea in a Sieve.

51.   'There was an Old Man at a Station'

There was an Old Man at a Station,
Who made a promiscuous oration;
But they said, 'Take some snuff! – You have talk'd quite enough,
You afflicting Old Man at a Station!'

52.   'There was an Old Man of Thames Ditton'

There was an Old Man of Thames Ditton,
Who called out for something to sit on;
But they brought him a hat, and said, 'Sit upon that,
You abruptious Old Man of Thames Ditton!'

53.   'There was an Old Person of Skye'

There was an Old Person of Skye,
Who waltz'd with a Bluebottle fly;
They buzz'd a sweet tune, to the light of the moon,
And entranced all the people of Skye.

54.   'There was a Young Person of Ayr'

There was a Young Person of Ayr,
Whose head was remarkably square;
On the top, in fine weather, she wore a gold feather,
Which dazzled the people of Ayr.

Robert Browning (1812–1889)

From *Pacchiarotto and How He Worked in Distemper* (1876)

55.   *House*

I

Shall I sonnet-sing you about myself?
  Do I live in a house you would like to see?
Is it scant of gear, has it store of pelf?
  'Unlock my heart with a sonnet-key?'

II

Invite the world, as my betters have done?
   'Take notice: this building remains on view,
Its suites of reception every one,
   Its private apartment and bedroom too;

III

'For a ticket, apply to the Publisher.'
   No: thanking the public, I must decline.
A peep through my window, if folk prefer;
   But, please you, no foot over threshold of mine!

IV

I have mixed with a crowd and heard free talk
   In a foreign land where an earthquake chanced:
And a house stood gaping, naught to balk
   Man's eye wherever he gazed or glanced.

V

The whole of the frontage shaven sheer,
   The inside gaped: exposed to day,
Right and wrong and common and queer,
   Bare, as the palm of your hand, it lay.

VI

The owner? Oh, he had been crushed, no doubt!
   'Odd tables and chairs for a man of wealth!
What a parcel of musty old books about!
   He smoked, – no wonder he lost his health!

VII

'I doubt if he bathed before he dressed.
   A brasier? – the pagan, he burned perfumes!
You see it is proved, what the neighbours guessed:
   His wife and himself had separate rooms.'

VIII

Friends, the goodman of the house at least
   Kept house to himself till an earthquake came:
'Tis the fall of its frontage permits you feast
   On the inside arrangement you praise or blame.

IX

Outside should suffice for evidence:
   And whoso desires to penetrate
Deeper, must dive by the spirit-sense –
   No optics like yours, at any rate!

X

'Hoity toity! A street to explore,
   Your house the exception! "*With this same key
Shakespeare unlocked his heart,*" once more!'
   Did Shakespeare? If so, the less Shakespeare he!

(1876)

56.   *Shop*

I

So, friend, your shop was all your house!
   Its front, astonishing the street,
Invited view from man and mouse
   To what diversity of treat
Behind its glass – the single sheet!

II

What gimcracks, genuine Japanese:
   Gape-jaw and goggle-eye, the frog;
Dragons, owls, monkeys, beetles, geese;
   Some crush-nosed human-hearted dog:
Queer names, too, such a catalogue!

III

I thought 'And he who owns the wealth
   Which blocks the window's vastitude,
– Ah, could I peep at him by stealth
   Behind his ware, pass shop, intrude
On house itself, what scenes were viewed!

IV

'If wide and showy thus the shop,
    What must the habitation prove?
The true house with no name a-top –
    The mansion, distant one remove,
    Once get him off his traffic-groove!

V

'Pictures he likes, or books perhaps;
    And as for buying most and best,
Commend me to these City chaps!
    Or else he's social, takes his rest
    On Sundays, with a Lord for guest.

VI

'Some suburb-palace, parked about
    And gated grandly, built last year:
The four-mile walk to keep off gout;
    Or big seat sold by bankrupt peer:
    But then he takes the rail, that's clear.

VII

'Or, stop! I wager, taste selects
    Some out o' the way, some all-unknown
Retreat: the neighbourhood suspects
    Little that he who rambles lone
    Makes Rothschild tremble on his throne!'

VIII

Nowise! Nor Mayfair residence
    Fit to receive and entertain, –
Nor Hampstead villa's kind defence
    From noise and crowd, from dust and drain, –
    Nor country-box was soul's domain!

IX

Nowise! At back of all that spread
    Of merchandise, woe's me, I find
A hole i' the wall where, heels by head,
    The owner couched, his ware behind,
    – In cupboard suited to his mind.

X

For why? He saw no use of life
   But, while he drove a roaring trade,
To chuckle 'Customers are rife!'
   To chafe 'So much hard cash outlaid
     Yet zero in my profits made!   50

XI

'This novelty costs pains, but — takes?
   Cumbers my counter! Stock no more!
This article, no such great shakes,
   Fizzes like wildfire? Underscore
     The cheap thing — thousands to the fore!'   55

XII

'Twas lodging best to live most nigh
   (Cramp, coffinlike as crib might be)
Receipt of Custom; ear and eye
   Wanted no outworld: 'Hear and see
     The bustle in the shop!' quoth he.   60

XIII

My fancy of a merchant-prince
   Was different. Through his wares we groped
Our darkling way to — not to mince
   The matter — no black den where moped
     The master if we interloped!   65

XIV

Shop was shop only: household-stuff?
   What did he want with comforts there?
'Walls, ceiling, floor, stay blank and rough,
   So goods on sale show rich and rare!
     "*Sell and scud home*" be shop's affair!'   70

XV

What might he deal in? Gems, suppose!
   Since somehow business must be done
At cost of trouble, — see, he throws
   You choice of jewels, everyone,
     Good, better, best, star, moon and sun!   75

XVI

Which lies within your power of purse?
　　This ruby that would tip aright
Solomon's sceptre? Oh, your nurse
　　Wants simply coral, the delight
　　Of teething baby, – stuff to bite!　　　　　　80

XVII

Howe'er your choice fell, straight you took
　　Your purchase, prompt your money rang
On counter, – scarce the man forsook
　　His study of the 'Times,' just swang
　　Till-ward his hand that stopped the clang, –　　85

XVIII

Then off made buyer with a prize,
　　Then seller to his 'Times' returned
And so did day wear, wear, till eyes
　　Brightened apace, for rest was earned:
　　He locked door long ere candle burned.　　　　90

XIX

And whither went he? Ask himself,
　　Not me! To change of scene, I think.
Once sold the ware and pursed the pelf,
　　Chaffer was scarce his meat and drink,
　　Nor all his music – money-chink.　　　　　　95

XX

Because a man has shop to mind
　　In time and place, since flesh must live,
Needs spirit lack all life behind,
　　All stray thoughts, fancies fugitive,
　　All loves except what trade can give?　　　　100

XXI

I want to know a butcher paints,
　　A baker rhymes for his pursuit,
Candlestick-maker much acquaints
　　His soul with song, or, haply mute,
　　Blows out his brains upon the flute!　　　　105

XXII

But – shop each day and all day long!
    Friend, your good angel slept, your star
Suffered eclipse, fate did you wrong!
    From where these sorts of treasures are,
    There should our hearts be – Christ, how far! 110

(1876)

from *Dramatic Idyls: Second Series* (1880)

57.   *Clive*

I and Clive were friends – and why not? Friends! I think you laugh, my lad.
Clive it was gave England India, while your father gives – egad,
England nothing but the graceless boy who lures him on to speak –
'Well, Sir, you and Clive were comrades –' with a tongue thrust in your cheek!
Very true: in my eyes, your eyes, all the world's eyes, Clive was man,   5
I was, am and ever shall be – mouse, nay, mouse of all its clan
Sorriest sample, if you take the kitchen's estimate for fame;
While the man Clive – he fought Plassy, spoiled the clever foreign game,
Conquered and annexed and Englished!

                      Never mind! As o'er my punch
(You away) I sit of evenings, – silence, save for biscuit-crunch,   10
Black, unbroken, – thought grows busy, thrids each pathway of old years,
Notes this forthright, that meander, till the long-past life appears
Like an outspread map of country plodded through, each mile and rood,
Once, and well remembered still: I'm startled in my solitude
Ever and anon by – what's the sudden mocking light that breaks   15
On me as I slap the table till no rummer-glass but shakes
While I ask – aloud, I do believe, God help me! – 'Was it thus?
Can it be that so I faltered, stopped when just one step for us –'
(Us, – you were not born, I grant, but surely some day born would be)
'– One bold step had gained a province' (figurative talk, you see)   20
'Got no end of wealth and honour, – yet I stood stock still no less?'
–'For I was not Clive,' you comment: but it needs no Clive to guess
Wealth were handy, honour ticklish, did no writing on the wall
Warn me 'Trespasser, 'ware man-traps!' Him who braves that notice – call
Hero! none of such heroics suit myself who read plain words,   25
Doff my hat, and leap no barrier. Scripture says the land's the Lord's:
Louts then – what avail the thousand, noisy in a smock-frocked ring,

All-agog to have me trespass, clear the fence, be Clive their king?
Higher warrant must you show me ere I set one foot before
T'other in that dark direction, though I stand for evermore   30
Poor as Job and meek as Moses. Evermore? No! By-and-by
Job grows rich and Moses valiant, Clive turns out less wise than I.
Don't object 'Why call him friend, then?' Power is power, my boy, and still
Marks a man, – God's gift magnific, exercised for good or ill.
You've your boot now on my hearth-rug, tread what was a tiger's skin: 35
Rarely such a royal monster as I lodged the bullet in!
True, he murdered half a village, so his own death came to pass;
Still, for size and beauty, cunning, courage – ah, the brute he was!
Why, that Clive, – that youth, that greenhorn, that quill-driving clerk, in fine, –
He sustained a siege in Arcot…But the world knows! Pass the wine.   40

Where did I break off at? How bring Clive in? Oh, you mentioned 'fear'!
Just so: and, said I, that minds me of a story you shall hear.

We were friends then, Clive and I: so, when the clouds, about the orb
Late supreme, encroaching slowly, surely, threatened to absorb
Ray by ray its noontide brilliance, – friendship might, with steadier eye   45
Drawing near, bear what had burned else, now no blaze – all majesty.
Too much bee's-wing floats my figure? Well, suppose a castle's new:
None presume to climb its ramparts, none find foothold sure for shoe
'Twixt those squares and squares of granite plating the impervious pile
As his scale-mail's warty iron cuirasses a crocodile.   50
Reels that castle thunder-smitten, storm-dismantled? From without
Scrambling up by crack and crevice, every cockney prates about
Towers – the heap he kicks now! turrets – just the measure of his cane!
Will that do? Observe moreover – (same similitude again) –
Such a castle seldom crumbles by sheer stress of cannonade: 55
'Tis when foes are foiled and fighting's finished that vile rains invade,
Grass o'ergrows, o'ergrows till night-birds congregating find no holes
Fit to build in like the topmost sockets made for banner-poles.
So Clive crumbled slow in London – crashed at last.

                                            A week before,
Dining with him, – after trying churchyard-chat of days of yore, –   60
Both of us stopped, tired as tombstones, head-piece, foot-piece, when they lean
Each to other, drowsed in fog-smoke, o'er a coffined Past between.
As I saw his head sink heavy, guessed the soul's extinguishment
By the glazing eyeball, noticed how the furtive fingers went
Where a drug-box skulked behind the honest liquor, – 'One more throw   65
Try for Clive!' thought I: 'Let's venture some good rattling question!' So –
'Come, Clive, tell us' – out I blurted – 'what to tell in turn, years hence,
When my boy – suppose I have one –asks me on what evidence

I maintain my friend of Plassy proved a warrior every whit
Worth your Alexanders, Caesars, Marlboroughs and – what said Pitt? – 70
Frederick the Fierce himself! Clive told me once' – I want to say –
'Which feat out of all those famous doings bore the bell away
– In his own calm estimation, mark you, not the mob's rough guess –
Which stood foremost as evincing what Clive called courageousness!
Come! what moment of the minute, what speck-centre in the wide 75
Circle of the action saw your mortal fairly deified?
(Let alone that filthy sleep-stuff, swallow bold this wholesome Port!)
If a friend has leave to question, – when were you most brave, in short?'

Up he arched his brows o' the instant – formidably Clive again.
'When was I most brave? I'd answer, were the instance half as plain 80
As another instance that's a brain-lodged crystal – curse it! – here
Freezing when my memory touches – ugh! – the time I felt most fear.
Ugh! I cannot say for certain if I showed fear – anyhow,
Fear I felt, and, very likely, shuddered, since I shiver now.'

'Fear!' smiled I. 'Well, that's the rarer: that's a specimen to seek, 85
Ticket up in one's museum, *Mind-Freaks, Lord Clive's Fear, Unique!*'

Down his brows dropped. On the table painfully he pored as though
Tracing, in the stains and streaks there, thoughts encrusted long ago.
When he spoke 'twas like a lawyer reading word by word some will,
Some blind jungle of a statement, – beating on and on until 90
Out there leaps fierce life to fight with.

                              'This fell in my factor-days.
Desk-drudge, slaving at Saint David's, one must game, or drink, or craze.
I chose gaming: and, – because your high-flown gamesters hardly take
Umbrage at a factor's elbow if the factor pays his stake, –
I was winked at in a circle where the company was choice, 95
Captain This and Major That, men high of colour, loud of voice,
Yet indulgent, condescending to the modest juvenile
Who not merely risked but lost his hard-earned guineas with a smile.

'Down I sat to cards, one evening, – had for my antagonist
Somebody whose name's a secret – you'll know why – so, if you list, 100
Call him Cock o' the Walk, my scarlet son of Mars from head to heel!
Play commenced: and, whether Cocky fancied that a clerk must feel
Quite sufficient honour came of bending over one green baize,
I the scribe with him the warrior, – guessed no penman dared to raise
Shadow of objection should the honour stay but playing end 105
More or less abruptly, – whether disinclined he grew to spend
Practice strictly scientific on a booby born to stare

At – not ask of – lace-and-ruffles if the hand they hide plays fair, –
Anyhow, I marked a movement when he bade me "Cut!"

                 'I rose.
"Such the new manoeuvre, Captain? I'm a novice: knowledge grows.
What, you force a card, you cheat, Sir?"

            'Never did a thunder-clap
Cause emotion, startle Thyrsis locked with Chloe in his lap,
As my word and gesture (down I flung my cards to join the pack)
Fired the man of arms, whose visage, simply red before, turned black.

'When he found his voice, he stammered "That expression once again!"

'"Well, you forced a card and cheated!"

             "'Possibly a factor's brain,
Busied with his all-important balance of accounts, may deem
Weighing words superfluous trouble: *cheat* to clerkly ears may seem
Just the joke for friends to venture: but we are not friends, you see!
When a gentleman is joked with, – if he's good at repartee,
He rejoins, as do I – Sirrah, on your knees, withdraw in full!
Beg my pardon, or be sure a kindly bullet through your skull
Lets in light and teaches manners to what brain it finds! Choose quick –
Have your life snuffed out or, kneeling, pray me trim yon candle-wick!"

'"Well, you cheated!"

       'Then outbroke a howl from all the friends around.
To his feet sprang each in fury, fists were clenched and teeth were ground.
"End it! no time like the present! Captain, yours were our disgrace!
No delay, begin and finish! Stand back, leave the pair a space!
Let civilians be instructed: henceforth simply ply the pen,
Fly the sword! This clerk's no swordsman? Suit him with a pistol, then!
Even odds! A dozen paces 'twixt the most and least expert
Make a dwarf a giant's equal: nay, the dwarf, if he's alert,
Likelier hits the broader target!"

          'Up we stood accordingly.
As they handed me the weapon, such was my soul's thirst to try
Then and there conclusions with this bully, tread on and stamp out
Every spark of his existence, that, – crept close to, curled about
By that toying tempting teasing fool-forefinger's middle joint, –
Don't you guess? – the trigger yielded. Gone my chance! and at the point
Of such prime success moreover: scarce an inch above his head

Went my ball to hit the wainscot. He was living, I was dead.
'Up he marched in flaming triumph – 'twas his right, mind! – up, within
Just an arm's length. "Now, my clerkling," chuckled Cocky with a grin
As the levelled piece quite touched me, "Now, Sir Counting-House, repeat
That expression which I told you proved bad manners! Did I cheat?"

'"Cheat you did, you knew you cheated, and, this moment, know as well.
As for me, my homely breeding bids you – fire and go to Hell!"
'Twice the muzzle touched my forehead. Heavy barrel, flurried wrist,
Either spoils a steady lifting. Thrice: then, "Laugh at Hell who list,
I can't! God's no fable either. Did this boy's eye wink once? No!
There's no standing him and Hell and God all three against me, – so,
I did cheat!"

      'And down he threw the pistol, out rushed – by the door
Possibly, but, as for knowledge if by chimney, roof or floor,
He effected disappearance – I'll engage no glance was sent
That way by a single starer, such a blank astonishment
Swallowed up their senses: as for speaking – mute they stood as mice.

'Mute not long, though! Such reaction, such a hubbub in a trice!
"Rogue and rascal! Who'd have thought it? What's to be expected next,
When His Majesty's Commission serves a sharper as pretext
For…But where's the need of wasting time now? Naught requires delay:
Punishment the Service cries for: let disgrace be wiped away
Publicly, in good broad daylight! Resignation? No, indeed
Drum and fife must play the Rogue's March, rank and file be free to speed
Tardy marching on the rogue's part by appliance in the rear
– Kicks administered shall right this wronged civilian, – never fear,
Mister Clive, for – though a clerk – you bore yourself – suppose we say –
Just as would beseem a soldier!"

                "Gentlemen, attention – pray!
First, one word!"

          'I passed each speaker severally in review.
When I had precise their number, names and styles, and fully knew
Over whom my supervision thenceforth must extend, – why, then –
'"Some five minutes since, my life lay – as you all saw, gentlemen –
At the mercy of your friend there. Not a single voice was raised
In arrest of judgement, not one tongue – before my powder blazed –
Ventured 'Can it be the youngster blundered, really seemed to mark
Some irregular proceeding? We conjecture in the dark,
Guess at random, – still, for sake of fair play – what if for a freak,
In a fit of absence, – such things have been! –if our friend proved weak

—What's the phrase? – corrected fortune! Look into the case, at least!'
Who dared interpose between the altar's victim and the priest?
Yet he spared me! You eleven! Whosoever, all or each,
To the disadvantage of the man who spared me, utters speech   180
– To his face, behind his back, – that speaker has to do with me:
Me who promise, if positions change and mine the chance should be,
Not to imitate your friend and waive advantage!"

                                                          'Twenty-five
Years ago this matter happened: and 'tis certain,' added Clive,
'Never, to my knowledge, did Sir Cocky have a single breath   185
Breathed against him: lips were closed throughout his life, or since his death,
For if he be dead or living I can tell no more than you.
All I know is – Cocky had one chance more; how he used it, – grew
Out of such unlucky habits, or relapsed, and back again
Brought the late-ejected devil with a score more in his train, –   190
That's for you to judge. Reprieval I procured, at any rate.
Ugh – the memory of that minute's fear makes gooseflesh rise! Why prate
Longer? You've my story, there's your instance: fear I did, you see!
'Well' – I hardly kept from laughing – 'if I see it, thanks must be
Wholly to your Lordship's candour. Not that – in a common case –   195
When a bully caught at cheating thrusts a pistol in one's face,
I should underrate, believe me, such a trial to the nerve!
'Tis no joke, at one-and-twenty, for a youth to stand nor swerve.
Fear I naturally look for – unless, of all men alive,
I am forced to make exception when I come to Robert Clive.   200
Since at Arcot, Plassy, elsewhere, he and death – the whole world knows –
Came to somewhat closer quarters.'

                                       Quarters? Had we come to blows,
Clive and I, you had not wondered – up he sprang so, out he rapped
Such a round of oaths – no matter! I'll endeavour to adapt
To our modern usage words he – well, 'twas friendly licence – flung 205
At me like so many fire-balls, fast as he could wag his tongue.

'You – a soldier? You – at Plassy? Yours the faculty to nick
Instantaneously occasion when your foe, if lightning-quick,
– At his mercy, at his malice, – has you, through some stupid inch
Undefended in your bulwark? Thus laid open, – not to flinch   210
– That needs courage, you'll concede me. Then, look here! Suppose the man,
Checking his advance, his weapon still extended, not a span
Distant from my temple, – curse him! – quietly had bade me "There!
Keep your life, calumniator! – worthless life I freely spare:
Mine you freely would have taken – murdered me and my good fame   215
Both at once – and all the better! Go, and thank your own bad aim

Which permits me to forgive you!" What if, with such words as these,
He had cast away his weapon? How should I have borne me, please?
Nay, I'll spare you pains and tell you. This, and only this, remained –
Pick his weapon up and use it on myself. I so had gained 220
Sleep the earlier, leaving England probably to pay on still
Rent and taxes for half India, tenant at the Frenchman's will.'

'Such the turn,' said I, 'the matter takes with you? Then I abate
– No, by not one jot nor tittle, – of your act my estimate.
Fear – I wish I could detect there: courage fronts me, plain enough – 225
Call it desperation, madness – never mind! for here's in rough
Why, had mine been such a trial, fear had overcome disgrace.
True, disgrace were hard to bear: but such a rush against God's face
– None of that for me, Lord Plassy, since I go to church at times,
Say the creed my mother taught me! Many years in foreign climes 230
Rub some marks away – not all, though! We poor sinners reach life's brink,
Overlook what rolls beneath it, recklessly enough, but think
There's advantage in what's left us – ground to stand on, time to call
"Lord, have mercy!" ere we topple over –do not leap, that's all!'

Oh, he made no answer, – re-absorbed into his cloud. I caught 235
Something like 'Yes – courage: only fools will call it fear.'

            If aught
Comfort you, my great unhappy hero Clive, in that I heard,
Next week, how your own hand dealt you doom, and uttered just the word
'Fearfully courageous!' – this, be sure, and nothing else I groaned.
I'm no Clive, nor parson either: Clive's worst deed –we'll hope condoned. 240

              (1880)

from *Jocsoseria* (1883)

58.   'Wanting is – what?'

   Wanting is – what?
   Summer redundant,
   Blueness abundant,
    – Where is the blot?
 Beamy the world, yet a blank all the same, 5
  – Framework which waits for a picture to frame:
 What of the leafage, what of the flower?

Roses embowering with naught they embower!
Come then, complete incompletion, O comer,
Pant through the blueness, perfect the summer!   10
    Breathe but one breath
    Rose-beauty above,
    And all that was death
    Grows life, grows love,
        Grows love!   15

from *Asolando: Fancies and Facts* (1889)

59.   *Speculative*

Others may need new life in Heaven –
    Man, Nature, Art – made new, assume!
Man with new mind old sense to leaven,
    Nature – new light to clear old gloom,
Art that breaks bounds, gets soaring-room.   5

I shall pray: 'Fugitive as precious –
    Minutes which passed, – return, remain!
Let earth's old life once more enmesh us,
    You with old pleasure, me – old pain,
So we but meet nor part again!'   10

60.   *Bad Dreams I*

Last night I saw you in my sleep:
    And how your charm of face was changed!
I asked 'Some love, some faith you keep?'
    You answered 'Faith gone, love estranged.'

Whereat I woke – a twofold bliss: 5
    Waking was one, but next there came
This other: 'Though I felt, for this,
    My heart break, I loved on the same.'

61.   *Bad Dreams II*

You in the flesh and here –
   Your very self! Now wait!
One word! May I hope or fear?
   Must I speak in love or hate?
Stay while I ruminate!

The fact and each circumstance
   Dare you disown? Not you!
That vast dome, that huge dance,
   And the gloom which overgrew
A – possibly festive crew!

For why should men dance at all –
   Why women – a crowd of both –
Unless they are gay? Strange ball –
   Hands and feet plighting troth,
Yet partners enforced and loth!

Of who danced there, no shape
   Did I recognize: thwart, perverse,
Each grasped each, past escape
   In a whirl or weary or worse:
Man's sneer met woman's curse,

While he and she toiled as if
   Their guardian set galley-slaves
To supple chained limbs grown stiff:
   Unmanacled trulls and knaves –
The lash for who misbehaves!

And a gloom was, all the while,
   Deeper and deeper yet
O'ergrowing the rank and file
   Of that army of haters – set
To mimic love's fever-fret.

By the wall-side close I crept,
   Avoiding the livid maze,
And, safely so far, outstepped
   On a chamber – a chapel, says
My memory or betrays –

Closet-like, kept aloof
　　　　From unseemly witnessing
　　What sport made floor and roof
　　　　Of the Devil's palace ring
　　While his Damned amused their king.   40

　　Ay, for a low lamp burned,
　　　　And a silence lay about
　　What I, in the midst, discerned
　　　　Though dimly till, past doubt,
　　'Twas a sort of throne stood out –   45

　　High seat with steps, at least:
　　　　And the topmost step was filled
　　By – whom? What vestured priest?
　　　　A stranger to me, – his guild,
　　His cult, unreconciled   50

　　To my knowledge how guild and cult
　　　　Are clothed in this world of ours:
　　I pondered, but no result
　　　　Came to – unless that Giaours
　　So worship the Lower Powers.   55

　　When suddenly who entered?
　　　　Who knelt – did you guess I saw?
　　Who – raising that face where centred
　　　　Allegiance to love and law
　　So lately – off-casting awe,   60

　　Down-treading reserve, away
　　　　Thrusting respect... but mine
　　Stands firm – firm still shall stay!
　　Ask Satan! for I decline
　　To tell – what I saw, in fine!   65

　　Yet here in the flesh you come –
　　　　Your same self, form and face, –
　　In the eyes, mirth still at home!
　　　　On the lips, that commonplace
　　Perfection of honest grace!   70

Yet your errand is – needs must be –
    To palliate – well, explain,
Expurgate in some degree
    Your soul of its ugly stain.
Oh, you – the good in grain –　　　　　　　　　　　75

How was it your white took tinge?
    'A mere dream' – never object!
Sleep leaves a door on hinge
    Whence soul, ere our flesh suspect,
Is off and away: detect　　　　　　　　　　　　80

Her vagaries when loose, who can!
    Be she pranksome, be she prude,
Disguise with the day began:
    With the night – ah, what ensued
From draughts of a drink hell-brewed?　　　　　85

Then She: 'What a queer wild dream!
    And perhaps the best fun is –
Myself had its fellow – I seem
    Scarce awake from yet. 'Twas this –
Shall I tell you? First, a kiss!　　　　　　　　　　90

'For the fault was just your own, –
    'Tis myself expect apology:
You warned me to let alone
    (Since our studies were mere philology)
That ticklish (you said) Anthology.　　　　　　　95

'So, I dreamed that I passed *exam*
    Till a question posed me sore:
"Who translated this epigram
    By – an author we best ignore?"
And I answered "Hannah More"!'　　　　　　　100

62.　　　　　　　　*Bad Dreams III*

This was my dream: I saw a Forest
    Old as the earth, no track nor trace
Of unmade man. Thou, Soul, explorest –
    Though in a trembling rapture – space
Immeasurable! Shrubs, turned trees,　　　　　　5

Trees that touch heaven, support its frieze
Studded with sun and moon and star:
While – oh, the enormous growths that bar
Mine eye from penetrating past
    Their tangled twine where lurks – nay, lives   10
Royally lone, some brute-type cast
    I' the rough, time cancels, man forgives.

On, Soul! I saw a lucid City
    Of architectural device
Every way perfect. Pause for pity,   15
    Lightning! nor leave a cicatrice
On those bright marbles, dome and spire,
Structures palatial, – streets which mire
Dares not defile, paved all too fine
For human footstep's smirch, not thine –   20
Proud solitary traverser,
    My Soul, of silent lengths of way –
With what ecstatic dread, aver,
    Lest life start sanctioned by thy stay!

Ah, but the last sight was the hideous!   25
    A City, yes, – a Forest, true, –
But each devouring each. Perfidious
    Snake-plants had strangled what I knew
Was a pavilion once: each oak
Held on his horns some spoil he broke   30
By surreptitiously beneath
    Upthrusting: pavements, as with teeth,
Griped huge weed widening crack and split
    In squares and circles stone-work erst.
Oh, Nature – good! Oh, Art – no whit   35
    Less worthy! Both in one – accurst!

63.   *Bad Dreams IV*

It happened thus: my slab, though new,
    Was getting weather-stained, – beside,
Herbage, balm, peppermint o'ergrew
    Letter and letter: till you tried
Somewhat, the Name was scarce descried.   5

That strong stern man my lover came:
  – Was he my lover? Call him, pray,
My life's cold critic bent on blame
  Of all poor I could do or say
To make me worth his love one day –   10

One far day when, by diligent
  And dutiful amending faults,
Foibles, all weaknesses which went
  To challenge and excuse assaults
Of culture wronged by taste that halts –   15

Discrepancies should mar no plan
  Symmetric of the qualities
Claiming respect from – say – a man
  That's strong and stern. 'Once more he pries
Into me with those critic eyes!'   20

No question! so – 'Conclude, condemn
  Each failure my poor self avows!
Leave to its fate all you contemn!
  There's Solomon's selected spouse:
Earth needs must hold such maids – choose them!'   25

Why, he was weeping! Surely gone
  Sternness and strength: with eyes to ground
And voice a broken monotone –
  'Only be as you were! Abound
In foibles, faults, – laugh, robed and crowned   30

'As Folly's veriest queen, – care I
  One feather-fluff? Look pity, Love,
On prostrate me – your foot shall try
  This forehead's use – mount thence above,
And reach what Heaven you dignify!'   35

Now, what could bring such change about?
  The thought perplexed: till, following
His gaze upon the ground, – why, out
  Came all the secret! So, a thing
Thus simple has deposed my king!   40

For, spite of weeds that strove to spoil
  Plain reading on the lettered slab,
My name was clear enough – no soil
  Effaced the date when one chance stab
Of scorn…if only ghosts might blab!   45

64.   *Inapprehensiveness*

We two stood simply friend-like side by side,
Viewing a twilight country far and wide,
Till she at length broke silence. 'How it towers
Yonder, the ruin o'er this vale of ours!
The West's faint flare behind it so relieves   5
Its rugged outline – sight perhaps deceives,
Or I could almost fancy that I see
A branch wave plain – belike some wind-sown tree
Chance-rooted where a missing turret was.
What would I give for the perspective glass   10
At home, to make out if 'tis really so!
Has Ruskin noticed here at Asolo
That certain weed-growths on the ravaged wall
Seem'... something that I could not say at all,
My thought being rather – as absorbed she sent   15
Look onward after look from eyes distent
With longing to reach Heaven's gate left ajar –
'Oh, fancies that might be, oh, facts that are!
What of a wilding? By you stands, and may
So stand unnoticed till the Judgement Day,   20
One who, if once aware that your regard
Claimed what his heart holds, – woke, as from its sward
The flower, the dormant passion, so to speak –
Then what a rush of life would startling wreak
Revenge on your inapprehensive stare   25
While, from the ruin and the West's faint flare,
You let your eyes meet mine, touch what you term
Quietude – that's an universe in germ –
The dormant passion needing but a look
To burst into immense life!'   30
                    'No, the book
Which noticed how the wall-growths wave' said she
'Was not by Ruskin.'
            I said 'Vernon Lee?'

65.   *The Lady and the Painter*

        SHE: Yet womanhood you reverence,
                    So you profess!
        HE: With heart and soul.

SHE: Of which fact this is evidence!
    To help Art-study, – for some dole 5
Of certain wretched shillings, – you
Induce a woman – virgin too –
To strip and stand stark-naked?
HE: True.

SHE: Nor feel you so degrade her? 10
HE: What
– (Excuse the interruption) – clings
Half-savage-like around your hat?
SHE: Ah, do they please you? Wild-bird-wings!
Next season, – Paris-prints assert, – 15
We must go feathered to the skirt:
My modiste keeps on the alert.

    Owls, hawks, jays –swallows most approve ...
HE: Dare I speak plainly?
SHE: Oh, I trust! 20
HE: Then, Lady Blanche, it less would move
   In heart and soul of me disgust
Did you strip off those spoils you wear,
And stand – for thanks, not shillings – bare,
To help Art like my Model there. 25
She well knew what absolved her – praise
   In me for God's surpassing good,
Who granted to my reverent gaze
   A type of purest womanhood.
You – clothed with murder of His best 30
Of harmless beings – stand the test!
What is it *you* know?
SHE: That you jest!

from *Uncollected Poems*

66.   *Lines for the Jubilee Window*

Fifty years' flight! Wherein should he rejoice
   Who hailed their birth, who as they die decays?
This – England echoes his attesting voice:
   'Wondrous and well – thanks, Ancient Thou of Days!'

(1887)

67.   *To Edward FitzGerald*

    I chanced upon a new book yesterday:
    I opened it, and, where my finger lay
      'Twixt page and uncut page, these words I read
    — Some six or seven at most — and learned thereby
    That you, FitzGerald, whom by ear and eye   5
      She never knew, 'thanked God my wife was dead.'

    Ay, dead! and were yourself alive, good Fitz,
    How to return you thanks would task my wits:
      Kicking you seems the common lot of curs —
    While more appropriate greeting lends you grace: 10
    Surely to spit there glorifies your face —
      Spitting — from lips once sanctified by Hers.

                          (1889)

68.   *Why I am a Liberal*

    'Why?' Because all I haply can and do,
      All that I am now, all I hope to be, —
      Whence comes it save from fortune setting free
    Body and soul the purpose to pursue,
    God traced for both? If fetters, not a few,   5
      Of prejudice, convention, fall from me,
      These shall I bid men — each in his degree
    Also God-guided — bear, and gaily too?

    But little do or can the best of us:
      THAT LITTLE IS ACHIEVED THROUGH LIBERTY.   10
    Who, then, dares hold — emancipated thus —
      His fellow shall continue bound? Not I,
    Who live, love, labour freely, nor discuss
      A brother's right to freedom. That is 'Why.'

                          (1885)

69.   *Suggestion for a Telegraphic Birthday Greeting*

>   Bancroft, the message-bearing wire,
>   Which flashes my 'All hail' today,
>   Moves slowlier than the heart's desire
>   That what hand pens, tongue's self might say.

(1890)

70.   *Conclusion of a Sonnet on 'Keely's Discovery'*

>   All we can dream of loveliness within, –
>   All ever hoped for by a will intense, –
>   This shall one day be palpable to sense
>   And earth become to heaven akin.

(1890)

Shirley Brooks (1816–1874)

71.   *Waggawocky*

A parody on "Jabberwocky, the Chattertonian poem" in Mr. Lewis Carroll's fairy book "Alice through the Looking Glass."

   Merely interpolating the note that the word "wabe" is explained by the Poet to mean "a grassplot round a sundial," but that it also means a Court of Justice, being derived from the Saxon *waube*, a wig-shop, Mr. Punch proceeds to dress the prophetic ode in plain English:—

>   'Twas Maytime, and the lawyer coves
>   Did gibe and jabber in the wabe,
>   All menaced were the Tichborne groves,
>   And their true lord, the Babe.
>
>   "Beware the Waggawock, my son,
>   The eyelid twitch, the knees' incline,
>   Beware the Baigent network, spun
>   For gallant Ballantine."

5

He took his ton-weight brief in hand,
    Long time the hidden clue he sought,
Then rested he by the Hawkins tree,
    And sat awhile in thought.

And as in toughish thought he rocks,
    The Waggawock, *sans* ruth or shame,
Came lumbering to the witness box,
    And perjured out his Claim.

"Untrue! untrue!" Then, through and through
    The weary weeks he worked the rack;
But March had youth, ere with the Truth
    He dealt the final whack.

"And hast thou slain the Waggawock?
    Come to my arms, my Beamish Boy!
O Coleridge, J.! Hoorah! hooray!"
    Punch chortled in his joy.

(1872)

George Eliot (1819–1880)

72.   *The Death of Moses*

Moses, who spake with God as with his friend,
And ruled his people with the twofold power
Of wisdom that can dare and still be meek,
Was writing his last word, the sacred name
Unutterable of that Eternal Will
Which was and is and evermore shall be.
Yet was his task not finished, for the flock
Needed its shepherd and the life-taught sage
Leaves no successor; but to chosen men,
The rescuers and guides of Israel,
A death was given called the Death of Grace,
Which freed them from the burden of the flesh
But left them rulers of the multitude
And loved companions of the lonely. This
Was God's last gift to Moses, this the hour
When soul must part from self and be but soul.

God spake to Gabriel, the messenger
Of mildest death that draws the parting life
Gently, as when a little rosy child
Lifts up its lips from off the bowl of milk   20
And so draws forth a curl that dipped its gold
In the soft white – thus Gabriel draws the soul.
"Go bring the soul of Moses unto me!"
And the awe-stricken angel answered, "Lord,
How shall I dare to take his life who lives   25
Sole of his kind, not to be likened once
In all the generations of the earth?"

Then God called Michaël, him of pensive brow
Snow-vest and flaming sword, who knows and acts:
"Go bring the spirit of Moses unto me!"   30
But Michaël with such grief as angels feel,
Loving the mortals whom they succour, pled:
"Almighty, spare me; it was I who taught
Thy servant Moses; he is part of me
As I of thy deep secrets, knowing them."   35

Then God called Zamaël, the terrible,
The angel of fierce death, of agony
That comes in battle and in pestilence
Remorseless, sudden or with lingering throes.
And Zamaël, his raiment and broad wings   40
Blood-tinctured, the dark lustre of his eyes
Shrouding the red, fell like the gathering night
Before the prophet. But that radiance
Won from the heavenly presence in the mount
Gleamed on the prophet's brow and dazzling pierced   45
Its conscious opposite: the angel turned
His murky gaze aloof and inly said:
"An angel this, deathless to angel's stroke."

But Moses felt the subtly nearing dark: –
"Who art thou? and what wilt thou?" Zamaël then: 50
"I am God's reaper; through the fields of life
I gather ripened and unripened souls
Both willing and unwilling. And I come
Now to reap thee." But Moses cried,
Firm as a seer who waits the trusted sign: 55
"Reap thou the fruitless plant and common herb –
Not him who from the womb was sanctified
To teach the law of purity and love."
And Zamaël baffled from his errand fled.

But Moses, pausing, in the air serene 60
Heard now that mystic whisper, far yet near,
The all-penetrating Voice, that said to him,
"Moses, the hour is come and thou must die."
"Lord, I obey; but thou rememberest
How thou, Ineffable, didst take me once 65
Within thy orb of light untouched by death."
Then the voice answered, "Be no more afraid:
With me shall be thy death and burial."
So Moses waited, ready now to die.

And the Lord came, invisible as a thought, 70
Three angels gleaming on his secret track,
Prince Michaël, Zamaël, Gabriel, charged to guard
The soul-forsaken body as it fell
And bear it to the hidden sepulchre
Denied for ever to the search of man. 75
And the Voice said to Moses: "Close thine eyes."
He closed them. "Lay thine hand upon thine heart,
And draw thy feet together." He obeyed.
And the Lord said, "O spirit! child of mine!
A hundred years and twenty thou hast dwelt 80
Within this tabernacle wrought of clay.
This is the end: come forth and flee to heaven."

But the grieved soul with plaintive pleading cried,
"I love this body with a clinging love:
The courage fails me, Lord, to part from it." 85

"O child, come forth! for thou shalt dwell with me
About the immortal throne where seraphs joy
In growing vision and in growing love."

Yet hesitating, fluttering, like the bird
With young wing weak and dubious, the soul 90
Stayed. But behold! upon the death-dewed lips
A kiss descended, pure, unspeakable –
The bodiless Love without embracing Love
That lingered in the body, drew it forth
With heavenly strength and carried it to heaven. 95

But now beneath the sky the watchers all,
Angels that keep the homes of Israel
Or on high purpose wander o'er the world
Leading the Gentiles, felt a dark eclipse:

The greatest ruler among men was gone. 100
And from the westward sea was heard a wail,
A dirge as from the isles of Javanim,
Crying, "Who now is left upon the earth
Like him to teach the right and smite the wrong?"
And from the East, far o'er the Syrian waste, 105
Came slowlier, sadlier, the answering dirge:
"No prophet like him lives or shall arise
In Israel or the world for evermore."

But Israel waited, looking toward the mount,
Till with the deepening eve the elders came 110
Saying, "His burial is hid with God.
We stood far off and saw the angels lift
His corpse aloft until they seemed a star
That burnt itself away within the sky."

The people answered with mute orphaned gaze 115
Looking for what had vanished evermore.
Then through the gloom without them and within
The spirit's shaping light, mysterious speech,
Invisible Will wrought clear in sculptured sound,
The thought-begotten daughter of the voice, 120
Thrilled on their listening sense: "He has no tomb.
He dwells not with you dead, but lives as Law."

(1875)

John Ruskin (1819–1900)

73. *Trust Thou Thy Love*

Trust thou thy Love: if she be proud, is she not sweet?
   Trust thou thy Love: if she be mute, is she not pure?
Lay thou thy soul full in her hands, low at her feet;—
   Fail, Sun and Breath!—yet, for thy peace, *she* shall endure.

Jean Ingelow (1820–1897)

74.
        Letters on Life and the Morning
        A Parson's Letter to a Young Poet

They said 'Too late, too late, the work is done;
Great Homer sang of glory and strong men
And that fair Greek whose fault all these long years
Wins no forgetfulness nor ever can;
For yet cold eyes upon her frailty bend,   5
For yet the world waits in the victor's tent
Daily, and sees an old man honourable,
His white head bowed, surprise to passionate tears
Awestruck Achilles; sighing, "I have endured
The like whereof no soul hath yet endured,   10
To kiss the hand of him that slew my son."

They said: 'We, rich by him, are rich by more;
One Æschylus found watchfires on a hill
That lit Old Night's three daughters to their work;
When the forlorn Fate leaned to their red light   15
And sat a-spinning, to her feet he came
And marked her till she span off all her thread.

O, it is late, good sooth, to cry for more:
The work once done, well done' they said, 'forbear!
A Tuscan afterward discovered steps   20
Over the line of life in its mid-way;
He climbed the wall of Heaven, beheld his love
Safe at her singing, and he left his foes
In a vale of shadow weltering, unassoiled
Immortal sufferers henceforth in both worlds.   25

Who may inherit next or who shall match
The Swan of Avon and go float with him
Down the long river of life aneath a sun
Not veiled, and high at noon?—the river of life
That as it ran reflected all its lapse   30
And rippling on the plumage of his breast?

Thou hast them, heed them, for thy poets now,
Albeit of tongue full sweet and majesty
Like even to theirs, are fallen on evil days,

Are wronged by thee of life, wronged of the world.　35
Look back they must and show thee thy fair past,
Or, choosing thy to-day, they may but chant
As they behold.

    The mother-glowworm broods
Upon her young, fast folded in the egg　40
And long before they come to life they shine—
The mother-age broods on her shining thought
That liveth, but whose life is hid. He comes
Her poet son, and lo you, he can see
The shining, and he takes it to his breast　45
And fashions for its wings that it may fly
And show its sweet light in the dusky world.
Mother, O Mother of our dusk to-day,
What hast thou lived for bards to sing of thee?
Lapsed water cannot flow above its source;　50
"*The kid must browse,*" they said, "*where she is tied.*"

Son of to-day, rise up, and answer them.
What! wilt thou let thy mother sit ashamed
And crownless?—Set the crown on her fair head:
She waited for thy birth, she cries to thee　55
'Thou art the man.' He that hath ears to hear,
To him the mother cries 'Thou art the man.'

She murmurs, for thy mother's voice is low—
'Methought the men of war were even as gods,
The old men of the ages. Now mine eyes　60
Retrieve the truth from ruined city walls
That buried it; from carved and curious homes
Full of rich garments and all goodly spoil,
Where having burned, battered, and wasted them,
They flung it. Give us, give us better gods　65
Than these that drink with blood upon their hands,
For I repent me that I worshipped them.
O that there might e a going up!
O to forget—and to begin again!'

Is not thy mother's rede at one with theirs　70
Who cry 'The work is done'? What though to thee,
Thee only, should the utterance shape itself
'O to forget, and to begin again,'
Only of thee be heard as that keen cry
Rending its way from some distracted heart　75

That yields it and so breaks? Yet list the cry
Begin for her again, and learn to sing;
But first, in all thy learning learn to be.
Is life a field? Then plough it up—re-sow
With worthier seed—Is life a ship? O heed 80
The southing of thy stars—Is life a breath?
Breathe deeper, draw life up from hour to hour,
Aye, from the deepest deep in they deep soul.

It may be God's first work is but to breathe
And fill the abysm with drifts of shining air 85
That slowly, slowly curdle into worlds.
A little space is measured out to us
Of His long leisure; breathe and grow therein,
For life, alas! is short, and *'when we die*
It is not for a little while.' 90

    They said,
'The work is done,' and is it therefore done?
Speak rather to thy mother thus: 'All-fair,
Lady of ages, beautiful To-day
And sorrowful To-day, thy children set 95
The crown of sorrow on their heads, their loss
Is like to be the loss of all: we hear
Lamenting, as of some that mourn in vain
Loss of high leadership, but where is he
That shall be great enough to lead thee now? 100

Where is thy Poet? thou hast wanted him.
Where? Thou has wakened as a child in the night
And found thyself alone. The stars have set,
There is great darkness, and the dark is void
Of music. Who shall set thy life afresh 105
And sing thee thy new songs? Whom wilt thou love
And lean on to break silence worthily—
Discern the beauty in thy goings—feel
The glory of thy yearning—thy self-scorn
Flatter to dim oblivion with a smile— 110
Own thy great want, that knew not its great name?
O who shall make to thee mighty amends
For thy lost childhood, joining two in one,
Thyself and Him? Behold Him, He is near:
God is thy Poet now. 115

75.   *Perdita*

'*I go beyond the commandment.*' So be it. Then mine be the blame,
The loss, the lack, the yearning, till life's last sand be run,—
I go beyond the commandment, yet Honour stands fast with her claim,
And what I have rued I shall rue; for what I have done—I have done.

Hush, hush! for what of the future; you cannot the base exalt,   5
There is no bridging a chasm over, that yawns with so sheer incline;
I will not any sweet daughter's cheek should pale for this mother's fault,
Nor son take leave to lower his life a-thinking on mine.

'*Will I tell you all?*' So! this, e'en this, will I do for your great love's sake;
Think what it costs. '*Then let there be silence—silence you'll count consent.*'   10
No, and no, and for ever no: rather to cross and to break,
And to lower your passion I speak—that other it was I meant.

That other I meant (but I know not how) to speak of, nor April days,
Nor a man's sweet voice that pleaded—O (but I promised this)—
He never talked of marriage, never; I grant him that praise;   15
And he bent his stately head, and I lost, and he won with a kiss.

He led me away—O, how poignant sweet the nightingale's note that noon—
I beheld, and each crispèd spire of grass to him for my sake was fair,
And warm winds flattered my soul, blowing straight from the soul of June,
And a lovely lie was spread on the fields, but the blue was bare.   20

When I looked up, he said: 'Love, fair love! O rather look in these eyes
With thine far sweeter than eyes of Eve when she stepped the valley unshod'—
For ONE might be looking through it, he thought, and he would not in any wise
I should mark it open, limitless, empty, bare 'neath the gaze of God.

Ah me! I was happy—yes, I was; 't is fit you should know it all,   25
While love was warm and tender and yearning, the rough winds troubled me not;
I heard them moan without in the forest; heard the chill rains fall—
But I thought my place was sheltered with him—I forgot, I forgot.

After came news of a wife; I think he was glad I should know,
To stay my pleading, 'take me to church and give me my ring;'   30
'You should have spoken before,' he had sighed, when I prayed him so,
For his heart was sick for himself and me, and this bitter thing.

But my dream was over me still,—I was half beguiled,
And he in his kindness left me seldom, O seldom, alone,
And yet love waxed cold, and I saw the face of my little child, 35
And then at the last I knew what I was, and what I had done.

'YOU *will give me the name of wife.* YOU *will give me a ring.*'—O peace!
You are not let to ruin your life because I ruined mine;
You will go to your people at home. There will be rest and release;
The bitter now will be sweet full soon—ay, and denial divine. 40

But spare me the ending. I did not wait to be quite cast away;
I left him asleep, and the bare sun rising shone red on my gown.
There was dust in the lane, I remember; prints of feet in it lay,
And honeysuckle trailed in the path that led on to the down.

I was going nowhere—I wandered up, then turned and dared to look back, 45
Where low in the valley he careless and quiet—quiet and careless slept.
'*Did I love him yet?*' I loved him. Ay, my heart on the upland track
Cried to him, sighed to him out by the wheat, as I walked, and I wept.

I knew of another alas, one that had been in my place,
Her little ones, she forsaken, were almost in need; 50
I went to her, and carried my babe, then all in my satins and lace
I sank at the step of her desolate door, a mourner indeed.

I cried, "'T is the way of the world, would I had never been born!'
'Ay, 't is the way of the world, but have you no sense to see
For all the way of the world,' she answers and laughs me to scorn, 55
'The world is made the world that it is by fools like you, like me?'

Right hard upon me, hard on herself, and cold as the cold stone,
But she took me in; and while I lay sick I knew I was lost,
Lost with the man I loved, or lost without him, making my moan
Blighted and rent of the bitter frost, wrecked, tempest tossed, lost, lost! 60

How am I fallen:—we that might make of the world what we would,
Some of us sink in deep waters. Ah! '*you would raise me again?*'
No, true heart,—you cannot, you cannot, and all in my soul that is good
Cries out against such a wrong. Let be, your quest is for ever in vain.

For I feel with another heart, I think with another mind, 65
I have worsened life, I have wronged the world, I have lowered the light;
But as for him, his words and his ways were after his kind,
He did but spoil where he could, and waste where he might.

For he was let to do it; I let him and left his soul
To walk mid the ruins he made of home in remembrance of love's despairs, 70
Despairs that harden the hearts of men and shadow their heads with dole,
And woman's fault, though never on earth, may be healed,—but what of theirs?

'T was fit you should hear it all—What, tears? they comfort me; now you will go,
Nor wrong your life for the nought you call 'a pair of beautiful eyes,'
'*I will not say I love you.*' Truly I will not, no. 75
'*Will I pity you?*' Ay, but the pang will be short, you shall wake and be wise.

'*Shall we meet?*' We shall meet on the other side, but not before.
I shall be pure and fair, I shall hear the sound of THE NAME,
And see the form of His face. You too will walk on that shore,
In the garden of the Lord God, where neither is sorrow nor shame. 80

Farewell, I shall bide alone, for God took my one white lamb,
I work for such as she was, and I will the while I last,
But there's no beginning again, ever I am what I am,
And nothing, nothing, nothing, can do away with the past.

76. *An Ancient Chess King*

Haply some Rajah first in the ages gone
  Amid his languid ladies fingered thee,
  While a black nightingale, sun-swart as he,
Sang his one wife, love's passionate oraison;
Haply thou may'st have pleased Old Prester John 5
  Among his pastures, when full royally
  He sat in tent, grave shepherds at his knee,
While lamps of balsam winked and glimmered on.
What doest thou here? Thy masters are all dead;
  My heart is full of ruth and yearning pain 10
  At sight of thee; O king that hast a crown
Outlasting theirs, and tell'st of greatness fled
  Through cloud-hung nights of unabated rain
  And murmurs of the dark majestic town.

77.   *The Long White Seam*

    As I came round the harbour buoy,
      The lights began to gleam,
    No wave the land-locked water stirred,
      The crags were white as cream;
    And I marked my love by candle-light 5
      Sewing her long white seam.
        It's aye sewing ashore, my dear,
          Watch and steer at sea,
        It's reef and furl, and haul the line,
          Set sail and think of thee. 10

    I climbed to reach her cottage door;
      O sweetly my love sings!
    Like a shaft of light her voice breaks forth,
      My soul to meet it springs
    As the shining water leaped of old, 15
      When stirred by angel wings.
        Aye longing to list anew,
          Awake and in my dream,
        But never a song she sang like this,
          Sewing her long white seam. 20

    Fair fall the lights, the harbour lights,
      That brought me in to thee,
    And peace drop down on that low roof
      For the sight that I did see,
    And the voice, my dear, that rang so clear 25
      All for the love of me.
        For O, for O, with brows bent low
          By the candle's flickering gleam,
        Her wedding gown it was she wrought,
          Sewing the long white seam. 30

                (1880)

Frederick Locker-Lampson (formerly Locker) (1821–1895)

78.
My Song

   You ask a Song,
Such as of yore, an autumn's eventide,
Some blest Boy-Poet caroll'd,—and then died.
   Nay, *I* have sung too long.

   Say, shall I fling 5
A sigh to Beauty at her window-pane?
I sang there once, may not I once again?
   Or tell me whom to sing.

   —The peer of Peers?
Lord of the wealth that gives his time employ: 10
Time to possess, but hardly to enjoy—
   He cannot need *my* tears.

   —The man of *Mind*,
Or Priest, who darkens what was never day?
I cannot sing them, yet I will not say 15
   Such guides are wholly blind.

   —The Orator?
He quiet lies where yon fresh hillock heaves:
'Twere well to sprinkle there those laurel-leaves
   He won, but never wore. 20

   Or shall I twine
The Cypress? Wreath of glory and of gloom.—
To march a gallant Soldier to his doom
   Needs fuller voice than mine.

   No Lay have I, 25
No murmur'd measure meet for your delight,
No Song of Love and Death, to make you quite
   Forget that we must die.

                    Something is wrong;
         The World is over-wise; or, more's the pity,   30
         These days are far too serious for a Ditty,
                    Yet take it,—take My Song.

                              (1876)

Matthew Arnold (1822–1888)

79.   *Geist's Grave*

         Four years!—and didst thou stay above
         The ground, which hides thee now, but four?
         And all that life, and all that love,
         Were crowded, Geist! into no more?

         Only four years those winning ways,   5
         Which make me for thy presence yearn,
         Call'd us to pet thee or to praise,
         Dear little friend! at every turn?

         That loving heart, that patient soul,
         Had they indeed no longer span,   10
         To run their course, and reach their goal,
         And read their homily to man?

         That liquid, melancholy eye,
         From whose pathetic, soul-fed springs
         Seem'd surging the Virgilian cry,   15
         The sense of tears in mortal things—

         That steadfast, mournful strain, consoled
         By spirits gloriously gay,
         And temper of heroic mould—
         What, was four years their whole short day?   20

         Yes, only four!—and not the course
         Of all the centuries yet to come,
         And not the infinite resource
         Of Nature, with her countless sum

Of figures, with her fulness vast
Of new creation evermore,
Can ever quite repeat the past,
Or just thy little self restore.

Stern law of every mortal lot!
Which man, proud man, finds hard to bear,
And builds himself I know not what
Of second life I know not where.

But thou, when struck thine hour to go,
On us, who stood despondent by,
A meek last glance of love didst throw,
And humbly lay thee down to die.

Yet would we keep thee in our heart—
Would fix our favourite on the scene,
Nor let thee utterly depart
And be as if thou ne'er hadst been.

And so there rise these lines of verse
On lips that rarely form them now;
While to each other we rehearse:
Such ways, such arts, such looks hadst thou!

We stroke thy broad brown paws again,
We bid thee to thy vacant chair,
We greet thee by the window-pane,
We hear thy scuffle on the stair.

We see the flaps of thy large ears
Quick raised to ask which way we go;
Crossing the frozen lake, appears
Thy small black figure on the snow!

Nor to us only art thou dear
Who mourn thee in thine English home;
Thou hast thine absent master's tear,
Dropt by the far Australian foam.

Thy memory lasts both here and there,
And thou shalt live as long as we.
And after that—thou dost not care!
In us was all the world to thee.

Yet, fondly zealous for thy fame,
Even to a date beyond our own
We strive to carry down thy name,
By mounded turf, and graven stone.

We lay thee, close within our reach,   65
Here, where the grass is smooth and warm,
Between the holly and the beech,
Where oft we watch'd thy couchant form,

Asleep, yet lending half an ear
To travellers on the Portsmouth road;—   70
There build we thee, O guardian dear,
Mark'd with a stone, thy last abode!

Then some, who through this garden pass,
When we too, like thyself, are clay,
Shall see thy grave upon the grass,   75
And stop before the stone, and say:

People who lived here long ago
Did by this stone, it seems, intend
To name for future times to know
The dachs-hound, Geist, their little friend.   80

(1881)

William Cory (formerly Johnson) (1823–1892)

80.   *Nuremberg Cemetery*

Outside quaint Albert Durer's town,
Where Freedom set her stony crown,
Whereof the gables red and brown
Curve over peaceful forts that screen
Spring bloom and garden lanes between   5
The scarp and courter-scarp, her feet
One highday of Saint Paraclete
Were led along the dolorous street
By stepping stones towards love and heaven,
And pauses of the soul twice seven.   10

Beneath the flowerless trees, where May,
Proud of her orchards' fine array,
Abates her claim and holds no sway,
Past iron tombs, the useless shields
Of cousins slain in Elsass fields, 15
The girl, with fair neck meekly bowed,

Moves bravely through a sauntering crowd,
Hastening, as she was bid, to breathe
Above the breathless, and enwreathe,
With pansies earned by spinster thrift, 20
And lilybells, a wooer's gift,
A stone which glimmers in the shade
Of yonder silent colonnade,
Over against the slates that hold
Marie in lines of slender gold, 25
A token wrought by fictive fingers,
A garland, last year's offering, lingers,
Hung out of reach, and facing north.
And lo! thereout a wren flies forth,
And Gertrude, straining on toetips, 30
Just touches with her prayerful lips
The warm home which a bird unskilled
In grief and hope knows how to build.

The maid can mourn, but not the wren.
Birds die, death's shade belongs to men. 35

(1877)

81.   *Sappho's Cursing*

Woman dead, lie there;
No recòrd of thee
Shall there ever be,
Since thou dost not share
Roses in Pieria grown. 5
In the deathful cave,
With the feeble troop
Of the folk that droop,
Lurk and flit and crave,
Woman severed and far-flown. 10

Coventry Patmore (1823–1896)

82.   *The Girl of All Periods: An Idyll*

"And even our women," lastly grumbles Ben,
"Leaving their nature, dress and talk like men!"
A damsel, as our train stops at Five Ashes,
Down to the station in a dog-cart dashes.
A footman buys her ticket, "Third class, parly;"   5
And, in huge-button'd coat and "Champagne Charley"
And such scant manhood else as use allows her,
Her two shy knees bound in a single trouser,
With, 'twixt her shapely lips, a violet
Perch'd as a proxy for a cigarette,   10
She takes her window in our smoking carriage,
And scans us, calmly scorning men and marriage.
Ben frowns in silence; older, I know better
Than to read ladies 'haviour in the letter.
This aping man is crafty Love's devising   15
To make the woman's difference more surprising;
And, as for feeling wroth at such rebelling,
Who'd scold the child for now and then repelling
Lures with "I won't!" or for a moment's straying
In its sure growth towards more full obeying?   20
"Yes, she had read the 'Legend of the Ages,'
And George Sand too, skipping the wicked pages."
And, whilst we talk'd, her protest firm and perky
Against mankind, I thought, grew lax and jerky;
And, at a compliment, her mouth's compressure   25
Nipt in its birth a little laugh of pleasure;
And smiles, forbidden her lips, as weakness horrid,
Broke, in grave lights, from eyes and chin and forehead;
And, as I push'd kind 'vantage 'gainst the scorner,
The two shy knees press'd shier to the corner;   30
And Ben began to talk with her, the rather
Because he found out that he knew her father,
Sir Francis Applegarth, of Fenny Compton,
And danced once with her sister Maude at Brompton;
And then he stared until he quite confused her,   35
More pleased with her than I, who but excused her;
And, when she got out, he, with sheepish glances,
Said he'd stop too, and call on old Sir Francis.

from *The Angel in the House*

CANTO IX.

The Friends

PRELUDES

II. *The Foreign Land*

A woman is a foreign land,
   Of which, though there he settle young,
A man will ne'er quite understand
   The customs, politics, and tongue.
The foolish hie them post-haste through,   5
   See fashions odd, and prospects fair,
Learn of the language, 'How d'ye do,'
   And go and brag that they've been there.
The most for leave to trade apply,
   For once, at Empire's seat, her heart,   10
Then get what knowledge ear and eye
   Glean chancewise in the life-long mart.
And certain others, few and fit,
   Attach them to the Court, and see
The Country's best, its accent hit,   15
   And partly sound its polity.

A London Fête

All night fell hammers, shock on shock;
With echoes Newgate's granite clang'd:
The scaffold built, at eight o'clock
They brought the man out to be hang'd.
Then came from all the people there   5
A single cry, that shook the air;
Mothers held up their babes to see,
Who spread their hands, and crow'd for glee;
Here a girl from her vesture tore
A rag to wave with, and join'd the roar;   10
There a man, with yelling tired,
Stopp'd, and the culprit's crime inquired;
A sot, below the doom'd man dumb,
Bawl'd his health in the world to come;

These blasphemed and fought for places;   15
Those, half-crush'd, cast frantic faces,
To windows, where, in freedom sweet,
Others enjoy'd the wicked treat.
At last, the show's black crisis pended;
Struggles for better standings ended;   20
The rabble's lips no longer curst,
But stood agape with horrid thirst;
Thousands of breasts beat horrid hope;
Thousands of eyeballs, lit with hell,
Burnt one way all, to see the rope   25
Unslacken as the platform fell.
The rope flew tight; and then the roar
Burst forth afresh; less loud, but more
Confused and affrighting than before.
A few harsh tongues for ever led   30
The common din, the chaos of noises,
But ear could not catch what they said.
As when the realm of the damn'd rejoices
At winning a soul to its will,
That clatter and clangour of hateful voices   35
Sicken'd and stunn'd the air, until
The dangling corpse hung straight and still.
The show complete, the pleasure past,
The solid masses loosen'd fast:
A thief slunk off, with ample spoil,   40
To ply elsewhere his daily toil;
A baby strung its doll to a stick;
A mother praised the pretty trick;
Two children caught and hang'd a cat;
Two friends walk'd on, in lively chat;   45
And two, who had disputed places,
Went forth to fight, with murderous faces.

85.   *The Scorched Fly*

Who sins in hope; who, sinning, says,
'Sorrow for sin God's judgment stays!'
Against God's Spirit he lies; quite stops
Mercy with insult; dares, and drops,
Like a scorch'd fly, that spins in vain   5
Upon the axis of its pain,
Then takes its doom, to limp and crawl,
Blind and forgot, from fall to fall.

86.   *The Year*

      The crocus, while the days are dark,
          Unfolds its saffron sheen;
      At April's touch, the crudest bark
          Discovers gems of green.

      Then sleep the seasons, full of might;   5
          While slowly swells the pod
      And rounds the peach, and in the night
          The mushroom bursts the sod.

      The Winter falls; the frozen rut
          Is bound with silver bars;   10
      The snow-drift heaps against the hut,
          And night is pierc'd with stars.

Sydney Thompson Dobell (1824–1874)

87.   *Perhaps*

Ten heads and twenty hearts! so that this me,
Having more room and verge, and striking less
The cage that galls us into consciousness,
Might drown the rings and ripples of to be
In the smooth deep of being: plenary   5
Round hours; great days, as if two days should press
Together, and their wine-press'd night accresce
The next night to so dead a parody
Of death as cures such living: of these ordain
My years; of those large years grant me not seven,   10
Nor seventy, no, nor only seventy sevens!
And then, perhaps, I might stand well in even
This rain of things; down-rain, up-rain, side-rain;
This rain from Earth and Ocean, air and heaven,
And from the Heaven within the Heaven of Heavens.   15

                        (1875)

William Allingham (1824–1889)

88.   *Writing*

    A man who keeps a diary, pays
    Due toll to many tedious days;
    But life becomes eventful—then
    His busy hand forgets the pen.
    Most books, indeed, are records less   5
    Of fulness than of emptiness.

———

    Men's wives' opinions, what are they to us?
    Much. M. to please his wife writes thus and thus;
    And books like M.'s are our Leviticus.
    N., too, to please his wife is shy or bold;   10
    And N. a lever of the world doth hold,
    Sways Fortune's mighty wheel as it is roll'd.

———

    Love first, Work second,
    Prudence be for third reckon'd.

———

    Some extol passion far above   15
    All other qualities in Love:
    Passion I fear, but long to prove
    The perfect *tenderness* of Love.

———

    Love's lips are always young;
    Love's lore is very old;   20
If you have ever loved, the key you hold
    To all that hath of Love been said or sung.

———

    Whenever I see from my loneliness
    Two to each other kindly press,
    I envy not, but in grateful mood   25
    Rejoice that earth holds thus much good.

———

O were I but rid of these ties,
  Adieu to vexation and sorrow!
O were I but rid of these ties—
  To go knotting up new ones to-morrow!   30

Some are so highly polish'd, they display
Only your own face when you turn their way.

89.   'I will not be a critic where I love.'

I will not be a critic where I love.
Love must love or not love—
So long as he's my sweetheart I will love him.
What care I what the world call this or that?
Have I such reason, that it cannot err,   5
Like God's? I am a poor weak human soul,
And love or hate, I cannot tell you why—
Friends have I, real, or they seem so now,
And while I'm in that notion I am theirs
Through good and evil—   10
If friendship, love, are nothing, what's life worth?
Some may endure to play at chilly chess
With men and women—I must hate and love!

90.   Æolian Harp

Is it all in vain?
Strangely throbbing pain,
Trembling joy of memory!
Bygone things, how shadowy
Within their graves they lie!   5

Shall I sit then by their graves,
Listening to the melancholy waves?
    I would fain.
But even these in vapours die:
    For nothing may remain.   10

　　　　One survivor in a boat
　　　　On the wide dim deep afloat,
　　　　When the sunken ship is gone,
　　　　Lit by late stars before the dawn,
　　　　The sea rolls vaguely, and the stars are dumb.　　　15
　　　　The ship is sunk full many a year.
　　　　　　Dream no more of loss or gain.
　　　　A ship was never here.
　　　　A dawn will never, never come.
　　　　　　—Is it all in vain?　　　20

91.　　　　　　　　*A Poet's Epitaph*

　　　　Body to purifying flame,
　　　　Soul to the Great Deep whence it came,
　　　　Leaving a song on earth below,
　　　　An urn of ashes white as snow.

　　　　　　　　———

　　　　What is your Heaven? describe it in a breath.　　　5
　　　　Pure health, fit work, beyond the gate of death.

(Sir) Francis Turner Palgrave (1824–1897)

92.　　　　　　　　*Eutopia*

　　　　There is a garden where lilies
　　　　　　And roses are side by side;
　　　　And all day between them in silence
　　　　　　The silken butterflies glide.

　　　　I may not enter the garden,　　　5
　　　　　　Though I know the road thereto;
　　　　And morn by morn to the gateway
　　　　　　I see the children go.

　　　　They bring back light on their faces;
　　　　　　But they cannot bring back to me　　　10
　　　　What the lilies say to the roses,
　　　　　　Or the songs of the butterflies be.

93.　　　　　　　*Père La Chaise*

    The field of death at Paris,
        You might think it a fold from afar;
    Like flocks the white tombs scatter'd
        That green enclosure star.

    There statesman, financier and poet,   5
        Love, glory, ambition and guile,
    Are laid 'neath their pompous inscriptions,
        And the stranger says 'Who?' with a smile.

    And some more proudly mock-modest
        Rest under their names alone;   10
    And all they will soon inherit
        Is but the name and the stone.

    There the passionate heart of de Musset
        Sleeps itself tranquil and pure;
    There Béranger, Heine, Bellini,   15
        Lie 'mid the brilliant obscure;

    He, whose melody echoes the music
        Of the old Sicilian shore;
    And they—in their lifetime too famous
        To be famous for evermore.   20

    But from the white mausolea
        The eye turns wearily soon,
    Drawn by the dark fascination
        Of the dreary *Fosse Commune*.

    Had these no story of passion?   25
        Had these no passion for fame,
    No deeds for remembrance or glory,
        Who lie without hillock or name?

    They shovel them in by fifties,
        And bid them lie down with a grin,   30
    Who could not buy a 'concession'—
        Sons of starvation and sin!

Here at last, by Mortality's favour,
   Fraternal and equal they lie:
And the child in vain seeks the mother   35
   With its cross to crown her, and die.

—In this best of worlds, O my brothers,
   Is surely something amiss!
Songs of advance and culture,
   Is your ultimate triumph this?   40

Is the soul's heart-hunger abolish'd,
   While agnostics their litany cry,
Or Science says, 'matter to matter,'
   With a smile that lurks in a sigh?—

The homage and incense of Paris   45
   On the famous and wealthy are shed;
But love and sorrow are kneeling
   O'er the undistinguish'd dead;

And the orphan sobs and wanders
   O'er the dust that will hide it soon   50
From the wolfish strife for existence,
   In the dreary *Fosse Commune*.

George MacDonald (1824–1905)

94.   *No End of No-Story*

There is a river
whose waters run asleep
run run ever
singing in the shallows
dumb in the hollows   5
sleeping so deep
and all the swallows
that dip their feathers
in the hollows
or in the shallows   10
are the merriest swallows
and the nests they make

with the clay they cake
with the water they shake
from their wings that rake   15
the water out of the shallows
or out of the hollows
will hold together
in any weather
and the swallows   20
are the merriest fellows
and have the merriest children
and are built very narrow
like the head of an arrow
to cut the air   25
and go just where
the nicest water is flowing
and the nicest dust is blowing
and each so narrow
like the head of an arrow   30
is a wonderful barrow
to carry the mud he makes
for his children's sakes
from the wet water flowing
and the dry dust blowing   35
to build his nest
for her he loves best
and the wind cakes it
the sun bakes it
into a nest   40
for the rest
of her he loves best
and all their merry children
each little fellow
with a beak as yellow   45
as the buttercups growing
beside the flowing
of the singing river
always and ever
growing and blowing   50
as fast as the sheep
awake or asleep
crop them and crop
and cannot stop
their yellowness blowing   55
nor yet the growing
of the obstinate daisies

the little white praises
they grow and they blow
they spread out their crown   60
and they praise the sun
and when he goes down
their praising is done
they fold up their crown
and sleep every one   65
till over the plain
he is shining amain
and they're at it again
praising and praising
such low songs raising   70
that no one can hear them
but the sun so near them
and the sheep that bite them
but do not fright them
are the quietest sheep   75
awake or asleep
with the merriest bleat
and the little lambs
are the merriest lambs
forgetting to eat   80
for the frolic in their feet
and the lambs and their dams
are the whitest sheep
with the woolliest wool
for the swallow to pull   85
when he makes his nest
for her he loves best
and they shine like snow
in the grasses that grow
by the singing river   90
that sings for ever
and the sheep and the lambs
are merry for ever
because the river
sings and they drink it   95
and the lambs and their dams
would any one think it
are bright and white
because of their diet
which gladdens them quiet   100
for what they bite
is buttercups yellow

and daisies white
and grass as green
as the river can make it 105
with wind as mellow
to kiss it and shake it
as never was known
but here in the hollows
beside the river 110
where all the swallows
are the merriest fellows
and the nests they make
with the clay they cake
in the sunshine bake 115
till they are like bone
and as dry in the wind
as a marble stone
dried in the wind
the sweetest wind 120
that blows by the river
flowing for ever
and who shall find
whence comes the wind
that blows on the hollows 125
and over the shallows
where dip the swallows
and comes and goes
and the sweet life blows
into the river 130
that sings as it flows
and the sweet life blows
into the sheep
awake or asleep
with the woolliest wool 135
and the trailingest tails
and never fails
gentle and cool
to wave the wool
and to toss the grass 140
as the lambs and the sheep
over it pass
and tug and bite
with their teeth so white
and then with the sweep 145
of their trailing tails
smooth it again

and it grows amain
and amain it grows
and the wind that blows 150
tosses the swallows
over the hollows
and over the shallows
and blows the sweet life
and the joy so rife 155
into the swallows
that skim the shallows
and have the yellowest children
and the wind that blows
is the life of the river 160
that flows for ever
and washes the grasses
still as it passes
and feeds the daisies
the little white praises 165
and buttercups sunny
with butter and honey
that whiten the sheep
awake or asleep
that nibble and bite 170
and grow whiter than white
and merry and quiet
on such good diet
watered by the river
and tossed for ever 175
by the wind that tosses
the wool and the grasses
and the swallow that crosses
with all the swallows
over the shallows 180
dipping their wings
to gather the water
and bake the cake
for the wind to make
as hard as a bone 185
and as dry as a stone
and who shall find
whence comes the wind
that blows from behind
and ripples the river 190
that flows for ever
and still as it passes

waves the grasses
and cools the daisies
the white sun-praises   195
that feed the sheep
awake or asleep
and give them their wool
for the swallows to pull
a little away   200
to mix with the clay
that cakes to a nest
for those they love best
and all the yellow children
soon to go trying   205
their wings at the flying
over the hollows
and over the shallows
with all the swallows
that do not know   210
whence the wind doth blow
that comes from behind
a blowing wind

(1893)

95.   *The Shortest and Sweetest of Songs*

            Come
            Home.

(1893)

John Askham (ca. 1825–1894)

96.   *A Dream: July 22nd*, 1881

Only a moment in a dream of night,
  That brought me less of pleasure than of pain;
  I saw and kissed my dear dead child again,
And straight the vision faded out of sight.

Shadows unreal are not so faint and slight 5
    As was that fleeting phantasm of the brain.
    Sobbing I woke, and, fast as summer rain,
Fell the hot drops as broke the dim wan light.
'Twas not a dream of heaven and blessedness
    That came unto me as I lay and slept; 10
    For, like myself, I thought my darling wept,
And not of heaven are tears and grief's excess.
    Only the sorrow and the tears were mine,
    Dear one! I know eternal bliss is thine.

Mortimer Collins (1827–1876)

97.   *The Positivists*

Life and the Universe show spontaneity;
Down with ridiculous notions of Deity!
    Churches and creeds are all lost in the mists;
    Truth must be sought with the Positivists.

Wise are their teachers beyond all comparison, 5
Comte, Huxley, Tyndall, Mill, Morley, and Harrison;
    Who will adventure to enter the lists,
    With such a squadron of Positivists?

Social arrangements are awful miscarriages;
Cause of all crime is our system of marriages; 10
    Poets with sonnets, and lovers with trysts,
    Kindle the ire of the Positivists.

Husbands and wives should be all one community,
Exquisite freedom with absolute unity;
    Wedding rings worse are than manacled wrists,— 15
    Such is the creed of the Positivists.

98.   *Couplets*

Imperfect utterance is our saddest taint,
And, when our hearts grow full, our lips grow faint.

What we call life is twilight: when 'tis done,
A door is opened, and we see the sun.

Joy is time's pander, Pleasure is time's thief,   5
But time's two conquerors are Toil and Grief.

Emily Pfeiffer (1827–1890)

99.   'Peace to the odalisque, whose morning glory'

Peace to the odalisque, whose morning glory
Is vanishing, to live alone in story;
Firm in her place, a dull-robed figure stands,
With wistful eyes, and earnest, grappling hands:
The working-woman, she whose soul and brain—   5
Her tardy right—are bought with honest pain.
Oh woman! sacrifice may still be thine—
More fruitful than the souls ye did resign
To sated masters; from your lives, so real,
Will shape itself a pure and high ideal,   10
That ye will seek with sad, wide-open eyes,
Till, finding nowhere, baffled love shall rise
To higher planes, where passion may look pale,
But charity's white light shall never fail.

(1873)

100.   *Any Husband to Many a Wife*

  I scarcely know my worthless picture,
  As seen in those soft eyes and clear;
  But oh, dear heart, I fear the stricture
  You pass on it when none are near.

  Deep eyes that smiling give denial 5
  To tears that you have shed in vain;
  Fond heart that summoned on my trial,
  Upbraids the witness of its pain.

  Eyes, tender eyes, betray me never!
  Still hold the flattered image fast 10
  Whereby I shape the fond endeavour
  To justify your faith at last.

       (1889)

101.   *Six Studies in Exotic Forms of Verse: Triolet*

  Warm from the wall she chose a peach,
   She took the wasps for councillors;
   She said: 'such little things can teach:'
  Warm from the wall she chose a peach;
  She waved the fruit within my reach, 5
   Then passed it to a friend of hers: —
  Warm from the wall she chose a peach,
   She took the wasps for councillors.

102.   *To Nature*

  IN HER ASCRIBED CHARACTER OF UNMEANING AND
     ALL-PERFORMING FORCE.

      I.

  O Nature! thou whom I have thought to love,
   Seeing in thine the reflex of God's face,
   A loathed abstraction would usurp thy place,—
  While Him they not dethrone, they but disprove.
  Weird Nature! can it be that joy is fled, 5

  And bald unmeaning lurks beneath thy smile?
   That beauty haunts the dust but to beguile,
And that with Order, Love and Hope are dead?
Pitiless Force, all-moving, all unmoved,
  Dread mother of unfather'd worlds, assuage   10
Thy wrath on us,—be this wild life reproved,
  And trampled into nothing in thy rage!
Vain prayer, although the last of human kind,—
Force is not wrath,—but only deaf and blind.

II.

Dread force, in whom of old we loved to see   15
  A nursing mother, clothing with her life
  The seeds of Love divine, with what sore strife
We hold or yield our thoughts of Love and thee!
Thou art not "calm," but restless as the ocean,
  Filling with aimless toil the endless years—   20
  Stumbling on thought, and throwing off the spheres,—
Churning the Universe with mindless motion.
Dull fount of joy, unhallow'd source of tears,
  Cold motor of our fervid faith and song,
Dead, but engendering life, love, pangs, and fears,   25
  Thou crownedst thy wild work with foulest wrong
When first thou lightedst on a seeming goal,
And darkly blunder'd on man's suffering soul.

III.

Blind Cyclop, hurling stones of destiny,
  And not in fury!—working bootless ill,   30
  In mere vacuity of mind and will—
Man's soul revolts against thy work and thee!
Slaves of a despot, conscienceless and *nil*,
  Slaves, by mad chance befool'd to think them free,
  We still might rise, and with one heart agree   35
To mar the ruthless "grinding of thy mill!"
Dead tyrant, tho' our cries and groans pass by thee,
  Man, cutting off from each new "tree of life"
Himself, its fatal flower, could still defy thee,
  In waging on thy work eternal strife,—   40
The races come and coming evermore,
Heaping with hecatombs thy dead-sea shore.

IV.

If we be fools of chance, indeed, and tend
   No whither, then the blinder fools in this:
     That, loving good, we live, in scorn of bliss,   45
Its wageless servants to the evil end.
If, at the last, man's thirst for higher things
   Be quench'd in dust, the giver of his life,
     Why press with growing zeal a hopeless strife,—
Why—born for creeping—should he dream of wings?   50
O Mother Dust! thou hast one law so mild,
   We call it sacred—all thy creatures own it—
The tie which binds the parent and the child,—
   Why has man's loving heart alone outgrown it?
Why hast thou travail'd so to be denied.   55
So trampled by a would-be matricide?

103.   *Past and Future*

Fair garden, where the man and woman dwelt,
   And loved and work'd, and where, in work's reprieve,
     The sabbath of each day, the restful eve,
They sat in silence with lock'd hands, and felt
The voice which compass'd them, a-near, a-far,   5
   Which murmur'd in the fountains and the breeze,
     Which breathed in spices from the laden trees,
And sent a silvery shout from each lone star.
Sweet dream of Paradise! and if a dream,
   One that has help'd us when our faith was weak;   10
We wake, and still it holds us, but would seem
   Before us, not behind,—the good we seek,—
The good from lowest root which waxes ever,
The golden age of science and endeavour.

104.   *To a Moth that Drinketh of the Ripe October*

I

A moth belated,—sun and zephyr-kist,—
   Trembling about a pale arbutus bell,
     Probing to wildering depths its honeyed cell,—
A noonday thief, a downy sensualist!
Not vainly, sprite, thou drawest careless breath,   5

Strikest ambrosia from the cool-cupped flowers,
　　　　And flutterest through the soft, uncounted hours,
　　To drop at last in unawaited death;—
　　'Tis something to be glad! and those fine thrills
　　　　Which move thee, to my lip have drawn the smile 10
　　Wherewith we look on joy. Drink! drown thine ills,
　　　　If ill have any part in thee; erewhile
　　May the pent force—thy bounded life—set free,
　　Fill larger sphere with equal ecstasy!

　　　　　　　　II

　　With what fine organs art thou dowered, frail elf! 15
　　　　Thy harp is pitched too high for dull annoy,
　　　　Thy life a love-feast, and a silent joy,
　　As mute and rapt as Passion's silent self.
　　I turn from thee, and see the swallow sweep
　　　　Like a winged will, and the keen-scented hound 20
　　　　That snuffs with rapture at the tainted ground,—
　　All things that freely course, that swim or leap,—
　　Then, hearing glad-voiced creatures men call dumb,
　　　　I feel my heart—oft sinking 'neath the weight
　　Of Nature's sorrow—lighten at the sum 25
　　　　Of Nature's joy; its half-unfolded fate
　　Breathes hope—for all but those beneath the ban,
　　The slavery accurst, of tyrant man!

105.　　　　　　　*A Chrysalis*

　　When gathering shells cast upwards by the waves
　　　　Of Progress, they who note its ebb and flow,
　　　　Its flux and re-flux, surely come to know
　　That the sea-level rises; that dark caves
　　Of ignorance are flooded, and foul graves 5
　　　　Of sin are cleansed; albeit the work is slow;
　　　　Till, seeing great from less for ever grow,
　　Law comes to mean for them the Love that saves!
　　And leaning down the ages, my dull ear,
　　　　Catching their slow-ascending harmonies, 10
　　I am uplift of them, and borne more near,
　　　　I feel within my flesh—laid pupa-wise—
　　A soul of worship, tho' of vision dim,
　　　　Which links me with wing-folded cherubim.

George Meredith (1828–1909)

106. *The Nuptials of Attila*

I

Flat as to an eagle's eye,
    Earth hung under Attila.
Sign for carnage gave he none.
In the peace of his disdain,
Sun and rain, and rain and sun,   5
Cherished men to wax again,
Crawl, and in their manner die.
On his people stood a frost.
Like the charger cut in stone,
Rearing stiff, the warrior host,   10
Which had life from him alone,
Craved the trumpet's eager note,
As the bridled earth the Spring.
Rusty was the trumpet's throat.
He let chief and prophet rave;   15
Venturous earth around him string
Threads of grass and slender rye,
Wave them, and untrampled wave.
O for the time when God did cry,
    Eye and have, my Attila!   20

II

Scorn of conquest filled like sleep
Him that drank of havoc deep
When the Green Cat pawed the globe:
When the horsemen from his bow
Shot in sheaves and made the foe   25
Crimson fringes of a robe,
Trailed o'er towns and fields in woe;
When they streaked the rivers red,
When the saddle was the bed.
    Attila, my Attila!   30

[II

War, the fire shut in his breast,
War, the torchfire he flung west.
Waned upon his people's face:
Waned like rocks of Danube's crest,
Wearing grey in flames that fly, 35
Leaving there a livid trace.
O for the time when God did cry,
    Eye and have, my Attila!]

III

He breathed peace and pulled a flower.
    Eye and have, my Attila! 40
This was the damsel Ildico,
Rich in bloom until that hour:
Shyer than the forest doe
Twinkling slim through branches green.
Yet the shyest shall be seen. 45
    Make the bed for Attila!

IV

Seen of Attila, desired,
She was led to him straightway:
Radiantly was she attired;
Rifled lands were her array, 50
Jewels bled from weeping crowns,
Gold of woeful fields and towns.
She stood pallid in the light.
How she walked, how withered white,
From the blessing to the board, 55
She who should have proudly blushed
Women whispered, asking why,
Hitting of a youth, and hushed.
Was it terror of her lord?
Was she childish? was she sly? 60
Was it the bright mantle's dye
Drained her blood to hues of grief
Like the ash that shoots the spark?
See the green tree all in leaf:
See the green tree stripped of bark!— 65
    Make the bed for Attila!

V

Round the banquet-table's load
Scores of iron horsemen rode;
Chosen warriors, keen and hard;
Grain of threshing battle-dints; 70
Attila's fierce body-guard,
Smelling war like fire in flints.
Grant them peace be fugitive!
Iron-capped and iron-heeled,
Each against his fellow's shield 75
Smote the spear-head, shouting, Live,
    Attila! my Attila!
Eagle, eagle of our breed,
Eagle, beak the lamb, and feed!
Have her, and unleash us! Live, 80
    Attila! my Attila!

VI

He was of the blood to shine
Bronze in joy, like shies that scorch.
Beaming with the goblet wine
In the wavering of the torch, 85
Looked he backward on his bride.
    Eye and have, my Attila!
Fair in her wide robe was she:
Where the robe and vest divide,
Fair she seemed surpassingly: 90
Soft, yet vivid as the stream
Danube rolls in the moonbeam
Through rock-barriers: but she smiled
Never, she sat cold as salt:
Open-mouthed as a young child 95
Wondering with a mind at fault.
    Make the bed for Attila!

VII

Under the thin hoop of gold
Whence in waves her hair outrolled,
'Twixt her brows the women saw 100
Shadows of a vulture's claw
Gript in flight: strange knots that sped
Closing and dissolving aye:
Such as wicked dreams betray

When pale dawn creeps o'er the bed. 105
They might show the common pang
Known to virgins, in whom dread
Hunts their bliss like famished hounds;
While the chiefs with roaring rounds
Tossed her to her lord, and sang 110
Praise of him whose hand was large,
Cheers for beauty brought to yield,
Chirrups of the trot afield,
Hurrahs of the battle-charge.

VIII

Those rock-faces hung with weed 115
Reddened: their great days of speed,
Slaughter, triumph, flood and flame,
Like a jealous frenzy wrought,
Scoffed at them and did them shame,
Quaffing idle, conquering naught. 120
O for the time when God decreed
    Earth the prey of Attila!
God called on thee in his wrath,
Trample it to mire! 'Twas done.
Swift as Danube clove our path 125
Down from East to Western sun.
Huns! behold your pasture, gaze,
Take, our king said: heel to flank
(Whisper it, the warhorse neighs!)
Forth we drove, and blood we drank 130
Fresh as dawn-dew: earth was ours:
Men were flocks we lashed and spurned:
Fast as windy flame devours,
Flame along the wind, we burned.
Arrow, javelin, spear, and sword! 135
Here the snows and there the plains;
On! our signal: onward poured
Torrents of the tightened reins,
Foaming over vine and corn
Hot against the city-wall. 140
Whisper it, you sound a horn
To the grey beast in the stall!
Yea, he whinnies at a nod.
O for sound of the trumpet-notes!
O for the time when thunder-shod, 145
He that scarce can munch his oats,

Hung on the peaks, brooded aloof,
Champed the grain of the wrath of God,
Pressed a cloud on the cowering roof,
Snorted out of the blackness fire! 150
Scarlet broke the sky, and down,
Hammering West with print of his hoof,
He burst out of the bosom of ire
Sharp as eyelight under thy frown,
    Attila, my Attila! 155

IX

Ravaged cities rolling smoke
Thick on cornfields dry and black,
Wave his banners, bear his yoke.
Track the lightning, and you track
Attila. They moan: 'tis he! 160
Bleed: 'tis he! Beneath his foot
Leagues are deserts charred and mute;
Where he passed, there passed a sea.
    Attila, my Attila!

X

—Who breathed on the king cold breath? 165
Said a voice amid the host,
He is Death that weds a ghost,
Else a ghost that weds with Death?
Ildico's chill little hand
Shuddering he beheld: austere 170
Stared, as one who would command
Sight of what has filled his ear:
Plucked his thin beard, laughed disdain.
Feast, ye Huns! His arm he raised,
Like the warrior, battle-dazed, 175
Joining to the fight amain.
    Make the bed for Attila!

XI

Silent Ildico stood up.
King and chief to pledge her well,
Shocked sword sword and cup on cup, 180
Clamouring like a brazen bell.
Silent stepped the queenly slave.

Fair, by heaven! she was to meet
On a midnight, near a grave,
Flapping wide the winding-sheet.   185

XII

Death and she walked through the crowd,
Out beyond the flush of light.
Ceremonious women bowed
Following her: 'twas middle night.
Then the warriors each on each   190
Spied, nor overloudly laughed;
Like the victims of the leech,
Who have drunk of a strange draught.

XIII

Attila remained. Even so
Frowned he when he struck the blow,   195
Brained his horse that stumbled twice,
On a bloody day in Gaul,
Bellowing, Perish omens! All
Marvelled at the sacrifice,
But the battle, swinging dim,   200
Rang off that axe-blow for him.
    Attila, my Attila!

XIV

Brightening over Danube wheeled
Star by star; and she, most fair,
Sweet as victory half-revealed,   205
Seized to make him glad and young;
She, O sweet as the dark sign
Given him oft in battles gone,
When the voice within said, Dare!
And the trumpet-notes were sprung   210
Rapturous for the charge in line:
She lay waiting: fair as dawn
Wrapped in folds of night she lay;
Secret, lustrous; flaglike there,
Waiting him to stream and ray,   215
With one loosening blush outflung,
Colours of his hordes of horse
Ranked for combat: still he hung
Like the fever-dreading air,

Cursed of heat; and as a corse
Gathers vultures, in his brain
Images of her eyes and kiss
Plucked at the limbs that could remain
Loitering nigh the doors of bliss.
    Make the bed for Attila!

XV

Passion on one hand, on one,
Destiny led forth the Hun.
Heard ye outcries of affright,
Voices that through many a fray,
In the press of flag and spear,
Warned the king of peril near?
Men were dumb, they gave him way,
Eager heads to left and right,
Like the bearded standard, thrust,
As in battle, for a nod
From their lord of battle-dust.
    Attila, my Attila!
Slow between the lines he trod.
Saw ye not the sun drop slow
On this nuptial day, ere eve
Pierced him on the couch aglow?
    Attila, my Attila?
Here and there his heart would cleave
Clotted memory for a space:
Some stout chief's familiar face,
Choicest of his fighting brood,
Touched him, as 'twere one to know
Ere he met his bride's embrace.
    Attila, my Attila!
Twisting fingers in a beard
Scant as winter underwood,
With a narrowed eye he peered;
Like the sunset's graver red
Up old pine-stems. Grave he stood
Eyeing them on whom was shed
Burning light from him alone.
    Attila, my Attila!
Red were they whose mouths recalled
Where the slaughter mounted high,
High on it, o'er earth appalled,
He; heaven's finger in their sight

Raising him on waves of dead:
Up to heaven his trumpets blown.
O for the time when God's delight
    Crowned the head of Attila!   265
Hungry river of the crag
Stretching hands for earth he came:
Force and Speed astride his name
Pointed back to spear and flag.
He came out of miracle cloud,   270
Lightning-swift and spectre-lean.
Now those days are in a shroud:
Have him to his ghostly queen.
    Make the bed for Attila!

XVI

One, with winecups overstrung,   275
Cried him farewell in Rome's tongue.
Who? for the great king turned as though
Wrath to the shaft's head strained the bow.
Nay, not wrath the king possessed,
But a radiance of the breast.   280
In that sound he had the key
Of his cunning malady.
Lo, where gleamed the sapphire lake,
Leo, with his Rome at stake,
Drew blank air to hues and forms;   285
Whereof Two that shone distinct,
Linked as orbed stars are linked,
Clear among the myriad swarms,
In a constellation, dashed
Full on horse and rider's eyes   290
Sunless light, but light it was—
Light that blinded and abashed,
Froze his members, bade him pause,
Caught him mid-gallop, blazed him home.
    Attila, my Attila!   295
What are streams that cease to flow?
What was Attila, rolled thence,
Cheated by a juggler's show?
Like that lake of blue intense,
Under tempest lashed to foam,   300
Lurid radiance, as he passed,
Filled him, and around was glassed,
When deep-voiced he uttered, Rome!

XVII

Rome! the word was: and like meat
Flung to dogs the word was torn.
Soon Rome's magic priests shall bleat
Round their magic Pope forlorn!
Loud they swore the king had sworn
Vengeance on the Roman cheat,
Ere he passed as, grave and still,
Danube through the shouting hill:
Sworn it by his naked life!
Eagle, snakes these women are:
Take them on the wing! but war,
Smoking war's the warrior's wife!
Then for plunder! then for brides
Won without a winking priest!—
Danube whirled his train of tides
Black toward the yellow East.
  Make the bed for Attila!

XVIII

Chirrups of the trot afield,
Hurrahs of the battle-charge,
How they answered, how they pealed,
When the morning rose and drew
Bow and javelin, lance and targe,
In the nuptial casement's view!
  Attila, my Attila!
Down the hillspurs, out of tents
Glimmering in mid-forest, through
Mists of the cool morning scents,
Forth from city-alley, court,
Arch, the bounding horsemen flew,
Joined along the plains of dew,
Raced and gave the rein to sport,
Closed and streamed like curtain-rents
Fluttered by a wind, and flowed
Into squadrons: trumpets blew,
Chargers neighed, and trappings glowed
Brave as the bright Orient's.
Look on the seas that run to greet
Sunrise: look on the leagues of wheat:
Look on the lines and squares that fret
Leaping to level the lance blood-wet.
Tens of thousands, man and steed,

Tossing like field-flowers in Spring; 345
Ready to be hurled at need
Whither their great lord may sling.
Finger Romeward, Romeward, King!
    Attila, my Attila!
Still the woman holds him fast 350
As a night-flag round the mast.

XIX

Nigh upon the fiery noon,
Out of ranks a roaring burst.
'Ware white women like the moon!
They are poison: they have thirst 355
First for love, and next for rule.
Jealous of the army, she?
Ho, the little wanton fool!
We were his before she squealed
Blind for mother's milk, and heeled 360
Kicking on her mother's knee.
His in life and death are we:
She but one flower of a field.
We have given him bliss tenfold
In an hour to match her night: 365
    Attila, my Attila!
Still her arms the master hold,
As on wounds the scarf winds tight.

XX

Over Danube day no more,
Like the warrior's planted spear, 370
Stood to hail the King: in fear
Western day knocked at his door.
    Attila, my Attila!
Sudden in the army's eyes
Rolled a blast of lights and cries: 375
Flashing through them: Dead are ye!
Dead, ye Huns, and torn piecemeal!
See the ordered army reel
Stricken through the ribs: and see,
Wild for speed to cheat despair, 380
Horsemen, clutching knee to chin,
Crouch and dart they know not where.
    Attila, my Attila!
Faces covered, faces bare,

Light the palace-front like jets 385
Of a dreadful fire within.
Beating hands and driving hair
Start on roof and parapets.
Dust rolls up; the slaughter din.
—Death to them who call him dead! 390
Death to them who doubt the tale!
Choking in his dusty veil,
Sank the sun on his death-bed.
    Make the bed for Attila!

XXI

'Tis the room where thunder sleeps. 395
Frenzy, as a wave to shore
Surging, burst the silent door,
And drew back to awful deeps,
Breath beaten out, foam-white. Anew
Howled and pressed the ghastly crew, 400
Like storm-waters over rocks.
    Attila, my Attila!
One long shaft of sunset red
Laid a finger on the bed.
Horror, with the snaky locks, 405
Shocked the surge to stiffened heaps,
Hoary as the glacier's head
Faced to the moon. Insane they look.
God it is in heaven who weeps
Fallen from his hand the Scourge he shook. 410
    Make the bed for Attila!

XXII

Square along the couch, and stark,
Like the sea-rejected thing
Sea-sucked white, behold their King.
    Attila, my Attila! 415
Beams that panted black and bright,
Scornful lightnings danced their sight:
Him they see an oak in bud,
Him an oaklog stripped of bark:
Him, their lord of day and night, 420
White, and lifting up his blood
Dumb for vengeance. Name us that,
Huddled in the corner dark,
Humped and grinning like a cat,

Teeth for lips!—'tis she! she stares, 425
Glittering through her bristled hairs.
Rend her! Pierce her to the hilt!
She is Murder: have her out!
What! this little fist, as big
As the southern summer fig! 430
She is Madness, none may doubt.
Death, who dares deny her guilt!
Death, who says his blood she spilt!
　　Make the bed for Attila!

XXIII

Torch and lamp and sunset-red 435
Fell three-fingered on the bed.
In the torch the beard-hair scant
With the great breast seemed to pant:
In the yellow lamp the limbs
Wavered, as the lake-flower swims: 440
In the sunset red the dead
Dead avowed him, dry blood-red.

XXIV

Hatred of that abject slave,
Earth, was in each chieftain's heart.
Earth has got him, whom God gave, 445
Earth may sing, and earth shall smart!
　　Attila, my Attila!

XXV

Thus their prayer was raved and ceased.
Then had Vengeance of her feast
Scent in their quick pang to smite 450
Which they knew not, but huge pain
Urged them from some victim slain
Swift, and blotted from the sight.
Each at each, a crouching beast,
Glared, and quivered for the word. 455
Each at each, and all on that,
Humped and grinning like a cat,
Head-bound with its bridal-wreath.
Then the bitter chamber heard
Vengeance in a cauldron seethe. 460
Hurried counsel rage and craft

Yelped to hungry men, whose teeth
Hard the grey lip-ringlet gnawed,
Gleaming till their fury laughed.
With the steel-hilt in the clutch, 465
Eyes were shot on her that froze
In their blood-thirst overawed;
Burned to rend, yet feared to touch.
She that was his nuptial rose,
She was of his heart's blood clad: 470
Oh! the last of him she had!—
Could a little fist as big
As the southern summer fig,
Push a dagger's point to pierce
Ribs like those? Who else! They glared 475
Each at each. Suspicion fierce
Many a black remembrance bared.
    Attila, my Attila!
Death, who dares deny her guilt!
Death, who says his blood she spilt! 480
Traitor he, who stands between!
Swift to hell, who harms the Queen!
She, the wild contention's cause,
Combed her hair with quiet paws.
    Make the bed for Attila! 485

XXVI

Night was on the host in arms.
Night, as never night before,
Hearkened to an army's roar
Breaking up in snaky swarms:
Torch and steel and snorting steed, 490
Hunted by the cry of blood,
Cursed with blindness, mad for day.
Where the torches ran a flood,
Tales of him and of the deed
Showered like a torrent spray. 495
Fear of silence made them strive
Loud in warrior-hymns that grew
Hoarse for slaughter yet unwreaked.
Ghostly Night across the hive,
With a crimson finger drew 500
Letters on her breast and shrieked.
Night was on them like the mould
On the buried half alive.

Night, their bloody Queen, her fold
Wound on them and struck them through. 505
    Make the bed for Attila!

XXVII

Earth has got him whom God gave,
Earth may sing, and earth shall smart!
None of earth shall know his grave.
They that dig with Death depart. 510
    Attila, my Attila!

XXVIII

Thus their prayer was raved and passed:
Passed in peace their red sunset:
Hewn and earthed those men of sweat
Who had housed him in the vast, 515
Where no mortal might declare,
There lies he—his end was there!
    Attila, my Attila!

XXIX

Kingless was the army left:
Of its head the race bereft. 520
Every fury of the pit
Tortured and dismembered it.
Lo, upon a silent hour,
When the pitch of frost subsides.
Danube with a shout of power 525
Loosens his imprisoned tides:
Wide around the frighted plains
Shake to hear his riven chains,
Dreadfuller than heaven in wrath,
As he makes himself a path: 530
High leap the ice-cracks, towering pile
Floes to bergs, and giant peers
Wrestle on a drifted isle;
Island on ice-island rears;
Dissolution battles fast: 535
Big the senseless Titans loom,
Through a mist of common doom
Striving which shall die the last:
Till a gentle-breathing morn
Frees the stream from bank to bank. 540

So the Empire built of scorn
Agonized, dissolved and sank.
Of the Queen no more was told
Than of leaf on Danube rolled.
    Make the bed for Attila! 545

107. *Lucifer in Starlight*

On a starred night Prince Lucifer uprose.
Tired of his dark dominion swung the fiend
Above the rolling ball in cloud part screened,
Where sinners hugged their spectre of repose.
Poor prey to his hot fit of pride were those. 5
And now upon his western wing he leaned,
Now his huge bulk o'er Afric's sands careened,
Now the black planet shadowed Arctic snows.
Soaring through wider zones that pricked his scars
With memory of the old revolt from Awe, 10
He reached a middle height, and at the stars,
Which are the brain of heaven, he looked, and sank.
Around the ancient track marched, rank on rank,
The army of unalterable law.

108. *Society*

Historic be the survey of our kind,
And how their brave Society took shape.
Lion, wolf, vulture, fox, jackal and ape,
The strong of limb, the keen of nose, we find,
Who, with some jars in harmony, combined, 5
Their primal instincts taming, to escape
The brawl indecent, and hot passions drape.
Convenience pricked conscience, that the mind.
Thus entered they the field of milder beasts,
Which in some sort of civil order graze, 10
And do half-homage to the God of Laws.
But are they still for their own ravenous feasts,
Earth gives the edifice they build no base:
They spring another flood of fangs and claws.

109.   *A Ballad of Past Meridian*

I

Last night returning from my twilight walk
I met the grey mist Death, whose eyeless brow
Was bent on me, and from his hand of chalk
He reached me flowers as from a withered bough:
O Death, what bitter nosegays givest thou!   5

II

Death said, I gather, and pursued his way.
Another stood by me, a shape in stone,
Sword-hacked and iron-stained, with breasts of clay,
And metal veins that sometimes fiery shone:
O Life, how naked and how hard when known!   10

III

Life said, As thou hast carved me, such am I.
Then memory, like the nightjar on the pine,
And sightless hope, a woodlark in night sky,
Joined notes of Death and Life till night's decline:
Of Death, of Life, those inwound notes are mine.   15

(1876)

110.   *King Harald's Trance*

I

Sword in length a reaping-hook amain
Harald sheared his field, blood up to shank:
    'Mid the swathes of slain,
    First at moonrise drank.

II

Thereof hunger, as for meats the knife,   5
Pricked his ribs, in one sharp spur to reach
    Home and his young wife,
    Nigh the sea-ford beach.

III

After battle keen to feed was he:
Smoking flesh the thresher washed down fast,   10
    Like an angry sea
    Ships from keel to mast.

IV

Name us glory, singer, name us pride
Matching Harald's in his deeds of strength;
    Chiefs, wife, sword by side,   15
    Foemen stretched their length!

V

Half a winter night the toasts hurrahed,
Crowned him, clothed him, trumpeted him high,
    Till awink he bade
    Wife to chamber fly.   20

VI

Twice the sun had mounted, twice had sunk,
Ere his ears took sound; he lay for dead;
    Mountain on his trunk,
    Ocean on his head.

VII

Clamped to couch, his fiery hearing sucked   25
Whispers that at heart made iron-clang:
    Here fool-woman clucked,
    There men held harangue.

VIII

Burial to fit their lord of war,
They decreed him: hailed the kingling: ha!   30
    Hateful! but this Thor
    Failed a weak lamb's baa.

IX

King they hailed a branchlet, shaped to fare,
Weighted so, like quaking shingle spume,
    When his blood's own heir   35
    Ripened in the womb!

X

Still he heard, and doglike, hoglike, ran
Nose of hearing till his blind sight saw:
    Woman stood with man
    Mouthing low, at paw.   40

XI

Woman, man, they mouthed; they spake a thing
Armed to split a mountain, sunder seas:
    Still the frozen king
    Lay and felt him freeze.

XII

Doglike, hoglike, horselike now he raced,   45
Riderless, in ghost across a ground
    Flint of breast, blank-faced,
    Past the fleshly bound.

XIII

Smell of brine his nostrils filled with might:
Nostrils quickened eyelids, eyelids hand: 50
    Hand for sword at right
    Groped, the great haft spanned.

XIV

Wonder struck to ice his people's eyes:
Him they saw, the prone upon the bier,
    Sheer from backbone rise,   55
    Sword uplifting peer.

XV

Sitting did he breathe against the blade,
Standing kiss it for that proof of life:
    Strode, as netters wade,
    Straightway to his wife.   60

XVI

Her he eyed: his judgement was one word,
Foulbed! and she fell: the blow clove two.
    Fearful for the third,
    All their breath indrew.

XVII

Morning danced along the waves to beach; 65
Dumb his chiefs fetched breath for what might hap:
    Glassily on each
    Stared the iron cap.

XVIII

Sudden, as it were a monster oak
Split to yield a limb by stress of heat, 70
    Strained he, staggered, broke
    Doubled at their feet.

III.   *England Before the Storm*

I

The day that is the night of days,
With cannon-fire for sun ablaze,
We spy from any billow's lift;
And England still this tidal drift!
Would she to sainted forethought vow 5
A space before the thunders flood,
That martyr of its hour might now
    Spare her the tears of blood.

II

Asleep upon her ancient deeds,
She hugs the vision plethora breeds, 10
And counts her manifold increase
Of treasure in the fruits of peace.
What curse on earth's improvident,
When the dread trumpet shatters rest,
Is wreaked, she knows, yet smiles content 15
    As cradle rocked from breast.

III

She, impious to the Lord of Hosts,
The valour of her offspring boasts,
Mindless that now on land and main
His heeded prayer is active brain. 20
No more great heart may guard the home,

Save eyed and armed and skilled to cleave
Yon swallower wave with shroud of foam,
   We see not distant heave.

IV

They stand to be her sacrifice, 25
The sons this mother flings like dice,
To face the odds and brave the Fates;
As in those days of starry dates,
When cannon cannon's counterblast
Awakened, muzzle muzzle bowled, 30
And high in swathe of smoke the mast
   Its fighting rag outrolled.

(1892)

Dante Gabriel Rossetti (1828–1882)

from *the House of Life*

XLV. Secret Parting

Because our talk was of the cloud-control
  And moon-track of the journeying face of Fate,
  Her tremulous kisses faltered at love's gate
And her eyes dreamed against a distant goal:
But soon, remembering her how brief the whole 5
  Of joy, which its own hours annihilate,
  Her set gaze gathered, thirstier than of late,
And as she kissed, her mouth became her soul.

Thence in what ways we wandered, and how strove
  To build with fire-tried vows the piteous home 10
  Which memory haunts and whither sleep may roam,—
They only know for whom the roof of Love
Is the still-seated secret of the grove,
  Nor spire may rise nor bell be heard therefrom.

113.

XLVIII. *Death-in-Love*

There came an image in Life's retinue
　　That had Love's wings and bore his gonfalon:
　　Fair was the web, and nobly wrought thereon,
O soul-sequestered face, thy form and hue!
Bewildering sounds, such as Spring wakens to, 5
　　Shook in its folds; and through my heart its power
　　Sped trackless as the immemorable hour
When birth's dark portal groaned and all was new.

But a veiled woman followed, and she caught
　　The banner round its staff, to furl and cling,– 10
　　Then plucked a feather from the bearer's wing,
And held it to his lips that stirred it not,
　　And said to me, "Behold, there is no breath:
I and this Love are one, and I am Death."

114.

LIX. *Love's Last Gift*

Love to his singer held a glistening leaf,
　　And said: "The rose-tree and the apple-tree
　　Have fruits to vaunt or flowers to lure the bee;
And golden shafts are in the feathered sheaf
Of the great harvest-marshal, the year's chief, 5
　　Victorious Summer; aye, and 'neath warm sea
　　Strange secret grasses lurk inviolably
Between the filtering channels of sunk reef.

All are my blooms; and all sweet blooms of love
　　To thee I gave while Spring and Summer sang; 10
　　But Autumn stops to listen, with some pang
From those worse things the wind is moaning of.
Only this laurel dreads no winter days:
Take my last gift; thy heart hath sung my praise.

115.

LXXXI. *Memorial Thresholds*

What place so strange,—though unrevealèd snow
　　With unimaginable fires arise
　　At the earth's end,—what passion of surprise
Like frost-bound fire-girt scenes of long ago?

Lo! this is none but I this hour; and lo! 5
    This is the very place which to mine eyes
    Those mortal hours in vain immortalize,
'Mid hurrying crowds, with what alone I know.

City, of thine a single simple door,
    By some new Power reduplicate, must be 10
    Even yet my life-porch in eternity,
Even with one presence filled, as once of yore:
Or mocking winds whirl round a chaff-strown floor
    Thee and thy years and these my words and me.

116.

LXXXVIII. *Hero's Lamp*

That lamp thou fill'st in Eros' name to-night,
    O Hero, shall the Sestian augurs take
    To-morrow, and for drowned Leander's sake
To Anteros its fireless lip shall plight.
Aye, waft the unspoken vow: yet dawn's first light 5
    On ebbing storm and life twice ebb'd must break;
    While 'neath no sunrise, by the Avernian Lake,
Lo where Love walks, Death's pallid neophyte.

That lamp within Anteros' shadowy shrine
    Shall stand unlit (for so the gods decree) 10
    Till some one man the happy issue see
Of a life's love, and bid its flame to shine:
Which still may rest unfir'd; for, theirs or thine,
    O brother, what brought love to them or thee?

117.

Astarte Syrica

(For a Picture)

Mystery: lo! betwixt the sun and moon
    Astarte of the Syrians: Venus Queen
    Ere Aphrodite was. In silver sheen
Her twofold girdle clasps the infinite boon
Of bliss whereof the heaven and earth commune: 5
    And from her neck's inclining flower-stem lean
    Love-freighted lips and absolute eyes that wean
The pulse of hearts to the spheres' dominant tune.

> Torch-bearing, her sweet ministers compel
>   All thrones of light beyond the sky and sea 10
>   The witnesses of Beauty's face to be:
> That face, of Love's all-penetrative spell
> Amulet, talisman, and oracle,—
>   Betwixt the sun and moon a mystery.

118.   *Proserpina*

(Per un Quadro)

> Lungi è la luce che in sù questo muro
>   Rifrange appena, un breve istante scorta
>   Del rio palazzo alla soprana porta.
> Lungi quei fiori d'Enna, O lido oscuro,
> Dal frutto tuo fatal che omai m'è duro. 5
>   Lungi quel cielo dal tartareo manto
>   Che quì mi cuopre: e lungi ahi lungi ahi quanto
> Le notti che sarán dai dì che furo.
>
> Lungi da me mi sento; e ognor sognando
>   Cerco e ricerco, e resto ascoltatrice; 10
>   E qualche cuore a qualche anima dice,
> (Di cui mi giunge il suon da quando in quando,
> Continuamente insieme sospirando,)—
>   'Oimè per te, Proserpina infelice!'

119.   *Proserpina*

(For a Picture)

> Afar away the light that brings cold cheer
>   Unto this wall,—one instant and no more
>   Admitted at my distant palace-door.
> Afar the flowers of Enna from this drear
> Dire fruit, which, tasted once, must thrall me here. 5
>   Afar those skies from this Tartarean grey
>   That chills me: and afar, how far away,
> The nights that shall be from the days that were.
>
> Afar from mine own self I seem, and wing
>   Strange ways in thought, and listen for a sign: 10

    And still some heart unto some soul doth pine,
    (Whose sounds mine inner sense is fain to bring,
    Continually together murmuring,)—
      'Woe's me for thee, unhappy Prosperine!'

120. *Dawn on the Night-journey*

    Till dawn the wind drove round me. It is past
      And still, and leaves the air to lisp of bird,
      And to the quiet that is almost heard
    Of the new-risen day, as yet bound fast
    In the first warmth of sunrise. When the last
      Of the sun's hours to-day shall be fulfilled,
      There shall another breath of time be stilled
    For me, which now is to my senses cast
As much beyond me as eternity,
      Unknown, kept secret. On the newborn air
The moth quivers in silence. It is vast,
Yea, even beyond the hills upon the sea,
      The day whose end shall give this hour as sheer
As chaos to the irrevocable Past.

121. *The Orchard-pit*

    Piled deep below the screening apple-branch
      They lie with bitter apples in their hands:
    And some are only ancient bones that blanch,
    And some had ships that last year's wind did launch,
      And some were yesterday the lords of lands.

    In the soft dell, among the apple-trees,
      High up above the hidden pit she stands,
    And there for ever sings, who gave to these,
    That lie below, her magic hour of ease,
      And those her apples holden in their hands.

    This in my dreams is shown me; and her hair
      Crosses my lips and draws my burning breath;
    Her song spread golden wings upon the air,
    Life's eyes are gleaming from her forehead fair,
      And from her breasts the ravishing eyes of Death.

Men say to me that sleep hath many dreams,
  Yet I knew never but this dream alone:
There, from a dried-up channel, once the stream's,
The glen slopes up; even such in sleep it seems
  As to my waking sight the place well known.   20

* * * * * *

My love I call her, and she loves me well:
  But I love her as in the maelstrom's cup
The whirled stone loves the leaf inseparable
That clings to it round all the circling swell,
  And that the same last eddy swallows up.   25

Gerald Massey (1828–1907)

122.   *Only a Dream*

As proper mode of quenching legal lust,
  A Roué takes unto Himself a Wife:
'Tis Cheaper when the bones begin to rust,
And there's no other Woman you can trust:
But, mind you, in return, Law says you must   5
  Provide her with the physical means of life:
And then the blindest beast may wallow and roll;
The twain are One flesh, never mind the Soul:
You may not cruelly beat her, but are free
To violate the life in sanctuary;   10
In virgin soil renew old seeds of Crime
To blast eternity as well as time:
  She must show black and blue, or no divorce
  Is granted by the Law of Physical Force.

(1889)

123.   *True Poets*

True Poets conquer Glory—do not woo
  It; do not beg their way to Fame;
Nor at her skirts in private bend and sue,
  Nor sow the public broadcast with their name:

They are the great High Priests of Heaven who 5
    Hold sacred as they feed their Altar-flame
Within the Temple: No man hears their cry
For recognition to the passers-by!

They toil on like old Noah with his Boat;
    "EL" hath forespoken it, and it shall be 10
Ready, although the need may seem remote:
    No sign that it will ever get to sea!
They fight the Deluge—keep the soul afloat—
    And still work on, and leave the issue free
With Him whose flood shall fall, or high-tide climb, 15
To launch the Vessel in His own good time.

Alone, in silence, secretly, they grow
    Invisibly, where no voice is raised to bless:
Creating in the dark like Hills below
    The ocean, shaped by Nature's strong caress: 20
Wave after wave sweeps over them; they know
    How many failures go to make success.
Their victory's in their work, not in the word
That waits to praise, as servant waits his Lord.

At last they mount from out the Lethean flood 25
    Beyond the cloud that covers and conceals
The present time, to join the Brotherhood
    Of minds that rise up lofty as the hills:
Heaven crowns them in majestic solitude;
    The world, that saw not once, in wonder kneels! 30
The less they wooed it all the more it heeds,
And still they mount the more their Age recedes.

124.   *A Peculiar Person*

You perfect, pure, original,
Writ in a tongue unknown to all;
Translated, in some other sphere,
You may be read; but will not here.

125.   *A Greek Reply*

"So many are your foes, their arrows shroud
The very Sun with an eclipsing cloud."
"We'll fight them in the dark then! and the horde
Illumine with the lightning of the Sword."

126.   *Womankind*

Dear things! we would not have you learn too much—
   Your Ignorance is so charming! We've a notion
That greater knowledge might not lend you such
   Sure aid to blind obedience and devotion.

127.   *An Angel in the House*

You have your Angel in the House! but look
On this, her likeness, mirrored in a book,
If but to learn how shadowy the Ideal
In presence of the living, loving Real.

Elizabeth ('Lizzie') Siddal (later Rossetti) (1829–1862)

128.   *The Lust of the Eyes*

I care not for my Lady's soul
   Though I worship before her smile;
I care not where be my Lady's goal
   When her beauty shall lose its wile.

Low sit I down at my Lady's feet
   Gazing through her wild eyes
Smiling to think how my love will fleet
   When their starlike beauty dies.

I care not if my Lady pray
    To our Father which is in Heaven 10
But for joy my heart's quick pulses play
    For to me her love is given.

Then who shall close my Lady's eyes
    And who shall fold her hands?
Will any hearken if she cries 15
    Up to the unknown lands?

129. *Dead Love*

Oh never weep for love that's dead
    Since love is seldom true
But changes his fashion from blue to red,
    From brightest red to blue,
And love was born to an early death 5
    And is so seldom true.

Then harbour no smile on your bonny face
    To win the deepest sigh.
The fairest words on truest lips
    Pass on and surely die, 10
And you will stand alone, my dear,
    When wintry winds draw nigh.

Sweet, never weep for what cannot be,
    For this God has not given.
If the merest dream of love were true 15
    Then, sweet we should be in heaven,
And this is only earth, my dear,
    Where true love is not given.

(wr. 1859?; pub. 1899)

Christina Rossetti (1830–1894)

130.
In an Artist's Studio

One face looks out from all his canvasses,
   One selfsame figure sits or walks or leans;
   We found her hidden just behind those screens,
That mirror gave back all her loveliness.
A queen in opal or in ruby dress, 5
   A nameless girl in freshest summer greens,
   A saint, an angel;—every canvass means
The same one meaning, neither more nor less.
He feeds upon her face by day and night,
   And she with true kind eyes looks back on him 10
Fair as the moon and joyful as the light:
   Not wan with waiting, not with sorrow dim;
Not as she is, but was when hope shone bright;
   Not as she is, but as she fills his dream.

131.
A Coast-Nightmare

I have a friend in ghostland—
   Early found, ah me, how early lost!—
Blood-red seaweeds drip along that coastland
   By the strong sea wrenched and tossed.
In every creek there slopes a dead man's islet, 5
   And such an one in every bay;
All unripened in the unended twilight:
   For there comes neither night nor day.

Unripe harvest there hath none to reap it
   From the watery misty place; 10
Unripe vineyard there hath none to keep it
   In unprofitable space.
Living flocks and herds are nowhere found there;
   Only ghosts in flocks and shoals:
Indistinguished hazy ghosts surround there 15
   Meteors whirling on their poles;
Indistinguished hazy ghosts abound there;
   Troops, yea swarms, of dead men's souls.—

Have they towns to live in?—
    They have towers and towns from sea to sea; 20
Of each town the gates are seven;
    Of one of these each ghost is free.
Civilians, soldiers, seamen,
    Of one town each ghost is free:
They are ghastly men those ghostly freemen: 25
    Such a sight may you not see.—

How know you that your lover
    Of death's tideless waters stoops to drink?—
Me by night doth mouldy darkness cover,
    It makes me quake to think: 30
All night long I feel his presence hover
    Thro' the darkness black as ink.

Without a voice he tells me
    The wordless secrets of death's deep:
If I sleep, his trumpet voice compels me 35
    To stalk forth in my sleep:
If I wake, he hunts me like a nightmare;
    I feel my hair stand up, my body creep:
Without light I see a blasting sight there,
    See a secret I must keep. 40

132.   *Two Thoughts of Death*

I.

Her heart that loved me once is rottenness
    Now and corruption; and her life is dead
    That was to have been one with mine she said.
The earth must lie with such a cruel stress
On her eyes where the white lids used to press; 5
    Foul worms fill up her mouth so sweet and red;
    Foul worms are underneath her graceful head.
Yet these, being born of her from nothingness
These worms are certainly flesh of her flesh.—
    How is it that the grass is rank and green, 10
And the dew dropping rose is brave and fresh
Above what was so sweeter far than they?
Even as her beauty hath passed quite away
    Their's too shall be as tho' it had not been.

2.

So I said underneath the dusky trees:
   But because I still loved her memory
   I stooped to pluck a pale anemone
And lo! my hand lighted upon heartsease
Not fully blown: while with new life from these
   Fluttered a starry moth that rapidly
   Rose toward the sun: sunlighted flashed on me
Its wings that seemed to throb like heart pulses.
Far far away it flew far out of sight,
   From earth and flowers of earth it passed away
As tho' it flew straight up into the light.
   Then my heart answered me: Thou fool to say
   That she is dead whose night is turned to day,
And whose day shall no more turn back to night.

133.   *Cor Mio*

Still sometimes in my secret heart of hearts
   I say "Cor mio" when I remember you,
   And thus I yield us both one tender due,
Welding one whole of two divided parts.
Ah Friend, too wise or unwise for such arts,
   Ah noble Friend, silent and strong and true,
   Would you have given me roses for the rue
For which I bartered roses in love's marts?
So late in autumn one forgets the spring,
   Forgets the summer with its opulence,
The callow birds that long have found a wing,
   The swallows that more lately got them hence:
Will anything like spring, will anything
   Like summer, rouse one day the slumbering sense?

My old admiration before I was twenty,—
Is predilect still, now promoted to se'enty!
My own demi-century plus an odd one
   Some weight to my judgment may fairly impart.
Accept this faint flash of a smouldering fun,
   The fun of a heavy old heart.

134.   *Yet a Little While*

> I dreamed and did not seek: today I seek
>   Who can no longer dream;
> But now am all behindhand, waxen weak,
>   And dazed amid so many things that gleam
>   Yet are not what they seem.
>
> I dreamed and did not work: today I work
>   Kept wide awake by care
> And loss, and perils dimly guessed to lurk;
>   I work and reap not, while my life goes bare
>   And void in wintry air.
>
> I hope indeed; but hope itself is fear
>   Viewed on the sunny side;
> I hope, and disregard the world that's here,
>   The prizes drawn, the sweet things that betide;
>   I hope, and I abide.

135.   *Yet a Little While*

> Heaven is not far, tho' far the sky
>   Overarching earth and main.
> It takes not long to live and die,
>   Die, revive, and rise again.
> Not long: how long? Oh, long re-echoing song!
> O Lord, how long?

136.   *Love Lies Bleeding*

> Love that is dead and buried, yesterday
>   Out of his grave rose up before my face;
>   No recognition in his look, no trace
> Of memory in his eyes dust-dimmed and grey.
> While I, remembering, found no word to say,
>   But felt my quickened heart leap in its place;
>   Caught afterglow, thrown back from long-set days,
> Caught echoes of all music passed away.
> Was this indeed to meet?—I mind me yet

> In youth we met when hope and love were quick, 10
>   We parted with hope dead, but love alive:
> I mind me how we parted then heart-sick,
>   Remembering, loving, hopeless, weak to strive:—
> Was this to meet? Not so, we have not met.

137.   *A Ballad of Boding*

There are sleeping dreams and waking dreams;
What seems is not always as it seems.

I looked out of my window in the sweet new morning,
And there I saw three barges of manifold adorning
Went sailing toward the East: 5
The first had sails like fire,
The next like glittering wire,
But sackcloth were the sails of the least;
And all the crews made music, and two had spread a feast.

The first choir breathed in flutes,   10
And fingered soft guitars;
The second won from lutes
Harmonious chords and jars,
With drums for stormy bars:
But the third was all of harpers and scarlet trumpeters;   15
Notes of triumph, then
An alarm again,
As for onset, as for victory, rallies, stirs,
Peace at last and glory to the vanquishers.

The first barge showed for figurehead a Love with wings;   20
The second showed for figurehead a Worm with stings;
The third, a Lily tangled to a Rose which clings.
The first bore for freight gold and spice and down;
The second bore a sword, a sceptre, and a crown;
The third, a heap of earth gone to dust and brown.   25
Winged Love meseemed like Folly in the face;
Stinged Worm meseemed loathly in his place;
Lily and Rose were flowers of grace.
Merry went the revel of the fire-sailed crew,
Singing, feasting, dancing to and fro: 30
Pleasures ever changing, ever graceful, ever new;
Sighs, but scarce of woe;

All the sighing
Wooed such sweet replying;
All the sighing, sweet and low, 35
Used to come and go
For more pleasure, merely so.
Yet at intervals some one grew tired
Of everything desired,
And sank, I knew not whither, in sorry plight, 40
Out of sight.

The second crew seemed ever
Wider-visioned, graver,
More distinct of purpose, more sustained of will;
With heads erect and proud, 45
And voices sometimes loud;
With endless tacking, counter-tacking,
All things grasping, all things lacking,
It would seem;
Ever shifting helm, or sail, or shroud, 50
Drifting on as in a dream.
Hoarding to their utmost bent,
Feasting to their fill,
Yet gnawed by discontent,
Envy, hatred, malice, on their road they went. 55
Their freight was not a treasure,
Their music not a pleasure;
The sword flashed, cleaving thro' their bands,
Sceptre and crown changed hands.

The third crew as they went 60
Seemed mostly different;
They toiled in rowing, for to them the wind was contrary,
As all the world might see.
They laboured at the oar,
While on their heads they bore 65
The fiery stress of sunshine more and more.
They laboured at the oar hand-sore,
Till rain went splashing,
And spray went dashing,
Down on them, and up on them, more and more. 70
Their sails were patched and rent,
Their masts were bent,
In peril of their lives they worked and went.
For them no feast was spread,
No soft luxurious bed 75

Scented and white,
No crown or sceptre hung in sight;
In weariness and painfulness,
In thirst and sore distress,
They rowed and steered from left to right   80
With all their might.
Their trumpeters and harpers round about
Incessantly played out,
And sometimes they made answer with a shout;
But oftener they groaned or wept,   85
And seldom paused to eat, and seldom slept.
I wept for pity watching them, but more
I wept heart-sore
Once and again to see
Some weary man plunge overboard, and swim   90
To Love or Worm ship floating buoyantly:
And there all welcomed him.

The ships steered each apart and seemed to scorn each other,
Yet all the crews were interchangeable;
Now one man, now another,   95
—Like bloodless spectres some, some flushed by health,—
Changed openly, or changed by stealth,
Scaling a slippery side, and scaled it well.
The most left Love ship, hauling wealth
Up Worm ship's side;   100
While some few hollow-eyed
Left either for the sack-sailed boat;
But this, tho' not remote,
Was worst to mount, and whoso left it once
Scarce ever came again,   105
But seemed to loathe his erst companions,
And wish and work them bane.

Then I knew (I know not how) there lurked quicksands full of dread,
Rocks and reefs and whirlpools in the water bed,
Whence a waterspout   110
Instantaneously leaped out,
Roaring as it reared its head.
Soon I spied a something dim,
Many-handed, grim,
That went flitting to and fro the first and second ship;   115
It puffed their sails full out
With puffs of smoky breath
From a smouldering lip,

And cleared the waterspout
Which reeled roaring round about 120
Threatening death.
With a horny hand it steered,
And a horn appeared
On its sneering head upreared
Haughty and high 125
Against the blackening lowering sky.
With a hoof it swayed the waves;
They opened here and there,
Till I spied deep ocean graves
Full of skeletons 130
That were men and women once
Foul or fair;
Full of things that creep
And fester in the deep
And never breathe the clean life-nurturing air. 135

The third bark held aloof
From the Monster with the hoof,
Despite his urgent beck,
And fraught with guile
Abominable his smile; 140
Till I saw him take a flying leap on to that deck.
Then full of awe,
With these same eyes I saw
His head incredible retract its horn
Rounding like babe's new born, 145
While silvery phosphorescence played
About his dis-horned head.
The sneer smoothed from his lip,
He beamed blandly on the ship;
All winds sank to a moan, 150
All waves to a monotone
(For all these seemed his realm),
While he laid a strong caressing hand upon the helm.

Then a cry well nigh of despair
Shrieked to heaven, a clamour of desperate prayer. 155
The harpers harped no more,
While the trumpeters sounded sore,
An alarm to wake the dead from their bed:
To the rescue, to the rescue, now or never,
To the rescue, O ye living, O ye dead, 160
Or no more help or hope for ever!—

The planks strained as tho' they must part asunder,
The masts bent as tho' they must dip under,
And the winds and the waves at length
Girt up their strength,   165
And the depths were laid bare,
And heaven flashed fire and volleyed thunder
Thro' the rain-choked air,
And sea and sky seemed to kiss
In the horror and the hiss   170
Of the whole world shuddering everywhere.

Lo! a Flyer swooping down
With wings to span the globe,
And splendour for his robe
And splendour for his crown.   175
He lighted on the helm with a foot of fire,
And spun the Monster overboard:
And that monstrous thing abhorred,
Gnashing with balked desire,
Wriggled like a worm infirm   180
Up the Worm
Of the loathly figurehead.
There he crouched and gnashed;
And his head re-horned, and gashed
From the other's grapple, dripped bloody red.   185

I saw that thing accurst
Wreak his worst
On the first and second crew:
Some with baited hook
He angled for and took,   190
Some dragged overboard in a net he threw,
Some he did to death
With hoof or horn or blasting breath.

I heard a voice of wailing
Where the ships went sailing,   195
A sorrowful voice prevailing
Above the sound of the sea,
Above the singers' voices,
And musical merry noises;
All songs had turned to sighing,   200
The light was failing,
The day was dying—
Ah me,
That such a sorrow should be!

There was sorrow on the sea and sorrow on the land 205
When Love ship went down by the bottomless quicksand
To its grave in the bitter wave.
There was sorrow on the sea and sorrow on the land
When Worm ship went to pieces on the rock-bound strand,
And the bitter wave was its grave. 210
But land and sea waxed hoary
In whiteness of a glory
Never told in story
Nor seen by mortal eye,
When the third ship crossed the bar 215
Where whirls and breakers are,
And steered into the splendours of the sky;
That third bark and that least
Which had never seemed to feast,
Yet kept high festival above sun and moon and star. 220

138. *Advent*

    Earth grown old, yet still so green,
        Deep beneath her crust of cold
Nurses fire unfelt, unseen:
        Earth grown old.

        We who live are quickly told: 5
Millions more lie hid between
        Inner swathings of her fold.

When will fire break up her screen?
        When will life burst thro' her mould?
Earth, earth, earth, thy cold is keen, 10
        Earth grown old.

139. *A Christmas Carol*

    In the bleak mid-winter
      Frosty wind made moan,
    Earth stood hard as iron,
      Water like a stone;
    Snow had fallen, snow on snow, 5

　　　　　Snow on snow,
　　　　In the bleak mid-winter
　　　　　　Long ago.

　　　　Our God, Heaven cannot hold Him
　　　　　　Nor earth sustain;
　　　　Heaven and earth shall flee away
　　　　　　When He comes to reign:
　　　　In the bleak mid-winter
　　　　　　A stable-place sufficed
　　　　The Lord God Almighty
　　　　　　Jesus Christ.

　　　　Enough for Him whom cherubim
　　　　　　Worship night and day,
　　　　A breastful of milk
　　　　　　And a mangerful of hay;
　　　　Enough for Him whom angels
　　　　　　Fall down before,
　　　　The ox and ass and camel
　　　　　　Which adore.

　　　　Angels and archangels
　　　　　　May have gathered there,
　　　　Cherubim and seraphim
　　　　　　Throng'd the air,
　　　　But only His mother
　　　　　　In her maiden bliss
　　　　Worshipped the Beloved
　　　　　　With a kiss.

　　　　What can I give Him,
　　　　　　Poor as I am?
　　　　If I were a shepherd
　　　　　　I would bring a lamb,
　　　　If I were a wise man
　　　　　　I would do my part,—
　　　　Yet what I can I give Him,
　　　　　　Give my heart.

140.   *Autumn Violets*

Keep love for youth, and violets for the spring:
    Or if these bloom when worn-out autumn grieves,
    Let them lie hid in double shade of leaves,
Their own, and others dropped down withering;
For violets suit when home birds build and sing,　　　　5
    Not when the outbound bird a passage cleaves;
    Not with dry stubble of mown harvest sheaves,
But when the green world buds to blossoming.
Keep violets for the spring, and love for youth,
    Love that should dwell with beauty, mirth, and hope:　　10
    Or if a later sadder love be born,
Let this not look for grace beyond its scope,
But give itself, nor plead for answering truth—
    A grateful Ruth tho' gleaning scanty corn.

141.   'A city plum is not a plum'

A city plum is not a plum;
A dumb-bell is no bell, though dumb;
A party rat is not a rat;
A sailor's cat is not a cat;
A soldier's frog is not a frog;　　　　5
A captain's log is not a log.

142.   'How many seconds in a minute?'

How many seconds in a minute?
Sixty, and no more in it.

How many minutes in an hour?
Sixty for sun and shower.

How many hours in a day?　　　　5
Twenty-four for work and play.

How many days in a week?
Seven both to hear and speak.

How many weeks in a month?
Four, as the swift moon runn'th.   10

How many months in a year?
Twelve the almanack makes clear.

How many years in an age?
One hundred says the sage.

How many ages in time?   15
No one knows the rhyme.

143.   'I planted a hand'

I planted a hand
   And there came up a palm,
I planted a heart
   And there came up balm.

Then I planted a wish,   5
   But there sprang a thorn,
While heaven frowned with thunder
   And earth sighed forlorn.

144.   'Stroke a flint, and there is nothing to admire'

Stroke a flint, and there is nothing to admire:
Strike a flint, and forthwith flash out sparks of fire.

145.   'Hollow-Sounding and Mysterious.'

There's no replying
To the Wind's sighing,
Telling, foretelling,
Dying, undying,
Dwindling and swelling,   5
Complaining, droning,
Whistling and moaning,
Ever beginning,

Ending, repeating,
Hinting and dinning,   10
Lagging and fleeting—
We've no replying
Living or dying
To the Wind's sighing.
What are you telling,   15
Variable Wind-tone?
What would be teaching,
O sinking, swelling,
Desolate Wind-moan?
Ever for ever   20
Teaching and preaching,
Never, ah never
Making us wiser—
The earliest riser
Catches no meaning,   25
The last who hearkens
Garners no gleaning
Of wisdom's treasure,
While the world darkens:—
Living or dying,   30
In pain, in pleasure,
We've no replying
To wordless flying
Wind's sighing.

146.   *Touching 'Never'*

Because you never yet have loved me, dear,
    Think you you never can nor ever will?
    Surely while life remains hope lingers still,
Hope the last blossom of life's dying year.
Because the season and mine age grow sere,   5
    Shall never Spring bring forth her daffodil,
    Shall never sweeter Summer feast her fill
Of roses with the nightingales they hear?
If you had loved me, I not loving you,
    If you had urged me with the tender plea   10
Of what our unknown years to come might do
(Eternal years, if Time should count too few),
    I would have owned the point you pressed on me,
Was possible, or probable, or true.

147.   *Passing and Glassing*

           All things that pass
              Are woman's looking-glass;
        They show her how her bloom must fade,
        And she herself be laid
        With withered roses in the shade;   5
           With withered roses and the fallen peach,
              Unlovely, out of reach
                 Of summer joy that was.

           All things that pass
              Are woman's tiring-glass;   10
        The faded lavender is sweet,
        Sweet the dead violet
        Culled and laid by and cared for yet;
           The dried-up violets and dried lavender
              Still sweet, may comfort her,   15
                 Nor need she cry Alas!

           All things that pass
              Are wisdom's looking-glass;
        Being full of hope and fear, and still
        Brimful of good or ill,
        According to our work and will;   20
           For there is nothing new beneath the sun;
              Our doings have been done,
                 And that which shall be was.

148.   'Earth has clear call of daily bells'

        Earth has clear call of daily bells,
           A chancel-vault of gloom and star,
           A rapture where the anthems are,
        A thunder when the organ swells:
        Alas, man's daily life—what else?—   5
        Is out of tune with daily bells.

        While Paradise accords the chimes
           Of Earth and Heaven, its patient pause
           Is rest fulfilling music's laws.
        Saints sit and gaze, where oftentimes   10
        Precursive flush of morning climbs
        And air vibrates with coming chimes.

149.   *'Endure hardness'*

    A cold wind stirs the blackthorn
        To burgeon and to blow,
    Besprinkling half-green hedges
        With flakes and sprays of snow.

    Thro' coldness and thro' keenness, 5
        Dear hearts, take comfort so:
    Somewhere or other doubtless
        These make the blackthorn blow.

150.   *'Sooner or later: yet at last'*

Sooner or later: yet at last
The Jordan must be past;

It may be he will overflow
His banks the day we go;

It may be that his cloven deep 5
Will stand up on a heap.

Sooner or later: yet one day
We all must pass that way;

Each man, each woman, humbled, pale,
Pass veiled within the veil; 10

Child, parent, bride, companion,
Alone, alone, alone.

For none a ransom can be paid,
A suretyship be made:

I, bent by mine own burden, must 15
Enter my house of dust;

I, rated to the full amount,
Must render mine account.

When earth and sea shall empty all
Their graves of great and small; 20

When earth wrapped in a fiery flood
Shall no more hide her blood;

When mysteries shall be revealed;
All secrets be unsealed;

When things of night, when things of shame, 25
Shall find at last a name,

Pealed for a hissing and a curse
Throughout the universe:

Then Awful Judge, most Awful God,
Then cause to bud Thy rod, 30

To bloom with blossoms, and to give
Almonds; yea, bid us live.

I plead Thyself with Thee, I plead
Thee in our utter need:

Jesus, most Merciful of Men, 35
Show mercy on us then;

Lord God of Mercy and of men,
Show mercy on us then.

151.   *'Balm in Gilead'*

Heartsease I found, where Love-lies-bleeding
 Empurpled all the ground:
Whatever flowers I missed unheeding,
 Heartsease I found.

 Yet still my garden mound 5
Stood sore in need of watering, weeding,
 And binding growths unbound.

Ah, when shades fell to light succeeding
 I scarcely dared look round:
"Love-lies-bleeding" was all my pleading, 10
 Heartsease I found.

152.   *Until the Day Break*

When will the day bring its pleasure?
    When will the night bring its rest?
Reaper and gleaner and thresher
    Peer toward the east and the west:—
    The Sower He knoweth, and He knoweth best.   5

Meteors flash forth and expire,
    Northern lights kindle and pale;
These are the days of desire,
    Of eyes looking upward that fail;
    Vanishing days as a finishing tale.   10

Bows down the crop in its glory
    Tenfold, fiftyfold, hundredfold;
The millet is ripened and hoary,
    The wheat ears are ripened to gold:—
    Why keep us waiting in dimness and cold?   15

The Lord of the harvest, He knoweth
    Who knoweth the first and the last:
The Sower Who patiently soweth,
    He scanneth the present and past:
    He saith, "What thou hast, what remaineth, hold fast."   20

Yet, Lord, o'er Thy toil-wearied weepers
    The storm-clouds hang muttering and frown:
On threshers and gleaners and reapers,
    O Lord of the harvest, look down;
    Oh for the harvest, the shout, and the crown!   25

"Not so," saith the Lord of the reapers,
    The Lord of the first and the last:
"O My toilers, My weary, My weepers,
    What ye have, what remaineth, hold fast.
    Hide in My heart till the vengeance be past."   30

153.   *An 'Immurata' Sister*

Life flows down to death; we cannot bind
    That current that it should not flee:
Life flows down to death, as rivers find
    The inevitable sea.

Men work and think, but women feel; 5
   And so (for I'm a woman, I)
   And so I should be glad to die
And cease from impotence of zeal,
And cease from hope, and cease from dread,
   And cease from yearnings without gain, 10
   And cease from all this world of pain,
And be at peace among the dead.

Hearts that die, by death renew their youth,
   Lightened of this life that doubts and dies;
Silent and contented, while the Truth 15
   Unveiled makes them wise.

Why should I seek and never find
   That something which I have not had?
   Fair and unutterably sad
The world hath sought time out of mind; 20
The world hath sought and I have sought,—
   Ah, empty world and empty I!
   For we have spent our strength for nought,
And soon it will be time to die.

Sparks fly upward toward their fount of fire, 25
   Kindling, flashing, hovering:—
Kindle, flash, my soul; mount higher and higher,
   Thou whole burnt-offering!

154.   *Monna Innominata No. 3*

"O ombre vane, fuor che ne l'aspetto!"—DANTE.
"Immaginata guida la conduce."—PETRARCA.

I dream of you to wake: would that I might
   Dream of you and not wake but slumber on;
   Nor find with dreams the dear companion gone,
As Summer ended Summer birds take flight.
In happy dreams I hold you full in sight, 5
   I blush again who waking look so wan;
   Brighter than sunniest day that ever shone,
In happy dreams your smile makes day of night.
Thus only in a dream we are at one,
   Thus only in a dream we give and take 10

The faith that maketh rich who take or give;
If thus to sleep is sweeter than to wake,
To die were surely sweeter than to live,
Tho' there be nothing new beneath the sun.

T. (Thomas) E. (Edward) Brown (1830–1897)

155.   *Opifex*

As I was carving images from clouds,
   And tinting them with soft ethereal dyes
   Pressed from the pulp of dreams, one comes, and cries:—
"Forbear!" and all my heaven with gloom enshrouds.

"Forbear!" Thou hast no tools wherewith to essay   5
   The delicate waves of that elusive grain:
   Wouldst have due recompense of vulgar pain?
The potter's wheel for thee, and some coarse clay!

"So work, if work thou must, O humbly skilled!
   Thou hast not known the Master; in thy soul   10
   His spirit moves not with a sweet control;
Thou art outside, and art not of the guild."

Thereat I rose, and from his presence passed,
   But, going, murmured:—"To the God above,
   Who holds my heart, and knows its store of love,   15
I turn from thee, thou proud iconoclast."

Then on the shore God stooped to me, and said:—
   "He spake the truth: even so the springs are set
   That move thy life, nor will they suffer let,
Nor change their scope; else, living, thou wert dead.   20

"This is thy life: indulge its natural flow,
   And carve these forms. They yet may find a place
   On shelves for them reserved. In any case,
I bid thee carve them, knowing what I know."

156.   *Ibant Obscuræ*

    To-night I saw three maidens on the beach,
        Dark-robed descending to the sea,
    So slow, so silent of all speech,
        And visible to me
    Only by that strange drift-light, dim, forlorn,   5
    Of the sun's wreck and clashing surges born.

    Each after other went,
        And they were gathered to his breast—
    It seemed to me a sacrament
        Of some stern creed unblest: 10
    As when to rocks, that cheerless girt the bay,
    They bound thy holy limbs, Andromeda.

157.   'High overhead'

      High overhead
      My little daughter
      Was going to bed:—
      Below
      In twenty fathoms of black water   5
      A cod went sulking slow—
    Perceived the light
    That sparkled on the height,
      Then swam
    Up to the filmy level,   10
     Brought's eye to bear
     With dull fixed stare,
       Then—'Damn!'
    He said—and 'Devil!—
I thought'—but what he thought who knows?   15
    One plunge, and off he goes
      East? North?
      Fares forth
To Lundy? Cardiff? But of that keen probe
That for an instant pierced the lobe   20
    Of his sad brain,
Tickling the phosphor-grit,
    How long will he retain
One bit?
    And then above   25

>   My little daughter kneels, and says her prayers.
>   Quite right!
>   My little love—
>   Good night!
>   Sweet pet!   30
>   Put out the light!
>   And so
>   I go
>   Downstairs—
>   And yet—and yet—   35
>   That cod!
>   O God!
>   O God!

                            (wr. 1877; pub. 1908)

158.   *I Bended unto Me*

> I bended unto me a bough of May,
> That I might see and smell:
> It bore it in a sort of way,
> It bore it very well.
> But, when I let it backward sway,   5
> Then it were hard to tell
> With what a toss, with what a swing,
> The dainty thing
> Resumed its proper level,
> And sent me to the devil.   10
> I know it did—you doubt it?
> I turned, and saw them whispering about it.

                            (wr. 1878; pub. 1900)

159.   *A Sermon at Clevedon*

                         GOOD FRIDAY

> Go on! Go on!
> Don't wait for me!
> *Isaac was Abraham's son—*
> Yes, certainly—
> *And as they clomb Moriah—*   5

I know! I know!
A type of the Messiah—
Just so! just so!
Perfectly right; and then the ram
Caught in the—*listening?* Why of course I am!
Wherefore, my brethren, that was counted—yes—
To Abraham for righteousness—
Exactly, so I said—
At least—but go a-head!
Now mark
The conduct of the Patriarch—
"Behold the wood!"
*Isaac exclaimed—*By Jove, an Oxford hood!
"But where"—
What long straight hair!
"Where is the lamb?"
You mean—the ram:
No, no! I beg your pardon!
There's the Churchwarden,
In the Clerk's pew—
Stick tipped with blue—
Now Justification—
"By Faith?" I fancy; Aye, the old equation;
Go it, Justice! Go it, Mercy!
Go it, Douglas! Go it, Percy!
I back the winner,
And have a vague conception of the sinner—
Limbs nude,
Horatian attitude,
Nursing his foot in Sublapsarian mood—
More power
To you my friend! you're good for half-an-hour.
Dry bones! dry bones!
But in my ear the long-drawn west wind moans,
Sweet voices seem to murmur from the wave;
And I can sit, and look upon the stones
That cover Hallam's grave.

from *Roman Women*

XII. 'Why does she stare at you like that? The glow'

Why does she stare at you like that? The glow
Flew sheeted,
As from the furnace seven times heated
For Shadrach, Meshech, and Abednego.
Is it immediate sense   5
Of difference?
Of complement? And so—
While we want sun and grapes,
This burning creature gapes
For ice and snow!   10

XIII. 'O Englishwoman on the Pincian'

O Englishwoman on the Pincian
I love you not, nor ever can—
Astounding woman on the Pincian!
I know your mechanism well-adjusted,
I see your mind and body have been trusted   5
To all the proper people:

I see you straight as is a steeple;
I see you are not old;
I see you are a rich man's daughter;
I see you know the use of gold,   10
But also know the use of soap-and-water;
And yet I love you not, nor ever can—
Distinguished woman on the Pincian!

You have no doubt of your pre-eminence,
Nor do I make pretence   15
To challenge it for my poor little slattern,
Whose costume dates from Saturn—
My wall-flower with the long, love-draggled fringes
But then the controversy hinges
On higher forms; and you must bear   20
Comparisons more noble. Stare, yes, stare—
I love you not, nor ever can,
You peerless woman on the Pincian.

No, you'll not see her on the Pincian,
My Roman woman, wife of Roman man!
Elsewhere you may—
And she is bright as is the day;
And she is sweet, that honest workman's wife,
Fulfilled with bounteous life;
Her body balanced like a spring
In equipoise of perfect natural grace;
Her soul unquestioning
Of all but genial cares; her face,
Her frock, her attitude, her pace
The confluence of absolute harmonies—
And you, my Lady Margaret,
Pray what have you to set
'Gainst splendours such as these?
No, I don't love you, and I never can,
Pretentious woman on the Pincian!

But morals—beautiful serenity
Of social life, the sugar and the tea,
The flannels and the soup, the coals,
The patent recipés for saving souls,
And other things: the chill dead sneer
Conventional, the abject fear
Of form-transgressing freedom—I admit
That you have these; but love you not a whit
The more, nor ever can,
Alarming female on the Pincian!

Come out, O woman, from this blindness!
Rome, too, has women full of loving-kindness,
Has noble women, perfect in all good
That makes the glory of great womanhood—
But they are Women! I have seen them bent
On gracious errand; seen how goodness lent
The grave, ineffable charm
That guards from possibility of harm
A creature so divinely made,
So softly swayed
With native gesture free—
The melting-point of passionate purity.
Yes—soup and flannels too,
And tickets for them—just like you—
Tracts, books, and all the innumerable channels
Through which your bounty acts—

Well—not the tracts,
But certainly the flannels—
Her I must love, but you I never can,
Unlovely woman on the Pincian.   70

And yet—
Remarkable woman on the Pincian!—
We owe a sort of debt
To you, as having gone with us of old
To those bleak islands, cold   75
And desolate and grim,
Upon the ocean's rim,
And shared their horrors with us—not that then
Our poor bewildered ken
Could catch the further issues, knowing only   80
That we were very lonely!
Ah well, you did us service in your station;
And how the progress of our civilisation
Has made you quite so terrible
It boots not ask; for still   85
You gave us stalwart scions,
Suckled the young sea-lions,
And smiled infrequent, glacial smiles
Upon the sulky isles—

For this and all His mercies——stay at home!   90
Here are the passion-flowers!
Here are the sunny hours!
O Pincian woman, do not come to Rome!

162.   *Dartmoor*

SUNSET AT CHAGFORD
HOMO LOQVITVR

Is it ironical, a fool enigma,
This sunset show?
The purple stigma,
Black mountain cut upon a saffron glow—
Is it a mammoth joke,   5
A riddle put for me to guess,
Which having duly honoured, I may smoke,
And go to bed,

And snore,
Having a soothing consciousness
Of something red?
Or is it more?
Ah, is it, is it more?

A dole, perhaps?
The scraps
Tossed from the table of the revelling gods?—
What odds!
I taste them—Lazarus
Was nourished thus!
But, all the same, it surely is a cheat—
Is this the stuff they eat?
A cheat! a cheat!

Then let the garbage be—
Some pig-wash! let it vanish down the sink
Of night! 'tis not for me.
I will not drink
Their draff,
While, throned on high, they quaff
The fragrant sconce—
Has Heaven no cloaca for the nonce?

Say 'tis an anodyne—
It never shall be mine.
I want no opiates—
The best of all their cates
Were gross to balk the meanest sense;
I want to be co-equal with their fates;
I will not be put off with temporal pretence:
I want to be awake, and know, not stand
And stare at waving of a conjuror's hand.

But is it speech
Wherewith they strive to reach
Our poor inadequate souls?
The round earth rolls;
I cannot hear it hum—
The stars are dumb—
The voices of the world are in my ear
A sensuous murmur. Nothing speaks
But man, my fellow—him I hear,
And understand; but beasts and birds

And winds and waves are destitute of words, 50
What is the alphabet
The gods have set?
What babbling! what delusion!
And in these sunset tints
What gay confusion! 55
Man prints
His meaning, has a letter
Determinate. I know that it is better
Than all this cumbrous hieroglyph—
The *For*, the *If* 60
Are growth of man's analysis:
The gods in bliss
Scrabble a baby jargon on the skies
For us to analyse!
Cumbrous? nay, idiotic— 65
A party-coloured symbolism,
The fragments of a shivered prism:
Man gives the swift demotic.

'Tis good to see
The economy 70
Of poor upstriving man!
Since time began,
He has been sifting
The elements; while God, on chaos drifting,
Sows broadcast all His stuff. 75
Lavish enough,
No doubt; but why this waste?
See! of these very sunset dyes
The virgin chaste
Takes one, and in a harlot's eyes 80
Another rots. They go by billion billions:
Each blade of grass
Ignores them as they pass;
The spiders in their foul pavilions,
Behold this vulgar gear, 85
And sneer;
Dull frogs
In bogs
Catch rosy gleams through rushes,
And know that night is near; 90
Wrong-headed thrushes
Blow bugles to it;
And a wrong-headed poet

Will strut, and strain the cogs
Of the machine, he blushes 95
To call his Muse, and maunder;
And, marvellous to relate!
These pseudo-messengers of state
Will wander
Where there is no intelligence to meet them, 100
Nor even a sensorium to greet them.
The very finest of them
Go where there's nought to love them
Or notice them: to cairns, to rocks
Where ravens nurse their young, 105
To mica-splints from granite-boulders wrung
By channels of the marsh, to stocks
Of old dead willows in a pool as dead.
Can anything be said
To these? The leech 110
Looks from its muddy lair,
And sees a silly something in the air—
Call you this *speech*?
O God, if it be speech,
Speak plainer, 115
If Thou would'st teach
That I shall be a gainer!
The age of picture-alphabets is gone:
We are not now so weak;
We are too old to con 120
The horn-book of our youth. Time lags—
O, rip this obsolete blazon into rags!
And speak! O, speak!

But, if I be a spectacle
In Thy great theatre, then do Thy will: 125
Arrange Thy instruments with circumspection;
Summon Thine angels to the vivisection!
But quick! O, quick!
For I am sick,
And very sad. 130
Thy pupils will be glad.
"See," Thou exclaim'st, "this ray!
How permanent upon the retina!
How odd that purple hue!
The pineal gland is blue. 135
I stick this probe
In the posterior lobe—

Behold the cerebellum
A smoky yellow, like old vellum!
Students will please observe   140
The structure of the optic nerve.
See! nothing could be finer—
That film of pink
Around the hippocampus minor.
Behold!   145
I touch it, and it turns bright gold.
Again!—as black as ink.
Another lancet—thanks!
That's Manx—
Yes, the delicate pale sea-green   150
Passing into ultra-marine—
A little blurred—in fact
This brain seems packed
With sunsets. Bring
That battery here; now put your   155
Negative pole beneath the suture—
That's just the thing.
Now then the other way—
I say! I say!
More chloroform!   160
(A little more will do no harm)
Now this is the most instructive of all
The phenomena, what in fact we may call
The most obvious justification
Of vivisection in general.   165
Observe (once! twice!
That's very nice)—
Observe, I say, the incipient relation
Of a quasi-moral activity
To this physical agitation!   170
Of course, you see...."
Yes, yes, O God,
I feel the prod
Of that dissecting knife.
Instructive, say the pupil angels, *very:*   175
And some take notes, and some take sandwiches and sherry;
And some are prying
Into the very substance of my brain—
I feel their fingers!
(My life! my life!)   180
Yes, yes! it lingers!
The sun, the sun—

Go on! go on!
Blue, yellow, red!
But please remember that I am not dead,
Nor even dying.   185

Sebastian Evans (1830–1909)

163.   *The Enigma Solved*

    Seest thou yon Sun in lustrous glory beaming,
        Shedding the rays of his unchanging essence
    With the same tenor evermore outstreaming?
        How can he shroud him, niggard of his presence?

    How can he choose, but with his force far-reaching,   5
        Shine on the world in plenitude supernal?
    'Tis the same law the dreams of elder teaching
        Feign to coerce the Almighty and Eternal!

    "Free," prate the Schools, "how free, the Force that acteth
        Even as it must, not wills, on mind and matter?   10
    Free, when it never addeth nor subtracteth,
        Fixed in perpetual Law that nought can shatter?

    If then Foreknowledge thus in Fate be folden,
        What thanks are due? And who is He that wants them?
    What be His blessings? Why are we beholden?   15
        'Tis but because He cannot choose He grants them!

    What are thy prayers? Wilt turn by supplication
        Him who remains the same from everlasting?"
    Down, down, delusive doubt! Faith's desolation,
        Sapping her fanes, her holy altars blasting!   20

    Shall the Creator need in any measure
        Aught of the creature—praises or devotion?
    'Tis enough praise that at His will and pleasure,
        He, without moving, giveth all things motion!

James Clerk Maxwell (1831–1879)

164.   *To the Chief Musician upon Nabla: A Tyndallic Ode*

I.

I come from fields of fractured ice,
  Whose wounds are cured by squeezing,
Melting they cool, but in a trice,
  Get warm again by freezing.
Here, in the frosty air, the sprays   5
  With fern-like hoar-frost bristle,
There, liquid stars their watery rays
  Shoot through the solid crystal.

II.

I come from empyrean fires—
  From microscopic spaces,   10
Where molecules with fierce desires,
  Shiver in hot embraces.
The atoms clash, the spectra flash,
  Projected on the screen,
The double D, magnesian b,   15
  And Thallium's living green.

III.

We place our eye where these dark rays
  Unite in this dark focus,
Right on the source of power we gaze,
  Without a screen to cloak us.   20
Then, where the eye was placed at first,
  We place a disc of platinum,
It glows, it puckers! will it burst?
  How ever shall we flatten him!

IV.

This crystal tube the electric ray   25
  Shows optically clean,
No dust or haze within, but stay!
  All has not yet been seen.
What gleams are these of heavenly blue?

   What air-drawn form appearing,
    What mystic fish, that, ghostlike, through
     The empty space is steering?

       V.

   I light this sympathetic flame,
    My faintest wish that answers,
   I sing, it sweetly sings the same,
    It dances with the dancers.
   I shout, I whistle, clap my hands,
    And stamp upon the platform,
   The flame responds to my commands,
    In this form and in that form.

       VI.

   What means that thrilling, drilling scream,
    Protect me! 'tis the siren:
   Her heart is fire, her breath is steam,
    Her larynx is of iron.
   Sun! dart thy beams! in tepid streams,
    Rise, viewless exhalations!
   And lap me round, that no rude sound
    May mar my meditations.

       VII.

   Here let me pause—These transient facts,
    These fugitive impressions,
   Must be transformed by mental acts,
    To permanent possessions.
   Then summon up your grasp of mind,
    Your fancy scientific,
   Till sights and sounds with thought combined,
    Become of truth prolific.

       VIII.

   Go to! prepare your mental bricks,
    Fetch them from every quarter,
   Firm on the sand your basement fix
    With best sensation mortar.
   The top shall rise to heaven on high—
    Or such an elevation,
   That the swift whirl with which we fly
    Shall conquer gravitation.

C. (Charles) S. (Stuart) Calverley (1831–1884)

165.   *'Forever'*

    Forever; 'tis a single word!
      Our rude forefathers deemed it two:
    Can you imagine so absurd
        A view?

    Forever! What abysms of woe   5
      The word reveals, what frenzy, what
    Despair! For ever (printed so)
        Did not.

    It looks, ah me! how trite and tame!
      It fails to sadden or appal   10
    Or solace—it is not the same
        At all.

    O thou to whom it first occurred
      To solder the disjoined, and dower
    Thy native language with a word   15
        Of power:

    We bless thee! Whether far or near
      Thy dwelling, whether dark or fair
    Thy kingly brow, is neither here
        Nor there.   20

    But in men's hearts shall be thy throne,
      While the great pulse of England beats.
    Thou coiner of a word unknown
        To Keats!

    And nevermore must printer do   25
      As men did long ago; but run
    'For' into 'ever,' bidding two
        Be one.

    Forever! passion-fraught, it throws
      O'er the dim page a gloom, a glamour: 30
    It's sweet, it's strange; and I suppose
        It's grammar.

> Forever! 'Tis a single word!
>   And yet our fathers deemed it two:
>   Nor am I confident they erred;   35
>   Are you?

                              (1872)

Isa (Craig) Knox (1831–1903)

166.   *The Box*

                    ST. MARK XIV.3.

> She brake the box, and on his head
> The costly spikenard freely shed:
>   Its fragrance filled the place;
> And he on whom it was bestowed,
> Who knew the gift from love had flowed,   5
>   Approved the lavish grace.
>
> He murmured at the waste, whose heart
> Already played the traitor's part:
>   The others murmured too;
> They nursed their small economies,   10
> They kept the bag before their eyes,
>   And hid their lord from view.
>
> Hid from their hearts that more and more
> He could increase the precious store
>   From which such gifts are shed –   15
> Freely the sweets of nature grow,
> But love must bid their fragrance flow,
>   And love the ointment spread.
>
> Look at the liberal world, and see
> Each blessing lavished boundlessly!   20
>   What, dost thou call it waste?
> The beauty of the wayside flower,
> The sweetness scattered every hour,
>   That all alike may taste?

    They who the costliest gifts have given,   25
Raising the fair-wrought towers to heaven,
      Whose precious stones endure,
Filling the place with prayer and psalm,
Anointing hearts with beauty's balm,
      Have most enriched the poor.   30

While they each gen'rous use who chide—
Whether they seek their greed to hide,
      Or but of sight too near,
Would save the cistern's scant supply,
And let the feeding fount run dry—   35
      Rob God's poor souls of cheer.

O generous heart, thy need fulfil,
Spend if thou wilt more freely still,
      And love's rich odours raise;
If all for love, and not for pride,   40
Surely thy Lord will take thy side,
      And crown thee with his praise.

          (1874)

167.   *The Building of the City*

Behold the city is building!—
Why do ye gazing stand?
It is not in the clouds: the city
Is in the midst of the land.

The little hills are round it,   5
And a river flows between;
And I say, 'Behold the vision,'
For the city ye have seen.

Ye know its chiefest places,
And its houses, street on street: 10
Ye know, I know, the faces
Of the men and women we meet.

Men groan within that city,
And sinful women snare;
Hell can have no uncleanness   15
Worse than is harboured there.

The river they have polluted
Till its waters foam with death,
And the foul stream bubbles daily
With the self-destroyer's breath.   20

And alas! in that cruel city
The children bear such woe,
That tender hearts are asking
If the earth be God's or no.

Yet here is the city building,   25
A labour of many days;
And her walls shall be salvation,
Her gates shall all be praise.

A river of life, her river,
Shall flow and shall not cease,   30
And they who dwell within her
Shall dwell in joy and peace.

I see the white walls rising
By the river, day by day,
They are building, building, building,   35
Everywhere and alway.

I see the builders going
On the white walls to and fro;
I am joined unto the builders,
With some I surely know.   40

One struck hands with another
With whom he had been at strife:
'Let us live, instead of striving
About the way of life.'

'How come you here?' said another,   45
'For you are not one of us.'
'Let him build,' said a master builder
'It will never be built but thus.'

Some said, 'We will build the city
With our gold and precious stones,'   50
And some 'We will build the city
With our flesh and with our bones.'

But when shall we behold it?
For death comes swiftly thus—
We shall walk unseen amidst it   55
And Christ in the midst of us.

(1874)

(Edward) Robert Bulwer Lytton (Earl of Lytton, Owen Meredith) (1831–1891)

168.   *Sorrento Revisited*

(1885.)

On the lizarded wall and the gold-orb'd tree
    Spring's splendour again is shining;
But the glow of its gladness awakes in me
    Only a vast repining.

To Sorrento, asleep on the soft blue breast   5
    Of the sea that she loves, and dreaming,
Lone Capri uplifts an ethereal crest
    In the luminous azure gleaming.

And the Sirens are singing again from the shore.
    'Tis the song that they sang to Ulysses;   10
But the sound of a song that is sung no more
    My soul in their music misses.

'Lewis Carroll' (Charles Lutwidge Dodgson) (1832–1898)

169.   *Poeta Fit, Non Nascitur*

'How shall I be a poet?
    How shall I write in rhyme:
You told me once "the very wish
    Partook of the sublime."

Then tell me how! Don't put me off
  With your "another time"!'

The old man smiled to see him,
  To hear his sudden sally;
He liked the lad to speak his mind
  Enthusiastically;
And thought 'There's no hum-drum in him,
  Nor any shilly-shally.'

'And would you be a poet
  Before you've been to school?
Ah, well! I hardly thought you
  So absolute a fool.
First learn to be spasmodic –
  A very simple rule.

'For first you write a sentence,
  And then you chop it small;
Then mix the bits, and sort them out
  Just as they chance to fall:
The order of the phrases makes
  No difference at all.

'Then, if you'd be impressive,
  Remember what I say,
That abstract qualities begin
  With capitals alway:
The True, the Good, the Beautiful–
  Those are the things that pay!

'Next, when you are describing
  A shape, or sound, or tint;
Don't state the matter plainly,
  But put it in a hint;
And learn to look at all things
  With a sort of mental squint.'

'For instance, if I wished, Sir,
  Of mutton-pies to tell,
Should I say "dreams of fleecy flocks
  Pent in a wheaten cell"?'
'Why, yes,' the old man said: 'that phrase
  Would answer very well.

'Then fourthly, there are epithets
    That suit with any word—
As well as Harvey's Reading Sauce   45
    With fish, or flesh, or bird—
Of these, "wild", "lonely", "weary", "strange",
    Are much to be preferred.'

'And will it do, O will it do
    To take them in a lump—   50
As "the wild man went his weary way
    To a strange and lonely pump"?'
'Nay, nay! You must not hastily
    To such conclusions jump.

'Such epithets, like pepper   55
    Give zest to what you write;
And, if you strew them sparely,
    They whet the appetite:
But if you lay them on too thick,
    You spoil the matter quite!   60

'Last, as to the arrangement:
    Your reader, you should show him,
Must take what information he
    Can get, and look for no im-
mature disclosure of the drift   65
    And purpose of your poem.

'Therefore, to test his patience—
    How much he can endure—
Mention no places, names, or dates,
    And evermore be sure   70
Throughout the poem to be found
    Consistently obscure.

'First fix upon the limit
    To which it shall extend:
Then fill it up with "Padding"   75
    (Beg some of any friend):
Your great SENSATION-STANZA
    You place towards the end.'

'And what is a Sensation,
   Grandfather, tell me, pray?   80
I think I never heard the word
   So used before to-day:
Be kind enough to mention one
   "Exempli gratiâ."'

And the old man, looking sadly   85
   Across the garden-lawn,
Where here and there a dew-drop
   Yet glittered in the dawn,
Said 'Go to the Adelphi,
   And see the "Colleen Bawn".   90

'The word is due to Boucicault—
   The theory is his,
Where Life becomes a Spasm,
   And History a Whiz:
If that is not Sensation,   95
   I don't know what it is.

'Now try your hand, ere Fancy
   Have lost its present glow—'
'And then,' his grandson added,
   'We'll publish it, you know: 100
Green cloth—gold-lettered at the back—
   In duodecimo!'

Then proudly smiled that old man
   To see the eager lad
Rush madly for his pen and ink   105
   And for his blotting-pad—
But, when he thought of *publishing*,
   His face grew stern and sad.

170.   'In winter, when the fields are white'

In winter, when the fields are white,
I sing this song for your delight—

In spring, when woods are getting green,
I'll try and tell you what I mean:

In summer, when the days are long,   5
Perhaps you'll understand the song:

In autumn, when the leaves are brown,
Take pen and ink, and write it down.

I sent a message to the fish:
I told them 'This is what I wish.'

The little fishes of the sea,
They sent an answer back to me.

The little fishes' answer was
'We cannot do it, Sir, because—'

I sent to them again to say
'It will be better to obey'.

The fishes answered, with a grin,
'Why, what a temper you are in!'

I told them once, I told them twice:
They would not listen to advice.

I took a kettle large and new,
Fit for the deed I had to do.

My heart went hop, my heart went thump:
I filled the kettle at the pump.

Then some one came to me and said
'The little fishes are in bed.'

I said to him, I said it plain,
'Then you must wake them up again.'

I said it very loud and clear:
I went and shouted in his ear.

But he was very stiff and proud:
He said, 'You needn't shout so loud!'

And he was very proud and stiff:
He said 'I'd go and wake them, if—'

I took a corkscrew from the shelf:
I went to wake them up myself.

And when I found the door was locked,
   I pulled and pushed and kicked and knocked.

And when I found the door was shut,
   I tried to turn the handle, but—   40

(wr. from 1869; pub. 1872)

171.   *The Hunting of the Snark*

FIT THE FIRST

THE LANDING

'Just the place for a Snark!' the Bellman cried,
   As he landed his crew with care;
Supporting each man on the top of the tide
   By a finger entwined in his hair.

'Just the place for a Snark! I have said it twice: 5
   That alone should encourage the crew.
Just the place for a Snark! I have said it thrice:
   What I tell you three times is true.'

The crew was complete: it included a Boots—
   A maker of Bonnets and Hoods—   10
A Barrister, brought to arrange their disputes—
   And a Broker, to value their goods.

A Billiard-marker, whose skill was immense,
   Might perhaps have won more than his share—
But a Banker, engaged at enormous expense,   15
   Had the whole of their cash in his care.

There was also a Beaver, that paced on the deck,
   Or would sit making lace in the bow:
And had often (the Bellman said) saved them from wreck
   Though none of the sailors knew how.   20

There was one who was famed for the number of things
   He forgot when he entered the ship:
His umbrella, his watch, all his jewels and rings,
   And the clothes he had bought for the trip.

He had forty-two boxes, all carefully packed,
    With his name painted clearly on each:
But, since he omitted to mention the fact,
    They were all left behind on the beach.

The loss of his clothes hardly mattered, because
    He had seven coats on when he came,
With three pair of boots—but the worst of it was,
    He had wholly forgotten his name.

He would answer to 'Hi' or to any loud cry,
    Such as 'Fry me!' or 'Fritter my wig!'
To 'What-you-may-call-um!' or 'What-was-his-name!'
    But especially 'Thing-um-a-jig!'

While, for those who preferred a more forcible word,
    He had different names from these:
His intimate friends called him 'Candle-ends',
    And his enemies 'Toasted-cheese'.

'His form is ungainly—his intellect small—'
    (So the Bellman would often remark)—
'But his courage is perfect! And that, after all,
    Is the thing that one needs with a Snark.'

He would joke with hyænas, returning their stare
    With an impudent wag of the head:
And he once went a walk, paw-in-paw, with a bear,
    'Just to keep up its spirits,' he said.

He came as a Baker: but owned, when too late—
    And it drove the poor Bellman half-mad—
He could only bake Bridecake—for which, I may state,
    No materials were to be had.

The last of the crew needs especial remark,
    Though he looked an incredible dunce:
He had just one idea—but, that one being 'Snark',
    The good Bellman engaged him at once.

He came as a Butcher: but gravely declared,
    When the ship had been sailing a week,
He could only kill Beavers. The Bellman looked scared,
    And was almost too frightened to speak:

But at length he explained, in a tremulous tone,
    There was only one Beaver on board;
And that was a tame one he had of his own,
    Whose death would be deeply deplored.

The Beaver, who happened to hear the remark,
    Protested, with tears in its eyes,
That not even the rapture of hunting the Snark
    Could atone for that dismal surprise!

It strongly advised that the Butcher should be
    Conveyed in a separate ship:
But the Bellman declared that would never agree
    With the plans he had made for the trip:

Navigation was always a difficult art,
    Though with only one ship and one bell:
And he feared he must really decline, for his part,
    Undertaking another as well.

The Beaver's best course was, no doubt, to procure
    A second-hand dagger-proof coat—
So the Baker advised it—and next, to insure
    Its life in some Office of note:

This the Baker suggested, and offered for hire
    (On moderate terms), or for sale,
Two excellent Policies, one Against Fire
    And one Against Damage From Hail.

Yet still, ever after that sorrowful day,
    Whenever the Butcher was by,
The Beaver kept looking the opposite way,
    And appeared unaccountably shy.

FIT THE SECOND

THE BELLMAN'S SPEECH

The Bellman himself they all praised to the skies—
    Such a carriage, such ease and such grace!
Such solemnity, too! One could see he was wise,
    The moment one looked in his face!

He had bought a large map representing the sea,
    Without the least vestige of land:
And the crew were much pleased when they found it to be
    A map they could all understand.

'What's the good of Mercator's North Poles and Equators,
    Tropics, Zones, and Meridian Lines?'
So the Bellman would cry: and the crew would reply
    'They are merely conventional signs!

'Other maps are such shapes, with their islands and capes!
    But we've got our brave Captain to thank'
(So the crew would protest) 'that he's bought *us* the best—
    A perfect and absolute blank!'

This was charming, no doubt: but they shortly found out
    That the Captain they trusted so well
Had only one notion for crossing the ocean,
    And that was to tingle his bell.

He was thoughtful and grave—but the orders he gave
    Were enough to bewilder a crew.
When he cried 'Steer to starboard, but keep her head larboard!'
    What on earth was the helmsman to do?

Then the bowsprit got mixed with the rudder sometimes:
    A thing, as the Bellman remarked,
That frequently happens in tropical climes,
    When a vessel is, so to speak, 'snarked'.

But the principal failing occurred in the sailing,
    And the Bellman, perplexed and distressed,
Said he *had* hoped, at least, when the wind blew due East,
    That the ship would *not* travel due West!

But the danger was past—they had landed at last,
    With their boxes, portmanteaus, and bags:
Yet at first sight the crew were not pleased with the view
    Which consisted of chasms and crags.

The Bellman perceived that their spirits were low,
    And repeated in musical tone
Some jokes he had kept for a season of woe—
    But the crew would do nothing but groan.

He served out some grog with a liberal hand,
  And bade them sit down on the beach:
And they could not but own that their Captain looked grand,
  As he stood and delivered his speech.

'Friends, Romans, and countrymen, lend me your ears!'   45
  (They were all of them fond of quotations:
So they drank to his health, and they gave him three cheers,
  While he served out additional rations).

'We have sailed many months, we have sailed many weeks,
  (Four weeks to the month you may mark),   50
But never as yet ('tis your Captain who speaks)
  Have we caught the least glimpse of a Snark!

'We have sailed many weeks, we have sailed many days,
  (Seven days to the week I allow),
But a Snark, on the which we might lovingly gaze,   55
  We have never beheld till now!

'Come, listen, my men, while I tell you again
  The five unmistakable marks
By which you may know, wheresoever you go,
  The warranted genuine Snarks.   60

'Let us take them in order. The first is the taste,
  Which is meagre and hollow, but crisp:
Like a coat that is rather too tight in the waist,
  With a flavour of Will-o'-the-Wisp.

'Its habit of getting up late you'll agree   65
  That it carries too far, when I say
That it frequently breakfasts at five-o'clock tea,
  And dines on the following day.

'The third is its slowness in taking a jest.
  Should you happen to venture on one,   70
It will sigh like a thing that is deeply distressed:
  And it always looks grave at a pun.

'The fourth is its fondness for bathing-machines,
  Which it constantly carries about,
And believes that they add to the beauty of scenes—   75
  A sentiment open to doubt.

'The fifth is ambition. It next will be right
    To describe each particular batch:
Distinguishing those that have feathers, and bite,
    From those that have whiskers, and scratch.   80

'For, although common Snarks do no manner of harm,
    Yet I feel it my duty to say
Some are Boojums—' The Bellman broke off in alarm,
    For the Baker had fainted away.

FIT THE THIRD

THE BAKER'S TALE

They roused him with muffins—they roused him with ice—
    They roused him with mustard and cress—
They roused him with jam and judicious advice—
    They set him conundrums to guess.

When at length he sat up and was able to speak,   5
    His sad story he offered to tell;
And the Bellman cried 'Silence! Not even a shriek!'
    And excitedly tingled his bell.

There was silence supreme! Not a shriek, not a scream,
    Scarcely even a howl or a groan,   10
As the man they called 'Ho!' told his story of woe
    In an antediluvian tone.

'My father and mother were honest, though poor—'
    'Skip all that!' cried the Bellman in haste.
'If it once becomes dark, there's no chance of a Snark—   15
    We have hardly a minute to waste!'

'I skip forty years,' said the Baker in tears,
    'And proceed without further remark
To the day when you took me aboard of your ship
    To help you in hunting the Snark.   20

'A dear uncle of mine (after whom I was named)
    Remarked, when I bade him farewell—'
'Oh, skip your dear uncle!' the Bellman exclaimed,
    As he angrily tingled his bell.

'He remarked to me then,' said that mildest of men,
    '"If your Snark *be* a Snark, that is right:
Fetch it home by all means—you may serve it with greens
    And it's handy for striking a light.

'"You may seek it with thimbles—and seek it with care—
    You may hunt it with forks and hope;
You may threaten its life with a railway-share;
    You may charm it with smiles and soap—"'

('That's exactly the method,' the Bellman bold
    In a hasty parenthesis cried,
'That's exactly the way I have always been told
    That the capture of Snarks should be tried!')

'"But oh, beamish nephew, beware of the day,
    If your Snark *be* a Boojum! For then
You will softly and suddenly vanish away,
    And never be met with again!"

'It is this, it is this that oppresses my soul,
    When I think of my uncle's last words:
And my heart is like nothing so much as a bowl
    Brimming over with quivering curds!

'It is this, it is this—' 'We have had that before!'
    The Bellman indignantly said.
And the Baker replied 'Let me say it once more.
    It is this, it is this that I dread!

'I engage with the Snark—every night after dark—
    In a dreamy delirious fight:
I serve it with greens in those shadowy scenes,
    And I use it for striking a light:

'But if ever I meet with a Boojum, that day,
    In a moment (of this I am sure),
I shall softly and suddenly vanish away—
    And the notion I cannot endure!'

FIT THE FOURTH

THE HUNTING

The Bellman looked uffish, and wrinkled his brow.
    'If only you'd spoken before!
It's excessively awkward to mention it now,
    With the Snark, so to speak, at the door!

'We should all of us grieve, as you well may believe, 5
    If you never were met with again—
But surely, my man, when the voyage began,
    You might have suggested it then?

'It's excessively awkward to mention it now—
    As I think I've already remarked' 10
And the man they called 'Hi!' replied, with a sigh,
    'I informed you the day we embarked.

'You may charge me with murder—or want of sense—
    (We are all of us weak at times):
But the slightest approach to a false pretence 15
    Was never among my crimes!

'I said it in Hebrew—I said it in Dutch—
    I said it in German and Greek:
But I wholly forgot (and it vexes me much)
    That English is what you speak!' 20

"Tis a pitiful tale' said the Bellman, whose face
    Had grown longer at every word:
'But, now that you've stated the whole of your case,
    More debate would be simply absurd.

'The rest of my speech' (he exclaimed to his men) 25
    'You shall hear when I've leisure to speak it.
But the Snark is at hand, let me tell you again!
    'Tis your glorious duty to seek it!

'To seek it with thimbles, to seek it with care;
    To pursue it with forks and hope; 30
To threaten its life with a railway-share;
    To charm it with smiles and soap!

'For the Snark's a peculiar creature, that wo'n't
    Be caught in a commonplace way.
Do all that you know, and try all that you don't:
    Not a chance must be wasted to-day!

'For England expects—I forbear to proceed:
    'Tis a maxim tremendous, but trite:
And you'd best be unpacking the things that you need
    To rig yourselves out for the fight.'

Then the Banker endorsed a blank cheque (which he crossed),
    And changed his loose silver for notes:
The Baker with care combed his whiskers and hair,
    And shook the dust out of his coats:

The Boots and the Broker were sharpening a spade—
    Each working the grindstone in turn:
But the Beaver went on making lace, and displayed
    No interest in the concern:

Though the Barrister tried to appeal to its pride,
    And vainly proceeded to cite
A number of cases, in which making laces
    Had been proved an infringement of right.

The maker of Bonnets ferociously planned
    A novel arrangement of bows:
While the Billiard-marker with quivering hand
    Was chalking the tip of his nose.

But the Butcher turned nervous, and dressed himself fine,
    With yellow kid gloves and a ruff—
Said he felt it exactly like going to dine,
    Which the Bellman declared was all 'stuff'.

'Introduce me, now there's a good fellow,' he said,
    'If we happen to meet it together!'
And the Bellman, sagaciously nodding his head,
    Said 'That must depend on the weather.'

The Beaver went simply galumphing about,
    At seeing the Butcher so shy:
And even the Baker, though stupid and stout,
    Made an effort to wink with one eye.

'Be a man!' said the Bellman in wrath, as he heard
    The Butcher beginning to sob. 70
'Should we meet with a Jubjub, that desperate bird,
    We shall need all our strength for the job!'

FIT THE FIFTH

THE BEAVER'S LESSON

They sought it with thimbles, they sought it with care;
    They pursued it with forks and hope;
They threatened its life with a railway-share;
    They charmed it with smiles and soap.

Then the Butcher contrived an ingenious plan 5
    For making a separate sally;
And had fixed on a spot unfrequented by man,
    A dismal and desolate valley.

But the very same plan to the Beaver occurred:
    It had chosen the very same place: 10
Yet neither betrayed, by a sign or a word,
    The disgust that appeared in his face.

Each thought he was thinking of nothing but 'Snark'
    And the glorious work of the day;
And each tried to pretend that he did not remark 15
    That the other was going that way.

But the valley grew narrower and narrower still,
    And the evening got darker and colder,
Till (merely from nervousness, not from good will)
    They marched along shoulder to shoulder. 20

Then a scream, shrill and high, rent the shuddering sky
    And they knew that some danger was near:
The Beaver turned pale to the tip of its tail,
    And even the Butcher felt queer.

He thought of his childhood, left far behind— 25
    That blissful and innocent state—
The sound so exactly recalled to his mind
    A pencil that squeaks on a slate!

"'Tis the voice of the Jubjub!' he suddenly cried.
   (This man, that they used to call 'Dunce'.)
'As the Bellman would tell you,' he added with pride,
   'I have uttered that sentiment once.

'Tis the note of the Jubjub! Keep count, I entreat.
   You will find I have told it you twice.
'Tis the song of the Jubjub! The proof is complete.
   If only I've stated it thrice.'

The Beaver had counted with scrupulous care,
   Attending to every word:
But it fairly lost heart, and outgrabe in despair,
   When the third repetition occurred.

It felt that, in spite of all possible pains,
   It had somehow contrived to lose count,
And the only thing now was to rack its poor brains
   By reckoning up the amount.

'Two added to one—if that could but be done',
   It said, 'with one's fingers and thumbs!'
Recollecting with tears how, in earlier years,
   It had taken no pains with its sums.

'The thing can be done,' said the Butcher, 'I think.
   The thing must be done, I am sure.
The thing shall be done! Bring me paper and ink,
   The best there is time to procure.'

The Beaver brought paper, portfolio, pens,
   And ink in unfailing supplies:
While strange creepy creatures came out of their dens,
   And watched them with wondering eyes.

So engrossed was the Butcher, he heeded them not,
   As he wrote with a pen in each hand,
And explained all the while in a popular style
   Which the Beaver could well understand.

'Taking Three as the subject to reason about—
   A convenient number to state—
We add Seven, and Ten, and then multiply out
   By One Thousand diminished by Eight.

'The result we proceed to divide, as you see,
    By Nine Hundred and Ninety and Two:
Then subtract Seventeen, and the answer must be
    Exactly and perfectly true.

'The method employed I would gladly explain,
    While I have it so clear in my head,
If I had but the time and you had but the brain—
    But much yet remains to be said.

'In one moment I've seen what has hitherto been
    Enveloped in absolute mystery,
And without extra charge I will give you at large
    A Lesson in Natural History.'

In his genial way he proceeded to say
    (Forgetting all laws of propriety,
And that giving instruction, without introduction,
    Would have caused quite a thrill in Society),

'As to temper the Jubjub's a desperate bird.
    Since it lives in perpetual passion:
Its taste in costume is entirely absurd—
    It is ages ahead of the fashion:

'But it knows any friend it has met once before:
    It never will look at a bribe:
And in charity-meetings it stands at the door,
    And collects—though it does not subscribe.

'Its flavour when cooked is more exquisite far
    Than mutton, or oysters, or eggs:
(Some think it keeps best in an ivory jar,
    And some, in mahogany kegs:)

'You boil it in sawdust: you salt it in glue:
    You condense it with locusts and tape:
Still keeping one principal object in view—
    To preserve its symmetrical shape.'

The Butcher would gladly have talked till next day,
    But he felt that the Lesson must end,
And he wept with delight in attempting to say
    He considered the Beaver his friend:

While the Beaver confessed, with affectionate looks
    More eloquent even than tears,
It had learned in ten minutes far more than all books
    Would have taught it in seventy years.

They returned hand-in-hand, and the Bellman, unmanned   105
    (For a moment) with noble emotion,
Said 'This amply repays all the wearisome days
    We have spent on the billowy ocean!'

Such friends, as the Beaver and Butcher became,
    Have seldom if ever been known;   110
In winter or summer, 'twas always the same—
    You could never meet either alone.

And when quarrels arose—as one frequently finds
    Quarrels will, spite of every endeavour—
The song of the Jubjub recurred to their minds,   115
    And cemented their friendship for ever!

FIT THE SIXTH

THE BARRISTER'S DREAM

They sought it with thimbles, they sought it with care;
    They pursued it with forks and hope;
They threatened its life with a railway-share;
    They charmed it with smiles and soap.

But the Barrister, weary of proving in vain   5
    That the Beaver's lace-making was wrong,
Fell asleep, and in dreams saw the creature quite plain
    That his fancy had dwelt on so long.

He dreamed that he stood in a shadowy Court,
    Where the Snark, with a glass in its eye,   10
Dressed in gown, bands, and wig, was defending a pig
    On the charge of deserting its sty.

The Witnesses proved, without error or flaw,
    That the sty was deserted when found:
And the Judge kept explaining the state of the law   15
    In a soft under-current of sound.

The indictment had never been clearly expressed,
    And it seemed that the Snark had begun,
And had spoken three hours, before any one guessed
    What the pig was supposed to have done.

The Jury had each formed a different view
    (Long before the indictment was read),
And they all spoke at once, so that none of them knew
    One word that the others had said.

'You must know—' said the Judge: but the Snark exclaimed 'Fudge!
    That statute is obsolete quite!
Let me tell you, my friends, the whole question depends
    On an ancient manorial right.

'In the matter of Treason the pig would appear
    To have aided, but scarcely abetted:
While the charge of Insolvency fails, it is clear,
    If you grant the plea "never indebted".

'The fact of Desertion I will not dispute:
    But its guilt, as I trust, is removed
(So far as relates to the costs of this suit)
    By the Alibi which has been proved.

'My poor client's fate now depends on your votes.'
    Here the speaker sat down in his place,
And directed the Judge to refer to his notes
    And briefly to sum up the case.

But the Judge said he never had summed up before;
    So the Snark undertook it instead,
And summed it so well that it came to far more
    Than the Witnesses ever had said!

When the verdict was called for, the Jury declined,
    As the word was so puzzling to spell;
But they ventured to hope that the Snark wouldn't mind
    Undertaking that duty as well.

So the Snark found the verdict, although, as it owned,
    It was spent with the toils of the day:
When it said the word 'GUILTY!' the Jury all groaned
    And some of them fainted away.

Then the Snark pronounced sentence, the Judge being quite
    Too nervous to utter a word:
When it rose to its feet, there was silence like night,   55
    And the fall of a pin might be heard.

'Transportation for life' was the sentence it gave,
    'And *then* to be fined forty pound.'
The Jury all cheered, though the Judge said he feared
    That the phrase was not legally sound.   60

But their wild exultation was suddenly checked
    When the jailer informed them, with tears,
Such a sentence would have not the slightest effect,
    As the pig had been dead for some years.

The Judge left the Court, looking deeply disgusted   65
    But the Snark, though a little aghast,
As the lawyer to whom the defence was intrusted,
    Went bellowing on to the last.

Thus the Barrister dreamed, while the bellowing seemed
    To grow every moment more clear: 70
Till he woke to the knell of a furious bell,
    Which the Bellman rang close at his ear.

FIT THE SEVENTH

THE BANKER'S FATE

They sought it with thimbles, they sought it with care;
    They pursued it with forks and hope;
They threatened its life with a railway-share;
    They charmed it with smiles and soap.

And the Banker, inspired with a courage so new   5
    It was matter for general remark,
Rushed madly ahead and was lost to their view
    In his zeal to discover the Snark.

But while he was seeking with thimbles and care,
    A Bandersnatch swiftly drew nigh   10
And grabbed at the Banker, who shrieked in despair,
    For he knew it was useless to fly.

He offered large discount—he offered a cheque
   (Drawn 'to bearer') for seven-pounds-ten:
But the Bandersnatch merely extended its neck   15
   And grabbed at the Banker again.

Without rest or pause—while those frumious jaws
   Went savagely snapping around—
He skipped and he hopped, and he floundered and flopped,
   Till fainting he fell to the ground.   20

The Bandersnatch fled as the others appeared
   Led on by that fear-stricken yell:
And the Bellman remarked 'It is just as I feared!'
   And solemnly tolled on his bell.

He was black in the face, and they scarcely could trace   25
   The least likeness to what he had been:
While so great was his fright that his waistcoat turned white—
   A wonderful thing to be seen!

To the horror of all who were present that day,
   He uprose in full evening dress,   30
And with senseless grimaces endeavoured to say
   What his tongue could no longer express.

Down he sank in a chair—ran his hands through hfais hair—
   And chanted in mimsiest tones
Words whose utter inanity proved his insanity,   35
   While he rattled a couple of bones.

'Leave him here to his fate—it is getting so late!'
   The Bellman exclaimed in a fright.
'We have lost half the day. Any further delay,
   And we sha'n't catch a Snark before night!'   40

FIT THE EIGHTH

THE VANISHING

They sought it with thimbles, they sought it with care;
   They pursued it with forks and hope;
They threatened its life with a railway-share;
   They charmed it with smiles and soap.

They shuddered to think that the chase might fail,
   And the Beaver, excited at last,
Went bounding along on the tip of its tail,
   For the daylight was nearly past.

'There is Thingumbob shouting!' the Bellman said.
   'He is shouting like mad, only hark!
He is waving his hands, he is wagging his head,
   He has certainly found a Snark!'

They gazed in delight, while the Butcher exclaimed
   'He was always a desperate wag!'
They beheld him—their Baker—their hero unnamed—
   On the top of a neighbouring crag,

Erect and sublime, for one moment of time,
   In the next, that wild figure they saw
(As if stung by a spasm) plunge into a chasm,
   While they waited and listened in awe.

'It's a Snark!' was the sound that first came to their ears,
   And seemed almost too good to be true.
Then followed a torrent of laughter and cheers:
   Then the ominous words 'It's a Boo—'

Then, silence. Some fancied they heard in the air
   A weary and wandering sigh
That sounded like '—jum!' but the others declare
   It was only a breeze that went by.

They hunted till darkness came on, but they found
   Not a button, or feather, or mark,
By which they could tell that they stood on the ground
   Where the Baker had met with the Snark.

In the midst of the word he was trying to say,
   In the midst of his laughter and glee,
He had softly and suddenly vanished away—
   For the Snark *was* a Boojum, you see.

(wr. 1875–6; pub. 1876)

172.   *Jabberwocky*

    'Twas brillig, and the slithy toves
       Did gyre and gimble in the wabe:
    All mimsy were the borogoves,
       And the mome raths outgrabe.

    'Beware the Jabberwock, my son!   5
       The jaws that bite, the claws that catch!
    Beware the Jubjub bird, and shun
       The frumious Bandersnatch!'

    He took his vorpal sword in hand:
       Long time the manxome foe he sought—   10
    So rested he by the Tumtum tree,
       And stood awhile in thought.

    And, as in uffish thought he stood,
       The Jabberwock, with eyes of flame,
    Came whiffling through the tulgey wood,   15
       And burbled as it came!

    One, two! One, two! And through and through
       The vorpal blade went snicker-snack!
    He left it dead, and with its head
       He went galumphing back.   20

    'And hast thou slain the Jabberwock?
       Come to my arms, my beamish boy!
    O frabjous day! Callooh! Callay!'
       He chortled in his joy.

    'Twas brillig, and the slithy toves   25
       Did gyre and gimble in the wabe:
    All mimsy were the borogoves,
       And the mome raths outgrabe.

(1872)

Joseph Skipsey (1832–1908)

173. *The Darling*

 Misfortune is a darling, ever
  Most faithful to the minstrel race;
 Let low-bred wretches shun them, never
  Yet acted she a part so base.

 True, oft by her the bard discovers 5
  He's stript of all he once possest;
 But then, just like your sculpture-lovers,
  She likes her idols naked, best.

174. *A Golden Lot*

 In the coal-pit, or the factory,
  I toil by night or day,
 And still to the music of labour
  I lilt my heart-felt lay;

 I lilt my heart-felt lay – 5
  And the gloom of the deep, deep mine,
 Or the din of the factory dieth away,
  And a Golden Lot is mine.

Richard Watson Dixon (1833–1900)

175. *The Mystery of the Body*

 Smiling with a pliant grace
 Rose on me a learned face:
 Smiled the soul when smiled the eyes? –
 Up when ran the traceries
 Of the forehead arching high, 5
 Did the inner faculty
 Tempering the hidden nerve

Mould the momentary curve,
Waking motions strange between
Spirit fine and fleshly screen?   10

May I then a likeness find
In the features of the mind
And the antic of the flesh?
Wherefore should the wrinkled mesh
Of the forehead arching high   15
Image the soul's pleasantry?

James Thomson (B. V.) (1834–1882)

176. *The City of Dreadful Night*

'Per me si va nella città dolente.'
            Dante

'Poi di tanto adoprar, di tanti moti
D'ogni celeste, ogni terrena cosa,
Girando senza posa,
Per tornar sempre là donde son mosse;
Uso alcuno, alcun frutto
Indovinar non so.'

'Sola nel mondo eterna, a cui si volve
Ogni creata cosa,
In te, morte, si posa
Nostra ignuda natura;
Lieta no, ma sicura
Dell' antico dolor…
Però ch' esser beato
Nega ai mortali e nega a' morti il fato.'
            Leopardi

PROEM

Lo, thus, as prostrate, 'In the dust I write
  My heart's deep languor and my soul's sad tears.'
Yet why evoke the spectres of black night
  To blot the sunshine of exultant years?

Why disinter dead faith from mouldering hidden? 5
Why break the seals of mute despair unbidden,
   And wail life's discords into careless ears?

Because a cold rage seizes one at whiles
   To show the bitter old and wrinkled truth
Stripped naked of all vesture that beguiles 10
   False dreams, false hopes, false masks and modes of youth;
Because it gives some sense of power and passion
In helpless impotence to try to fashion
   Our woe in living words howe'er uncouth.

Surely I write not for the hopeful young, 15
   Or those who deem their happiness of worth,
Or such as pasture and grow fat among
   The shows of life and feel nor doubt nor dearth,
Or pious spirits with a God above them
To sanctify and glorify and love them, 20
   Or sages who foresee a heaven on earth.

For none of these I write, and none of these
   Could read the writing if they deigned to try:
So may they flourish, in their due degrees,
   On our sweet earth and in their unplaced sky. 25
If any cares for the weak words here written,
It must be some one desolate, Fate-smitten,
   Whose faith and hope are dead, and who would die.

Yes, here and there some weary wanderer
   In that same city of tremendous night, 30
Will understand the speech, and feel a stir
   Of fellowship in all-disastrous fight;
'I suffer mute and lonely, yet another
Uplifts his voice to let me know a brother
   Travels the same wild paths though out of sight.' 35

O sad Fraternity, do I unfold
   Your dolorous mysteries shrouded from of yore?
Nay, be assured; no secret can be told
   To any who divined it not before:
None uninitiate by many a presage 40
Will comprehend the language of the message,
   Although proclaimed aloud for evermore.

I

The City is of Night; perchance of Death,
    But certainly of Night; for never there
Can come the lucid morning's fragrant breath
    After the dewy dawning's cold grey air;
The moon and stars may shine with scorn or pity;
The sun has never visited that city,
    For it dissolveth in the daylight fair.

Dissolveth like a dream of night away;
    Though present in distempered gloom of thought
And deadly weariness of heart all day.
    But when a dream night after night is brought
Throughout a week, and such weeks few or many
Recur each year for several years, can any
    Discern that dream from real life in aught?

For life is but a dream whose shapes return,
    Some frequently, some seldom, some by night
And some by day, some night and day: we learn,
    The while all change and many vanish quite,
In their recurrence with recurrent changes
A certain seeming order; where this ranges
    We count things real; such is memory's might.

A river girds the city west and south,
    The main north channel of a broad lagoon,
Regurging with the salt tides from the mouth;
    Waste marshes shine and glister to the moon
For leagues, then moorland black, then stony ridges;
Great piers and Causeways, many noble bridges,
    Connect the town and islet suburbs strewn.

Upon an easy slope it lies at large,
    And scarcely overlaps the long curved crest
Which swells out two leagues from the river marge.
    A trackless wilderness rolls north and west,
Savannahs, savage woods, enormous mountains,
Bleak uplands, black ravines with torrent fountains;
    And eastward rolls the shipless sea's unrest.

The city is not ruinous, although
    Great ruins of an unremembered past,
With others of a few short years ago
    More sad, are found within its precincts vast.

The street-lamps always burn; but scarce a casement
In house or palace front from roof to basement
   Doth glow or gleam athwart the mirk air cast.

The street-lamps burn amidst the baleful glooms,   85
   Amidst the soundless solitudes immense
Of rangèd mansions dark and still as tombs.
   The silence which benumbs or strains the sense
Fulfils with awe the soul's despair unweeping:
Myriads of habitants are ever sleeping,   90
   Or dead, or fled from nameless pestilence!

Yet as in some necropolis you find
   Perchance one mourner to a thousand dead,
So there; worn faces that look deaf and blind
   Like tragic masks of stone. With weary tread,   95
Each wrapt in his own doom, they wander, wander,
Or sit foredone and desolately ponder
   Through sleepless hours with heavy drooping head.

Mature men chiefly, few in age or youth,
   A woman rarely, now and then a child: 100
A child! If here the heart turns sick with ruth
   To see a little one from birth defiled,
Or lame or blind, as preordained to languish
Through youthless life, think how it bleeds with anguish
   To meet one erring in that homeless wild.   105

They often murmur to themselves, they speak
   To one another seldom, for their woe
Broods maddening inwardly and scorns to wreak
   Itself abroad; and if at whiles it grow
To frenzy which must rave none heeds the clamour,   110
Unless there waits some victim of like glamour,
   To rave in turn, who lends attentive show.

The City is of Night, but not of Sleep;
   There sweet sleep is not for the weary brain;
The pitiless hours like years and ages creep,   115
   A night seems termless hell. This dreadful strain
Of thought and consciousness which never ceases,
Or which some moments' stupor but increases,
   This, worse than woe, makes wretches there insane.

They leave all hope behind who enter there: 120
    One certitude while sane they cannot leave,
One anodyne for torture and despair;
    The certitude of Death, which no reprieve
Can put off long; and which, divinely tender,
But waits the outstretched hand to promptly render 125
    That draught whose slumber nothing can bereave.

II

Because he seemed to walk with an intent
    I followed him; who, shadowlike and frail,
Unswervingly though slowly onward went,
    Regardless, wrapt in thought as in a veil: 130
Thus step for step with lonely sounding feet
We travelled many a long dim silent street.

At length he paused: a black mass in the gloom,
    A tower that merged into the heavy sky;
Around, the huddled stones of grave and tomb: 135
    Some old God's-acre now corruption's sty:
He murmured to himself with dull despair,
Here Faith died, poisoned by this charnel air.

Then turning to the right went on once more,
    And travelled weary roads without suspense; 140
And reached at last a low wall's open door,
    Whose villa gleamed beyond the foliage dense:
He gazed, and muttered with a hard despair,
Here Love died, stabbed by its own worshipped pair.

Then turning to the right resumed his march, 145
    And travelled streets and lanes with wondrous strength,
Until on stooping through a narrow arch
    We stood before a squalid house at length:
He gazed, and whispered with a cold despair,
Here Hope died, starved out in its utmost lair. 150

When he had spoken thus, before he stirred,
    I spoke, perplexed by something in the signs
Of desolation I had seen and heard
    In this drear pilgrimage to ruined shrines:
When Faith and Love and Hope are dead indeed, 155
Can Life still live? By what doth it proceed?

As whom his one intense thought overpowers,
    He answered coldly, Take a watch, erase
The signs and figures of the circling hours,
    Detach the hands, remove the dial-face;   160
The works proceed until run down; although
Bereft of purpose, void of use, still go.

Then turning to the right paced on again,
    And traversed squares and travelled streets whose glooms
Seemed more and more familiar to my ken;   165
    And reached that sullen temple of the tombs;
And paused to murmur with the old despair,
Here Faith died, poisoned by this charnel air.

I ceased to follow, for the knot of doubt
    Was severed sharply with a cruel knife: 170
He circled thus for ever tracing out
    The series of the fraction left of Life;
Perpetual recurrence in the scope
Of but three terms, dead Faith, dead Love, dead Hope.

III

Although lamps burn along the silent streets;   175
    Even when moonlight silvers empty squares
The dark holds countless lanes and close retreats;
    But when the night its sphereless mantle wears
The open spaces yawn with gloom abysmal,
The sombre mansions loom immense and dismal,   180
    The lanes are black as subterranean lairs.

And soon the eye a strange new vision learns:
    The night remains for it as dark and dense,
Yet clearly in this darkness it discerns
    As in the daylight with its natural sense;   185
Perceives a shade in shadow not obscurely,
Pursues a stir of black in blackness surely,
    Sees spectres also in the gloom intense.

The ear, too, with the silence vast and deep
    Becomes familiar though unreconciled;   190
Hears breathings as of hidden life asleep,
    And muffled throbs as of pent passions wild,
Far murmurs, speech of pity or derision;
But all more dubious than the things of vision,
    So that it knows not when it is beguiled.   195

No time abates the first despair and awe,
    But wonder ceases soon; the weirdest thing
Is felt least strange beneath the lawless law
    Where Death-in-Life is the eternal king;
Crushed impotent beneath this reign of terror,
Dazed with such mysteries of woe and error,
    The soul is too outworn for wondering.

IV

He stood alone within the spacious square
    Declaiming from the central grassy mound,
With head uncovered and with streaming hair,
    As if large multitudes were gathered round:
A stalwart shape, the gestures full of might,
The glances burning with unnatural light: —

As I came through the desert thus it was,
As I came through the desert: All was black,
In heaven no single star, on earth no track;
A brooding hush without a stir or note,
The air so thick it clotted in my throat;
And thus for hours; then some enormous things
Swooped past with savage cries and clanking wings:
    But I strode on austere;
    No hope could have no fear.

As I came through the desert thus it was,
As I came through the desert: Eyes of fire
Glared at me throbbing with a starved desire;
The hoarse and heavy and carnivorous breath
Was hot upon me from deep jaws of death;
Sharp claws, swift talons, fleshless fingers cold
Plucked at me from the bushes, tried to hold:
    But I strode on austere;
    No hope could have no fear.

As I came through the desert thus it was,
As I came through the desert: Lo you, there,
That hillock burning with a brazen glare;
Those myriad dusky flames with points a-glow
Which writhed and hissed and darted to and fro;
A Sabbath of the Serpents, heaped pell-mell
For Devil's roll-call and some *fête* of Hell:
    Yet I strode on austere;
    No hope could have no fear.

As I came through the desert thus it was,
As I came through the desert: Meteors ran
And crossed their javelins on the black sky-span;
The zenith opened to a gulf of flame,
The dreadful thunderbolts jarred earth's fixed frame;   240
The ground all heaved in waves of fire that surged
And weltered round me sole there unsubmerged:
   Yet I strode on austere;
   No hope could have no fear.

As I came through the desert thus it was,   245
As I came through the desert: Air once more,
And I was close upon a wild sea-shore;
Enormous cliffs arose on either hand,
The deep tide thundered up a league-broad strand;
White foambelts seethed there, wan spray swept and flew;   250
The sky broke, moon and stars and clouds and blue:
   And I strode on austere;
   No hope could have no fear.

As I came through the desert thus it was,
As I came through the desert: On the left   255
The sun arose and crowned a broad crag-cleft;
There stopped and burned out black, except a rim,
A bleeding eyeless socket, red and dim;
Whereon the moon fell suddenly south-west,
And stood above the right-hand cliffs at rest: 260
   Still I strode on austere;
   No hope could have no fear.

As I came through the desert thus it was
As I came through the desert: From the right
A shape came slowly with a ruddy light;   265
A woman with a red lamp in her hand,
Bareheaded and barefooted on that strand;
O desolation moving with such grace!
O anguish with such beauty in thy face!
   I fell as on my bier,   270
   Hope travailed with such fear.

As I came through the desert thus it was,
As I came through the desert: I was twain,
Two selves distinct that cannot join again;
One stood apart and knew but could not stir,   275
And watched the other stark in swoon and her;

And she came on, and never turned aside,
Between such sun and moon and roaring tide:
   And as she came more near
   My soul grew mad with fear.

As I came through the desert thus it was,
As I came through the desert: Hell is mild
And piteous matched with that accursèd wild;
A large black sign was on her breast that bowed,
A broad black band ran down her snow-white shroud;
That lamp she held was her own burning heart,
Whose blood-drops trickled step by step apart:
   The mystery was clear;
   Mad rage had swallowed fear.

As I came through the desert thus it was,
As I came through the desert: By the sea
She knelt and bent above that senseless me;
Those lamp-drops fell upon my white brow there,
She tried to cleanse them with her tears and hair;
She murmured words of pity, love, and woe,
She heeded not the level rushing flow:
   And mad with rage and fear,
   I stood stone bound so near.

As I came through the desert thus it was,
As I came through the desert: When the tide
Swept up to her there kneeling by my side,
She clasped that corpse-like me, and they were borne
Away, and this vile me was left forlorn;
I know the whole sea cannot quench that heart,
Or cleanse that brow, or wash those two apart:
They love; their doom is drear,
   Yet they nor hope nor fear;
   But I, what do I here?

V

How he arrives there none can clearly know;
   Athwart the mountains and immense wild tracts,
Or flung a waif upon that vast sea-flow,
   Or down the river's boiling cataracts:
To reach it is as dying fever-stricken;
To leave it, slow faint birth intense pangs quicken;
   And memory swoons in both the tragic acts.

But being there one feels a citizen;
   Escape seems hopeless to the heart forlorn:
Can Death-in-Life be brought to life again?
   And yet release does come; there comes a morn
When he awakes from slumbering so sweetly 320
That all the world is changed for him completely,
   And he is verily as if new-born.

He scarcely can believe the blissful change,
   He weeps perchance who wept not while accurst;
Never again will he approach the range 325
   Infected by that evil spell now burst:
Poor wretch! who once hath paced that dolent city
Shall pace it often, doomed beyond all pity,
   With horror ever deepening from the first.

Though he possess sweet babes and loving wife, 330
   A home of peace by loyal friendships cheered,
And love them more than death or happy life,
   They shall avail not; he must dree his weird;
Renounce all blessings for that imprecation,
Steal forth and haunt that builded desolation, 335
   Of woe and terrors and thick darkness reared.

VI

I sat forlornly by the river-side,
   And watched the bridge-lamps glow like golden stars
Above the blackness of the swelling tide,
   Down which they struck rough gold in ruddier bars; 340
And heard the heave and plashing of the flow
Against the wall a dozen feet below.

Large elm-trees stood along that river-walk;
   And under one, a few steps from my seat,
I heard strange voices join in stranger talk, 345
   Although I had not heard approaching feet:
These bodiless voices in my waking dream
Flowed dark words blending with the sombre stream: –

And you have after all come back; come back.
I was about to follow on your track. 350
And you have failed: our spark of hope is black.

That I have failed is proved by my return:
The spark is quenched, nor ever more will burn.
But listen; and the story you shall learn.

I reached the portal common spirits fear, 355
And read the words above it, dark yet clear,
'Leave hope behind, all ye who enter here:'

And would have passed in, gratified to gain
That positive eternity of pain,
    Instead of this insufferable inane. 360

A demon warder clutched me, Not so fast;
First leave your hopes behind! – But years have passed
Since I left all behind me, to the last:

You cannot count for hope with all your wit,
This bleak despair that drives me to the Pit: 365
How could I seek to enter void of it?

He snarled, What thing is this which apes a soul,
And would find entrance to our gulf of dole
Without the payment of the settled toll?

Outside the gate he showed an open chest: 370
Here pay their entrance fees the souls unblest;
Cast in some hope, you enter with the rest.

This is Pandora's box; whose lid shall shut,
And Hell-gate too, when hopes have filled it; but
They are so thin that it will never glut. 375

I stood a few steps backwards, desolate;
And watched the Spirits pass me to their fate,
And fling off hope, and enter at the gate.

When one casts off a load he springs upright,
Squares back his shoulders, breathes with all his might, 380
And briskly paces forward strong and light:

But these, as if they took some burden, bowed;
The whole frame sank; however strong and proud
Before, they crept in quite infirm and cowed.

And as they passed me, earnestly from each
A morsel of his hope I did beseech,
To pay my entrance; but all mocked my speech.

Not one would cede a tittle of his store,
Though knowing that in instants three or four
He must resign the whole for evermore.

So I returned. Our destiny is fell;
For in this Limbo we must ever dwell,
Shut out alike from Heaven and Earth and Hell.

The other sighed back, Yea; but if we grope
With care through all this Limbo's dreary scope,
We yet may pick up some minute lost hope;

And, sharing it between us, entrance win,
In spite of fiends so jealous for gross sin:
Let us without delay our search begin.

VII

Some say that phantoms haunt those shadowy streets,
   And mingle freely there with sparse mankind;
And tell of ancient woes and black defeats,
And murmur mysteries in the grave enshrined:
   But others think them visions of illusion,
Or even men gone far in self-confusion;
   No man there being wholly sane in mind.

And yet a man who raves, however mad,
   Who bares his heart and tells of his own fall,
Reserves some inmost secret good or bad:
   The phantoms have no reticence at all:
The nudity of flesh will blush though tameless,
The extreme nudity of bone grins shameless,
   The unsexed skeleton mocks shroud and pall.

I have seen phantoms there that were as men
   And men that were as phantoms flit and roam;
Marked shapes that were not living to my ken,
   Caught breathings acrid as with Dead Sea foam:
The City rests for man so weird and awful,
That his intrusion there might seem unlawful,
   And phantoms there may have their proper home.

VIII

While I still lingered on that river-walk,
    And watched the tide as black as our black doom,
I heard another couple join in talk,
    And saw them to the left hand in the gloom
Seated against an elm bole on the ground,
Their eyes intent upon the stream profound.

'I never knew another man on earth
    But had some joy and solace in his life,
    Some chance of triumph in the dreadful strife:
My doom has been unmitigated dearth.'

'We gaze upon the river, and we note
The various vessels large arid small that float,
Ignoring every wrecked and sunken boat.'

'And yet. I asked no splendid dower, no spoil
    Of sway or fame or, rank or even wealth;
    But homely love with common food and health,
And nightly sleep to balance daily toil.'

'This all-too humble soul would arrogate
Unto itself some signalising hate
From the supreme indifference of Fate!'

'Who is most wretched in this dolorous place?
    I think myself; yet I would rather be
    My miserable self than He, than He
Who formed such creatures to His own disgrace.

'The vilest thing must be less vile than Thou
    From whom it had its being, God and Lord!
    Creator of all woe and sin! abhorred,
Malignant and implacable! I vow

'That not for all Thy power furled and unfurled,
    For all the temples to Thy glory built,
    Would I assume the ignominious guilt
Of having made such men in such a world.'

'As if a Being, God or Fiend, could reign,
At once so wicked, foolish, and insane,
As to produce men when He might refrain!

'The world rolls round for ever like a mill;
It grinds out death and life and good and ill;
It has no purpose, heart or mind or will.

'While air of Space and Time's full river flow
The mill must blindly whirl unresting so: 460
It may be wearing out, but who can know?

'Man might know one thing were his sight less dim;
That it whirls not to suit his petty whim,
That it is quite indifferent to him.

'Nay, does it treat him harshly as he saith?   465
It grinds him some slow years of bitter breath,
Then grinds him back into eternal death.'

IX

It is full strange to him who hears and feels,
   When wandering there in some deserted street,
The booming and the jar of ponderous wheels,   470
   The trampling clash of heavy ironshod feet:
Who in this Venice of the Black Sea rideth?
Who in this city of the stars abideth
   To buy or sell as those in daylight sweet?

The rolling thunder seems to fill the sky   475
   As it comes on; the horses snort and strain,
The harness jingles, as it passes by;
   The hugeness of an overburthened wain:
A man sits nodding on the shaft or trudges
Three parts asleep beside his fellow-drudges: 480
And so it rolls into the night again.

What merchandise? whence, whither, and for whom?
   Perchance it is a Fate-appointed hearse,
Bearing away to some mysterious tomb
   Or Limbo of the scornful universe   485
The joy, the peace, the life-hope, the abortions
Of all things good which should have been our portions,
   But have been strangled by that City's curse.

X

The mansion stood apart in its own ground;
   In front thereof a fragrant garden-lawn,
High trees about it, and the whole walled round:
   The massy iron gates were both withdrawn;
And every window of its front shed light,
Portentous in that City of the Night.

But though thus lighted it was deadly still
   As all the countless bulks of solid gloom:
Perchance a congregation to fulfil
   Solemnities of silence in this doom,
Mysterious rites of dolour and despair
Permitting not a breath of chant or prayer?

Broad steps ascended to a terrace broad
   Whereon lay still light from the open door;
The hall was noble, and its aspect awed,
   Hung round with heavy black from dome to floor;
And ample stairways rose to left and right
Whose balustrades were also draped with night.

I paced from room to room, from hall to hall,
   Nor any life, throughout the maze discerned;
But each was hung with its funereal pall,
   And held a shrine, around which tapers burned,
With picture or with statue or with bust,
All copied from the same fair form of dust:

A woman very young and very fair;
   Beloved by bounteous life and joy and youth,
And loving these sweet lovers, so that care
   And age and death seemed not for her in sooth:
Alike as stars, all beautiful and bright,
These shapes lit up that mausoléan night.

At length I heard a murmur as of lips,
   And reached an open oratory hung
With heaviest blackness of the whole eclipse;
   Beneath the dome a fuming censer swung;
And one lay there upon a low white bed,
With tapers burning at the foot and head:

    The Lady of the images: supine, 525
       Deathstill, lifesweet, with folded palms she lay:
    And kneeling there as at a sacred shrine
       A young man wan and worn who seemed to pray:
    A crucifix of dim and ghostly white
    Surmounted the large altar left in night: – 530

    The chambers of the mansion of my heart,
    In every one whereof thine image dwells,
    Are black with grief eternal for-thy sake.

    The inmost oratory of my soul,
    Wherein thou ever dwellest quick or dead, 535
    Is black with grief eternal for thy sake.

    I kneel beside thee and I clasp the cross,
    With eyes for ever fixed upon that face,
    So beautiful and dreadful in its calm.

    I kneel here patient as thou liest there; 540
    As patient as a statue carved in stone,
    Of adoration and eternal grief.

    While thou dost not awake I cannot move;
    And something tells me thou wilt never wake,
    And I alive feel turning into stone. 545

    Most beautiful were Death to end my grief,
    Most hateful to destroy the sight of thee,
    Dear vision better than all death or life.

    But I renounce all choice of life or death,
    For either shall be ever at thy side, 550
    And thus in bliss or woe be ever well. –

    He murmured thus and thus in monotone,
       Intent upon that uncorrupted face,
    Entranced except his moving lips alone:
       I glided with hushed footsteps from the place. 555
    This was the festival that filled with light
    That palace in the City of the Night.

XI

What men are they who haunt these fatal glooms,
    And fill their living mouths with dust of death,
And make their habitations in the tombs,   560
    And breathe eternal sighs with mortal breath,
And pierce life's pleasant veil of various error
To reach that void of darkness and old terror
    Wherein expire the lamps of hope and faith?

They have much wisdom yet they are not wise,   565
    They have much goodness yet they do not well,
(The fools we know have their own Paradise,
    The wicked also have their proper Hell);
They have much strength but still their doom is stronger,
Much patience but their time endureth longer,   570
    Much valour but life mocks it with some spell.

They are most rational and yet insane:
    An outward madness not to be controlled;
A perfect reason in the central brain,
    Which has no power, but sitteth wan and cold,   575
And sees the madness, and foresees as plainly
The ruin in its path, and trieth vainly
    To cheat itself refusing to behold.

And some are great in rank and wealth and power,
    And some renowned for genius and for worth;   580
And some are poor and mean, who brood and cower
    And shrink from notice, and accept all dearth
Of body, heart and soul, and leave to others
All boons of life: yet these and those are brothers,
    The saddest and the weariest men on earth.   585

XII

Our isolated units could be brought
    To act together for some common end?
For one by one, each silent with his thought,
    I marked a long loose line approach and wend
Athwart the great cathedral's cloistered square,   590
And slowly vanish from the moonlit air.

Then I would follow in among the last:
    And in the porch a shrouded figure stood,
Who challenged each one pausing ere he passed,
    With deep eyes burning through a blank white hood: 595

Whence come you in the world of life and light
To this our City of Tremendous Night? –

From pleading in a senate of rich lords
For some scant justice to our countless hordes
Who toil half-starved with scarce a human right: 600
I wake from daydreams to this real night.

From wandering through many a solemn scene
Of opium visions, with a heart serene
And intellect miraculously bright:
I wake from daydreams to this real night. 605

From making hundreds laugh and roar with glee
By my transcendent feats of mimicry,
And humour wanton as an elfish sprite:
I wake from daydreams to this real night.

From prayer and fasting in a lonely cell, 610
Which brought an ecstasy ineffable
Of love and adoration and delight:
I wake from daydreams to this real night.

From ruling on a splendid kingly throne
A nation which beneath my rule has grown 615
Year after year in wealth and arts and might:
I wake from daydreams to this real night.

From preaching to an audience fired with faith
The Lamb who died to save our souls from death,
Whose blood hath washed our scarlet sins wool-white: 620
I wake from daydreams to this real night.

From drinking fiery poison in a den
Crowded with tawdry girls and squalid men,
Who hoarsely laugh and curse and brawl and fight:
I wake from daydreams to this real night. 625

From picturing with all beauty and all grace
First Eden and the parents of our race,
A luminous rapture unto all men's sight:
I wake from daydreams to this real night.

From writing a great work with patient plan 630
To justify the ways of God to man,
And show how ill must fade and perish quite:
I wake from daydreams to this real night.

From desperate fighting with a little band
Against the powerful tyrants of our land, 635
To free our brethren in their own despite:
I wake from daydreams to this real night.

Thus, challenged by that warder sad and stern,
   Each one responded with his countersign,
Then entered the cathedral; and in turn 640
   I entered also, having given mine;
But lingered near until I heard no more,
And marked the closing of the massive door.

XIII

Of all things human which are strange and wild
   This is perchance the wildest and most strange, 645
And showeth man most utterly beguiled,
   To those who haunt that sunless City's range;
That he bemoans himself for aye, repeating
How Time is deadly swift, how life is fleeting,
   How naught is constant on the earth but change. 650

The hours are heavy on him and the days;
   The burden of the months he scarce can bear;
And often in his secret soul he prays
   To sleep through barren periods unaware,
Arousing at some longed-for date of pleasure; 655
Which having passed and yielded him small treasure,
   He would outsleep another term of care.

Yet in his marvellous fancy he must make
   Quick wings for Time, and see it fly from us;
This Time which crawleth like a monstrous snake, 660
   Wounded and slow and very venomous;
Which creeps blindwormlike round the earth and ocean,
Distilling poison at each painful motion,
   And seems condemned to circle ever thus.

And since he cannot spend and use aright 665
    The little time here given him in trust,
But wasteth it in weary undelight
    Of foolish toil and trouble, strife and lust,
He naturally claimeth to inherit
The everlasting Future, that his merit 670
    May have full scope; as surely is most just.

O length of the intolerable hours,
    O nights that are as æons of slow pain,
O Time, too ample for our vital powers,
    O Life, whose woeful vanities remain 675
Immutable for all of all our legions
Through all the centuries and in all the regions,
    Not of your speed and variance *we* complain.

We do not ask a longer term of strife,
    Weakness and weariness and nameless woes; 680
We do not claim renewed and endless life
    When this which is our torment here shall close,
An everlasting conscious inanition!
We yearn for speedy death in full fruition,
    Dateless oblivion and divine repose. 685

XIV

Large glooms were gathered in the mighty fane,
    With tinted moongleams slanting here and there;
And all was hush: no swelling organ-strain,
    No chant, no voice or murmuring of prayer;
No priests came forth, no tinkling censers fumed, 690
And the high altar space was unillumed.

Around the pillars and against the walls
    Leaned men and shadows; others seemed to brood
Bent or recumbent in secluded stalls.
    Perchance they were not a great multitude 695
Save in that city of so lonely streets
Where one may count up every face he meets.

All patiently awaited the event
    Without a stir or sound, as if no less
Self-occupied, doomstricken, while attent. 700
    And then we heard a voice of solemn stress
From the dark pulpit, and our gaze there met
Two eyes which burned as never eyes burned yet:

Two steadfast and intolerable eyes
   Burning beneath a broad and rugged brow;   705
The head behind it of enormous size.
   And as black fir-groves in a large wind bow,
Our rooted congregation, gloom-arrayed,
By that great sad voice deep and full were swayed: —

O melancholy Brothers, dark, dark, dark!   710
O battling in black floods without an ark!
   O spectral wanderers of unholy Night!
My soul hath bled for you these sunless years,
With bitter blood-drops running down like tears:
   Oh, dark, dark, dark, withdrawn from joy and light!   715

My heart is sick with anguish for your bale;
Your woe hath been my anguish; yea, I quail
   And perish in your perishing unblest.
And I have searched the highths and depths, the scope
Of all our universe, with desperate hope   720
   To find some solace for your wild unrest.

And now at last authentic word I bring,
Witnessed by every dead and living thing;
   Good tidings of great joy for you, for all:
There is no God; no Fiend with names divine   725
Made us and tortures us, if we must pine,
   It is to satiate no Being's gall.

It was the dark delusion of a dream,
That living Person conscious and supreme,
   Whom we must curse for cursing us with life;   730
Whom we must curse because the life He gave
Could not be buried in the quiet grave,
   Could not be killed by poison or by knife.

This little life is all we must endure,
The grave's most holy peace is ever sure,   735
   We fall asleep and never wake again;
Nothing is of us but the mouldering flesh,
Whose elements dissolve and merge afresh
   In earth, air, water, plants, and other men.

We finish thus; and all our wretched race   740
Shall finish with its cycle, and give place
   To other beings, with their own time-doom:
Infinite æons ere our kind began;

Infinite æons after the last man
    Has joined the mammoth in earth's tomb and womb.   745

We bow down to the universal laws,
Which never had for man a special clause
    Of cruelty or kindness, love or hate:
If toads and vultures are obscene to sight,
If tigers burn with beauty and with might,   750
    Is it by favour or by wrath of Fate?

All substance lives and struggles evermore
Through countless shapes continually at war;
    By countless interactions interknit:
If one is born a certain day on earth,
All times and forces tended to that birth,   755
    Not all the world could change or hinder it.

I find no hint throughout the Universe
Of good or ill, of blessing or of curse;
    I find alone Necessity Supreme;   760
With infinite Mystery, abysmal, dark,
Unlighted ever by the faintest spark
    For us the flitting shadows of a dream.

O Brothers of sad lives! they are so brief;
A few short years must bring us all relief: 765
    Can we not bear these years of labouring breath?
But if you would not this poor life fulfil,
Lo, you are free to end it when you will,
    Without the fear of waking after death. –

The organ-like vibrations of his voice   770
    Thrilled through the vaulted aisles and died away;
The yearning of the tones which bade rejoice
    Was sad and tender as a requiem lay:
Our shadowy congregation rested still
As brooding on that 'End it when you will.'   775

XV

Wherever men are gathered, all the air
    Is charged with human feeling, human thought;
Each shout and cry, and laugh, each curse and prayer,
    Are into its vibrations surely wrought;
Unspoken passion, wordless meditation,   780
    Are breathed into it with our respiration;
It is with our life fraught and overfraught.

So that no man there breathes earth's simple breath,
    As if alone on mountains or wide seas;
But nourishes warm life or hastens death   785
    With joys and sorrows, health and foul disease,
Wisdom and folly, good and evil labours,
Incessant of his multitudinous neighbours;
    He in his turn affecting all of these.

That City's atmosphere is dark and dense,   790
    Although not many exiles wander there,
With many a potent evil influence,
    Each adding poison to the poisoned air;
Infections of unutterable sadness,
Infections of incalculable madness,   795
    Infections of incurable despair.

XVI

Our shadowy congregation rested still,
    As musing on that message we had heard
And brooding on that 'End it when you will;'
    Perchance awaiting yet some other word;   800
When keen as lightning through a muffled sky
Sprang forth a shrill and lamentable cry: –

The man speaks sooth, alas! the man speaks sooth:
    We have no personal life beyond the grave;
There is no God; Fate knows nor wrath nor ruth: 805
    Can I find here the comfort which I crave?

In all eternity I had one chance,
    One few years' term of gracious human life:
The splendours of the intellect's advance,
    The sweetness of the home with babes and wife;   810

The social pleasures with their genial wit;
    The fascination of the worlds of art,
The glories of the worlds of nature, lit
    By large imagination's glowing heart;

The rapture of mere being, full of health;   815
    The careless childhood and the ardent youth,
The strenuous manhood winning various wealth,
    The reverend age serene with life's long truth:

All the sublime prerogatives of Man;
    The storied memories of the times of old,   820
The patient tracking of the world's great plan
    Through sequences and changes myriadfold.

This chance was never offered me before;
    For me the infinite Past is blank and dumb:
This chance recurreth never, nevermore;   825
    Blank, blank for me the infinite To-come.

And this sole chance was frustrate from my birth,
    A mockery, a delusion; and my breath
Of noble human life upon this earth
    So racks me that I sigh for senseless death.   830

My wine of life is poison mixed with gall,
    My noonday passes in a nightmare dream,
I worse than lose the years which are my all:
    What can console me for the loss supreme?

Speak not of comfort where no comfort is,   835
    Speak not at all: can words make foul things fair?
Our life's a cheat, our death a black abyss:
    Hush and be mute envisaging despair. —

This vehement voice came from the northern aisle
    Rapid and shrill to its abrupt harsh close;   840
And none gave answer for a certain while,
    For words must shrink from these most wordless woes;
At last the pulpit speaker simply said,
With humid eyes and thoughtful drooping head: —

My Brother, my poor Brothers, it is thus;   845
This life itself holds nothing good for us,
    But it ends soon and nevermore can be;
And we knew nothing of it ere our birth,
And shall know nothing when consigned to earth:
    I ponder these thoughts and they comfort me.   850

XVII

How the moon triumphs through the endless nights!
    How the Stars throb and glitter as they wheel
Their thick processions of supernal lights
    Around the blue vault obdurate as steel!

And men regard with passionate awe and yearning 855
The mighty marching and the golden burning,
   And think the heavens respond to what they feel.

Boats gliding like dark shadows of a dream,
   Are glorified from vision as they pass
The quivering moonbridge on the deep black stream; 860
   Cold windows kindle their dead glooms of glass
To restless crystals; cornice, dome, and column
Emerge from chaos in the splendour solemn;
   Like faëry lakes gleam lawns of dewy grass.

With such a living light these dead eyes shine, 865
   These eyes of sightless heaven, that as we gaze
We read a pity, tremulous, divine,
   Or cold, majestic scorn in their pure rays:
Fond man! they are not haughty, are not tender;
There is no heart or mind in all their splendour, 870
   They thread mere puppets all their marvellous maze.

If we could near them with the flight unflown,
   We should but find them worlds as sad as this,
Or suns all self-consuming like our own
   Enringed by planet worlds as much amiss: 875
They wax and wane through fusion and confusion;
The spheres eternal are a grand illusion,
   The empyréan is a void abyss.

XVIII

I wandered in a suburb of the north,
   And reached a spot whence three close lanes led down, 880
Beneath thick trees and hedgerows winding forth
   Like deep brook channels, deep and dark and lown:
The air above was wan with misty light,
The dull grey south showed one vague blur of white.

I took the left-hand lane and slowly trod 885
   Its earthen footpath, brushing as I went
The humid leafage; and my feet were shod
   With heavy languor, and my frame downbent,
With infinite sleepless weariness outworn,
So many nights I thus had paced forlorn. 890

After a hundred steps I grew aware
    Of something crawling in the lane below;
It seemed a wounded creature prostrate there
    That sobbed with pangs in making progress slow,
The hind limbs stretched to push, the fore limbs then   895
To drag; for it would die in its own den.

But coming level with it I discerned
    That it had been a man; for at my tread
It stopped in its sore travail and half-turned,
    Leaning upon its right, and raised its head,   900
And with the left hand twitched back as in ire
Long grey unreverend locks befouled with mire.

A haggard filthy face with bloodshot eyes,
    An infamy for manhood to behold.
He gasped all trembling, What, you want my prize?   905
    You leave, to rob me, wine and lust and gold
And all that men go mad upon, since you
Have traced my sacred secret of the clue?

You think that I am weak and must submit;
    Yet I but scratch you with this poisoned blade,   910
And you are dead as if I clove with it
    That false fierce greedy heart. Betrayed! betrayed!
I fling this phial if you seek to pass,
And you are forthwith shrivelled up like grass.

And then with sudden change, Take thought! take thought!   915
    Have pity on me! it is mine alone,
If you could find, it would avail you naught;
    Seek elsewhere on the pathway of your own:
For who of mortal or immortal race
The lifetrack of another can retrace?   920

Did you but know my agony and toil!
    Two lanes diverge up yonder from this lane;
My thin blood marks the long length of their soil;
    Such clue I left, who sought my clue in vain:
My hands and knees are worn both flesh and bone;   925
I cannot move but with continual moan.

But I am in the very way at last,
    To find the long-lost broken golden thread
Which reunites my present with my past,
    If you but go your own way. And I said,   930

I will retire as soon as you have told
Whereunto leadeth this lost thread of gold.

And so you know it not! he hissed with scorn;
    I feared you, imbecile! It leads me back
From this accursed night without a morn,   935
    And through the deserts which have else no track,
And through vast wastes of horror-haunted time,
To Eden innocence in Eden's clime:

And I become a nursling soft and pure,
    An infant cradled on its mother's knee,   940
Without a past, love-cherished and secure;
    Which if it saw this loathsome present Me,
Would plunge its face into the pillowing breast,
And scream abhorrence hard to lull to rest.

He turned to grope; and I retiring brushed   945
    Thin shreds of gossamer from off my face,
And mused, His life would grow, the germ uncrushed;
    He should to antenatal night retrace,
And hide his elements in that large womb
Beyond the reach of man-evolving Doom.   950

And even thus, what weary way were planned,
    To seek oblivion through the far-off gate
Of birth, when that of death is close at hand!
    For this is law, if law there be in Fate:
What never has been, yet may have its when;   955
The thing which has been, never is again.

XIX

The mighty river flowing dark and deep,
    With ebb and flood from the remote sea-tides
Vague-sounding through the City's sleepless sleep,
    Is named the River of the Suicides;   960
For night by night some lorn wretch overweary,
And shuddering from the future yet more dreary,
    Within its cold secure oblivion hides.

One plunges from a bridge's parapet,
    As by some blind and sudden frenzy hurled;   965
Another wades in slow with purpose set
    Until the waters are above him furled;
Another in a boat with dreamlike motion

Glides drifting down into the desert ocean,
    To starve or sink from out the desert world.

They perish from their suffering surely thus,
    For none beholding them attempts to save,
The while each thinks how soon, solicitous,
    He may seek refuge in the self-same wave;
Some hour when tired of ever-vain endurance
Impatience will forerun the sweet assurance
    Of perfect peace eventual in the grave.

When this poor tragic-farce has palled us long,
    Why actors and spectators do we stay? –
To fill our so-short *rôles* out right or wrong;
    To see what shifts are yet in the dull play
For our illusion; to refrain from grieving
Dear foolish friends by our untimely leaving:
    But those asleep at home, how blest are they!

Yet it is but for one night after all:
    What matters one brief night of dreary pain?
When after it the weary eyelids fall
    Upon the weary eyes and wasted brain;
And all sad scenes and thoughts and feelings vanish
In that sweet sleep no power can ever banish,
    That one best sleep which never wakes again.

XX

I sat me weary on a pillar's base,
    And leaned against the shaft; for broad moonlight
O'erflowed the peacefulness of cloistered space,
    A shore of shadow slanting from the right:
The great cathedral's western front stood there,
A wave-worn rock in that calm sea of air.

Before it, opposite my place of rest,
    Two figures faced each other, large, austere;
A couchant sphinx in shadow to the breast,
    An angel standing in the moonlight clear;
So mighty by magnificence of form,
They were not dwarfed beneath that mass enorm.

Upon the cross-hilt of a naked sword
    The angel's hands, as prompt to smite, were held;   1005
His vigilant, intense regard was poured
    Upon the creature placidly unquelled,
Whose front was set at level gaze which took
No heed of aught, a solemn trance-like look.

And as I pondered these opposèd shapes   1010
    My eyelids sank in stupor, that dull swoon
Which drugs and with a leaden mantle drapes
    The outworn to worse weariness. But soon
A sharp and clashing noise the stillness broke,
And from the evil lethargy I woke.   1015

The angel's wings had fallen, stone on stone,
    And lay there shattered; hence the sudden sound:
A warrior leaning on his sword alone
    Now watched the sphinx with that regard profound;
The sphinx unchanged looked forthright, as aware   1020
Of nothing in the vast abyss of air.

Again I sank in that repose unsweet,
    Again a clashing noise my slumber rent;
The warrior's sword lay broken at his feet:
    An unarmed man with raised hands impotent   1025
Now stood before the sphinx, which ever kept
Such mien as if with open eyes it slept.

My eyelids sank in spite of wonder grown;
    A louder crash upstartled me in dread:
The man had fallen forward, stone on stone,   1030
    And lay there shattered, with his trunkless head
Between the monster's large quiescent paws,
Beneath its grand front changeless as life's laws.

The moon had circled westward full and bright,
    And made the temple-front a mystic dream,   1035
And bathed the whole enclosure with its light,
    The sworded angel's wrecks, the sphinx supreme:
I pondered long that cold majestic face
Whose vision seemed of infinite void space.

XXI

Anear the centre of that northern crest   1040
    Stands out a level upland bleak and bare,
From which the city east and south and west
    Sinks gently in long waves; and thronèd there
An Image sits, stupendous, superhuman,
    The bronze colossus of a wingèd Woman,   1045
Upon a graded granite base foursquare.

Low-seated she leans forward massively,
    With cheek on clenched left hand, the forearm's might
Erect, its elbow on her rounded knee;
    Across a clasped book in her lap the right   1050
Upholds a pair of compasses; she gazes
With full set eyes, but wandering in thick mazes
    Of sombre thought beholds no outward sight.

Words cannot picture her; but all men know
    That solemn sketch the pure sad artist wrought   1055
Three centuries and threescore years ago,
    With phantasies of his peculiar thought:
The instruments of carpentry and science
Scattered about her feet, in strange alliance
    With the keen wolf-hound sleeping undistraught;   1060

Scales, hour-glass, bell, and magic-square above;
    The grave and solid infant perched beside,
With open winglets that might bear a dove,
    Intent upon its tablets, heavy-eyed;
Her folded wings as of a mighty eagle,   1065
But all too impotent to lift the regal
    Robustness of her earth-born strength and pride;

And with those wings, and that light wreath which seems
    To mock her grand head and the knotted frown
Of forehead charged with baleful thoughts and dreams,   1070
    The household bunch of keys, the housewife's gown
Voluminous, indented, and yet rigid
As if a shell of burnished metal frigid,
    The feet thick-shod to tread all weakness down;

The comet hanging o'er the waste dark seas,   1075
    The massy rainbow curved in front of it,
Beyond the village with the masts and trees;
    The snaky imp, dog-headed, from the Pit,

Bearing upon its batlike leathern pinions
Her name unfolded in the sun's dominions,   1080
    The 'MELENCOLIA' that transcends all wit.

Thus has the artist copied her, and thus
    Surrounded to expound her form sublime,
Her fate heroic and calamitous;
    Fronting the dreadful mysteries of Time,   1085
Unvanquished in defeat and desolation,
Undaunted in the hopeless conflagration
    Of the day setting on her baffled prime.

Baffled and beaten back she works on still,
    Weary and sick of soul she works the more,   1090
Sustained by her indomitable will:
    The hands shall fashion and the brain shall pore,
And all her sorrow shall be turned to labour,
Till Death the friend-foe piercing with his sabre
    That mighty heart of hearts ends bitter war.   1095

But as if blacker night could dawn on night,
    With tenfold gloom oh moonless night unstarred,
A sense more tragic than defeat and blight,
    More desperate than strife with hope debarred,
More fatal than the adamantine Never   1100
Encompassing her passionate endeavour,
    Dawns glooming in her tenebrous regard:

The sense that every struggle brings defeat
    Because Fate holds no prize to crown success;
That all the oracles are dumb or cheat   1105
    Because they have no secret to express;
That none can pierce the vast black veil uncertain
Because there is no light beyond the curtain;
    That all is vanity and nothingness.

Titanic from her high throne in the north,   1110
    The City's sombre Patroness and Queen,
In bronze sublimity she gazes forth
    Over her Capital of teen and threne,
Over the river with its isles and bridges,
The marsh and moorland, to the stern rock-ridges,   1115
    Confronting them with a coëval mien.

The moving moon and stars from east to west
   Circle before her in the sea of air;
Shadows and gleams glide round her solemn rest.
   Her subjects often gaze up to her there: 1120
The strong to drink new strength of iron endurance,
The weak new terrors; all, renewed assurance
   And confirmation of the old despair.

177.   *In the Room*

           '*ceste insigne fable et tragicque comedie*'—RABELAIS

                       I

The sun was down, and twilight grey
   Filled half the air; but in the room,
Whose curtain had been drawn all day,
   The twilight was a dusky gloom:
Which seemed at first as still as death,   5
   And void; but was indeed all rife
With subtle thrills, the pulse and breath
   Of multitudinous lower life.

                      II

In their abrupt and headlong way
   Bewildered flies for light had dashed   10
Against the curtain all the day,
   And now slept wintrily abashed;
And nimble mice slept, wearied out
   With such a double night's uproar;
But solid beetles crawled about   15
   The chilly hearth and naked floor.

                     III

And so throughout the twilight hour
   That vaguely murmurous hush and rest
There brooded; and beneath its power
   Life throbbing held its throbs supprest: 20
Until the thin-voiced mirror sighed,
   I am all blurred with dust and damp,
So long ago the clear day died,
   So long has gleamed nor fire nor lamp.

IV

Whereon the curtain murmured back,
    Some change is on us, good or ill;
Behind me and before is black
    As when those human things lie still:
But I have seen the darkness grow
    As grows the daylight every morn;
Have felt out there long shine and glow,
    In here long chilly dusk forlorn.

V

The cupboard grumbled with a groan,
    Each new day worse starvation brings:
Since *he* came here I have not known
    Or sweets or cates or wholesome things:
But now! a pinch of meal, a crust,
    Throughout the week is all I get.
I am so empty; it is just
    As when they said we were to let.

VI

What is become, then, of our Man?
    The petulant old glass exclaimed;
If all this time he slumber can,
    He really ought to be ashamed.
I wish we had our Girl again,
    So gay and busy, bright and fair:
The girls are better than these men,
    Who only for their dull selves care.

VII

It is so many hours ago—
    The lamp and fire were both alight—
I saw him pacing to and fro,
    Perturbing restlessly the night.
His face was pale to give one fear,
    His eyes when lifted looked too bright;
He muttered; what, I could not hear:
    Bad words though; something was not right.

VIII

The table said, He wrote so long
 That I grew weary of his weight;
The pen kept up a cricket song,
 It ran and ran at such a rate:
And in the longer pauses he
 With both his folded arms downpressed
And stared as one who does not see,
 Or sank his head upon his breast.

IX

The fire-grate said, I am as cold
 As if I never had a blaze;
The few dead cinders here I hold,
 I held unburned for days and days.
Last night he made them flare; but still
 What good did all his writing do?
Among my ashes curl and thrill
 Thin ghosts of all those papers too.

X

The table answered, Not quite all;
 He saved and folded up one sheet,
And sealed it fast, and let it fall;
 And here it lies now white and neat.
Whereon the letter's whisper came,
 My writing is closed up too well;
Outside there's not a single name,
 And who should read me I can't tell.

XI

The mirror sneered with scornful spite,
 (That ancient crack which spoiled her looks
Had marred her temper), Write and write!
 And read those stupid, worn-out books!
That's all he does, read, write, and read,
 And smoke that nasty pipe which stinks:
He never takes the slightest heed
 How any of us feels or thinks.

XII

But Lucy fifty times a day
    Would come and smile here in my face,   90
Adjust a tress that curled astray,
    Or tie a ribbon with more grace:
She looked so young and fresh and fair,
    She blushed with such a charming bloom,
It did one good to see her there,   95
    And brightened all things in the room.

XIII

She did not sit hours stark and dumb
    As pale as moonshine by the lamp;
To lie in bed when day was come,
    And leave us curtained chill and damp.   100
She slept away the dreary dark,
    And rose to greet the pleasant morn;
And sang as gaily as a lark
    While busy as the flies sun-born.

XIV

And how she loved us every one;   105
    And dusted this and mended that,
With trills and laughs and freaks of fun,
    And tender scoldings in her chat!
And then her bird, that sang as shrill
    As she sang sweet; her darling flowers   110
That grew there in the window-sill,
    Where she would sit at work for hours.

XV

It was not much she ever wrote;
    Her fingers had good work to do;
Say, once a week a pretty note;   115
    And very long it took her too.
And little more she read, I wis;
    Just now and then a pictured sheet,
Besides those letters she would kiss
    And croon for hours, they were so sweet.   120

XVI

She had her friends too, blithe young girls,
    Who whispered, babbled, laughed, caressed,
And romped and danced with dancing curls,
    And gave our life a joyous zest.
But with this dullard, glum and sour,   125
    Not one of all his fellow-men
Has ever passed a social hour;
    We might be in some wild beast's den.

XVII

This long tirade aroused the bed,
    Who spoke in deep and ponderous bass,   130
Befitting that calm life he led,
    As if firm-rooted in his place:
In broad majestic bulk alone,
    As in thrice venerable age,
He stood at once the royal throne,   135
    The monarch, the experienced sage:

XVIII

I know what is and what has been;
    Not anything to me comes strange,
Who in so many years have seen
    And lived through every kind of change.   140
I know when men are good or bad,
    When well or ill, he slowly said;
When sad or glad, when sane or mad,
    And when they sleep alive or dead.

XIX

At this last word of solemn lore   145
    A tremor circled through the gloom,
As if a crash upon the floor
    Had jarred and shaken all the room:
For nearly all the listening things
    Were old and worn, and knew what curse   150
Of violent change death often brings,
    From good to bad, from bad to worse;

XX

They get to know each other well,
    To feel at home and settled down;
Death bursts among them like a shell,   155
    And strews them over all the town.
The bed went on, This man who lies
    Upon me now is stark and cold;
He will not any more arise,
    And do the things he did of old.   160

XXI

But we shall have short peace or rest;
    For soon up here will come a rout,
And nail him in a queer long chest,
    And carry him like luggage out.
They will be muffled all in black,   165
    And whisper much, and sigh and weep:
But he will never more come back,
    And some one else in me must sleep.

XXII

Thereon a little phial shrilled,
    Here empty on the chair I lie: 170
I heard one say, as I was filled,
    With half of this a man would die.
The man there drank me with slow breath,
    And murmured, Thus ends barren strife:
O sweeter, thou cold wine of death,   175
    Than ever sweet warm wine of life.

XXIII

One of my cousins long ago,
    A little thing, the mirror said,
Was carried to a couch to show,
    Whether a man was really dead.   180
Two great improvements marked the case:
    He did not blur her with his breath,
His many-wrinkled, twitching face
    Was smooth old ivory: verdict, Death.—

XXIV

It lay, the lowest thing there, lulled 185
    Sweet-sleep-like in corruption's truce;
The form whose purpose was annulled,
    While all the other shapes meant use.
It lay, the *he* become now *it*,
    Unconscious of the deep disgrace, 190
Unanxious how its parts might flit
    Through what new forms in time and space.

XXV

It lay and preached, as dumb things do,
    More powerfully than tongues can prate;
Though life be torture through and through, 195
    Man is but weak to plain of fate:
The drear path crawls on drearier still
    To wounded feet and hopeless breast?
Well, he can lie down when he will,
    And straight all ends in endless rest. 200

XXVI

And while the black night nothing saw,
    And till the cold morn came at last,
That old bed held the room in awe
    With tales of its experience vast.
It thrilled the gloom; it told such tales 205
    Of human sorrows and delights,
Of fever moans and infant wails,
    Of births and deaths and bridal nights.

(wr. 1867–8; pub. 1872)

Roden (Berkeley Wriothesley) Noel (1834–1894)

178.   *At Court*

    Beholding with a listless eye
    A gaily-apparelled train
    Of many ladies passing by,
    With a delightful pain
    My heart was taken unaware 5
    In very sweet suspense;

Amid the crowd unfair and fair
A hallowed influence
Stole on me, like some fountain sweet
That mantles in the brine 10
Of unrefreshing seas to greet
A mariner's lips that pine;
Stole on me from a girlish face
That passed among the rest;
Like hers whom I may ne'er embrace, 15
Hers who hath never blest
These many pallid latter years,
Nor may for evermore
Shine on my soul for all my tears,
As in the days of yore.... 20
Was it ever heard that a hallowed face
Of one whom hearts enwound
Faded slowly, and left no trace
In death's chill mist profound,
Yet later unto living eyes, 25
That yearned with mute despair,
Dawned faint again with sweet surprise,
And the old loving air?
Because so warm a human love
With tremulous living breath 30
Had power to charm, and melt and move
Inviolable Death!
Nay, that hath never, never been;
She may not come again,
My sister, my long-lost Kathleen, 35
Into our world of pain!
For well I know the girlish face!
Her child, her very own,
Left here, lest we whom she forsook
Might wither all alone! 40
And so in sooth she blooms anew
To bless our later time,
Beautiful now as when she blew
About my boyish prime.
Fair child! thou risest from a grave; 45
To me thy silken hair
Seems radiant with flowers that wave
Above thy mother there.
Thy face is toward the dawning bright;
And One will lead thee on, 50
Tranquil for ever in the light,
Until the day be done!

179.   *A Vision of the Desert*

    Methought I saw the morning bloom
    A solemn wilderness illume,
    Desert sand and empty air:
    Yet in a moment I was aware
    Of One who grew from forth the East,   5
    Mounted upon a vasty Beast.
    It swung with silent, equal stride,
    With a mighty shadow by the side:
    The tawny, tufted hair was frayed;
    The long, protruding snout was laid   10
    Level before it; looking calm away
    From that imperial rising of the Day.
    Methought a very awful One
    Towered speechless thereupon:
    All the figure like a cloud   15
    An ample mantle did enshroud,
    Folding heavily dark and white,
    Concealing all the face from sight,
    Save where through storm-like rifts there came
    A terrible gleam of eyes like flame.   20

    Then I beheld how on his arm
    A child was lying without alarm.
    With innocent rest it lay asleep;
    Awakening soon to laugh and leap;
    Yet well I knew, whatever passed,   25
    The arm that held would hold it fast.
    Nor ever then it sought to know
    Whose tender strength encircled so,
    Living incuriously wise
    Under the terrible flame of eyes.   30
    In those sweet early morning hours
    It played with dewy, wreathing flowers,
    Drinking oft from a little flask
    Under the mantle: I heard it ask:
    Yea, and at other times the cooling cup   35
    Gentle and merciful He tilted up.

    But when the sun began to burn,
    I saw the child more restless turn,
    Seeking to view the silent One:
    Then, growing graver thereupon,   40
    It whispered "Father!" but I never heard

If any lips in answer stirred.
Yet if no answer reached the child,
I know not why he lay and smiled,
Raising his little arms on high   45
In a solemn rapture quietly!

   The shadow moved, and growing less,
A blue blaze ruled the wilderness.
The child, alert with life and fire,
Gazed all around with infinite desire.   50
Erect he sat, contented now no more
To nestle, and feed upon the homely store:
He searched the lessening distance whence they came;
He peered into the clear cærulean flame;
His hand would mingle with the shaggy hair   55
Of that enormous Living Thing which bare,
Whose feet were planted in the powdery ground
With ne'er a pause, with ne'er a sound.
Yon fascinating, wondrous Infinite
His clear young eyes explored with keen delight: 60
He gazed into the muffled Countenance,
Undazzled with the rifted radiance:
Then, giving names to all that he espied,
He murmured with a bright triumphant pride,
"I hold their secret: lo! I am satisfied."   65
Oh! it was rare to see the lovely child,
As with a gaze ecstatical he smiled,
Following with eager, splendour-beaming eyes
A bird magnificent, who sailed the skies
On vast expanded plumes of sanguine white,   70
Enamoured of transcendent azure light,
Higher and higher soaring to the sun;
Claiming a share in his dominion;
Elate with ardour, like unwearying youth,
Imperially at home in awful realms of Truth!   75

   But ah! the sun beat fierce and merciless
Upon the boundless, barren wilderness.
Then soon, responsive to a slakeless thirst,
Behold upon his ravished sight there burst
A vision of a far-off lake most fair,   80
Where many a palm was dallying with air,
And soft mimosa: how alluringly
Smiled the sweet water in a blinding sky!
Can he not hear a gentle turtle coo
Among light leaves, yea, very wavelets blue   85

Lapping among green reeds upon the shore,
Calling him to abide for evermore?
Ah! how doth he impetuous entreat,
And chide the silent, never-lingering feet!
Yet was it strange—for as the feet advanced,   90
The lake receded, and the waters danced
An eerie dance with all the belts of trees,
And mingled with them, till the sand with these
On the horizon made a marge that wavered,
And all blew sidelong, thin white flame that quavered—   95
Then one low whispered, "'Tis the Devil's water!"
While in his ear there pealed cruel, unearthly laughter.
On this the child fell ill with fever,
Made many a vain yet wild endeavour
To fling himself from forth the grasp   100
That held with ne'er-relaxing clasp,
Murmuring, "None holds me fast;
I am a plaything of the blast."
But the Rider from the girdled store
Ministered to him as before.   105

   And while the shadow veered by stealth,
A measure of his primal health
The boy resumed: an air that fanned
Blew veritably o'er the sand;
And little birds before them flew,   110
Vested in a sober hue,
A paly brown, to suit the home
Where 'tis their destiny to roam.
Yet I am sure that ne'er a bird
Fluting more soft and sweet was heard   115
Among the lawns of Paradise,
Than these in such a humble guise,
Who, without any rest or haste,
Travel warbling o'er the waste.
Moreover in the sterile soil   120
Some spots of verdure, while the travellers toil,
Arise; yea, even the sweet oases,
That vanished with the feigning, undulating graces,
Were fair and real delight, however fleeing,
With law distinct of transitory being;   125
Only illusion for deluding eyes,
That yearn for what nor waste nor world supplies,
Some dim ideal of the soul,
That ever loves, and grows toward the illimitable whole.

But ever, as they two solitary range, 130
And as the immeasurable horizons change,
Upon the child more burdensome doth lie
Sense of impenetrable mystery.
Erst he imagined that he chose to go;
But now he feels, whether he will or no 135
One carries him: he joyed to be in life
For possibilities of boundless strife,
Wresting resplendent secrets bold from all:
Now the unmasked immensities appal,
Weighing incumbent on the sense and thought, 140
As on a dwindling grain of dust, as on a thing of nought!
A moment looking toward the shrouded Fac
Now is he fain his timid eyes to abase:
"Father, unveil!" he tremulously cries,
Fearing he asks impossibilities. 145

Yet hearken! voices musical
Like dew upon the desert fall,
Rising and falling,
Calling, calling!
Very plaintive, sweet, and low, 150
As the lonely pilgrims go:
Are they spirits of the wild,
Calling, answering low and mild?
Is it a voice of one departed,
Plaining gentle, unquiet-hearted, 155
Vainly hungering to enfold
His belovèd as of old?
Severed from our living kind,
In a feeble, wandering wind
Wandering ever? none can tell 160
Whence the mystic murmurs well:
But oft an Arab, roaming far
Over sands of Saharâ,
Hears the sweet mysterious measure
With a solemn-hearted pleasure, 165
Saying, "No wind among the stones
Breathes the rare unearthly tones!"
And howsoe'er it be, they tell
The soul of things ineffable,
Of a life beyond our death or birth, 170
Of a universe beyond the earth!

Monotonously weary seemed the way,
While light declining faded slowly away.
Some haze obscured a gradual westering sun,
And all the oppressive firmament was wan.   175
In it voluminous appears to form
From the horizon a continent of storm,
A ponderous bulk of gathering indigo,
Tinged in its formidable overflow
With hues of livid purple poison-flowers.   180
In ghastlier whiteness for the night that
    lowers,
Strewing forlorn the desolate desert pale,
Some grinning skeletons of men assail
My vision; while a monstrous bird of prey
From a putrescent corse rends fierce away   185
The clinging flesh with horrid sound of tearing,
Its beak abruptly plunging, pulling, baring;
Bald-headed, hideous neck low crouched betwixt
The pressure of strong talons curved, infixed:
Now the proud brain, like fearful Madness, mangling,   190
Like Sin now with the reeking bosom wrangling;
Like ignorance, disease, war, tyranny, starvation,
Eating the vitals of a noble fallen nation!
This creature, as they pass, a moment glaring
Voracious-eyed, with vasty vans that cover—   195
A little further on obscene doth hover
A grey hyena, and he laughs a peal
Of beastly laughter, scraping up a meal
Loathsome from forth the sand: there is a howl
Dolefully borne from where the lean wolves prowl!   200
Then silence falls upon the deepening gloom,
And sultry air forebodes the smothering Simoom.
Looking toward the child with deep dismay,
I noted his fair ringlets grown to grey,
And sparse like withered bents upon his head: 205
His pale, worn countenance was drawn with dread;
Yet in his eyes there burned a grand resolve,
No sights of terror lightly might dissolve.
And now I heard him murmur, "Mighty Father!
I trust thee; yea, to thee I cling the rather,   210
Albeit I may not see thine awful face!"
Then I was sure he felt the strong embrace
Tighten around him, though a Skeleton
Came stalking from the night to lead them on:

A far-off murmur swelled into a wildering roar;
A hurricane of flame and sand whirled like a conqueror!
And when the o'erwhelming terrible death-tempest on them broke,
The shrinking child crept nestling close under the Father's cloak.
Then darkness swallowed the portentous plain
When faint it dawned upon mine eyes again,
Lo ! there was moonlight in a sky serene:
All lay at peace beneath the melancholy sheen.
No voice was heard, no living thing was seen.
Yet ere I was aware, that awful Apparition
Once more emerged upon my mortal vision—
The shrouded, dim, unutterable Form,
With eyes that flame as through the rifts of storm,
Mounted on that colossal Living Thing,
Bearing the child now, softly slumbering—
While all confused immeasurable shadow fling.
Peacefully lay the boy's pale, silent head:
And, looking long, I knew that he was dead.
Then all my wildered anguish forced a way
Through my wild lips: "Reveal, O Lord, I pray,
Whither thou carriest him!" I cried aloud:
No sound responded from the shadowy shroud;
Only methought that something like a hand
Was raised to point athwart the shadowy land;
And while afar the dwindling twain were borne,
I, gazing all around with eyes forlorn,
Divined the bloom of some unearthly morn!

Where was he carried? to an isle of calm,
Lulled with sweet water and the pensile palm?
Vanishing havens on the pilgrimage
Surely some more abiding home presage!
Or must the Sire attain always alone
The happy land, with never a living son?
O! awful, silent, everlasting One!
If thou must roam those islands of the West,
Ever with some dead child upon thy breast,
Who would have hailed the glory, being blest,
Eternity were one long moan for rest!
For do we not behold thee morn by morn,
Issuing from the East with one newborn,
Carrying him silently, none knoweth whither,
Knowing only all we travel swiftly thither?

William Morris (1834–1896)

180.   Tr. *The Odyssey of Homer (Book I)*

BOOK I

THE ARGUMENT

THE GODS ORDAIN THE RETURN OF ODYSSEUS: PALLAS GOES TO ITHACA AND IN THE LIKENESS OF MENTES HEARTENS UP TELEMACHUS, AND BIDS HIM CALL A MEETING OF MEN TO LAY HIS GRIEVANCE AGAINST THE WOOERS, AND THEN TO TAKE SHIP TO PYLOS AND SPARTA SEEKING TIDINGS OF HIS FATHER.

Tell me, O Muse, of the Shifty, the man who wandered afar,
After the Holy Burg, Troy-town, he had wasted with war;
He saw the towns of menfolk, and the mind of men did he learn;
As he warded his life in the world, and his fellow-farers' return,
Many a grief of heart on the deep-sea flood he bore,   5
Nor yet might he save his fellows, for all that he longed for it sore.
They died of their own souls' folly, for witless as they were
They ate up the beasts of the Sun, the Rider of the Air,
And he took away from them all their dear returning day;
O Goddess, O daughter of Zeus, from whencesoever ye may,   10
Gather the tale, and tell it, yea even to us at the last!

Now all the other heroes, who forth from the warfare passed
And fled from sheer destruction and 'scaped each man his bane,
Saved from the sea and the battle, at home they sat full fain;
But him alone, Odysseus, sore yearning after the strife   15
To get him back to his homestead, sore yearning for his wife,
Did the noble nymph Calypso, the Godhead's glory, hoard
In the hollow rocky places; for she longed for him for lord,
Yea and e'en when the circling seasons had brought the year to hand,
Wherein the Gods had doomed it that he should reach his land,   20
E'en Ithaca his homestead, not even then was he,
Though amidst his kin and his people, of heavy trouble free.

Know now, that of all the Godfolk there was none but pitied him,
Save that Poseidon only was with ceaseless wrath abrim
Against the God-like Hero from his house and his home shut out.   25

But he to the Æthiopians e'en now was gone about,
The far-dwellers outmost of menfolk; and these are sundered atwain,
Some dwell where the High-rider setteth, and some where he riseth again.
There then of bulls and of rams would he gather an hundred-fold,

And he sat him adown rejoicing and noble feast did hold. 30
But the rest in the hall were gathered of Zeus the Olympian lord.
So the Father of Gods and of men amidst them took up the word,
For mindful in heart was he of Ægistheus the noble one,
He that was slain of Orestes far-famed, Agamemnon's son.
Thus then to the deathless he spake, these things remembering still. 35

"Out on it! how do the menfolk to the Gods lay all their ill,
And say that of us it cometh; when they themselves indeed
Gain griefs from their own souls' folly beyond the fateful meed.
E'en as of late Ægistheus must wed Atrides' wife
In Doom's despite, and must slay him returning home from the strife. 40
Though his end. therefrom he wotted, and thereof we warned him plain,
Sending him Hermes withal, the keen-eyed Argus-bane,
Bidding him slay not the man, nor woo the wife to his bed.
'For vengeance shall come from Orestes for the son of Atreus dead
When the child is waxen a man and longeth his land to win:' 45
So spake Hermes, but nought prevailed with Ægistheus herein,
Despite of his goodly counsel. But now for all hath he paid."

Therewith the Grey-eyed, the Goddess Athene, answered and said:
"O Father, O Son of Cronos, O Highest of all that is high!
In a doom and a death most fitting indeed that man doth lie, 50
And e'en so may all men perish such deeds as this who earn!
But lo for the wise Odysseus as now my heart doth burn.
Luckless, aloof from his folk, long-lasting woe bears he
In an isle of the circling Ocean, and the navel of the Sea,
In an isle by trees grown over: in that house a Goddess dwells, 55
Daughter of Atlas the baleful, who knoweth all ocean wells
Whereso they be, and moreover he holdeth in his hand
The long-wrought pillars that sunder the heavens from the earthly land.
There the hapless man in sorrow this Atlas' Daughter hoards
And his heart for ever wooeth with soft and wheedling words 60
That of Ithaca nought he may mind him; but Odysseus longeth to see,
If it were but the smoke a-leaping from the land where he would be;
And now he yearneth for death. Nor yet doth thy dear heart
Heed aught of this, Olympian. But Odysseus for his part
Wrought he not holy deeds, and gifts to give thee joy 65
By the side of the ships of the Argives before wide-spreading Troy?
Then why doth thine anger O Zeus so sore against him drift?"

But to her made answer Zeus, the Lord that driveth the lift:
"O thou my child! what a word from the wall of thy teeth hath sped!
How should I ever forget Odysseus' goodlihead? 70
Whose mind overgoes all mortals, and hallowed gifts hath he given

To the deathless folk of the Gods, the lords of the wide-spread heaven.
But Poseidon Girdler of Earth his anger will not slake
Because of the eye bereft, and the blinded Cyclops' sake,
Polyphemus great as a god, whose might is far before   75
All others of the Cyclops: but him Thoosa bore
Daughter of Phorcys, the lord of the untilled salt-sea plain;
For with Poseidon she lay in the hollow rocks of the main.
Now therefore the Shaker of Earth, though the man he will not slay,
From the father-land of his folk still driveth him ever to stray.   80
But come! let us compass his ways, and bring his returning about,
So that at last Poseidon may let his wrath die out:
For nought is his might so mighty that one 'gainst all may strive,
E'en he alone contending with the Gods for ever alive."

181.   Tr. *The Aeneids of Virgil (Books I and VI)*

BOOK I

THE ARGUMENT

ÆNEAS AND HIS TROJANS BEING DRIVEN TO LIBYA BY A TEMPEST, HAVE GOOD WELCOME OF DIDO, QUEEN OF CARTHAGE.

Lo I am he who led the song through slender reed to cry,
And then, come forth from out the woods, the fields that are thereby
In woven verse I bade obey the hungry tillers' need:
Now I, who sang their merry toil, sing Mars and dreadful deed.

I sing of arms, I sing of him, who from the Trojan land
Thrust forth by Fate, to Italy and that Lavinian strand
First came: all tost about was he on earth and on the deep
By heavenly night for Juno's wrath, that had no mind to sleep:
And plenteous war he underwent ere he his town might frame   5
And set his Gods in Latian earth, whence is the Latin name,
And father-folk of Alba-town, and walls of mighty Rome.
Say, Muse, what wound of godhead was whereby all this must come,
How grieving, she, the Queen of Gods, a man so pious drave
To win such toil, to welter on through such a troublous wave: 10
—Can anger in immortal minds abide so fierce and fell?

There was a city of old time where Tyrian folk did dwell,
Called Carthage, facing far away the shores of Italy
And Tiber-mouth; fulfilled of wealth and fierce in arms was she,
And men say Juno loved her well o'er every other land,   15

Yea e'en o'er Samos: there were stored the weapons of her hand,
And there her chariot: even then she cherished the intent
To make her Lady of all Lands, if Fate might so be bent;
Yea had she heard how such a stem from Trojan blood should grow,
As, blooming fair, the Tyrian towers should one day overthrow,   20
That thence a folk, kings far and wide, most noble lords of fight,
Should come for bane of Libyan land: such web the Parcæ dight.
The Seed of Saturn, fearing this, and mindful how she erst
For her beloved Argive walls by Troy the battle nursed—
—Nay neither had the cause of wrath nor all those hurts of old   25
Failed from her mind: her inmost heart still sorely did enfold
That grief of body set at nought in Paris' doomful deed,
The hated race, and honour shed on heaven-rapt Ganymede—
So set on fire, that Trojan band o'er all the ocean tossed,
Those gleanings from Achilles' rage, those few the Greeks had lost,   30
She drave far off the Latin Land: for many a year they stray
Such wise as Fate would drive them on by every watery way.
—Lo, what there was to heave aloft in fashioning of Rome!

Now out of sight of Sicily the Trojans scarce were come
And merry spread their sails abroad and clave the sea with brass,   35
When Juno's heart, who nursed the wound that never thence would pass,
Spake out:
        "And must I, vanquished, leave the deed I have begun,
Nor save the Italian realm a king who comes of Teucer's son?
The Fates forbid it me forsooth! And Pallas, might not she
Burn up the Argive fleet and sink the Argives in the sea   40
For Oïleus' only fault and fury that he wrought?
She hurled the eager fire of Jove from cloudy dwelling caught,
And rent the ships and with the wind the heaped-up waters drew,
And him a-dying, and all his breast by wildfire smitten through,
The whirl of waters swept away on spiky crag to bide.   45
While I, who go forth Queen of Gods, the very Highest's bride
And sister, must I wage a war for all these many years
With one lone race? What! is there left a soul that Juno fears
Henceforth? or will one suppliant hand gifts on mine altar lay?"

So brooding in her fiery heart the Goddess went her way   50
Unto the fatherland of storm, full fruitful of the gale,
Æolia hight, where Æolus is king of all avail,
And far adown a cavern vast the bickering of the winds
And roaring tempests of the world with bolt and fetter binds:
They set the mountains murmuring much, a-growling angrily   55
About their bars, while Æolus sits in his burg on high,
And, sceptre-holding, softeneth them, and strait their wrath doth keep:

Yea but for that the earth and sea, and vault of heaven the deep,
They eager-swift would roll away and sweep adown of space:
For fear whereof the Father high in dark and hollow place   60
Hath hidden them, and high above a world of mountains thrown,
And given them therewithal a king, who, taught by law well known,
Now draweth, and now casteth loose the reins that hold them in:
To whom did suppliant Juno now in e'en such words begin:

"The Father of the Gods and men hath given thee might enow,   65
O Æolus, to smooth the sea, and make the storm-wind blow.
Hearken! a folk, my very foes, saileth the Tyrrhene main
Bearing their Troy to Italy, and Gods that were but vain:
Set on thy winds, and overwhelm their sunken ships at sea,
Or prithee scattered cast them forth, things drowned diversedly.   70
Twice seven nymphs are in my house of body passing fair:
Of whom indeed Deïopea is fairest fashioned there.
I give her thee in wedlock sure, and call her all thine own
To wear away the years with thee, for thy deserving shown
To me this day; of offspring fair she too shall make thee sire."   75

To whom spake Æolus: "O Queen, to search out thy desire
Is all thou needest toil herein; from me the deed should wend.
Thou mak'st my realm; the sway of all, and Jove thou mak'st my friend,
Thou givest me to lie with Gods when heavenly feast is dight,
And o'er the tempest and the cloud thou makest me of might."   80

Therewith against the hollow hill he turned him spear in hand
And hurled it on the flank thereof, and as an ordered band
By whatso door the winds rush out o'er earth in whirling blast,
And driving down upon the sea its lowest deeps upcast.
The East, the West together there, the Afric, that doth hold   85
A heart fulfilled of stormy rain, huge billows shoreward rolled.
Therewith came clamour of the men and whistling through the shrouds,
And heaven and day all suddenly were swallowed by the clouds
Away from eyes of Teucrian men; night on the ocean lies,
Pole thunders unto pole, and still with wildfire glare the skies,   90
And all things hold the face of death before the seamen's eyes.

Now therewithal Æneas' limbs grew weak with chilly dread,
He groaned, and lifting both his palms aloft to heaven, he said:
"O thrice and four times happy ye, that had the fate to fall
Before your fathers' faces there by Troy's beloved wall!   95

BOOK VI

THE ARGUMENT

ÆNEAS COMETH TO THE SIBYL OF CUMÆ, AND BY HER IS LED INTO THE UNDER-WORLD, AND THERE BEHOLDETH MANY STRANGE THINGS, & IN THE END MEETETH HIS FATHER, ANCHISES, WHO TELLETH HIM OF THE DAYS TO COME.

So spake he weeping, and his host let loose from every band,
Until at last they draw anigh Cumæ's Eubœan strand.
They turn the bows from off the main; the tothèd anchors' grip
Makes fast the keels; the shore is hid by many a curvèd ship.
Hot-heart the youthful company leaps on the Westland's shore;   5
Part falleth on to seek them out the seed of fiery store
That flint-veins hide; part runneth through the dwellings of the deer,
The thicket steads, and each to each the hidden streams they bare.

But good Æneas seeks the house where King Apollo bides,
The mighty den, the secret place set far apart, that hides   10
The awful Sibyl, whose great soul and heart he seeketh home,
The Seer of Delos, showing her the hidden things to come:
And so the groves of Trivia and golden house they gain.

Now Dædalus, as tells the tale, fleeing from Minos' reign,
Durst trust himself to heaven on wings swift hastening, and swim forth   15
Along the road ne'er tried before unto the chilly north;
So light at last o'er Chalcis' towers he hung amid the air,
Then, come adown to earth once more, to thee he hallowed here,
O Phœbus, all his wingèd oars, and built thee mighty fane:
Androgeus' death was on the doors; then paying of the pain   20
By those Cecropians; bid, alas, each year to give in turn
Seven bodies of their sons;—lo there, the lots drawn from the urn.
But facing this the Gnosian land draws up amid the sea:
There is the cruel bull-lust wrought, and there Pasiphaë
Embraced by guile: the blended babe is there, the twiformed thing,   25
The Minotaur, that evil sign of Venus' cherishing;
And there the tangled house and toil that ne'er should be undone:
But ruth of Dædalus himself a queen's love-sorrow won,
And he himself undid the snare and winding wilderment,
Guiding the blind feet with the thread. Thou, Icarus, wert blent   30
Full oft with such a work be sure, if grief forbade it not;
But twice he tried to shape in gold the picture of thy lot,
And twice the father's hands fell down.
                                Long had their eyes read o'er
Such matters, but Achates, now, sent on a while before,
Was come with that Deïphobe, the Glaucus' child, the maid   35

Of Phœbus and of Trivia, and such a word she said:
"The hour will have no tarrying o'er fair shows for idle eyes;
'Twere better from an unyoked herd seven steers to sacrifice,
And e'en so many hosts of ewes in manner due culled out."

She spake; her holy bidding then the warriors go about, 40
Nor tarry; into temple high she calls the Teucrian men,
Where the huge side of Cumæ's rock is carven in a den,
Where are an hundred doors to come, an hundred mouths to go,
Whence e'en so many awful sounds, the Sibyl's answers flow.
But at the threshold cried the maid: "Now is the hour awake 45
For asking—Ah, the God, the God!"
                                And as the word she spake
Within the door, all suddenly her visage and her hue
Were changed, and all her sleekèd hair, and gasping breath she drew,
And with the rage her wild heart swelled, and greater was she grown,
Nor mortal-voiced; for breath of God upon her heart was blown 50
As He drew nigher:
                "Art thou dumb of vows and prayers, forsooth,
Trojan Æneas, art thou dumb? unprayed, the mighty mouth
Of awe-mazed house shall open not."
                              Even such a word she said,
Then hushed: through hardened Teucrian bones swift ran the chilly dread,
And straight the king from inmost heart the flood of prayers doth pour: 55
"Phœbus, who all the woe of Troy hast pitied evermore,
Who Dardan shaft and Paris' hands in time agone didst speed
Against Achilles' body there, who me withal didst lead
Over the seas that go about so many a mighty land,
Through those Massylian folks remote, and length of Syrtes' sand, 60
Till now I hold that Italy that ever drew aback;
And now perchance a Trojan fate we, even we may lack.
Ye now, O Gods and Goddesses, to whom a stumbling-stone
Was Ilium in the days of old, and Dardan folk's renown,
May spare the folk of Pergamus. But thou, O holiest, 65
O Maid that knowest things to come, grant thou the Latin rest
To Teucrian men, and Gods of Troy, the straying wayworn powers!
For surely now no realm I ask but such as Fate makes ours.
To Phœbus and to Trivia then a temple will I raise,
A marble world; in Phœbus' name will hallow festal days: 70
Thee also in our realm to be full mighty shrines await,
There will I set thine holy lots and hidden words of fate
Said to my folk, and hallow there well-chosen men for thee,
O Holy One: But give thou not thy songs to leaf of tree,
Lest made a sport to hurrying gales confusedly they wend; 75
But sing them thou thyself, I pray!"

                    Therewith his words had end.
Meanwhile the Seer-maid, not yet tamed to Phœbus, raves about
The cave, still striving from her breast to cast the godhead out;
But yet the more the mighty God her mouth bewildered wears,
Taming her wild heart, fashioning her soul with weight of fears.　　　80
At last the hundred mighty doors fly open, touched of none,
And on the air the answer floats of that foreseeing one:

"O Thou, who dangers of the sea hast throughly worn away,
Abides thee heavier toil of earth: the Dardans on a day
Shall come to that Lavinian land,—leave fear thereof afar:　　　85
Yet of their coming shall they rue. Lo, war, war, dreadful war!
And Tiber bearing plenteous blood upon his foaming back.
Nor Simoïs there, nor Xanthus' stream, nor Dorian camp shall lack:
Yea, once again in Latin land Achilles is brought forth,
God-born no less: nor evermore shall mighty Juno's wrath　　　90
Fail Teucrian men. Ah, how shalt thou, fallen on evil days,
To all Italian lands and folks thine hands beseeching raise!
Lo, once again a stranger bride brings woeful days on Troy,
Once more the wedding of a foe.
But thou, yield not to any ill, but set thy face, and wend　　　95
The bolder where thy fortune leads; the dawn of perils' end,
Whence least thou mightest look for it, from Greekish folk shall come."

Suchwise the Seer of Cumæ sang from out her inner home
The dreadful double words, wherewith the cavern moans again,
As sooth amid the mirk she winds: Apollo shakes the rein　　　100
Over the maddened one, and stirs the strings about her breast;
But when her fury lulled awhile and maddened mouth had rest,
Hero Æneas thus began:
                          "No face of any care,
O maiden, can arise on me in any wise unware:
Yea, all have I forecast; my mind hath worn through everything.　　　105
One prayer I pray, since this they call the gateway of the King
Of Nether-earth, and Acheron's o'erflow this mirky mere:
O let me meet the eyes and mouth of my dead father dear;
O open me the holy gate, and teach me where to go!
I bore him on these shoulders once from midmost of the foe,　　　110
From flame and weapons thousandfold against our goings bent;
My yoke-fellow upon the road o'er every sea he went,
'Gainst every threat of sea and sky a hardy heart he held,
Though worn and feeble past decay and feebleness of eld.
Yea, he it was who bade me wend, a suppliant, to thy door,　　　115
And seek thee out: O holy one, cast thou thy pity o'er
Father and son! All things thou canst, nor yet hath Hecaté

Set thee to rule Avernus' woods an empty Queen to be.
Yea, Orpheus wrought with Thracian harp and strings of tuneful might
To draw away his perished love from midmost of the night.   120
Yea, Pollux, dying turn for turn, his brother borrowed well,
And went and came the road full oft—Of Theseus shall I tell?
Or great Alcides? Ah, I too from highest Jove am sprung."

182.   *The Story of Sigurd the Volsung*

And that was at eve of the day; and lo now, Signy the white
Wan-faced and eager-eyed stole through the beginning of night
To the place where the builders built, and the thralls with lingering hands
Had roofed in the grave of Sigmund and hidden the glory of lands,
But over the head of Sinfiotli for a space were the rafters bare.   5
Gold then to the thralls she gave, and promised them days full fair
If they held their peace for ever of the deed that then she did:
And nothing they gainsayed it; so she drew forth something hid,
In wrappings of wheat-straw winded, and into Sinfiotli's place
She cast it all down swiftly; then she covereth up her face,   10
And beneath the winter starlight she wended swift away.
But her gift do the thralls deem victual, and the thatch on the hall they lay,
And depart, they too, to their slumber, now dight was the dwelling of death.

Then Sigmund hears Sinfiotli, how he cries through the stone and saith:
"Best unto babe is mother, well sayeth the elder's saw;   15
Here hath Signy sent me swine's-flesh in windings of wheaten straw."

And again he held him silent of bitter words or of sweet;
And quoth Sigmund, "What hath betided? is an adder in the meat!"
Then loud his fosterling laughed: "Yea, a worm of bitter tooth,
The serpent of the Branstock, the sword of thy days of youth!   20
I have felt the hilts aforetime; I have felt how the letters run
On each side of the trench of blood and the point of that glorious one.
O mother, O mother of kings! we shall live and our days shall be sweet!
I have loved thee well aforetime, I shall love thee more when we meet."

Then Sigmund heard the sword-point smite on the stone wall's side,   25
And slowly mid the darkness therethrough he heard it gride
As against it bore Sinfiotli: but he cried out at the last:
"It biteth, O my fosterer! it cleaves the earth-bone fast!
Now learn we the craft of the masons that another day may come
When we build a house for King Siggeir, a strait unlovely home."   30

Then in the grave-mound's darkness did Sigmund the King upstand,
And unto that saw of battle he set his naked hand;
And hard the gift of Odin home to their breasts they drew;
Sawed Sigmund, sawed Sinfiotli, till the stone was cleft atwo,
And they met and kissed together: then they hewed and heaved full hard   35
Till lo, through the bursten rafters the winter heavens bestarred!
And they leap out merry-hearted; nor is there need to say
A many words between them of whither was the way.

For they took the night-watch sleeping, and slew them one and all,
And then on the winter fagots they made them haste to fall,   40
They pile the oak-trees cloven, and when the oak-beams fail
They bear the ash and the rowan, and build a mighty bale
About the dwelling of Siggeir, and lay the torch therein.
Then they drew their swords and watched it till the flames began to win
Hard on to the mid-hall's rafters, and those feasters of the folk,   45
As the fire-flakes fell among them, to their last of days awoke.
By the gable-door stood Sigmund, and fierce Sinfiotli stood
Red-lit by the door of the women in the lane of blazing wood:
To death each doorway opened, and death was in the hall.

Then amid the gathered Goth-folk 'gan Siggeir the King to call: 50
"Who lit the fire I burn in, and what shall buy me peace?
Will ye take my heaped up treasure, or ten years of my fields' increase,
Or half of my father's kingdom? O toilers at the oar,
O wasters of the sea-plain, now labour ye no more!
But take the gifts I bid you, and lie upon the gold,   55
And clothe your limbs in purple and the silken women hold!"

But a great voice cried o'er the fire: "Nay, no such men are we,
No tuggers at the hawser, no wasters of the sea:
We will have the gold and the purple when we list such things to win;
But now we think on our fathers, and avenging of our kin.   60
Not all King Siggeir's kingdom, and not all the world's increase
For ever and for ever, shall buy thee life and peace.
For now is the tree-bough blossomed that sprang from murder's seed;
And the death-doomed and the buried are they that do the deed;
Now when the dead shall ask thee by whom thy days were done,   65
Thou shalt say by Sigmund the Volsung, and Sinfiotli, Signy's son."

183.   *Atalanta's Race*

THE ARGUMENT

ATALANTA, DAUGHTER OF KING SCHŒNEUS, NOT WILLING TO LOSE HER VIRGIN'S ESTATE, MADE IT A LAW TO ALL SUITORS THAT THEY SHOULD RUN A RACE WITH HER IN THE PUBLIC PLACE, AND IF THEY FAILED TO OVERCOME HER SHOULD DIE UNREVENGED; AND THUS MANY BRAVE MEN PERISHED. AT LAST CAME MILANION, THE SON OF AMPHIDAMAS, WHO, OUTRUNNING HER WITH THE HELP OF VENUS, GAINED THE VIRGIN AND WEDDED HER.

  Through thick Arcadian woods a hunter went,
Following the beasts up, on a fresh spring day;
But since his horn-tipped bow but seldom bent,
Now at the noontide nought had happed to slay,
Within a vale he called his hounds away   5
Hearkening the echoes of his lone voice cling
About the cliffs and through the beech-trees ring.

  But when they ended, still awhile he stood,
And but the sweet familiar thrush could hear,
And all the day-long noises of the wood,   10
And o'er the dry leaves of the vanished year
His hounds' feet pattering as they drew anear,
And heavy breathing from their heads low hung,
To see the mighty cornel bow unstrung.

  Then smiling did he turn to leave the place,   15
But with his first step some new fleeting thought
A shadow cast across his sun-burnt face;
I think the golden net that April brought
From some warm world his wavering soul had caught;
For, sunk in vague sweet longing, did he go   20
Betwixt the trees with doubtful steps and slow.

  Yet howsoever slow he went, at last
The trees grew sparser, and the wood was done;
Whereon one farewell backward look he cast,
Then, turning round to see what place was won,   25
With shaded eyes looked underneath the sun,
And o'er green meads and new-turned furrows brown
Beheld the gleaming of King Schœneus' town.

    So thitherward he turned, and on each side
The folk were busy on the teeming land,   30
And man and maid from the brown furrows cried,
Or midst the newly-blossomed vines did stand,
And as the rustic weapon pressed the hand
Thought of the nodding of the well-filled ear,
Or how the knife the heavy bunch should shear.   35

    Merry it was: about him sung the birds,
The spring flowers bloomed along the firm dry road,
The sleek-skinned mothers of the sharp-horned herds
Now for the barefoot milking-maidens lowed;
While from the freshness of his blue abode,   40
Glad his death-bearing arrows to forget,
The broad sun blazed, nor scattered plagues as yet.

    Through such fair things unto the gates he came,
And found them open, as though peace were there;
Wherethrough, unquestioned of his race or name,   45
He entered, and along the streets 'gan fare,
Which at the first of folk were well-nigh bare;
But pressing on, and going more hastily,
Men hurrying too he 'gan at last to see.

    Following the last of these, he still pressed on,   50
Until an open space he came unto,
Where wreaths of fame had oft been lost and won,
For feats of strength folk there were wont to do.
And now our hunter looked for something new,
Because the whole wide space was bare, and stilled   55
The high seats were, with eager people filled.

    There with the others to a seat he gat,
Whence he beheld a broidered canopy,
'Neath which in fair array King Schœneus sat
Upon his throne with councillors thereby;   60
And underneath his well-wrought seat and high,
He saw a golden image of the sun,
A silver image of the Fleet-foot One.

    A brazen altar stood beneath their feet
Whereon a thin flame flickered in the wind,   65
Nigh this a herald clad in raiment meet
Made ready even now his horn to wind,

By whom a huge man held a sword, entwined
With yellow flowers; these stood a little space
From off the altar, nigh the starting-place.   70

And there two runners did the sign abide
Foot set to foot: a young man slim and fair,
Crisp-haired, well knit, with firm limbs often tried
In places where no man his strength may spare;
Dainty his thin coat was, and on his hair   75
A golden circlet of renown he wore,
And in his hand an olive garland bore.

But on this day with whom shall he contend?
A maid stood by him like Diana clad
When in the woods she lists her bow to bend,   80
Too fair for one to look on and be glad,
Who scarcely yet has thirty summers had,
If he must still behold her from afar;
Too fair to let the world live free from war.

She seemed all earthly matters to forget;   85
Of all tormenting lines her face was clear,
Her wide grey eyes upon the goal were set
Calm and unmoved, as though no soul were near;
But her foe trembled as a man in fear,
Nor from her loveliness one moment turned   90
His anxious face with fierce desire that burned.

Now through the hush there broke the trumpet's clang
Just as the setting sun made eventide.
Then from light feet a spurt of dust there sprang,
And swiftly were they running side by side;   95
But silent did the thronging folk abide
Until the turning-post was reached at last,
And round about it still abreast they passed.

But when the people saw how close they ran,
When halfway to the starting-point they were,   100
A cry of joy broke forth, whereat the man
Headed the white-foot runner, and drew near
Unto the very end of all his fear;
And scarce his straining feet the ground could feel,
And bliss unhoped for o'er his heart 'gan steal.   105

But midst the loud victorious shouts he heard
Her footsteps drawing nearer, and the sound
Of fluttering raiment, and thereat afeard
His flushed and eager face he turned around,
And even then he felt her past him bound   110
Fleet as the wind, but scarcely saw her there
Till on the goal she laid her fingers fair.

There stood she breathing like a little child
Amid some warlike clamour laid asleep,
For no victorious joy her red lips smiled,   115
Her cheek its wonted freshness did but keep;
No glance lit up her clear grey eyes and deep,
Though some divine thought softened all her face
As once more rang the trumpet through the place.

But her late foe stopped short amidst his course,   120
One moment gazed upon her piteously,
Then with a groan his lingering feet did force
To leave the spot whence he her eyes could see;
And, changed like one who knows his time must be
But short and bitter, without any word   125
He knelt before the bearer of the sword;

Then high rose up the gleaming deadly blade,
Bared of its flowers, and through the crowded place
Was silence now, and midst of it the maid
Went by the poor Wretch at a gentle pace,   130
And he to hers upturned his sad white face;
Nor did his eyes behold another sight
Ere on his soul there fell eternal night.

So was the pageant ended, and all folk
Talking of this and that familiar thing   135
In little groups from that sad concourse broke,
For now the shrill bats were upon the wing,
And soon dark night would slay the evening,
And in dark gardens sang the nightingale
Her little-heeded, oft-repeated tale.   140

And with the last of all the hunter went,
Who, wondering at the strange sight he had seen
Prayed an old man to tell him what it meant,
Both why the vanquished man so slain had been,

And if the maiden were an earthly queen, 145
Or rather what much more she seemed to be,
No sharer in the world's mortality.

"Stranger," said he, "I pray she soon may die
Whose lovely youth has slain so many an one!
King Schœneus' daughter is she verily, 150
Who when her eyes first looked upon the sun
Was fain to end her life but new begun,
For he had vowed to leave but men alone
Sprung from his loins when he from earth was gone.

"Therefore he bade one leave her in the wood, 155
And let wild things deal with her as they might,
But this being done, some cruel God thought good
To save her beauty in the world's despite:
Folk say that her, so delicate and white
As now she is, a rough root-grubbing bear 160
Amidst her shapeless cubs at first did rear.

"In course of time the woodfolk slew her nurse,
And to their rude abode the youngling brought,
And reared her up to be a kingdom's curse,
Who grown a woman, of no kingdom thought, 165
But armed and swift, mid beasts destruction wrought,
Nor spared two shaggy centaur kings to slay
To whom her body seemed an easy prey.

"So to this city, led by fate, she came
Whom known by signs, whereof I cannot tell, 170
King Schœneus for his child at last did claim,
Nor otherwhere since that day doth she dwell,
Sending too many a noble soul to hell—
What! thine eyes glisten! What then, thinkest thou
Her shining head unto the yoke to bow? 175

"Listen, my son, and love some other maid,
For she the saffron gown will never wear,
And on no flower-strewn couch shall she be laid,
Nor shall her voice make glad a lover's ear:
Yet if of Death thou hast not any fear, 180
Yea, rather, if thou lovest him utterly,
Thou still mayst woo her ere thou com'st to die,

"Like him that on this day thou sawest lie dead;
For, fearing as I deem the sea-born one,
The maid has vowed e'en such a man to wed   185
As in the course her swift feet can outrun,
But whoso fails herein, his days are done:
He came the nighest that was slain to-day,
Although with him I deem she did but play.

"Behold, such mercy Atalanta gives   190
To those that long to win her loveliness;
Be wise! be sure that many a maid there lives
Gentler than she, of beauty little less,
Whose swimming eyes thy loving words shall bless,
When in some garden, knee set close to knee,   195
Thou sing'st the song that love may teach to thee."

So to the hunter spake that ancient man,
And left him for his own home presently:
But he turned round, and through the moonlight wan
Reached the thick wood, and there 'twixt tree and tree   200
Distraught he passed the long night feverishly,
'Twixt sleep and waking, and at dawn arose
To wage hot war against his speechless foes.

There to the hart's flank seemed his shaft to grow,
As panting down the broad green glades he flew,   205
There by his horn the Dryads well might know
His thrust against the bear's heart had been true,
And there Adonis' bane his javelin slew,
But still in vain through rough and smooth he went,
For none the more his restlessness was spent.   210

So wandering, he to Argive cities came,
And in the lists with valiant men he stood,
And by great deeds he won him praise and fame,
And heaps of wealth for little-valued blood;
But none of all these things, or life, seemed good   215
Unto his heart, where still unsatisfied
A ravenous longing warred with fear and pride.

Therefore it happed when but a month had gone
Since he had left King Schœneus' city old,
In hunting-gear again, again alone   220
The forest-border meads did he behold,

Where still mid thoughts of August's quivering gold
Folk hoed the wheat, and clipped the vine in trust
Of faint October's purple-foaming must.

 And once again he passed the peaceful gate,   225
While to his beating heart his lips did lie,
That owning not victorious love and fate,
Said, half aloud: "And here too must I try,
To win of alien men the mastery,
And gather for my head fresh meed of fame   230
And cast new glory on my father's name."

 In spite of that, how beat his heart, when first
Folk said to him: "And art thou come to see
That which still makes our city's name accurst
Among all mothers for its cruelty?   235
Then know indeed that fate is good to thee,
Because to-morrow a new luckless one
Against the whitefoot maid is pledged to run."

 So on the morrow with no curious eyes
As once he did, that piteous sight he saw,   240
Nor did that wonder in his heart arise
As toward the goal the conquering maid 'gan draw,
Nor did he gaze upon her eyes with awe,
Too full the pain of longing filled his heart
For fear or wonder there to have a part.   245

 But O, how long the night was ere it went!
How long it was before the dawn begun
Showed to the wakening birds the sun's intent
That not in darkness should the world be done!
And then, and then, how long before the sun   250
Bade silently the toilers of the earth
Get forth to fruitless cares or empty mirth!

 And long it seemed that in the market-place
He stood and saw the chaffering folk go by,
Ere from the ivory throne King Schœneus' face   255
Looked down upon the murmur royally,
But then came trembling that the time was nigh
When he midst pitying looks his love must claim,
And jeering voices must salute his name.

But as the throng he pierced to gain the throne, 260
His alien face distraught and anxious told
What hopeless errand he was bound upon,
And, each to each, folk whispered to behold
His godlike limbs; nay, and one woman old
As he went by must pluck him by the sleeve 265
And pray him yet that wretched love to leave.

For sidling up she said: "Canst thou live twice,
Fair son? canst thou have joyful youth again,
That thus thou goest to the sacrifice
Thyself the victim? nay then, all in vain 270
Thy mother bore her longing and her pain,
And one more maiden on the earth must dwell
Hopeless of joy, nor fearing death and hell.

"O fool, thou knowest not the compact then
That with the three-formed Goddess she has made 275
To keep her from the loving lips of men,
And in no saffron gown to be arrayed,
And therewithal with glory to be paid,
And love of her the moonlit river sees
White 'gainst the shadow of the formless trees. 280

"Come back, and I myself will pray for thee
Unto the sea-born framer of delights,
To give thee her who on the earth may be
The fairest stirrer up to death and fights,
To quench with hopeful days and joyous nights 285
The flame that doth thy youthful heart consume;
Come back, nor give thy beauty to the tomb."

How should he listen to her earnest speech?
Words, such as he not once or twice had said
Unto himself, whose meaning scarce could reach 290
The firm abode of that sad hardihead?
He turned about, and through the market-stead
Swiftly he passed, until before the throne
In the cleared space he stood at last alone.

Then said the King: "Stranger, what dost thou here? 295
Have any of my folk done ill to thee?
Or art thou of the forest men in fear?
Or art thou of the sad fraternity

 Who still will strive my daughter's mates to be,
Staking their lives to win to earthly bliss   300
The lonely maid, the friend of Artemis?"

 "O King," he said, "thou sayest the word indeed;
Nor will I quit the strife till I have won
My sweet delight, or death to end my need.
And know that I am called Milanion,   305
Of King Amphidamas the well-loved son:
So fear not that to thy old name, O King,
Much loss or shame my victory will bring."

 "Nay, Prince," said Schœneus, "welcome to this land
Thou wert indeed, if thou wert here to try   310
Thy strength 'gainst someone mighty of his hand;
Nor would we grudge thee well-won mastery.
But now, why wilt thou come to me to die,
And at my door lay down thy luckless head,
Swelling the band of the unhappy dead,   315

 "Whose curses even now my heart doth fear?
Lo, I am old, and know what life can be,
And what a bitter thing is death anear.
O Son! be wise, and hearken unto me,
And if no other can be dear to thee,   320
At least as now, yet is the world full wide,
And bliss in seeming hopeless hearts may hide:

 "But if thou losest life, then all is lost."
"Nay, King," Milanion said, "thy words are vain.
Doubt not that I have counted well the cost.   325
But say, on what day wilt thou that I gain
Fulfilled delight, or death to end my pain?
Right glad were I if it could be to-day,
And all my doubts at rest for ever lay."

 "Nay," said King Schœneus, "thus it shall not be,   330
But rather shalt thou let a month go by,
And weary with thy prayers for victory
What God thou know'st the kindest and most nigh.
So doing, still perchance thou shalt not die:
And with my goodwill wouldst thou have the maid   335
For of the equal Gods I grow afraid.

"And until then, O Prince, be thou my guest,
And all these troublous things awhile forget."
"Nay," said he, "couldst thou give my soul good rest,
And on mine head a sleepy garland set, 340
Then had I 'scaped the meshes of the net,
Nor shouldst thou hear from me another word;
But now, make sharp thy fearful heading sword.

"Yet will I do what son of man may do,
And promise all the Gods may most desire, 345
That to myself I may at least be true;
And on that day my heart and limbs so tire,
With utmost strain and measureless desire,
That, at the worst, I may but fall asleep
When in the sunlight round that sword shall sweep." 350

He went therewith, nor anywhere would bide,
But unto Argos restlessly did wend;
And there, as one who lays all hope aside,
Because the leech has said his life must end,
Silent farewell he bade to foe and friend, 355
And took his way unto the restless sea,
For there he deemed his rest and help might be.

Upon the shore of Argolis there stands
A temple to the Goddess that he sought,
That, turned unto the lion-bearing lands, 360
Fenced from the east, of cold winds hath no thought,
Though to no homestead there the sheaves are brought,
No groaning press torments the close-clipped murk,
Lonely the fane stands, far from all men's work.

Pass through a close, set thick with myrtle trees, 365
Through the brass doors that guard the holy place,
And entering, hear the washing of the seas
That twice a-day rise high above the base,
And with the south-west urging them, embrace
The marble feet of her that standeth there 370
That shrink not, naked though they be and fair.

Small is the fane through which the seawind sings
About Queen Venus' well-wrought image white,
But hung around are many precious things,
The gifts of those who, longing for delight, 375

Have hung them there within the Goddess' sight,
And in return have taken at her hands
The living treasures of the Grecian lands.

And thither now has come Milanion,
And showed unto the priests' wide open eyes 380
Gifts fairer than all those that there have shone,
Silk cloths, inwrought with Indian fantasies,
And bowls inscribed with sayings of the wise
Above the deeds of foolish living things,
And mirrors fit to be the gifts of kings. 385

And now before the Sea-born One he stands,
By the sweet veiling smoke made dim and soft,
And while the incense trickles from his hands,
And while the odorous smoke-wreaths hang aloft,
Thus doth he pray to her: "O Thou, who oft 390
Hast holpen man and maid in their distress,
Despise me not for this my wretchedness!

"O Goddess, among us who dwell below,
Kings and great men, great for a little while,
Have pity on the lowly heads that bow, 395
Nor hate the hearts that love them without guile;
Wilt thou be worse than these, and is thy smile
A vain device of him who set thee here,
An empty dream of some artificer?

"O Great One, some men love, and are ashamed; 400
Some men are weary of the bonds of love;
Yea, and by some men lightly art thou blamed,
That from thy toils their lives they cannot move,
And mid the ranks of men their manhood prove.
Alas! O Goddess, if thou slayest me 405
What new immortal can I serve but thee?

"Think then, will it bring honour to thy head
If folk say: 'Everything aside he cast
And to all fame and honour was he dead,
And to his one hope now is dead at last, 410
Since all unholpen he is gone and past:
Ah, the Gods love not man, for certainly,
He to his helper did not cease to cry.'

"Nay, but thou wilt help; they who died before
Not single-hearted as I deem came here, 415
Therefore unthanked they laid their gifts before
Thy stainless feet, still shivering with their fear,
Lest in their eyes their true thought might appear,
Who sought to be the lords of that fair town,
Dreaded of men and winners of renown. 420

"O Queen, thou knowest I pray not for this;
O set us down together in some place
Where not a voice can break our heaven of bliss,
Where nought but rocks and I can see her face,
Softening beneath the marvel of thy grace, 425
Where not a foot our vanished steps can track—
The golden age, the golden age come back!

"O fairest, hear me now who do thy will,
Plead for thy rebel that she be not slain,
But live and love and be thy servant still; 430
Ah, give her joy and take away my pain,
And thus two long-enduring servants gain.
An easy thing this is to do for me,
What need of my vain words to weary thee!

"But none the less, this place will I not leave 435
Until I needs must go my death to meet,
Or at thy hands some happy sign receive
That in great joy we twain may one day greet
Thy presence here and kiss thy silver feet,
Such as we deem thee, fair beyond all words, 440
Victorious o'er our servants and our lords."

Then from the altar back a space he drew,
But from the Queen turned not his face away,
But 'gainst a pillar leaned, until the blue
That arched the sky, at ending of the day, 445
Was turned to ruddy gold and changing grey,
And clear but low, the nigh-ebbed windless sea
In the still evening murmured ceaselessly.

And there he stood when all the sun was down,
Nor had he moved, when the dim golden light, 450
Like the far lustre of a godlike town,
Had left the world to seeming hopeless night,

    Nor would he move the more when wan moonlight
Streamed through the pillars for a little while,
And lighted up the white Queen's changeless smile.   455

    Nought noted he the shallow-flowing sea
As step by step it set the wrack a-swim;
The yellow torchlight nothing noted he
Wherein with fluttering gown and half-bared limb
The temple damsels sung their midnight hymn;   460
And nought the doubled stillness of the fane
When they were gone and all was hushed again.

    But when the waves had touched the marble base,
And steps the fish swim over twice a-day,
The dawn beheld him sunken in his place   465
Upon the floor; and sleeping there he lay,
Not heeding aught the little jets of spray
The roughened sea brought nigh, across him cast,
For as one dead all thought from him had passed.

    Yet long before the sun had showed his head,   470
Long ere the varied hangings on the wall
Had gained once more their blue and green and red,
He rose as one some well-known sign doth call
When war upon the city's gates doth fall,
And scarce like one fresh risen out of sleep,   475
He 'gan again his broken watch to keep.

    Then he turned round; not for the sea-gull's cry
That wheeled above the temple in his flight,
Not for the fresh south wind that lovingly
Breathed on the new-born day and dying night,   480
But some strange hope 'twixt fear and great delight
Drew round his face, now flushed, now pale and wan,
And still constrained his eyes the sea to scan.

    Now a faint light lit up the southern sky,
Not sun nor moon, for all the world was grey,   485
But this a bright cloud seemed, that drew anigh,
Lighting the dull waves that beneath it lay
As toward the temple still it took its way,
And still grew greater, till Milanion
Saw nought for dazzling light that round him shone.   490

But as he staggered with his arms outspread,
Delicious unnamed odours breathed around;
For languid happiness he bowed his head,
And with wet eyes sank down upon the ground,
Nor wished for aught, nor any dream he found   495
To give him reason for that happiness,
Or make him ask more knowledge of his bliss.

   At last his eyes were cleared, and he could see
Through happy tears the Goddess face to face
With that faint image of Divinity,   500
Whose well-wrought smile and dainty changeless grace
Until that morn so gladdened all the place;
Then he, unwitting, cried aloud her name
And covered up his eyes for fear and shame.

   But through the stillness he her voice could hear   505
Piercing his heart with joy scarce bearable,
That said: "Milanion, wherefore dost thou fear?
I am not hard to those who love me well;
List to what I a second time will tell,
And thou mayest hear perchance, and live to save   510
The cruel maiden from a loveless grave.

   "See, by my feet three golden apples lie—
Such fruit among the heavy roses falls,
Such fruit my watchful damsels carefully
Store up within the best loved of my walls,   515
Ancient Damascus, where the lover calls
Above ray unseen head and faint and light
The rose-leaves flutter round me in the night.

   "And note, that these are not alone most fair
With heavenly gold, but longing strange they bring 520
Unto the hearts of men, who will not care,
Beholding these, for any once-loved thing
Till round the shining sides their fingers cling.
And thou shalt see thy well-girt swiftfoot maid
By sight of these amidst her glory stayed.   525

   "For bearing these within a scrip with thee,
When first she heads thee from the starting-place
Cast down the first one for her eyes to see,
And when she turns aside make on apace,

  And if again she heads thee in the race   530
Spare not the other two to cast aside
If she not long enough behind will bide.

  "Farewell, and when has come the happy time
That she Diana's raiment must unbind,
And all the world seems blessed with Saturn's clime,   535
And thou with eager arms about her twined
Beholdest first her grey eyes growing kind,
Surely, O trembler, thou shalt scarcely then
Forget the Helper of unhappy men."

  Milanion raised his head at this last word,   540
For now so soft and kind she seemed to be
No longer of her Godhead was he feared;
Too late he looked; for nothing could he see
But the white image glimmering doubtfully
In the departing twilight cold and grey,   545
And those three apples on the steps that lay.

  These then he caught up quivering with delight,
Yet fearful lest it all might be a dream;
And though aweary with the watchful night,
And sleepless nights of longing, still did deem   550
He could not sleep; but yet the first sunbeam
That smote the fane across the heaving deep
Shone on him laid in calm untroubled sleep.

  But little ere the noontide did he rise,
And why he felt so happy scarce could tell   555
Until the gleaming apples met his eyes.
Then leaving the fair place where this befell
Oft he looked back as one who loved it well,
Then homeward to the haunts of men 'gan wend
To bring all things unto a happy end.   560

  Now has the lingering month at last gone by,
Again are all folk round the running place,
Nor other seems the dismal pageantry
Than heretofore, but that another face
Looks o'er the smooth course ready for the race;   565
For now, beheld of all, Milanion
Stands on the spot he twice has looked upon.

But yet—what change is this that holds the maid?
Does she indeed see in his glittering eye
More than disdain of the sharp shearing blade,   570
Some happy hope of help and victory?
The others seemed to say: "We come to die,
Look down upon us for a little while,
That dead, we may bethink us of thy smile."

 But he—what look of mastery was this   575
He cast on her? why were his lips so red?
Why was his face so flushed with happiness?
So looks not one who deems himself but dead,
E'en if to death he bows a willing head;
So rather looks a God well pleased to find   580
Some earthly damsel fashioned to his mind.

 Why must she drop her lids before his gaze,
And even as she casts adown her eyes
Redden to note his eager glance of praise,
And wish that she were clad in other guise?   585
Why must the memory to her heart arise
Of things unnoticed when they first were heard,
Some lover's song, some answering maiden's word?

 What makes these longings, vague, without a name,
And this vain pity never felt before,   590
This sudden languor, this contempt of fame,
This tender sorrow for the time past o'er,
These doubts that grow each minute more and more?
Why does she tremble as the time grows near,
And weak defeat and woeful victory fear?   595

 Now while she seemed to hear her beating heart,
Above their heads the trumpet blast rang out
And forth they sprang; and she must play her part.
Then flew her white feet, knowing not a doubt,
Though slackening once, she turned her head about,   600
But then she cried aloud and faster fled
Than e'er before, and all men deemed him dead.

 But with no sound he raised aloft his hand,
And thence what seemed a ray of light there flew
And past the maid rolled on along the sand;   605
Then trembling she her feet together drew

And in her heart a strong desire there grew
To have the toy; some God she thought had given
That gift to her, to make of earth a heaven.

   Then from the course with eager steps she ran, 610
And in her odorous bosom laid the gold.
But when she turned again, the great-limbed man,
Now well ahead she failed not to behold,
And mindful of her glory waxing cold,
Sprang up and followed him in hot pursuit, 615
Though with one hand she touched the golden fruit.

   Note too, the bow that she was wont to bear
She laid aside to grasp the glittering prize,
And o'er her shoulder from the quiver fair
Three arrows fell and lay before her eyes 620
Unnoticed, as amidst the people's cries
She sprang to head the strong Milanion,
Who now the turning-post had well-nigh won.

   But as he set his mighty hand on it
White fingers underneath his own were laid, 625
And white limbs from his dazzled eyes did flit,
Then he the second fruit cast by the maid:
She ran awhile, and then as one afraid
Wavered and stopped, and turned and made no stay,
Until the globe with its bright fellow lay. 630

   Then, as a troubled glance she cast around,
Now far ahead the Argive could she see,
And in her garment's hem one hand she wound
To keep the double prize, and strenuously
Sped o'er the course, and little doubt had she 635
To win the day, though now but scanty space
Was left betwixt him and the winning place.

   Short was the way unto such wingèd feet,
Quickly she gained upon him, till at last
He turned about her eager eyes to meet 640
And from his hand the third fair apple cast.
She wavered not, but turned and ran so fast
After the prize that should her bliss fulfil,
That in her hand it lay ere it was still.

 Nor did she rest, but turned about to win 645
Once more, an unblest woeful victory:
And yet—and yet—why does her breath begin
To fail her, and her feet drag heavily?
Why fails she now to see if far or nigh
The goal is? why do her grey eyes grow dim? 650
Why do these tremors run through every limb?

 She spreads her arms abroad some stay to find
Else must she fall, indeed, and findeth this,
A strong man's arms about her body twined.
Nor may she shudder now to feel his kiss, 655
So wrapped she is in new unbroken bliss:
Made happy that the foe the prize hath won,
She weeps glad tears for all her glory done.

 Shatter the trumpet, hew adown the posts!
Upon the brazen altar break the sword, 660
And scatter incense to appease the ghosts
Of those who died here by their own award.
Bring forth the image of the mighty Lord,
And her who unseen o'er the runners hung,
And did a deed for ever to be sung. 665

 Here are the gathered folk; make no delay,
Open King Schœneus' well-filled treasury,
Bring out the gifts long hid from light of day,
The golden bowls o'erwrought with imagery,
Gold chains, and unguents brought from over sea, 670
The saffron gown the old Phœnician brought,
Within the temple of the Goddess wrought.

 O ye, O damsels, who shall never see
Her, that Love's servant bringeth now to you,
Returning from another victory, 675
In some cool bower do all that now is due!
Since she in token of her service new
Shall give to Venus offerings rich enow,
Her maiden zone, her arrows and her bow.

 So when his last word's echo died away, 680
The growing wind at end of that wild day
Alone they heard, for silence bound them all;
Yea, on their hearts a weight had seemed to fall,
As unto the scarce-hoped felicity

The tale grew round— the end of life so nigh, 685
The aim so little, and the joy so vain—
For as a child's unmeasured joy brings pain
Unto a grown man holding grief at bay,
So the old fervent story of that day
Brought pain half-sweet, to these: till now the fire 690
Upon the hearth sent up a flickering spire
Of ruddy flame, as fell the burned-through logs,
And, waked by sudden silence, grey old dogs,
The friends of this or that man, rose and fawned
On hands they knew; withal once more there dawned 695
The light of common day on those old hearts,
And all were ready now to play their parts,
And take what feeble joy might yet remain
In place of all they once had hoped to gain.

   Now on the second day that these did meet 700
March was a-dying through soft days and sweet
Too hopeful for the wild days yet to be;
But in the hall that ancient company,
Not lacking younger folk that day at least,
Softened by spring were gathered at the feast, 705
And as the time drew on, throughout the hall
A horn was sounded, giving note to all
That they at last the looked-for tale should hear.

   Then spake a Wanderer: "O kind hosts and dear,
Hearken a little unto such a tale 710
As folk with us will tell in every vale
About the yule-tide fire, whenas the snow
Deep in the passes, letteth men to go
From place to place: now there few great folk be,
Although we upland men have memory 715
Of ills kings did us; yet as now indeed
Few have much wealth, few are in utter need.
Like the wise ants a kingless, happy folk
We long have been, not galled by any yoke,
But the white leaguer of the winter tide 720
Whereby all men at home are bound to bide.
—Alas, my folly! how I talk of it,
As though from this place where to-day we sit
The way thereto were short. Ah, would to God
Upon the snow-freed herbage now I trod! 725
But pardon, sirs; the time goes swiftly by,
Hearken a tale of conquering destiny."

Chants for Socialists:

184.   (i) *The Voice of Toil*

I heard men saying, Leave hope and praying,
All days shall be as all have been;
To-day and to-morrow bring fear and sorrow,
The never-ending toil between.

When Earth was younger mid toil and hunger, 5
In hope we strove, and our hands were strong;
Then great men led us, with words they fed us,
And bade us right the earthly wrong.

Go read in story their deeds and glory,
Their names amidst the nameless dead; 10
Turn then from lying to us slow-dying
In that good world to which they led;

Where fast and faster our iron master,
The thing we made, for ever drives,
Bids us grind treasure and fashion pleasure 15
For other hopes and other lives.

Where home is a hovel and dull we grovel,
Forgetting that the world is fair;
Where no babe we cherish, lest its very soul perish;
Where mirth is crime, and love a snare. 20

Who now shall lead us, what God shall heed us
As we lie in the hell our hands have won?
For us are no rulers but fools and befoolers,
The great are fallen, the wise men gone.

I heard men saying, Leave tears and praying, 25
The sharp knife heedeth not the sheep;
Are we not stronger than the rich and the wronger,
When day breaks over dreams and sleep?

Come, shoulder to shoulder ere the world grows older!
Help lies in nought but thee and me; 30
Hope is before us, the long years that bore us
Bore leaders more than men may be.

> Let dead hearts tarry and trade and marry,
> And trembling nurse their dreams of mirth,
> While we the living our lives are giving
> To bring the bright new world to birth. 35
>
> Come, shoulder to shoulder ere Earth grows older!
> The Cause spreads over land and sea;
> Now the world shaketh, and fear awaketh,
> And joy at last for thee and me. 40

185.   (ii) *All for the Cause*

> Hear a word, a word in season, for the day is drawing nigh,
> When the Cause shall call upon us, some to live, and some to die!
>
> He that dies shall not die lonely, many an one hath gone before;
> He that lives shall bear no burden heavier than the life they bore.
>
> Nothing ancient is their story, e'en but yesterday they bled, 5
> Youngest they of earth's beloved, last of all the valiant dead.
>
> E'en the tidings we are telling was the tale they had to tell,
> E'en the hope that our hearts cherish, was the hope for which they fell.
>
> In the grave where tyrants thrust them, lies their labour and their pain,
> But undying from their sorrow springeth up the hope again. 10
>
> Mourn not therefore, nor lament it, that the world outlives their life;
> Voice and vision yet they give us, making strong our hands for strife.
>
> Some had name, and fame, and honour, learn'd they were, and wise and strong;
> Some were nameless, poor, unlettered, weak in all but grief and wrong.
>
> Named and nameless all live in us; one and all they lead us yet, 15
> Every pain to count for nothing, every sorrow to forget.
>
> Hearken how they cry, "O happy, happy ye that ye were born
> In the sad slow night's departing, in the rising of the morn.
>
> "Fair the crown the Cause hath for you, well to die or well to live
> Through the battle, through the tangle, peace to gain or peace to give." 20

Ah, it may be! Oft meseemeth, in the days that yet shall be,
When no slave of gold abideth 'twixt the breadth of sea to sea,

Oft, when men and maids are merry, ere the sunlight leaves the earth,
And they bless the day beloved, all too short for all their mirth,

Some shall pause awhile and ponder on the bitter days of old,   25
Ere the toil of strife and battle overthrew the curse of gold;

Then 'twixt lips of loved and lover solemn thoughts of us shall rise;
We who once were fools defeated, then shall be the brave and wise.

There amidst the world new-builded shall our earthly deeds abide,
Though our names be all forgotten, and the tale of how we died.   30

Life or death then, who shall heed it, what we gain or what we lose?
Fair flies life amid the struggle, and the Cause for each shall choose.

Hear a word, a word in season, for the day is drawing nigh,
When the Cause shall call upon us, some to live, and some to die!

186.   (iii) *The March of the Workers*

What is this, the sound and rumour? What is this that all men hear,
Like the wind in hollow valleys when the storm is drawing near,
Like the rolling on of ocean in the eventide of fear?
                   'Tis the people marching on.

Whither go they, and whence come they? What are these of whom ye tell?   5
In what country are they dwelling 'twixt the gates of heaven and hell?
Are they mine or thine for money? Will they serve a master well?
                   Still the rumour's marching on.

         Hark the rolling of the thunder!
         Lo the sun! and lo thereunder   10
         Riseth wrath, and hope, and wonder,
                   And the host comes marching on.

Forth they come from grief and torment; on they wend toward health and mirth,
All the wide world is their dwelling, every corner of the earth.
Buy them, sell them for thy service! Try the bargain what 'tis worth,   15
                   For the days are marching on.

These are they who build thy houses, weave thy raiment, win thy wheat,
Smooth the rugged, fill the barren, turn the bitter into sweet,
All for thee this day—and ever. What reward for them is meet
                      Till the host comes marching on? 20

      Hark the rolling of the thunder!
      Lo the sun! and lo thereunder
      Riseth wrath, and hope, and wonder,
                  And the host comes marching on.

Many a hundred years passed over have they laboured deaf and blind; 25
Never tidings reached their sorrow, never hope their toil might find.
Now at last they've heard and hear it, and the cry comes down the wind,
                      And their feet are marching on.

O ye rich men hear and tremble! for with words the sound is rife:
"Once for you and death we laboured; changed henceforward is the strife. 30
We are men, and we shall battle for the world of men and life;
                      And our host is marching on."

      Hark the rolling of the thunder!
      Lo the sun! and lo thereunder
      Riseth wrath, and hope, and wonder, 35
                  And the host comes marching on.

"Is it war, then? Will ye perish as the dry wood in the fire?
Is it peace? Then be ye of us, let your hope be our desire.
Come and live! for life awaketh, and the world shall never tire;
                      And hope is marching on." 40

"On we march then, we the workers, and the rumour that ye hear
Is the blended sound of battle and deliv'rance drawing near;
For the hope of every creature is the banner that we bear,
                      And the world is marching on."

      Hark the rolling of the thunder! 45
      Lo the sun! and lo thereunder
      Riseth wrath, and hope, and wonder,
                  And the host comes marching on.

187.   *A Garden by the Sea*

I know a little garden-close,
Set thick with lily and red rose,
Where I would wander if I might
From dewy morn to dewy night,
And have one with me wandering.   5

And though within it no birds sing,
And though no pillared house is there,
And though the apple-boughs are bare
Of fruit and blossom, would to God
Her feet upon the green grass trod,   10
And I beheld them as before.

There comes a murmur from the shore,
And in the close two fair streams are,
Drawn from the purple hills afar,
Drawn down unto the restless sea: 15
Dark hills whose heath-bloom feeds no bee,
Dark shore no ship has ever seen,
Tormented by the billows green
Whose murmur comes unceasingly
Unto the place for which I cry.   20

For which I cry both day and night,
For which I let slip all delight,
Whereby I grow both deaf and blind,
Careless to win, unskilled to find,
And quick to lose what all men seek.   25

Yet tottering as I am and weak,
Still have I left a little breath
To seek within the jaws of death
An entrance to that happy place,
To seek the unforgotten face,   30
Once seen, once kissed, once reft from me
Anigh the murmuring of the sea.

188.   *Tapestry Trees*

    OAK
    I am the Roof-tree and the Keel;
    I bridge the seas for woe and weal.

    FIR
    High o'er the lordly oak I stand,
    And drive him on from land to land.

    ASH
    I heft my brother's iron bane;
    I shaft the spear, and build the wain.

    YEW
    Dark down the windy dale I grow,
    The father of the fateful Bow.

    POPLAR
    The war-shaft and the milking-bowl
    I make, and keep the hay-wain whole.

    OLIVE
    The King I bless; the lamps I trim;
    In my warm wave do fishes swim.

    APPLE-TREE
    I bowed my head to Adam's will;
    The cups of toiling men I fill.

    VINE
    I draw the blood from out the earth;
    I store the sun for winter mirth.

    ORANGE-TREE
    Amidst the greenness of my night,
    My odorous lamps hang round and bright.

    FIG-TREE
    I who am little among trees
    In honey-making mate the bees.

    MULBERRY-TREE
    Love's lack hath dyed my berries red:
    For Love's attire my leaves are shed.

PEAR-TREE
High o'er the mead-flowers' hidden feet
I bear aloft my burden sweet.

BAY
Look on my leafy boughs, the Crown
Of living song and dead renown!

189.   *The Flowering Orchard*

SILK EMBROIDERY

Lo silken my garden, and silken my sky,
And silken my apple-boughs hanging on high;
All wrought by the Worm in the peasant carle's cot
On the Mulberry leafage when summer was hot!

190.   *The Forest*

PEAR-TREE
By woodman's edge I faint and fail;
By craftsman's edge I tell the tale.

CHESTNUT-TREE
High in the wood, high o'er the hall,
Aloft I rise when low I fall.

OAK-TREE
Unmoved I stand what wind may blow.
Swift, swift before the wind I go.

191.   *Pomona*

I am the ancient Apple-Queen,
As once I was so am I now.
For evermore a hope unseen,
Betwixt the blossom and the bough.

> Ah, where's the river's hidden Gold! 5
> And where the windy grave of Troy?
> Yet come I as I came of old,
> From out the heart of Summer's joy.

192. *For the Briar Rose*

> THE BRIARWOOD
> The fateful slumber floats and flows
> About the tangle of the rose;
> But lo! the fated hand and heart
> To rend the slumbrous curse apart!
>
> THE COUNCIL ROOM
> The threat of war, the hope of peace,
> The Kingdom's peril and increase
> Sleep on and bide the latter day,
> When fate shall take her chain away.
>
> THE GARDEN COURT
> The maiden pleasance of the land
> Knoweth no stir of voice or hand,
> No cup the sleeping waters fill,
> The restless shuttle lieth still.
>
> THE ROSEBOWER
> Here lies the hoarded love, the key
> To all the treasure that shall be;
> Come feted hand the gift to take,
> And smite this sleeping world awake.

193. *Drawing near the Light*

> Lo, when we wade the tangled wood,
> In haste and hurry to be there,
> Nought seem its leaves and blossoms good,
> For all that they be fashioned fair.
>
> But looking up, at last we see 5
> The glimmer of the open light,
> From o'er the place where we would be:
> Then grow the very brambles bright.

So now, amidst our day of strife,
With many a matter glad we play, 10
When once we see the light of life
Gleam through the tangle of to-day.

194. *Verses for Pictures*

DAY
I am Day; I bring again
Life and glory, Love and pain:
Awake, arise! from death to death
Through me the World's tale quickeneth.

SPRING
Spring am I, too sort of heart
Much to speak ere I depart:
Ask the Summer-tide to prove
The abundance of my love.

SUMMER
Summer looked for long am I;
Much shall change or e'er I die.
Prithee take it not amiss
Though I weary thee with bliss.

AUTUMN
Laden Autumn here I stand
Worn of heart, and weak of hand:
Nought but rest seems good to me,
Speak the word that sets me free.

WINTER
I am Winter, that do keep
Longing safe amidst of sleep:
Who shall say if I were dead
What should be remembered?

NIGHT
I am Night: I bring again
Hope of pleasure, rest from pain:
Thoughts unsaid 'twixt Life and Death
My fruitful silence quickeneth.

195. *The Roots of the Mountains*

I–SONG

(FROM CHAPTER VI)

In hay-tide, through the day new-born,
    Across the meads we come;
Our hauberks brush the blossomed corn
    A furlong short of home.

Ere yet the gables we behold
    Forth flasheth the red sun,
And smites our fallow helms and cold
    Though all the fight be done.

In this last mead of mowing-grass
    Sweet doth the clover smell,
Crushed neath our feet red with the pass
    Where hell was blent with hell.

And now the willowy stream is nigh,
    Down wend we to the ford;
No shafts across its fishes fly,
    Nor flasheth there a sword.

But lo! what gleameth on the bank
    Across the water wan,
As when our blood the mouse-ear drank
    And red the river ran?

Nay, hasten to the ripple clear,
    Look at the grass beyond!
Lo ye the dainty band and dear
    Of maidens fair and fond!

Lo how they needs must take the stream!
    The water hides their feet;
On fair kind arms the gold doth gleam,
    And midst the ford we meet.

Up through the garden two and two,
    And on the flowers we drip;
Their wet feet kiss the morning dew
    As lip lies close to lip.

Here now we sing; here now we stay:
   By these gray walls we tell
The love that lived from out the fray,   35
   The love that fought and fell.

II–A LAY OF TIME PAST

(FROM CHAPTER IX)

'Tis over the hill and over the dale
   Men ride from the city fast and far,
If they may have a soothfast tale,
   True tidings of the host of war.

And first they hap on men-at-arms,   5
   All clad in steel from head to foot:
Now tell true tale of the new-come harms,
   And the gathered hosts of the mountain-root.

Fair sirs, from murder-carles we flee,
   Whose fashion is as the mountain-trolls';   10
No man can tell how many they be,
   And the voice of their host as the thunder rolls.

They were weary men at the ending of day,
   But they spurred nor stayed for longer word.
Now ye, O merchants, whither away?   15
   What do ye there with the helm and the sword?

O we must fight for life and gear,
   For our beasts are spent and our wains are stayed,
And the host of the Mountain-men draws near,
   That maketh all the world afraid.   20

They left the chapmen on the hill,
   And through the eve and through the night
They rode to have true tidings still,
   And were there on the way when the dawn was bright.

O damsels fair, what do ye then   25
   To loiter thus upon the way,
And have no fear of the Mountain-men,
   The host of the carles that strip and slay?

O riders weary with the road,
   Come eat and drink on the grass hereby!   30
And lay you down in a fair abode
   Till the mid-day sun is broad and high;

Then unto you shall we come aback,
   And lead you forth to the Mountain-men,
To note their plenty and their lack,   35
   And have true tidings there and then.

'Tis over the hill and over the dale
   They ride from the mountain fast and far;
And now have they learned a soothfast tale,
   True tidings of the host of war.   40

It was summer-tide and the Month of Hay,
   And men and maids must fare afield;
But we saw the place where the bow-staves lay,
   And the hall was hung with spear and shield.

When the moon was high we drank in the hall,   45
   And they drank to the guests and were kind and blithe,
And they said: Come back when the chestnuts fall,
   And the wine-carts wend across the hythe.

Come oft and o'er again, they said;
   Wander your ways; but we abide   50
For all the world in the little stead;
   For wise are we, though the world be wide.

Yea, come in arms if ye will, they said;
   And despite your host shall we abide
For life or death in the little stead;   55
   For wise are we, though the world be wide.

196.   *Love Fulfilled*

Hast thou longed through weary days
For the sight of one loved face?
Hast thou cried aloud for rest,
Mid the pain of sundering hours;
Cried aloud for sleep and death,   5
Since the sweet unhoped for best

Was a shadow and a breath?
O, long now, for no fear lowers
O'er these faint feet-kissing flowers.
O, rest now; and yet in sleep 10
All thy longing shalt thou keep.

Thou shalt rest and have no fear
Of a dull awaking near,
Of a life for ever blind,
Uncontent and waste and wide. 15
Thou shalt wake and think it sweet
That thy love is near and kind.
Sweeter still for lips to meet;
Sweetest that thine heart doth hide
Longing all unsatisfied 20
With all longing's answering
Howsoever close ye cling.

Thou rememberest how of old
E'en thy very pain grew cold,
How thou might'st not measure bliss 25
E'en when eyes and hands drew nigh.
Thou rememberest all regret
For the scarce remembered kiss,
The lost dream of how they met,
Mouths once parched with misery. 30
Then seemed Love born but to die,
Now unrest, pain, bliss are one,
Love, unhidden and alone.

197. *Love's Gleaning-Tide*

Draw not away thy hands, my love,
With wind alone the branches move,
And though the leaves be scant above
      The Autumn shall not shame us.

Say: Let the world wax cold and drear, 5
What is the worst of all the year
But life, and what can hurt us, dear,
      Or death, and who shall blame us?

> Ah, when the summer comes again
> How shall we say, we sowed in vain? 10
> The root was joy, the stem was pain,
>   The ear a nameless blending.
>
> The root is dead and gone, my love,
> The stem's a rod our truth to prove;
> The ear is stored for nought to move 15
>   Till heaven and earth have ending.

198.   *Mine and Thine (from a Flemish poem of the fourteenth century)*

> Two words about the world we see,
> And nought but Mine and Thine they be.
> Ah! might we drive them forth and wide
> With us should rest and peace abide;
> All free, nought owned of goods and gear, 5
> By men and women though it were.
> Common to all all wheat and wine
> Over the seas and up the Rhine.
> No manslayer then the wide world o'er
> When Mine and Thine are known no more. 10
>
> Yea, God, well counselled for our health,
> Gave all this fleeting earthly wealth
> A common heritage to all,
> That men might feed them therewithal,
> And clothe their limbs and shoe their feet 15
> And live a simple life and sweet.
> But now so rageth greediness
> That each desireth nothing less
> Than all the world, and all his own;
> And all for him and him alone. 20

John (Byrne) Leicester Warren, Lord de Tabley (1835–1895) (G. F. Preston, W. P. Lancaster)

199.　　　　　　　*The Pilgrim Cranes*

    The pilgrim cranes are moving to their south,
        The clouds are herded pale and rolling slow.
    One flower is withered in the warm wind's mouth,
        Whereby the gentle waters always flow.

    The cloud-fire wanes beyond the lighted trees.　　　　5
        The sudden glory leaves the mountain dome.
    Sleep into night, old anguish mine, and cease
        To listen for a step that will not come.

200.　　　　　　　*A Song of Faith Forsworn*

    Take back your suit.
    It came when I was weary and distraught
    With hunger. Could I guess the fruit you brought?
    I ate in mere desire of any food,
    Nibbled its edge and nowhere found it good.　　　　5
    Take back your suit.

    Take back your love,
    It is a bird poached from my neighbour's wood:
    Its wings are wet with tears, its beak with blood.
    'Tis a strange fowl with feathers like a crow:　　　　10
    Death's raven, it may be, for all we know.
    Take back your love.

    Take back your gifts.
    False is the hand that gave them; and the mind
    That planned them, as a hawk spread in the wind　　　　15
    To poise and snatch the trembling mouse below.
    To ruin where it dares—and then to go.
    Take back your gifts.

Take back your vows.
Elsewhere you trimmed and taught these lamps to burn;
You bring them stale and dim to serve my turn.
You lit those candles in another shrine,
Guttered and cold you offer them on mine.
Take back your vows.

Take back your words.
What is your love? Leaves on a woodland plain,
Where some are running and where some remain:
What is your faith? Straws on a mountain height,
Dancing like demons on Walpurgis night.
Take back your words.

Take back your lies.
Have them again: they wore a rainbow face,
Hollow with sin and leprous with disgrace;
Their tongue was like a mellow turret bell
To toll hearts burning into wide-lipped hell.
Take back your lies.

Take back your kiss.
Shall I be meek, and lend my lips again
To let this adder daub them with his stain?
Shall I turn cheek to answer, when I hate?
You kiss like Judas in the garden gate!
Take back your kiss.

Take back delight,
A paper boat launched on a heaving pool
To please a child, and folded by a fool;
The wild elms roared: it sailed—a yard or more.
Out went our ship but never came to shore.
Take back delight.

Take back your wreath.
Has it done service on a fairer brow?
Fresh, was it folded round her bosom snow?
Her cast-off weed my breast will never wear:
Your word is "love me." My reply "despair!"
Take back your wreath.

Circe

This the house of Circe, queen of charms—
A kind of beacon-cauldron poised on high,
Hooped round with ember-clasping iron bars,
Sways in her palace porch, and smoulderingly
Drips out in blots of fire and ruddy stars; 5
But out behind that trembling furnace air,
The lands are ripe and fair,
Hush are the hills and quiet to the eye.
The river's reach goes by
With lamb and holy tower and squares of corn, 10
And shelving interspace
Of holly bush and thorn,
And hamlets happy in an Alpine morn,
And deep-bowered lanes with grace
Of woodbine newly born. 15
But inward o'er the hearth a torch-head stands
Inverted, slow green flames of fulvous hue,
Echoed in wave-like shadows over her.
A censer's swing-chain set in her fair hands
Dances up wreaths of intertwisted blue 20
In clouds of fragrant frankincense and myrrh.
A giant tulip head and two pale leaves
Grew in the midmost of her chamber there,
A flaunting bloom, naked and undivine,
Rigid and bare, 25
Gaunt as a tawny bond-girl born to shame,
With freckled cheeks and splotched side serpentine,
A gipsy among flowers,
Unmeet for bed or bowers,
Virginal where pure-handed damsels sleep: 30
Let it not breathe a common air with them,
Lest when the night is deep,
And all things have their quiet in the moon,
Some birth of poison from its leaning stem
Waft in between their slumber-parted lips, 35
And they cry out or swoon,
Deeming some vampire sips,
Where riper Love may come for nectar boon!

And near this tulip, reared across a loom,
Hung a fair web of tapestry half done, 40
Crowding with folds and fancies half the room:
Men eyed as gods and damsels still as stone,

Pressing their brows alone,
In amethystine robes,
Or reaching at the polished orchard globes, 45
Or rubbing parted love-lips on their rind,
While the wind
Sows with sere apple leaves their breast and hair.
And all the margin there
Was arabesqued and bordered intricate 50
With hairy spider things
That catch and clamber,
And salamander in his dripping cave
Satanic ebon-amber;
Blind worm, and asp, and eft of cumbrous gait, 55
And toads who love rank grasses near a grave,
And the great goblin moth, who bears
Between his wings the ruined eyes of death;
And the enamelled sails
Of butterflies, who watch the morning's breath. 60
And many an emerald lizard with quick ears
Asleep in rocky dales.
And for an outer fringe embroidered small,
A ring of many locusts, horny-coated,
A round of chirping tree-frogs merry-throated, 65
And sly, fat fishes sailing, watching all.

(1893)

Sir Alfred Comyns Lyall (1835–1911)

from *Studies at Delhi* (1876)

202.   I. *The Hindu Ascetic*

Here as I sit by the Jumna bank,
Watching the flow of the sacred stream,
Pass me the legions, rank on rank,
And the cannon roar, and the bayonets gleam.

Is it a god or a king that comes? 5
Both are evil, and both are strong;
With women and worshipping, dancing and drums,
Carry your gods and your kings along.

Fanciful shapes of a plastic earth,
These are the visions that weary the eye;   10
These I may 'scape by a luckier birth,
Musing, and fasting, and hoping to die.

When shall these phantoums flicker away?
Like the smoke of the guns on the wind-swept hill.
Like the sounds and colours of yesterday: 15
And the soul have rest, and the air be still.

II. *Badminton*

203.

Hardly a shot from the gate we stormed,
Under the Moree battlement's shade;
Close to the glacis our game was formed,
There had the fight been, and there we played.

Lightly the demoiselles tittered and leapt,   5
Merrily capered the players all;
North, was the garden where Nicholson slept,
South, was the sweep of a battered wall.

Near me a Musalmán, civil and mild,
Watched as the shuttlecocks rose and fell;   10
And he said, as he counted his beads and smiled,
"God smite their souls to the depths of hell."

Alfred Austin (1835–1913)

204.

At the Gate of the Convent

I

Beside the Convent Gate I stood,
   Lingering to take farewell of those
To whom I owed the simple good
   Of three days' peace, three nights' repose.

II

My sumpter-mule did blink and blink;
    Was nothing more to munch or quaff;
Antonio, far too wise to think,
    Leaned vacantly upon his staff.

III

It was the childhood of the year:
    Bright was the morning, blithe the air;
And in the choir I plain could hear
    The monks still chanting matin prayer.

IV

The throstle and the blackbird shrilled,
    Loudly as in an English copse,
Fountain-like note that, still refilled,
    Rises and falls, but never stops.

V

As lush as in an English chase,
    The hawthorn, guessed by its perfume,
With folds on folds of snowy lace
    Blindfolded all its leaves with bloom.

VI

Scarce seen, and only faintly heard,
    A torrent, 'mid far snow-peaks born,
Sang kindred with the gurgling bird,
    Flowed kindred with the foaming thorn.

VII

The chanting ceased, and soon instead
    Came shuffling sound of sandalled shoon;
Each to his cell and narrow bed
    Withdrew, to pray and muse till noon.

VIII

Only the Prior—for such their Rule—
    Into the morning sunshine came.
Antonio bared his locks; the mule
    Kept blinking, blinking, just the same.

IX

I thanked him with a faltering tongue;
    I thanked him with a flowing heart.
"This for the poor." His hand I wrung,   35
    And gave the signal to depart.

X

But still in his he held my hand,
    As though averse that I should go.
His brow was grave, his look was bland,
    His beard was white as Alpine snow.   40

XI

And in his eye a light there shone,
    A soft, subdued, but steadfast ray,
Like to those lamps that still burn on
    In shrines where no one comes to pray.

XII

And in his voice I seemed to hear   45
    The hymns that novice-sisters sing,
When only anguished Christ is near,
    And earth and life seem vanishing.

XIII

"Why do you leave us, dear my son?
    Why from calm cloisters backward wend,   50
Where moil is much and peace is none,
    And journeying hath nor bourne nor end?

XIV

"Read I your inmost soul aright,
    Heaven hath to you been strangely kind;
Gave gentle cradle, boyhood bright,   55
    A fostered soul, a tutored mind.

XV

"Nor wealth did lure, nor penury cramp,
    Your ripening soul; it lived and throve,
Nightly beside the lettered lamp,
    Daily in field, and glade, and grove.   60

XVI

"And when the dawn of manhood brought
    The hour to choose to be of those
Who serve for gold, or sway by thought,
    You doubted not, and rightly chose.

XVII

"Loving your Land, you face the strife;
    Loved by the Muse, you shun the throng;
And blend within your dual life
    The patriot's pen, the poet's song.

XVIII

"Hence now, in gaze mature and wise,
    Dwells scorn of praise, dwells scorn of blame;
Calm consciousness of surer prize
    Than dying noise of living fame.

XIX

"Have you not loved, been loved, as few
    Love, or are loved, on loveless earth?
How often have you felt its dew?
    Say, have you ever known its dearth?

XX

"I speak of love divorced from pelf,
    I speak of love unyoked and free,
Of love that deadens sense of self,
    Of love that loveth utterly.

XXI

"And this along your life hath flowed
    In full and never-failing stream,
Fresh from its source, unbought, unowed,
    Beyond your boyhood's fondest dream."

XXII

He paused. The cuckoo called. I thought
    Of English voices, English trees.
The far-off fancy instant brought
    The tears; and he, misled by these,

XXIII

With hand upon my shoulder, said,
    "You own 'tis true. The richest years
Bequeath the beggared heart, when fled,
    Only this legacy of tears.

XXIV

"Why is it that all raptures cloy?
    Though men extol, though women bless,
Why are we still chagrined with joy,
    Dissatisfied with happiness?

XXV

"Yes, the care-flouting cuckoo calls,
    And yet your smile betokens grief,
Like meditative light that falls
    Through branches fringed with autumn leaf.

XXVI

"Whence comes this shadow? You are now
    In the full summer of the soul.
The answer darkens on your brow:
    'Winter the end, and death the goal.'

XXVII

"Yes, vain the fires of pride and lust
    Fierce in meridian pulses burn:
Remember, Man, that thou art dust,
    And unto dust thou shalt return.

XXVIII

"Rude are our walls, our beds are rough,
    But use is hardship's subtle friend.
He hath got all that hath enough;
    And rough feels softest, in the end.

XXIX

"While luxury hath this disease,
    It ever craves and pushes on.
Pleasures, repeated, cease to please,
    And rapture, once 'tis reaped, is gone.

XXX

"My flesh hath long since ceased to creep,
    Although the hairshirt pricketh oft.
A plank my couch; withal, I sleep
    Soundly as he that lieth soft.   120

XXXI

"And meagre though may be the meal
    That decks the simple board you see,
At least, my son, we never feel
    The hunger of satiety.

XXXII

"You have perhaps discreetly drunk: 125
    O, then, discreetly, drink no more!
Which is the happier, worldling, monk,
    When youth is past, and manhood o'er?

XXXIII

"Of life beyond I speak not yet.
    'Tis solitude alone can e'er,   130
By hushing controversy, let
    Man catch earth's undertone of prayer.

XXXIV

"Your soul which Heaven at last must reap,
    From too much noise hath barren grown;
Long fallow silence must it keep,   135
    Ere faith revive, and grace be sown.

XXXV

"Let guide and mule alone return.
    For you I will prepare a cell,
In whose calm silence you will learn,
    Living or dying, All is well!"   140

XXXVI

Again the cuckoo called; again
    The merle and mavis shook their throats;
The torrent rambled down the glen,
    The ringdove cooed in sylvan cotes.

XXXVII

The hawthorn moved not, but still kept 145
    As fixedly white as far cascade;
The russet squirrel frisked and leapt
    From breadth of sheen to breadth of shade.

XXXVIII

I did not know the words had ceased,
    I thought that he was speaking still, 150
Nor had distinguished sacred priest
    From pagan thorn, from pagan rill.

XXXIX

Not that I had not harked and heard;
    But all he bade me shun or do,
Seemed just as sweet as warbling bird, 155
    But not more grave and not more true.

XL

So deep yet indistinct my bliss,
    That when his counsels ceased to sound,
That one sweet note I did not miss
    From other sweet notes all around. 160

XLI

But he, misreading my delight,
    Again with urging accents spoke.
Then I, like one that's touched at night,
    From the deep swoon of sweetness woke.

XLII

And just as one that, waking, can 165
    Recall the thing he dreamed, but knows
'Twas of the phantom world that man
    Visits in languors of repose;

XLIII

So, though I straight repictured plain
    All he had said, it seemed to me, 170
Recalled from slumber, to retain
    No kinship with reality.

XLIV

"Father, forgive!" I said; "and look!
    Who taught its carolling to the merle?
Who wed the music to the brook?
    Who decked the thorn with flakes of pearl?   175

XLV

"'Twas He, you answer, that did make
    Earth, sea, and sky: He maketh all;
The gleeful notes that flood the brake,
    The sad notes wailed in Convent stall.   180

XLVI

"And my poor voice He also made;
    And like the brook, and like the bird,
And like your brethren mute and staid,
    I too can but fulfil His word.

XLVII

"Were I about my loins to tie   185
    A girdle, and to hold in scorn
Beauty and Love, what then were I
    But songless stream, but flowerless thorn?

XLVIII

"Why do our senses love to list
    When distant cataracts murmur thus?   190
Why stealeth o'er your eyes a mist
    When belfries toll the Angelus?

XLIX

"It is that every tender sound
    Art can evoke, or Nature yield,
Betokens something more profound,   195
    Hinted, but never quite revealed.

L

"And though it be the self-same Hand
    That doth the complex concert strike,
The notes, to those that understand,
    Are individual, and unlike.   200

LI

"Allow my nature. All things are,
    If true to instinct, well and wise.
The dewdrop hinders not the star;
    The waves do not rebuke the skies.

LII

"So leave me free, good Father dear,
    While you on humbler, holier chord
Chant your secluded Vespers here,
    To fling my matin notes abroad.

LIII

"While you with sacred sandals wend
    To trim the lamp, to deck the shrine,
Let me my country's altar tend,
    Nor deem such worship less divine.

LIV

"Mine earthly, yours celestial love:
    Each hath its harvest; both are sweet.
You wait to reap your Heaven, above;
    I reap the Heaven about my feet.

LV

"And what if I—forgive your guest
    Who feels, so frankly speaks, his qualm—
Though calm amid the world's unrest,
    Should restless be amid your calm?

LVI

"But though we two be severed quite,
    Your holy words will sound between
Our lives, like stream one hears at night,
    Louder, because it is not seen.

LVII

"Father, farewell! Be not distressed;
    And take my vow, ere I depart,
To found a Convent in my breast,
    And keep a cloister in my heart."

LVIII

The mule from off his ribs a fly
    Flicked, and then zigzagged down the road.
Antonio lit his pipe, and I
    Behind them somewhat sadly strode.

LIX

Just ere the Convent dipped from view,
    Backward I glanced: he was not there.
Within the chapel, well I knew,
    His lips were now composed in prayer.

LX

But I have kept my vow. And when
    The cuckoo chuckleth o'er his theft,
When throstles sing, again, again,
    And runnels gambol down the cleft,

LXI

With these I roam, I sing with those,
    And should the world with smiles or jeers
Provoke or lure, my lids I close,
    And draw a cowl about my ears.

205. *Love's Blindness*

Now do I know that love is blind, for I
Can see no beauty on this beauteous earth,
No life, no light, no hopefulness, no mirth,
Pleasure nor purpose, when thou art not nigh.
Thy absence exiles sunshine from the sky,
Seres Spring's maturity, checks Summer's birth,
Leaves linnet's pipe as sad as plover's cry,
And makes me in abundance find but dearth.
But when thy feet flutter the dark, and thou
With orient eyes dawnest on my distress,
Suddenly sings a bird on every bough,
The heavens expand, the earth grows less and less,
The ground is buoyant as the ether now,
And all looks lovely in thy loveliness.

F. (Frances) Ridley Havergal (1836–1879)

206.   *An Indian Flag*

    The golden gates were opening
        For another welcome guest;
    For a ransomed heir of glory
        Was entering into rest:

    The first in far Umritsur   5
        Who heard the joyful sound,
    The first who came to Jesus
        Within its gloomy bound.

    The wonderers and the watchers
        Around his dying bed,   10
    Saw Christ's own fearless witness
        Safe through the valley led.

    And they whose faithful sowing
        Had not been all in vain,
    Knew that the angels waited   15
        Their sheaf of ripened grain.

    He spoke: 'Throughout the city
        How many a flag is raised
    Where loveless deities are owned,
        And powerless gods are praised!   20

    'I give my house to Jesus,
        That it may always be
    A flag for Christ, the Son of God,
        Who gave Himself for me.'

    And now in far Umritsur   25
        That flag is waving bright,
    Amid the heathen darkness,
        A clear and shining light.

    A house where all may gather
        The words of peace to hear,   30
    And seek the only Saviour
        Without restraint or fear;

Where patient toil of teaching,
    And kindly deeds abound;
Where holy festivals are kept,   35
    And holy songs resound.

First convert of Umritsur,
    Well hast thou led the way;
Now, who will rise and follow?
    Who dares to answer, 'Nay'?   40

O children of salvation!
    O dwellers in the light!
Have ye no 'flag for Jesus,'
    Far-waving, fair, and bright?

Will ye not band together,   45
    And, working hand in hand,
Set up a 'flag for Jesus,'
    In that wide heathen land?

In many an Indian city,
    Oh, let a standard wave,   50
Our gift of love and honour,
    To Him who came to save;

To Him beneath whose banner
    Of wondrous love we rest;
Our Friend, the Friend of sinners,   55
    The Greatest and the Best.

207.   *A Worker's Prayer*

Lord, speak to me, that I may speak
    In living echoes of Thy tone;
As Thou hast sought, so let me seek
    Thy erring children, lost and lone.

O lead me, Lord, that I may lead   5
    The wandering and the wavering feet;
O feed me, Lord, that I may feed
    Thy hungering ones with manna sweet.

> O strengthen me, that while I stand
>   Firm on the Rock and strong in Thee, 10
> I may stretch out a loving hand
>   To wrestlers with the troubled sea.
>
> O teach me, Lord, that I may teach
>   The precious things Thou dost impart;
> And wing my words, that they may reach 15
>   The hidden depths of many a heart.
>
> O give Thine own sweet rest to me,
>   That I may speak with soothing power
> A word in season, as from Thee,
>   To weary ones in needful hour. 20
>
> O fill me with Thy fulness, Lord,
>   Until my very heart o'erflow
> In kindling thought and glowing word,
>   Thy love to tell, Thy praise to show.
>
> O use me, Lord, use even me, 25
>   Just *as* Thou wilt, and *when*, and *where*;
> Until Thy blessèd Face I see,
>   Thy rest, Thy joy, Thy glory share.

208.   *Consecration Hymn*

'Here we offer and present unto Thee, O Lord, ourselves, our souls and bodies, to be a reasonable, holy, and lively sacrifice unto Thee.'

> Take my life, and let it be
> Consecrated, Lord, to Thee.
>
> Take my moments and my days;
> Let them flow in ceaseless praise.
>
> Take my hands, and let them move 5
> At the impulse of Thy love.
>
> Take my feet, and let them be
> Swift and 'beautiful' for Thee.
>
> Take my voice, and let me sing
> Always, only, for my King. 10

Take my lips, and let them be
Filled with messages from Thee.

Take my silver and my gold;
Not a mite would I withhold.

Take my intellect, and use
Every power as Thou shalt choose.

Take my will, and make it Thine;
It shall be no longer mine.

Take my heart, it *is* Thine own;
It shall be Thy royal throne.

Take my love; my Lord, I pour
At Thy feet its treasure-store.

Take myself, and I will be
Ever, *only*, ALL for Thee.

Thomas Ashe (1836–1889)

209. *Pall-Bearing*

I remember, they sent
  Some one to me, who said,
'You were his friend while he lived:
  Be so now he is dead.'

So I went next day to the house;
  And a woman nodded to me,
As I sat alone in thought:–
  Said, 'Sir, would you like to see

The poor dead body upstairs,
  Before we rivet the lid?'
But I said, 'I would rather not:
  For the look would never be hid

'From my sight, day after day,
   From my soul, year after year.
Enough to look on the pall:
   Enough to follow the bier.'

So the mourners gather'd at last;
   And the poor dead body was put
In a hearse with mournful plumes,
   And the door of the hearse was shut.

And when the mourners were all
   In the coaches, ready to start,
The sorrowing parent came
   To me, and whisper'd apart.

He smiled as well as he could;
   And the import of what he said
Was, that I should bear at the feet,
   And his son would bear at the head.

He was ever my friend;
   And I was happy to be
Of ever so little use
   To one who had so loved me.

But, what a weight, O God!
   Was that one coffin to bear!
Like a coffin of lead!
   And I carry it everywhere

About, wherever I go!
   If I lift the slightest thing,
That requires an effort to lift,
   The effort at once will bring

The whole weight into my hands,
   And I carry the corpse at the feet;
And feel as if it would drop,
   And slip out of its winding-sheet.

I have made a vow in my heart,
   Whatever the friends may say,
Never to carry a corpse
   Again, to my dying day.

(1871)

210.

To Two Bereaved

> You must be sad; for though it is to Heaven,
> 'Tis hard to yield a little girl of seven.
> Alas, for me, 'tis hard my grief to rule,
> Who only met her as she went to school;
> Who never heard the little lips so sweet 5
> Say even "good morning," though our eyes would meet
> As whose would fain be friends! How must you sigh,
> Sick for your loss, when even so sad am I,
> Who never clasp'd the small hands any day!
> Fair flowers thrive round the little grave, I pray. 10

211.

To the Maids, Who Will Marry

> You merry maids, with yellow hair, or jet,
> Blown loose or bound or deftly loop'd in net,
> With eyes all hues, and sunny-brow'd and wise,
> With looks too hard, or tender, in your eyes,
> Since 'tis your love, your winning airs divine, 5
> Your fingers laid, or rosy lip, on mine,
> Have been my bliss through bitter years I've known,
> Why will you leave me islanded and lone?
> Why, one by one, thus will you launch away
> On that strange sea whose strand's a wedding-day? 10

(Jane) Ellice Hopkins (1836–1904)

212.

Life in Death

> I heard him in the autumn winds,
>   I felt him in the cadent star,
> And in the shattered mirror of the wave,
>   That still in death a rapture finds,
>   I caught his image faint and far; 5
> And musing in the twilight on the grave,
>   I heard his footstep stealing by,
>   Where the long churchyard grasses sigh.

> But never might I see his face,
>   Though everywhere I found Death's hand,
> And his large language all things living spake;
>   And ever heavy with the grace
>   Of bygone things through all the land
> The song of birds or distant church-bells brake.
>   'I will arise and seek his face,'
>   I said, 'ere wrapped in his embrace.'
>
> 'For Death is king of life,' I cried,
>   'Beauty is but his pomp and state;
> His kiss is on the apple's crimson cheek,
>   And with the grape his feet are dyed,
>   Treading at noon the purple vat;
> And flowers, more radiant hued, more quickly seek
>   His face, betraying, in disguise
>   Their young blooms are but autumn dyes.'
>
> Then I arose ere dawn, and found
>   A faded lily. 'Lo, 'tis He!
> I will surprise him in his golden bed,
>   Where, muffled close from light and sound,
>   He sleeps the day up.' Noiselessly
> I drew the faded curtains from his head,
>   And, peeping, found, not Death below,
>   But fairy life set all arow.
>
> A chrysalis next I chanced upon:
>   'Death in this dusty shroud has dwelt!'
> But stooping saw a wingèd Thing, sun-kist,
>   Crusted with jewels Life had won
>   From Death's dim dust; and as I knelt,
> Some passion shook the jewels into mist,
>   Some ecstasy of coming flight,
>   And lo, he passed in morning light.
>
> And as I paced, still questioning,
>   Behold, a dead bird at my feet;
> The faded violets of his filmy eyes,
>   And tender loosened throat, to sing
>   No more to us his nocturns sweet,
> Told me that death at length before me lies.
>   But gazing, quick I turned in fear,
>   Not Death, but teeming Life was there.

        Then haply Death keeps house within?
          And with the scalpel of keen thought
I traced the chemic travail of the brain,
          The throb and pulse of Life's machine,
          And mystic force with force still caught
In the embrace that maketh one of twain;
          And all the beatings, swift and slow,
          Of Life's vibration to and fro.

        And still I found the downward swing,
          Decay, but ere I cried 'Lo, here!'
The upward stroke rang out glad life and breath;
          And still dead winters changed with spring,
          And graves the new birth's cradle were;
And still I grasped the flying skirts of Death,
          And still he turned, and, beaming fair,
          The radiant face of Life was there!

213. *A Vision of Womanhood*

Out in the desert, half-submerged, a sphinx
Gazed at her awful mirrored loveliness,
In dull deep waters sunk of Lethe, fed
By the dark river of the unknown source;
Gazed at the pure high face that answered hers,
As moon to moon, and lovely moulded curves
Of motherhood that shaped the pure white breast,
And deemed she saw herself, nor knew
That just below the shining surfaces
The woman sickened into unclean beast,
Bestial, with ravening claws and murderous strength;
And all around were strewn the bones of men,
And eyeless sockets filled with desert dust
Of those who cursed her with a dying curse.

Then a great Angel, standing in the sun,
Smote those dull Lethe-waters and they fled,
And all her hidden shame to her lay bare;
And in her agony she knew herself
To be half woman and half beast unclean,
That grew to her and made one shuddering flesh
With her, inextricably one with death.
And all her being burned as in a furnace,

And the cold stone was fused about her heart
Into warm blood and sweat of agony;
While men awe-stricken gazed upon her woe, 25
And every kingdom wailed because of her,
And all the land was darkened for her sake.
Then as one dead before her feet I fell,
Made one with her intolerable shame.

Æons or hours did that deep trance endure? 30
When the dark veil of that abysmal sleep
Was rent in twain by a loud trumpet sound,
And starting up, I saw a temple vast,
And many worshippers therein were bowed.
But on the upturned faces, I beheld 35
The light of a new world, and homage high,
As that a queen may render to her king,
Who owning a subjection yet remains
A majesty—such pure manhood on them lay.
And high above all worshippers enthroned, 40
Lo, the Egyptian woman who abode
With Death in desert places; and behold
The beast was slain, the deathful riddle solved
That slew the man; and throned upon men's hearts—
A wall of fire to guard her round about— 45
A perfect woman in her weakness rose,
And in her arms the future's child divine.

W. (William) S. (Schwenk) Gilbert (1836–1911)

214. 'If you're anxious for to shine in the high aesthetic line'
(Bunthorne's Recital and Song from *Patience*)

As soon as he is alone, BUNTHORNE *changes his manner and becomes intensely melodramatic.*

RECIT. AND SONG—BUNTHORNE

Am I alone,
    And unobserved? I am!
Then let me own
    I'm an æsthetic sham!
This air severe 5

                    Is but a mere
                        Veneer!
                  This cynic smile
                     Is but a wile
                        Of guile!   10
                  This costume chaste
                   Is but a good taste
                       Misplaced!
                    Let me confess!
            A languid love for lilies does *not* blight me!   15
            Lank limbs and haggard cheeks do *not* delight me!
                 I do *not* care for dirty greens
                      By any means.
                 I do *not* long for all one sees
                      That's Japanese.   20
                 I am *not* fond of uttering platitudes
                      In stained-glass attitudes.
                 In short, my mediævalism's affectation,
                 Born of a morbid love of admiration!

                              SONG

If you're anxious for to shine in the high aesthetic line as a man of culture rare,
You must get up all the germs of the transcendental terms, and plant them everywhere.
You must lie upon the daisies and discourse in novel phrases of your complicated
     state of mind,
The meaning doesn't matter if it's only idle chatter of a transcendental kind.
                    And every one will say,   5
                    As you walk your mystic way,
"If this young man expresses himself in terms too deep for *me*,
Why what a singularly deep young man this deep young man must be!"
Be eloquent in praise of the very dull old days which have long since passed away,
And convince 'em, if you can, that the reign of good Queen Anne was Culture's
     palmiest day.   10
Of course you will pooh-pooh whatever's fresh and new, and declare it's crude and mean,
For Art stopped short in the cultivated sport of the Empress Josephine.
                    And every one will say,
                    As you walk your mystic way,
"If that's not good enough for him which is good enough for *me*,   15
Why what a very cultivated kind of youth this kind of youth must be!"
Then a sentimental passion of a vegetable fashion must excite your languid spleen,
An attachment *à la* Plato for a bashful young potato, or a not-too-French French bean!
Though the Philistines may jostle, you will rank as an apostle in the high aesthetic band,
If you walk down Piccadilly with a poppy or a lily in your mediæval hand.   20

                    And everyone will say,
                        As you walk your flowery way,
"If he's content with a vegetable love which would certainly not suit *me*,
Why what a most particularly pure young man this pure young man must be!"

H. (Henry) Cholmondeley Pennell (1836–?)

215.   *'Faite À Peindre'*

'Made to be painted' – a Millais might give
    A fortune to study that exquisite face –
The face is a fortune – a Lawrence might live
    Anew in each line of that figure's still grace.

The pose is perfection, a model each limb,   5
    From the delicate foot to the classical head;
But the almond blue eyes, with their smiling, look dim,
    And lips to be *loved* want a trifle more red.

Statuesque? no, a Psyche, let's say, in repose, –
    A Psyche whose cupid beseeches in vain,–   10
We sigh as the nightingale sighs to the rose
    That declines (it's averred) to give sighs back again....

If the wind shook the rose? then a shower would fall
    Of sweet-scented petals to gather who list;
If a sigh shook my Psyche? she'd yawn, that is all,   15
    She's made to be painted – and not to be kist.

                              (1884)

Algernon Charles Swinburne (1837–1909)

216.   *Fragment on Death*

And Paris be it or Helen dying,
    Who dies soever, dies with pain.
He that lacks breath and wind for sighing,
    His gall bursts on his heart; and then

> He sweats, God knows what sweat! again, 5
> No man may ease him of his grief;
>   Child, brother, sister, none were fain
> To bail him thence for his relief.
>
> Death makes him shudder, swoon, wax pale,
>   Nose bend, veins stretch, and breath surrender, 10
> Neck swell, flesh soften, joints that fail
>   Crack their strained nerves and arteries slender.
>   O woman's body found so tender,
> Smooth, sweet, so precious in men's eyes,
>   Must thou too bear such count to render? 15
> Yes; or pass quick into the skies.

(1878)

217.   *Ballad of the Lords of Old Time*
                    (after the former argument)

> What more? Where is the third Calixt,
>   Last of that name now dead and gone,
> Who held four years the Papalist?
>   Alfonso king of Aragon,
>   The gracious lord, duke of Bourbon, 5
> And Arthur, duke of old Britaine?
>   And Charles the Seventh, that worthy one?
> Even with the good knight Charlemain.
>
> The Scot too, king of mount and mist,
>   With half his face vermilion, 10
> Men tell us, like an amethyst
>   From brow to chin that blazed and shone;
>   The Cypriote king of old renown,
> Alas! and that good king of Spain,
>   Whose name I cannot think upon? 15
> Even with the good knight Charlemain.
>
> No more to say of them I list;
>   'Tis all but vain, all dead and done:
> For death may no man born resist,
>   Nor make appeal when death comes on. 20
>   I make yet one more question;

>   Where's Lancelot, king of far Bohain?
>   Where's he whose grandson called him son?
>   Even with the good knight Charlemain.
>
>   Where is Guesclin, the good Breton?
>   The lord of the eastern mountain-chain
>   And the good late duke of Alençon?
>   Even with the good knight Charlemain.

(1878)

218.   *Nephelidia*

> From the depth of the dreamy decline of the dawn through a
>   notable nimbus of nebulous noonshine,
>   Pallid and pink as the palm of the flag-flower that flickers with
>   fear of the flies as they float,
> Are they looks of our lovers that lustrously lean from a marvel
>   of mystic miraculous moonshine,
>   These that we feel in the blood of our blushes that thicken
>   and threaten with throbs through the throat?
> Thicken and thrill as a theatre thronged at appeal of an actor's
>   appalled agitation,
>   Fainter with fear of the fires of the future than pale with the
>   promise of pride in the past;
> Flushed with the famishing fullness of fever that reddens with
>   radiance of rathe recreation,
>   Gaunt as the ghastliest of glimpses that gleam through the
>   gloom of the gloaming when ghosts go aghast?
> Nay, for the nick of the tick of the time is a tremulous touch on
>   the temples of terror,
>   Strained as the sinews yet strenuous with strife of the dead
>   who is dumb as the dust-heap of death:
> Surely no soul is it, sweet as the spasm of erotic emotional
>   exquisite error,
>   Bathed in the balms of beatified bliss, beatific itself by
>   beatitude's breath.
> Surely no spirit or sense of a soul that was soft to the spirit and soul
>   of our senses
>   Sweetens the stress of suspiring suspicion that sobs in the
>   semblance and sound of a sigh;
> Only this oracle opens Olympian, in mystical moods and
>   triangular tenses –

'Life is the lust of a lamp for the light that is dark till the
    dawn of the day when we die'.
Mild is the mirk and monotonous music of memory,
    melodiously mute as it may be,
  While the hope in the heart of a hero is bruised by the
    breach of men's rapiers, resigned to the rod;
Made meek as a mother whose bosom-beats bound with the
    bliss-bringing bulk of a balm-breathing baby,
  As they grope through the grave-yard of creeds, under skies
    growing green at a groan for the grimness of God.   20
Blank is the book of his bounty beholden of old, and its binding
    is blacker than bluer:
  Out of blue into black is the scheme of the skies, and their
    dews are the wine of the bloodshed of things;
Till the darkling desire of delight shall be free as a fawn that is
    freed from the fangs that pursue her,
  Till the heart-beats of hell shall be hushed by a hymn from the
    hunt that has harried the kennel of kings.

(1880)

219.   *The Higher Pantheism in a Nutshell*

One, who is not, we see: but one, whom we see not, is:
Surely this is not that: but that is assuredly this.

What, and wherefore, and whence? for under is over and under:
If thunder could be without lightning, lightning could be without thunder.

Doubt is faith in the main: but faith, on the whole, is doubt: 5
We cannot believe by proof: but could we believe without?

Why, and whither, and how? for barley and rye are not clover:
Neither are straight lines curves: yet over is under and over.

Two and two may be four: but four and four are not eight:
Fate and God may be twain: but God is the same thing as fate.   10

Ask a man what he thinks, and get from a man what he feels:
God, once caught in the fact, shows you a fair pair of heels.

Body and spirit are twins: God only knows which is which:
The soul squats down in the flesh, like a tinker drunk in a ditch.

More is the whole than a part: but half is more than the whole:
Clearly, the soul is the body: but is not the body the soul?

One and two are not one: but one and nothing is two:
Truth can hardly be false, if falsehood cannot be true.

Once the mastodon was: pterodactyls were common as cocks:
Then the mammoth was God: now is He a prize ox.

Parallels all things are: yet many of these are askew:
You are certainly I: but certainly I am not you.

Springs the rock from the plain, shoots the stream from the rock:
Cocks exist for the hen: but hens exist for the cock.

God, whom we see not, is: and God, who is not we see:
Fiddle, we know, is diddle: and diddle, we take it, is dee.

(1880)

220. *Sonnet: Hope and Fear*

Beneath the shadow of dawn's aerial cope,
   With eyes enkindled as the sun's own sphere,
   Hope from the front of youth in godlike cheer
Looks Godward, past the shades where blind men grope
Round the dark door that prayers nor dreams can ope,
   And makes for joy the very darkness dear
   That gives her wide wings play; nor dreams that fear
At noon may rise and pierce the heart of hope.
Then, when the soul leaves off to dream and yearn,
May truth first purge her eyesight to discern
   What once being known leaves time no power to appal;
Till youth at last, ere yet youth be not, learn
   The kind wise word that falls from years that fall—
"Hope thou not much, and fear thou not at all."

(1882)

221. *A Midsummer Holiday*

ON THE VERGE.

Here begins the sea that ends not till the world's end. Where we stand,
Could we know the next high sea-mark set beyond these waves that gleam,
We should know what never man hath known, nor eye of man hath scanned.
Nought beyond these coiling clouds that melt like fume of shrines that steam
Breaks or stays the strength of waters till they pass our bounds of dream. 5
Where the waste Land's End leans westward, all the seas it watches roll
Find their border fixed beyond them, and a world-wide shore's control:
These whereby we stand no shore beyond us limits: these are free.
Gazing hence, we see the water that grows iron round the Pole,
From the shore that hath no shore beyond it set in all the sea. 10

Sail on sail along the sea-line fades and flashes; here on land
Flash and fade the wheeling wings on wings of mews that plunge and scream.
Hour on hour along the line of life and time's evasive strand
Shines and darkens, wanes and waxes, slays and dies: and scarce they seem
More than motes that thronged and trembled in the brief noon's breath and beam. 15
Some with crying and wailing, some with notes like sound of bells that toll,
Some with sighing and laughing, some with words that blessed and made us whole,
Passed, and left us, and we know not what they were, nor what were we.
Would we know, being mortal? Never breath of answering whisper stole
From the shore that hath no shore beyond it set in all the sea. 20

Shadows, would we question darkness? Ere our eyes and brows be fanned
Round with airs of twilight, washed with dews from sleep's eternal stream,
Would we know sleep's guarded secret? Ere the fire consume the brand,
Would it know if yet its ashes may requicken? yet we deem
Surely man may know, or ever night unyoke her starry team, 25
What the dawn shall be, or if the dawn shall be not: yea, the scroll
Would we read of sleep's dark scripture, pledge of peace or doom of dole.
Ah, but here man's heart leaps, yearning toward the gloom with venturous glee,
Though his pilot eye behold nor bay nor harbour, rock nor shoal,
From the shore that hath no shore beyond it set in all the sea. 30

Friend, who knows if death indeed have life or life have death for goal?
Day nor night can tell us, nor may seas declare nor skies unroll
What has been from everlasting, or if aught shall alway be.
Silence answering only strikes response reverberate on the soul
From the shore that hath no shore beyond it set in all the sea. 35

(1884)

from *A Century of Roundels*

I. *To Catullus*

My brother, my Valerius, dearest head
Of all whose crowning bay-leaves crown their mother
Rome, in the notes first heard of thine I read
    My brother.

No dust that death or time can strew may smother
Love and the sense of kinship inly bred
From loves and hates at one with one another.

To thee was Cæsar's self nor dear nor dread,
Song and the sea were sweeter each than other:
How should I living fear to call thee dead
    My brother?

(1883)

II. *In Guernsey*

(*To Theodore Watts*)

(III.)

Across and along, as the bay's breadth opens, and o'er us
Wild autumn exults in the wind, swift rapture and strong
Impels us, and broader the wide waves brighten before us
    Across and along.

The whole world's heart is uplifted, and knows not wrong;
The whole world's life is a chant to the sea-tide's chorus;
Are we not as waves of the water, as notes of the song?
Like children unworn of the passions and toils that wore us,
We breast for a season the breadth of the seas that throng,
Rejoicing as they, to be borne as of old they bore us
    Across and along.

224.   *A Sequence of Sonnets on the Death of Robert Browning*

I.

The clearest eyes in all the world they read
    With sense more keen and spirit of sight more true
    Than burns and thrills in sunrise, when the dew
Flames, and absorbs the glory round it shed,
As they the light of ages quick and dead,
    Closed now, forsake us: yet the shaft that slew
    Can slay not one of all the works we knew,
Nor death discrown that many-laurelled head.

The works of words whose life seems lightning wrought,
And moulded of unconquerable thought,
    And quickened with imperishable flame,
Stand fast and shine and smile, assured that nought
    May fade of all their myriad-moulded fame,
    Nor England's memory clasp not Browning's name.

(1889)

II

Death, what hast thou to do with one for whom
    Time is not lord, but servant? What least part
    Of all the fire that fed his living heart,
Of all the light more keen than sundawn's bloom
That lit and led his spirit, strong as doom
    And bright as hope, can aught thy breath may dart
    Quench? Nay, thou knowest he knew thee what thou art,
A shadow born of terror's barren womb,
That brings not forth save shadows. What art thou,
To dream, albeit thou breathe upon his brow,
    That power on him is given thee,—that thy breath
Can make him less than love acclaims him now,
    And hears all time sound back the word it saith?
    What part hast thou then in his glory, Death?

III

A graceless doom it seems that bids us grieve:
    Venice and winter, hand in deadly hand,
    Have slain the lover of her sunbright strand
And singer of a stormbright Christmas Eve.
A graceless guerdon we that loved receive

For all our love, from that the dearest land
      Love worshipped ever. Blithe and soft and bland, 35
Too fair for storm to scathe or fire to cleave,
Shone on our dreams and memories evermore
The domes, the towers, the mountains and the shore
      That gird or guard thee, Venice: cold and black
Seems now the face we loved as he of yore. 40
      We have given thee love—no stint, no stay, no lack:
      What gift, what gift is this thou hast given us back?

                          IV

But he—to him, who knows what gift is thine,
   Death? Hardly may we think or hope, when we
      Pass likewise thither where to-night is he, 45
Beyond the irremeable outer seas that shine
And darken round such dreams as half divine
      Some sunlit harbour in that starless sea
      Where gleams no ship to windward or to lee,
To read with him the secret of thy shrine. 50

There too, as here, may song, delight, and love,
The nightingale, the sea-bird, and the dove,
      Fulfil with joy the splendour of the sky
Till all beneath wax bright as all above:
      But none of all that search the heavens, and try 55
      The sun, may match the sovereign eagle's eye.

                                                  (1889)

                          V

Among the wondrous ways of men and time
      He went as one that ever found and sought
      And bore in hand the lamp-like spirit of thought
To illume with instance of its fire sublime 60
The dusk of many a cloudlike age and clime.
      No spirit in shape of light and darkness wrought,
      No faith, no fear, no dream, no rapture, nought
That blooms in wisdom, nought that burns in crime,
No virtue girt and armed and helmed with light, 65
No love more lovely than the snows are white,
      No serpent sleeping in some dead soul's tomb,
No song-bird singing from some live soul's height,
      But he might hear, interpret, or illume
      With sense invasive as the dawn of doom. 70

VI

What secret thing of splendour or of shade
   Surmised in all those wandering ways wherein
   Man, led of love and life and death and sin,
Strays, climbs, or cowers, allured, absorbed, afraid,
Might not the strong and sunlike sense invade
   Of that full soul that had for aim to win
   Light, silent over time's dark toil and din,
Life, at whose touch death fades as dead things fade?
O spirit of man, what mystery moves in thee
That he might know not of in spirit, and see
   The heart within the heart that seems to strive,
The life within the life that seems to be,
   And hear, through all thy storms that whirl and drive,
   The living sound of all men's souls alive?

VII

He held no dream worth waking: so he said,
   He who stands now on death's triumphal steep,
   Awakened out of life wherein we sleep
And dream of what he knows and sees, being dead.
But never death for him was dark or dread:
   "Look forth" he bade the soul, and fear not. Weep,
   All ye that trust not in his truth, and keep
Vain memory's vision of a vanished head
As all that lives of all that once was he
Save that which lightens from his word: but we,
   Who, seeing the sunset-coloured waters roll,
Yet know the sun subdued not of the sea,
   Nor weep nor doubt that still the spirit is whole,
   And life and death but shadows of the soul.

(1890)

(Julia) Augusta Webster (1837–1894)

225.   *The Flowing Tide*

The slow green wave comes curling from the bay
   And leaps in spray along the sunny marge,
And steals a little more and more away,
   And drowns the dulse, and lifts the stranded barge.

Leave me, strong tide, my smooth and yellow shore;
But the clear waters deepen more and more:
   Leave me my pathway of the sands, strong tide;
   Yet are the waves more fair than all they hide.

226.
The Lovers

And we are lovers, lovers he and I:
   Oh sweet dear name that angels envy us;
Lovers for now, lovers for by and by,
   And God to hear us call each other thus.
Flow softly, river of our life, and fair;
We float together to the otherwhere:
   Storm, river of our life, if storm must be,
   We brunt thy tide together to that sea.

227.
We Two

The road slopes on that leads us to the last,
   And we two tread it softly, side by side;
'Tis a blithe count the milestones we have passed,
   Step fitting step, and each of us for guide.
My love, and I thy love, our road is fair,
And fairest most because the other's there:
   Our road is fair, adown the harvest hill,
   But fairest that we two are we two still.

We Two

We two, we two! the children's smiles are dear—
   Thank God how dear the bonny children's smiles!—
But 'tis we two among our own ones here,
   We two along life's way through all the whiles.
To think if we had passed each other by;
And he not he apart, and I not I!
   And oh to think if we had never known;
   And I not I and he not he alone!

228. Where Home Was

'Twas yesterday; 'twas long ago:
  And for this flaunting grimy street,
And for this crowding to and fro,
  And thud and roar of wheels and feet,
    Were elm-trees and the linnet's trill,
    The little gurgles of the rill,
And breath of meadow-flowers that blow
  Ere roses make the summer sweet.

'Twas long ago; 'twas yesterday:
  Our peach would just be new with leaves,
The swallow pair that used to lay
    Their glimmering eggs beneath our eaves
    Would flutter busy with their brood,
    And, haply, in our hazel-wood,
Small village urchins hide at play,
  And girls sit binding blue-bell sheaves.

Was the house here, or there, or there?
  No landmark tells. All changed; all lost;
As when the waves that fret and tear
    The fore-shores of some level coast
    Roll smoothly where the sea-pinks grew.
    All changed, and all grown old anew;
And I pass over, unaware,
  The memories I am seeking most.

But where these huddled house-rows spread,
  And where this thickened air hangs murk
And the dim sun peers round and red
    On stir and haste and cares and work,
    For me were baby's daisy-chains,
    For me the meetings in the lanes,
The shy good-morrows softly said
  That paid my morning's lying lurk.

Oh lingering days of long ago,
  Not until now you passed away.
Years wane between and we unknow;
    Our youth is always yesterday.
    But, like a traveller home who craves
    For friends and finds forgotten graves,
I seek you where you dwelt, and, lo,
  Even farewells not left to say.

229.   *The Flood of Is in Brittany*

Crests of foam where the milch-kine fed,
   Where the green corn whitened and tanned;
Crests of foam and breakers ahead,
   And the deeps run smooth over rocks and sand.
Will the flood-tide back at the churchyard slope?   5
   Mercy, God, from thy sea!
'Twill check at the church and the graves. There's hope.
   Christ, let some land yet be!
   The surf came sprinkling over the graves:
     Then, human speed to the speed of waves,   10
And the drowning sank to the blessèd dead.

Fly who can! No moment to breathe:
   If the homes wreck, life is worth most.
Sound from the front of surges that seethe!
   'Tis the sea rolling in from the other coast.   15
Sea from the west! Sea from the south!
   "Husband! snatched in the tide!"
"Child, thy mother?" "She kissed my mouth,
   And sat with baby and cried,
For she could not carry him any more."   20
   "Brother, farewell, lest neither reach shore."
Flood, flood right and left! Is there footing beneath?

Grallon rode, rode, and said no word,
   Till the white foam splashed at his knee.
"Cling more close, my tender pet-bird;   25
   No fear but stout Gael save thee and me."
St. Gwenolé rode behind the king,
   Muttered low in his prayer,
"Can God will the life of this wanton thing,
   She that scoffed everywhere?"   30
   Foremost and fastest the great tide raced;
   Dahut, clasped firm to her father's waist,
Prayed in her terror, and never stirred.

Speed of horse to the flood-tide's speed:
   And the high land seemed ever more far.   35
Grallon cried out, and patted his steed,
   "Hurry thee, Gael, or we drown where we are."
Spake St. Gwenolé, riding at Grallon's hand,
   "Gael bears weight of sin:
She that has brought God's doom on thy land   40
   Sits him; the tide will win."

Quoth Grallon, "Thou'rt holy, and I forgive;
  None else could have spoken thus and live."
But proud fair Dahut gave scarcely heed.

Gael forced through amid the brunt   45
  Where the waves lashed at side and flanks.
St. Gwenolé's horse plunged on to the front,
  St. Gwenolé cried, "Douarnenez banks!
We'd reach them yet, if Gael bore one.
    Grallon, God bids, obey: 50
Thy kingdom drowns for the sins she has done;
    Cast the sinner away."
  King Grallon spoke slowly, "She's my child."
    Fair Dahut lifted her head and smiled;
And 'twas "Wait till Douarnenez, priest, for my thanks."   55

Dead and drowning came on with the scud;
  And the swimmers clutched wrack and drift;
Mark's hill tore and slipped with a thud,
  And the sea made a whirling pool in the rift.
Gwenolé's horse had the water shoal;   60
    Grallon's kept losing his feet,
Swam, but once shrieked like a human soul:
    Grallon's had two in seat.
  On a moment's ground Grallon gave him halt,
    Looked back. Oh, the Heavens for Dahut's fault   65
No city, no landmarks—bare trackless flood.

"Heart! dear father: Gael must swim."
  It was Dahut's voice at his ear.
Close she sat and clinging to him
  She the thing of the world he held dear.   70
Her little fingers were knitted so tight,
    Grallon needed his strength:
But 'twixt such a two was no equal strife;
    'Twas but a minute's length.
  "Father!" she cried, and then, "Murderer!"   75
    Then fell. So her sins were revenged on her;
And the flood-tide stayed at a low rock rim.

230.   *Mother and Daughter*
An Uncompleted Sonnet-Sequence (I, IX, X, XI)

I

Young laughters, and my music! Aye till now
   The voice can reach no blending minors near;
   'Tis the bird's trill because the spring is here
And spring means trilling on a blossomy bough;
'Tis the spring joy that has no why or how,
   But sees the sun and hopes not nor can fear —
   Spring is so sweet and spring seems all the year.
Dear voice, the first-come birds but trill as thou.

Oh music of my heart, be thus for long:
Too soon the spring bird learns the later song;
   Too soon a sadder sweetness slays content;
Too soon! There comes new light on onward day,
There comes new perfume o'er a rosier way:
   Comes not again the young spring joy that went.

(1881)

IX

Oh weary hearts! Poor mothers that look back!
   So outcasts from the vale where they were born
   Turn on their road and, with a joy forlorn,
See the far roofs below their arid track:
So in chill buffets while the sea grows black
   And windy skies, once blue, are tost and torn,
   We are not yet forgetful of the morn,
And praise anew the sunshine that we lack.

Oh, sadder than pale sufferers by a tomb
   That say 'My dead is happier, and is more,'
   Are they who dare no 'is' but tell what's o'er —
   Thus the frank childhood, those the lovable ways —
   Stirring the ashes of remembered days
For yet some sparks to warm the livelong gloom.

X

Love's Counterfeit

Not Love, not Love, that worn and footsore thrall
   Who, crowned with withered buds and leaves gone dry,   30
     Plods in his chains to follow one passed by,
Guerdoned with only tears himself lets fall.
Love is asleep and smiling in his pall,
   And this that wears his shape and will not die
     Was once his comrade shadow, Memory –   35
His shadow that now stands for him in all.

And there are those who, hurrying on past reach,
   See the dim follower and laugh, content,
     'Lo, Love pursues me, go where'er I will!'
Yet, longer gazing, some may half beseech,   40
   'This *must* be Love that wears his features still:
Or else when was the moment that Love went?'

XI

Love's Mourner

'Tis men who say that through all hurt and pain
   The woman's love, wife's, mother's, still will hold,
   And breathes the sweeter and will more unfold   45
For winds that tear it, and the sorrowful rain.
So in a thousand voices has the strain
   Of this dear patient madness been retold,
   That men call woman's love. Ah! they are bold,
Naming for love that grief which *does* remain.   50

Love faints that looks on baseness face to face:
   Love pardons all; but by the pardonings dies,
     With a fresh wound of each pierced through the breast.
And there stand pityingly in Love's void place
   Kindness of household wont familiar-wise.   55
     And faith to Love – faith to our dead at rest.

(1882)

Sarah ('Sadie') Williams (1837/8–1868)

from *Nature Apostate*

231.   *The Life of a Leaf*

I. THE BUD

Close within a downy cover
   Here at rest I lie,
Half awake and half in slumber
   While the storms go by.

Sometimes vague impatient strivings
   Stir my life within;
Hopes of being something worthy,
   Longing to begin.

Then again a soft contentment
   Broodeth o'er my state;
When the time comes I am ready,
   Until then I wait.

II. THE LEAFLET

Is this then life? 'Tis glorious, so fair!
   The sweet soft breezes playing round our rest,
The summer fragrance growing everywhere,
   The happy birds low cooing in their nest.

What meant the fear with which we put on life?
   It is all good, and hope comes after joy;
Come anything in this delightsome strife,
   Storms cannot daunt us, sunshine cannot cloy.

III. SUMMER LEAF

Kiss me, kiss me, kingly sun,
   Till I glow with crimson light,
Till along my veins shall run
   Liquid lustre glistening bright.

　　　　　Let thy touch so piercing sweet 5
　　　　　　　Hold me close and thrill me through,
　　　　　Till I faint with languid heat,
　　　　　　　Till for rest from thee I sue;
　　　　　Hear me not, O king of light!
　　　　　　　Let me die within thy sight. 10

IV. AUTUMN LEAF

　　　　　I wonder what has vanished from the world,
　　　　　　　It was so bright a little while ago;
　　　　　And now we leaves upon the branches curled
　　　　　　　Hang wearily, just swaying to and fro.

232.　　　　　　　*President Lincoln*

　　　　　"They killed him then? the cowards—be it so!
　　　　　　　Henceforth he is immortal— President,
　　　　　Until the dead shall waken: none may know
　　　　　　　His term of office now, nor how 'tis spent.

　　　　　"His life is rounded off and perfect now; 5
　　　　　　　It reached its fitting climax when great Death
　　　　　Herself stooped down to crown the victor's brow,
　　　　　　　And set the seal of silence on his breath.

　　　　　"Nor foe nor friend can fret him into speech;
　　　　　　　He shines as calmly as some distant star, 10
　　　　　Whose light these lower worlds of ours can reach,
　　　　　　　While not a cloud doth e'er extend so far.

　　　　　"Silent and grand, embalmed in suffering,
　　　　　　　What monarch ever lay in state like this?
　　　　　We dare not weep, we hear the angels sing, 15
　　　　　　　Exultant, as they welcome him to bliss."

Charlotte Elliot ('Florenz') (1839–1880)

233. *The Pythoness*

'Bind up her loose hair in the fillet, and wipe the cold dew from her cheek,
For the force of the spirit has left her outwearied, and nerveless, and weak.'
So murmured the pitying maidens, and soothed me, and laid me to rest,
And lightly the leopard-skin mantle drew over my shivering breast;
Then bent their warm faces to kiss me, with tenderness mingled with awe, 5
Revering the god in his priestess, whose word is obeyed as a law
By the tyrant, the terror of nations. A word from my lips, and the land
Shall have rest, and the weapon uplifted shall fall from the threatening hand;
Though gifts may be heaped on the altar, rich goblet and gold-embossed shield,
The gods give no promise of favour, and keep what they will unrevealed. 10
Shall I glory in this, that decreeing the close or beginning of strife,
I, who speak what I know not, am chosen controller of death and of life?
Nay; I, who was voiceless, am fated to be as a flute which is blown
By the powerful breath of immortals, to music which is not its own:
Soon, soon, strained to tones superhuman, unfitted for use or delight, 15
The tremulous flute will lie shattered, cast out from remembrance and sight.
My maidens have left me to slumber; but tears scorch my eyelids instead—
Tears, bitter with passionate envy of those either living or dead;
Not as I, who exist in illusion, with body and soul rent apart,
Possessed by a terrible spirit, pierced through by a fiery dart, 20
Caught up by a whirlwind, tormented with light too intense for my brain,
Till the vision is past, and I waken remembering nought but the pain.
O mighty and cruel Apollo, thy gift is despair and the grave!
My life, like a wreck on the ocean, is tossed to and fro by the wave.

O fair, pleasant home of my childhood!—dear valley, thy shadows are cool; 25
All pale in the languor of noontide the lily bends over the pool,
The laurel and cistus are fettered by tangles of blossoming weeds,
The rose leans her cheek to the ivy, the asphodel shines through the reeds;
Wild bees, with low rapturous murmurs, drink deep at the hyacinth's heart,
And over the mystical lotus bright legions of dragon-flies dart. 30
And there dwelt my woodland companions, my tender-voiced soft-breasted dove,
Which perched on my shoulder, with flutterings and murmurs of pleasure and love;
And my gentle white fawn, the fleet-footed, whose breath was so wondrously sweet,
For he fed upon rose-leaves, and ever he lay on the moss at my feet,
And his wild, wistful eyes shone like jewels, as if he delighted to hear 35
The dream-woven songs which I fashioned and sang when no other was near.

I pine for the breeze of the forest, I thirst for the spring cold as ice,
Instead of these fumes of rich incense, this draught mixed with dream-giving spice;
I long for my infancy's slumber, untroubled by phantoms of dread;
I long for cool dews of the morning, to drop on my fever-hot head; 40
I long—how I long—to be cradled once more in the valley's soft breast,
And, lulled by my childhood's lost music, to sink like a babe into rest.

★ ★ ★

The day died in flames on the mountains, and stealthily, hiding the skies
With a film of thick-gathering darkness, night fell on the earth by surprise;
But flashes of wild summer lightning played over the tops of the pines, 45
And glanced on the streams—which meandered in slender and silvery lines,
'Mid alder, and willow, and hazel—and shone in my face, as I fled
Alone through the depths of the forest, all panting and trembling with dread.
Astray in the darkness, I threaded the briery paths of the wood,
Then burst through the thicket. Before me, terrific and glorious, stood— 50
Oh horror! the oak of Apollo—the haunted, the fearful, the vast;
Whose roots search the earth's deep foundations, whose limbs are as steel in the blast:
Pale visions that may not be uttered, dwell under its branches at night,
And strike the beholder with madness, and wither his limbs and his sight.
The hand of the god was upon me, the power that is mighty to form 55
My life at his will, as the cloud-wreaths are shaped by the power of the storm;
And my heart fainted in me for terror, since nowhere unmarked could I flee
From the doom that pursued me. Then, dimly, I saw in the shade of the tree
The priest of the temple; and onward he came, and drew near, and his gaze
Sought me out and subdued and enthralled me, and pierced me with glittering rays, 60
Which drew forth my soul from my body, with force that I could not resist,
Then grew into flames, and enwound me in meshes of fiery mist;
My eyelids drooped under the pressure, a shock of unbearable pain
Thrilled through me, as keen as a sword-thrust; then darkness fell over my brain.

★ ★ ★

Great Delphi! in desolate grandeur thy cliffs stand all bare to the sky, 65
As barren of beauty and freshness, as lonely and mournful as I.
The scream of the wandering eagle rings over thy echoing rocks;
The vultures flock hitherward, scenting the flesh of the sacrificed ox;
But the murmurous voice of the woodland shall never more breathe in my ear,
Nor Philomel's passionate music melt stones into tenderness here; 70
My soul has resigned its communion with all that it cherished and loved;
From dreams of a happier future, for ever and ever removed.
No love-lay shall thrill with my praises the balmy and sensitive air,
No hand shall twine garlands of jasmine to star the deep night of my hair,
No eye shall grow soft at my presence, nor watch me with rapturous glance, 75
Amid the bright circle of maidens move swift through the rhythmical dance,—
No bridegroom shall woo me, no taper of marriage be lighted for me,
No children with flower-like faces shall smile away care at my knee.

But surely the night will bring slumber, and surely the grave will bring rest,
And my spirit be lapped in Elysium in balm-breathing isles of the blest;   80
And as summer, and sunshine, and beauty are born of the elements' strife,
My life, which brought death, be transmuted at last into death which brings life.
For luminous visions surround me, and exquisite forms hover near,
Caress me with soft spirit-touches, and murmur strange words in my ear:
Through air which seems empty to others, bright spirit-shapes cluster and throng:—   85
Already I mix with their essence, already I join in their song.

(1867; reprinted 1878)

Walter Pater (1839–1894)

234.   *Style*

Since all progress of mind consists for the most part in differentiation, in the resolution of an obscure and complex object into its component aspects, it is surely the stupidest of losses to confuse things which right reason has put asunder, to lose the sense of achieved distinctions, the distinction between poetry and prose, for instance, or, to speak more exactly, between the laws and characteristic excellences of verse and prose composition. On the other hand, those who have dwelt most emphatically on the distinction between prose and verse, prose and poetry, may sometimes have been tempted to limit the proper functions of prose too narrowly; and this again is at least false economy, as being, in effect, the renunciation of a certain means or faculty, in a world where after all we must needs make the most of things. Critical efforts to limit art *a priori*, by anticipations regarding the natural incapacity of the material with which this or that artist works, as the sculptor with solid form, or the prose-writer with the ordinary language of men, are always liable to be discredited by the facts of artistic production; and while prose is actually found to be a coloured thing with Bacon, picturesque with Livy and Carlyle, musical with Cicero and Newman, mystical and intimate with Plato and Michelet and Sir Thomas Browne, exalted or florid, it may be, with Milton and Taylor, it will be useless to protest that it can be nothing at all, except something very tamely and narrowly confined to mainly practical ends—a kind of "good round-hand;" as useless as the protest that poetry might not touch prosaic subjects as with Wordsworth, or an abstruse matter as with Browning, or treat contemporary life nobly as with Tennyson. In subordination to one essential beauty in all good literary style, in all literature as a fine art, as there are many beauties of poetry so the beauties of prose are many, and it is the business of criticism to estimate them as such; as it is good in the criticism of verse to look for those hard, logical, and quasi-prosaic excellences which that too has, or needs. To find in the poem, amid the flowers, the allusions, the mixed perspectives, of *Lycidas* for instance, the thought, the logical structure:—how wholesome! how delightful! as to identify in prose what we call the poetry, the imaginative power, not treating it as out of place and a kind of vagrant intruder, but by way of an estimate of its rights, that is, of its achieved powers, there.

Dryden, with the characteristic instinct of his age, loved to emphasise the distinction between poetry and prose, the protest against their confusion with each other, coming with somewhat diminished effect from one whose poetry was so prosaic. In truth, his sense of prosaic excellence affected his verse rather than his prose, which is not only fervid, richly figured, poetic, as we say, but vitiated, all unconsciously, by many a scanning line. Setting up correctness, that humble merit of prose, as the central literary excellence, he is really a less correct writer than he may seem, still with an imperfect mastery of the relative pronoun. It might have been foreseen that, in the rotations of mind, the province of poetry in prose would find its assertor; and, a century after Dryden, amid very different intellectual needs, and with the need therefore of great modifications in literary form, the range of the poetic force in literature was effectively enlarged by Wordsworth. The true distinction between prose and poetry he regarded as the almost technical or accidental one of the absence or presence of metrical beauty, or, say! metrical restraint; and for him the opposition came to be between verse and prose of course—but, as the essential dichotomy in this matter, between imaginative and unimaginative writing, parallel to De Quincey's distinction between "the literature of power and the literature of knowledge," in the former of which the composer gives us not fact, but his peculiar sense of fact, whether past or present, or prospective, it may be, as often in oratory.

Dismissing then, under sanction of Wordsworth, that harsher opposition of poetry to prose, as savouring in fact of the arbitrary psychology of the last century, and with it the prejudice that there can be but one only beauty of prose style, I propose here to point out certain qualities of all literature as a fine art, which, if they apply to the literature of fact, apply still more to the literature of the imaginative sense of fact, while they apply indifferently to verse and prose, so far as either is really imaginative—certain conditions of true art in both alike, which conditions may also contain in them the secret of the proper discrimination and guardianship of the peculiar excellences of either.

John Todhunter (1839–1916)

235. *Snake-Charm*

I

Into this dusky bower
Of sylvan quiet
Where roses and rank vines
Only run riot,
Whence comest thou, dark Shape, at this sweet hour,   5
Into this lonely bower?

2

'I am the spectral form
 Of hopes forgotten,
Birth-strangled babes of joy
 Left to grow rotten, 10
Corpses of unborn deeds, devoured still warm
 By sloth's corrupting swarm.'

3

Welcome, thou dismal guest,
 Sit down beside me,
Lie by me all night long, 15
 Sting me and chide me.
At dawn I'll gather fruits to lull thy rest,
 Thou serpent of the breast!

John Addington Symonds (1840–1893)

236.   *Personality*

I

I know not what I am.—Oh dreadful thought!—
 Nor know I what my fellow-creatures are:
 Between me and the world without, a bar
 Impalpable of adamant is wrought.
Each self, from its own self concealed, is caught 5
 Thus in a cage of sense, sequestered far
 From comradeship, calling as calleth star
 To star across blank intermediate nought.
His own self no man sees, and none hath seen
 His brother's self. Nay, lovers, though they sigh 10
 'There is no room for ought to come between
'Our blended souls in this felicity,'
 Starting from sleep, shall find a double screen
 Built 'twixt two sundered selves—and both must die.

II

    Yea, both shall carry with them to the void 15
        Without, the void more terrible within,
        Tormented haply by the smart of sin,
        And cursing what their wilful sense enjoyed.
    Yet were they free to take or to avoid?
        Who knows!—Amid the dull chaotic din 20
        Of wrangling schools which argument can win
        Conviction, when blind faith hath been destroyed?
    Freedom or servitude?—So fooled is man
        By blind self-ignorance, he cannot say
        If will alone beneath heaven's azure span 25
    Its self-determined impulses obey;
        Or if each impulse, wild as wind at play,
        Be but a cog-wheel in the cosmic plan.

237.   *The Will*

    Blame not the times in which we live,
    Nor Fortune frail and fugitive;
    Blame not thy parents, nor the rule
    Of vice or wrong once learned at school;
        But blame thyself, O man! 5

    Although both heaven and earth combined
    To mould thy flesh and form thy mind,
    Though every thought, word, action, will,
    Was framed by powers beyond thee, still
        Thou art thyself, O man! 10

    And self to take or leave is free,
    Feeling its own sufficiency:
    In spite of science, spite of fate,
    The judge within thee soon or late
        Will blame but thee, O man! 15

    Say not, 'I would, but could not—He
    'Should bear the blame, who fashioned me—
    'Call you mere change of motive choice?'—
    Scorning such pleas, the inner voice
        Cries, 'Thine the deed, O man!' 20

238.   *A Dream of Burial in Mid Ocean*

  Down through the deep deep grey-green seas, in sleep,
    Plunged my drowsed soul; and ever on and on,
    Hurrying at first, then where the faint light shone
    Through fathoms twelve, with slackening fall did creep:
Nor touched the bottom of that bottomless steep,   5
    But with a slow sustained suspension,
    Buoyed 'mid the watery wildernesses wan,
    Like a thin cloud in air, voyaged the deep.
Then all those dreadful faces of the sea,
    Horned things abhorred and shapes intolerable,   10
    Fixing glazed lidless eyes, swam up to me,
And pushed me with their snouts, and coiled and fell
    In spiral volumes writhing horribly—
    Jagged fins grotesque, fanged ghastly jaws of hell.

239.   *An Invitation to the Sledge*

    Come forth, for dawn is breaking;
      The sun hath touched the snow:
    Our blithe sledge-bells are calling,
      And Christian waits below.

    All day o'er snow-drifts gliding   5
      'Twixt grey-green walls of ice,
    We'll chase the winter sunlight
      Adown the precipice.

    Above black swirling death-waves
      We will not shrink nor blanch,   10
    Though the bridge that spans the torrent
      Be built by an avalanche.

    We'll talk of love and friendship
      And hero-hearted men,
    Mid the stems of spangled larches   15
      In the fairy-frosted glen.

    With flight as swift as swallows
      We'll sweep the curdled lake,
    Where the groans of prisoned kelpies
      Make the firm ice-pavement quake.   20

> We'll thread the sombre forest,
>   Where giant pines are crowned
> With snow-caps on their branches
>   Bent to the snowy ground.
>
> Strong wine of exultation, 25
>   Free thoughts that laugh at death,
> Shall warm our wingèd spirits
>   Though the shrill air freeze our breath.
>
> With many a waif of music
>   And memory-wafted song, 30
> With the melody of faces
>   Loved when the world was young,
>
> With clear Hellenic stories
>   And names of old romance,
> We'll wake our soul's deep echoes 35
>   While the hills around us dance;
>
> Dance to the arrowy motion
>   Of our sledge so firm and free,
> Skimming the beaten snow-track
>   As a good ship skims the sea. 40
>
> Like love, like all that's joyous,
>   Like youth, like life's delight,
> This day is dawning o'er us
>   Between a night and a night.
>
> O friend, 'tis ours to clasp it! 45
>   Come forth! No better bliss
> For hearts by hope uplifted
>   Hath heaven or earth than this!

240.   *Love in Dreams*

> Love hath his poppy-wreath,
>   Not Night alone.
> I laid my head beneath
>   Love's lilied throne:
> Then to my sleep he brough 5
>   This anodyne—

            The flower of many a thought
                And fancy fine:
            A form, a face, no more;
                Fairer than truth;   10
            A dream from death's pale shore;
                The soul of youth:
            A dream so dear, so deep,
                All dreams above,
            That still I pray to sleep—   15
                Bring Love back, Love!

(William) Cosmo Monkhouse (1840–1901)

241.   *Her Face*

                              I

            Had I a painter's skill,
            There are no changeless lines
            That could its grace imprison,
            But as I laboured still
            To trace its sweet confines,   5
            Ever some quick spontaneous light,
            As of a star,
            Or sun new-risen,
            Would change the cold to warm, the dull to bright,
            And all my labour mar.   10

                              II

            Ever some secret missed,
            Some swift-escaping glow,
            Some one look in the eyes,
            Some strange smile never kissed,
            Would melt as melting snow;   15
            That even were my pencil quicker
            Than wind or wing,
            Or could it rise
            And fall as shadows to the leaves' least flicker,
            It were a useless thing.   20

III

Only but yesterday
She was as cold as ice,
As any marble still,
Her eyes were pale and gray
As though for sacrifice;
I little ever thought to see her so;
But as I came,
Her loving will
Filled her sweet features, as an afterglow
Fills the gray skies with flame.

IV

'Tis ever strange to me,
When she is sad at heart,
Where her deep dimples go,
And a like mystery
When back again they start.
How can my hand move quicker than my eyes,
Which are too slow
To disentwine
The least of all the sweet intricacies
Of her face which is mine?

V

And yet I sometimes think
'Tis just because I love her
I cannot draw her face,
Because upon the brink
I hang till all is over,
The fingers waiting for the soul's release.
If for the space
I see my love
My mouth is voiceless till the vision cease,
How shall my fingers move?

VI

But if I sing of her
When she is far removed
May I not limn her too?
Ah, if much worth ye were
My songs, if my beloved

Would quicken ye with music of her face.
Each day anew
Some song I sing,
Yet of her loveliness not one small grace
Makes it a precious thing.   60

VII

Natheless I know her well—
Though she change e'en as much
As light within a flower,
And aye her face can tell,
Because there is none such   65
In any land beyond the farthest sea,
And hour by hour
I wonder why
She ever thought to give it all to me—
To me so utterly.   70

VIII

Yet many a portrait fair
Of other lovely ones
Have I seen like to her.
I seem to hear the air
Sweet with her very tones.   75
Yet what to me were such things to possess!
Ay, though they stir
With life and speak!
Wanting that little one unruly tress
That strays upon her cheek.   80

IX

She is beyond all art
Of any sweetest word,
Of brush however fine;
And yet I wrong my heart
Who hath a chamber stored   85
With many a face of her and perfect all.
Ah, joy divine,
When quite alone,
To steal and turn them slowly from the wall,
Tenderly, one by one.   90

242.   *Under the Oak*

(To W. E. H.)

Soft the windblow and sunshine
In this garden which is mine,
Scarce a hundred yards in girth,
Yet a part of all the earth!
World for carpet, roof of skies,   5
Walls of Nature's tapestries,
Nought between the sun and me
Save the curtain of a tree.

Here as 'neath the oak I sit,
Whisperings come out of it;   10
Summer-fancies, half desires,
Breaths that fan forgotten fires,
Trembling little waifs of song
Seeking words to make them strong,
Life that dies without a sorrow,   15
Butterflies of no to-morrow,
Odours of a bygone day,
All the sweets that will not stay,
All the sweets that never cloy,
Unembodied souls of joy,   20
Sing and flutter, flash and go,
With a ceaseless interflow;
Till at last some happier seed,
Finds the rest its brothers need,
Strikes a root and grows and climbs,   25
Buds in words and flowers in rhymes.

Who shall tell me how it came!
Was it in the winnowed flame
Golden-dripping through the leaves
Like the grain of heavenly sheaves?   30
From the voice of throstle clear
Was it filtered through the ear?
Came it thus, or did it come
Borne upon the wild bees' hum,
That a moment buzzed around   35
With a circle charmed of sound?
Or did zephyr in a dell,
Steal it with a scent as well

From some hidden flower bell,
To instil its life in me 40
With a subtle chemistry?

    Little knew I, but a sense,
Solemn, delicate, intense,
Filled my spirit with a bliss,
Sweeter, holier, than a kiss. 45
Liquid, radiant, unthought,
That at once all being brought
Into rarer harmony,
Beast and bird and sun and tree,
Air and perfume, God and me. 50

    Just as one whose birthright lost,
Wander-struck and passion-tost,
After many a loveless day
Sails at length into a bay
Where he thinks his bones to lay; 55
Finds indeed an end to strife,
Not in dying, but in life,
Friends and kindred, birthright, all,
With dear love for coronal.

    So at length I seemed at home, 60
Underneath that distant dome,
Where the spirit holds at ease
Frank communion with the trees;
Comrade of the boundless wind,
Linked in universal mind 65
With all things which live or are,
From the daisy to the star,
Part for once of nature's plan
Not the lonely exile—Man.

243.   *The Christ upon the Hill: A Ballad*

PART I

A couple old sat o'er the fire,
    And they were bent and gray;
They burned the charcoal for their Lord,
    Who lived long leagues away.

Deep in the wood the old pair dwelt, 5
    Far from the paths of men,
And saw no face but their poor son's,
    And a wanderer's now and then.

The son, alas! Had grown apace,
    And left his wits behind; 10
He was as helpless as the air,
    As empty as the wind.

With puffing lips and shambling feet,
    And eyes a-staring wide,
He whistled ever as he went, 15
    And little did beside.

He whistled high, he whistled low,
    He whistled sharp and sweet;
He brought the redbreast to his hand,
    And the brown hare to his feet. 20

Without a fear of beast or bird,
    He wandered all the day;
But when the light began to fail
    His courage passed away.

He feared the werewolf in the wood, 25
    The dragon in the dell,
And home he fled as if pursued
    By all the hosts of hell.

"Ah! we are old," the woman said,
    "And soon shall we be gone, 30
And what will our poor Michael do
    When he is left alone?

"We are forgotten of all men;
    And he is dead, I fear,
That good old priest, who used to come 35
    And shrive us thrice a year.

"We have no kin," the mother said,
    "We have no friend," said she;
The father gazed upon the fire,
    And not a word said he. 40

Again she spoke, "No friend or kin,
    'Death, only Death,' is near;
And he will take us both away,
    And leave our Michael here.

"And who shall give him bite or sup? 45
    And who shall keep him neat?
Ah! what were Heaven if we must weep
    Before God's mercy-seat!"

And when the woman ceased, the man
    A little waited still, 50
And then he said, "We have one friend—
    The Christ upon the Hill."

PART II

The Christ upon the Hill – so gaunt
    And lean and stark and drear;
It made the heart with pity start, 55
    It smote the soul with fear.

High reared against a cliff it stood,
    Just where the great roads met;
And many a knee had worn the stone
    Wherein the Rood was set. 60

For deadly was the pass beyond,
    And all men paused to pray
For courage, or to pour their thanks
    For dangers passed away.

But not for fear of beast or fiend, 65
    But boding deeper ill,
The charcoal-burner and his wife
    Slow climbed the weary hill.

Before the Rood their simple son
    Lay stretched upon the ground, 70
And crumbled black bread for the birds
    That hopped and pecked around.

(For he had gone before with feet
    As wild and light as air,
And borne the basket on his back 75
    That held their frugal fare.)

And they were faint, and, ere they prayed,
    They sat them down to eat;
And much they marvelled at their son,
    Who never touched his meat,   80

But, now the birds were flown away,
    Sat up, and only gazed
Upon the Christ upon the cross,
    As one with wonder dazed.

Full long he sat and never moved;   85
    But then he gave a cry,
And caught his mother by the wrist
    And said, "I heard a sigh."

"It is an image made of wood,
    It has no voice," she said;   90
"Twas but the wind you heard, my son,"
    But Michael shook his head,

And gazed again, so earnestly
    His face grew almost wise;
And now he cried again, and said,   95
    "Look, how he closed his eyes!"

"'Tis but the shadow of a bird
    That passed across his face,"
The mother said; "see, even now
    It hovers near the place."   100

And then the father said, "My son,
    The image is of wood;
And do you think a man could live
    Without a taste of food?"

"No food?" the silly youth replied,   105
    And pointed to a wren,
Who with a crumb upon Christ's lip
    Had just alighted then.

And now the old man held his peace,
    And the woman ceased to strive,   110
For still he shook his silly head,
    And said, "The man's alive."

"It is God's will," they said, and knelt,
    And knew not what to say;
But when they rose they felt as though   115
    All fear had passed away.

And they could smile when Michael left
    His dinner on the stone;
He said, "The birds will feed the Christ
    When they are quite alone."   120

PART III

The couple sat before the fire,
    More old, and sad, and poor,
For there was winter at the heart,
    And winter at the door.

It shook the roof with shocks of wind;   125
    It caked the pane with snow;
The candle flickered on the sill,
    Like a soul that longed to go.

'Twas Michael's beacon, – gone to feed
    The Christ upon the Hill;   130
And midnight long had passed and gone,
    And he was absent still.

And now and then they turned a log,
    And now they dropped a word:
"'Twas all the wind," the mother said;   135
    The father said, "The bird."

"I hoped that it was God himself,"
    The mother muttered low;
"It must have been the fiend," he said,
    "For to deceive him so."   140

And then the mother cried aloud,
    "What matter it?" she said;
"Or wind, or bird, or fiend, or God,
    For he is dead – is dead!"

"Hark!" cried the man, and through the storm   145
    A note came high and clear;
It was the whistle of their son,
    That sound they longed to hear.

And then a cry for help, and out
    Into the snow they ran;
And there was Michael. On his back
    He bore a helpless man.

"He lives, he lives," he wildly cried;
    "His wounds are dripping still;"
And surely, red from hand and side
    There ran a tiny rill.

They brought Him in and laid Him down,
    Upon the warm hearthstone;
It was the Christ, but not of wood,
    But made of flesh and bone.

They washed His wounds, and at their touch
    They turned to purple scars,
Like a young moon upon the breast,
    On hands and feet like stars.

They brought to moisten His dry lips
    They hoarded flask of wine;
They wrapped Him round with blankets warm,
    And waited for a sign.

And soon without the help of hand
    He rose upon His feet,
And like a friend beside the fire
    He took the vacant seat.

He sat up in the chair then,
    And straight began to shine,
Until His face and raiment poured
    A glory most divine.

The thorns upon His forehead
    Broke out in leaves of gold;
The blood-drops turned to berries,
    Like rubies rich and bold.

The blankets that bewrapped Him
    Flowed into folds of white,
Bestarred with gold and jewels
    Which sparkled in the light.

The very chair He sat on 185
    Became a crystal throne;
The oaken stool beneath His feet
    Turned to a jasper stone.

He stretched an arm to Michael,
    And touched him with His hand, 190
And he arose beside the throne
    An angel, bright and grand.

And then His lips were opened,
    And strong and sweet and clear,
Like water from a fountain, 195
    His voice was good to hear.

"I am the King of Glory;
    I am your brother too;
And even as you do to Me,
    So do I unto you. 200

"You took Me in and clothed Me;
    You washed My body pierced;
You gave me of your wine to drink
    When I was sore athirst.

"And you have suffered also, 205
    And you must suffer still;
I suffered upon Calvary;
    I suffer on the Hill.

"But I am Prince of Sorrow,
    And I am Lord of Care; 210
I come to bring you comfort,
    And save you from despair.

"Your son, your only son, is safe
    And beautiful to see;
And though you miss him for a while, 215
    You know he is with Me.

"And I will give him peace and joy
    As no man every knew–
A little grief, a little pain,
    And I will come for you." 220

He rose, His arms around their son;
    And through the open door
They only saw a whirl of snow,
    And heard the tempest roar.

244. *Any Soul to Any Body*

So we must part, my body, you and I
    Who've spent so many pleasant years together.
'Tis sorry work to lose your company
    Who clove to me so close, whate'er the weather,
From winter unto winter, wet or dry;
    But you have reached the limit of your tether,
And I must journey on my way alone,
And leave you quietly beneath a stone.

They say that you are altogether bad
    (Forgive me, 'tis not my experience),
And think me very wicked to be sad
    At leaving you, a clod, a prison, whence
To get quite free I should be very glad.
    Perhaps I may be so, some few days hence,
But now, methinks, 'twere graceless not to spend
    A tear or two on my departing friend.

Now our long partnership is near completed,
    And I look back upon its history;
I greatly fear I have not always treated
    You with the honesty you showed to me.
And I must own that you have oft defeated
    Unworthy schemes by your sincerity,
And by a blush or stammering tongue have tried
To make me think again before I lied.

'Tis true you're not so handsome as you were,
    But that's not your fault and is partly mine.
You might have lasted longer with more care,
    And still looked something like your first design;
And even now, with all your wear and tear,
    'Tis pitiful to think I must resign
You to the friendless grave, the patient prey
Of all the hungry legions of Decay.

But you must stay, dear body, and I go.
    And I was once so very proud of you;
You made my mother's eyes to overflow   35
    When first she saw you, wonderful and new.
And now, with all your faults, 'twere hard to find
    A slave more willing or a friend more true.
Ay—even they who say the worst about you
Can scarcely tell what I shall do without you.   40

(Henry) Austin Dobson (1840–1921)

245.   *The Ballad of Prose and Rhyme*

When the ways are heavy with mire and rut,
    In November fogs, in December snows,
When the North Wind howls, and the doors are shut,—
    There is place and enough for the pains of prose;
    But whenever a scent from the whitethorn blows,   5
And the jasmine-stars at the casement climb,
    And a Rosalind-face at the lattice shows,
Then hey!—for the ripple of laughing rhyme!

When the brain gets dry as an empty nut,
    When the reason stands on its squarest toes,   10
When the mind (like a beard) has a 'formal cut,'—
    There is place and enough for the pains of prose;
    But whenever the May-blood stirs and glows,
And the young year draws to the 'golden prime,'
    And Sir Romeo sticks in his ear a rose,—   15
Then hey!—for the ripple of laughing rhyme!

In a theme where the thoughts have a pedant-strut,
    In a changing quarrel of 'Ayes' and 'Noes,'
In a starched procession of 'If' and 'But,'—
    There is place and enough for the pains of prose;   20
    But whenever a soft glance softer grows
And the light hours dance to the trysting-time,
    And the secret is told 'that no one knows,'—
Then hey!—for the ripple of laughing rhyme!

ENVOY.

In the work-a-day world,—or its needs and woes, 25
There is place and enough for the pains of prose;
But whenever the May-bells clash and chime,
Then hey!—for the ripple of laughing rhyme!

(1878)

246.   *The Poet and the Critics*

If those who wield the Rod forget,
'Tis truly—*Quis custodiet?*

A certain Bard (as Bards will do)
Dressed up his Poems for Review.
His Type was plain, his Title clear; 5
His Frontispiece by FOURDRINIER.
Moreover, he had on the Back
A sort of sheepskin Zodiac;—
A Mask, a Harp, an Owl,—in fine,
A neat and 'classical' Design. 10
But the *in*-Side?—Well, good or bad,
The Inside was the best he had:
Much Memory,—more Imitation;—
Some Accidents of Inspiration;—
Some Essays in that finer Fashion 15
Where Fancy takes the place of Passion;—
And some (of course) more roughly wrought
To catch the Advocates of Thought.

In the less-crowded Age of ANNE,
Our Bard had been a favoured Man; 20
Fortune, more chary with the Sickle,
Had ranked him next to GARTH or TICKELL;—
He might have even dared to hope
A Line's Malignity from POPE!
But now, when Folks are hard to please, 25
And Poets are as thick as—Peas,
The Fates are not so prone to flatter,
Unless, indeed, a Friend ... No Matter.

The Book, then, had a minor Credit:
The Critics took, and doubtless read it.   30
Said A.—*These little Songs display
No lyric Gift; but still a Ray,—
A Promise. They will do no Harm.*
'Twas kindly, if not *very* warm.
Said B.— *The Author may, in Time,*   35
*Acquire the Rudiments of Rhyme:
His Efforts now are scarcely Verse.*
This, certainly, could not be worse.

Sorely discomfited, our Bard
Worked for another ten Years—hard.   40
Meanwhile the World, unmoved, went on;
New Stars shot up, shone out, were gone;
Before his second Volume came
His Critics had forgot his Name:
And who, forsooth, is bound to know   45
Each Laureate *in embryo!*
They tried and tested him, no less,—
The sworn Assayers of the Press.
Said A.—*The Author may, in Time ....*
Or much what B. had said of Rhyme.   50
Then B.—*These little Songs display ....*
And so forth, in the sense of A.
Over the Bard I throw a Veil.

There is no MORAL to this Tale.

(1879)

247.   *On the Hurry of this Time*

(To F. G.)

With slower pen men used to write,
Of old, when 'letters' were 'polite';
  In ANNA'S, or in GEORGE'S days,
  They could afford to turn a phrase,
Or trim a straggling theme aright.   5

They knew not steam; electric light
Not yet had dazed their calmer sight;—
  They meted out both blame and praise
    With slower pen.

>   Too swiftly now the Hours take flight! 10
>   What's read at morn is dead at night:
>   Scant space have we for Art's delays,
>   Whose breathless thought so briefly stays,
>   We may not work—ah! would we might!—
>   With slower pen. 15
>
>   (1882)

248.   *In After Days*

>   In after days when grasses high
>   O'er-top the stone where I shall lie,
>   Though ill or well the world adjust
>   My slender claim to honoured dust,
>   I shall not question or reply. 5
>
>   I shall not see the morning sky;
>   I shall not hear the night-wind sigh;
>   I shall be mute, as all men must
>   In after days!
>
>   But yet, now living, fain were I 10
>   That some one then should testify,
>   Saying—'He held his pen in trust
>   To Art, not serving shame or lust.'
>   Will none?—Then let my memory die
>   In after days! 15
>
>   (1884)

249.   *A Garden Song*

                    (To W. E. H.)

>   Here, in this sequestered close,
>   Bloom the hyacinth and rose;
>   Here beside the modest stock
>   Flaunts the flaring hollyhock;
>   Here, without a pang, one sees 5
>   Ranks, conditions, and degrees.

       All the seasons run their race
       In this quiet resting place;
       Peach, and apricot, and fig
       Here will ripen, and grow big;   10
       Here is store and overplus,—
       More had not Alcinoüs!

       Here, in alleys cool and green,
       Far ahead the thrush is seen;
       Here along the southern wall   15
       Keeps the bee his festival;
       All is quiet else—afar
       Sounds of toil and turmoil are.

       Here be shadows large and long;
       Here be spaces meet for song;   20
       Grant, O garden-god, that I,
       Now that none profane is nigh,—
       Now that mood and moment please,—
       Find the fair Pierides!

                  (1885)

Harriet Eleanor Hamilton King (1840–1920)

250.   *A Mid May Mystery*

       A silver dream of waters to the East,
       A golden dream of meadows to the West,
       A rosy dream of blossoms to the South,
       A shadowy dream of elm-trees to the North.

       The East lies charmed and stilly through the white   5
       Midnight wherein the maythorns meet the moon;
       The strewn pear-blossom and the daisies light
       The long grass and the edges of the pool.

       The West lies all one sloping spread of gold
       Down the wide meadows to the setting sun;   10
       A sea of buttercups, beneath whose fold
       The earth lies warm and laughs with living light.

A little gust of wind may stir and pass
Among the wilderness of apple-trees;
All the deep sky above, all the deep grass   15
Below, is filled with bloom innumerable.

Tall stands the wall of trees within the line
Of its own shadow, ever dusk and dim,
Down at its feet th' unfading laurustine,
And the blue iris weave a mist of flowers.   20

Four walls of dreams, and what should they uphold
But the blue dome of heaven in all its height?
And what of sunny space should they enfold
But all the open glory of the day?

And yet not so,—a measured sanctuary   25
Is theirs, and passing feet may enter in;
The gates of it are seen as men go by,
And some have dwelling there, and some have life.

They do indeed encompass and enclose
A very pleasure-house of cedar shade,   30
With gleam of lawns and crimson tulip-glows,
And flutter of white robes and youthful feet.

But whereof are they boundaries, and for whom?
Are they from inside or from outside set?
Spread from some conscious centre in their room,   35
Or built round guarded treasure hidden there?

The jewel lighting up the inmost shrine,
The soul that outward weaves its sanctuary,
Both are the same, and both seem half-divine
In the throbbing air mixed by the nightingales.   40

What name, what form?—A lamp?—a hearth of home?—
A poet's heart?—a rose of man's desire?
Or of a full-blown hour not twice to come,
The crowning, still more radiant and more fair?

Here set beyond the chance of time and change,   45
Awhile at least to sense and sight revealed,
That which makes all the sunlight rapture-strange,
That which makes all the moonlight magical.

More white than folded lilies of the East,
More golden than the meadows of the West, 50
More rosy than the orchards of the South,
More shadowy than the dark dream of the North.

251.
Working-Girls in London

'Is not this the time of flowers,
    And of birds that sing?'
'Here we know the days and hours,
    Not the Spring.'

'Is not this the age for pleasure, 5
    And for holidays?'
'We have neither ease nor leisure,
    Work always.'

'Are not ripe fruits now in season,
    Honey, cream, and cake?' 10
'Daily bread for us is reason
    Thanks to make.'

'Are not these the days for playing
    On the garden-grass?'
'We, our daily work delaying, 15
    Starve, alas!'

'Are not these the nights for wearing
    Robes of gossamer?'
'Summer finds us burdens bearing,
    Spite of her.' 20

'Are not cool streams lowing whitely,
    Water-lily lit?'
'Here within close walls we nightly
    Stifling sit.'

'Is not this the month for lying 25
    In the green leaves' shade?'
'Summer breezes fresh are flying,
    Fast we fade.'

'Will not Love come here to-morrow,
    For bridegroom and bride?' 30
'Here Love meaneth pain and sorrow
    Multiplied.'

'Is not this the time of roses,
    Opening red and bright?'
'In the Chapel one reposes, 35
    Shut and white.'

'If of good things life bereft us,
    What avails the rest?'
'Still the better things are left us,
    And the best.' 40

'Are not some among you living
    Who can cheer the way?'
'Yes, their lives in service giving,
    Day by day.'

'Would you not with your rich neighbour 45
    Change, and cast off care?'
'Christ our poverty and labour
    Chose to share.'

'Refuge have you none, unholpen,
    From the strife and din?'
'Yes, the Church stands always open, 50
    Hushed within.'

'Is there not one hour suspended
    From the hard world's wrong?'
'Softly sounds when day is ended 55
    Evensong.'

'Would you for fine houses rather
    Leave your chambers bare?'
'Still in secret speaks Our Father
    To us there.' 60

'Are the days not long and dreary,
    And the years afar?'
'Leaning on Thy breast Thy weary
    Children are.'

'In your conflict have you never 65
    Recompense for loss?'
'Yes, One Presence with us ever
    Bears our cross.'

'O young feet, ye can but falter
    On your road at length!' 70
'Still we kneel before the Altar
    For fresh strength.'

'Have not some, O faithful daughters,
    Sunk beneath the wave?'
'One we know in the deep waters, 75
    Swift to save.'

'Are there not dark hours, too lonely
    For all help, at last?'
'Through the darkest ones Christ only
    Holds us fast.' 80

W. (Wilfrid) S. (Scawen) Blunt (1840–1922)

252.   *He is Not a Poet*

I would not, if I could, be called a poet.
I have no natural love of the "chaste muse."
If aught be worth the doing I would do it;
And others, if they will, may tell the news.
I care not for their laurels but would choose   5
On the world's field to fight or fall or run.
My soul's ambition will not take excuse
To play the dial rather than the sun.
The faith I held I hold, as when a boy
I left my books for cricket-bat and gun.   10
The tales of poets are but scholars' themes.
In my hot youth I held it that a man
With heart to dare and stomach to enjoy
Had better work to his hand in any plan
Of any folly, so the thing were done,   15
Than in the noblest dreaming of mere dreams.

253. *On the Shortness of Time*

If I could live without the thought of death,
Forgetful of time's waste, the soul's decay,
I would not ask for other joy than breath
With light and sound of birds and the sun's ray.
I could sit on untroubled day by day   5
Watching the grass grow, and the wild flowers range
From blue to yellow and from red to grey
In natural sequence as the seasons change.
I could afford to wait, but for the hurt
Of this dull tick of time which chides my ear.   10
But now I dare not sit with loins ungirt
And staff unlifted, for death stands too near.
I must be up and doing—ay, each minute.
The grave gives time for rest when we are in it.

254. *Chanclebury Ring*

Say what you will, there is not in the world
A nobler sight than from this upper Down.
No rugged landscape here, no beauty hurled
From its Creator's hand as with a frown;
But a green plain on which green hills look down   5
Trim as a garden plot. No other hue
Can hence be seen, save here and there the brown
Of a square fallow, and the horizon's blue.
Dear checker-work of woods, the Sussex Weald!
If a name thrills me yet of things of earth,   10
That name is thine. How often I have fled
To thy deep hedgerows and embraced each field,
Each lag, each pasture,—fields which gave me birth
And saw my youth, and which must hold me dead.

from *The Love Lyrics of Proteus*

255.   *Song (Love Me a Little)*

Love me a little, love me as thou wilt,
   Whether a draught it be of passionate wine
   Poured with both hands divine,
Or just a cup of water spilt
   On dying lips and mine.   5
Give me the love thou wilt,
The purity, the guilt,
   So it be thine.

Love me a little. Let it be thy cheek
   With its red signals. That were dear to kiss.   10
   Or, if thou mayest not this,
A finger-tip my own to seek
   At nightfall when none guess.
Eyes have the wit to speak,
And sighs send messages: 15
   Even give less.

Love me a little. Let it be in words
   Of happy omen heralding thy choice,
   Or in a veiled sad voice
Of warning, like a frightened bird's.   20
   How should I not rejoice,
Though swords be crossed with swords
And discord mar love's chords
   And tears thy voice?

Love me a little. All my world thou art.   25
   Thy much were Heaven: thy little Earth shall be.
   If not Eternity,
Then Time be mine, the human part,
   A single hour with thee.
Love as thou wilt and art,   30
With all or half a heart,
   So thou love me.

256.   *At a Funeral*

I loved her too, this woman who is dead.
   Look in my face. I have a right to go
And see the place where you have made her bed
   Among the snow.

I loved her too whom you are burying.
   I have a right to stand beside her bier,
And to my handful of the dust I fling,
   That she may hear.

I loved her; and it was not for the eyes
   Which you have shut, nor for her yellow hair,
Nor for the face which in your bosom lies.
   Let it lie there!

Nor for the wild-birds' music of her voice,
   Which we shall hear in dreams till we too sleep;
Nor for the rest, which made the world rejoice,
   The angels weep.

It was not for the payment of sweet love,
   Though love is often straitened for a kiss,
Nor for the hope of other joys above,
   But only this,

That she had laid her hand upon my heart
   Once in the summer time when we were young,
And that her finger-tips had left a smart,
   And that my tongue

Had spoken words which might not be unspoken
   Lest they should make a by-word of love's truth,
And I had sworn that love should be the token
   Of my youth.

And so I gave her all, and long ago
   The treasure of my youth was put in pawn;
And she was little richer that I know
   When that was gone.

But I have lived a beggar since that day
   And hide my face it may be from men's eyes;
For often I have seen them shrink away,
   As in surprise

That such a loathsome cripple should be found
    To walk abroad in daylight with the rest,
And scarce a rag to cover up the wound
    Upon his breast.   40

Yet no man stopped to ask how this might be,
    Or I had scared them, and let loose my tongue,
How I had bought myself this misery
    When I was young.

Yet I have loved her. This must be my pay,   45
    The pension I have earned me with these tears;
The right to kneel beside her grave to-day,
    Despite these years,

With all her kisses burning on my cheek,
    As when I left her and our love was dead,   50
And our lips trembled though they did not speak;
    The night I fled;

The right to bid you stand aside, nor be
    A witness of our meeting. Did you love
In joy as I have loved in misery?   55
    You did not prove

Your love was stronger than the strength of death,
    Or she had never died upon your hand.
I would have fed her breathing with my breath;
    I would have fanned   60

A living wind of Heaven to her lips;
    I would have stolen life from Paradise.
And she is dead, and you have seen eclipse
    Within those eyes.

If I could know that you had loved her well;   65
    If I could hold it for a certainty
That you had sold your life as I did sell;
    If I could see

The blackness of your soul, and with my tongue
    Taste the full bitterness of tears unshed;   70
If I should find your very heart was wrung
    And maimed and dead;

If I should feel your hand's grasp crumble mine,
   And hug the pain when I should grasp in turn;
If I could dip my fingers in the brine
   Of eyes that burn;

If I could hear your voice call back the dead
   With such a mighty cry of agony
That she should turn and listen in the bed
   Where she doth lie,

And all the heavens should together roll,
   Thinking they heard the angel's trumpet tone,
I could forget it that you bought a soul
   Which was my own;

I could forget that she forgot her vows,
   That aught was bartered for the wealth of love;
I could untell the story of my woes,
   Till God above

Should hold her guiltless and condone the wrong
   Done to His justice; I could take your hand
And call you brother, as we went along
   To take our stand

Before His judgment-seat with her again
   Where we are hurrying,—for we could not keep
Our place unchallenged in the ranks of men
   Who do not weep.

from *The Idler's Calendar*

I. *October: Gambling at Monaco*

A jewelled kingdom set impregnable
   In gardens green which front the violet sea,
A happy fortress shut and guarded well,
   And cradled ever on the mountain's knee:
   Here Monsieur Blanc, sad prince of industry,
Has reared the palace which men call his hell:
   And here in autumn days, when winds blow free,
Pleasure shall lead us to sin's citadel.

  Alas for vice! Yet, who dares moralize,
   In the hushed rooms, where fortune reigns alway?
  Her solemn priest, with chink of coin, replies
   "Messieurs, faites votre jeu. Le jeu est fait."
  Who dares be wise, lest wisdom's self be vexed?
   For all who come to preach remain to play.
  Nay, leave poor vice, say I, her pleasant text,
   Nor grudge her Heaven in this world with the next.

258.
II. *November: Across Country*

  November's here. Once more the pink we don,
   And on old Centaur, at the coverside,
  Sit changing pleasant greetings one by one
   With friend and neighbour. Half the county's pride
   Is here to-day. Squire, parson, peer, bestride
  Their stoutest nags, impatient to be gone.
   Here, schoolboys on their earliest ponies ride,
  And village lads on asses, not out-done.

  But hark! That sounds like music. Ay, by God!
   He's off across the fallow. "No, sirs, no;
  "Not yet a minute, just another rod!
   "Then let him have it. Ho, there, tallyho!"
  Now that's worth seeing! Look! He's topped the wall,
   Leaving his whole field pounded in a row.
  A first flight place to-day was worth a fall.
  So forward each, and Heaven for us all!

from *From the Arabic*

259.
I. *The Camel-Rider*

There is no thing in all the world but love,
No jubilant thing of sun or shade worth one sad tear.
Why dost thou ask my lips to fashion songs
Other than this, my song of love to thee?

See where I lie and pluck the thorns of grief,
Dust on my head and fire, as one who mourns his slain.
Are they not slain, my treasures of dear peace?
This their red burial is, sand heaped on sand.

Here came I in the morning of my joys.
Before the dawn was born, through the dark downs I rode.
The low stars led me on as with a voice,
Stars of the scorpion's tail in the deep South.

Sighing I came, and scattering wide the sand.
No need had I to urge her speed with hand or heel,
The creature I bestrode. She knew my haste,
And knew the road I sought, the road to thee.

Jangling her bells aloud in wantonness,
And sighing soft, she too, her sighs to my soul's sighs.
Behind us the wind followed thick with scents
Of incense blossoms and the dews of night.

The thorn trees caught at us with their crook'd hands;
The hills in blackness hemmed us in and hid the road;
The spectres of the desert howled and warned;
I heeded nothing of their words of woe.

Thus till the dawn I sped in my desire,
Breasting the ridges, slope on slope, till morning broke;
And lo! the sun revealed to me no sign,
And lo! the day was widowed of my hope.

Where are the tents of pleasure and dear love,
Set in the Vale of Thyme, where winds in Spring are fain?
The highways of the valley, where they stood
Strong in their flocks, are there. But where are they?

The plain was dumb, as emptied of all voice;
No bleat of herds, no camels roaring far below
Told of their presence in the pastures void,
Of the waste places which had been their homes.

I climbed down from my watch-tower of the rocks,
To where the tamarisks grow, and the dwarf palms, alarmed.
I called them with my voice, as the deer calls,
Whose young the wolves have hunted from their place.

I sought them in the foldings of the hill,
In the deep hollows shut with rocks, where no winds blow.
I sought their footstep under the tall cliffs,
Shut from the storms, where the first lambs are born.

The tamarisk boughs had blossomed in the night, 45
And the white broom which bees had found, the wild bees' brood.
But no dear signal told me of their life,
No spray was torn in all that world of flowers.

Where are the tents of pleasure and dear love,
For which my soul took ease for its delight in Spring, 50
The black tents of hex people beautiful
Beyond the beauty of the sons of kings?

The wind of war has swept them from their place,
Scattering them wide as quails, whom the hawk's hate pursues;
The terror of the sword importunate 55
Was at their backs, nor spared them as they flew.

The summer wind has passed upon their fields;
The rain has purged their hearth-stones, and made smooth their floors;
Low in the valley lie their broken spears,
And the white bones which are their tale forlorn. 60

Where are the sons of Saba in the South,
The men of mirth and pride to whom my songs were sung,
The kinsmen of her soul who is my soul,
The brethren of her beauty whom I love?

She mounted her tall camel in the waste, 65
Loading it high for flight with her most precious things;
She went forth weeping in the wilderness,
Alone with fear on that far night of ill.

She fled mistrusting, as the wild roe flees,
Turning her eyes behind her, while fear fled before; 70
No other refuge knew she than her speed,
And the black land that lies where night is born.

Under what canopy of sulphurous heaven,
Dark with the thunderclouds unloosing their mad tongues,
Didst thou lie down aweary of thy burden, 75
In that dread place of silence thou hadst won?

Close to what shelter of what naked rooks,
Carved with what names of terror of what kings of old,
Near to what monstrous shapes unmerciful,
Watching thy death, didst thou give up thy soul?   80

Or dost thou live by some forgotten well,
Waiting thy day of ransom to return and smile,
As the birds come when Spring is in the heaven,
And dost thou watch me near while I am blind?

Blind in my tears, because I only weep,   85
Kindling my soul to fire because I mourn my slain,
My kindred slain, and thee, and my dear peace,
Making their burial thus, sand heaped on sand.

For see, there nothing is in all the world
But only love worth any strife or song or tear.   90
Ask me not then to sing or fashion songs
Other than this, my song of love to thee.

Mathilde Blind (1841–1896)

260. *Green Leaves and Sere*

Three tall poplars beside the pool
   Shiver and moan in the gusty blast,
The carded clouds are blown like wool,
   And the yellowing leaves fly thick and fast.

The leaves, now driven before the blast,   5
   Now flung by fits on the curdling pool,
Are tossed heaven-high and dropped at last
   As if at the whim of a jabbering fool.

O leaves, once rustling green and cool!
   Two met here where one moans aghast   10
With wild heart heaving towards the past:
   Three tall poplars beside the pool.

261.   *The Forest Pool*

Lost amid gloom and solitude,
A pool lies hidden in the wood,
A pool the autumn rain has made
Where flowers with their fair shadows played.

Bare as a beggar's board, the trees
Stand in the water to their knees;
The birds are mute, but far away
I hear a bloodhound's sullen bay.

Blue-eyed forget-me-nots that shook,
Kissed by a little laughing brook,
Kissed too by you with lips so red,
Float in the water drowned and dead.

And dead and drowned 'mid leaves that rot,
Our angel-eyed Forget-me-not,
The love of unforgotten years,
Floats corpse-like in a pool of tears.

                    Delamere Forest.

from *Love in Exile*

262.   VI. 'Many will love you; you were made for love'

Many will love you; you were made for love;
For the soft plumage of the unruffled dove
    Is not so soft as your caressing eyes.
You will love many; for the winds that veer
Are not more prone to shift their compass, dear,
    Than your quick fancy flies.

Many will love you; but I may not, no;
Even though your smile sets all my life aglow,
    And at your fairness all my senses ache.
You will love many; but not me, my dear,
Who have no gift to give you but a tear
    Sweet for your sweetness' sake.

263.   X. 'On Life's long round by chance I found'

On life's long round by chance I found
    A dell impearled with dew,
Where hyacinths, gushing from the ground,
    Lent to the earth heaven's native hue
        Of holy blue.   5

I sought that plot of azure light
    Once more in gloomy hours;
But snow had fallen overnight
And wrapped in mortuary white
    My fairy ring of flowers.   10

264.   XIII. 'We met as strangers on life's lonely way'

We met as strangers on life's lonely way,
    And yet it seemed we knew each other well;
There was no end to what thou hadst to say,
    Or to the thousand things I found to tell.
My heart, long silent, at thy voice that day   5
    Chimed in my breast like to a silver bell.

How much we spoke, and yet still left untold
    Some secret half revealed within our eyes:
Didst thou not love me once in ages old?
    Had I not called thee with importunate cries,   10
And, like a child left sobbing in the cold,
    Listened to catch from far thy fond replies?

We met as strangers, and as such we part;
    Yet all my life seems leaving me with thine;
Ah, to be clasped once only heart to heart,   15
    If only once to feel that thou wert mine!
These lips are locked, and yet I know thou art
    That all in all for which my soul did pine.

265.   Manchester by Night

O'er this huge town, rife with intestine wars,
Whence as from monstrous sacrificial shrines
Pillars of smoke climb heavenward, Night inclines
Black brows majestical with glimmering stars.
Her dewy silence soothes life's angry jars:　　　　　　　　　　5
And like a mother's wan white face, who pines
Above her children's turbulent ways, so shines
The moon athwart the narrow cloudy bars.

Now toiling multitudes that hustling crush
Each other in the fateful strife for breath,　　　　　　　　　　10
And, hounded on by divers hungers, rush
Across the prostrate ones that groan beneath,
Are swathed within the universal hush,
As life exchanges semblances with death.

266.   Haunted Streets

Lo, happily walking in some clattering street—
Where throngs of men and women dumbly pass.
Like shifting pictures seen within a glass
Which leave no trace behind—one seems to meet,
In roads once trodden by our mutual feet,　　　　　　　　　　5
A face projected from that shadowy mass
Of faces, quite familiar as it was,
Which beaming on us stands out clear and sweet.

The face of faces we again behold
That lit our life when life was very fair,　　　　　　　　　　10
And leaps our heart towards eyes and mouth and hair;
Oblivious of the undying love grown cold,
Or body sheeted in the churchyard mould,
We stretch out yearning hands and grasp—the air.

267.   *Scarabæus Sisyphus*

    I've watched thee, Scarab! Yea, an hour in vain
        I've watched thee, slowly toiling up the hill,
        Pushing thy lump of mud before thee still
    With patience infinite and stubborn strain.
    Strive as thou mayest, spare neither time nor pain,   5
        To screen thy burden from all chance of ill;
        Push, push, with all a beetle's force of will,
    Thy ball, alas! rolls ever down again.

    Toil without end! And why? That after thee
        Dim hosts of groping Scarabs too shall climb   10
    This self-same height? Accursèd progeny
        Of Sisyphus, what antenatal crime
    Has doomed us too to roll incessantly
        Life's Stone, recoiling from the Alps of time?

268.   *A Fantasy*

    I was an Arab,
        I loved my horse;
    Swift as an arrow
        He swept the course.

    Sweet as a lamb   5
        He came to hand;
    He was the flower
        Of all the land.

    Through lonely nights
        I rode afar;   10
    God lit His lights—
        Star upon star.

    God's in the desert;
        His breath the air:
    Beautiful desert,
        Boundless and bare!   15

Free as the wild wind,
  Light as a foal;
Ah, there is room there
  To stretch one's soul.

Far reached my thought,
  Scant were my needs:
A few bananas
  And lotus seeds.

Sparkling as water
  Cool in the shade,
Ibrahim's daughter,
  Beautiful maid.

Out of thy Kulleh,
  Fairest and first,
Give me to drink,
  Quencher of thirst.

I am athirst, girl;
  Parched with desire,
Love in my bosom
  Burns as a fire.

Green thy oasis,
  Waving with Palms;
Oh, be no niggard,
  Maid, with thy alms.

Kiss me with kisses,
  Buds of thy mouth,
Sweeter than Cassia
  Fresh from the South.

Bind me with tresses,
  Clasp with a curl;
And in caresses
  Stifle me, girl.

I was an Arab
  Ages ago!
Hence this home-sickness
  And all my woe.

269.   *The Message*

From side to side the sufferer tossed
   With quick impatient sighs;
Her face was bitten as by frost,
The look as of one hunted crossed
   The fever of her eyes.   5

All seared she seemed with life and woe,
   Yet scarcely could have told
More than a score of springs or so;
Her hair had girlhood's morning glow,
   And yet her mouth looked old.   10

Not long for her the sun would rise,
   Nor that young slip of moon,
Wading through London's smoky skies,
Would dwindling meet those dwindling eyes,
   Ere May was merged in June.   15

May was it somewhere? Who, alas!
   Could fancy it was May?
For here, instead of meadow grass,
You saw, through naked panes of glass,
   Bare walls of whitish gray.   20

Instead of songs, where in the quick
   Leaves hide the blackbirds' nests,
You heard the moaning of the sick,
And tortured breathings harsh and thick
   Drawn from their labouring chests.   25

She muttered, "What's the odds to me?"
   With an old cynic's sneer;
And looking up, cried mockingly,
"I hate you, nurse! Why, can't you see
   You'll make no convert here?"   30

And then she shook her fist at Heaven,
   And broke into a laugh!
Yes, though her sins were seven times seven
Let others pray to be forgiven—
   She scorned such canting chaff.   35

Oh, it was dreadful, sir! Far worse
   In one so young and fair;
Sometimes she'd scoff and swear and curse;
Call me bad names, and vow each nurse
   A fool for being there.   40

And then she'd fall back on her bed,
   And many a weary hour
Would lie as rigid as one dead;
Her white throat with the golden head
   Like some torn lily flower.   45

We could do nothing, one and all
   How much we might beseech;
Her girlish blood had turned to gall;
Far lower than her body's fall
   Her soul had sunk from reach.   50

Her soul had sunk into a slough
   Of evil past repair.
The world had been against her; now
Nothing in heaven or earth should bow
   Her stubborn knees in prayer.   55

Yet I felt sorry all the same,
   And sometimes, when she slept,
With head and hands as hot as flame,
I watched beside her, half in shame,
   Smoothed her bright hair and wept.   60

To die like this—'twas awful, sir!
   To know I prayed in vain;
And hear her mock me, and aver
That if her life came back to her
   She'd live her life again.   65

Was she a wicked girl? What then?
   She didn't care a pin!
She was not worse than all those men
Who looked so shocked in public, when
   They made and shared her sin.   70

"Shut up, nurse, do! Your sermons pall;
   Why can't you let me be?
Instead of worrying o'er my fall,
I wish, just wish, you sisters all
   Turned to the likes of me.' 75

I shuddered! I could bear no more,
   And left her to her fate;
She was too cankered at the core;
Her heart was like a bolted door,
   Where Love had knocked too late. 80

I left her in her savage spleen,
   And hoarsely heard her shout,
"What does the cursed sunlight mean
By shining in upon this scene?
   Oh, shut the sunlight out!" 85

Sighing, I went my round once more,
   Full heavy for her sin;
Just as Big Ben was striking four,
The sun streamed through the open door,
   As a young girl came in. 90

She held a basket full of flowers—
   Cowslip and columbine;
A lilac bunch from rustic bowers,
Strong-scented after morning showers,
   Smelt like some cordial wine. 95

There, too, peeped Robin-in-the-hedge,
   There daisies pearled with dew,
Wild parsley from the meadow's edge,
Sweet-william and the purple vetch,
   And hyacinth's heavenly blue. 100

But best of all the spring's array,
   Green boughs of milk-white thorn;
Their petals on each perfumed spray
Looked like the wedding gift of May
   On nature's marriage morn. 105

And she who bore those gifts of grace
    To our poor patients there,
Passed like a sunbeam through the place:
Dull eyes grew brighter for her face,
    Angelically fair.						110

She went the round with elf-like tread,
    And with kind words of cheer,
Soothing as balm of Gilead,
Laid wild flowers on each patient's bed,
    And made the flowers more dear.				115

At last she came where Nellie Dean
    Still moaned and tossed about—
"What does the cursed sunlight mean
By shining in upon this scene?
    Will no one shut it out?"					120

And then she swore with rage and pain,
    And moaning tried to rise;
It seemed her ugly words must stain
The child who stood with heart astrain,
    And large blue listening eyes.				125

Her fair face did not blush or bleach.
    She did not shrink away;
Alas! she was beyond the reach
Of sweet or bitter human speech—
    Deaf as the flowers of May.					130

Only her listening eyes could hear
    That hardening in despair,
Which made that other girl, so near
In age to her, a thing to fear
    Like fever-tainted air.					135

She took green boughs of milk-white thorn
    And laid them on the sheet,
Whispering appealingly, "Don't scorn
My flowers! I think, when one's forlorn,
    They're like a message, Sweet.'				140

How heavenly fresh those blossoms smelt,
    Like showers on thirsty ground!
The sick girl frowned as if repelled,
And with hot hands began to pelt
    And fling them all around.   145

But then some influence seemed to stay
    Her hands with calm control;
Her stormy passions cleared away,
The perfume of the breath of May
    Had passed into her soul.   150

A nerve of memory had been thrilled,
    And, pushing back her hair,
She stretched out hungry arms half filled
With flower and leaf, and panting shrilled,
    "Where are you, mother, where?"   155

And then her eyes shone darkly bright
    Through childhood in a mist,
As if she suddenly caught sight
Of some one hidden in the light
    And waited to be kissed.   160

"Oh, mother dear!" we heard her moan,
    "Have you not gone away?
I dreamed, dear mother, you had gone,
And left me in the world alone,
    In the wild world astray.   165

"It was a dream; I'm home again!
    I hear the ivy-leaves
Tap-tapping on the leaded pane!
Oh, listen! how the laughing rain
    Runs from our cottage eaves!   170

"How very sweet the things do smell!
    How bright our pewter shines;
I am at home; I feel so well:
I think I hear the evening bell
    Above our nodding pines.   175

"The firelight glows upon the brick,
   And pales the rising moon;
And when your needles flash and click,
My heart, my heart, that felt so sick,
   Throbs like a hive in June. 180

"If only father would not stay
   And gossip o'er his brew;
Then, reeling homewards, lose his way,
Come staggering in at break of day
   And beat you black and blue! 185

"Yet he can be as good as gold,
   When mindful of the farm,
He tills the field and tends the fold:
But never fear; when I'm grown old
   I'll keep him out of harm. 190

"And then we'll be as happy here
   As kings upon their throne!
I dreamed you'd left me, mother dear;
That you lay dead this many a year
   Beneath the churchyard stone. 195

"Mother, I sought you far and wide,
   And ever in my dream,
Just out of reach you seemed to hide;
I ran along the streets and cried,
   'Where are you, mother, where?' 200

"Through never-ending streets in fear
   I ran and ran forlorn;
And through the twilight yellow-drear
I saw blurred masks of loafers leer,
   And point at me in scorn. 205

"How tired, how deadly tired, I got;
   I ached through all my bones!
The lamplight grew one quivering blot,
And like one rooted to the spot,
   I dropped upon the stones. 210

"A hard bed make the stones and cold,
    The mist a wet, wet sheet;
And in the mud, like molten gold,
The snaky lamplight blinking rolled
    Like guineas at my feet. 215

"Surely there were mothers when
    A voice hissed in my ear,
'A sovereign! Quick; Come on!' –and then
A knowing leer! There were but men,
    And not a creature near. 220

"I went—I could not help it. Oh,
    I didn't want to die;
With now a kiss and now a blow,
Strange men would come, strange men would go
    I didn't care—not I. 225

"Sometimes my life was like a tale
    Read in a story-book;
Our blazing nights turned daylight pale,
Champagne would fizz like ginger-ale,
    Red wine flow like a brook. 230

"Then like a vane my dream would veer:
    I walked the street again;
And through the twilight yellow-drear
Blurred clouds of faces seemed to peer,
    And drift across the rain." 235

She started with a piercing scream
    And wildly rolling eye:
"Ah me! it was no evil dream
To pass with the first market-team—
    That thing of shame am I. 240

"Where were you that you could not come?
    Were you so far above–
Far as the moon above a slum?
Yet, mother, you were all the sum
    I had of human love. 245

"Ah yes! you've sent this branch of May,
    A fair light from the past.
The town is dark—I went astray.
Forgive me, mother! Lead the way;
I'm going home at last."   250

In eager haste she tried to rise,
    And struggled up in bed,
With luminous, transfigured eyes,
As if they glassed the opening skies,
    Fell back, sir, and was dead.   255

270.   *Autumn Tints*

Coral-coloured yew-berries
    Strew the garden ways,
Hollyhocks and sunflowers
    Make a dazzling blaze
    In these latter days.   5

Marigolds by cottage doors
    Flaunt their golden pride,
Crimson-punctured bramble leaves
    Dapple far and wide
    The green mountain-side.   10

Far away, on hilly slopes
    Where fleet rivulets run,
Miles and miles of tangled fern,
    Burnished by the sun,
    Glow a copper dun.   15

For the year that's on the wane,
    Gathering all its fire,
Flares up through the kindling world
    As, ere they expire
    Flames leap high and higher.   20

271.   *A Winter Landscape*

All night, all day, in dizzy, downward flight,
   Fell the wild-whirling, vague, chaotic snow,
   Till every landmark of the earth below,
Trees, moorlands, roads, and each familiar sight
Were blotted out by the bewildering white;   5
   And winds, now shrieking loud, now whimpering low,
   Seemed lamentations for the world-old woe
That death must swallow life, and darkness light.

But all at once the rack was blown away,
   The snowstorm hushing ended in a sigh;   10
   Then like a flame the crescent moon on high
Leaped forth among the planets; pure as they,
Earth vied in whiteness with the Milky Way:
   Herself a star beneath the starry sky.

272.   *Mourning Women*

All veiled in black, with faces hid from sight,
   Crouching together in the jolting cart,
   What forms are these that pass alone, apart,
In abject apathy to life's delight?
The motley crowd, fantastically bright,   5
   Shifts gorgeous through each dazzling street and mart
   Only these sisters of the suffering heart
Strike discords in this symphony of light,
Most wretched woman! whom your prophet dooms
   To take love's penalties without its prize!   10
Yes; you shall bear the unborn in your wombs,
   And water dusty death with streaming eyes,
   And, wailing, beat your breasts among the tombs;
   But souls ye have none fit for Paradise.

from *The Ascent of Man*

273. I. 'Struck out of dim fluctuant forces and
shock of electrical vapour'

Struck out of dim fluctuant forces and shock of electrical vapour,
Repelled and attracted the atoms flashed mingling in union primeval,
And over the face of the waters far heaving in limitless twilight
Auroral pulsations thrilled faintly, and, striking the blank heaving surface,
The measureless speed of their motion now leaped into light on the waters. 5
And lo, from the womb of the waters, upheaved in volcanic convulsion,
Ribbed and ravaged and rent there rose bald peaks and the rocky
Heights of confederate mountains compelling the fugitive vapours
To take a form as they passed them and float as clouds through the azure;
Mountains, the broad-bosomed mothers of torrents and rivers perennial, 10
Feeding the rivers and plains with patient persistence, till slowly,
In the swift passage of æons recorded in stone by Time's graver,
There germ grey films of the lichen and mosses and palm-ferns gigantic,
And jungle of tropical forest fantastical branches entwining,
And limitless deserts of sand and wildernesses primeval. 15

274. II. *Motherhood*

From out the font of being, undefiled,
   A life hath been upheaved with struggle and pain;
   Safe in her arms a mother holds again
That dearest miracle—a new-born child.
To moans of anguish terrible and wild— 5
   As shrieks the night-wind through an ill-shut pane—
   Pure heaven succeeds; and after fiery strain
Victorious woman smiles serenely mild.

Yea, shall she not rejoice, shall not her frame
   Thrill with a mystic rapture! At this birth, 10
The soul now kindled by her vital flame
   May it not prove a gift of priceless worth?
Some saviour of his kind whose starry fame
   Shall bring a brightness to the darkened earth.

Robert Buchanan (T. Maitland) (1841–1901)

275.   *The Cities*

    I took my staff and wandered o'er the mountains,
    And came among the heaps of gold and silver,
    The gorgeous desolation of the Cities.

    My trouble grew tenfold when I beheld
    The agony and burden of my fellows,   5
    The pains of sick men and the groans of hungry.

    I saw the good man tear his hair and weep;
    I saw the bad man tread on human necks
    Prospering and blaspheming: and I wondered.

    The silken-natured woman was a bond-slave;   10
    The gross man foul'd her likeness in high places;
    The innocent were heart-wrung: and I wondered.

    The gifts of earth are given to the base;
    The monster of the Cities spurned the martyr;
    The martyr died, denying: and I wondered.   15

                                (1874)

Rosa Mulholland (Lady Gilbert) (1841–1921)

276.   *Poverty*

    I had a dream of Poverty by night,
      And saw the holy palmer wending by
      With pensive mien and radiant upturned eye,
    Drinking the tender moon's approving light.

    I saw her take the hills and climb the height,   5
      While broad below the city murmured nigh,
      Spangling the dusk with lamps of revelry
    That made the mellow planets pale to sight.

Yet kept my love her face toward the stars
Till broke the dawn against the mountain ridge   10
   And angels met her on the misty way;

Then heaven looked forth on her through golden bars,
Then gleamed her feet along a rosy bridge,
   Then passed she noiseless into eternal day.

Margaret Veley (1843–1887)

277.   *A Game of Piquet*

See, as you turn a page
Of Holbein's Dance of Death,
Across the narrow stage,
Drawing a hurried breath,
The sons of men go by,   5
Like a bewildered dream,
Beneath a changeless sky
An ever-changing stream.
Swiftly as driven clouds
They pass in love and strife,   10
And all the shifting crowds
Are busy with their life,
Eager, intent, and much
            Perplexed.
Then comes the deadly touch—   15
            What next?

We do not paint Death now,
As did those men of old,
(And, truly, I allow
They make my blood run cold,)   20
Yet the old fancy lives
In spite of growth and change,
And to our sorrow gives
Its humour grim and strange.
The bitter wine that when   25
We meet our mocking chance
Is stamped from souls of men
In Death's fantastic dance.

As when the cry of Love,
        Or Hate,   30
Rings to the heaven above
        Too late.

We need not paint the scene,
The skull, the grasping hand,
For that which once has been   35
Our hearts will understand.
A flower may be the sign
That calls your vision back,
Or just a pencil line
In some old almanac.   40
A pack of cards for me,
Where smiling queen and knave
Can bid me turn and see
A shadow and a grave,
Nor to my dying day   45
        Forget
How once I used to play
        Piquet.

Once, in a quaint old place!
My dreamy thoughts recall   50
Its somewhat faded grace
Of painting on the wall,
Pink roses ribbon-tied.
And pairs of snowy doves
Tall vases side by side,   55
And lightly flying Loves,
Such as our poets sing,
Or sang, some time ago,
Dan Cupid on the wing
With quiver, shafts, and bow—   60
But Love had there no need
        Of darts,
He simply gave the lead
        In Hearts.

Into the sunlit room   65
To break the half-played game,
With heavy stroke of doom,
The grief of parting came.
Strong in my happy love
I faced the bitter pain,   70

And swore by heaven above
We two would meet again.
Silent I saw her stand,
Pallid, in trouble sore,
While from her hanging hand 75
Slipped downward to the floor
Black cards, whose ominous
      Array
Fate had not suffered us
      To play. 80

I bade a brave farewell
Without a thought of fear,
Ah God! I could not tell
That evil day was near,
When Life's glad music sank 85
To sobs, and died away,
When Earth's high mountains shrank
To one low heap of clay.
When I, aghast and sad,
Stood silent and apart, 90
When all Creation had
A sepulchre for heart.
No love the unknown land
      Invades,
And Death played out the hand 91
      Of Spades.

278.   *A Japanese Fan*

How time flies! Have we been talking
      For an hour?
Have we been so long imprisoned
      By the shower
In this old oak-panelled parlour? 5
      Is it noon?
Don't you think the rain is over
      Rather soon?

Since the heavy drops surprised us,
      And we fled 10
Here for shelter, while it darkened
      Overhead;

Since we leaned against the window,
    Saw the flash
Of the lightning, heard the rolling
    Thunder crash;
You have looked at all the treasures
    Gathered here,
Out of other days and countries
    Far and near;
At those glasses, thin as bubbles,
    Opal bright—
At the carved and slender chessmen
    Red and white—
At the long array of china
    Cups and plates—
(Do you really understand them?
    Names and dates?)
At the tapestry, where dingy
    Shepherds stand,
Holding grim and faded damsels
    By the hand,
All the while my thoughts were busy
    With the fan
Lying here—bamboo and paper
    From Japan.
It is nothing—very common—
    Be it so;
Do you wonder why I prize it?
    Care to know?
Shall I teach you all the meaning,
    The romance
Of the picture you are scorning
    With a glance?

From Japan! I let my fancy
    Swiftly fly;
Now if we set sail to-morrow,
    You and I,
If the waves were liquid silver,
    Fair the breeze,
If we reached that wondrous island
    O'er the seas,
Should we find that every woman
    Was so white,
And had slender upward eyebrows
    Black as night?

Should we then perhaps discover
    Why, out there,
People spread a mat to rest on
    In mid air?   60

Here's a lady, small of feature,
    Narrow-eyed,
With her hair of ebon straightness
    Queerly tied;
In her hand are trailing flowers   65
    Rosy sweet,
And her silken robe is muffled
    Round her feet.
She looks backward with a conscious
    Kind of grace,   70
As she steps from off the carpet
    Into space;
Though she plants her foot on nothing
    Does not fall,
And in fact appears to heed it   75
    Not at all.
See how calmly she confronts us
    Standing there—
Will you say she is not lovely?
    Do you dare?   80
I will not! I honour beauty
    Where I can,
Here's a woman one might die for!
    —In Japan.

Read the passion of her lover—   85
    All his soul
Hotly poured in this fantastic
    Little scroll.
See him swear his love, and vengeance
    Read his fate —   90
You don't understand the language?
    I'll translate.

'Long ago,' he says, 'when summer
    Filled the earth
With its beauty, with the brightness   95
    Of its mirth;
When the leafy boughs were woven
    Far above;

                    In the noonday I beheld her,
                            Her—my love!   100
                    Oftentimes I met her, often
                            Saw her pass,
                    With her dusky raiment trailing
                            On the grass.
                    I would follow, would approach her,   105
                            Dare to speak,
                    Till at last the sudden colour
                            Flushed her cheek.
                    Through the sultry heat we lingered
                            In the shade;   110
                    And the fan of pictured paper
                            That she swayed
                    Seemed to mark the summer's pulses,
                            Soft and slow,
                    And to thrill me as it wavered   115
                            To and fro.
                    For I loved her, loved her, loved her,
                            And its beat
                    Set my passion to a music
                            Strangely sweet.   120

                    Sunset came, and after sunset
                            When the dusk
                    Filled the quiet house with shadows;
                            And the musk
                    From the dim and dewy garden   125
                            Where it grows,
                    Mixed its perfume with the jasmine
                            And the rose;
                    When the western splendour faded,
                            And the breeze   130
                    Went its way, with good-night whispers
                            Through the trees.
                    Leaning out we watched the dying
                            Of the light,
                    Till the bats came forth with sudden   135
                            Ghostly flight.
                    They were shadows, wheeling, flitting
                            Round my joy,
                    While she spoke and while her slender
                            Hands would toy   140
                    With her fan, which as she swayed it
                            Might have been

Fairy wand, or fitting sceptre
    For a queen.
When she smiled at me, half pausing   145
    In her play,
All the gloom of gathering twilight
    Turned to day!

Though to talk too much of heaven
    Is not well—   150
Though agreeable people never
    Mention hell—
Yet the woman who betrayed me—
    Whom I kissed—
In that bygone summer taught me   155
    Both exist.
I was ardent, she was always
    Wisely cool,
So my lady played the traitor,
    I—the fool'—   160
Oh, your pardon! But remember,
    If you please,
I'm translating—this is only
    Japanese.

'Japanese?' you say, and eye me   165
    Half in doubt;
Let us have the lurking question
    Spoken out.
Is all this about the lady
    Really said   170
In that little square of writing
    Near her head?
I will answer, on my honour,
    As I can,
Every syllable is written   175
    On the fan.
Yes, and you could learn the language
    Very soon—
Shall I teach you on some August
    Afternoon?   180

You are wearied. There is little
    Left to say;
For the disappointed hero
    Goes his way,

And such pain and rapture never 185
    More will know.
But he smiles—all this was over
    Long ago.
I am not a blighted being—
    Scarcely grieve— 190
I can laugh, make love, do most things
    But believe!

Yet the old days come back strangely
    As I stand
With the fan she swayed so softly 195
    In my hand.
I can almost see her, touch her,
    Hear her voice,
Till, afraid of my own madness,
    I rejoice 200
That beyond my help or harming
    Is her fate—
Past the reach of passion—is it
    Love—or hate?

This is tragic! Are you laughing? 205
    So am I!
Let us go—the clouds have vanished
    From the sky.
Yes, and you'll forget this folly?
    Time it ceased, 210
For you do not understand me
    In the least.
You have smiled and sighed politely
    Quite at ease,—
And my story might as well be 215
    Japanese!

279.   *A Town Garden*

A plot of ground—the merest scrap—
    Deep, like a dry, forgotten well,
A garden caught in a brick-built trap,
    Where men make money, buy and sell;
And struggling through the stagnant haze, 5

Dim flowers, with sapless leaf and stem,
Look up with something of the gaze
   That homesick eyes have cast on them.

There is a rose against the wall,
   With scanty, smoke-incrusted leaves;
Fair showers on happier roses fall—
   On this, foul droppings from the eaves.
It pines, but you need hardly note;
   It dies by inches in the gloom;
Shoots in the spring-time, as if by rote;
   Long has forgotten to dream of bloom.

The poorest blossom, and it were classed
   With colour and name—but never a flower!
It blooms with the roses whose bloom is past,
   Of every hue, and place, and hour.
They live before me as I look—
   The damask buds that breathe and glow,
Pink wild roses, down by a brook,
   Lavish clusters of airy snow.

Could one transplant you—(far on high
   A murky sunset lights the tiles)—
And set you 'neath the arching sky,
   In the green country, many miles,
Would you strike deep and suck up strength,
   Washed with rain and hung with pearls,
Cling to the trellis, a leafy length,
   Sweet with blossom for June and girls?

Yet no! Who needs you in those bowers?
   Who prizes gifts that all can give?
Bestow your life instead of flowers,
   And slowly die that dreams may live.
Prisoned and perishing, your dole
   Of lingering leaves shall not be vain—
Worthy to wreathe the hemlock bowl,
   Or twine about the cross of pain!

Edward Dowden (1843–1893)

280. *Burdens*

Are sorrows hard to bear,—the ruin
   Of flowers, the rotting of red fruit,
A love's decease, a life's undoing,
   And summer slain, and song-birds mute,
And skies of snow and bitter air?
These things, you deem, are hard to bear.

But ah the burden, the delight
   Of dreadful joys! Noon opening wide,
Golden and great; the gulfs of night,
   Fair deaths, and rent veils cast aside,
Strong soul to strong soul rendered up,
And silence filling like a cup.

(wr. 1872; pub. 1876)

Sonnets:

281. *A Disciple (The Inner Life)*

Master, they argued fast concerning Thee,
Proved what Thou art, denied what Thou art not,
Till brows were on the fret, and eyes grew hot,
And lip and chin were thrust out eagerly;
Then through the temple-door I slipped to free
My soul from secret ache in solitude,
And sought this brook, and by the brookside stood
The world's Light, and the Light and Life of me.
It is enough, O Master, speak no word!
The stream speaks, and the endurance of the sky
Outpasses speech: I seek not to discern
Even what smiles for me Thy lips have stirred;
Only in Thy hand still let my hand lie,
And let the musing soul within me burn.

282.   *Seeking God (The Inner Life)*

    I said "I will find God," and forth I went
    To Seek Him in the clearness of the sky,
    But over me stood unendurably
    Only a pitiless, sapphire firmament
    Ringing the world,—blank splendour; yet intent   5
    Still to find God, "I will go seek," said I,
    "His way upon the waters," and drew nigh
    An ocean marge weed-strewn and foam-besprent;
    And the waves dashed on idle sand and stone,
    And very vacant was the long, blue sea;   10
    But in the evening as I sat alone,
    My window open to the vanishing day,
    Dear God! I could not choose but kneel and pray,
    And it sufficed that I was found of Thee.

Mary Montgomerie Lamb ('Violet Fane', Mrs Sinclair) (1843–1905)

283.   *Victoria*

    21st June 1887

Queen of so many nations that the sun
    Sets not upon the boundaries of thy sway,–
    Whom men of varied clime and creed obey,–
Mother of many Princes,–wife of one
Who,–now these fleet-foot fifty years are run   5
    Whereof the festival is held to-day,–
    Sees not thy golden tresses turn'd to grey,
But,–in eternal slumber, slumbers on;–
How many glorious images unite
    'Round thine illustrious name!–The Dragon's head   10
Beneath St. George's heel:–the Lion's might:–
    Britannia:–India's Empress,–robed in red,
Crown'd and enthroned!–Then lo! thou com'st in sight,–
    A lonely woman,–sable garmented.

284.   *At Christie's*

> They scowl and simper here in rows,
>   Or seem to look with pleading eyes
> Upon the crowd that comes and goes,
>   And talks and stares, and bids and buys;
>
> Brave knights and squires, and belted earls,
>   In boots and spurs, and coats-of-mail;
> And ladies fair, in lace and pearls,
>   And ruff, and coiff, and farthingale.
>
> The founders of a noble race,
>   Whose blood in righteous cause was shed,
> Find here a brief abiding-place,
>   Exiled and disinherited.
>
> Kinsman and kinswoman are they,
>   Brother and sister, bride and groom,
> All waiting here in brave array
>   To meet their unexpected doom;
>
> For they that did so long abide
>   Beneath one roof, by right of birth,
> Must now dissever and divide,
>   And be as wand'rers on the earth.
>
> In what hot haste they came to town
>   From their long sojourn in the shires!
> And as they sped by dale and down,
>   And fiash'd past rivers, fields, and spires,
>
> I wonder, did they, in amaze
>   At such swift progress, call to mind
> Those good old jog-trot pillion-days
>   That seem to lie so far behind?
>
> And (for they all have human eyes
>   That from these walls look sadly down)
> I wonder, did they realise
>   The purport of this trip to town?

Or merely deem some lucky chance
    Released them from their dull abode,
And sent them forth to dine and dance,   35
    And see the plays, and learn the mode?

In mouldy vault, 'neath sculptured tomb,
    They sleep who bore these forms in life,
Kinsman and comrade, bride and groom,
    Brother and sister, man and wife.   40

But since their bones are brown and bare,
    And worms have spun across their eyes,
And holland sarks are what they wear
    In lieu of all these braveries,

And since they turn not in their graves   45
    For very horror and dismay,
To see themselves, like negro slaves,
    Set up for auction here to-day,

Whilst these, their sad-eyed portraits, gaze
    With looks of passionate appeal,   50
As though regretful of the days
    When arm could smite and heart could feel,

I hold these for the truer men,
    More keen of soul, more clear of sight,
In closer touch with human ken   55
    Of what is wrong and what is right.

285.   *The Siren*

"My voice is sweeter than the lute,
    My form is passing fair,
My lips are like the scarlet fruit
    The coral branches bear.

"My teeth are whiter than the pearls   5
    Men seek beneath the brine,
And when I shake my dripping curls
    Far brighter jewels shine;

"My russet curls, whose golden tips
　　Half hide a breast that swells
As pink and pearly as the lips
　　That laugh on spike-back'd shells;

"My eyes reflect the glimmer cast
　　When seas lie calm and deep,
Where, under rotting spar and mast,
　　The silent sailors sleep.

"Oft have I dragged them from the sands,–
　　They cannot make demur,–
And pull'd the gold rings from their hands:
　　They neither speak nor stir,

"So stark they lie! Yet one, alone,
　　Awoke to find me fair,—
(This harp is made of his breast-bone,
　　Its strings were once his hair!)

"A merry moon we pass'd, and more,
　　And then upon him came
Some wanton mem'ry of the shore,
　　He breathed a woman's name;

"Wherefore I made him sleep again,
　　So sound, he could not stir;
But first I suck'd his heart and brain,
　　Lest he should dream of her.

"Before he slept he spake strange words;
　　These were the words he said:
'Your song is blither than the birds',
　　Your lips are ripe and red,

"'Your breast is white, your eyes are blue,
　　Yet you cannot understand,
Or love your love as the maidens do
　　That live upon the land.'

"So, since, whene'er the sun is low,
　　And length'ning shadows fall,
And straying lovers come and go
　　Along the grey sea-wall,

"Amongst the rocks I crouch me down 45
    To hear what they may say,
And learn this thing I have not known—
    To love the land-girls' way!

"But oft I hear them moan and sigh,
    And often weep for woe; 50
The summer nights are going by,
    Yet this is all I know!

"So, mine must be the wiser way,
    For all my sweetheart said!
I made far merrier than they 55
    The moon that I was wed!

"And he was mine,—my very own!
    I clasp'd him firm and fair!...
(This harp is made of his breast-bone,
    Its strings were once his hair!)" 60

Arthur O'Shaughnessy (1844–1881)

286. *Ode*

We are the music makers,
    And we are the dreamers of dreams,
Wandering by lone sea-breakers,
    And sitting by desolate streams;—
World-losers and world-forsakers, 5
    On whom the pale moon gleams:
Yet we are the movers and shakers
    Of the world for ever, it seems.

With wonderful deathless ditties
We build up the world's great cities, 10
    And out of a fabulous story
    We fashion an empire's glory:
One man with a dream, at pleasure,
    Shall go forth and conquer a crown;
And three with a new song's measure 15
    Can trample a kingdom down.

We, in the ages lying
   In the buried past of the earth,
Built Nineveh with our sighing,
   And Babel itself in our mirth;
And o'erthrew them with prophesying
   To the old of the new world's worth;
For each age is a dream that is dying,
   Or one that is coming to birth.

A breath of our inspiration
Is the life of each generation;
   A wondrous thing of our dreaming
   Unearthly, impossible seeming—
The soldier, the king, and the peasant
   Are working together in one,
Till our dream shall become their present,
   And their work in the world be done.

They had no vision amazing
Of the goodly house they are raising;
   They had no divine foreshowing
   Of the land to which they are going:
But on one man's soul it hath broken,
   A light that doth not depart;
And his look, or a word he hath spoken,
   Wrought flame in another man's heart.

And therefore to-day is thrilling
With a past day's late fulfilling;
   And the multitudes are enlisted
   In the faith that their fathers resisted,
And, scorning the dream of to-morrow,
   Are bringing to pass, as they may,
In the world, for its joy or its sorrow,
   The dream that was scorned yesterday.

But we, with our dreaming and singing,
   Ceaseless and sorrowless we!
The glory about us clinging
   Of the glorious futures we see,
Our souls with high music ringing:
   O men! it must ever be
That we dwell, in our dreaming and singing,
   A little apart from ye.

For we are afar with the dawning
   And the suns that are not yet high,
And out of the infinite morning
   Intrepid you hear us cry—   60
How, spite of your human scorning,
   Once more God's future draws nigh,
And already goes forth the warning
   That ye of the past must die.

Great hail! we cry to the comers   65
   From the dazzling unknown shore;
Bring us hither your sun and your summers,
   And renew our world as of yore;
You shall teach us your song's new numbers,
   And things that we dreamed not before: 70
Yea, in spite of a dreamer who slumbers,
   And a singer who sings no more.

Gerard Manley Hopkins (1844–1889)

287.   *A Trio of Triolets*

(a)

Λέγεταί τι καινόν;

'No news in the *Times* to-day,'
Each man tells his next-door neighbour.
He, to see if what they say,
'No news in the *Times* to-day,'
Is correct, must plough his way   5
Through that: after three hours' labour,
'No news in the *Times* to-day,'
Each man tells his next-door neighbour.

(b)

Cockle's Antibilious Pills

'When you ask for Cockle's Pills,
Beware of spurious imitations.'   10
Yes, when you ask for every ill's
Cure, when you ask for Cockle's Pills,

Some hollow counterfeit that kills
Would fain mock that which heals the nations.
Oh, when you ask for Cockle's Pills   15
Beware of heartless imitations.

(c)

'The Child is Father to the Man' (Wordsworth)

'The child is father to the man.'
How can he be? The words are wild.
Suck any sense from that who can:
'The child is father to the man.'   20
No; what the poet did write ran,
'The man is father to the child.'
'The child is father to the man'!
How *can* he be? The words are wild.

288.   *The Wreck of the Deutschland*

December 6. 7. 1875

*to the
happy memory of five Franciscan nuns,
exiles by the Falck Laws,
drowned between midnight and morning of
December 7*

PART THE FIRST

1

Thou mastering me
God! giver of breath and bread;
Wórld's stránd, swáy of the séa;
Lord of living and dead;
Thou hast bóund bónes and véins in me, fástened me flésh,   5
And áfter it álmost únmade, what with dréad,
Thy doing: and dost thou touch me afresh?
Óver agáin I féel thy fínger and fínd thée.

2

   I did say yes
  O at líghtning and láshed ród;
 Thou heardst me, truer than tongue, confess
  Thy terror, O Christ, O God;
Thou knówest the wálls, áltar and hóur and níght:
The swoon of a heart that the sweep and the hurl of thee trod
  Hárd dówn with a horror of height:
And the midriff astrain with leaning of, laced with fire of stress.

3

   The frown of his face
  Before me, the hurtle of hell
 Behind, where, where was a, where was a place?—
  I whirled out wings that spell
And fled with a fling of the heart to the heart of the Host.—
My heart, but you were dovewinged, I can tell,
  Cárrier-wítted, I am bóld to bóast,
To flash from the flame to the flame then, tower from the grace to the grace.

4

   I am sóft síft
  In an hourglass—at the wall
 Fast, but mined with a motion, a drift,
  And it crowds and it combs to the fall;
I stéady as a wáter in a wéll, to a póise, to a páne,
But roped with, always, all the way down from the tall
  Fells or flanks of the voel, a vein
Of the góspel próffer, a préssure, a prínciple, Chríst's gíft.

5

   I kiss my hand
  To the stars, lovely-asunder
 Starlight, wafting him out of it; and
  Glow, glory in thunder;
Kiss my hand to the dappled-with-damson west:
Since, thóugh he is únder the wórld's spléndour and wónder,
  His mýstery múst be instréssed, stressed;
For I greet him the days I meet him, and bless when I understand.

6

      Not out of his bliss
    Springs the stress felt
Nor first from heaven (and few know this)
      Swings the stroke dealt—
Stroke and a stress that stars and storms deliver,   45
That guilt is hushed by, hearts are flushed by and melt—
    But it rídes tíme like ríding a ríver
(And here the faithful waver, the faithless fable and miss).

7

      It dates from day
    Of his going in Galilee;   50
Warm-laid grave of a womb-life grey;
      Manger, maiden's knee;
The dense and the driven Passion, and frightful sweat:
Thence the discharge of it, there its swelling to be,
    Though félt befóre, though in high flood yét—   55
What none would have known of it, only the heart, being hard at bay,

8

      Is out with it! Oh,
    We lash with the best or worst
Word last! How a lush-kept plush-capped sloe
      Will, mouthed to flesh-burst,   60
Gush!—flush the man, the being with it, sour or sweet
Brim, in a flásh, fúll!—Híther then, lást or fírst,
    To hero of Calvary, Christ,'s feet—
Never ask if méaning it, wánting it, wárned of it—mén gó.

9

      Be adored among men,   65
    God, three-numberèd form;
Wring thy rebel, dogged in den,
      Man's malice, with wrecking and storm.
Beyónd sáying swéet, past télling of tóngue,
    Thou art lightning and love, I found it, a winter and warm;   70
      Father and fondler of heart thou hast wrung:
Hast thy dark descending and most art merciful then.

           10

           With an anvil-ding
       And with fire in him forge thy will
    Or rather, rather then, stealing as Spring   75
           Through him, melt him but master him still:
Whether át ónce, as ónce at a crásh Pául,
Or as Áustin, a língering-óut swéet skíll,
       Make mercy in all of us, out of us all
Mástery, bút be adóred, bút be adóred Kíng.   80

           PART THE SECOND

                 11

           'Some find me a swórd; sóme
       The flánge and the ráil; fláme,
    Fang, or flood' goes Death on drum,
           And stórms búgle his fáme.
But *wé* dréam we are róoted in éarth—Dúst!   85
Flesh falls within sight of us: we, though our flower the same,
       Wave with the meadow, forget that there must
The sóur scýthe crínge, and the bléar sháre cóme.

                 12

           —On Saturday sailed from Bremen,
       American-outward-bound,   90
    Take settler and seamen, tell men with women,
           Two hundred souls in the round—
O Father, not under thy feathers nor ever as guessing
The goal was a shoal, of a fourth the doom to be drowned;
       Yet *did* the dark side of the bay of thy blessing   95
Not vault them, the million of rounds of thy mercy not reeve even them in?

                 13

           Into the snows she sweeps,
       Hurling the Haven behind,
    The Deutschland, on Sunday; and so the sky keeps,
           For the infinite air is unkind,   100
And the sea flint-flake, black-backed in the regular blow,
Sitting Eastnortheast, in cursed quarter, the wind;
       Wíry and white-fíery and whírlwind-swivellèd snów
Spins to the widow-making unchilding unfathering deeps.

14

      She drove in the dark to leeward, 105
        She struck—not a reef or a rock
  But the combs of a smother of sand: night drew her
        Dead to the Kentish Knock;
And she beat the bank down with her bows and the ride of her keel;
    The breakers rolled on her beam with ruinous shock; 110
       And, canvass and compass, the whorl and the wheel
Idle for ever to waft her or wind her with, these she endúred.

15

      Hope had grown grey hairs,
        Hope had mourning on,
  Trénched with téars, cárved with cáres, 115
        Hope was twelve hours gone;
And frightful a nightfall folded rueful a day
Nor rescue, only rocket and lightship, shone,
       And lives at last were washing away:
To the shrouds they took,—they shook in the hurling and horrible airs. 120

16

      One stirred from the rigging to save
        The wild woman-kind below,
  With a rope's end round the man, handy and brave—
        He was pitched to his death at a blow,
For all his dreadnought breast and braids of thew: 125
    They could téll him for hóurs, dándled the tó and the fró
       Through the cobbled foam-fleece. What could he do
With the burl of the fóuntains of aír, búck and the flóod of the wave?

17

      They fought with God's cold—
        And they could not, and fell to the deck 130
  (Crushed them) or water (and drowned them) or rolled
        With the searomp over the wreck.
Night roared, with the heartbreak hearing a heartbroke rabble,
The woman's wailing, the crying of child without check—
      Till a líoness aróse bréasting the bábble, 135
A próphetess tówered in the túmult, a vírginal tóngue tóld.

18

    Ah, touched in your bower of bone,
      Are you! turned, for an exquisite smart,
  Have you! make words break from me here all alone,
      Do you!—móther of béing in me, héart.   140
O unteachably after evil, but uttering truth,
  Why, tears! is it? tears; such a melting, a madrigal start!
    Never-eldering revel and river of youth,
What can it be, this glee? the good you have there of your own?

19

    Sister, a sister calling   145
      A master, her master and mine!—
  And the inboard seas run swirling and hawling;
      The rash smart sloggering brine
Blínds her; but shé that wéather sees óne thing, óne;
Has óne fetch ín her: she réars hersélf to divíne   150
    E'ars, and the cáll of the táll nún
To the mén in the tóps and the táckle rode óver the stórm's brawling.

20

    She was first of a five and came
    Of a coifèd sisterhood.
  (O Deutschland, double a desperate name!   155
      O wórld wíde of its góod!
But Gertrude, lily, and Luther, are two of a town,
  Chríst's líly, and béast of the wáste wóod:
    From lífe's dáwn it is dráwn dówn,
Ábel is Cáin's brother and bréasts they have súcked the sáme.)   160

21

    Loathed for a love men knew in them,
      Banned by land of their birth,
    Rhíne refúsed them, Thámes would rúin them;
      Surf, snow, river and earth
Gnashed: but thou art above, thou Orion of light;   165
  Thy unchancelling poising palms were weighing the worth,
    Thou mártyr-máster: in thý síght
Storm flákes were scróll-leaved flówers, lily shówers—sweet héaven was astréw in them.

22

   Five! the finding and sake
    And cipher of suffering Christ.
  Márk, the márk is of mán's máke
   And the word of it Sacrificed,
But he scores it in scarlet himself on his own bespoken,
 Before-time-taken, dearest prizèd and priced—
   Stigma, signal, cinquefoil token
For léttering of the lámb's fléece, rúddying of the róse-fláke.

23

   Joy fall to thee, father Francis,
    Drawn to the Life that died;
  With the gnarls of the nails in thee, niche of the lance, his
    Lovescape crucified
And seal of his seraph-arrival! and these thy daughters
 And five-livèd and leavèd favour and pride,
   Are sísterly séaled in wíld wáters,
To bathe in his fall-gold mercies, to breathe in his all-fire glances

24

   Away in the loveable west,
    On a pastoral forehead of Wales,
  I was under a roof here, I was at rest,
    And they the prey of the gales;
She to the black-about air, to the breaker, the thickly
 Falling flakes, to the throng that catches and quails,
   Was cálling 'O Chríst, Chríst, come quíckly':
The cross to her she calls Christ to her, christens her wild-worst Best.

25

   The majesty! what did she mean?
    Breathe, arch and original Breath.
  Is it lóve in her of the béing as her lóver had béen?
    Breathe, body of lovely Death.
They were élse-mínded then, áltogéther, the mén
 Wóke thee with a *We are périshing* in the wéather of Gennésaréth.
   Or ís it that she críed for the crówn thén,
The keener to come at the comfort for feeling the combating keen?

26

   For how to the heart's cheering
    The down-dugged ground-hugged grey
  Hovers off, the jay-blue heavens appearing
     Of pied and peeled May!
Blue-beating and hoary-glow height; or night, still higher,   205
 With bélled fíre and the móth-soft Mílky Wáy.
   What bý your méasure is the héaven of desíre,
The tréasure never éyesight gót, nor was éver guessed whát for the héaring?

27

   Nó, but it was nót thése.
    The jáding and the jár of the cárt,   210
  Time's tásking, it is fáthers that ásking for éase
     Of the sódden-with-its-sórrowing héart,
Not danger, electrical-horror; then, further, it finds
 The appéaling of the Pássion is ténderer in práyer apárt:
   Other, I gather, in measure her mind's   215
Búrden, in wínd's búrly and béat of endrágonèd séas.

28

   But how shall I... Make me room there;
    Reach me a ... Fancy, come faster—
  Strike you the sight of it? look at it loom there,
     Thing that she ... There then! the Master,   220
Ípse, the ónly one, Chríst, Kíng, Héad:
 He was to cure the extremity where he had cast her;
   Do, deal, lord it with living and dead;
Let him ride, her pride, in his triumph, despatch and have done with his doom there.

29

   Ah! thére was a héart right!   225
    There was single eye!
  Réad the unshápeable shóck níght
     And knew the who and the why;
Wording it how but by him that present and past,
 Heaven and earth are word of, worded by?—   230
   The Símon-Péter of a sóul! to the blást
Tárpeïan-fást, but a blówn béacon of líght.

30

Jésu, héart's líght,
Jésu, máid's són,
Whát was the féast fóllowed the níght
Thou hadst glóry of thís nún?—
Féast of the óne wóman withóut stáin.
For so conceivèd, so to conceive thee is done;
But here was heart-throe, birth of a brain,
Wórd, that héard and képt thee and úttered thee óutríght.

31

Well, shé has thée for the pain, for the
Pátience; but píty of the rést of them!
Heart, go and bleed at a bitterer vein for the
Comfortless unconfessed of them—
No not uncomforted: lovely-felicitous Providence,
Fínger of a ténder of, O of a féathery délicacy, the bréast of the
Maiden could obey so, be a bell to, ring óf it, and
Stártle the poor shéep back! is the shípwreck then a hárvest,
does témpest carry the gráin for thee?

32

I admíre thee, máster of the tídes,
Of the Yóre-flood, of the yéar's fáll;
The recúrb and the recóvery of the gúlf's sídes,
The gírth of it and the whárf of it and the wáll;
Stánching, quénching ócean of a mótionable mínd;
Gróund of béing and gránite of it: pást áll
Grásp Gód, thróned behínd
Déath, with a sóvereignty that héeds but hídes, bódes but abídes;

33

With a mércy that oútrídes
The all of water, an ark
For the lístener; for the língerer with a lóve glídes
Lówer than déath and the dárk;
A véin for the vísiting of the pást-prayer, pént in príson,
The-last-breath penitent spirits—the uttermost mark
Our passion-plungèd giant risen,
The Christ of the Father compassionate, fetched in the storm of his strides.

34

    Now burn, new born to the world,
      Double-naturèd name,
  The heaven-flúng, heart-fléshed, máiden-fúrled
    Míracle-in-Máry-of-fláme,
Mid-numberèd he in three of the thunder-throne!   270
Not a dóomsday dázzle in his cóming nor dárk as he cáme;
    Kínd, but róyally recláiming his ówn;
A released shówer, let flásh to the shíre, not a líghtning of fíre hard húrled.

35

    Dáme, at óur dóor
      Drówned, and among óur shóals,   275
  Remémber us in the róads, the heaven-háven of the rewárd:
    Our kíng back, Oh, upon Énglish sóuls!
Let him éaster in us, be a dáyspring to the dímness of us, be a crímson-cresseted east,
  More bríghtening her, ráre-dear Brítain, as his réign rólls,
    Príde, rose, prínce, hero of us, hígh-príest,   280
Oür héart's charity's héarth's fíre, oür thóughts' chivalry's thróng's Lórd.

Brân Maenefa

289.   *The Silver Jubilee*

To James First Bishop of Shrewsbury on the
25th Year of his Episcopate July 28 1876

Though no high-hung bells or din
Of braggart bugles cry it in—
   What is sound? Nature's round
Makes the Silver Jubilee.

Five and twenty years have run   5
Since sacred fountains to the sun
   Sprang, that but now were shut,
Showering Silver Jubilee.

Feasts, when we shall fall asleep,
Shrewsbury may see others keep;   10
   None but you this her true,
This her Silver Jubilee.

   Not today we need lament
   Your wealth of life is some way spent:
    Toil has shed round your head   15
   Silver but for Jubilee.

   Then for her whose velvet vales
   Should have pealed with welcome, Wales,
    Let the chime of a rhyme
   Utter Silver Jubilee.   20

290. 'Hope holds to Christ the mind's own mirror out'

   Hope holds to Christ the mind's own mirror out
   To take His lovely likeness more and more.
   It will not well, so she would bring about
  { A growing burnish brighter
  { An ever brighter burnish than before
   And turns to wash it from her welling eyes   5
   And breathes the blots off all with sighs on sighs.

   Her glass is blest but she as good as blind
   Holds till hand aches and wonders what is there;
   Her glass drinks light, she darkles down behind,
   All of her glorious gainings unaware.   10
   I told you that she turned her mirror dim
  { At times, but then she sees herself, not Him.
  { Betweenwhiles, but she sees herself not Him.

291. *The Starlight Night*

Look at the stars! look, look up at the skies!
 O look at all the fire-folk sitting in the air!
 The bright bóroughs, the circle-citadels there!
Down in dim woods the diamond delves! the elves'-eyes!
The grey lawns cold where gold, where quickgold lies!   5
 Wind-beat whitebeam! airy abeles set on a flare!
 Flake-doves sent floating forth at a farmyard scare!—
Ah well! it is all a purchase, all is a prize.

Buy then! bid then!—What?—Prayer, pátience, alms, vows.
Look, look: a May-mess, like on orchard boughs! 10
  Look! March-bloom, like on mealed-with-yellow sallows!
These are indeed the barn; withindoors house
The shocks. This piece-bright paling shuts the spouse
  Christ home, Christ and his mother and all his hallows.

292. *The Lantern Out of Doors*

Sometimes a lantern moves along the night.
  That interests our eyes. And who goes there?
  I think; where from and bound, I wonder, where,
With, all down darkness wide, his wading light?
Men go by me whom either beauty bright 5
  In mould or mind or what not else makes rare:
  They rain against our much-thick and marsh air
Rich beams, till death or distance buys them quite.

Déath or distance soon consumes them: wind,
  What most I may eye after, be in at the end 10
I cannot, and out of sight is out of mind.

Christ minds: Christ's interest, what to avow or amend
  There, éyes them, heart wánts, care haúnts, foot fóllows kínd,
Their ránsom, théir rescue, ánd first, fást, last friénd.

293. *In the Valley of the Elwy*

Í remémber a house where all were good
  To me, God knows, deserving no such thing:
  Cómforting smell bréathed at very entering,
Fetched fresh, as I suppose, off some sweet wood.
That cordial air made those kind people a hood 5
  All over, as a bevy of eggs the mothering wíng
  Will, or mild nights the new mórsels of Spring:
Why, it séemed of cóurse; séemed of ríght it shóuld.

Lóvely the woods, wáters, méadows, combes, vales,
All the air things wear that build this world of Wales; 10
  Ónly the inmate does not correspond:

God, lóver of souls, swáying considérate scales,
Complete thy creature dear O where it fails,
   Being mighty a master, being a father and fond.

294.   *The Caged Skylark*

As a dare-gale skylark scanted in a dúll cáge,
   Man's mounting spirit in his bone-house, mean house, dwells—
      That bird beyond the remembering hís free fells,
This in drudgery, day-labouring-out life's age.

Though aloft on turf or perch or poor low stage   5
   Both sing sometímes the sweetest, sweetest spells,
      Yet both droop deadly sómetimes in their cells
Or wring their barriers in bursts of fear or rage.

Not that the sweet-fowl, song-fowl, needs no rest—
Why, hear him, hear him babble and drop down to his nest,   10
   But his ówn nést, wíld nést, no prison.

Man's spirit will be flesh-bound when found at best,
But úncúmberèd: meadow-dówn is nót distréssed
   For a ráinbow fóoting it nor hé for his bónes rísen.

295.   *Hurrahing in Harvest*

Summer énds now; now, bárbarous in béauty, the stóoks ríse
Around; up above, what wind-walks! what lovely behaviour
Of sílk-sack clóuds! has wilder, wílful-wávier
Méal-drift moulded ever and melted acróss skíes?

I wálk, I líft up, Í lift úp heart, éyes,   5
Down all that glory in the heavens to glean our Saviour;
And, éyes, heárt, what looks, what lips yet gáve you á
Rápturous love's greeting of realer, of rounder replies?

And the azurous hung hills are his wórld-wíelding shoulder
Majestic—as a stallion stalwart, very-violet-sweet!—   10
These things, these things were here and but the beholder
Wánting; whích two whén they ónce méet,
The héart réars wíngs bóld and bolder
And hurls for him, O half hurls earth for him off under his feet.

296.   *Harry Ploughman*

Hard as hurdle arms, with a broth of goldish flue
Breathed round; the rack of ribs; the scooped flank; lank
                        { knee-nave;
Rope-over thigh;   { kneebank; and barrelled shank—
            Héad and fóot, shóuldér and shánk—
By a grey eye's heed steered well, one crew, fall to;   5
                        { barrowy brawn, his thew
Stánd at stress. Each limb's { barrowy-brawnèd thew
That onewhere curded, onewhere sucked or sank—
                    Sóared ór sánk—,
Though as a beechbole firm, finds his, as at a rollcall, rank
And features, ín flesh, whát deed he each must do—   10
                His sínew-sérvice whére dó.
He leans to it, Harry bends, look. Back, elbow, and liquid waist
In him, all quail to the wallowing o' the plough. 'S cheek crímsons; curls
                    { in a wind liftéd, windláced—
Wag or crossbridle,   { Windloft or windlaced—
                    { Wind-lilylocks-laced;
                    { See his wínd-lílylócks-láced—;   15
Chúrlsgrace too, chíld of Amansstrength, how it hángs or húrls
{ Them
{ These—broád ín bluff híde his frówning féet lashed! ráced
                                { cold fúrls—
With, along them, cragiron under and { flame-fúrls—
                { With-a-fountain's shining-shot furls.
                { With-a-wét-shéen-shót fúrls.

297.   *Tom's Garland: on the Unemployed*

Tom—gárlanded with squat and surly stéel
Tom; then Tom's fallowbootfellow píles pí ck
By him and rips out rockfire homeforth—sturdy Dick;
Tom Heart-at-ease, Tòm Navvy; he is all for his méal
Sure, 's bed now. Low be it: lustily he his lòw lót (féel   5
That ne'er need hunger, Tom; Tom seldom sick,
Seldomer heartsóre; that treads through, prickproof, thick
Thousands of thorns, thoughts) swíngs though. Commonweal
Little Í reck ho! lacklevel in, if all had bread:
What! cóuntry is honour enough in all us—lordly head,   10
With heaven's lights high hung round, or, mother-gróund

  That mammocks, mighty foot. But nő way sped,
  Nor mind nor mainstrength; gőld go garlanded
  With, perilous, O nó; nor yet plod safe shod sound;
      Ùndenizened, be͡yond bound
  Of earth's glory, e͡arth's ease, all; noone, nowhere,
  In wide the world's weal; răre gŏld, bŏld stĕel, băre
      In both; càre, but shàre cắre—
  This, by Despăir, bred Hangdog dull; by Rage,
  Manwolf, worse; and their packs infest the age.

298.   *Epithalamion*

  Hark, hearer, hear what I do; lend a thought now, make believe
  We are leaf-whelmed somewhere with the hood
  Of some branchy bunchy bushybowered wood,
  Southern dean or Lancashire clough or Devon cleave,
  { That leans along
  { Leaning on the loins of hills, where a candycoloured,
    where a gluegold-brown
  Marbled river, boisterously beautiful, between
  Roots and rocks is danced and dandled, all in froth and
    waterblowballs, down.
  We are there, when we hear a shout
  That the hanging honeysuck, the dogeared hazels in the cover
  Makes dither, makes hover
  And the riot of a rout
  Of, it must be, boys from the town
  Bathing: it is summer's sovereign good.

  By there comes a listless stranger: beckoned by the noise
  He drops towards the river: unseen
  Sees the bevy of them, how the boys
  With dare and with downdolfinry and bellbright bodies
    huddling out,
  Are earthworld, airworld, waterworld thorough hurled, all by
    turn and turn about.

  This garland of their gambol flashes in his breast
  Into such a sudden zest
  Of summertime joys
  That he hies to a pool neighbouring; sees it is the best
  There; sweetest, freshest, shadowiest;

Fairyland; silk-beech, scrolled ash, packed sycamore, wild
    wychelm, hornbeam fretty overstood 30
By Rafts and rafts of flake-leaves light, dealt so, painted on
    the air,
Hang as still as hawk or hawkmoth, as the stars or as the
    angels there,
Like the thing that never knew the earth, never off roots 35
Rose. Here he feasts: lovely all is! Nó more: off with—down
    he dings
His bleachèd both and woolwoven wear:
Careless these in coloured wisp
All lie tumbled-to; then with loop-locks 40
Forward falling, forehead frowning, lips crisp
Over fingerteasing task, his twiny boots
Fast he opens, last he off wrings
Till walk the world he can with bare his feet
And come where lies a coffer, burly all of blocks 45
Built of chancequarrièd, selfquainèd hoār-huskèd rocks
And the water warbles over into, filleted with glassy grassy
    quicksilvery shivès and shoots
And with heavenfallen freshness down from moorland still
    brims, 50
Dark or daylight, on and on. Here he will then, here he will
    the fleet
Flinty kindcold element let break across his limbs,
Long. Where we leave him, froliclavish, while he looks about
    him, laughs, swims. 55

Enough now; since the sacred matter that I mean
I should be wronging longer leaving it to float
Upon this only gambolling and echoing-of-earth note
What is .... the delightful dean?
Wedlock. What the water? Spousal love 60

. . . .

    to Everard, as I surmise,
Sparkled first in Amy's eyes

. . . .

                turns
Father, mother, brothers, sisters, friends
Into fairy trees, wildflowers, woodferns 65
Rankèd round the bower

. . . .

299.　　　　　'What shall I do for the land that bred me'

        What shall I do for the land that bred me,
        Her homes and fields that folded and fed me?
        Be under her banner and live for her honour:
        Under her banner I'll live for her honour.
            Chorus. Under her banner we live for her honour.　　　　5

        Not the pleasure, the pay, the plunder,
        But country and flag, the flag I am under—
        There is the shilling that finds me willing
        To follow a banner and fight for honour.
            Chorus. We follow her banner, we fight for her honour.　　　10

        Call me England's fame's fond lover,
        Her fame to keep, her fame to recover.
        Spend me or end me what God shall send me,
        But under her banner I live for her honour.
            Chorus. Under her banner we march for her honour.　　　15

        Where is the field I must play the man on?
        O welcome there their steel or cannon.
        Immortal beauty is death with duty,
        If under her banner I fall for her honour.
            Chorus. Under her banner we fall for her honour.　　　20

300.　　　　'The shepherd's brow, fronting forked lightning, owns'

        The shepherd's brow, fronting forked lightning, owns
        The horror and the havoc and the glory
        Of it. Angels fall, they are towers, from heaven—a story
        Of just, majestical, and giant groans.
        But man—we, scaffold of score brittle bones;　　　　5
        Who breathe, from groundlong babyhood to hoary
        Age gasp; whose breath is our *memento mori*—
        What bass is *our* viol for tragic tones?
        He! Hand to mouth he lives, and voids with shame;
        And, blazoned in however bold the name,　　　　10
        Man Jack the man is, just; his mate a hussy.
        And I that die these deaths, that feed this flame,
        That ... in smooth spoons spy life's masque mirrored: tame
        My tempests there, my fire and fever fussy.

301.

Felix Randal

Félix Rándal the fárrier, O is he déad then? my dúty máll énded,
Who have watched his mould of man, big-bóned and hardy-handsome
Pining, píning, till time when reason rámbled in it and some
Fatal four disorders, fléshed there, all conténded?

Síckness bróke him. Impatient, he cursed at first, but mended   5
Being anointed and all; though a heavenlier heart began some
Mónths éarlier, since I had our swéet repríeve and ránsom
Téndered to him. Áh well, God rést him áll road éver he offénded!

This séeing the síck endéars them tó us, us tóo it endéars.
My tongue had taught thee comfort, touch had quenched thy tears,   10
Thy tears that touched my heart, child, Félix, poor Felix Randal;

How far from then forethought of, all thy more boisterous years,
When thou at the random grím fórge, pówerful amídst péers,
Didst fettle for the great grey drayhorse his bright and battering sandal!

302.

Spelt from Sibyl's Leaves

Earnest, earthless, equal, attuneable, |vaulty, voluminous,...
    stupendous
Evening strains to be tíme's vást, |womb-of-all, home-of-all,
    hearse-of-all night.
Her fond yellow hornlight wound to the west, |her wild hollow
    hoarlight hung to the height
Waste; her earliest stars, earlstars, |stárs principal, overbend us,
Fíre-féaturing héaven. For éarth |her béing has unbóund; her dápple
    is at énd, as–   5
Tray or aswarm, all throughther, in throngs; |self ín self stéepèd and
    páshed—qúite
Disremembering, dísmémbering |áll now. Heart, you round me right
With: Óur évening is óver us; óur night |whélms, whélms, ánd will
    énd us.
Only the beakleaved boughs dragonish |damask the tool-smooth
    bleak light; black,
Ever so black on it. Óur tale, O óur oracle! |Lét life, wáned, ah lét life
    wínd   10
Off hér once skéined stained véined varíety |upon, áll on twó spools;
    párt, pen, páck

Now her áll in twó flocks, twó folds—bláck, white; |ríght, wrong;
 réckon but, réck but, mínd
But thése two; wáre of a wórld where bút these |twó tell, éach off
 the óther; of a ráck
Where, selfwrung, selfstrung, sheathe- and shelterless, |thóughts
 against thoughts ín groans grínd.

303.   'Thee, God, I come from, to thee go'

       Thee, God, I come from, to thee go,
       All dáy long I like fountain flow
       From thy hand out, swayed about
       Mote-like in thy mighty glow.

       What I know of thee I bless,   5
       As acknowledging thy stress
       On my being and as seeing
       Something of thy holiness.

       Once I turned from thee and hid,
       Bound on what thou hadst forbid;   10
       Sow the wind I would; I sinned:
       I repent of what I did.

       Bad I am, but yet thy child.
       Father, be thou reconciled.
       Spare thou me, since I see   15
       With thy might that thou art mild.

               { left with me }
       I have life { before   me } still
       And thy purpose to fulfill;
       Yea a debt to pay thee yet: 20
       Help me, sir, and so I will.

       But thou bidst, and just thou art,
       Me shew mercy from my heart
       Towards my brother, every other
       Man my mate and counterpart.   25

             . . . .

       Jesus Christ sacrificed
       On the cross

        Moulded, he, in maiden's womb,
        Lived and died and from the tomb
        Rose in power and is our   30
        Judge that comes to deal our doom.

304.   'Repeat that, repeat'

Repeat that, repeat,
Cuckoo, bird, and open ear wells, heart-springs, delightfully sweet,
With a ballad, with a ballad, a rebound
Off trundled timber and scoops of the hillside ground, hollow
    hollow hollow ground:
The whóle lándscape flushes on a sudden at a sound   5

305.   *To his Watch*

    Mortal my mate, bearing my rock-a-heart,
    Warm beat with cold beat[,] company, shall I
    Earlier or you fail at our force and lie
    The ruins of, rifled, once a world of art?
    The telling time our task is; time's some part,   5
    Not all, but we were framed to fail and die—
    One spell and well that one. There, ah thereby
{ Is comfort's carol of all or woe's worst smart.
{ Is sweetest comfort's carol or worst woe's smart.
    Field-flown, the departed day no morning brings   10
    Saying 'This was yours' with her, but new one, worse,
    And then that last and shortest...

306.   *Spring*

Nothing is so beautiful as Spring—
    When weeds, in wheels, shoot long and lovely and lush;
    Thrush's eggs look little low heavens, and thrush
Through the echoing timber does so rinse and wring

The ear, it strikes like lightnings to hear him sing;   5
    The glassy peartree leaves and blooms, they brush
    The descending blue; that blue is all in a rush
With richness; the racing lambs too have fair their fling.

What is all this juice and all this joy?
    A strain of the earth's sweet being in the beginning
In Eden garden. – Have, get, before it cloy,

Before it cloud, Christ, lord, and sour with sinning,
Innocent mind and Mayday in girl and boy,
    Most, O maid's child, thy choice and worthy the winning.

307.   *To R. B.*

The fine delight that fathers thought; the strong
Spur, live and lancing like the blowpipe flame,
Breathes once and, quenchèd faster than it came,
Leaves yet the mind a mother of immortal song.
Nine months she then, nay years, nine years she long
Within her wears, bears, cares and combs the same:

The widow of an insight lost she lives, with aim
Now known and hand at work now never wrong.
Sweet fire the sire of muse, my soul needs this;
I want the one rapture of an inspiration.
O then if in my lagging lines you miss
The roll, the rise, the carol, the creation,
My winter world, that scarcely breathes that bliss
Now, yields you, with some sighs, our explanation.

Andrew Lang (1844–1912)

308.   *Ballade of Blue China*

There's a joy without canker or cark,
There's a pleasure eternally new,
'Tis to gloat on the glaze and the mark
Of China that's ancient and blue;
Unchipp'd all the centuries through
It has pass'd since the chime of it rang,
And they fashion'd it, figure and hue,
In the reign of the Emperor Hwang.

These dragons (their tails, you remark,
Into bunches of gillyflowers grew),— 10
When Noah came out of the ark,
Did these lie in wait for his crew?
They snorted, they snapp'd, and they slew,
They were mighty of fin and of fang,
And their portraits Celestials drew, 15
In the reign of the Emperor Hwang.

Here's a pot with a cot in a park,
In a park where the peach-blossoms blew,
Where the lovers eloped in the dark,
Loved, died, and were changed into two 20
Bright birds, that eternally flew
Through the boughs of the may as they sang
'Tis a tale was undoubtedly true
In the reign of the Emperor Hwang.

ENVOY

Come, snarl at my ecstasies, do, 25
Kind critic, your "tongue has a tang,"
But—a sage never heeded a shrew
In the reign of the Emperor Hwang.

309. *The Haunted Homes of England*

The Haunted Homes of England,
   How eerily they stand,
While through them flit their ghosts – to wit,
   The Monk with the Red Hand;
The Eyeless Girl – an awful spook – 5
   To stop the boldest breath,
The boy that inked his copybook,
   And so got 'wopped' to death!

Call them not shams – from haunted Glamis
   To haunted Woodhouselea, 10
I mark in hosts the grisly ghosts
   I hear the fell Banshie!
I know the spectral dog that howls
   Before the death of squires;
In my 'Ghosts'-guide' addresses hide 15
   For Podmore and for Myers!

  I see the Vampire climb the stairs
   From vaults below the church;
  And hark! the Pirate's spectre swears!
   O Psychical Research,   20
  Canst *thou* not hear what meets my ear,
   The viewless wheels that come?
  The wild Banshie that wails to thee?
   The Drummer with his drum?

  O Haunted Homes of England,   25
   Though tenandess ye stand,
  With none content to pay the rent,
   Through all the shadowy land,
  Now, Science true will find in you
   A sympathetic perch,   30
  And take you all, both Grange and Hall,
   For Psychical Research!

       (1894)

310.   *The Last Chance*

  Within the streams, Pausanias saith,
   That down Cocytus valley flow,
  Girdling the grey domain of Death,
   The spectral fishes come and go;
  The ghosts of trout flit to and fro.   5
   Persephone, fulfil my wish,
  And grant that in the shades below
   My ghost may land the ghosts of fish.

       (1888)

311.   *Good-bye*

  Kiss me, and say good-bye;
   Good-bye, there is no word to say but this,
   Nor any lips left for my lips to kiss,
  Nor any tears to shed, when these tears dry;
  Kiss me, and say good-bye.   5

Farewell, be glad, forget;
    There is no need to say "forget," I know,
    For youth is youth and time will have it so,
And though your lips are pale, and your eyes wet,
Farewell, you must forget.   10

You shall bring home your sheaves,
    Many, and heavy, and with blossoms twined
    Of memories that go not out of mind;
Let this one sheaf be twined with poppy leaves
When you bring home your sheaves.   15

In garnered loves of thine,
    The ripe good fruit of many hearts and years,
    Somewhere let this lie, grey and salt with tears;
It grew too near the sea wind, and the brine
Of life, this love of mine.   20

This sheaf was spoiled in spring,
    And over-long was green, and early sere,
    And never gathered gold in the late year
From autumn suns, and moons of harvesting,
But failed in frosts of spring.   25

Yet was it thine, my sweet,
    This love, though weak as young corn withered,
    Whereof no man may gather and make bread;
Thine, though it never knew the summer heat;
Forget not quite, my sweet.   30

Caroline (née Fitzroy), Lady Lindsay (1844–1912)

312.   *To My Own Face*

A greeting to thee, O most trusty friend!
That hast so steadfastly companioned me.
What other, say, in this can equal thee,
Who cam'st to life with me, with me shalt end?
Poor face of mine ! Right often dost thou lend   5
A smile to hide some smileless thoughts that be
Bound deep in heart, and oft thy kind eyes see
My soul's great grief and bid their ears attend.

Ah, childish fairness, seeming near, yet far,
Prized tenderly by dear ones pass'd away, 10
Fain I'd recall it! Next, an oval grace
Of girlhood; for thy woman's sorrows are
Stamped now on lips and forehead day by day,
Yet God's own image thou—O human face!

313. *Of a Bird-Cage*

*One of those made in Germany by convicts
sentenced to penal servitude*

A tiny prison built by prisoned hands
To coop some bright-wing'd thing; a mimic cell,
Wrought amid sighs by one who knew full well
The smart and pressure of enforcèd bands,
When high-soul'd courage failed him to assuage 5
The close-laid torture of a life-locked cage.

Perchance he wept his own deep grief and pain.
Alas, each day the sun rose high to set
In clouds of golden hope! And yet, and yet,
Time mattered naught. Him freedom called in vain, 10
As in the future she might beckon it—
That bird now free—who captive here should sit.

Thus with vague sympathy was each space barr'd,
Yet none less sure. Here shall the creature eat,
Here drink, here restless perch in cold or heat, 15
Setting to melody the sentence hard
Fate spells the words of. Plane the cramping floor,
Bend down the latch, and firmly bolt the door!

Samuel Waddington (1844–1923)

314. *Soul and Body*

Where wert thou, Soul, ere yet my body born
  Became thy dwelling place? Didst thou on earth,
  Or in the clouds, await this body's birth?
Or by what chance upon that winter's morn

    Didst thou this body find, a babe forlorn?   5
      Didst thou in sorrow enter, or in mirth?
      Or for a jest, perchance, to try its worth
    Thou tookest flesh, ne'er from it to be torn?

    Nay, Soul, I will not mock thee; well I know
      Thou wert not on the earth, nor in the sky;   10
    For with my body's growth thou too didst grow;
      But with that body's death wilt thou too die?
    I know not; and thou canst not tell me, so
      In doubt we'll go together—thou and I.

Edward Carpenter (1844–1929)

315.　　　　　*In a Manufacturing Town*

As I walked restless and despondent through the gloomy city,
    And saw the eager unresting to and fro—as of ghosts in some sulphurous Hades;
    And saw the crowds of tall chimneys going up, and the pall of smoke covering the sun,
        covering the earth, lying heavy against the very ground;
    And saw the huge refuse-heaps writhing with children picking them over,
    And the ghastly half-roofless smoke-blackened houses, and the black river flowing below;
As I saw these, and as I saw again far away the Capitalist quarter,
    With its villa residences and its high-walled gardens and its well-appointed carriages, and
        its face turned away from the wriggling poverty which made it rich;
    As I saw and remembered its drawing-room airs and affectations, and its wheezy pursy
        Church-going and its gas-reeking heavy-furnished rooms and its scent-bottles, and its
        other abominations—
I shuddered:
For I felt stifled, like one who lies half-conscious—knowing not clearly the shape of the
    evil—in the grasp of some heavy nightmare.

Then out of the crowd descending towards me came a little ragged boy:
Came—from the background of dirt disengaging itself—an innocent wistful child-face,
    begrimed like the rest but strangely pale, and pensive before its time.
And in an instant (it was as if a trumpet had been blown in that place) I saw it all clearly,
    the lie I saw and the truth, the false dream and the awakening.
For the smoke-blackened walls and the tall chimneys, and the dreary habitations of the
    poor, and the drearier habitations of the rich, crumbled and conveyed themselves away
    as if by magic;

And instead, in the backward vista of that face, I saw the joy of free open life under the sun:
The green sun-delighting earth and rolling sea I saw,
The free sufficing life—sweet comradeship, few needs and common pleasures—the needless endless burdens all cast aside,
Not as a sentimental vision, but as a fact and a necessity existing,
I saw
In the backward vista of that face.
Stronger than all combinations of Capital, wiser than all the Committees representative of Labor, the simple need and hunger of the human heart.
Nothing more is needed.
All the books of political economy ever written, all the proved impossibilities, are of no account.
The smoke-blackened walls and tall chimneys duly crumble and convey themselves away;
The falsehood of a gorged and satiated society curls and shrivels together like a withered leaf,
Before the forces which lie, dormant in the pale and wistful face of a little child.

Robert Bridges (1844–1930)

316.   *Eros*

    Why hast thou nothing in thy face?
    Thou idol of the human race,
    Thou tyrant of the human heart,
    The flower of lovely youth that art;
    Yea, and that standest in thy youth   5
    An image of eternal Truth,
    With thy exuberant flesh so fair,
    That only Pheidias might compare,
    Ere from his chaste marmoreal form
    Time had decayed the colours warm;   10
    Like to his gods in thy proud dress
    Thy starry sheen of nakedness.

    Surely thy body is thy mind,
    For in thy face is nought to find,
    Only thy soft unchristen'd smile,   15
    That shadows neither love nor guile,
    But shameless will and power immense,
    In secret sensuous innocence.

O king of joy, what is thy thought?
I dream thou knowest it is nought, 20
And wouldst in darkness come, but thou
Makest the light where'er thou go.
Ah yet no victim of thy grace,
None who e'er long'd for thy embrace,
Hath cared to look upon thy face. 25

317.   *London Snow*

When men were all asleep the snow came flying,
In large white flakes falling on the city brown,
Stealthily and perpetually settling and loosely lying,
    Hushing the latest traffic of the drowsy town;
Deadening, muffling, stifling its murmurs failing; 5
Lazily and incessantly floating down and down:
    Silently sifting and veiling road, roof and railing;
Hiding difference, making unevenness even,
Into angles and crevices softly drifting and sailing.
    All night it fell, and when full inches seven 10
It lay in the depth of its uncompacted lightness,
The clouds blew off from a high and frosty heaven;
    And all woke earlier for the unaccustomed brightness
Of the winter dawning, the strange unheavenly glare:
The eye marvelled—marvelled at the dazzling whiteness; 15
    The ear hearkened to the stillness of the solemn air;
No sound of wheel rumbling nor of foot falling,
And the busy morning cries came thin and spare.
    Then boys I heard, as they went to school, calling,
They gathered up the crystal manna to freeze 20
Their tongues with tasting, their hands with snowballing;
    Or rioted in a drift, plunging up to the knees;
Or peering up from under the white-mossed wonder,
'O look at the trees!' they cried, 'O look at the trees!'
    With lessened load a few carts creak and blunder, 25
Following along the white deserted way,
A country company long dispersed asunder:
    When now already the sun, in pale display
Standing by Paul's high dome, spread forth below
His sparkling beams, and awoke the stir of the day. 30
    For now doors open, and war is waged with the snow;
And trains of sombre men, past tale of number,
Tread long brown paths, as toward their toil they go:

But even for them awhile no cares encumber
Their minds diverted; the daily word is unspoken,   35
The daily thoughts of labour and sorrow slumber
At the sight of the beauty that greets them, for the charm they have broken.

Lucy Knox (1845–1884)

318. *Sonnet: A Cry to Men*

Say to men, women starve, and will they heed?
Say to them women drudge and faint and die
And sin, discrowning womanhood for aye;
Beseech men piteously to mind their need
Of wisdom, who must little children feed;   5
Implore them for her sake who stands on high
Enthroned, yet nestled in each heart, to try
If those (her sisters) may be saved indeed;
Saved from starvation, saved from overstrain,
Bloom ere they fade, not wither incomplete,   10
So low, so fall'n, such dust beneath the feet!
Say this to man, and wilt thou speak in vain?
Time, like a mist, thine answer from thee veils,
Yet cry, weak voice; cry while thy strength avails!

(1872)

L. (Louisa) S. Bevington (Mrs Guggenberger) (1845–1895)

319. *Three*

What of our time?

(Oracle.)

A fog and a blur,
A hum and a whirr,
And large mellow lights that are slowly dawning;
Lo! elements mixed,   5

　　　　　　Lo! centres unfixed,
　　A hope, and a fear; a chance, and a warning.

　　What of our time?

　　　　　　　(Pessimist.)

　　　　　The reign of the worse,
　　　　　　The breath of a curse,　　　　　　　　　　　10
　　Ash-fruit of man's pride and the knowledge he stole
　　　　　　False witness and fell,
　　　　　　Swift sliding to hell,
　　The shudder of heaven and the glare of the goal.

　　What of our time?　　　　　　　　　　　　　　　15

　　　　　　　(Optimist.)

　　　　　The reign of the best
　　　　　　By sympathy's test;
　　The travail of ages repaid in an age;
　　　　　　The finding of law
　　　　　　Where no prophet foresaw;　　　　　　　20
　　Glad glance of man's eye on his destiny's page.

　　What is our time?

　　　　　　　(Oracle.)

　　　　　A question of "When?"
　　　　　　An echoed "Amen,"
　　Vague answering around and below and above;　　25
　　　　　　The hour of the sure,
　　　　　　Yet the hour of the pure,
　　And a blank new seal on the title of love.

　　What is our time?

　　　　　　　(Pessimist.)

　　　　　The death-hour of art;　　　　　　　　　　30
　　　　　　The rending apart
　　Of the truth of man's thought from the hope of his life.
　　　　　　The cloud of death-dust
　　　　　　From a pageant of lust,
　　The triumph of force, and the mocking of strife.　　35

　　What is our time?

(Optimist.)

The birth-hour of man,
The dawn of his plan
Whose purpose is life, yet whose cradle a grave;
The time of bold truth,　　　　　　　　　　40
And of counsel for youth,
And a sword given into the hand of the brave.

What of our time?

(Oracle.)

Lo! the present re-cast
In the fire of the past,
And the future is his who will venture the flame;　　45
Thou child of the hour,
Thy will is its power,
Go claim it, and guide it, and give it thy name.

What is our time?　　　　　　　　　　　　　　　　50

(Pessimist.)

The great sneer of God
At his animate clod,
The oneness of angel, and poet, and beast;
The quenching of prayer
In the lull of despair,　　　　　　　　　　55
The moan of the woman, the whine of the priest.

What is our time?

(Optimist.)

A greeting of bands,
A meeting of hands,
And barriers broken that hindered the deed;　　60
The idol thrown low
That the Loving may grow
Where the shadow lay dark and the victims yet bleed.

What of the time?

(Oracle.)

Not yet have ye read,
Not yet have ye said,
It is less than your word, it is more than your thought;
Not good and not ill,
But eternal and still;—
What it was; what it shall be; unfound,—and unsought.

320. 'Egoisme À Deux'

When the great universe hung nebulous
   Betwixt the unprevented and the need,
Was it foreseen that you and I should be?—
      Was it decreed?

While time leaned onward through eternities,
   Unrippled by a breath and undistraught,
Lay there at leisure Will that we should breathe?—
      Waited a Thought?

When the warm swirl of chaos-elements
   Fashioned the chance that woke to sentient strife,
Did there a Longing seek, and hasten on
      Our mutual life?

That flux of many accidents but now
   That brought you near and linked your hand in mine,—
That fused our souls in love's most final faith,—
      Was it divine?

321. Stanza

The sweetest song that a poet sings,
Though to your dull ear it be speech with wings,
He, singing, hears with a pent distress,
'Tis a cypher that stands for his speechlessness.

322.   *Revolution*

        Ah, yes! You must meet it, and brave it;
        Too laggard—too purblind to save it;
      Who recks of your doubting and fearing
                  Phrase-bound "Evolution?"

        Do you not hear the sea sounding it?   5
        Do you not feel the fates founding it?
      Do you not know it for nearing?
                  Its name—Revolution.

        What! stem it, and stay it, and spare it?
        Or will you defy it, and dare it?   10
      Then this way or that you must change you
                  For swift restitution.

        Do you not see men deserving it?
        Do you not hear women nerving it?
      Down with old Mammon! and range you   15
                  To aid Revolution!

        The last hour has struck of our waiting,
        The last of your bloodless debating,
      The wild-fire of spirit is speeding
                  Us on to solution.   20

        Do you not thrill at the uttering?
        Do you not breathe the breeze fluttering
      Round the brave flag of our pleading?
                  The world's Revolution!

323.   *Am I to Lose You?*

   "Am I to lose you now?" The words were light;
     You spoke them, hardly seeking a reply,
     That day I bid you quietly "Good-bye,"
   And sought to hide my soul away from sight.
   The question echoed, dear, through many a night,—   5
     My question, not your own—most wistfully;
       "Am I to lose him?"—asked my heart of me;
   "Am I to lose him now, and lose him quite?"

And only you can tell me. Do you care
   That sometimes we in quietness should stand
   As fellow-solitudes, hand firm in hand,
And thought with thought and hope with hope compare?
What is your answer? Mine must ever be,
   "I greatly need your friendship: leave it me."

324. Love and Language

Love that is alone with love
   Makes solitudes of throngs;
Then why not songs of silences,—
   Sweet silences of songs?
Parts need words: the perfect whole
   Is silent as the dead;
When I offered you my soul
   Heard you what I *said*?

325. Twilight

Grey the sky, and growing dimmer,
   And the twilight lulls the sea;
Half in vagueness, half in glimmer,
   Nature shrouds her mystery.

What have all the hours been spent for?
   Why the on and on of things?
Why eternity's procession
   Of the days and evenings?

Hours of sunshine, hours of gloaming,
   Wing their unexplaining flight,
With a measured punctuation
   Of unconsciousness, at night.

Just at sunset was translucence,
   When the west was all aflame;
So I asked the sea a question,
   And an answer nearly came.

Is there nothing but Occurrence?
    Though each detail seem an Act,
Is that whole we deem so pregnant
    But unemphasizèd Fact?   20

Or, when dusk is in the hollows
    Of the hill-side and the wave,
Are things just so much in earnest
    That they cannot but be grave?

Nay, the lesson of the Twilight   25
    Is as simple as 'tis deep;
Acquiescence, acquiescence,
    And the coming on of sleep.

Eugene Lee-Hamilton (1845–1907)

326.   Introduction to *Imaginary Sonnets*

My spirit stood and listened in its awe
    Beside the great abyss where seethes the Past,
    And caught the voices that were upward cast
By, those whom Fate whirled on like floating straw;

While, in the glimmering depth, I vaguely saw,   5
    Lashed to some frail remainder of a mast,
    The wretches drifting faster and more fast,
Sucked down for ever in the whirlpool's maw:

And these wild voices of despair and fear,
    Of love and hate, from out the deep abyss   10
I treasured up, just as they struck the ear,—

Appeals which rise above the roar and hiss
    Of story's turbid current high and clear;
And by-and-bye I rhymed them into this.

327.   *What the Sonnet Is*

Fourteen small broidered berries on the hem
Of Circe's mantle, each of magic gold;
   Fourteen of lone Calypso's tears that roll'd
Into the sea, for pearls to come of them;

Fourteen clear signs of omen in the gem
   With which Medea human fate foretold;
   Fourteen small drops, which Faustus, growing old,
Craved of the Fiend, to water Life's dry stem.

It is the pure white diamond Dante brought
   To Beatrice; the sapphire Laura wore
When Petrarch cut it sparkling out of thought;

The ruby Shakespeare hewed from his heart's core;
   The dark, deep emerald that Rossetti wrought
For his own soul, to wear for evermore.

328.   *Lethe*

I had a dream of Lethe,—of the brink
   Of sluggish waters, whither strong men bore
   Dead pallid loves; while others, old and sore,
Brought but their tottering selves, in haste to drink:

And having drunk, they plunged, and seemed to sink
   Their load of love or guilt for evermore,
   Reaching with radiant brow the sunny shore
That lay beyond, no more to think and think.

Oh, who will give me, chained to Memory's strand,
   A draught of Lethe, salt with final tears,
Were it one drop within the hollow hand?

Oh, who will rid me of the wasted years,
   The thought of life's fair structure vainly planned,
And each false hope that mocking reappears?

329.   *On Leonardo's Head of Medusa*

The livid and unutterable head,
    Fresh cut, lies welt'ring in its mane of snakes;
    A slowly writhing tangle which still takes
Its time to die, round temples that are dead;

While through the lips, wet as with froth of lead,
    Like the last breath of horror which forsakes
    Evil's cut throat, a poisonous vapour makes
Its way from Hell to Heaven, vague and dread.

Already blind, the dying vipers grope,
    Writhing in vain to leave the head they loathe,
Now that it lies there, gory, dead and wan;

Each strangling each in coils of creeping rope,
    Till death invades them from the brows they clothe,
And they coagulate. A toad looks on.

330.   *To My Wheeled Bed*

Hybrid of rack and of Procrustes' bed,
    Thou thing of wood, of leather, and of steel,
    Round which, by day and night, at head and heel,
Crouch shadowy Tormentors, dumb and dread;

Round which the wingless Hours, with feet of lead
    For ever crawl, in spite of fierce appeal,
    And the dark Terrors dance their silent reel;
What will they do with thee when I am dead?

Last men should ask, who find thee stowed away
    In some old lumber room, what wretch was he
Who used so strange an engine night and day,

Fain would I have thee shivered utterly;
    For, please the Fates, no other son of clay
Will ever need so dire a bed as thee.

331.   *Henry I to the Sea*

(1120)

O Sea, take all, since thou hast taken him
    Whose life to me was life. Let one wide wave
    Now sweep this land, and make a single grave
For king and people. Let the wild gull skim

Where now is England, and the sea-fish swim
    In every drowned cathedral's vaulted nave,
    As in a green and pillared ocean cave,
Submerged for ever and for ever dim.

And if the shuddering pilot ventures there
    And sees their pinnacles, like rocks to shun,
Above the waves, and green with tidal hair,

Then let him whisper that this thing was done
    By God, the Lord of Oceans, at the prayer
Of England's king, who mourned his only son.

332.   *Ipsissimus*

Thou priest that art behind the screen
    Of this confessional, give ear:
I need God's help, for I have seen
    What turns my vitals limp with fear.
O Christ, O Christ, I must have done
More mortal sin than any one
    Who says his prayers in Venice here!

And yet by stealth I only tried
    To kill my enemy, God knows;
And who on earth has yet denied
    A man the right to kill his foes?
He won the race of the Gondoliers;
I hate him and the skin he wears;
    I hate him and the shade he throws.

I hate him through each day and hour;
    All ills that curse me seem his fault;
He makes my daily soup taste sour,
    He makes my daily bread taste salt.

And so I hung upon his track
At dusk, to stab him in the back
   In some lone street archway vault.

But oh, give heed!—As I was stealing
   Upon his heels, with knife grasped tight,
There crept across my soul a feeling
   That I myself was kept in sight.
Each time I turned, dodge as I would,
A masked and unknown watcher stood,
   Who baffled all my plans that night.

What mask is this, I thought and thought,
   Who dogs me thus, when least I care?
His figure is nor tall nor short,
   And yet has a familiar air.
But oh, despite this watcher's eye,
I'll reach my man yet, by-and-by,
   And snuff his life out yet, elsewhere!

And though compelled to thus defer,
   I schemed another project soon;
I armed my boat with a hidden spur,
   To run him down in the lagoon.
At dusk I saw him row one day
Where lone and wide the waters lay,
   Reflecting scarce the dim white moon.

No boat, as far as sight could strain,
   Loomed on the solitary sea;
I saw my oar each minute gain
   Upon my death-doomed enemy....
When lo, a black-masked gondolier,
Silent and spectre-like, drew near,
   And stepped between my deed and me.

He seemed to rise from out the flood,
   And hovered near, to mar my game;
I knew him and his cursed hood,
   His cursed mask: he was the same.
So balked once more, enraged and cowed,
Back through the still lagoon I rowed
   In mingled wonder, wrath, and shame.

Oh, were I not to come and pray
    Thee for thy absolution here
In the confessional to-day,
    My very ribs would burst with fear. 60
Leave not, good Father, in the lurch,
An honest son of Mother Church,
    Whose faith is firm and soul sincere.

Behind St Luke's, as the dead men know,
    A pale apothecary dwells, 65
Who deals in death both quick and slow,
    And baleful philtres, withering spells.
He sells alike to rich and poor
Who know what knocks to give his door,
    The yellow powder that rings the knells. 70

Well then, I went and knocked the knock
    With cautious hand, as I'd been taught;
The door revolved with silent lock,
    And I went in, suspecting naught.
But oh, the self-same form stood masked 75
Behind the counter, and unasked
    In silence proffered what I sought.

My knees and hands like aspens shook:
    I spilt the powder on the ground;
I dared not turn, I dared not look; 80
    My palsied tongue would make no sound.
Then through the door I fled at last,
With feet that seemed more slow than fast,
    And dared not even once turn round.

And yet I am an honest man, 85
    Who only sought to kill his foe:
Could I sit down and see each plan
    That I took up frustrated so?
God wot, as every scheme was balked,
And in the sun my man still walked, 90
    I felt my hatred grow and grow.

I thought, "At dusk, with stealthy tread
    I'll seek his dwelling, and I'll creep
Upstairs, and hide beneath his bed,
    And in the night I'll strike him deep." 95

And so I went; but at his door
The figure, masked just as before,
    Sat on the step, as if asleep.

Bent, spite all fear, upon my task,
    I tried to pass: there was no space.   100
Then rage prevailed; I snatched the mask
    From off the baffling figure's face....
And (oh, unutterable dread!)
The face was mine,—mine white and dead,—
    Stiff with some frightful death's grimace. 105

What sins are mine, oh, luckless wight!
    That fate should play me such a trick,
And make me see a sudden sight
    That turns both soul and body sick?
Stretch out thy hands, thou Priest unseen,   110
That sittest there behind the screen,
    And give me absolution quick!

O God, O God, his hands are dead!
    His hands are mine, oh, monstrous spell!
I feel them clammy on my head: 115
    Is he my own dead self as well?
Those hands are mine,—their scars, their shape:
O God, O God, there's no escape,
    And seeking Heaven, I fall on Hell!

Alexander Anderson ('Surfaceman') (1845–1909)

333.   *Reading the Book*

I sat by night and read the Book,
Till doubt was mingled with my look,

And dimness lay before my eyes,
As mists in hollows form and rise.

"So dark, so very dark," I said,   5
And shut the Book and bow'd my head;

Then lo! I felt a wondrous light
Behind me, making all things bright;

While a clear voice, like some refrain,
Said—"Ope the Book, and read again."

I open'd up its leaves, and lo!
Each page was living with the glow

Of some great Presence undefin'd,
Yet standing in its place behind.

Methought that as I read the Word
Each leaf turn'd of its own accord,

And all the meaning fair and clear,
As pebbles through the stream appear,

Lay to my eyes, that saw beneath
Each sentence lie without its sheath.

I raised my head, and spoke in fear—
"This is God's Book, and very clear."

Then, lo! the light behind me fled,
But left a clear, sweet voice that said—

"Read thou not like to him who sees
Evolving mists of mysteries,

But like to him whose heart perceives
God's finger turning o'er the leaves!"

The San' Man

San' man frae the quarry hole,
    Bring a pouk o' san';
Stan' ahint my back, an' tak'
    A neivefu' in your han'.
Here's a fechtin', restless wean,
    To every mischief gi'en;
Fling a handfu' in his face,
    And gar him rub his een.

I hae done what mithers may
    To please this glow'rin' fule—
Made a stable for his horse
    By turnin' up the stule;
Tied the cart-string roun' its neck—
    I did the same yestreen—
Yet he rocks and coonts his taes,
    An' winna rub his een.

I hae sat frae six to eicht,
    This rogue upon my knee;
I may sit anither hoor,
    For onything I see.
No a sign o' sleep ava,
    What can a' this mean?
San' man frae the quarry hole,
    Come an' fill his een.

Ben he comes wi' lang slow steps,
    Seen an' heard by náne,
Hauds a gowpenfu' o' san'
    Richt aboon the wean.
Drap, drap, the san' rins doon,
    Through fingers lang an' lean;
San' man, tak' away your han',
    See, he rubs his een.

What a rubbin' wi' his neive,
    Row'd as if to fecht;
What a raxin' oot o' legs,
    Then an unco weicht.
Soun' at last, although he focht
    Wi' a' his micht an' main—
Ready wi' his creddly ba',
    Here's a sleepin' wean.

In this restless age o' oors,
    Seam'd wi' speirin' doot,
Mony a san' man ane could name
    Stogs an' slings aboot.
We, wha are but bearded weans,
    Wunner what they mean,
When they fling their creeds aboot,
    An' gar us rub oor een.

335. Move Upward

"Move upward, working out the brute,
    And let the ape and tiger die."—Tennyson

Ay, in heaven's name, let us move upward still
    In this time-changing planet of ours,
And bring to the task what the gods still ask—
    The best of our years and our pow'rs.
Let us make this great century, whirling around,   5
    A footstool to lift up the foot,
Whereon we may cry, looking upward to God—
    "We are all this way from the brute."

Is the dream of the poet forever to be
    Like the myth of the Greek, or at least   10
The skeleton dress'd up in costliest gold,
    And set in the midst of the feast?
Is the double meaning forever to wind
    Like the coil of the snake round our speech?
And the Dead Sea fable still utter its truth   15
    As we mimic and chatter to each?

But questions are weapons an infant can lift,
    Let us marry the fruitfuller act,
And widen our being to let in the light,
    And the strength of the deed-giving fact.   20
Is it not enough we have come from God?
    But since Time took his birthright in years,
We have bred with the brute, and our offspring has been
    The sucklings of bloodshed and tears.

It were time, then, to burst from the links we have forged   25
    To fetter the soul in the breast,
Though the wrench should bring with it the best of our blood,
    And we faint as a pilgrim for rest.
Heart! but each has some task he must close with his life
    When he slips from this world's wide plan,   30
And the highest a man can shape out for himself
    Is to move himself upward to man.

Ay, move himself up to that nature of his
    Which, though trampled and trod in the dust,
Still shows, as a jewel may gleam through the sand,   35
    The finger of God through its crust.

Let him, then, so alive with miraculous breath,
    Make the best of his energies join,
Till he lift himself up in the light of the Christ
    To the clear, true ring of the coin.   40

There be some who squat down by the world's rough path,
    As if life were a burden to shirk,
Heeding not the great watchword it thunders to all—
    "Up, shoulder to shoulder, and work!"
But sit in their darkness to wince at the truth,   45
    As an owl at the light sits and blinks,
And for ever propound each his question to solve,
    Like a nineteenth-century Sphinx.

"Move upward from what?" they break in, with a croak,
    And I answer at once in reply—   50
"From the sham that has flung our soul under its heel,
    And the words that are wrap to a lie—
From the thought that still grovels and hides in the dust,
    As a viper may do, until blind
It springs up to find venom to add to its own,   55
    In the plague-spots seen in our kind.

Ay, battle with this as a fighter strikes out,
    When he stands with his back to the wall,
With no help but the strength that is in his right arm,
    And the eye that has glances for all.   60
Shame on us, then, who stand with our face to the front,
    And modell'd in God's mighty shape,
If we roughen our soul with the dust of the earth,
    To give better foothold for the ape.

God! to look on this manifold, wonderful earth,   65
    As Novalis look'd on men,
And feel the old reverence grow upward within
    To the pitch of the Hebrew's again—
To have the rapt soul and the calm, deep eye
    That can look upon all without fear,   70
And the firm, steady beat of the heart that can feel
    When the footsteps of God are anear.

It may be that we may, fighting upward to this,
    Grow footsore and faint in the heat,
But the moving oneself up to heights in this life   75
    Spreads no carpeted way for the feet.

Let us think of those grand, true souls who have left
    Guiding posts on each side of the way,
And press ever on with our eyes to the light
    They have left as a part of their day.   80

Ay, in Heaven's name, let us move upward, then,
    To the grand, true ring of the man,
Giving to this one task all the best of our years,
    And the strength to reach up to the plan.
Let the *"Ernst ist das Leben"* of Schiller speak on,   85
    Till we seize and place under our foot
The head of the ape, crying upward to God,
    "Lo! at last we are free from the brute!"

336.   *Song of the Engine*

In the shake and rush of the engine,
    In the full, deep breath of his chest,
In the swift, clear clank of the gleaming crank,
    In his soul that is never at rest,
In the spring and ring of the bending rail,   5
    As he thunders and hurtles along,
A strong world's melody fashions itself,
    And this smoke demon calls it his song.

"Hurrah! for my path I devour in my wrath,
    As I rush to the cities of men   10
With a load I lay down like a slave at their feet,
    Then turn and come backward again.
Hurrah! for the rush of the yielding air
    That gives way to my wild, fierce springs
As I keep to the rail, while my heart seems to burst   15
    In a wild, mad craving for wings.

I rush by hills where the shepherds are seen
    Like a speck as they walk on their side;
I roar through glens and by rocks that shake
    As I quicken the speed of my stride.   20
I glide by woods and by rock-bound streams
    That hurry and race in their glee,
But swift as they run, with their face to the sun,
    They can never keep pace with me.

I tear through caverns of sudden dark,   25
    Like that in which first I lay,
Ere the cunning of man had alit on a plan
    To drag me up to the day.
I rush with a shriek, which is all I can speak,
    A wild protest against fear;   30
But I come to the light with a snort of delight,
    And my black breath far in the rear.

I crash along bridges that span the hills,
    And catch at a glimpse below
The roof-thatch'd cot and the low white wall   35
    Lying white in the sun's last glow.
Or it may be the gleam of some dull, broad stream
    Creeping slowly onward beneath,
While within its breast for a moment I catch
    The shadow and film of my breath.   40

I rush over roofs in my madness of flight,
    But not like the demon of old;
I leave them unturn'd, for the arches in air
    Bear me up, and my feet keep their hold.
At times, too, I catch, when I check my speed,   45
    The long, wide lane of the street,
And hear, 'twixt the snorts of my own fierce breath,
    The clamour and hurry of feet.

Then I snatch a look at the puppets beneath,
    But to snort and rush onward again,   50
With a fear at my heart almost quenching its heat,
    For heavens! these must be men—
Ay, men, I could bend like the willow, but who,
    With a thought that from nothing will shrink,
Have hurl'd me down with their hands on my throat,   55
    And bound me in rivet and link.

I rush by village, and cottage, and farm;
    I thunder sudden and quick
Upon handfuls of men who leap out of my way,
    And lean on their shovel and pick.   60
There is one brown fellow among them who sings
    The terrible sweep of my limb;
The fool! dare he mimic this music of mine,
    And such pitiful music in him?

I flare through the night when the stars are bright,
    With the lights of the city for mark;
With bound upon bound I shake the ground,
    As I feel for the rail in the dark.
And I know that the stars whisper each to each,
    As downward they flicker and peer,
'What is this that these fellows have hit on below,
    That seems like a meteor from here?'

For my great eye glistens and gleams in the front,
    As if to give light to my tread,
While behind like the fires of a Vulcan flung out,
    Three others glare thirsty and red.
And the flame licking round the fierce life in my heart,
    Let loose for a moment upsprings,
And darts through the whirls of my breath overhead,
    Till it makes me a demon with wings.

I send through the city's wild heart shocks of life,
    But to feel them come back like a wave;
I loom broad and swart in wild traffic's rough mart,
    I kneel to men like a slave.
I gather from all the four ends of the earth,
    What profit and use there may be—
Did the Greek ever dream, in his talk with the gods,
    Of a wild beast of burden like me?

But often my own wild thoughts leap far ahead,
    And I question myself with a moan—
'Will I ripen and grow into sinew and limb
    With the higher race that comes on?
Or shall I grow white with the hour of the years
    That, falling, cankers and wears—
Turning feeble of limb with the things that benumb,
    And steal the vigour from theirs?

Were this worthy end for a being like mine,
    Begot in the frenzy of thought,
And sent as the type of the soul of this age,
    Setting time and distance at nought?
No, if there be death, let it come in the end,
    For my iron-girt bosom will beat,
Till the judgment-bolts flung from the right hand of God
    Smite the pathway from under my feet.'"

Thus he snorts and sings as he thunders by me,　　　　105
　　This wild smoke-demon of ours,
While from end to end the rail quivers and bends
　　To his thousand Hercules' powers.
And his great breath mixes and whirls with the clouds,
　　While he whoops as if mad with glee:　　　　110
"Did the Greek ever dream in his talk with the gods
　　Of a black beast of burden like me?"

337.　　　　　　　　*The Violet*

On the down line, and close beside the rail,
　　A tender violet grew,
A sister spirit, when the stars grew pale,
　　Gave it a drink of dew.

And so its azure deepen'd day by day,　　　　5
　　And sweet it was to see,
As I went up and down the four-feet way,
　　The flower peep up at me.

I grew to like it—such a tiny thing,
　　So free from human stains,　　　　10
Bending and swaying to each rush and swing
　　Of passing pitiless trains.

And when we came at times to make repair
　　Beside the place, I took
A living heed to let it blossom there,　　　　15
　　To cheer me with its look.

For fancy working in its quiet ways,
　　Sometimes would change the flower
Into a maiden of these iron days,
　　When might was right and power.　　　　20

And up and down the lints of gleaming rail
　　With echoing clank and shock,
Rode the stern engines in their suits of mail,
　　Like knights with spears of smoke.

I crown'd her queen of beauty at their call,
    And as I knelt beside
My bud, it look'd up, as if knowing all,
    And shook with modest pride.

Then restless fancy changing, it became
    A martyr firm and high,
Bound to the stake and lick'd with tongues of flame,
    With bigots scowling nigh.

Next, a young poet with his soul aglow
    With passionate dreams of truth,
And thoughts akin to those that angels know,
    Who have eternal youth.

A nature all unfitted for the time,
    Born but to droop and fade,
Like long sweet cadences of fairy rhyme
    Within the summer shade.

All these and more my little flower did seem,
    As to and fro I went,
Not early light or when the sun's soft beam,
    That to the west half spent.

It made itself a presence in my thought,
    Seen of the inner eye,
So pure and sweet, and yet so near the spot
    Where wild trains thunder by.

But one sweet morning, when the young sunshine
    Laid long soft arms of light
Around the earth, I found the flower of mine
    Stricken as with some blight.

For like a fallen spot of heaven grown pale,
    It lent its drooping head
Against the cold touch of the careless rail,
    Wither'd, and shrunk, and dead.

Thus some rare soul, toiling for purer gains,
    Sinks in the night alone,
While the hoarse world, like the iron trains,
    Unheeding, thunders on.

Emily H. (Henrietta) Hickey (1845–1924)

338.   *Her Dream*

    Fold your arms around me, Sweet,
    As against your heart my heart doth beat.

    Kiss me, Love, till it fade, the fright
    Of the dreadful dream I dreamt last night.

    Oh, thank God, it is you, it is you,   5
    My own love, fair and strong and true.

    We two are the same that, yesterday,
    Played in the light and tost the hay.

    My hair you stroke, O dearest one,
    Is alive with youth and bright with the sun.   10

    Tell me again, Love, how I seem
    'The prettiest queen of curds and cream.'

    Fold me close and kiss me again;
    Kiss off the shadow of last night's pain.

    I dreamt last night, as I lay in bed,   15
    That I was old and that you were dead.

    I knew you had died long time ago,
    And I well recalled the moan and woe.

    You had died in your beautiful youth, my sweet;
    You had gone to rest with untired feet;   20

    And I had prayed to come to you,
    To lay me down and slumber too.

    But it might not be, and the days went on,
    And I was all alone, alone.

    The women came so neighbourly,   25
    And kissed my face and wept with me;

And the men stood still to see me pass,
And smiled grave smiles, and said, *'Poor lass!'*

Sometimes I seemed to hear your feet,
And my grief-numbed heart would wildly beat;

And I stopt and named my darling's name—
But never a word of answer came.

The men and women ceased at last
To pity pain that was of the past;

For pain is common, and grief, and loss;
And many come home by Weeping Cross

Why do I tell you this, my dear?
Sorrow is gone now you are here.

You and I we sit in the light,
And fled is the horror of yesternight.

The time went on, and I saw one day
My body was bent and my hair was grey.

But the boys and girls a-whispering
Sweet tales in the sweet light of the spring,

Never paused in the tales they told
To say, *'He is dead and she is old.'*

There's a place in the churchyard where, I thought,
Long since my lover had been brought:

It had sunk with years from a high green mound
To a level no stranger would have found:

But I, I always knew the spot;
How could I miss it, know it not?

Darling, darling, draw me near,
For I cannot shake off the dread and fear.

Hold me so close I scarce can breathe;
And kiss me, for, lo, above, beneath,

The blue sky fades, and the green grass dries,
And the sunshine goes from my lips and eyes.

O God—that dream—it has not fled—
One of us old, and one of us dead!

339.   *A Sea Story*

Silence. A while ago
    Shrieks went up piercingly;
But now is the ship gone down;
    Good ship, well manned, was she.
There's a raft that's a chance of life for one,
    This day upon the sea.

A chance for one of two;
    Young, strong, are he and he,
Just in the manhood prime,
    The comelier, verily,
For the wrestle with wind and weather and wave
    In the life upon the sea.

One of them has a wife
    And little children three;
Two that can toddle and lisp;
    And a suckling on the knee;
Naked, they'll go and hunger sore,
    If he be lost at sea.

One has a dream of home,
    A dream that well may be;
He never has breathed it yet;
    She never has known it, she.
But some one will be sick at heart,
    If he be lost at sea.

"Wife and kids and home!—
    Wife, kids nor home has he!—
Give us a chance, Bill!" Then,
    "All right, Jem!" Quietly
A man gives up his life for a man,
    This day upon the sea.

William Canton (1845–1926)

340.   *Sea-Pictures I*

Blithe morning; sun and sea! Zone beyond zone,
Blue frolic waves and gold clouds softly blown.
One half the globe a sapphire glass which swings
Doubling the sun.

     No sail. No wink of wings.   5
No haze of land.

    Look! who comes wafted here—
What lone yet all unfearful mariner?
You cannot see him? No; he mocks the sight—
Mid such immensities so mere a mite.   10

Look close! That tiniest speck of brownish red,
Perched on his single subtle spider-thread!

Trust, little aeronaut, thy filmy sail.
Blow wind! the reef and palm-tree shall not fail.

Alexander MacGregor Rose (1846–1898)

341.   *Tour Abroad of Wilfrid the Great*

    By Jean Baptiste Trudeau.

W'en Queen Victoria calls her peup's
 For mak' some Jubilee,
She sen' for men from all de worl' –
 And from her colonie.

But mos' of all, she sen' dis word   5
 To dis Canadian shore,
"If Wilfrid Laurier do not come,
 I will be glad no more."

Den Wilfrid not hard-hearted, he
    Lif w'at you call de hat,
An' say, "Ma reine, you mus' not fret,
    For little t'ing lak' dat.

"To Londres, on de day in June
    You mention, I will come,
And show you w'at is lak' de French-
    Canadian gentilhomme."

So Wildred sailed across de sea,
    An' Queen Victoria met,
An' w'en she's see him, ah! she is
    Jus' tickle half to deat'!

An' w'en he's kneel, as etiquette
    Demand, for be correc',
She tak' a sword into her han'
    An' hit him on de neck.

An' w'en she do, she smile on him,
    An' dese de words she say:
"Rise up, my true Canadian Knight –
    Sir Wilfrid Laurier!

"An' on dose grand Imperial plans
    Which I have now in view,
For guidance, counsel, an' advice
    I'll always look to you."

Den Wilfrid kiss de Royal han',
    An' back off on de door,
An' bow as only Frenchman can,
    An' smile an' bow some more.

Nex' day, it was a glorious sight,
    At half-pas' twelve o'clock,
To see Sir Wilfrid ride in state,
    An' in chapeau de coque.

Lords Solsby, Roberts, and Cecil Rhodes,
    An' Chamberlain an' dose
Were w'at you call "not in it," for
    Sir Wilfrid was de boss.

Oui, certainement, excep' de Queen
    Herself dat glorious day,
De greates' man on Angleterre
    Was Wilfrid Laurier.

VISITS PARIS.

Sir Wilfrid cross de Channel den,
    Mak' visit La Patrie,
An' mak' fine speeches two or three
    In de city of Paree.

An' shak' de han', an' drink de vin
    Mit Faure de Presiden',
An' show him what de kin' of man
    Dis contrie represen'.

An' w'en Dir Wilfrid's voice dey hear,
    An' his fine shape dey see,
De men of France was hall surprise,
    De ladies hall epris.

Den Monsieur Faure he rise an say,
    "Sir Wilfrid Laurier,
In de Legion d'Honneur you are
    Un grand officier."

An' to Sir Wilfrid, front dem hall,
    He mak' some fine address,
An' den ribbon wit' de star
    He pin upon his breas'.

En bref, our Wilfrid capture France,
    He's capture Anglan', too;
I t'ink he will annex dem both
    To Canada – don' you?

SIR WILFRID'S RETURN.

Sir Wilfrid, tired of Jubilee
    An' glorie an' eclat,
He says, "Dese contrie dey ees not
    Lak' my own Canada.

"I wan' my own dear lan' for see
    An' de St. Laurent gran',
An' hear again de French he spik
    Mon bonhomme habitan!"   80

Den to the Queen an' Monsieur Faure
    Hees "au revoirs" he say,
"I mus' go back on ole Kebec,
    An' Mo'real dis day.

"An' I mus go an help toujours,   85
    Lor' Aberdeen mak' law,
An' keep dem Tory boodler from
    De safe in Ottawa.

"An' help Sir Olivair, Sir Deek
    An' Tarte mak' politique,   90
An' keep Sir Tuppair an' hees gang
    From play some crooked trique."

So, on de "Labrador" he sail,
    On Canada he come,
We hall be glad his face to see,   95
    An' he ees glad be home.

An' hall de Angleesh, Ireesh, Franch
    'Roun hees triomphan' car,
Say, "Bienvenu! Come, spok to us
    Upon de Champ de Mars."   100

Sir Wilfrid tole us dat he drink
    Dose vins mit' Monsieur Faure,
An' dine on Windsor – so he tole
    Us on de Champ de Mars.

Den hall de peup' dey mak' big cheer,   105
    De cannon dey mak' shoot,
We hall be on one grand hoorau,
    De steamboats on a toot.

So we hall sing, "God bless de Queen!
    An' Monsieur Faure, alway!   110
Because dey treat all same lak' prince,
    Our Wilfrid Laurier."

342.   'Kaiser and Co. or, Hoch der Kaiser'

Being Wilhelm der Grosser's estimate of himself and partner,
translated from the original Hoch-deutsch.

> Der Kaiser auf der Vaterland
> Und Gott on high all dings gommand,
> Ve two! Ach! don'd you understandt?
>   Meinself – und Gott.
>
> He reigns in Heafen, und always shall,   5
> Und mein own Embire don'd vas small;
> Ein noble bair, I dink you call
>   Meinself – und Gott.
>
> While some men sing der power divine,
> Mein soldiers sing der "Wacht am Rhein,"   10
> Und drink der healt in Rhenish wein,
>   Auf me – und Gott.
>
> Dere's France dot swaggers all aroundt,
> She ausgespieldt – she's no aggoundt,
> To mooch ve dinks she don't amoundt: 15
>   Meinself – und Gott.
>
> She vill not dare to fight again,
> But if she should, I'll show her blain
> Dot Elsass und (in French) Lorraine
>   Are Mein – und Gott's.   20
>
> Von Bismarck was a man auf might,
> Und dought he vas glean oud auf sight,
> But ach! he vas nicht goot to fight
>   Mit me – und Gott.
>
> Ve knock him like ein man auf sdraw,   25
> Ve let him know whose vill vas law,
> Und dot ve don'd vould sdandt his jaw,
>   Meinself – und Got.
>
> Ve send him oudt in big disgrace,
> Ve gif him insuldt to his face,   30
> Und put Caprivi in his place,
>   Meinself – und Gott.

Und ven Caprivi get svelled headt,
Ve very brombtly on him set,
Und toldt him to get vp and get –
    Meinself – und Gott.   35

Dere's Grandma dinks she's nicht shmall beer,
Mit Boers und dings she interfere;
She'll learn none runs dis hemisphere
    But Me – und Gott.   40

She dinks, goot frau, some ships she's got,
Und soldiers mit der sgarlet coat,
Ach! ve could knock dem – pouf! like dot,
    Meinself – und Gott.

Dey say dat badly fooled I vas   45
At Betersburg by Nicholas,
Und dat I act shust like ein ass
    Und dupe, Herr Gott.

Vell, maybe yah und maybe nein,
Und maybe Czar mit France gombine   50
To take dem lands about der Rhein
    From me – und Gott.

But dey may try dot leedle game,
Und make der breaks; but all der same,
Dey only vill increase der fame   55
    Auf me – und Gott.

In dimes auf beace, brebared for wars
I bear der helm and sbear auf Mars,
Und care nicht for ten dousand Czars,
    Meinself – und Gott.   60

In short, I humour efery whim,
Mit aspect dark and visage grim,
Gott pulls mit me und I mit Him –
    Meinself – und Gott.

'Michael Field' (Katherine Harris Bradley, 1846–1914, and Edith Emma Cooper, 1862–1913)

343.
Cyclamens

    They are terribly white:
    There is snow on the ground,
And a moon on the snow at night;
The sky is cut by the winter light;
Yet I, who have all these things in ken,   5
Am struck to the heart by the chiselled white
    Of this handful of cyclamen.

344.
Irises

    In a vase of gold
    And scarlet, how cold
  The flicker of wrinkled grays
In this iris-sheaf! My eyes fill with wonder
At the tossed, moist light, at the withered scales under   5
  And among the uncertain sprays.

    The wavings of white
    On the cloudy light,
  And the finger-marks of pearl;
The facets of crystal, the golden feather,   10
The way that the petals fold over together,
  The way that the buds unfurl!

345.
La Gioconda

Leonardo Da Vinci

The Louvre

Historic, side-long, implicating eyes;
A smile of velvet's lustre on the cheek;
Calm lips the smile leads upward; hand that lies
Glowing and soft, the patience in its rest
Of cruelty that waits and doth not seek   5

For prey; a dusky forehead and a breast
Where twilight touches ripeness amorously:
Behind her, crystal rocks, a sea and skies
Of evanescent blue on cloud and creek;
Landscape that shines suppressive of its zest   10
For those vicissitudes by which men die.

(1892)

346.   *A Portrait*

Bartolommeo Veneto

The Städel'sche Institut at Frankfurt

A crystal, flawless beauty on the brows
Where neither love nor time has conquered space
On which to live; her leftward smile endows
The gazer with no tidings from the face;
About the clear mounds of the lip it winds with silvery pace   5
And in the umber eyes it is a light
Chill as a glowworm's when the moon embrowns an August night.

She saw her beauty often in the glass,
Sharp on the dazzling surface, and she knew
The haughty custom of her grace must pass: 10
Though more persistent in all charm it grew
As with a desperate joy her hair across her throat she drew
In crinkled locks stiff as dead, yellow snakes . . .
Until at last within her soul the resolution wakes

   She will be painted, she who is so strong   15
In loveliness, so fugitive in years:
Forth to the field she goes and questions long
Which flowers to choose of those the summer bears;
She plucks a violet larkspur,—then a columbine appears
Of perfect yellow,—daisies choicely wide;   20
These simple things with finest touch she gathers in her pride.

Next on her head, veiled with well-bleachen white
And bound across the brow with azure-blue,
She sets the box-tree leaf and coils it tight
In spiky wreath of green, immortal hue;   25

Then, to the prompting of her strange, emphatic insight true,
    She bares one breast, half-freeing it of robe,
And hangs green-water gem and cord beside the naked globe.

    So was she painted and for centuries
    Has held the fading field-flowers in her hand
    Austerely as a sign. O fearful eyes
    And soft lips of the courtesan who planned
To give her fragile shapeliness to art, whose reason spanned
    Her doom, who bade her beauty in its cold
And vacant eminence persist for all men to behold!

    She had no memories save of herself
    And her slow-fostered graces, naught to say
    Of love in gift or boon; her cruel pelf
    Had left her with no hopes that grow and stay;
She found default in everything that happened night or day,
    Yet stooped in calm to passion's dizziest strife
And gave to art a fair, blank form, unverified by life.

    Thus has she conquered death: her eyes are fresh,
    Clear as her frontlet jewel, firm in shade
    And definite as on the linen mesh
    Of her white hood the box-tree's sombre braid,
That glitters leaf by leaf and with the year's waste will not fade.
    The small, close mouth, leaving no room for breath,
In perfect, still pollution smiles—Lo, she has conquered death!

347.   'Thanatos, thy praise I sing'

    Thanatos, thy praise I sing,
    Thou immortal, youthful king!
    Glorious offerings I will bring;
    For men say thou hast no shrine,
    And I find thou art divine
    As no other god: thy rage
    Doth preserve the Golden Age,
    What we blame is thy delay;
    Cut the flowers ere they decay!

Come, we would not derogate, 10
Age and nipping pains we hate,
Take us at our best estate:
While the head burns with the crown,
In the battle strike us down!
At the bride-feast do not think 15
From thy summons we should shrink;
We would give our latest kiss
To a life still warm with bliss.

Come and take us to thy train
Of dead maidens on the plain 20
Where white lilies have no stain;
Take us to the youths, that thou
Lov'st to choose, of fervid brow,
Unto whom thy dreaded name
Hath been simply known as Fame: 25
With these unpolluted things
Be our endless revellings.

(1893)

348.   'A girl'

A girl,
Her soul a deep-wave pearl
Dim, lucent of all lovely mysteries;
A face flowered for heart's ease,
A brow's grace soft as seas 5
Seen through faint forest-trees:
A mouth, the lips apart,
Like aspen-leaflets trembling in the breeze
From her tempestuous heart.
Such: and our souls so knit, 10
I leave a page half-writ—
The work begun
Will be to heaven's conception done,
If she come to it.

(1893)

349.   *Renewal*

As the young phoenix, duteous to his sire,
Lifts in his beak the creature he has been,
And, laying o'er the corse broad vans for screen,
Bears it to solitudes, erects a pyre,
And, soon as it is wasted by the fire,   5
Grides with disdainful claw the ashes clean;
Then spreading unencumbered wings serene
Mounts to the aether with renewed desire:

So joyously I lift myself above
The life I buried in hot flames to-day;   10
The flames themselves are dead – and I can range
Alone through the untarnished sky I love,
And I trust myself, as from the grave one may,
To the enchanting miracles of change.

(1898)

350.   *Constancy*

'*I am pure! I am pure! I am pure!*'

I love her with the seasons, with the winds,
As the stars worship, as anemones
Shudder in secret for the sun, as bees
Buzz round an open flower: in all kinds
My love is perfect, and in each she finds   5
Herself the goal; then why, intent to tease
And rob her delicate spirit of its ease,
Hastes she to range me with inconstant minds?
If she should die, if I were left at large
On earth without her – I, on earth, the same   10
Quick mortal with a thousand cries, her spell
She fears would break. And I confront the charge
As sorrowing, and as careless of my fame
As Christ intact before the infidel.

(1898)

351.   "Ἐγων δ' ἐμαύτα τοῦτο σύνοιδα."

Tiresias: but that I know by experience

Climbing the hill a coil of snakes
Impedes Tiresias' path; he breaks
His staff across them — idle thrust
That lays the female in the dust,
But dooms the prophet to forego   5
His manhood, and, as woman, know
The unfamiliar, sovereign guise
Of passion he had dared despise.

Ah, not in the Erinnys' ground
Experience so dire were found   10
As that to the enchanter known
When womanhood was round him thrown:
He trembled at the quickening change,
He trembled at his vision's range,
His finer sense for bliss and dole,   15
His receptivity of soul;
But when love came, and, loving back,
He learnt the pleasure men must lack,
It seemed that he had broken free
Almost from his mortality.   20

Seven years he lives as woman, then
Resumes his cruder part 'mong men,
Till him indignant Hera becks
To judge betwixt the joys of sex,
For the great Queen in wrath has heard   25
By her presumptuous lord averred
That, when he sought her in his brave,
Young godhead, higher bliss he gave
Than the unutterable lure
Of her veiled glances could procure   30
For him, as balmy-limbed and proud
She drew him to Olympia's cloud.
'In marriage who hath more delight?'
She asks; then quivers and grows white,
As sacrilegious lips reveal   35
What woman in herself must feel—
And passes an avenging hand
Across his subtle eyelids bland.

Deep-bosomed Queen, fain would'st thou hide
The mystic raptures of the bride! 40
When man's strong nature draweth nigh
'Tis as the lightning to the sky,
The blast to idle sail, the thrill
Of springtide when the saplings fill.
Though fragrant breath the sun receives 45
From the young rose's softening leaves,
Her plaited petals once undone
The rose herself receives the sun.

Tiresias, ere the goddess smite,
Look on me with unblinded sight, 50
That I may learn if thou hast part
In womanhood's secluded heart:
Medea's penetrative charm
Own'st thou to succour and disarm,
Hast thou her passion inly great 55
Heroes to mould and subjugate?
Can'st thou divine how sweet to bring
Apollo to thy blossoming
As Daphne; or, as just a child
Gathering a bunch of tulips wild, 60
To feel the flowery hillside rent
Convulsive for thy ravishment?
Thou need'st not to unlock thine eyes,
Thy slow ironic smile replies:
Thou hast been woman, and although 65
The twining snakes with second blow
Of golden staff thou did'st assail,
And, crushing at a stroke the male,
Had'st virtue from thy doom to break,
And lost virility re-take — 70
Thou hast been woman, and her deep,
Magnetic mystery dost keep;
Thou hast been woman, and can'st see
Therefore into futurity:
It is not that Zeus gave thee power 75
To look beyond the transient hour,
For thou hast trod the regions dun,
Where life and death are each begun;
Thy spirit from the gods set free
Hath communed with Necessity. 80
Tilphusa's fountain thou may'st quaff
And die, but still thy golden staff

Will guide thee with perceptive hand
Among the Shades to understand
The terrors of remorse and dread, 85
And prophesy among the dead.

(1889)

James Logie Robertson (1846–1922)

352.   *The White Winter – Hughie Snawed Up*

'Jam satis terris nivis atque diræ
Grandinis misit Pater.'
– Car. i.2.
'Enough already of dire snow and hail has the
Father [of the gods] sent upon the earth'.
(Horace, Odes I. 2).

Man, but it's vexin'! There's the Law
For five months noo been white wi' snaw;
An', when we lookit for a thaw,
    An' lowser weather,
It's gaitherin' for anither fa', 5
    As black as ever!

It's no' alane that fother's dear,
Yowes stervin', an' the lambin' near,
An' Winter owre the Ochils drear
    Drivin' unstintit, – 10
But, Lordsake! what's come owre the year?
    An' what's ahint it?

Wha kens but what oor aixle tree
'S been slew'd aboot, or dung ajee,   *dashed aside*
An' aff thro' space awa' we flee 15
    In a daft orbit?
Whilk mak's the seasons, as we see,
    Be sair disturbit.

Wha kens but what we've seen the heel
O' Simmer in a last fareweel? 20
Nae mair green gowany braes to speel   *flowery hillsides to climb*

> Wi' joyfu' crook,
> Nor dip in Devon, whaur a wiel   *pool*
>   Invites to dook!

> What aince has been may be aince mair,   25
> An' aince — as learnèd clerks declare —
> This planet's fortune was to fare,
>   In ages auld,
> Thro' regions o' the frigid air,
>   Past kennin' cauld.   30

> Nae doot but this was centuries gane,
> When human cretur' there was nane,
> An' this auld warld, her liefu' lane,   *rightful course*
>   Bowl'd thro' the nicht,
> Wi' tangles hingin' fra a mune   *icicles* 35
>   That was her licht.

> An eldritch scene that licht display'd!
> There lay the continents array'd,
> Like corpses o' the lately dead,
>   In a cauld sheet,   40
> Wi' icebergs sittin' at their head
>   An' at their feet!

> What aince has been may happen twice, —
> It's weel kenn'd *we* hae little ch'ice;
> An' if it be the Age o' Ice   45
>   Return'd aince mair —
> Faith, tak' this present for a spice,
>   It offers fair!

> The snaw a' owre lies sax feet deep;
> Ae half oor time we're howkin' sheep;   *hooking (out of drifts)* 50
> We haena haen a blanket sleep
>   Sin' the New Year;
> An' here we're at oor hin'most neep,   *turnip*
> An' term-time, near!

> It's juist as bad wi' ither folk: 55
> A shepherd's missin' wi' his flock;
> An eagle's ravagin' the Knock;
>   An' nearer hame,
> A dearth o' whisky's at the Crook,
>   An' aumries toom.   *store-cupboards empty* 60

The gates are blockit up a' roun' 's,
Silent are a' the seas an' soun's,
An' at the very trons in toons,   *market-places in towns*
  It's hoch deep lyin':
In fac', the Winter's broken boun's,   65
  There's nae denyin'.

It may be – for we're grown sae wice,
We're no' juist to be smoor'd like mice,   *smothered*
It may be that by some device
  We'll fricht the snaw,   *frighten off* 70
An' gie this threaten'd Age o' Ice
  The ca' awa'!

Some braw electrical machine
Amang the cluds may intervene,
Send licht an' heat, an' change the scene   75
  The warld throughoot;
An' burn oor skins, an' blind oor een,
  Wi't a', nae doot!

Come back, come back, oor ain auld sun,
Thy auld-appointed path to run;   80
An' a' the freits that were begun   *omens*
  To shore us ill   *threaten*
Shall, in the crackin' of a gun,
  Flee owre the hill.

Then, as of auld, when skies are clear,   85
An' springin' corn begins to breer,
Those joys your shepherd's heart shall cheer
  That charm'd of yore;
An' life on Devon be as dear
  As heretofore!   90

353.   *The Discovery of America*

(*Seen from the Ochils through the perspective of four centuries*)

All the mill-horses of Europe
  Were plodding round and round;
All the mills were droning
  The same old sound.

The drivers were dozing, the millers 5
    Were deaf—as millers will be;
When, startling them all, without warning
    Came a great shout from the sea!

It startled them all. The horses,
    Lazily plodding round, 10
Started and stopp'd; and the mills dropp'd
    Like a mantle their sound.

The millers look'd over their shoulders,
    The drivers open'd their eyes:
A silence, deeper than deafness, 15
    Had fallen out of the skies.

'Halloa there!'—this time distinctly
    It rose from the barren sea;
And Europe, turning in wonder,
    Whisper'd, 'What can it be?' 20

'Come down, come down to the shore here!'
    And Europe was soon on the sand;—
It was the great Columbus
    Dragging his prize to land.

(1891)

Alice Meynell (née Thompson) (1847–1922)

354.   *A Song of Derivations*

I come from nothing; but from where
Come the undying thoughts I bear?
    Down, through long links of death and birth,
    From the past poets of the earth,
My immortality is there. 5

I am like the blossom of an hour.
But long, long vanished sun and shower
    Awoke my breath i' the young world's air;
    I track the past back everywhere
Through seed and flower and seed and flower. 10

Or I am like a stream that flows
Full of the cold springs that arose
   In morning lands, in distant hills;
   And down the plain my channel fills
With melting of forgotten snows.   15

Voices, I have not heard, possessed
My own fresh songs; my thoughts are blessed
   With relics of the far unknown.
   And mixed with memories not my own
The sweet streams throng into my breast.   20

Before this life began to be,
The happy songs that wake in me
   Woke long ago and far apart.
   Heavily on this little heart
Presses this immortality.   25

355.   *Builders of Ruins*

We build with strength the deep tower wall
   That shall be shattered thus and thus.
And fair and great are court and hall,
   But *how* fair — this is not for us,
Who know the lack that lurks in all.   5

We know, we know how all too bright
   The hues are that our painting wears,
And how the marble gleams too white; —
   We speak in unknown tongues, the years
Interpret everything aright,   10

And crown with weeds our pride of towers,
   And warm our marble through with sun,
And break our pavements through with flowers,
   With an Amen when all is done,
Knowing these perfect things of ours.   15

O days, we ponder, left alone,
   Like children in their lonely hour,
And in our secrets keep your own,
   As seeds the colour of the flower.
To-day they are not all unknown,   20

The stars that 'twixt the rise and fall,
   Like relic-seers, shall one by one
Stand musing o'er our empty hall;
   And setting moons shall brood upon
The frescoes of our inward wall.   25

And when some midsummer shall be,
   Hither will come some little one
(Dusty with bloom of flowers is he),
   Sit on a ruin i' the late long sun,
And think, one foot upon his knee.   30

And where they wrought, these lives of ours,
   So many-worded, many-souled,
A North-west wind will take the towers,
   And dark with colour, sunny and cold,
Will range alone among the flowers.   35

And here or there, at our desire,
   The little clamorous owl shall sit
Through her still time; and we aspire
   To make a law (and know not it)
Unto the life of a wild briar.   40

Our purpose is distinct and dear,
   Though from our open eyes 'tis hidden.
Thou, Time to come, shalt make it clear,
   Undoing our work; we are children chidden
With pity and smiles of many a year.   45

Who shall allot the praise, and guess
   What part is yours and what is ours? —
O years that certainly will bless
   Our flowers with fruits, our seeds with flowers,
With ruin all our perfectness.   50

Be patient, Time, of our delays,
   Too happy hopes, and wasted fears,
Our faithful ways, our wilful ways;
   Solace our labours, O our seers
The seasons, and our bards the days;   55

        And make our pause and silence brim
           With the shrill children's play, and sweets
    Of those pathetic flowers and dim,
           Of those eternal flowers my Keats,
        Dying, felt growing over him!   60

356.   Renouncement

I must not think of thee; and, tired yet strong,
  I shun the thought that lurks in all delight –
  The thought of thee – and in the blue Heaven's height,
And in the sweetest passage of a song.

O just beyond the fairest thoughts that throng   5
  This breast, the thought of thee waits, hidden yet bright;
  But it must never, never come in sight;
I must stop short of thee the whole day long.

But when sleep comes to close each difficult day,
  When night gives pause to the long watch I keep,   10
  And all my bonds I needs must loose apart,

Must doff my will as raiment laid away, –
  With the first dream that comes with the first sleep
  I run, I run, I am gathered to thy heart.

357.   'I Am the Way'

    Thou art the Way.
Hadst Thou been nothing but the goal,
    I cannot say
If Thou hadst ever met my soul.

    I cannot see—   5
I, child of process—if there lies
    An end for me,
Full of repose, full of replies.

    I'll not reproach
The road that winds, my feet that err.   10
    Access, Approach
Art Thou, Time, Way, and Wayfarer.

        (1896)

358. *The Lady Poverty*

The Lady Poverty was fair:
But she has lost her looks of late,
With change of times and change of air.
Ah slattern! she neglects her hair,
Her gown, her shoes; she keeps no state 5
As once when her pure feet were bare.

Or—almost worse, if worse can be—
She scolds in parlours, dusts and trims,
Watches and counts. O is this she
Whom Francis met, whose step was free, 10
Who with Obedience carolled hymns,
In Umbria walked with Chastity?

Where is her ladyhood? Not here,
Not among modern kinds of men;
But in the stony fields, where clear 15
Through the thin trees the skies appear,
In delicate spare soil and fen,
And slender landscape and austere.

(1896)

359. *Cradle-Song at Twilight*

The child not yet is lulled to rest.
   Too young a nurse, the slender Night
So laxly holds him to her breast
   That throbs with flight.

He plays with her, and will not sleep. 5
   For other playfellows she sighs;
An unmaternal fondness keep
   Her alien eyes.

(1895)

360.   *After a Parting*

    Farewell has long been said; I have forgone thee;
        I never name thee even.
    But how shall I learn virtues and yet shun thee?
        For thou art so near Heaven
    That Heavenward meditations pause upon thee.   5

    Thou dost beset the path to every shrine;
        My trembling thoughts discern
    Thy goodness in the good for which I pine;
        And, if I turn from but one sin, I turn
    Unto a smile of thine.   10

    How shall I thrust thee apart
        Since all my growth tends to thee night and day–
    To thee faith, hope, and art?
        Swift are the currents setting all one way;
    They draw my life, my life, out of my heart.   15

George R. (Robert) Sims (1847–1922)

361.   *A Garden Song*

    I scorn the doubts and cares that hurt
        The world and all its mockeries,
    My only care is now to squirt
        The ferns among my rockeries.

    In early youth and later life   5
        I've seen an up and seen a down,
    And now I have a loving wife
        To help me peg verbena down.

    Of joys that come to womankind
        The loom of fate doth weave her few,   10
    But here are summer joys entwined
        And bound with golden feverfew,

I've learnt the lessons one and all
    With which the world its sermon stocks,
Now, heedless of a rise or fall,   15
    I've Brompton and I've German stocks.

In peace and quiet pass our days,
    With nought to vex our craniums,
Our middle beds are all ablaze
    With red and white geraniums.   20

And like a boy I laugh when she,
    In Varden hat and Varden hose,
Comes slyly up the lawn at me
    To squirt me with the garden hose.

Let him who'd have the peace he needs   25
    Give all his worldly mumming up,
Then dig a garden, plant the seeds,
    And watch the product coming up.

(1879)

L. (Laura) Ormiston Chant (1848–1923)

362.
Hope's Song

We are standing on the threshold, sisters,
    Of the new and brighter day,
And the hideous night of savage customs
    Passes, with the dark, away.

Pale your faces are with weeping, sisters.   5
    Haggard with your weary watch,
And your voices fainter grow and weaker,
    Till we scarce your tones can catch.

But the rose light of the dawning, sisters,
    Flushing up the golden skies,   10
Will such rapture bring to you and beauty,
    Heaven will nestle in your eyes.

And your hearts grow young again, rejoicing
    In the warm life-giving power
Of the reign of love, and truth, and justice,   15
    And the gladness of the hour.

You have borne the burden, O my sisters,
    Through long dynasties of pain,
Of the scoff and scorn of being women,
    That shall ne'er return again.   20

'Twas the winter of the world, my sisters,
    Spring was coming, spring has come,
And the patient anguish of the women
    Sowed the seed for Harvest Home.

Still the east winds blow of hate and scorning,   25
    Still the savage mars the man,
Still these human brutes, or men, or women,
    Crush and ruin where they can.

But their numbers lessen surely, sisters,
    Sink the east wind's blighting chills,   30
In the glorious prophecy of summer
    Coming o'er the eternal hills.

I am singing to you, O my sisters,
    In the early morn of spring,
And the coldness of the gloomy shadows   35
    Makes me tremble as I sing.

But from where I with my song am soaring,
    High above the earth below,
I can hear the singing of the angels,
    And their psalm ye soon shall know.   40

Song of fruits celestial from the flowers
    Of goodwill for evermore;
And a tranquil reign of peace and beauty,
    Summer light on sea and shore.

Man and woman in one aim united,   45
    Dual force of unity;
Equal glory, equal progress blended
    In their one humanity.

>   Deepest love and kindest, in the union
>   Of two equals, strong and free;   50
>   Highest hope and loftiest aim, the impress
>   Of the race that soon shall be.
>
>   *All* the nerve-force of the human storehouse
>   For the world's work and the age;
>   And no longer half by custom wasted   55
>   In an endless tutelage.
>
>   Oh, take comfort, dear and honoured sisters,
>   Patriots ye for country, home;
>   With the angels welcome ye the morning,
>   Heaven in earth, the kingdom come   60

                                (1887)

W. (William) E. (Ernest) Henley (1849–1903)

from *In Hospital*

363.   I. *Enter Patient*

> The morning mists still haunt the stony street;
> The northern summer air is shrill and cold;
> And lo, the Hospital, grey, quiet, old,
> Where Life and Death like friendly chafferers meet.
> Thro' the loud spaciousness and draughty gloom   5
> A small, strange child—so agèd yet so young!—
> Her little arm besplinted and beslung,
> Precedes me gravely to the waiting-room.
> I limp behind, my confidence all gone.
> The grey-haired soldier-porter waves me on,   10
> And on I crawl, and still my spirits fail:
> A tragic meanness seems so to environ
> These corridors and stairs of stone and iron,
> Cold, naked, clean—half-workhouse and half-jail.

364.   II. *Waiting*

    A square, squat room (a cellar on promotion),
        Drab to the soul, drab to the very daylight;
        Plasters astray in unnatural-looking tinware;
        Scissors and lint and apothecary's jars.

    Here, on a bench a skeleton would writhe from,   5
        Angry and sore, I wait to be admitted:
        Wait till my heart is lead upon my stomach,
        While at their ease two dressers do their chores.

    One has a probe—it feels to me a crowbar.
        A small boy sniffs and shudders after bluestone.   10
        A poor old tramp explains his poor old ulcers.
        Life is (I think) a blunder and a shame.

365.   XXIII. *Music*

    Down the quiet eve,
    Thro' my window with the sunset
    Pipes to me a distant organ
    Foolish ditties;

    And, as when you change   5
    Pictures in a magic lantern,
    Books, beds, bottles, floor, and ceiling
    Fade and vanish,

    And I'm well once more. . . .
    August flares adust and torrid,   10
    But my heart is full of April
    Sap and sweetness.

    In the quiet eve
    I am loitering, longing, dreaming . . .
    Dreaming, and a distant organ   15
    Pipes me ditties.

    I can see the shop,
    I can smell the sprinkled pavement,
    Where she serves—her chestnut chignon
    Thrills my senses!   20

O, the sight and scent,
Wistful eve and perfumed pavement!
In the distance pipes an organ . . .
The sensation

Comes to me anew,   25
And my spirit for a moment
Thro' the music breathes the blessèd
Airs of London.

366.   XXIV. *Suicide*

Staring corpselike at the ceiling,
   See his harsh, unrazored features,
   Ghastly brown against the pillow,
   And his throat—so strangely bandaged!

Lack of work and lack of victuals,   5
   A debauch of smuggled whisky,
   And his children in the workhouse
   Made the world so black a riddle

That he plunged for a solution;
   And, although his knife was edgeless,   10
   He was sinking fast towards one,
   When they came, and found, and saved him.

Stupid now with shame and sorrow,
   In the night I hear him sobbing.
   But sometimes he talks a little.   15
   He has told me all his troubles.

In his broad face, tanned and bloodless,
   White and wild his eyeballs glisten;
   And his smile, occult and tragic,
   Yet so slavish, makes you shudder!   20

367.   XXVIII. *Discharged*

 Carry me out
 Into the wind and the sunshine,
 Into the beautiful world.

 O, the wonder, the spell of the streets!
 The stature and strength of the horses,　　5
 The rustle and echo of footfalls,
 The flat roar and rattle of wheels!
 A swift tram floats huge on us . . .
 It's a dream?
 The smell of the mud in my nostrils　　10
 Blows brave—like a breath of the sea!

 As of old,
 Ambulant, undulant drapery,
 Vaguely and strangely provocative,
 Flutters and beckons. O, yonder—　　15
 Is it?—the gleam of a stocking!
 Sudden, a spire
 Wedged in the mist! O, the houses,
 The long lines of lofty, grey houses,
 Cross-hatched with shadow and light!　　20
 These are the streets. . . .
 Each is an avenue leading
 Whither I will!

 Free . . . !
 Dizzy, hysterical, faint,　　25
 I sit, and the carriage rolls on with me
 Into the wonderful world.

 THE OLD INFIRMARY, EDINBURGH, 1873–75

368.   'On the way to Kew'

 On the way to Kew,
 By the river old and gray,
 Where in the Long Ago
 We laughed and loitered so,
 I met a ghost to-day,　　5

A ghost that told of you —
A ghost of low replies
And sweet, inscrutable eyes
Coming up from Richmond
As you used to do.   10

By the river old and gray,
The enchanted Long Ago
Murmured and smiled anew.
On the way to Kew,
March had the laugh of May,   15
The bare boughs looked aglow,
And old, immortal words
Sang in my breast like birds,
Coming up from Richmond
As I used with you.   20

With the life of Long Ago
Lived my thought of you.
By the river old and gray
Flowing his appointed way
As I watched I knew   25
What is so good to know —
Not in vain, not in vain,
Shall I look for you again
Coming up from Richmond
On the way to Kew.   30

Henry Bellyse Baildon (1849–1907)

369.　　　　　　　　*Alone in London*

By her fault or by ill-fate,
Left in great London, desolate
Of helpers and of comforters,
Without one heart to beat with hers, —
Without one hand in tenderness   5
And sympathy her hand to press, —
A lone soul, left dispassionate,
Without one link of love or hate.

From her lodging poor and bare,
And high up in the smoke-dim air,
With cheerless heart, with aimless feet,
She descendeth to the street,
Where the people, coming, going,
Ceaseless as a river's flowing,
Seemed as imperturbable,
As though no heart-warm tear could well
Into those dry eyes, – no sob
Ever could those set lips rob
Of their sternness, – with blind stare
They passed a woman in despair.

With hopeless heart, with weary feet,
She wanders on from street to street,
   Restless as a withered leaf
Fallen from its parent tree;
   Goaded by a sleepless grief,
Dogged by dull perplexity,
Passing along, in dumb despair,
Deserted street and silent square.

Into the shadow black and deep
   Of a doorway she doth shrink,
Crouching there, she cannot weep,
   Waiting there, she cannot think.
As a tide on river wall
   Lappeth ever wearily,
Round her soul despair doth call
   Constantly and drearily;
As round ancient gable peaks
A ghostly night-wind wails and shrieks,
So again and yet again
Rise the bitter gusts of pain.

Steps are heard upon the stone:
One cometh down the street alone,
And upon the footsteps follow,
'Mid the dark roofs, echoes hollow,
On he comes, all unaware
Of the dark misery lurking there;
He pauseth not, but passes on, –
She speaketh not, and he is gone.
She thinks, 'He would but reckon me
The vile thing that I would not be,

Silence again. A wild intent
The pang woke in her as it went;
She goes, nought with her, down the street,
But haunting echoes of her feet.

. . . .

She stands where, far below, is heard 55
The river's one unchanging word;
She stands and listens, and doth know,
Beneath the waters seaward go.
Like an incantation drear
She hears them wash by wharf and pier. 60

Will none come to save her yet?
Her foot is on the parapet;
Upward to a starless heaven
One last, hopeless look is given:
On each hand stretches black and far 65
The line of roofs irregular,
And beneath, a vast night-wall,
Based in gloom funereal.

The blackness floweth up to meet
The wanderer's world-weary feet, 70
And afar, below it all,
Still the river seems to call,
'Mortal, since thou wouldst not live,
Come, for I have rest to give;
Over thee and thy dark woes 75
Silently my waves shall close,
Spreading changeless over all,
Like a mighty funeral pall.'

A moment, agonized and mute,
Rigid, yet irresolute 80
She stands; then, with a bitter cry,
Rent from her soul's last agony,
Sheer down the black abyss she falls; —

The river washes by its walls.

(1877)

W. (William) H. (Hurrell) Mallock (1849–1923)

370.   *Every Man His Own Poet:*
                  or, The Inspired Singer's Recipe Book

INTRODUCTION

To have attempted in former times a work of this description, would have seemed, we cannot deny, to savour either of presumption or of idiotcy, or more probably of both. And rightly. But we live in times of progress. The mystery of yesterday is the common-place of to-day; the Bible, which was Newton's oracle, is Professor Huxley's jest-book; and students at the University now lose a class for not being familiar with opinions, which but twenty years ago they would have been expelled for dreaming of. Everything is moving onward swiftly and satisfactorily; and if, when we have made all faiths fail, we can only contrive to silence the British Association, and so make all knowledge vanish away, there will lack nothing but the presence of a perfect charity to turn the nineteenth century into a complete kingdom of heaven. Amongst changes, then, so great and so hopeful—amongst the discoveries of the rights of women, the infallibility of the Pope, and the physical basis of life, it may well be doubted if the great fathers of ancient song would find, if they could come back to us, anything out of the way or ludicrous in a recipe-book for concocting poetry.

Some, indeed, object that poetry is not progressive. But on what grounds this assertion is based, it is not possible to conjecture. Poetry is as much progressive as anything else in these days of progress. Free-thought itself shews scarcely more strikingly those three great stages which mark advance and movement. For poetry, like Free-thought, was first a work of inspiration, secondly of science, and lastly now of trick. At its first stage it was open to only here and there a genius; at its next to all intelligent men; and at its third to all the human race. Thus, just as there is no boy now, but can throw stones at the windows which Bishop Colenso has broken, so there is scarcely even a young lady but can raise flowers from the seed stolen out of Mr. Tennyson's garden.

And surely, whatever, in this its course of change, poetry may have lost in quality, is more than made up for by what it has gained in quantity. For in the first place it is far pleasanter to the tastes of a scientific generation, to understand how to make bad poetry than to wonder at good; and secondly, as the end of poetry is pleasure, that we should make it each for ourselves is the very utmost that we can desire, since it is a fact in which we all agree, that no man's verses please him so much as his own.

OF THE NATURE OF POETRY

Poetry as practised by the latest masters, is the art of expressing what is too foolish, too profane, or too indecent to be expressed in any other way. And thus, just as a consummate cook will prepare a most delicate repast out of the most poor materials, so will the modern poet concoct us a most popular poem from the weakest emotions, and the most tiresome platitudes. The only difference is, that the cook would prefer good materials if he could get them, whilst the modern poet will take the bad from choice. As far, however, as the nature of materials goes, those which the two artists work with are the same—*viz.*, animals, vegetables, and spirits. It was the practice of Shakespeare and other earlier masters to make use of all these together, mixing them in various proportions. But the moderns have found that it is better and far easier to employ each separately. Thus Mr. Swinburne uses very little else but animal matter in the composition of his dishes, which it must be confessed are somewhat unwholesome in consequence: whilst the late Mr. Wordsworth, on the contrary, confined himself almost exclusively to the confection of primrose pudding, and flint soup, flavoured with the lesser-celandine; and only now and then a beggar-boy boiled down in it to give it a colour. The robins and drowned lambs which he was wont to use, when an additional piquancy was needed, were employed so sparingly that they did not destroy in the least the general vegetable tone of his productions; and these form in consequence an unimpeachable lenten diet. It is difficult to know what to say of Mr. Tennyson, as the milk and water of which his books are composed chiefly, make it almost impossible to discover what was the original nature of the materials he has boiled down in it. Mr. Shelley, too, is perhaps somewhat embarrassing to classify; as, though spirits are what he affected most, he made use of a large amount of vegetable matter also. We shall be probably not far wrong in describing his material as a kind of methyllated spirits; or pure psychic alcohol, strongly tinctured with the barks of trees, and rendered below proof by a quantity of sea-water. In this division of the poets, however, into animalists, spiritualists, and vegetarians, we must not be discouraged by any such difficulties as these; but must bear in mind that in whatever manner we may neatly classify anything, the exceptions and special cases will always far outnumber those to which our rule applies.

But in fact, at present, mere theory may be set entirely aside: for although in the case of action, the making and adhering to a theory may be the surest guide to inconsistency and absurdity, in poetry these results can be obtained without such aid.

The following recipes, compiled from a careful analysis of the best authors, will be found, we trust, efficient guides for the composition of genuine poems. But the tyro must bear always in mind that there is no royal road to anything, and that not even the most explicit directions will make a poet all at once of even the most fatuous, the most sentimental, or the most profane.

RECIPES

The following are arranged somewhat in the order in which the student is recommended to begin his efforts. About the more elaborate ones, which come later, he may use his own discretion as to which he will try first; but he must previously have had some training in the simpler compositions, with which we deal before all others. These form as it were a kind of palæstra of folly, a very short training in which will suffice to break down that stiffness and self-respect in the soul, which is so incompatible with modern poetry. Taking, therefore, the silliest and commonest of all kinds of verse, and the one whose sentiments come most readily to hand in vulgar minds, we begin with directions,

HOW TO MAKE AN ORDINARY LOVE POEM

Take two large and tender human hearts, which match one another perfectly. Arrange these close together, but preserve them from actual contact by placing between them some cruel barrier. Wound them both in several places, and insert through the openings thus made a fine stuffing of wild yearnings, hopeless tenderness, and a general admiration for stars. Then completely cover up one heart with a sufficient quantity of chill church-yard mould, which may be garnished according to taste with dank waving weeds or tender violets: and promptly break over it the other heart.

HOW TO MAKE A PATHETIC MARINE POEM

This kind of poem has the advantage of being easily produced, yet being at the same time pleasing, and not unwholesome. As, too, it admits of no variety, the chance of going wrong in it is very small. Take one midnight storm, and one fisherman's family, which, if the poem is to be a real success, should be as large and as hungry as possible, and must contain at least one innocent infant. Place this last in a cradle, with the mother singing over it, being careful that the babe be dreaming of angels, or else smiling sweetly. Stir the father well up in the storm until he disappears. Then get ready immediately a quantity of cruel crawling foam, in which serve up the father directly on his re-appearance, which is sure to take place in an hour or two, in the dull red morning. This done, a charming saline effervescence will take place amongst the remainder of the family. Pile up the agony to suit the palate, and the poem will be ready for perusal.

HOW TO WRITE AN EPIC POEM LIKE MR. TENNYSON

(The following, apart from its intrinsic utility, forms in itself a great literary curiosity, being the original directions from which the Poet Laureate composed the Arthurian Idylls.)

To compose an epic, some writers instruct us first to catch our hero. As, however, Mr. Carlyle is the only person on record who has ever performed this feat, it will be best for the rest of mankind to be content with the nearest approach to a hero available, namely a prig. These animals are very plentiful, and easy to catch, as they delight in being run after. There are however many different kinds, not all equally fit for the present purpose, and amongst which it is very necessary to select the right one. Thus, for instance, there is the scientific and atheistical prig, who may be frequently observed eluding notice between the covers of the "Westminster Review;" the Anglican prig, who is often caught exposing himself in the "Guardian;" the Ultramontane prig, who abounds in the "Dublin Review;" the scholarly prig, who twitters among the leaves of the "Academy;" and the Evangelical prig, who converts the heathen, and drinks port wine. None of these, and least of all the last, will serve for the central figure, in the present class of poem. The only one entirely suitable is the blameless variety. Take, then, one blameless prig. Set him upright in the middle of a round table, and place beside him a beautiful wife, who cannot abide prigs. Add to these, one marred goodly man; and tie the three together in a bundle with a link or two of Destiny. Proceed, next, to surround this group with a large number of men and women of the nineteenth century, in fancy-ball costume, flavoured with a great many very possible vices, and a few impossible virtues. Stir these briskly about for two volumes, to the great annoyance of the blameless prig, who is, however, to be kept carefully below swearing-point, for the whole time. If he once boils over into any natural action or exclamation, he is forthwith worthless, and you must get another. Next break the wife's reputation into small pieces; and dust them well over the blameless prig. Then take a few vials of tribulation and wrath, and empty these generally over the whole ingredients of your poem: and, taking the sword of the heathen, cut into small pieces the greater part of your minor characters. Then wound slightly the head of the blameless prig; remove him suddenly from the table, and keep in a cool barge for future use.

HOW TO WRITE A POEM LIKE MR. MATTHEW ARNOLD

Take one soulfull of involuntary unbelief, which has been previously well flavoured with self-satisfied despair. Add to this one beautiful text of Scripture. Mix these well together; and as soon as ebullition commences grate in finely a few regretful allusions to the New Testament and the lake of Tiberias, one constellation of stars, half-a-dozen allusions to the nineteenth century, one to Goethe, one to Mont Blanc, or the Lake of Geneva; and one also, if possible, to some personal bereavement. Flavour the whole with a mouthful of "faiths" and "infinites," and a mixed mouthful of "passions," "finites," and "yearnings." This class of poem is concluded usually with some question, about which we have to observe only that it shall be impossible to answer.

HOW TO WRITE A POEM LIKE MR. BROWNING

Take rather a coarse view of things in general. In the midst of this, place a man and a woman, her and her ankles, tastefully arranged on a slice of Italy, or the country about Pornic. Cut an opening across the breast of each, until the soul becomes visible, but be very careful that none of the body be lost during the operation. Pour into each breast as much as it will hold of the new strong wine of love: and, for fear they should take cold by exposure, cover them quickly up with a quantity of obscure classical quotations, a few familar allusions to an unknown period of history, and a half-destroyed fresco by an early master, varied every now and then with a reference to the fugues or toccatas of a quite-forgotten composer.

If the poem be still intelligible, take a pen and remove carefully all the necessary particles.

HOW TO WRITE A MODERN PRE-RAPHAELITE POEM

Take a packet of fine selected early English, containing no words but such as are obsolete and unintelligible. Pour this into about double the quantity of entirely new English, which must have never been used before, and which you must compose yourself, fresh as it is wanted. Mix these together thoroughly till they assume a colour quite different from any tongue that was ever spoken, and the material will be ready for use.

Determine the number of stanzas of which your poem shall consist, and select a corresponding number of the most archaic or most peculiar words in your vocabulary, allotting one of these to each stanza; and pour in the other words round them, until the entire poem is filled in.

This kind of composition is usually cast in shapes. These, though not numerous—amounting in all to something under a dozen—it would take too long to describe minutely here: and a short visit to Mr. —'s shop in King street, where they are kept in stock, would explain the whole of them. A favourite one, however, is the following, which is of very easy construction. Take three damozels, dressed in straight night-gowns. Pull their hair-pins out, and let their hair tumble all about their shoulders. A few stars may be sprinkled into this with advantage. Place an aureole about the head of each, and give each a lily in her hand, about half the size of herself. Bend their necks all different ways, and set them in a row before a stone wall, with an apple-tree between each and some large flowers at their feet. Trees and flowers of the right sort are very plentiful in church windows. When you have arranged all these objects rightly, take a cast of them in the softest part of your brain, and pour in your word-composition as above described.

This kind of poem is much improved by what is called a burden. This consists of a few jingling words, generally of an archaic character, about which we have only to be careful that they have no reference to the subject of the poem they are to ornament. They are inserted without variation between the stanzas.

In conclusion we would remark to beginners that this sort of composition must be attempted only in a perfectly vacant atmosphere; so that no grains of common-sense may injure the work whilst in progress.

HOW TO WRITE A NARRATIVE POEM LIKE MR. MORRIS

Take about sixty pages-full of the same word-mixture as that described in the preceding; and dilute it with a double quantity of mild modern Anglo-Saxon. Pour this composition into two vessels of equal size, and into one of these empty a small mythological story. If this does not put your readers to sleep soon enough, add to it the rest of the language, in the remaining vessel.

HOW TO WRITE A SATANIC POEM, LIKE THE LATE LORD BYRON

(This recipe is inserted for the benefit of those poets who desire to attain what is called originality. This is only to be got by following some model of a past generation, which has ceased to be made use of by the public at large. We do not however recommend this course, feeling sure that all writers in the end will derive far more real satisfaction from producing fashionable, than original verses; which two things it is impossible to do at one and the same time.)

Take a couple of fine deadly sins; and let them hang before your eyes until they become racy. Then take them down, dissect them, and stew them for some time in a solution of weak remorse; after which they are to be devilled with mock-despair.

HOW TO WRITE A PATRIOTIC POEM LIKE MR. SWINBURNE

Take one blaspheming patriot, who has been hung or buried for some time, together with the oppressed country belonging to him. Soak these in a quantity of rotten sentiment, till they are completely sodden; and in the mean while get ready an indefinite number of Christian kings and priests. Kick these till they are nearly dead; add copiously broken fragments of the Catholic church, and mix all together thoroughly. Place them in a heap upon the oppressed country; season plentifully with very coarse expressions; and on the top carefully arrange your patriot, garnished with laurel or with parsley: surround with artificial hopes for the future, which are never meant to be tasted. This kind of poem is cooked in verbiage, flavoured with Liberty, the taste of which is much heightened by the introduction of a few high gods, and the game of Fortune. The amount of verbiage which Liberty is capable of flavouring, is practically infinite.

CONCLUSION

We regret to have to offer this work to the public in its present incomplete state, the whole of that part treating of the most recent section of modern poetry, *viz.*, the blasphemous and the obscene, being entirely wanting. It was found necessary to issue this from an eminent publishing firm in Holywell street, Strand, where by an unforeseen casualty, the whole of the first edition was seized by the police, and is at present in the hands of the Society for the Suppression of Vice. We incline however to trust that this loss will have but little effect; as indecency and profanity are things in which, even to the dullest, external instruction is a luxury, rather than a necessity. Those of our readers, who, either from sense, self-respect, or other circumstances, are in need of a special training in these subjects, will find excellent professors of them in any public-house, during the late hours of the evening; where the whole sum and substance of the fieriest school of modern poetry is delivered nightly; needing only a little dressing and flavouring with artificial English to turn it into very excellent verse.

371. *Christmas Thoughts, by a Modern Thinker*

(After Mr. Matthew Arnold)

The windows of the church are bright;
   'Tis Christmas Eve; a low wind breathes;
And girls with happy eyes to-night
   Are hanging up the Christmas wreaths;

And village voices by-and-by   5
   Will reach my windows through the trees,
With wild, sweet music: 'Praise on high
   To God: on earth, good-will and peace.'

Oh, happy girls, that hang the wreaths!
   Oh, village fiddlers, happy ye!   10
Christmas to you still truly breathes
   Good-will and peace; but not to me.

Yes, gladness is your simple rôle,
   Ye foolish girls, ye labouring poor;
But joy would ill beseem my soul—   15
   To sigh, my part is, and endure.

For once as Rousseau stood, I stand
   Apart, made picturesque by grief—
One of a small world-weary band,
   The orphans of a dead belief.   20

Through graveyards lone we love to stray,
    And sadly the sad tombs explore,
And contradict the texts which say
    That we shall rise once more.

Out faith is dead, of course; and grief
    Fills its room up; and Christmas pie
And turkey cannot bring relief
    To such as Obermann and I.

Ah, Obermann, and might I pass
    This English Christmas-tide with thee,
Far by those inland waves whose glass
    Brightens and breaks by Meillerie;

Or else amongst the sternest dells
    Alp shags with pine, we'd mix our sighs,
Mourn at the sound of Christmas bells,
    Sniff at the smell of Christmas pies.

But thou art dead; and long, dank grass
    And wet mould cool thy tired, hot brain;
Thou art lain down, and now, alas!
    Of course you won't get up again.

Yet, Obermann, 'tis better so;
    For if, sad slumberer, after all
You were to re-arise, you know
    'Twould make us feel so very small.

Best bear our grief this manlier way,
    And make our grief be balm to grief;
For if in faith sweet comfort lay,
    There lurks sweet pride in unbelief.

Wherefore, remembering this, once more
    Unto my childhood's church I'll go,
And bow my head at that low door
    I passed through standing, long ago.

I'll sit in the accustomed place,
    And make, while all the unlearnèd stare,
A mournful, atheistic face
    At their vain noise of unheard prayer.

> Then, while they hymn the heavenly birth
>   And angel voices from the skies,
> My thoughts shall go where Weimar's earth
>   For ever darkens Goethe's eyes;   60
>
> Till sweet girls' glances from their books
>   Shall steal towards me, and they sigh:
> 'How intellectual he looks,
>   And yet how wistful! And his eye
>
> Has that vain look of baffled prayer!'   65
>   And then when church is o'er I'll run,
> Comb misery into all my hair,
>   And go and get my portrait done.

(1893)

Edmund Gosse (1849–1928)

372. *Lying in the Grass*

> Between two golden tufts of summer grass,
> I see the world through hot air as through glass,
> And by my face sweet lights and colours pass.
>
> Before me, dark against the fading sky,
> I watch three mowers mowing, as I lie: 5
> With brawny arms they sweep in harmony.
>
> Brown English faces by the sun burnt red,
> Rich glowing colour on bare throat and head,
> My heart would leap to watch them, were I dead!
>
> And in my strong young living as I lie,   10
> I seem to move with them in harmony—
> A fourth is mowing, and that fourth am I.
>
> The music of the scythes that glide and leap,
> The young men whistling as their great arms sweep,
> And all the perfume and sweet sense of sleep,   15

The weary butterflies that droop their wings,
The dreamy nightingale that hardly sings,
And all the lassitude of happy things,

Is mingling with the warm and pulsing blood,
That gushes through my veins a languid flood, 20
And feeds my spirit as the sap a bud.

Behind the mowers, on the amber air,
A dark-green beech-wood rises, still and fair,
A white path winding up it like a stair.

And see that girl, with pitcher on her head, 25
And clean white apron on her gown of red,—
Her even-song of love is but half-said:

She waits the youngest mower. Now he goes;
Her cheeks are redder than a wild blush-rose:
They climb up where the deepest shadows close. 30

But though they pass, and vanish, I am there.
I watch his rough hands meet beneath her hair,
Their broken speech sounds sweet to me like prayer.

Ah! now the rosy children come to play,
And romp and struggle with the new-mown hay; 35
Their clear high voices sound from far away.

They know so little why the world is sad,
They dig themselves warm graves and yet are glad;
Their muffled screams and laughter make me mad!

I long to go and play among them there; 40
Unseen, like wind, to take them by the hair.
And gently make their rosy cheeks more fair.

The happy children! full of frank surprise,
And sudden whims and innocent ecstasies;
What godhead sparkles from their liquid eyes! 45

No wonder round those urns of mingled clays
That Tuscan potters fashioned in old days,
And coloured like the torrid earth ablaze,

We find the little gods and loves portrayed,
Through ancient forests wandering undismayed,   50
And fluting hymns of pleasure unafraid.

They knew, as I do now, what keen delight
A strong man feels to watch the tender flight
Of little children playing in his sight;

What pure sweet pleasure, and what sacred love,   55
Comes drifting down upon us from above,
In watching how their limbs and features move.

I do not hunger for a well-stored mind
I only wish to live my life, and find
My heart in unison with all mankind.   60

My life is like the single dewy star
That trembles on the horizon's primrose-bar,—
A microcosm where all things living are.

And if, among the noiseless grasses, Death
Should come behind and take away my breath   65
I should not rise as one who sorroweth;

For I should pass; but all the world would be
Full of desire and young delight and glee,
And why should men be sad through loss of me?

The light is flying; in the silver-blue   70
The young moon shines from her bright window through:
The mowers are all gone, and I go too.

Philip Bourke Marston (1850–1887)

Sonnets:

No Death

373.

I saw in dreams a mighty multitude,—
   Gathered, they seemed, from North, South, East, and West,
   And in their looks such horror was exprest
As must forever words of mine elude.

As if transfixed by grief, some silent stood,   5
   While others wildly smote upon the breast,
   And cried out fearfully, "No rest, no rest!"
Some fled, as if by shapes unseen pursued.

Some laughed insanely. Others shrieking, said:
   "To think but yesterday we might have died;   10
For then God had not thundered, 'Death is dead!'"
They gashed themselves till they with blood were red.
   "Answer, O God; take back this curse!" they cried,
But "Death is dead," was all the voice replied.

374. *Flower Fairies*

Flower fairies—have you found them,
   When the summer's dusk is falling,
With the glow-worms watching round them;
   Have you heard them softly calling?

Silent stand they through the moonlight,   5
   In their flower shapes, fair and quiet,
But they hie them forth by moonlight
   Ready then to sing and riot.

I have heard them; I have seen them,—
   Light from their bright petals raying;   10
And the trees bent down to screen them,
   Great, wise trees, too old for playing.

Hundreds of them, all together,—
   Flashing flocks of flying fairies,—
Crowding through the summer weather,   15
   Seeking where the coolest air is.

And they tell the trees that know them,
   As upon their boughs they hover,
Of the things that chance below them,—
   How the rose has a new lover.   20

And the gay Rose laughs, protesting,
   "Neighbor Lily is as fickle."
Then they search where birds are nesting,
   And their feathers softly tickle.

Then away they all dance, sweeping, 25
    Having drunk their fill of gladness.
But the trees, their night-watch keeping,
    Thrill with tender, pitying sadness;

For they know of bleak December,
    When each bough left cold and bare is,— 30
When they only shall remember
    The bright visits of the fairies,—

When the roses and the lilies
    Shall be gone, to come back never
From the land where all so still is 35
    That they sleep and sleep forever.

375. Grief's Aspects

Grief does not come alike to all, I know.
    To some, grief cometh like an armèd man,
    Crying, 'Arise, and strive with me who can!'
And some are brought to heavenly peace through woe,
And watch a new life from the old life grow; 5
    And some there be who strive beneath the ban,
    And, having struggled hotly for a span,
Tread on the fallen body of their foe.

My grief has taken hold of me, and led
    My feet to lands of any spring unknown. 10
There has he bound me in strong chains, and said,
    'Behold, we are forevermore alone!
Drink from my hand thy wine, and eat my bread
    At last, I have thee solely for my own.'

Robert Louis (formerly Lewis) Balfour Stevenson (1850–1894)

376.   'The tropics vanish, and meseems that I'

    The tropics vanish, and meseems that I,
    From Halkerside, from topmost Allermuir,
    Or steep Caerketton, dreaming gaze again.
    Far set in fields and woods, the town I see
    Spring gallant from the shallows of her smoke,   5
    Cragged, spired, and turreted, her virgin fort
    Beflagged. About, on seaward-drooping hills,
    New folds of city glitter. Last, the Forth
    Wheels ample waters set with sacred isles,
    And populous Fife smokes with a score of towns.   10

    There, on the sunny frontage of a hill,
    Hard by the house of kings, repose the dead,
    My dead, the ready and the strong of word.
    Their works, the salt-encrusted, still survive;
    The sea bombards their founded towers; the night   15
    Thrills pierced with their strong lamps. The artificers,
    One after one, here in this grated cell,
    Where the rain erases and the rust consumes,
    Fell upon lasting silence. Continents
    And continental oceans intervene;   20
    A sea uncharted, on a lampless isle,
    Environs and confines their wandering child
    In vain. The voice of generations dead
    Summons me, sitting distant, to arise,
    My numerous footsteps nimbly to retrace,   25
    And, all mutation over, stretch me down
    In that devoted city of the dead.

377.   *Fragment*

    Thou strainest through the mountain fern,
    A most exiguously thin
        Burn.
    For all thy foam, for all thy din,

>   Thee shall the pallid lake inurn,　　　　　　　　　　　5
>   With well-a-day for Mr Swin-
>   Burne!
>   Take then this quarto in thy fin
>   And, O thou stoker huge and stern,
>   The whole affair, outside and in,　　　　　　　　　　10
>   Burn!
>   But save the true poetic kin,
>   The works of Mr Robert Burn!
>   And William Wordsworth upon Tin-
>   Tern!　　　　　　　　　　　　　　　　　　　　15

　　　　　　　　　(wr. 1884?; pub. 1916)

378.　　　　　　　　*The Light-Keeper*

I

> The brilliant kernel of the night,
> The flaming lightroom circles me:
> I sit within a blaze of light
> Held high above the dusky sea.
> Far off the surf doth break and roar　　　　　　　　　　5
> Along bleak miles of moonlit shore,
> Where through the tides the tumbling wave
> Falls in an avalanche of foam
> And drives its churnèd waters home
> Up many an undercliff and cave.　　　　　　　　　　　10
>
> The clear bell chimes: the clockworks strain:
> The turning lenses flash and pass,
> Frame turning within glittering frame
> With frosty gleam of moving glass:
> Unseen by me, each dusky hour　　　　　　　　　　　15
> The sea-waves welter up the tower
> Or in the ebb subside again;
> And ever and anon all night,
> Drawn from afar by charm of light,
> A sea-bird beats against the pane.　　　　　　　　　　20
>
> And lastly when dawn ends the night
> And belts the semi-orb of sea,
> The tall, pale pharos in the light
> Looks white and spectral as may be.

The early ebb is out: the green 25
Straight belt of seaweed now is seen,
That round the basement of the tower
Marks out the interspace of tide;
And watching men are heavy-eyed,
And sleepless lips are dry and sour. 30

The night is over like a dream:
The sea-birds cry and dip themselves;
And in the early sunlight, steam
The newly-bared and dripping shelves,
Around whose verge the glassy wave 35
With lisping wash is heard to lave;
While, on the white tower lifted high,
With yellow light in faded glass
The circling lenses flash and pass
And sickly shine against the sky. 40

II

As the steady lenses circle
With a frosty gleam of glass;
And the clear bell chimes,
And the oil brims over the lip of the burner,
Quiet and still at his desk, 45
The lonely Light-Keeper
Holds his vigil.

Lured from afar,
The bewildered seagull beats
Dully against the lantern; 50
Yet he stirs not, lifts not his head
From the desk where he reads,
Lifts not his eyes to see
The chill blind circle of night
Watching him through the panes. 55
This is his country's guardian,
The outmost sentry of peace.
This is the man,
Who gives up all that is lovely in living
For the means to live. 60

Poetry cunningly gilds
The life of the Light-Keeper,
Held on high in the blackness

In the burning kernel of night:
The seaman sees and blesses him; 65
The Poet, deep in a sonnet,
Numbers his inky fingers
Fitly to praise him;
Only we behold him,
Sitting, patient and stolid, 70
Martyr to a salary.

379.   'My house, I say. But hark to the sunny doves'

My house, I say. But hark to the sunny doves
That make my roof the arena of their loves,
That gyre about the gable all day long
And fill the chimneys with their murmurous song:
Our house, they say; and *mine,* the cat declares 5
And spreads his golden fleece upon the chairs;
And *mine* the dog, and rises stiff with wrath
If any alien foot profane the path.
So too the buck that trimmed my terraces,
Our whilome gardener, called the garden his; 10
Who now, deposed, surveys my plain abode
And his late kingdom, only from the road.

(1887)

380.   *Browning*

Browning makes the verses:
    Your servant the critique.
Browning wouldn't sing at all:
    I fancy I could speak.
Although the book was clever 5
    (To give the Deil his due)
I wasn't pleased with Browning
    Nor he with my review.

(wr. 1875?; pub. 1915)

381.   'So live, so love, so use that fragile hour'

So live, so love, so use that fragile hour,
That when the dark hand of the shining power
Shall one from other, wife or husband, take,
The poor survivor may not weep and wake.

(wr. *c*.1885; pub. 1916)

from *A Child's Garden of Verses*

382.   VI. *Block City*

What are you able to build with your blocks?
Castles and palaces, temples and docks.
Rain may keep raining, and others go roam,
But I can be happy and building at home.

Let the sofa be mountains, the carpet be sea,   5
There I'll establish a city for me:
A kirk and a mill and a palace beside,
And a harbour as well where my vessels may ride.

Great is the palace with pillar and wall,
A sort of a tower on the top of it all,   10
And steps coming down in an orderly way
To where my toy vessels lie safe in the bay.

This one is sailing and that one is moored:
Hark to the song of the sailors on board!
And see on the steps of my palace, the kings   15
Coming and going with presents and things!

Now I have done with it, down let it go!
All in a moment the town is laid low.
Block upon block lying scattered and free,
What is there left of my town by the sea?   20

Yet as I saw it, I see it again,
The kirk and the palace, the ships and the men,
And as long as I live and where'er I may be,
I'll always remember my town by the sea.

383.   XVII. *The Land of Nod*

From breakfast on through all the day
At home among my friends I stay;
But every night I go abroad
Afar into the Land of Nod.

All by myself I have to go,   5
With none to tell me what to do—
All alone beside the streams
And up the mountain-sides of dreams.

The strangest things are there for me,
Both things to eat and things to see,   10
And many frightening sights abroad
Till morning in the Land of Nod.

Try as I like to find the way,
I never can get back by day,
Nor can remember plain and clear   15
The curious music that I hear.

384.   XVIII. *My Shadow*

I have a little shadow that goes in and out with me,
And what can be the use of him is more than I can see.
He is very, very like me from the heels up to the head;
And I see him jump before me, when I jump into my bed.

The funniest thing about him is the way he likes to grow—   5
Not at all like proper children, which is always very slow;
For he sometimes shoots up taller like an india-rubber ball,
And he sometimes gets so little that there's none of him at all.

He hasn't got a notion of how children ought to play,
And can only make a fool of me in every sort of way.   10
He stays so close beside me, he's a coward you can see;
I'd think shame to stick to nursie as that shadow sticks to me!

One morning, very early, before the sun was up,
I rose and found the shining dew on every buttercup;
But my lazy little shadow, like an arrant sleepy-head,   15
Had stayed at home behind me and was fast asleep in bed.

Elizabeth Rachel Chapman (1850–? [post 1897])

385.   *A Woman's Strength*

You ought to be stronger than I, dear,
    You, who are a man—
And yet I am stronger than you, dear,—
    Who proves it? I can.

You know how to walk upon thorns, dear,   5
    Quite placid the while;
But I, who have tenderer feet, dear,
    Can do it, and smile.

You watch the red stream as it runs, dear,
    You know whence it flows,   10
And say, 'It is only my heart's blood,'
    Or, 'Thus the world goes.'

But I, when I see my blood running,
    Exclaim with delight,
'Look, look at the beautiful colour!'   15
    I laugh at the sight.

You feel the earth opening beside you,
    You stand on the brink,
And wait with all stoical calmness,
    Preparing to sink.   20

I stretch out my arms to the chasm,
    I hug the abyss;
Its fathomless depth and its darkness,
    I hail with a kiss.

I stoop to pick flowers on the edge, dear!   25
    The people around—
Who guess it is not so with you—think
    I stand on firm ground.

Who says you are stronger than I, dear,
    You, who are a man?   30
I think I shall bear off the palm, dear,
    Gainsay it who can.

> Hold! Hold! Do not move! Do not cancel
>   The effort of years!
> My strength, do you see? if you touched me,   35
>   Might melt into tears.

(1887)

(The Revd. Canon) Hardwick Drummond Rawnsley (1851–1920)

386.   *The Jet Worker*

> Close prisoner in his narrow dusty room,
> He bends and breathes above his whirring wheel;
> The treadle murmurs sad beneath his heel,
> And sad he works his jewels of the tomb,
> Emblems of sorrow from the darkened womb   5
> Of woods on which the Deluge set its seal—
> Offerings from death to death: he needs must feel
> A little of his craft's incessant gloom.
> But, as the pewter disk to brightness runs,
> On Iris wings light shoots across the dusk,   10
> And leaps out joyous from the heart of jet.
> Lord of the Iris bow and thousand suns,
> By wheels of work, if men will only trust,
> In darkest souls Thy light and life are set.

Francis William Bourdillon (1852–1921)

387.   *The Night has a Thousand Eyes*

> The night has a thousand eyes,
>   And the day but one;
> Yet the light of the bright world dies
>   With the dying sun.

> The mind has a thousand eyes,
>   And the heart but one;
> Yet the light of a whole life dies
>   When love is done.

F. (Francis) B. (Burdett) Money-Coutts (1852–1923)

388.   *The Inquest*

> Not labour kills us; no, nor joy:
>   The incredulity and frown,
> The interference and annoy,
>   The small attritions wear us down.
>
> The little gnat-like buzzings shrill,
>   The hurdy-gurdies of the street,
> The common curses of the will–
>   These wrap the cerements round our feet.
>
> And more than all, the look askance
>   Of loving souls that cannot gauge
> The numbing touch of circumstance,
>   The heavy toll of heritage.
>
> It is not Death, but Life that slays:
>   The night less mountainously lies
> Upon our lids, than foolish day's
>   Importunate futilities!

William Renton (*fl.* 1852–post 1905)

389.   *Cloud Groupings*

I

> Those clouds at even are swollen and pieced
>   With a hundred milky paps at least;
> And wait the sun's last thirsty tremors shooting high
>   To tint them ruddier and to lip them dry.

II

Two clouds sail through the noonday space,
One fair, the other dusky in the face.
In such sweet equipoise they move,
The cloud beneath sleeps like the shadow of the cloud above.

III

Sweet are the pencillings of April skies,
Soft lashes upon closing April eyes:
Drabbled and flustered films, depending sheer
From streaky cloud, or washed on wrinkled slice
Of sandlike murk upreared to precipice.
Not such, these pointing streaks; yet not less dear;
Calm, unimpeached, while cloudlets pass and flee,
Pure silver skiffs on immemorial sea.

(1876)

390. *Moon and Candle-light*

Beneath our eaves the moonbeams play,
    Where trumps of white convolvulus
Lean out askance, and have their say
    Half to the moon and half to us.
The foam-white tassel nestles still,
    Where the taperlight has laid,
In its corner by the sill,
    A black tassel for a shade.
It has laid the shadowy clasp
    Of the high-barred baby-chair
On the milkwhite casement hasp.
    The moon clasps and holds it there
With a darker, of her own
    Milkwhite standing casement bar:
Dusky hands, thus all alone,
    Clasped in each as lovers' are.
Through the sea of mellow space,
    Where the moon and candle-light,
Taking tender heart of grace,
    Mingle hands of holy white,
The moon looks between the bars
    On the bar-flecked baby-seat,
Thinks—*She!*—to wile away the scars.

                    The taper smiles on her defeat.
                Smiles, too, a steady shadow down   25
                    Between the fore and hinder stays
                Of the moon's dais: with a frown
                    The table greets the carpet grays.
                The moon turns to hide her smile ..
                    Creep up the light two spokes of dust,   30
                Like light-streaks in a dusty aisle,
                    Beneath the chair—midway, are thrust
                On the table shade in black.
                    The taper shrugs and hums a tune,
                Two black crutches stumble back   35
                    On the wainscot to the moon.
                    ... So the shadows make a raft
                    Of the chamber gear to-night:
                Play cross-purpose fore and aft
                    By the moon and candle-light.   40

                                (1876)

391.   *The Fork of the Road*

            An utter moorland, high, and wide, and flat;
            A beaten roadway, branching out in grave distaste;
            And weather-beaten and defaced,
            Pricking its ears along the solitary waste—
            A signpost; pointing this way, pointing that.   5

                                (1876)

Herbert Edwin Clarke (1852–?)

392.   *Age*

            All the strong spells of Passion slowly breaking
                        Its chains undone;
            A troubled sleep that dreams to peaceful waking
                        A haven won.
            A fire burnt out unto the last dead ember,   5
                        Left black and cold;

A fiery August unto still September
   Yielding her gold.
A dawn serene the windy midnight over,
   The darkness past;   10
Now, with no clouds nor mists her face to own
   The Day at last.
Thou hast thy prayed-for peace, O soul, and quit
   From storm and strife;—
Now yearn for ever for the noise and riot   15
   That made thy Life.

393.   *A City Rhyme*

Under the lamps the tide flows on
Of faces haggard, and wild, and wan;
 Faces weary with toil and care,
Some that are dreaming of days that are gone,
 Some that are pallid with pleasures that were;— 5
 How they gleam in the gas-lamps' glare!

A tide of sorrow, and sin, and pain,
Flowing for ever in mist and in rain,
 Under the lamps that flicker and flash,
Like thoughts that torture a fevered brain.—   10
 The sky's tears fall with a ceaseless plash;
The wind is howling for prey in vain.—

Rain in the country!—The ground smells sweet,
And a tenderer green is upon the wheat;
 But here in the city, when rain falls fast,   15
Under the lamps, in the crowded street,
 The watcher trembles with heart aghast,
As the tide of wretchedness rushes past.

O yearning bosoms, O hearts that fail!
O women with work and with weeping pale!   20
 O men with sullen and downcast eyes!
Who start betimes as the wild wind's wail
 Sounds in your ears like an infant's cries,—
Where find ye comfort? Can aught avail?

I am a shadow that followeth 25
Such one of you, and behold he saith
  Low mournful words as he passes by;—
The name of that shadow is mighty Death;—
  I am their comforter,—even I,—
Their only comforter 'neath the sky. 30

To each broken heart, and each toil-worn breast,
I bring sweet slumber, and peace most blest;
  I come to each as a welcome friend.
Sharp of all things for the weary is best,
  And best of all sleeps the sleep without end, 35
To these who shall never on earth find rest.

Aye, ye have never that men may see
Friend or deliverer save but he;
  Of the sons of men there are none that hear.
Cry to them,—cry that they set you free;— 40
  Cry aloud,—shall they listen? shall they turn ear?
'Say! cease your crying,—it shall not be!

Annie Matheson (1853–1924)

394.   *A Song for Women*

Within a dreary narrow room
  That looks upon a noisome street,
  Half fainting with the stifling heat
A starving girl works out her doom.
    Yet not the less in God's sweet air 5
    The little birds sing free of care,
    And hawthorns blossom everywhere.

Swift ceaseless toil scarce wins her bread:
  From early dawn till twilight falls,
  Shut in by four dull ugly walls, 10
The hours crawl round with murderous tread.
    And all the while, in some still place,
    Where intertwining boughs embrace,
    The blackbirds build, time flies apace.

With envy of the folk who die,
   Who may at last their leisure take,
   Whose longed-for sleep none roughly wake,
Tired hands the restless needle ply.
    But far and wide in meadows green
    The golden buttercups are seen,
    And reddening sorrel nods between.

Too pure and proud to soil her soul,
   Or stoop to basely gotten gain,
   By days of changeless want and pain
The seamstress earns a prisoner's dole.
    While in the peaceful fields the sheep
    Feed, quiet; and through heaven's blue deep
    The silent cloud-wings stainless sweep.

And if she be alive or dead
   That weary woman scarcely knows,
   But back and forth her needle goes
In tune with throbbing heart and head.
    Lo, where the leaning alders part,
    White-bosomed swallows, blithe of heart,
    Above still waters skim and dart.

O God in heaven! shall I, who share
   That dying woman's womanhood,
   Taste all the summer's bounteous good
Unburdened by her weight of care?
    The white moon-daisies star the grass,
    The lengthening shadows o'er them pass:
    The meadow pool is smooth as glass.

(1890)

Oscar (Fingal O'Flahertie Wills) Wilde (1854–1900)

395. *Poems in Prose: The Artist*

One evening there came into his soul the desire to fashion an image of *The Pleasure that abideth for a Moment*. And he went forth into the world to look for bronze. For he could only think in bronze.

But all the bronze of the whole world had disappeared, nor anywhere in the whole world was there any bronze to be found, save only the bronze of the image of *The Sorrow that endureth for Ever*.

Now this image he had himself, and with his own hands, fashioned, and had set it on the tomb of the one thing he had loved in life. On the tomb of the dead thing he had most loved had he set this image of his own fashioning, that it might serve as a sign of the love of man that dieth not, and a symbol of the sorrow of man that endureth for ever. And in the whole world there was no other bronze save the bronze of this image.

And he took the image he had fashioned, and set it in a great furnace, and gave it to the fire.

And out of the bronze of the image of *The Sorrow that endureth for Ever* he fashioned an image of *The Pleasure that abideth for a Moment*.

396. *On the Sale by Auction of Keats' Love Letters*

    These are the letters which Endymion wrote
        To one he loved in secret, and apart.
        And now the brawlers of the auction mart
    Bargain and bid for each poor blotted note,
    Ay! for each separate pulse of passion quote   5
        The merchant's price. I think they love not art
        Who break the crystal of a poet's heart
    That small and sickly eyes may glare and gloat.

    Is it not said that many years ago,
        In a far Eastern town, some soldiers ran   10
        With torches through the midnight, and began
    To wrangle for mean raiment, and to throw
        Dice for the garments of a wretched man,
    Not knowing the God's wonder, or His woe?

(1886)

397.   *Symphony in Yellow*

An omnibus across the bridge
  Crawls like a yellow butterfly,
  And, here and there, a passer-by
Shows like a little restless midge.

Big barges full of yellow hay   5
  Are moved against the shadowy wharf,
  And, like a yellow silken scarf,
The thick fog hangs along the quay.

The yellow leaves begin to fade
  And flutter from the Temple elms,   10
  And at my feet the pale green Thames
Lies like a rod of rippled jade.

              from *Fantaisies décoratives*

398.   II. *Les Ballons*

Against these turbid turquoise skies
  The light and luminous balloons
  Dip and drift like satin moons,
Drift like silken butterflies;

Reel with every windy gust,   5
  Rise and reel like dancing girls,
  Float like strange transparent pearls,
Fall and float like silver dust.

Now to the low leaves they cling,
  Each with coy fantastic pose,   10
  Each a petal of a rose
Straining at a gossamer string.

Then to the tall trees they climb,
  Like thin globes of amethyst,
  Wandering opals keeping tryst   15
With the rubies of the lime.

399.   *The Harlot's House*

           We caught the tread of dancing feet,
           We loitered down the moonlit street,
           And stopped beneath the harlot's house.

           Inside, above the din and fray,
           We heard the loud musicians play
           The 'Treues Liebes Herz' of Strauss.

           Like strange mechanical grotesques,
           Making fantastic arabesques,
           The shadows raced across the blind.

           We watched the ghostly dancers spin
           To sound of horn and violin,
           Like black leaves wheeling in the wind.

           Like wire-pulled automatons,
           Slim silhouetted skeletons
           Went sidling through the slow quadrille.

           They took each other by the hand,
           And danced a stately saraband;
           Their laughter echoed thin and shrill.

           Sometimes a clockwork puppet pressed
           A phantom lover to her breast,
           Sometimes they seemed to try to sing.

           Sometimes a horrible marionette
           Came out, and smoked its cigarette
           Upon the steps like a live thing.

           Then, turning to my love, I said,
           'The dead are dancing with the dead,
           The dust is whirling with the dust.'

           But she—she heard the violin,
           And left my side, and entered in:
           Love passed into the house of lust.

           Then suddenly the tune went false,
           The dancers wearied of the waltz,
           The shadows ceased to wheel and whirl.

And down the long and silent street,
The dawn, with silver-sandalled feet,
Crept like a frightened girl.

400.   *The Ballad of Reading Gaol*

I

He did not wear his scarlet coat,
   For blood and wine are red,
And blood and wine were on his hands
   When they found him with the dead,
The poor dead woman whom he loved,
   And murdered in her bed.

He walked amongst the Trial Men
   In a suit of shabby gray;
A cricket cap was on his head,
   And his step seemed light and gay;
But I never saw a man who looked
   So wistfully at the day.

I never saw a man who looked
   With such a wistful eye
Upon that little tent of blue
   Which prisoners call the sky,
And at every drifting cloud that went
   With sails of silver by.

I walked, with other souls in pain,
   Within another ring,
And was wondering if the man had done
   A great or little thing,
When a voice behind me whispered low,
   '*That fellow's got to swing.*'

Dear Christ! the very prison walls
   Suddenly seemed to reel,
And the sky above my head became
   Like a casque of scorching steel;
And, though I was a soul in pain,
   My pain I could not feel.

I only knew what hunted thought
    Quickened his step, and why
He looked upon the garish day
    With such a wistful eye;
The man had killed the thing he loved,　　　　　　　　　35
    And so he had to die.

Yet each man kills the thing he loves,
    By each let this be heard,
Some do it with a bitter look,
    Some with a flattering word,　　　　　　　　　　　40
The coward does it with a kiss,
    The brave man with a sword!

Some kill their love when they are young,
    And some when they are old;
Some strangle with the hands of Lust,　　　　　　　　45
    Some with the hands of Gold:
The kindest use a knife, because
    The dead so soon grow cold.

Some love too little, some too long,
    Some sell, and others buy;　　　　　　　　　　　　50
Some do the deed with many tears,
    And some without a sigh:
For each man kills the thing he loves,
    Yet each man does not die.

He does not die a death of shame　　　　　　　　　　55
    On a day of dark disgrace,
Nor have a noose about his neck,
    Nor a cloth upon his face,
Nor drop feet foremost through the floor
    Into an empty space.　　　　　　　　　　　　　　60

He does not sit with silent men
    Who watch him night and day;
Who watch him when he tries to weep,
    And when he tries to pray;
Who watch him lest himself should rob　　　　　　　65
    The prison of its prey.

He does not wake at dawn to see
    Dread figures throng his room,
The shivering Chaplain robed in white,
    The Sheriff stern with gloom,　　　　　　　　　　70

And the Governor all in shiny black,
    With the yellow face of Doom.

He does not rise in piteous haste
    To put on convict-clothes,
While some coarse-mouthed Doctor gloats, and notes
    Each new and nerve-twitched pose,
Fingering a watch whose little ticks
    Are like horrible hammer-blows.

He does not know that sickening thirst
    That sands one's throat, before
The hangman with his gardener's gloves
    Slips through the padded door,
And binds one with three leathern thongs,
    That the throat may thirst no more.

He does not bend his head to hear
    The Burial Office read,
Nor, while the terror of his soul
    Tells him he is not dead,
Cross his own coffin, as he moves
    Into the hideous shed.

He does not stare upon the air
    Through a little roof of glass:
He does not pray with lips of clay
    For his agony to pass;
Nor feel upon his shuddering cheek
    The kiss of Caiaphas.

II

Six weeks our guardsman walked the yard,
    In the suit of shabby grey:
His cricket cap was on his head,
    And his step seemed light and gay,
But I never saw a man who looked
    So wistfully at the day.

I never saw a man who looked
    With such a wistful eye
Upon that little tent of blue
    Which prisoners call the sky,
And at every wandering cloud that trailed
    Its ravelled fleeces by.

He did not wring his hands, as do
    Those witless men who dare
To try to rear the changeling Hope
    In the cave of black Despair:
He only looked upon the sun,
    And drank the morning air.

He did not wring his hands nor weep,
    Nor did he peek or pine,
But he drank the air as though it held
    Some healthful anodyne;
With open mouth he drank the sun
    As though it had been wine!

And I and all the souls in pain,
    Who tramped the other ring,
Forgot if we ourselves had done
    A great or little thing,
And watched with gaze of dull amaze
    The man who had to swing.

And strange it was to see him pass
    With a step so light and gay,
And strange it was to see him look
    So wistfully at the day,
And strange it was to think that he
    Had such a debt to pay.

   .   .   .   .   .

For oak and elm have pleasant leaves
    That in the spring-time shoot:
But grim to see is the gallows-tree,
    With its adder-bitten root,
And, green or dry, a man must die
    Before it bears its fruit!

The loftiest place is that seat of grace
    For which all worldlings try:
But who would stand in hempen band
    Upon a scaffold high,
And through a murderer's collar take
    His last look at the sky?

It is sweet to dance to violins
    When Love and Life are fair:
To dance to flutes, to dance to lutes
    Is delicate and rare:
But it is not sweet with nimble feet
    To dance upon the air!

So with curious eyes and sick surmise
    We watched him day by day,
And wondered if each one of us
    Would end the self-same way,
For none can tell to what red Hell
    His sightless soul may stray.

At last the dead man walked no more
    Amongst the Trial Men,
And I knew that he was standing up
    In the black dock's dreadful pen,
And that never would I see his face
    In God's sweet world again.

Like two doomed ships that pass in storm
    We had crossed each other's way:
But we made no sign, we said no word,
    We had no word to say;
For we did not meet in the holy night,
    But in the shameful day.

A prison wall was round us both,
    Two outcast men we were:
The world had thrust us from its heart,
    And God from out His care:
And the iron gin that waits for Sin
    Had caught us in its snare.

III

In Debtors' Yard the stones are hard,
    And the dripping wall is high,
So it was there he took the air
    Beneath the leaden sky,
And by each side a Warder walked,
    For fear the man might die.

Or else he sat with those who watched
    His anguish night and day;
Who watched him when he rose to weep,
    And when he crouched to pray;
Who watched him lest himself should rob   185
    Their scaffold of its prey.

The Governor was strong upon
    The Regulations Act:
The Doctor said that Death was but
    A scientific fact: 190
And twice a day the Chaplain called,
    And left a little tract.

And twice a day he smoked his pipe,
    And drank his quart of beer:
His soul was resolute, and held   195
    No hiding-place for fear;
He often said that he was glad
    The hangman's hands were near.

But why he said so strange a thing
    No Warder dared to ask: 200
For he to whom a watcher's doom
    Is given as his task,
Must set a lock upon his lips,
    And make his face a mask.

Or else he might be moved, and try   205
    To comfort or console:
And what should Human Pity do
    Pent up in Murderers' Hole?
What word of grace in such a place
    Could help a brother's soul?   210

.   .   .   .   .

With slouch and swing around the ring
    We trod the Fools' Parade!
We did not care: we knew we were
    The Devil's Own Brigade:
And shaven head and feet of lead   215
    Make a merry masquerade.

We tore the tarry rope to shreds
  With blunt and bleeding nails;
We rubbed the doors, and scrubbed the floors,
  And cleaned the shining rails:
And, rank by rank, we soaped the plank,
  And clattered with the pails.

We sewed the sacks, we broke the stones,
  We turned the dusty drill:
We banged the tins, and bawled the hymns,
  And sweated on the mill:
But in the heart of every man
  Terror was lying still.

So still it lay that every day
  Crawled like a weed-clogged wave:
And we forgot the bitter lot
  That waits for fool and knave,
Till once, as we tramped in from work,
  We passed an open grave.

With yawning mouth the yellow hole
  Gaped for a living thing;
The very mud cried out for blood
  To the thirsty asphalte ring:
And we knew that ere one dawn grew fair
  Some prisoner had to swing.

Right in we went, with soul intent
  On Death and Dread and Doom:
The hangman, with his little bag,
  Went shuffling through the gloom:
And each man trembled as he crept
  Into his numbered tomb.

     .   .   .   .   .

That night the empty corridors
  Were full of forms of Fear,
And up and down the iron town
  Stole feet we could not hear,
And through the bars that hide the stars
  White faces seemed to peer.

He lay as one who lies and dreams
    In a pleasant meadow-land,
The watchers watched him as he slept,
    And could not understand
How one could sleep so sweet a sleep
    With a hangman close at hand.

But there is no sleep when men must weep
    Who never yet have wept:
So we—the fool, the fraud, the knave—
    That endless vigil kept,
And through each brain on hands of pain
    Another's terror crept.

Alas! it is a fearful thing
    To feel another's guilt!
For, right within, the sword of Sin
    Pierced to its poisoned hilt,
And as molten lead were the tears we shed
    For the blood we had not spilt.

The Warders with their shoes of felt
    Crept by each padlocked door,
And peeped and saw, with eyes of awe,
    Grey figures on the floor,
And wondered why men knelt to pray
    Who never prayed before.

All through the night we knelt and prayed,
    Mad mourners of a corse!
The troubled plumes of midnight were
    The plumes upon a hearse:
And bitter wine upon a sponge
    Was the savour of Remorse.

         .   .   .   .   .

The grey cock crew, the red cock crew,
    But never came the day:
And crooked shapes of Terror crouched,
    In the corners where we lay:
And each evil sprite that walks by night
    Before us seemed to play.

They glided past, they glided fast,
    Like travellers through a mist:
They mocked the moon in a rigadoon
    Of delicate turn and twist,
And with formal pace and loathsome grace
    The phantoms kept their tryst.

With mop and mow, we saw them go,
    Slim shadows hand in hand:
About, about, in ghostly rout
    They trod a saraband:
And the damned grotesques made arabesques,
    Like the wind upon the sand!

With the pirouettes of marionettes,
    They tripped on pointed tread:
But with flutes of Fear they filled the ear,
    As their grisly masque they led,
And loud they sang, and long they sang,
    For they sang to wake the dead.

'Oho!' they cried, *'The world is wide,*
    But fettered limbs go lame!
And once, or twice, to throw the dice
    Is a gentlemanly game,
But he does not win who plays with Sin
    In the secret House of Shame.'

No things of air these antics were,
    That frolicked with such glee:
To men whose lives were held in gyves,
    And whose feet might not go free,
Ah! wounds of Christ! they were living things,
    Most terrible to see.

Around, around, they waltzed and wound;
    Some wheeled in smirking pairs;
With the mincing step of a demirep
    Some sidled up the stairs:
And with subtle sneer, and fawning leer,
    Each helped us at our prayers.

The morning wind began to moan,
    But still the night went on:
Through its giant loom the web of gloom
    Crept till each thread was spun:

And, as we prayed, we grew afraid
    Of the Justice of the Sun.   330

The moaning wind went wandering round
    The weeping prison-wall:
Till like a wheel of turning steel
    We felt the minutes crawl:
O moaning wind! what had we done   335
    To have such a seneschal?

At last I saw the shadowed bars,
    Like a lattice wrought in lead,
Move right across the whitewashed wall
    That faced my three-plank bed,   340
And I knew that somewhere in the world
    God's dreadful dawn was red.

At six o'clock we cleaned our cells,
    At seven all was still,
But the sough and swing of a mighty wing   345
    The prison seemed to fill,
For the Lord of Death with icy breath
    Had entered in to kill.

He did not pass in purple pomp,
    Nor ride a moon-white steed.   350
Three yards of cord and a sliding board
    Are all the gallows' need:
So with rope of shame the Herald came
    To do the secret deed.

We were as men who through a fen   355
    Of filthy darkness grope:
We did not dare to breathe a prayer,
    Or to give our anguish scope:
Something was dead in each of us,
    And what was dead was Hope.   360

For Man's grim Justice goes its way,
    And will not swerve aside:
It slays the weak, it slays the strong,
    It has a deadly stride:
With iron heel it slays the strong,   365
    The monstrous parricide!

We waited for the stroke of eight:
   Each tongue was thick with thirst:
For the stroke of eight is the stroke of Fate
   That makes a man accursed,   370
And Fate will use a running noose
   For the best man and the worst.

We had no other thing to do,
   Save to wait for the sign to come:
So, like things of stone in a valley lone,   375
   Quiet we sat and dumb:
But each man's heart beat thick and quick,
   Like a madman on a drum!

With sudden shock the prison-clock
   Smote on the shivering air,   380
And from all the gaol rose up a wail
   Of impotent despair,
Like the sound that frightened marshes hear
   From some leper in his lair.

And as one sees most fearful things   385
   In the crystal of a dream,
We saw the greasy hempen rope
   Hooked to the blackened beam,
And heard the prayer the hangman's snare
   Strangled into a scream.   390

And all the woe that moved him so
   That he gave that bitter cry,
And the wild regrets, and the bloody sweats,
   None knew so well as I:
For he who lives more lives than one   395
   More deaths than one must die.

IV

There is no chapel on the day
   On which they hang a man:
The Chaplain's heart is far too sick,
   Or his face is far too wan,   400
Or there is that written in his eyes
   Which none should look upon.

So they kept us close till nigh on noon,
   And then they rang the bell,
And the Warders with their jingling keys
   Opened each listening cell,
And down the iron stair we tramped,
   Each from his separate Hell.

Out into God's sweet air we went,
   But not in wonted way,
For this man's face was white with fear,
   And that man's face was grey,
And I never saw sad men who looked
   So wistfully at the day.

I never saw sad men who looked
   With such a wistful eye
Upon that little tent of blue
   We prisoners called the sky,
And at every careless cloud that passed
   In happy freedom by.

But there were those amongst us all
   Who walked with downcast head,
And knew that, had each got his due,
   They should have died instead:
He had but killed a thing that lived,
   Whilst they had killed the dead.

For he who sins a second time
   Wakes a dead soul to pain,
And draws it from its spotted shroud,
   And makes it bleed again,
And makes it bleed great gouts of blood,
   And makes it bleed in vain!

   .   .   .   .   .

Like ape or clown, in monstrous garb
   With crooked arrows starred,
Silently we went round and round,
   The slippery asphalte yard;
Silently we went round and round
   And no man spoke a word.

Silently we went round and round,
    And through each hollow mind
The Memory of dreadful things
    Rushed like a dreadful wind,
And Horror stalked before each man,
    And Terror crept behind.

    .   .   .   .   .

The Warders strutted up and down,
    And kept their herd of brutes,
Their uniforms were spick and span,
    And they wore their Sunday suits,
But we knew the work they had been at,
    By the quicklime on their boots.

For where a grave had opened wide,
    There was no grave at all:
Only a stretch of mud and sand
    By the hideous prison-wall,
And a little heap of burning lime,
    That the man should have his pall.

For he has a pall, this wretched man,
    Such as few men can claim:
Deep down below a prison-yard,
    Naked for greater shame,
He lies, with fetters on each foot,
    Wrapt in a sheet of flame!

And all the while the burning lime
    Eats flesh and bone away,
It eats the brittle bone by night,
    And the soft flesh by day,
It eats the flesh and bone by turns,
    But it eats the heart alway.

    .   .   .   .   .

For three long years they will not sow
    Or root or seedling there:
For three long years the unblessed spot
    Will sterile be and bare,
And look upon the wondering sky
    With unreproachful stare.

They think a murderer's heart would taint
    Each simple seed they sow.
It is not true! God's kindly earth
    Is kindlier than men know,
And the red rose would but blow more red,
    The white rose whiter blow.

Out of his mouth a red, red rose!
    Out of his heart a white!
For who can say by what strange way,
    Christ brings His will to light,
Since the barren staff the pilgrim bore
    Bloomed in the great Pope's sight?

But neither milk-white rose nor red
    May bloom in prison air;
The shard, the pebble, and the flint,
    Are what they give us there:
For flowers have been known to heal
    A common man's despair.

So never will wine-red rose or white,
    Petal by petal, fall
On that stretch of mud and sand that lies
    By the hideous prison-wall,
To tell the men who tramp the yard
    That God's Son died for all.

  .   .   .   .   .

Yet though the hideous prison-wall
    Still hems him round and round,
And a spirit may not walk by night
    That is with fetters bound,
And a spirit may but weep that lies
    In such unholy ground,

He is at peace—this wretched man—
    At peace, or will be soon:
There is no thing to make him mad,
    Nor does Terror walk at noon,
For the lampless Earth in which he lies
    Has neither Sun nor Moon.

They hanged him as a beast is hanged:
    They did not even toll
A requiem that might have brought
    Rest to his startled soul,
But hurriedly they took him out,　　　　　　　　　　　　515
    And hid him in a hole.

They stripped him of his canvas clothes,
    And gave him to the flies:
They mocked the swollen purple throat,
    And the stark and staring eyes:　　　　　　　　　　520
And with laughter loud they heaped the shroud
    In which their convict lies.

The Chaplain would not kneel to pray
    By his dishonoured grave:
Nor mark it with that blessed Cross　　　　　　　　　525
    That Christ for sinners gave,
Because the man was one of those
    Whom Christ came down to save.

Yet all is well; he has but passed
    To life's appointed bourne:　　　　　　　　　　　　530
And alien tears will fill for him
    Pity's long-broken urn,
For his mourners will be outcast men,
    And outcasts always mourn.

V

I know not whether Laws be right,　　　　　　　　　535
    Or whether Laws be wrong;
All that we know who lie in gaol
    Is that the wall is strong;
And that each day is like a year,
    A year whose days are long.　　　　　　　　　　　540

But this I know, that every Law
    That men have made for Man,
Since first Man took his brother's life,
    And the sad world began,
But straws the wheat and saves the chaff　　　　　　545
    With a most evil fan.

This too I know—and wise it were
    If each could know the same—
That every prison that men build
    Is built with bricks of shame,   550
And bound with bars lest Christ should see
    How men their brothers maim.

With bars they blur the gracious moon,
    And blind the goodly sun:
And they do well to hide their Hell,   555
    For in it things are done
That Son of God nor son of Man
    Ever should look upon!

    .   .   .   .   .

The vilest deeds like poison weeds,
    Bloom well in prison-air;   560
It is only what is good in Man
    That wastes and withers there:
Pale Anguish keeps the heavy gate,
    And the Warder is Despair.

For they starve the little frightened child   565
    Till it weeps both night and day:
And they scourge the weak, and flog the fool,
    And gibe the old and grey,
And some grow mad, and all grow bad,
    And none a word may say.   570

Each narrow cell in which we dwell
    Is a foul and dark latrine,
And the fetid breath of living Death
    Chokes up each grated screen,
And all, but Lust, is turned to dust   575
    In Humanity's machine.

The brackish water that we drink
    Creeps with a loathsome slime,
And the bitter bread they weigh in scales
    Is full of chalk and lime,   580
And Sleep will not lie down, but walks
    Wild-eyed, and cries to Time.

    .   .   .   .   .

But though lean Hunger and green Thirst
    Like asp with adder fight,
We have little care of prison fare,
    For what chills and kills outright
Is that every stone one lifts by day
    Becomes one's heart by night.

With midnight always in one's heart,
    And twilight in one's cell,
We turn the crank, or tear the rope,
    Each in his separate Hell,
And the silence is more awful far
    Than the sound of a brazen bell.

And never a human voice comes near
    To speak a gentle word:
And the eye that watches through the door
    Is pitiless and hard:
And by all forgot, we rot and rot,
    With soul and body marred.

And thus we rust Life's iron chain
    Degraded and alone:
And some men curse, and some men weep,
    And some men make no moan:
But God's eternal Laws are kind
    And break the heart of stone.

    .   .   .   .   .   .

And every human heart that breaks,
    In prison-cell or yard,
Is as that broken box that gave
    Its treasure to the Lord,
And filled the unclean leper's house
    With the scent of costliest nard.

Ah! happy they whose hearts can break
    And peace of pardon win!
How else may man make straight his plan
    And cleanse his soul from Sin?
How else but through a broken heart
    May Lord Christ enter in?

    .   .   .   .   .   .

And he of the swollen purple throat,
    And the stark and staring eyes,
Waits for the holy hands that took
    The Thief to Paradise;
And a broken and a contrite heart
    The Lord will not despise.

The man in red who reads the Law
    Gave him three weeks of life,
Three little weeks in which to heal
    His soul of his soul's strife,
And cleanse from every blot of blood
    The hand that held the knife.

And with tears of blood he cleansed the hand,
    The hand that held the steel:
For only blood can wipe out blood,
    And only tears can heal:
And the crimson stain that was of Cain
    Became Christ's snow-white seal.

VI

In Reading gaol by Reading town
    There is a pit of shame,
And in it lies a wretched man
    Eaten by teeth of flame,
In a burning winding-sheet he lies,
    And his grave has got no name.

And there, till Christ call forth the dead,
    In silence let him lie:
No need to waste the foolish tear,
    Or heave the windy sigh:
The man had killed the thing he loved,
    And so he had to die.

And all men kill the thing they love,
    By all let this be heard,
Some do it with a bitter look,
    Some with a flattering word,
The coward does it with a kiss,
    The brave man with a sword!

401.   *Requiescat*

    Tread lightly, she is near
        Under the snow,
    Speak gently, she can hear
        The daisies grow.

    All her bright golden hair   5
        Tarnished with rust,
    She that was young and fair
        Fallen to dust.

    Lily-like, white as snow,
        She hardly knew   10
    She was a woman, so
        Sweetly she grew.

    Coffin-board, heavy stone,
        Lie on her breast,
    I vex my heart alone,   15
        She is at rest.

    Peace, Peace, she cannot hear
        Lyre or sonnet,
    All my life's buried here,
        Heap earth upon it.   20

          Avignon.

Fiona MacLeod (William Sharp) (1855–1905)

402.   *Lullaby*

Lennavan-mo,
Lennavan-mo,
Who is it swinging you to and fro,
With a long low swing and a sweet low croon,
And the loving words of the mother's rune?   5

Lennavan-mo,
Lennavan-mo,
Who is it swinging you to and fro?
I am thinking it is an angel fair,
The Angel that looks on the gulf from the lowest stair
And swings the green world upward by its leagues of sunshine hair.

Lennavan-mo,
Lennavan-mo,
Who swingeth you and the Angel to and fro?
It is He whose faintest thought is a world afar,
It is He whose wish is a leaping seven-moon'd star,
It is He, Lennavan-mo,
To whom you and I and all things flow.

Lennavan-mo,
Lennavan-mo,
It is only a little wee lass you are, Eilidh-mo-chree,
But as this wee blossom has roots in the depths of the sky,
So you are at one with the Lord of Eternity—
Bonnie wee lass that you are,
My morning-star,
Eilidh-mo-chree, Lennavan-mo,
    Lennavan-mo.

403. *Prayer of Women*

O Spirit that broods upon the hills
And moves upon the face of the deep,
And is heard in the wind,
Save us from the desire of men's eyes,
And the cruel lust of them.
Save us from the springing of the cruel seed
In that narrow house which is as the grave
For darkness and loneliness ...
That women carry with them with shame, and weariness, and long pain,
Only for the laughter of man's heart,
And for the joy that triumphs therein,
And the sport that is in his heart,
Wherewith he mocketh us,
Wherewith he playeth with us,
Wherewith he trampleth upon us ...
Us, who conceive and bear him;

Us, who bring him forth;
Who feed him in the womb, and at the breast, and at the knee:
Whom he calleth mother and wife,
And mother again of his children and his children's children.   20
Ah, hour of the hours,
When he looks at our hair and sees it is grey;
And at our eyes and sees they are dim;
And at our lips straightened out with long pain;
And at our breasts, fallen and seared as a barren hill;   25
And at our hands, worn with toil!
Ah, hour of the hours,
When, seeing, he seeth all the bitter ruin and wreck of us—
All save the violated womb that curses him—
All save the heart that forbeareth ... for pity—   30
All save the living brain that condemneth him—
All save the spirit that shall not mate with him—
All save the soul he shall never see
Till he be one with it, and equal;
He who hath the bridle, but guideth not;   35
He who hath the whip, yet is driven;
He who as a shepherd calleth upon us,
But is himself a lost sheep, crying among the hills!
O Spirit, and the Nine Angels who watch us,
And Thy Son, and Mary Virgin,   40
Heal us of the wrong of man:
We whose breasts are weary with milk,
Cry, cry to Thee, O Compassionate!

(Juliana Mary Louisa) May Probyn (1856–1909)

404.   *Changes*

> Only a cottage border,
>   And a scent of mignonette,
> And beans and peas in order,
>   And a row of beehives set.
> A pipkin and a platter   5
>   Laid out for an evening meal;
> A cage, and a magpie's chatter,
>   And the whirr of a spinning wheel.
> Only a woman hearkening

>   For a step along the lane—
> A shadow the doorway darkening—
>   A kiss and a kiss again.
>
>   *   *   *
>
> Only a church bell tolling,
>   And a funeral winding slow,
> And a sound of earth-sods rolling
>   On a coffin-lid below.
> Only the grass grown wavy
>   On a grave, where the swallows flit—
> And a cradle, and a baby,
>   And no mother rocking it.

10

15

20

Margaret L. (Louisa) (Bradley) Woods (1856–1945)

from *Aeromancy*

405.   VI. 'I hear the incantation of the bells'

> I hear the incantation of the bells,
> And since that Hour made me her neophyte,
> I know what occult power within them dwells
> To mock at Time's inviolable might.
>
> A power to make invisible things seen,
> And tumult calm and morning in dull night,
> To set the day with stars, and like a screen
>
> Rolled back, the curtain of a peopled stage,
> Uplift a tenuous moment's painted scene
> From Life's loud pageant and mute pilgrimage.

5

10

(1896)

Eliza Keary (1857–1882)

406.   *Doctor Emily*

Her room, bare of all beauty.
She in the gloom of the dull hour,
Midwinter's afternoon,
By the fire, grey and low,
Left of her hours ago,   5
Now with a little glow
And new stir in it just made by her,
Weary, come in alone,
Musing, "Did I ever wince
At sorrow, or pain of my profession, the parish doctor,   10
Chosen eleven years since,
As now? Though there has been torture enough, I trow,
Only a word or two just heard
Have set my heart throbbing so—
Can it rest again?   15
Matched with this, it was scarcely pain
That I felt by the dying man yonder,
All agony of sympathy,
As I watched the cruel death-blow
Dealt, long gathered up of want, sin, and woe.   20
It was thus I heard—walking
From the blank house with friends, talking
Of this sorrow and of some
Hope, might we cherish, in the long years to come,
When sin and pain,   25
Bound with health's chain,
Not even one should lie
Shut up in misery:
I still continually
Shadowed by *his* last sigh,   30
As we spoke;
One, silent till then alone, broke
On our converse: "Friend,
You are over sad, we must embrace the whole, the end
Each serves, *must* serve, purpose   35
Better or worse. Are not all
Fitted in due places they cannot fall
From, glory or shame,
Fulness of pleasure, inextinguishable flame?

All cannot win, 40
Or the *same* goal reach,
Since some by virtue, some by vice teach,
But why quail at each miserable wail,
And yet forget the praise
That from endless days 45
Swells through the universe?
Let the curse lie
In its own place—needed, verily.
Whereat we,
Chilled through our very pain as to death, 50
"Not that *He* wills it," cry,
"Say 'tis not that you mean."
And gasped for his reply,
This that came pityingly, "He!
Him I know not, but the things that be." 55

Chilled as to death whilst here alone
I ponder, ah! and he is not one
Saying thus we know, nor are they few;
And these are they we love,
Towards whom our hopes move, 60
With whom we would prove
That we can friendly seek, and sympathize, and do;
These, who, whate'er betide,
We find, all tested, still on the generous side,
Who reach strong hands 65
Of help and kindliness to brother lands,
Would shatter lawless might,
Who claim us, all, for right in the name of right.
What small cloud in their fair, deep sky do we see?
"Him, one I know not, but the things that be." 70
One in the hidden, in the finite
Lost, loss infinite.
Seek we the True that we dare,
They say, we dare face, be it foul, be it fair?
It, not *He*, then. Has it a heart, this, the True? 75
Faithless and hopeless; must we be loveless too?

But 'tis the age of woman, they say,
All say it, of her full message,
Presage of good, do we deem? Ah! blind,
Weak, awe-stricken, what do we strive 80
For? All that we *are* to *give*.
Are we a message to this scorching age

Whilst our tears rain upon it?
Want and woe and sin,
Searching that cannot find—　　　　　　　　　　　　　85
Would that we could win
Some influence from the skies!
Was not Christ born of Mary for mankind?
Alas! our eyes are dim,
Pining for Him.　　　　　　　　　　　　　　　　90
Lo! we are broken with fears
Lest *One* belied,
Love should be crucified
Through countless years.

Must they not see that seek　　　　　　　　　　　　95
Then? Can there be aught
Empty of Him, forgot,
Or does His promise break?
Some approach there must be.
And we, shall we　　　　　　　　　　　　　　　100
Who, fearfully, think
That we feel Him, tremble on His brink,
Have such fear of a deep
As to be prisoned in pain lest loved feet graze the steep?
Can light quench light?　　　　　　　　　　　　105
May not the near the far?
Obscure our vision of it—
Nay, He is far and near,
Yea, who is more than light.
Can He fail? we will not fear.　　　　　　　　　　110

Seek on, then, spurn
Giants of thought, old thoughts, turn
Still to new days. Hew
The immense tree with the strong axes two,
Even as visions of old　　　　　　　　　　　　　115
Tell how the giants hewed:
And lo! it fell, and lo! it stood, and lo! it grew.
Watching the while, we
Smile of sorrow and hope,
Saying God speed,　　　　　　　　　　　　　　120
As loved faiths stricken from life
Thicken around us, darkening our skies,
Praying God speed,
Till the new dawn arise.
Yet we are home-birds, we must sing from home, place　　125

Of sure refuge for our faltering race,
Low from the yearning of the Father's breast,
Wooing you hitherward,
Where love is Lord.
Children, come home, we seek His face;   130
When will ye come?
Home—not for rest—
Measureless labour, 'tensest sacrifice,
Price of the very life—"

So, musing this wise   135
With tears and sighs,
Into the night, till night had set,
Watching her, musing yet,
When "Doctor" a voice cries
From without, a weak child's voice, "come quick,   140
Come to us, sister. Mother fell sick
At noon, and she dies in the dawn alone."
She, "Ready, I am ready,
I am coming, little one."

407.   *Old Age*

    Such a wizened creature,
      Sitting alone;
      Every kind of ugliness thrown
    Into each feature.

    "I wasn't always so,"   5
      Said the wizened
      One; "sweet motions unimprisoned
    Were mine long ago."

    And again, "I shall be—
      At least something
      Out of this outside me, shall wing   10
    Itself fair and free."

John Davidson (1857–1909)

408.
London

Athwart the sky a lowly sigh
   From west to east the sweet wind carried;
The sun stood still on Primrose Hill;
   His light in all the city tarried:
The clouds on viewless columns bloomed
Like smouldering lilies unconsumed.

"Oh sweetheart, see! how shadowy,
   Of some occult magician's rearing,
Or swung in space of heaven's grace
   Dissolving, dimly reappearing,
Afloat upon ethereal tides
St. Paul's above the city rides!"

A rumour broke through the thin smoke
   Enwreathing abbey, tower, and palace,
The parks, the squares, the thoroughfares,
   The million-peopled lanes and alleys,
An ever-muttering prisoned storm,
The heart of London beating warm.

409.
Piper, Play!

Now the furnaces are out,
   And the aching anvils sleep;
Down the road the grimy rout
   Tramples homeward twenty deep.
      Piper, play! Piper, play!
         Though we be o'erlaboured men,
      Ripe for rest, pipe your best!
         Let us foot it once again!

Bridled looms delay their din;
   All the humming wheels are spent;
Busy spindles cease to spin;
   Warp and woof must rest content.

Piper, play! Piper, play!
    For a little we are free!
  Foot it girls and shake your curls,
    Haggard creatures though we be!

Racked and soiled the faded air
  Freshens in our holiday;
Clouds and tides our respite share;
  Breezes linger by the way.
    Piper, rest! Piper, rest!
      Now, a carol of the moon!
    Piper, piper, play your best!
      Melt the sun into your tune!

We are of the humblest grade;
  Yet we dare to dance our fill:
Male and female were we made—
  Fathers, mothers, lovers still!
    Piper—softly; soft and low;
      Pipe of love in mellow notes,
    Till the tears begin to flow,
      And our hearts are in our throats.

Nameless as the stars of night
  Far in galaxies unfurled,
Yet we wield unrivalled might,
  Joints and hinges of the world!
    Night and day! Night and day!
      Sound the song the hours rehearse!
    Work and play! Work and play!
      The order of the universe!

Now the furnaces are out,
  And the aching anvils sleep;
Down the road a merry rout
  Dances homeward, twenty deep.
    Piper, play! Piper, play!
      Wearied people though we be,
    Ripe for rest, pipe your best!
      For a little we are free!

410.   *Serenade*

                        (1250 A.D.)

With stars, with trailing galaxies,
    Like a white-rose bower in bloom,
Darkness garlands the vaulted skies,
    Day's ethereal tomb;
A whisper without from the briny west   5
    Thrills and sweetens the gloom;
Within, Miranda seeks her rest
    High in her turret-room.

Armies upon her walls encamp
    In silk and silver thread;   10
Chased and fretted, her silver lamp
    Dimly lights her bed;
And now the silken screen is drawn,
    The velvet coverlet spread;
And the pillow of down and snowy lawn   15
    Mantles about her head.

With violet-scented rain
    Sprinkle the rushy floor;
Let the tapestry hide the tinted pane,
    And cover the chamber door;   20
But leave a glimmering beam,
    Miranda belamour,
To touch and gild my waking dream,
    For I am your troubadour.

I sound my throbbing lyre,   25
    And sing to myself below;
Her damsel sits beside the fire
    Crooning a song I know;
The tapestry shakes on the wall,
    The shadows hurry and go,   30
The silent flames leap up and fall,
    And the muttering birch-logs glow.

Deep and sweet she sleeps,
    Because of her love for me;
And deep and sweet the peace that keeps   35
    My happy heart in fee!
Peace on the heights, in the deeps,

    Peace over hill and lea,
   Peace through the star-lit steeps,
    Peace on the starlit sea,   40
   Because a simple maiden sleeps
    Dreaming a dream of me!

411.   *A Ballad of Euthanasia*

  In magic books she read at night,
   And found all things to be
  A spectral pageant brought to light
   By nameless sorcery.

  "Bethink you, now, my daughter dear,"   5
   The King of Norway cried,
  "'Tis summer, and your twentieth year—
   High time you were a bride!

  "The sunlight lingers o'er the wold
   By night; the stars above   10
  With passion throb like hearts of gold;
   The whole world is in love."

  The scornful princess laughed and said,
   "This love you praise, I hate.
  Oh, I shall never, never wed;   15
   For men degenerate.

  "The sun grows dim on heaven's brow;
   The world's worn blood runs cold;
  Time staggers in his dotage now;
   Nature is growing old.   20

  "Deluded by the summertime,
   Must I with wanton breath
  Whisper and sigh? I trow not!—I
   Shall be the bride of Death."

  Fair princes came with gems of price, 25
   And kings from lands afar.
  "Jewels!" she said. "I may not wed
   Till Death comes with a star."

At midnight when she ceased to read,
    She pushed her lattice wide,
And saw the crested rollers lead
    The vanguard of the tide.

The mighty host of waters swayed,
    Commanded by the moon;
The Wind a marching music made;
    The surges chimed in tune.

But she with sudden-startled ears
    O'erheard a ghostly sound—
Or drums that beat, or trampling feet,
    Above or underground.

The mountain-side was girt about
    With forests dark and deep.
"What meteor flashes in and out
    Thridding the darksome steep?"

Soon light and sound reached level ground,
    And lo, in blackest mail,
Along the shore a warrior
    Rode on a war-horse pale!

And from his helm as on he came
    A crescent lustre gleamed;
The charger's hoofs were shod with flame:
    The wet sand hissed and steamed.

"He leaves me! Nay; he turns this way
    From elfin lands afar.
"'Tis Death," she said. "He comes to wed
    His true love with a star!

"No ring for me, no blushing groom,
    No love with all its ills,
No long-drawn life! I am the wife
    Of Death, whose first kiss kills."

The rider reached the city wall;
    Over the gate he dashed;
Across the roofs the fire-shod hoofs
    Like summer-lightning flashed.

Before her bower the pale horse pawed
    The air, unused to rest;
The sable groom, he whispered "Come!"
    And stooped his shining crest.

She sprang behind him; on her brow
    He placed his glowing star.
Back o'er the roofs the fire-shod hoofs
    Like lightning flashed afar.

Through hissing sand and shrivelled grass
    And flowers singed and dead,
By wood and lea, by stream and sea,
    The pale horse panting sped.

At last as they beheld the morn
    His sovereignty resume,
Deep in an ancient land forlorn
    They reached a marble tomb.

They lighted down and entered in:
    The tears, they brimmed her eyes;
She turned and took a lingering look,
    A last look at the skies;

Then went with Death. Her lambent star
    The sullen darkness lit
In avenues of sombre yews,
    Where ghosts did peer and flit.

But soon the way grew light as day;
    With wonderment and awe,
A golden land, a silver strand,
    And grass-green hills she saw.

In gown and smock good country folk
    In fields and meadows worked;
The salt seas wet the ruddy net
    Where glistering fishes lurked.

The meads were strewn with purple flowers,
    With every flower that blows;
And singing loud o'er cliff and cloud
    The larks, the larks arose!

"The sun is bright on heaven's brow,
  The world's fresh blood runs fleet;
Time is as young as ever now,
  Nature as fresh and sweet,"

Her champion said; then through the wood 105
  He led her to a bower;
He doffed his sable casque and stood
  A young man in his flower!

"Lo! I am Life, your lover true!"
  He kissed her o'er and o'er. 110
And still she wist not what to do,
  And still she wondered more.

And they were wed. The swift years sped
  Till children's children laughed;
And joy and pain and joy again 115
  Mixed in the cup they quaffed.

Upon their golden wedding day,
  He said, "How now, dear wife?"
Then she: "I find the sweetest kind
  Of Death is Love and Life." 120

412. *Insomnia*

He wakened quivering on a golden rack
  Inlaid with gems: no sign of change, no fear
  Or hope of death came near;
Only the empty ether hovered black
  About him stretched upon his living bier, 5
Of old by Merlin's Master deftly wrought:
  Two Seraphim of Gabriel's helpful race
  In that far nook of space
With iron levers wrenched and held him taut.

The Seraph at his head was Agony; 10
  Delight, more terrible, stood at his feet:
  Their sixfold pinions beat
The darkness, or were spread immovably
  Poising the rack, whose jewelled fabric meet

To strain a god, did fitfully unmask 15
    With olive light of chrysoprases dim
  The smiling Seraphim
Implacably intent upon their task.

413.   *A Ballad of an Artist's Wife*

"Sweet wife, this heavy-hearted age
    Is nought to us; we two shall look
To Art, and fill a perfect page
    In Life's ill-written doomsday book."

He wrought in colour; blood and brain 5
    Gave fire and might; and beauty grew
And flowered with every magic stain
    His passion on the canvas threw.

They shunned the world and worldly ways:
    He laboured with a constant will; 10
But few would look, and none would praise,
    Because of something lacking still.

After a time her days with sighs
    And tears o'erflowed; for blighting need
Bedimmed the lustre of her eyes, 15
    And there were little mouths to feed.

"My bride shall ne'er be commonplace,"
    He thought, and glanced; and glanced again:
At length he looked her in the face;
    And lo, a woman old and plain! 20

About this time the world's heart failed—
    The lusty heart no fear could rend;
In every land wild voices wailed,
    And prophets prophesied the end.

"To-morrow or to-day," he thought, 25
    "May be Eternity; and I
Have neither felt nor fashioned aught
    That makes me unconcerned to die.

"With care and counting of the cost
   My life a sterile waste has grown,
Wherein my better dreams are lost
   Like chaff in the Sahara sown.

"I must escape this living tomb!
   My life shall yet be rich and free,
And on the very stroke of Doom
   My soul at last begin to be.

"Wife, children, duty, household fires
   For victims of the good and true!
For me my infinite desires,
   Freedom and things untried and new!

"I would encounter all the press
   Of thought and feeling life can show,
The sweet embrace, the aching stress
   Of every earthly joy and woe;

"And from the world's impending wreck
   And out of pain and pleasure weave
Beauty undreamt of, to bedeck
   The Festival of Doomsday Eve."

He fled, and joined a motley throng
   That held carousal day and night;
With love and wit, with dance and song,
   They snatched a last intense delight.

Passion to mould an age's art,
   Enough to keep a century sweet,
Was in an hour consumed; each heart
   Lavished a life in every beat.

Amazing beauty filled the looks
   Of sleepless women; music bore
New wonder on its wings; and books
   Throbbed with a thought unknown before.

The sun began to smoke and flare
   Like a spent lamp about to die;
The dusky moon tarnished the air;
   The planets withered in the sky.

Earth reeled and lurched upon her road;
    Tigers were cowed, and wolves grew tame;
Seas shrank, and rivers backward flowed,
    And mountain-ranges burst in flame.

The artist's wife, a soul devout,
    To all these things gave little heed;
For though the sun was going out,
    There still were little mouths to feed.

And there were also shrouds to stitch,
    And chares to do; with all her might,
To feed her babes, she served the rich
    And kept her useless tears till night.

But by-and-by her sight grew dim;
    Her strength gave way; in desperate mood
She laid her down to die. "Tell him,"
    She sighed, "I fed them while I could."

The children met a wretched fate;
    Self-love was all the vogue and vaunt,
And charity gone out of date;
    Wherefore they pined and died of want.

Aghast he heard the story: "Dead!
    All dead in hunger and despair!
I courted misery," he said;
    "But here is more than I can bear."

Then, as he wrought, the stress of woe
    Appeared in many a magic stain;
And all adored his work, for lo,
    Tears mingled now with blood and brain!

"Look, look!" they cried; "this man can weave
    Beauty from anguish that appals;"
And at the feast of Doomsday Eve
    They hung his pictures in their halls,

And gazed; and came again between
    The faltering dances eagerly;
They said, "The loveliest we have seen,
    The last, of man's work, we shall see!"

Then was there neither death nor birth;
   Time ceased; and through the ether fell
The smoky Sun, the leprous earth—
   A cinder and an icicle.

No wrathful vials were unsealed;   105
   Silent, the first things passed away:
No terror reigned; no trumpet pealed
   The dawn of Everlasting Day.

The bitter draught of sorrow's cup
   Passed with the seasons and the years;   110
And Wisdom dried for ever up
   The deep, old fountain-head of tears.

Out of the grave and ocean's bed
   The artist saw the people rise;
And all the living and the dead   115
   Were borne aloft to Paradise.

He came where on a silver throne
   A spirit sat for ever young;
Before her Seraphs worshipped prone,
   And Cherubs silver censers swung.   120

He asked, "Who may this martyr be?
   What votaress of saintly rule?"
A Cherub said, "No martyr; she
   Had one gift; she was beautiful."

Then came he to another bower   125
   Where one sat on a golden seat,
Adored by many a heavenly Power
   With golden censers smoking sweet.

"This was some gallant wench who led
   Faint-hearted folk and set them free?"   130
"Oh, no! a simple maid," they said,
   "Who spent her life in charity."

At last he reached a mansion blest
   Where on a diamond throne, endued
With nameless beauty, one possessed   135
   Ineffable beatitude.

     The praises of this matchless soul
        The sons of God proclaimed aloud;
     From diamond censers odours stole;
        And Hierarchs before her bowed.   140

     "Who was she?" God himself replied:
        "In misery her lot was cast;
     She lived a woman's life, and died
        Working My work until the last."

     It was his wife. He said, "I pray   145
        Thee, Lord, despatch me now to Hell."
     But God said, "No; here shall you stay,
        And in her peace for ever dwell."

414.   *Holiday at Hampton Court*

     Scales of pearly cloud inlay
        North and south the turquoise sky,
     While the diamond lamp of day
        Quenchless burns, and time on high
     A moment halts upon his way   5
        Bidding noon again good-bye.

     Gaffers, gammers, huzzies, louts,
        Couples, gangs, and families
     Sprawling, shake, with Babel-shouts
        Bluff King Hal's funereal trees;   10
     And eddying groups of stare-abouts
        Quiz the sandstone Hercules.

     When their tongues and tempers tire,
        Harry and his little lot
     Condescendingly admire   15
        Lozenge-bed and crescent-plot,
     Aglow with links of azure fire,
        Pansy and forget-me-not.

     Where the emerald shadows rest
        In the lofty woodland aisle,   20
     Chaffing lovers quaintly dressed
        Chase and double many a mile
     Indifferent exiles in the west
        Making love in cockney style.

Now the echoing palace fills; 25
    Men and women, girls and boys
Trample past the swords and frills,
    Kings and Queens and trulls and toys;
Or listening loll on window-sills,
    Happy amateurs of noise! 30

That for pictured rooms of state!
    Out they hurry, wench and knave,
Where beyond the palace-gate
    Dusty legions swarm and rave,
With laughter, shriek, inane debate, 35
    Kentish fire and comic stave.

Voices from the river call;
    Organs hammer tune on tune;
Larks triumphant over all
    Herald twilight coming soon, 40
For as the sun begins to fall
Near the zenith gleams the moon.

415.
Matinées I & II

I

Night went down; the twilight ceased;
    The moon withdrew her phantom flame;
In pearl and silver out of the east,
    Pallid and vigilant, morning came:
By heath and hill with trumpets shrill 5
    The orient wind declared his name:—

"Morning! Morning! Mighty, alone,
    Light, the light, whose titles are
Courage and hope, ascends his throne
    Over the head of every star: 10
Terror and pain are chained and slain,
    And mournful shadows flee afar."

II

From the night-haunt where vapours crowd
    The airy outskirts of the earth
A winding caravan of cloud 15
    Rose when the morning's punctual hearth

Began to charm the winds and skies
With odours fresh and golden dyes.

It made a conquest of the sun,
    And tied his beams; but, in the game
Of hoodman-blind, the rack, outdone,
    Beheld the brilliant captive claim
Forfeit on forfeit, as he pressed
The mountains to his burning breast.

Above the path by vapours trod
    A ringing causey seemed to be,
Whereby the orient, silver-shod,
    Rode out across the Atlantic sea,
An embassy of valour sent
Under the echoing firmament.

And while the hearkener divined
    A clanging cavalcade on high,
This rush and trample of the wind
    Arose among the tree-tops nigh,
For mystery is the craft profound,
The sign, and ancient trade of sound.

An unseen roadman breaking flint,
    If echo and the winds conspire
To dedicate his morning's stint,
    May beat a tune out, dew and fire
So wrought that heaven might lend an ear,
And Ariel hush his harp to hear.

416.   *The Last Ballad*

By coasts where scalding deserts reek,
    The apanages of despair;
In outland wilds, by firth and creek,
    O'er icy bournes of silver air;

In storm or calm delaying not,
    To every noble task addressed,
Year after year, Sir Lancelot
    Fulfilled King Arthur's high behest.

He helped the helpless ones; withstood
   Tyrants and sanctioners of vice;
He rooted out the dragon brood,
   And overthrew false deities.

Alone with his own soul, alone
   With life and death, with day and night,
His thought and strength grew great and shone
   A tongue of flame, a sword of light.

And yet not all alone. On high,
   When midnight set the spaces free,
And brimming stars hung from the sky
   Low down, and spilt their jewellery,

Behind the nightly squandered fire,
   Through a dark lattice only seen
By love, a look of rapt desire
   Fell from a vision of the Queen.

From heaven she bent when twilight knit
   The dusky air and earth in one;
He saw her like a goddess sit
   Enthroned upon the noonday sun.

In passages of gulfs and sounds,
   When wild winds dug the sailor's grave,
When clouds and billows merged their bounds,
   And the keel climbed the slippery wave,

A sweet sigh laced the tempest; nay,
   Low at his ear he heard her speak;
Among the hurtling sheaves of spray
   Her loosened tresses swept his cheek.

And in the revelry of death,
   If human greed of slaughter cast
Remorse aside, a violet breath,
   The incense of her being passed

Across his soul, and deeply swayed
   The fount of pity; o'er the strife
He curbed the lightning of his blade,
   And gave the foe his forfeit life.

Low on the heath, or on the deck, 45
    In bloody mail or wet with brine,
Asleep he saw about her neck
    The wreath of gold and rubies shine;

He saw her brows, her lovelit face,
    And on her cheek one passionate tear; 50
He felt in dreams the rich embrace,
    The beating heart of Guinevere.

"Visions that haunt my couch, my path,
    Although the waste, unfathomed sea
Should rise against me white with wrath 55
    I must behold her verily,

"Once ere I die," he said, and turned
    Westward his faded silken sails
From isles where cloudy mountains burned,
    And north to Severn-watered Wales. 60

Beside the Usk King Arthur kept
    His Easter court, a glittering rout.
But Lancelot, because there swept
    A passion of despair throughout

His being, when he saw once more 65
    The sky that canopied, the tide
That girdled Guinevere, forbore
    His soul's desire, and wandered wide

In unknown seas companionless,
    Eating his heart, until by chance 70
He drifted into Lyonesse,
    The wave-worn kingdom of romance.

He leapt ashore and watched his barque
    Unmastered stagger to its doom;
Then doffed his arms and fled baresark 75
    Into the forest's beckoning gloom.

The exceeding anguish of his mind
    Had broken him. "King Arthur's trust,"
He cried; "ignoble, fateful, blind!
    Her love and my love, noxious lust! 80

"Dupes of our senses! Let us eat
   In caverns fathoms underground,
Alone, ashamed! To sit at meat
   In jocund throngs?—the most profound

"Device of life the mountebank,   85
   Vendor of gilded ashes! Steal
From every sight to use the rank
   And loathsome needs that men conceal;

"And crush and drain in curtained beds
   The clusters called of love; but feed   90
With garlanded uplifted heads;
   Invite the powers that sanction greed

"To countenance the revel; boast
   Of hunger, thirst; be drunken; claim
Indulgence to the uttermost,   95
   Replenishing the founts of shame!"

He gathered berries, efts, and snails,
   Sorrel, and new-burst hawthorn leaves;
Uprooted with his savage nails
   Earth-nuts; and under rocky eaves   100

Shamefast devoured them, out of sight
   In darkness, lest the eye of beast,
Or bird, or star, or thing of night
   Uncouth, unknown, should watch him feast.

At noon in twilight depths of pine   105
   He heard the word Amaimon spoke;
He saw the pallid, evil sign
   The wred-eld lit upon the oak.

The viper loitered in his way;
   The minx looked up with bloodshot leer;   110
Ill-meaning fauns and lamiæ
   With icy laughter flitted near.

But if he came upon a ring
   Of sinless elves, and crept unseen
Beneath the brake to hear them sing,   115
   And watch them dancing on the green,

They touched earth with their finger-tips;
    They ceased their roundelay; they laid
A seal upon their elfin lips
    And vanished in the purple shade.

At times he rent the dappled flank
    Of some fair creature of the chase,
Mumbled its flesh, or growling drank
    From the still-beating heart, his face

And jowl ruddled, and in his hair
    And beard, blood-painted straws and burs,
While eagles barked screening the air,
    And wolves that were his pensioners.

Sometimes at night his mournful cry
    Troubled all waking things; the mole
Dived to his deepest gallery;
    The vixen from the moonlit knoll

Passed like a shadow underground,
    And the mad satyr in his lair
Whined bodeful at the world-old sound
    Of inarticulate despair.

Sir Lancelot, beloved of men!
    The ancient earth gat hold of him;
A year was blotted from his ken
    In the enchanted forest dim.

At Easter when the thorn beset
    The bronzing wood with silver sprays,
And hyacinth and violet
    Empurpled all the russet ways;

When buttercup and daffodil
    A stainless treasure-trove unrolled,
And cowslips had begun to fill
    Their chalices with sweeter gold,

He heard a sound of summer rush
    By swarthy grove and kindled lawn;
He heard, he sighed to hear the thrush
    Singing alone before the dawn.

Forward he stalked with eyes on fire
    Like one who keeps in sound and sight
An angel with celestial lyre   155
    Descanting rapturous delight.

He left behind the spell-bound wood;
    He saw the branchless air unfurled;
He climbed a hill and trembling stood
    Above the prospect of the world.   160

With lustre in its bosom pent
    From many a shining summer day
And harvest moon, the wan sea leant
    Against a heaven of iron-grey.

Inland on the horizon beat   165
    And flickered, drooping heavily,
A fervid haze, a vaporous heat,
    The dusky eyelid of the sky.

White ways, white gables, russet thatch
    Fretted the green and purple plain;   170
The herd undid his woven latch;
    The bleating flock went forth again;

The skylarks uttered lauds and prime;
    The sheep-bells rang from hill to hill;
The cuckoo pealed his mellow chime;   175
    The orient bore a burden shrill.

His memory struggled half awake;
    Dimly he groped within to see
What star, what sun, what light should break
    And set his darkened spirit free.   180

But from without deliverance came:
    Afar he saw a horseman speed,
A knight, a spirit clad in flame
    Riding upon a milkwhite steed.

For now the sun had quenched outright   185
    The clouds and all their working charms,
Marshalled his legionary light,
    And fired the rider's golden arms.

Softly the silver billows flowed;
    Beneath the hill the emerald vale 190
Dipped seaward; on the burnished road
    The milkwhite steed, the dazzling mail

Advanced and flamed against the wind;
    And Lancelot, his body rent
With the fierce trial of his mind 195
    To know, reeled down the steep descent.

Remembrances of battle plied
    His soul with ruddy beams of day.
"A horse! a lance! to arms!" he cried,
    And stood there weeping in the way. 200

"Speak!" said the knight. "What man are you?"
    "I know not yet. Surely of old
I rode in arms, and fought and slew
    In jousts and battles manifold."

Oh, wistfully he drew anear, 205
    Fingered the reins, the jewelled sheath;
With rigid hand he grasped the spear,
    And shuddering whispered, "Life and death,

"Love, lofty deeds, renown—did these
    Attend me once in days unknown?" 210
With courtesy, with comely ease,
    And brows that like his armour shone,

The golden knight dismounting took
    Sir Lancelot by the hand and said,
"Your voice of woe, your lonely look 215
    As of a dead man whom the dead

"Themselves cast out—whence are they, friend?"
    Sir Lancelot a moment hung
In doubt, then knelt and made an end
    Of all his madness, tensely strung 220

In one last effort to be free
    Of evil things that wait for men
In secret, strangle memory,
    And shut the soul up in their den.

"Spirit," he said, "I know your eyes:
   They bridge with light the heavy drift
Of years. ... A woman said, 'Arise;
   And if you love the Queen, be swift!'

"The token was an emerald chased
   In gold, once mine. Wherefore I rode
At dead of night in proudest haste
   To Payarne where the Queen abode.

"A crafty witch gave me to drink:
   Almost till undern of the morn
Silent, in darkness. ... When I think
   It was not Guinevere, self-scorn

"Cuts to the marrow of my bones,
   A blade of fire. Can wisdom yield
No mood, no counsel, that atones
   For wasted love! ... Heaven had revealed

"That she should bear a child to me
   My bed-mate said. ... Yet am I mad?
The offspring of that treachery!
   The maiden knight! You—Galahad,

"My son, who make my trespass dear!"
   His look released his father's thought—
The darkling orbs of Guinevere;
   For so had Lancelot's passion wrought.

With tenderer tears than women shed
   Sir Galahad held his father fast.
"Now I shall be your squire," he said.
   But Lancelot fought him long. At last

The maiden gently overpowered
   The man. Upon his milkwhite steed
He brought him where a castle towered
   Midmost a green enamelled mead;

And clothed his body, clothed his heart
   In human garniture once more.
"My father, bid me now depart.
   I hear beside the clanging shore,

"Above the storm, or in the wind,
　　Outland, or on the old Roman street,
A chord of music intertwined
　　From wandering tones deep-hued and sweet.

"Afar or near, at noon, at night,   265
　　The braided sound attends and fills
My soul with peace, as heaven with light
　　O'erflows when morning crowns the hills.

"And with the music, seen or hid,
　　A blood-rose on the palace lawn,   270
A fount of crimson, dark amid
　　The stains and glories of the dawn;

"Above the city's earthly hell
　　A token ominous of doom,
A cup on fire and terrible   275
　　With thunders in its ruddy womb;

"But o'er the hamlet's fragrant smoke,
　　The dance and song at eventide,
A beating heart, the gentle yoke
　　Of life the bridegroom gives the bride;   280

"A ruby shadow on the snow;
　　A flower, a lamp—through every veil
And mutable device I know,
　　And follow still the Holy Grail

"Until God gives me my new name   285
　　Empyreal, and the quest be done."
Then like a spirit clad in flame,
　　He kissed his father and was gone.

Long gazed Sir Lancelot on the ground
　　Tormented till benign repose   290
Enveloped him in depths profound
　　Of sweet oblivion. When he rose

The bitterest was past. "And I
　　Shall follow now the Holy Grail,
Seen, or unseen, until I die: 295
　　My very purpose shall avail

"My soul," he said. By day, by night,
   He rode abroad, his vizor up;
With sun and moon his vehement sight
   Fought for a vision of the cup—   300

In vain. For evermore on high
   When darkness set the spaces free,
And brimming stars hung from the sky
   Low down, and spilt their jewellery,

Behind the nightly squandered fire,   305
   Through a dim lattice only seen
By love, a look of rapt desire
   Fell from a vision of the Queen.

From heaven she bent when twilight knit
   The dusky air and earth in one;   310
He saw her like a goddess sit
   Enthroned upon the noonday sun.

Wherefore he girt himself again:
   In lawless towns and savage lands,
He overthrew unrighteous men,   315
   Accomplishing the King's commands.

In passages of gulfs and sounds
   When wild winds dug the sailor's grave,
When clouds and billows merged their bounds,
   And the keel climbed the slippery wave,   320

A sweet sigh laced the tempest; nay,
   Low at his ear he heard her speak;
Among the hurtling sheaves of spray
   Her loosened tresses swept his cheek.

And in the revelry of death,   325
   If human greed of slaughter cast
Remorse aside, a violet breath,
   The incense of her being passed

Across his soul, and deeply swayed
   The fount of pity; o'er the strife   330
He curbed the lightning of his blade,
   And gave the foe his forfeit life.

His love, in utter woe annealed,
    Escaped the furnace, sweet and clear—
His love that on the world had sealed
    The look, the soul of Guinevere.

417.   *The Last Rose*

"Oh, which is the last rose?"
A blossom of no name.
At midnight the snow came;
At daybreak a vast rose,
In darkness unfurled,
O'er-petaled the world.

Its odourless pallor,
Blossomed forlorn,
Till radiant valour
Established the morn—
Till the night
Was undone
In her fight
With the sun.

The brave orb in state rose
And crimson he shone first;
While from the high vine
Of heaven the dawn burst,
Staining the great rose
From sky-line to sky-line.

The red rose of morn
A white rose at noon turned;
But at sunset reborn,
All red again soon burned.
Then the pale rose of noonday
Re-bloomed in the night,
And spectrally white
In the light
Of the moon lay.

But the vast rose
Was scentless,
And this is the reason:
When the blast rose

Relentless,
And brought in due season 35
The snow-rose, the last rose
Congealed in its breath,
There came with it treason;
The traitor was Death.

In lee-valleys crowded, 40
The sheep and the birds
Were frozen and shrouded
In flights and in herds.
In highways
And byways 45

The young and the old
Were tortured and maddened
And killed by the cold.
But many were gladdened
By the beautiful last rose, 50
The blossom of no name
That came when the snow came,
In darkness unfurled—
The wonderful vast rose
That filled all the world. 55

(1899)

Jane Barlow (1857–1917)

418. *Expectation*

Fleet wheels had whirled for us, deep hedgerows threading,
Till where, down labyrinthine lanes enfolden,
The grey, green-mantled church stood, half withholden
From passing eyes by elms full-fledged for shedding
Midsummer shade, noon-shrunken, softly spreading 5
O'er swarded path a dappled pavement, golden
And beryl-flecked, to a door, whose dusk-arch olden
Let glimpse in hesitant gleams, the sill's gloom dreading.
A knot of children, snowy-bibbed, blue-skirted,
Hung round the gate, from devious ways diverted; 10

Shawled crone's slow halt and girl's light foot one goal
Had found thereby. *Grand weather for whose wedding?*
Methought: and straight a daw from ivied steading
Swooped startled, as a bell began to—toll.

A Mary F. Robinson (Mme Darmesteter, Mme Duclaux) (1857–1944)

419. *To my Muse*

The vast Parnassus never knew thy face,
   O Muse of mine, O frail and tender elf
   That dancest in a moonbeam to thyself
Where olives rustle in a lonely place!

And yet . . . thou hast a sort of Tuscan grace;   5
   Thou may'st outlive me! Some unborn Filelf
   One day may range thee on his studious shelf
With Lenau, Leopardi, and their race.

And so, some time, the sole sad scholar's friend,
   The melancholy comrade of his dreams,   10
   Thou may'st, O Muse, escape a little while
The none the less inevitable end:
   Take heart, therefore, and sing the thing that seems,
     And watch the world's disaster with a smile.

420. *Sonnet:* 'God sent a poet to reform His earth'

God sent a poet to reform His earth.
But when he came and found it cold and poor,
Harsh and unlovely, where each prosperous boor
Held poets light for all their heavenly birth,
He thought—Myself can make one better worth   5
The living in than this—full of old lore,
Music and light and love, where Saints adore
And Angels, all within mine own soul's girth.

But when at last he came to die, his soul
Saw earth (flying past to Heaven), with new love, 10
And all the unused passion in him cried:
O God, your Heaven I know and weary of.
Give me this world to work in and make whole.
God spoke: Therein, thou fool, hast lived and died!

421. *The Idea*

    Beneath this world of stars and flowers
        That rolls in visible deity,
    I dream another world is ours
        And is the soul of all we see.

    It hath no form, it hath no spirit; 5
        It is perchance the Eternal Mind;
    Beyond the sense that we inherit
        I feel it dim and undefined.

    How far below the depth of being,
        How wide beyond the starry bound 10
    It rolls unconscious and unseeing,
        And is as Number or as Sound.

    And through the vast fantastic visions
        Of all this actual universe,
    It moves unswerved by our decisions, 15
        And is the play that we rehearse.

(1888)

422. *Personality*

(A SESTINA)

As one who goes between high garden walls,
Along a road that never has an end,
With still the empty way behind, in front,
Which he must pace for evermore alone—
So, even so, is Life to every soul, 5
Walled in with barriers which no Love can break.

And yet, ah me! how often would we break
Through fence and fold, and overleap the walls,
To link ourselves to some belovèd soul;
Hearing her answering voice until the end,   10
Going her chosen way, no more alone,
But happy comrades, seeing Heaven in front.

But, ah, the barrier's high! and still my front
I dash against the stones in vain, nor break
A passage through, but still remain alone.   15
Sometimes I hear across high garden walls
A voice the wind brings over, or an end
Of song that sinks like dew into my soul.

Since others sing, let me forget, my Soul,
How dreary-long the road goes on in front,   20
And tow'rds how flat, inevitable an end.
Come, let me look for daisies, let me break
The gillyflowers that shelter in the walls—
But, ah! it is so sad to be alone!

For ever, irremediably alone,   25
Not only I or thou, but every soul,
Each cased and fastened with invisible walls.
Shall we go mad with it? or bear a front
Of desperate courage doomed to fail and break?
Or trudge in sullen patience till the end?   30

Ah, hope of every heart, there *is* an end!
An end when each shall be no more alone,
But strong enough and bold enough to break
This prisoning self and find that larger Soul
(Neither of thee nor me) enthroned in front   35
Of Time, beyond the world's remotest walls!

I trust the end; I sing within my walls,
Sing all alone, to bid some listening soul
Wait till the day break, watch for me in front!

423.   *A Pastoral of Parnassus*

"*Ma io perchè venirvi? O chi 'l concede?*"

At morning dawn I left my sheep
    And sought the mountains all aglow;
The shepherds said, "The way is steep:
        Ah, do not go!"

I left my pastures fresh with rain,
    My water-courses edged with bloom,
A larger breathing space to gain
        And singing room.

Then of a reed I wrought a flute,
    And as I went I sang and played.
But though I sang, my heart was mute
        And sore afraid.

Because the great hill and the sky
    Were full of glooms and glorious
Beyond all light or dark that I
        Imagined thus.

A sudden sense, a second sight,
    Showed God, who burns in every briar.
Then sudden voices, strong and bright,
        Flashed up like fire.

And turning where that music rang
    I saw aloft, and far away,
The watching poets; and they sang
        Through night and day.

And very sweet—ah, sweet indeed—
    Their voices sounded high and deep.
I blew an echo on my reed
        As one asleep.

I heard. My heart grew cold with dread,
    For what would happen if they heard?
Would not these nightingales strike dead
        Their mocking-bird?

      Then from the mountain's steepest crown,
         Where white cliffs pierce the tender grass,
      I saw an arm reach slowly down,   35
         Heard some word pass.

      "The end is come," I thought, "and still
         I am more happy, come what may,
      To die upon Parnassus-hill
         Than live away."   40

      Then hands and faces luminous
         And holy voices grew one flame—
      "Come up, poor singer, and sing with us!"
         They sang; I came.

      So ended all my wandering;   45
         This is the end and this is sweet—
      All night, all day, to listen and sing
         Below their feet.

                (1891)

424.   *The Bookworm*

      The whole day long I sit and read
      Of days when men were men indeed
         And women knightlier far:
      I fight with Joan of Arc; I fall
      With Talbot; from my castle-wall   5
         I watch the guiding star . . .

      But when at last the twilight falls
      And hangs about the book-lined walls
         And creeps across the page,
      Then the enchantment goes, and I   10
      Close up my volumes with a sigh
         To greet a narrower age.

      Home through the pearly dusk I go
      And watch the London lamplight glow
         Far off in wavering lines: 15
      A pale grey world with primrose gleams,
      And in the West a cloud that seems
         My distant Apennines.

O Life! so full of truths to teach,
Of secrets I shall never reach,   20
   O world of Here and Now;
Forgive, forgive me, if a voice,
A ghost, a memory be my choice
   And more to me than Thou!

(1893)

425.　　　　　　　　*Rispetti*

My mother bore me 'neath the streaming moon,
  And all the enchanted light is in my soul.
I have no place amid the happy noon,
  I have no shadow there nor aureole.

Ah, lonely whiteness in a clouded sky,   5
You are alone, nor less alone am I;
Ah, moon, that makest all the roses grey,
The roses I behold are wan as they!

Constance (Caroline Woodhill) Naden (1858–1889)

from *Evolutional Erotics*

426.　　　　　　*Solomon Redivivus*

What am I? Ah, you know it,
  I am the modern Sage,
Seer, savant, merchant, poet—
  I am, in brief, the Age.

Look not upon my glory   5
  Of gold and sandal-wood,
But sit and hear a story
  From Darwin and from Buddh.

Count not my Indian treasures,
    All wrought in curious shapes,
My labours and my pleasures,
    My peacocks and my apes;

For when you ask me riddles,
    And when I answer each,
Until my fifes and fiddles
    Burst in and drown our speech,

Oh then your soul astonished
    Must surely faint and fail,
Unless, by me admonished,
    You hear our wondrous tale.

We were a soft Amœba
    In ages past and gone,
Ere you were Queen of Sheba,
    And I King Solomon.

Unorganed, undivided,
    We lived in happy sloth,
And all that you did I did,
    One dinner nourished both:

Till you incurred the odium
    Of fission and divorce—
A severed pseudopodium
    You strayed your lonely course.

When next we met together
    Our cycles to fulfil,
Each was a bag of leather,
    With stomach and with gill.

But our Ascidian morals
    Recalled that old mischance,
And we avoided quarrels
    By separate maintenance.

Long ages passed—our wishes
    Were fetterless and free,
For we were jolly fishes,
    A-swimming in the sea.

We roamed by groves of coral,   45
    We watched the youngsters play—
The memory and the moral
    Had vanished quite away.

Next, each became a reptile,
    With fangs to sting and slay;   50
No wiser ever crept, I'll
    Assert, deny who may.

But now, disdaining trammels
    Of scale and limbless coil,
Through every grade of mammals   55
    We passed with upward toil.

Till, anthropoid and wary
    Appeared the parent ape,
And soon we grew less hairy,
    And soon began to drape.   60

So, from that soft Amœba,
    In ages past and gone,
You've grown the Queen of Sheba,
    And I King Solomon.

427.   *Poet and Botanist*

Fair are the bells of this bright-flowering weed;
    Nectar and pollen treasuries, where grope
    Innocent thieves; the Poet lets them ope
And bloom, and wither, leaving fruit and seed
To ripen; but the Botanist will speed   5
    To win the secret of the blossom's hope,
    And with his cruel knife and microscope
Reveal the embryo life, too early freed.

Yet the mild Poet can be ruthless too,
    Crushing the tender leaves to work a spell   10
        Of love or fame; the record of the bud
    He will not seek, but only bids it tell
His thoughts, and render up its deepest hue
    To tinge his verse as with his own heart's blood.

428.   *The Nebular Theory*

    This is the genesis of Heaven and Earth.
      In the beginning was a formless mist
      Of atoms isolate, void of life; none wist
    Aught of its neighbour atom, nor any mirth,
    Nor woe, save its own vibrant pang of dearth;   5
      Until a cosmic motion breathed and hissed
      And blazed through the black silence; atoms kissed,
    Clinging and clustering, with fierce throbs of birth,
    And raptures of keen torment, such as stings
      Demons who wed in Tophet; the night swarmed   10
      With ringèd fiery clouds, in glowing gyres
    Rotating: æons passed: the encircling rings
      Split into satellites; the central fires
    Froze into suns; and thus the world was formed.

429.   *Speech and Silence*

    When some sweet voice flows forth in foreign speech,
      The soul shines through the words, and makes them clear,
      And all we see interprets all we hear,
    For smiles and frowns have wondrous power to teach:
    And voiceless grief our inmost heart can reach,   5
      With calm, deep gaze, too sad for hope or fear:
      Our eyes are wet for those who shed no tear,
    And lips that Death has silenced, yet may preach.

    In stillness we must win our deepest lore,
      Or 'mid the speechless chant of earth and sea: 10
      Truth is a spirit, bodiless and free;
    Imaged in words, 'tis perfect truth no more,
      For all our lofty visions fade and flee,
    And song begins, when ecstasy is o'er.

430.   *Love's Mirror*

    I live with love encompassed round,
      And glowing light that is not mine,
      And yet am sad; for, truth to tell,
      It is not I you love so well;

    Some fair Immortal, robed and crowned,   5
       You hold within your heart's dear shrine.

Cast out the Goddess! let me in;
   Faulty I am, yet all your own,
   But this bright phantom you enthrone
Is such as mortal may not win.   10

And yet this beauty that you see
   Is like to mine, though nobler far;
Your radiant guest resembles me
   E'en as the sun is like a star.

Then keep her in your heart of hearts,   15
   And let me look upon her face,
   And learn of that transcendent grace,
Till all my meaner self departs,

And, while I love you more and more,
   My spirit, gazing on the light,   20
   Becomes, in loveliness and might,
The glorious Vision you adore.

431.
The Lady Doctor

Saw ye that spinster gaunt and grey,
Whose aspect stern might well dismay
   A bombardier stout-hearted?
The golden hair, the blooming face,
And all a maiden's tender grace   5
   Long, long from her have parted.

A Doctor she—her sole delight
To order draughts as black as night,
   Powders, and pills, and lotions;
Her very glance might cast a spell   10
Transmuting Sherry and Moselle
   To chill and acrid potions.

Yet if some rash presumptuous man
Her early life should dare to scan,
   Strange things he might discover;   15
For in the bloom of sweet seventeen

She wandered through the meadows green
    To meet a boyish lover.

She did not give him Jesuit's bark,
To brighten up his vital spark,
    Nor ipecacuanha,
Nor chlorodyne, nor camomile,
But blushing looks, and many a smile,
    And kisses sweet as manna.

But ah! the maiden's heart grew cold,
Perhaps she thought the youth too bold,
    Perhaps his views had shocked her;
In anger, scorn, caprice, or pride,
She left her old companion's side
    To be a Lady Doctor.

She threw away the faded flowers,
Gathered amid the woodland bowers,
    Her lover's parting token:
If suffering bodies we relieve,
What need for wounded souls to grieve?
    Why mourn, though hearts be broken?

She cared not, though with frequent moan
He wandered through the woods alone
    Dreaming of past affection:
She valued at the lowest price
Men neither patients for advice
    Nor subjects for dissection.

She studied hard for her degree;
At length the coveted M.D.
    Was to her name appended;
Joy to that Doctor, young and fair,
With rosy cheeks and golden hair,
    Learning with beauty blended.

Diseases man can scarce endure
A lady's glance may quickly cure,
    E'en though the pains be chronic;
Where'er that maiden bright was seen
Her eye surpassed the best quinine,
    Her smile became a tonic.

But soon, too soon, the hand of care 55
Sprinkled with snow her golden hair,
   Her face grew worn and jaded;
Forgotten was each maiden wile,
She scarce remembered how to smile,
   Her roses all were faded. 60

And now, she looks so grim and stern,
We wonder any heart could burn
   For one so uninviting;
No gentle sympathy she shows,
She seems a man in woman's clothes, 65
   All female graces slighting.

Yet blame her not, for she has known
The woe of living all alone,
   In friendless, dreary sadness;
She longs for what she once disdained, 70
And sighs to think she might have gained
   A home of love and gladness.

Moral

Fair maid, if thine unfettered heart
Yearn for some busy, toilsome part,
   Let that engross thee only; 75
But oh! if bound by love's light chain,
Leave not thy fond and faithful swain
   Disconsolate and lonely.

432. ## Moonlight and Gas

The poet in theory worships the moon,
   But how can he linger, to gaze on her light?
With proof-sheets and copy the table is strewn,
   A poem lies there, to be finished to-night.
He silently watches the queen of the sky, 5
   But orbs more prosaic must dawn for him soon—
The gas must be lighted; he turns with a sigh,
   Lets down his Venetians and shuts out the moon.

"This is but a symbol," he sadly exclaims,
    "Heaven's glory must yield to the lustre of earth;
More golden, less distant, less pure are the flames
    That shine for the world over sorrow and mirth.
When Wisdom sublime sheds her beams o'er the night,
    I turn with a sigh from the coveted boon,
And choosing instead a more practical light
    Let down my venetians and shut out the moon."

He sits to his desk and he mutters "Alas,
    My muse will not waken, and yet I must write!"
But great is Diana: venetians and gas
    Have not been sufficient to banish her quite.
She peeps through the blinds and is bright as before,
    He smiles and he blesses the hint opportune,
And feels he can still, when his labour is o'er,
    Draw up his venetians and welcome the moon.

433.   *The Two Artists*

"Edith is fair," the painter said,
    "Her cheek so richly glows,
My palette ne'er could match the red
    Of that pure damask rose.

"Perchance, the evening rain-drops light,
    Soft sprinkling from above,
Have caught the sunset's colour bright,
    And borne it to my love.

"In distant regions I must seek
    For tints before unknown,
Ere I can paint the brilliant cheek
    That blooms for me alone."

All this his little sister heard,
    Who frolicked by his side;
To check such theories absurd,
    That gay young sprite replied:

"Oh, I can tell you where to get
    That pretty crimson bloom,
For in a bottle it is set
    In Cousin Edith's room.

"I'm sure that I could find the place,
    If you want some to keep;
I watched her put it on her face—
    She didn't see me peep!

"So nicely she laid on the pink,   25
    As well as *you* could do,
And really, I almost think
    She is an artist, too."

The maddened painter tore his hair,
    And vowed he ne'er would wed,   30
And never since, to maiden fair,
    A tender word has said.

Bright ruby cheeks, and skin of pearl,
    He knows a shower may spoil,
And when he wants a blooming girl   35
    Paints one himself in oil.

434.   *The Pantheist's Song of Immortality*

Bring snow-white lilies, pallid heart-flushed roses,
    Enwreathe her brow with heavy-scented flowers;
In soft undreaming sleep her head reposes,
    While, unregretted, pass the sunlit hours.

Few sorrows did she know—and all are over;   5
    A thousand joys—but they are all forgot:
Her life was one fair dream of friend and lover;
    And were they false—ah, well, she knows it not.

Look in her face, and lose thy dread of dying;
    Weep not, that rest will come, that toil will cease: 10
Is it not well, to lie as she is lying,
    In utter silence, and in perfect peace?

Canst thou repine that sentient days are numbered?
    Death is unconscious Life, that waits for birth:
So didst thou live, while yet thy embryo slumbered,   15
    Senseless, unbreathing, e'en as heaven and earth.

Then shrink no more from Death, though Life be gladness,
    Nor seek him, restless in thy lonely pain:
The law of joy ordains each hour of sadness,
    And firm or frail, thou canst not live in vain.

What though thy name by no sad lips be spoken,
    And no fond heart shall keep thy memory green?
Thou yet shalt leave thine own enduring token,
    For earth is not as though thou ne'er hadst been.

See yon broad current, hasting to the ocean,
    Its ripples glorious in the western red:
Each wavelet passes, trackless; yet its motion
    Has changed for evermore the river bed.

Ah, wherefore weep, although the form and fashion
    Of what thou seemest, fades like sunset flame?
The uncreated Source of toil and passion,
    Through everlasting change abides the same.

Yes, thou shalt die: but these almighty forces,
    That meet to form thee, live for evermore:
They hold the suns in their eternal courses,
    And shape the tiny sand-grains on the shore.

Be calmly glad, thine own true kindred seeing
    In fire and storm, in flowers with dew impearled;
Rejoice in thine imperishable being,
    One with the Essence of the boundless world.

Dollie (Caroline) (Mrs Ernest) Radford (née Maitland) (1858–1920)

435. *Two Songs*

Winds blow cold in the bright March weather,
    Yet I heard her sing in the street to-day,
And the tattered garments scarce hung together
    Round her tiny form as she turned away.
She was too little to know or care
Why she and her mother were singing there.

Skies are fair when the buds are springing,
   When the March sun rises up fresh and strong,
And a little maid, with her mother, singing,
   Smiled in my face as she skipped along,   10
She was too happy to wonder why
   She laughed and sang as she passed me by.

Stars are bright, and the moon rejoices
   To pierce the clouds with her broken light,
But the air is heavy with childish voices,   15
   Two songs ring through the clear March night—
Songs which the night with burning tears
Sings out again to the coming years.

436.   *From the Suburbs*

It rushes home, our own express,
So cheerfully, no one would guess
      The weight it carries

Of tired husbands, back from town,
For each of whom, in festal gown,   5
      A fond wife tarries.

For each of whom a better half,
At even, serves the fatted calf,
      In strange disguises,

At anxious boards of all degree,   10
Down to the simple 'egg at tea,'
      Which love devises.

For whom all day, disconsolate,
Deserted villas have to wait,
      Detached and Semi—   15

Barred by their own affairs, which are
As hard to pass through as the far
      Famed Alpine Gemmi.

Sometimes as I at leisure roam,
Admiring my suburban home,   20
      I wonder sadly

If men will always come and go
In these vast numbers, to and fro,
        So fast and madly.

I muse on what the spell can be,
Which causes this activity:
        Who of our Sages

The potent charm has meted out
To tall and thin, to short and stout,
        Of varying ages.

I think, when other fancy flags,
The magic lies within the bags
        Which journey ever

In silent, black mysterious ways,
With punctual owners, all their days
        And fail them never.

In some perhaps sweet flowers lie,
Sweet flowers which shape a destiny
        To pain or pleasure,

Or lady's glove, or ringlet bright,
Or many another keepsake light,
        Which true knights treasure.

May be—may be—Romance is rife,
Despite our busy bustling life,
        And rules us gaily,

And shows no sign of weariness,
But in our very own express,
        Does travel daily.

Edith Nesbit (Mrs Bland, Mrs Tucker) (1858–1924)

437.　　　　　　　　*Under Convoy*

Too many the questions, too subtle
　　The doubts that bewilder my brain!
Too strong is the strength of old custom
　　For iron convention's cold reign;
Too doubtful the issue of conflict, 5
　　Too leafless the crown and too vain!

Driven blindly by wind and by current,
　　Too weak to be strong as I would,
Too good to be bad as my promptings,
　　Too bad to be valued as good, 10
I would do the work that I cannot—
　　And will not, the work that I could.

As a swimmer alone in mid-ocean
　　Breasts wave after green wave, until
He sees the horizon unbroken 15
　　By any coast-line—so I still
Swam blindly through life, not perceiving
　　The infinite stretch of life's ill.

But wave after wave crowds upon me—
　　I am tired, I can face them no more— 20
Let me sink—or not sink—you receive me,
　　And I rest in your arms as before,
Which were waiting, O Love, to receive me,
　　Fulfilling the troth that you swore.

And so you are left me—what matters 25
　　Of Freedom, or Duty, or Right?
Let my chance of a life-work be ended,
　　End my chance of a soul's worthy fight!
End my chance to oppose—ah, how vainly!—
　　Vast wrong with its mass and its might! 30

Hold me fast—kiss me close—and persuade me
   'Tis better to lean upon you
Than to play out my part unsupported,
   My share in the world's work to do.
'Tis better be safe and ignoble   35
   Than be free, and be wretched, and true.

And you think that you offer a haven,
   As you do, for the storm-blown and tossed,
And you know not how under your kisses
   The soul of me shrinks and is lost: 40
And you save me my ease as a woman,
   —And the life of a soul is the cost!

(1889)

438.   *Inspiration*

I wandered in the enchanted wood,
   And as I wandered there, I sang
A song I never understood,
   Though sweet the music rang.

I held a lily white and fair,   5
   Its perfume was a song divine,
A song like moonlight and clear air,
   No rose-hued cloud like mine.

Beneath pale moon and wind-winged skies
   My lips were dumb as one drew near,   10
Folded warm wings across my eyes
   And whispered in my ear.

He left a flame-flower in my hand,
   And bade me sing as heretofore
The song I could not understand;   15
   But I can sing no more.

His secret seals my dumb lips fast,
   My lily withered 'neath his wing;
But now I understand at last
   The song I used to sing.   20

Among His Books

439.

A silent room—gray with a dusty blight
    Of loneliness;
A room with not enough of life or light
    Its form to dress.

Books enough though! The groaning sofa bears 5
    A goodly store—
Books on the window-seat, and on the chairs,
    And on the floor.

Books of all sorts of soul, all sorts of age,
    All sorts of face— 10
Black-letter, vellum, and the flimsy page
    Of commonplace.

All bindings, from the cloth whose hue distracts
    One's weary nerves,
To yellow parchment, binding rare old tracts 15
    It serves—deserves.

Books on the shelves, and in the cupboard books,
    Worthless and rare—
Books on the mantelpiece—where'er one looks
    Books everywhere! 20

Books! books! the only things in life I find
    Not wholly vain.
Books in my hands—books in my heart enshrined—
    Books in my brain.

My friends are they: for children and for wife 25
    They serve me too;
For these alone, of all dear things in life,
    Have I found true.

They do not flatter, change, deny, deceive—
    Ah no—not they! 30
The same editions which one night you leave
    You find next day.

You don't find railway novels where you left
    Your Elzevirs!
Your Aldines don't betray you—leave bereft   35
    Your lonely years!

And yet this common book of Common Prayer
    My heart prefers,
Because the names upon the fly-leaf there
    Are mine and hers.   40

It's a dead flower that makes it open so—
    Forget-me-not—
The Marriage Service ... well, my dear, you know
    Who first forgot.

Those were the days when in the choir we two   45
    Sat—used to sing—
When I believed in God, in love, in you—
    In everything.

Through quiet lanes to church we used to come,
    Happy and good,   50
Clasp hands through sermon, and go slowly home
    Down through the wood.

Kisses? A certain yellow rose no doubt
    That porch still shows,
Whenever I hear kisses talked about   55
    I smell that rose!

No—I don't blame you—since you only proved
    My choice unwise,
And taught me books should trusted be and loved,
    Not lips and eyes!   60

And so I keep your book—your flower—to show
    How much I care
For the dear memory of what, you know,
    You never were.

(1888)

440.   *The Forest Pool*

Lean down and see your little face
    Reflected in the forest pool,
Tall foxgloves grow about the place,
    Forget-me-nots grow green and cool.
Look deep and see the naiad rise   5
To meet the sunshine of your eyes.

Lean down and see how you are fair,
    How gold your hair, your mouth how red;
See the leaves dance about your hair
    The wind has left unfilleted.   10
What naiad of them can compare
With you for good and dear and fair?

Ah! look no more—the water stirs,
    The naiad weeps your face to see,
Your beauty is more rare than hers,   15
    And you are more beloved than she.
Fly! fly, before she steals the charms
The pool has trusted to her arms.

(Sir) William Watson (1858–1935)

441.   *Imaginary Inscription*
    (on a rock resembling colossal human features)

The seafowl build in wrinkles of my face.
    Ages ere man was, man was mocked by me.
Kings fall, gods die, worlds crash. At my throne's base,
    In showers of bright white thunder, breaks the sea.

(1882)

442.   *The Metropolitan Underground Railway*

       Here were a goodly place wherein to die;—
          Grown latterly to sudden change averse,
       All violent contrasts fain avoid would I
          On passing from this world into a worse.

                    (1879)

Elizabeth ('Bessie') Craigmyle (*fl.* 1886)

443.   *Catullian Hendecasyllabics*

    Long ago, the Roman poet Catullus,
    Seeking to give some gift to future ages,
    More than his rhymes of very doubtful moral,
    Left, for a torture to us modern rhymsters,
    This most difficult form of all verse-cadence.   5
    English Sapphics Macaulay calls a failure,
    Swinburne-anapæsts drive a man half crazy;
    Why should we, who are neither Greek nor Latin,
    Fetter ourselves within these ancient metres?
    They are but fit for light love-tales and stories,   10
    Fit for praising the blossom of a girl's mouth,
    Or the creaming froth of the rich Falernian;
    Fit for songs in temple of Aphrodité,
    Not the glorious battle-crash of the Iliad.

444.   *Beginning Work*

         8th Jan., 1884.

    Hands that I love have touched my key before,
    Feet that I love passed through this fast-shut door.

    Two went before: and both have passed away.
    Their work is done: and mine begins to-day.

Now the fair head the Eastern sunbeams crown,
On the dark hair the Western rays pour down.

Here, where they lived and worked, with longing vain,
My heart cries out for them in bitter pain.

While all about me, in the sunlit air,
Linger the echoes of a once-heard prayer.

Teacher, I thank you, while my eyes are wet,
For lessons learnt I shall not soon forget.

Your careless pupil keeps a love most true;
A very tender memory of you.

Dear friend! no word of sorrow would I say,
Though it could bring you to my side to-day.

Nor by a wish would strive to keep you here—
Love casts out selfishness as well as fear.

No need to think that I am desolate;
We both can trust, and I can work and wait.

Enough if, at the last, you say, with tears,
"You have grown worthier in the waiting years."

445. *My Bookcase*

How many volumes do I miss!
   I wish, among folks' duties,
That they would rank returning books.
   But those morocco beauties
Are never touched except by me,
   And really, though I know it's
A shame, I do rejoice to think
   That no one borrows poets.

To those lost books my fancy clings,
   O'er them my memory grovels,
I swear in spirit when I see
   The gaps among the novels.

The Thackeray I "loved and lost,"
    I mourn with sorrow tender,
Whoever has it also has
    The curses of the lender.

The second shelf I frankly own
    A motley, queer collection,
Half-filled with grave philosophers,
    In spite of Kant's defection.
But Calverley and Kingsley sit
    Tucked in among the Germans,
And "Ouida" snugly nestles next
    My only book of sermons.

Spencer keeps cheerful company
    With "How I caught a Tartar,"
Near them the book I treasure most,
    My well-belovèd "Sartor."
Montgomery by Macaulay stands,
    The scorned beside the scorner,
And dear Mark Twain with Rabelais
    Is chatting in the corner.

Homer! This same old copy shone,
    Star of my childish vision,
To read it for myself was once
    The height of my ambition.
Full fifteen years ago, I made
    That blot upon the binding,
Trying to print my name in Greek,
    And difficulty finding.

Dear books! you answer questioning
    Without a why or wherefore.
Our friendship never had a jar;
    You seem to know and care for
The tender touches that I give
    To every well-worn cover,
And, as I love you, friends of mine,
    I could not love a lover.

446. Heaven and Earth

"'Let me not to the marriage of true minds admit impediment.' But is it not from the perfect union of intellectual sympathy in such that the most bitter human pain can come?"

SHE.

Since here I dwelt the years are seven,
Thou on earth, and I in heaven.

The saints are happy. I only know
The love of a life lies far below.

For gates of pearl and city of gold,   5
Give me the home of days of old.

Through song and harpings I strain my ear,
For my children's prayer I cannot hear.

Still thou art first. If I sin in this,
The pitying Christ will forgive, I wis.   10

One face is sad 'mid the angel mirth;
I in heaven, and thou on earth.

Still works in my heart the old love-leaven,
Thou on earth, and I in heaven.

HE.

Ah! Heaven is full: but here is dearth.   15
Thou in heaven, and I on earth.

Is it well with you? Do you never miss
Homejoy, and sorrow, and daily kiss?

Forgive me. Doubt will have its birth;
Thou in heaven, and I on earth.   20

Man's trust cannot cling as a woman's cleaves,
Through faith in some woman a man believes.

What matters the three years' path we trod,
If death can sunder the joined of God?

Over those years did ever brood
The beauty of your womanhood.

The touch of your lips made day of night;
Sweet saint, had I known you half aright,

I had seen a glory round your hair—
God's angel with me unaware.

I was blind and deaf till my angel fled;
What hope or help lies with the dead?

Though I cried to you in my bitterest need,
Though I wept my heart out, you would not heed.

What life, that goes unloved, would take
Friendship or love, that Death can break?

What were it to find, past Death's abyss,
A great gulf set 'twixt that life and this?

Better to hunger, long, and crave,
Than take God's best this side the grave.

Make that life climax all in this,
Leave heaven to teach the highest bliss.

But love and longing are little worth;
Thou in heaven, and I on earth.

447.   *Clasped Hands*

In the hurry of life they pass us by,
   And the hands we have touched but a moment before
     Drop lightly from ours, and so it ends,
And we acquiesce without knowing why;
   But the spirit clasps hands for the Evermore
     With those who in deed and in truth are friends.

448.   *Love's Resurrection*

I made a grave for Love two years ago,
   With tearless eyes I covered up my dead,
And over it I piled the winter snow.
   "Love has no resurrection"—So I said.

Ah! friend, can I forget? How changed I seem!   5
   Now, when our Northern spring-tide wakes the land,
I stand beside the grave; and yet I dream
   Love's resurrection very near at hand.

449.   *A Woman's 'Yes'*

"Veni, vidi," but *non "vici."*

I met her walking in the park,
   Observed the night was wet,
And slipped by slow gradations to
   The night when first we met.

Told her I saw, and straightway then   5
   Proceeded to adore,
And though six weeks had passed since that
   I only loved the more.

I said, with easy grace, that I
   Had read her through and through,   10
And by her eyes I fancied she
   Had learnt to love me too.

Then whispered low, (I trusted she
   Like feelings would confess),
"Ah! do you think me foolish, dear?"   15
   She answered promptly, "Yes."

450.   *Dream of the Pine*

               "*Ein Fichten-baum steht einsam.*"

          A pine-tree standeth lonely
               On a far Norland height,
          It slumbereth, while around it
               The snow falls thick and white.

          And of a palm it dreameth   5
               That, in a southern land,
          Lonely and silent standeth
               Amid the scorching sand.

                              —(Heine.)

451.   *The End of the Story*

          So the old story ends,
               Endeth for ever here.
               Once our two souls came near,
               Each was to other dear,
          We were more than lovers—friends.   5

          Ah ! all this *once* hath been.
               For while we twain did stand,
               Hand clasped in either hand,
               Was earthquake in Love's land,
          And a chasm yawned between.   10

          No rift too deep to cross;
               We had bridged it, had we tried,
               But now the gulf is wide,
               We shiver on either side,
          Neither can pass across.   15

          Were she a man, why then,
               No need of a magic wand,
               We should clasp each other's hand
               And he would understand,
          And all would come right again.   20

Were I a woman, she,
   Knowing she did me wrong,
   Being as sweet as strong,
   Would own her fault ere long;
Now, it will never be.   25

No more regretful talk.
   We saw Love's face turn gray
   With death. He lies to-day,
   Crushed down beneath the clay,
But still Love's ghost will walk.   30

I have paid him each grave-rite,
   For hardening memories sought,
   Have heaped above him ought
   Of bitter word and thought,
But the ghost comes forth at night.   35

They will haunt me all my days,
   Her turn of head and throat,
   Her tresses as they float,
   Her voice's clear low note,
And all her gracious ways.   40

No meeting while we live.
   In the dark, where life makes end,
   Where both our footsteps wend,
   I shall seek and find my friend,
And say, at last, "Forgive."   45

J. (James) K. (Kenneth) Stephen (1859–1892)

452.   *A Parodist's Apology*

If I've dared to laugh at you, Robert Browning,
   'Tis with eyes that with you have often wept:
You have oftener left me smiling or frowning,
   Than any beside, one bard except.

But once you spoke to me, storm-tongued poet,
    A trivial word in an idle hour;
But thrice I looked on your face and the glow it
    Bore from the flame of the inward power.

But you'd many a friend you never knew of,
    Your words lie hid in a hundred hearts,
And thousands of hands that you've grasped but few of
    Would be raised to shield you from slander's darts.

For you lived in the sight of the land that owned you,
    You faced the trial, and stood the test:
They have piled you a cairn that would fain have stoned you:
    You have spoken your message and earned your rest.

453.   *Steam-launches on the Thames*

Shall we, to whom the stream by right belongs,
Who travel silent, save, perchance, for songs;
Whose track's a ripple,—leaves the Thames a lake,
Nor frights the swan—scarce makes the rushes shake;
Who harmonize, exemplify, complete
And vivify a scene already sweet:
Who travel careless on, from lock to lock,
Oblivious that the world contains a clock,
With pace commensurate to our desires,
Propelled by other force than Stygian fire's;
Shall we be driven hence to leave a place
For these, who bring upon our stream disgrace:
The rush, the roar, the stench, the smoke, the steam,
The nightmare striking through our heavenly dream;
The scream as shrill and hateful to the ear
As when a peacock vents his rage and fear;
Which churn to fury all a glassy reach,
And heave rude breakers on a pebbly beach:
Which half o'erwhelm with waves our frailer craft,
While graceless shop-boys chuckle fore and aft:
Foul water-toadstools, noisome filth-stained shapes,
Fit only to be manned by dogs and apes:
Blots upon nature: scars that mar her smile:
Obscene, obtrusive, execrable, vile?

454. *The Philosopher and the Philanthropist*

  Searching an infinite Where,
  Probing a bottomless When,
   Dreamfully wandering,
   Ceaselessly pondering,
  What is the Wherefore of men: 5
  Bartering life for a There,
  Selling his soul for a Then,
   Baffling obscurity,
   Conning futurity,
  Usefulest, wisest of men!   10

  Grasping the Present of Life,
  Seizing a definite Now,
   Labouring thornfully,
   Banishing scornfully
  Doubts of his Whither and How: 15
  Spending his substance in Strife,
  Working a practical How,
   Letting obscurity
   Rest on futurity,
  Usefuler, wiser, I trow.   20

A. (Alfred) E. (Edward) Housman (1859–1936)

455. 'Oh who is that young sinner with handcuffs on his wrists?'

XVIII

Oh who is that young sinner with the handcuffs on his wrists?
And what has he been after that they groan and shake their fists?
And wherefore is he wearing such a conscience-stricken air?
Oh they're taking him to prison for the colour of his hair.

'Tis a shame to human nature, such a head of hair as his;   5
In the good old time 'twas hanging for the colour that it is;
Though hanging isn't bad enough and flaying would be fair
For the nameless and abominable colour of his hair.

Oh a deal of pains he's taken and a pretty price he's paid
To hide his poll or dye it of a mentionable shade;   10
But they've pulled the beggar's hat off for the world to see and stare,
And they're haling him to justice for the colour of his hair.

Now 'tis oakum for his fingers and the treadmill for his feet
And the quarry-gang on Portland in the cold and in the heat,
And between his spells of labour in the time he has to spare   15
He can curse the God that made him for the colour of his hair.

                                        (wr. 1895; pub. 1937)

456.   'The laws of God, the laws of man'

    The laws of God, the laws of man,
    He may keep that will and can;
    Not I: let God and man decree
    Laws for themselves and not for me;
    And if my ways are not as theirs   5
    Let them mind their own affairs.
    Their deeds I judge and much condemn,
    Yet when did I make laws for them?
    Please yourselves, say I, and they
    Need only look the other way.   10
    But no, they will not; they must still
    Wrest their neighbour to their will,
    And make me dance as they desire
    With jail and gallows and hell-fire.
    And how am I to face the odds   15
    Of man's bedevilment and God's?
    I, a stranger and afraid
    In a world I never made.
    They will be master, right or wrong;
    Though both are foolish, both are strong.   20
    And since, my soul, we cannot fly
    To Saturn nor to Mercury,
    Keep we must, if keep we can,
    These foreign laws of God and man.

                                    (wr. 1900; pub. 1922)

457.   'Yonder see the morning blink'

Yonder see the morning blink:
    The sun is up, and up must I,
To wash and dress and eat and drink
And look at things and talk and think
    And work, and God knows why.   5

Oh often have I washed and dressed
    And what's to show for all my pain?
Let me lie abed and rest:
Ten thousand times I've done my best
    And all's to do again.   10

from *A Shropshire Lad*

458.   II. 'Loveliest of trees, the cherry now'

Loveliest of trees, the cherry now
Is hung with bloom along the bough,
And stands about the woodland ride
Wearing white for Eastertide.

Now, of my threescore years and ten,   5
Twenty will not come again,
And take from seventy springs a score,
It only leaves me fifty more.

And since to look at things in bloom
Fifty springs are little room,   10
About the woodlands I will go
To see the cherry hung with snow.

459.   XVI. 'It nods and curtseys and recovers'

It nods and curtseys and recovers
    When the wind blows above,
The nettle on the graves of lovers
    That hanged themselves for love.

>   The nettle nods, the wind blows over,   5
>   The man, he does not move,
>   The lover of the grave, the lover
>   That hanged himself for love.

460.   XXXIX. 'My dreams are of a field afar'

>   My dreams are of a field afar
>   And blood and smoke and shot.
>   There in their graves my comrades are,
>   In my grave I am not.
>
>   I too was taught the trade of man   5
>   And spelt the lesson plain;
>   But they, when I forgot and ran,
>   Remembered and remain.

461.   XL. 'Into my heart an air that kills'

>   Into my heart an air that kills
>   From yon far country blows:
>   What are those blue remembered hills,
>   What spires, what farms are those?
>
>   This is the land of lost content,   5
>   I see it shining plain,
>   The happy highways where I went
>   And cannot come again.

Francis Thompson (1859–1907)

462.   *The Hound of Heaven*

>   I fled Him, down the nights and down the days;
>   I fled Him, down the arches of the years;
>   I fled Him, down the labyrinthine ways
>   Of my own mind; and in the mist of tears

I hid from Him, and under running laughter. 5
    Up vistaed hopes I sped;
    And shot, precipitated,
Adown Titanic glooms of chasmèd fears,
  From those strong Feet that followed, followed after.
    But with unhurrying chase, 10
    And unperturbèd pace,
  Deliberate speed, majestic instancy,
    They beat—and a Voice beat
    More instant than the Feet—
  'All things betray thee, who betrayest Me.' 15

    I pleaded, outlaw-wise,
By many a hearted casement, curtained red,
  Trellised with intertwining charities;
(For, though I knew His love Who followèd,
    Yet was I sore adread 20
Lest, having Him, I must have naught beside)
But, if one little casement parted wide,
  The gust of His approach would clash it to:
  Fear wist not to evade, as Love wist to pursue.
Across the margent of the world I fled, 25
  And troubled the gold gateways of the stars,
  Smiting for shelter on their clangèd bars;
    Fretted to dulcet jars
And silvern chatter the pale ports o' the moon.
I said to Dawn: Be sudden—to Eve: Be soon; 30
With thy young skiey blossoms heap me over
    From this tremendous Lover—
Float thy vague veil about me, lest He see!
  I tempted all His servitors, but to find
My own betrayal in their constancy, 35
In faith to Him their fickleness to me,
  Their traitorous trueness, and their loyal deceit.
To all swift things for swiftness did I sue;
  Clung to the whistling mane of every wind.
    But whether they swept, smoothly fleet, 40
    The long savannahs of the blue;
      Or whether, Thunder-driven,
    They clanged his chariot 'thwart a heaven,
Plashy with flying lightnings round the spurn o' their feet:—
  Fear wist not to evade as Love wist to pursue. 45
    Still with unhurrying chase,
    And unperturbèd pace,
  Deliberate speed, majestic instancy,

>   Came on the following Feet,
>   And a Voice above their beat—
>   'Naught shelters thee, who wilt not shelter Me.'

> I sought no more that after which I strayed
>   In face of man or maid;
> But still within the little children's eyes
>   Seems something, something that replies.
> *They* at least are for me, surely for me!
> I turned me to them very wistfully;
> But just as their young eyes grew sudden fair
>   With dawning answers there,
> Their angel plucked them from me by the hair.
> 'Come then, ye other children, Nature's—share
> With me' (said I) 'your delicate fellowship;
>   Let me greet you lip to lip,
>   Let me twine with you caresses,
>   Wantoning
>   With our Lady-Mother's vagrant tresses,
>   Banqueting
>   With her in her wind-walled palace,
>   Underneath her azured daïs,
>   Quaffing, as your taintless way is,
>   From a chalice
> Lucent-weeping out of the dayspring.'
>   So it was done:
> *I* in their delicate fellowship was one—
> Drew the bolt of Nature's secrecies.
>   I knew all the swift importings
>   On the wilful face of skies;
>   I knew how the clouds arise
>   Spumèd of the wild sea-snortings;
>   All that's born or dies
>   Rose and drooped with; made them shapers
> Of mine own moods, or wailful or divine;
>   With them joyed and was bereaven.
>   I was heavy with the even,
>   When she lit her glimmering tapers
>   Round the day's dead sanctities.
>   I laughed in the morning's eyes.
> I triumphed and I saddened with all weather,
>   Heaven and I wept together,
> And its sweet tears were salt with mortal mine;
> Against the red throb of its sunset-heart

50

55

60

65

70

75

80

85

90

   I laid my own to beat,
   And share commingling heat;
But not by that, by that, was eased my human smart.
In vain my tears were wet on Heaven's grey cheek.
For ah! we know not what each other says,
   These things and I; in sound *I* speak—
Their sound is but their stir, they speak by silences.
Nature, poor stepdame, cannot slake my drouth;
   Let her, if she would owe me,
Drop yon blue bosom-veil of sky, and show me
   The breasts o' her tenderness:
Never did any milk of hers once bless
    My thirsting mouth.
    Nigh and nigh draws the chase,
    With unperturbèd pace,
   Deliberate speed, majestic instancy;
    And past those noisèd Feet
    A Voice comes yet more fleet—
  'Lo! naught contents thee, who content'st not Me.'

Naked I wait Thy love's uplifted stroke!
My harness piece by piece Thou hast hewn from me,
   And smitten me to my knee;
   I am defenceless utterly.
   I slept, methinks, and woke,
And, slowly gazing, find me stripped in sleep.
In the rash lustihead of my young powers,
   I shook the pillaring hours
And pulled my life upon me; grimed with smears,
I stand amid the dust o' the mounded years—
My mangled youth lies dead beneath the heap.
My days have crackled and gone up in smoke,
Have puffed and burst as sun-starts on a stream.
   Yea, faileth now even dream
The dreamer, and the lute the lutanist;
Even the linked fantasies, in whose blossomy twist
I swung the earth a trinket at my wrist,
Are yielding; cords of all too weak account
For earth with heavy griefs so overplussed.
   Ah! is Thy love indeed
A weed, albeit an amaranthine weed,
Suffering no flowers except its own to mount?
   Ah! must—
   Designer infinite!—

Ah! must Thou char the wood ere Thou canst limn with it? 135
My freshness spent its wavering shower i' the dust;
And now my heart is as a broken fount,
Wherein tear-drippings stagnate, spilt down ever
      From the dank thoughts that shiver
Upon the sighful branches of my mind. 140
    Such is; what is to be?
The pulp so bitter, how shall taste the rind?
I dimly guess what Time in mists confounds;
Yet ever and anon a trumpet sounds
From the hid battlements of Eternity; 145
Those shaken mists a space unsettle, then
Round the half-glimpsèd turrets slowly wash again.
    But not ere him who summoneth
    I first have seen, enwound
With glooming robes purpureal, cypress-crowned; 150
His name I know, and what his trumpet saith.
Whether man's heart or life it be which yields
    Thee harvest, must Thy harvest-fields
    Be dunged with rotten death?

    Now of that long pursuit 155
    Comes on at hand the bruit;
That Voice is round me like a bursting sea:
    'And is thy earth so marred,
    Shattered in shard on shard?
    Lo, all things fly thee, for thou fliest Me! 160

    'Strange, piteous, futile thing!
Wherefore should any set thee love apart?
Seeing none but I makes much of naught' (He said),
'And human love needs human meriting:
    How hast thou merited— 165
Of all man's clotted clay the dingiest clot?
    Alack, thou knowest not
How little worthy of any love thou art!
Whom wilt thou find to love ignoble thee,
    Save Me, save only Me? 170
All which I took from thee I did but take,
    Not for thy harms,
But just that thou might'st seek it in My arms.
    All which thy child's mistake
Fancies as lost, I have stored for thee at home: 175
    Rise, clasp My hand, and come!'

    Halts by me that footfall:
      Is my gloom, after all,
Shade of His hand, outstretched caressingly?
    'Ah, fondest, blindest, weakest,   180
      I am He Whom thou seekest!
Thou dravest love from thee, who dravest Me.'

463.   *Memorat Memoria*

Come you living or dead to me, out of the silt of the Past,
With the sweet of the piteous first, and the shame of the shameful last?
Come with your dear and dreadful face through the passes of Sleep,
The terrible mask, and the face it masked—the face you did not keep?
You are neither two nor one—I would you were one or two,   5
For your awful self is embalmed in the fragrant self I knew:
And Above may ken, and Beneath may ken, what I mean by these words of whirl,
But by my sleep that sleepeth not,—O Shadow of a Girl!—
Naught here but I and my dreams shall know the secret of this thing:—
For ever the songs I sing are sad with the songs I never sing,   10
Sad are sung songs, but how more sad the songs we dare not sing!

Ah, the ill that we do in tenderness, and the hateful horror of love!
It has sent more souls to the unslaked Pit than it ever will draw above.
I damned you, girl, with my pity, who had better by far been thwart,
And drave you hard on the track to hell, because I was gentle of heart.   15
I shall have no comfort now in scent, no ease in dew, for this;
I shall be afraid of daffodils, and rose-buds are amiss;
You have made a thing of innocence as shameful as a sin,
I shall never feel a girl's soft arms without horror of the skin.
My child ! what was it that I sowed, that I so ill should reap?   20
You have done this to me. And I, what I to you?—It lies with Sleep.

464.   *A Dead Astronomer*

           STEPHEN PERRY, S. J.

    Starry amorist, starward gone,
      Thou art—what thou didst gaze upon!
    Passed through thy golden garden's bars,
    Thou seest the Gardener of the Stars.
      She, about whose moonèd brows   5

Seven stars make seven glows,
Seven lights for seven woes;
She, like thine own Galaxy,
All lustres in one purity:—
What said'st thou, Astronomer, 10
When thou did'st discover *her*?
When thy hand its tube let fall,
Thou found'st the fairest Star of all!

465. *To the Dead Cardinal of Westminster*

(HENRY EDWARD MANNING: DIED JANUARY 1892)

I will not perturbate
Thy Paradisal state
    With praise
    Of thy dead days;

To the new-heavened say, 5
'Spirit, thou wert fine clay':
    This do,
    Thy praise who knew.

Therefore my spirit clings
Heaven's porter by the wings, 10
    And holds
    Its gated golds

Apart, with thee to press
A private business;—
    Whence, 15
    Deign me audience.

Anchorite, who didst dwell
With all the world for cell,
    My soul
    Round me doth roll 20

A sequestration bare.
Too far alike we were,
    Too far
    Dissimilar.

For its burning fruitage I 25
Do climb the tree o' the sky;
    Do prize
  Some human eyes.

You smelt the Heaven-blossoms,
And all the sweet embosoms 30
    The dear
  Uranian year.

Those Eyes my weak gaze shuns,
Which to the suns are Suns,
    Did 35
  Not affray your lid.

The carpet was let down
(With golden moultings strown)
    For you
  Of the angels' blue. 40

But I, ex-Paradised,
The shoulder of your Christ
    Find high
  To lean thereby.

So flaps my helpless sail, 45
Bellying with neither gale,
    Of Heaven
  Nor Orcus even.

Life is a coquetry
Of Death, which wearies me, 50
    Too sure
  Of the amour;

A tiring-room where I
Death's divers garments try,
    Till fit 55
  Some fashion sit.

It seemeth me too much
I do rehearse for such
    A mean
  And single scene. 60

The sandy glass hence bear—
Antique remembrancer:
    My veins
  Do spare its pains.

With secret sympathy
My thoughts repeat in me
    Infirm
  The turn o' the worm

Beneath my appointed sod;
The grave is in my blood;
    I shake
  To winds that take

Its grasses by the top;
The rains thereon that drop
    Perturb
  With drip acerb

My subtly answering soul;
The feet across its knoll
    Do jar
  Me from afar.

As sap foretastes the spring;
As Earth ere blossoming
    Thrills
  With far daffodils,

And feels her breast turn sweet
With the unconceivèd wheat:
    So doth
  My flesh foreloathe

The abhorrèd spring of Dis,
With seething presciences
    Affirm
  The preparate worm.

I have no thought that I,
When at the last I die,
    Shall reach
  To gain your speech.

But you, should that be so,
May very well, I know,
     May well
  To me in hell

With recognizing eyes
Look from your Paradise—
     'God bless
  Thy hopelessness!'

Call, holy soul, O call
The hosts angelical,
     And say,—
  'See, far away

'Lies one I saw on earth;
One stricken from his birth
     With curse
  Of destinate verse.

'What place doth He ye serve
For such sad spirit reserve,—
     Given,
  In dark lieu of Heaven,

'The impitiable Dæmon,
Beauty, to adore and dream on,
     To be
  Perpetually

'Hers, but she never his?
He reapeth miseries;
     Foreknows
  His wages woes;

'He lives detachèd days;
He serveth not for praise;
     For gold
  He is not sold;

'Deaf is he to world's tongue;
He scorneth for his song
     The loud
  Shouts of the crowd;

'He asketh not world's eyes;
Not to world's ears he cries;
  Saith,—"These
  Shut, if ye please!"

'He measureth world's pleasure,
World's ease, as Saints might measure;
  For hire
  Just love entire

'He asks, not grudging pain;
And knows his asking vain,
  And cries—
  "Love! Love!" and dies,

'In guerdon of long duty,
Unowned by Love or Beauty;
  And goes—
  Tell, tell, who knows!

'Aliens from Heaven's worth,
Fine beasts who nose i' the earth,
  Do there
  Reward prepare.

'But are *his* great desires
Food but for nether fires?
  Ah me,
  A mystery!

'Can it be his alone,
To find when all is known,
  That what
  He solely sought

'Is lost, and thereto lost
All that its seeking cost?
  That he
  Must finally,

'Through sacrificial tears,
And anchoretic years,
  Tryst
  With the sensualist?'

So ask; and if they tell
The secret terrible,   170
    Good friend,
I pray thee send

Some high gold embassage
To teach my unripe age.
    Tell!   175
Lest my feet walk hell.

466. *The End of It*

She did not love to love, but hated him
For making her to love; and so her whim
From passion taught misprision to begin.
And all this sin
Was because love to cast out had no skill   5
Self, which was regent still.
Her own self-will made void her own self's will.

467. *The Singer Saith of his Song*

The touches of man's modern speech
Perplex her unacquainted tongue;
There seems through all her songs a sound
    Of falling tears. She is not young.

Within her eyes' profound arcane   5
    Resides the glory of her dreams;
Behind her secret cloud of hair
    She sees the Is beyond the Seems.

Her heart sole-towered in her steep spirit,
    Somewhat sweet is she, somewhat wan: 10
And she sings the songs of Sion
    By the streams of Babylon.

468.   *Poems on Children: Daisy*

    Where the thistle lifts a purple crown
        Six foot out of the turf,
    And the harebell shakes on the windy hill—
        O the breath of the distant surf!—

    The hills look over on the South,   5
        And southward dreams the sea;
    And with the sea-breeze hand in hand
        Came innocence and she.

    Where 'mid the gorse the raspberry
        Red for the gatherer springs,   10
    Two children did we stray and talk
        Wise, idle, childish things.

    She listened with big-lipped surprise,
        Breast-deep mid flower and spine:
    Her skin was like a grape whose veins   15
        Run snow instead of wine.

    She knew not those sweet words she spake,
        Nor knew her own sweet way;
    But there's never a bird, so sweet a song
        Thronged in whose throat that day.   20

    Oh, there were flowers in Storrington
        On the turf and on the spray;
    But the sweetest flower on Sussex hills
        Was the Daisy-flower that day!

    Her beauty smoothed earth's furrowed face.   25
        She gave me tokens three:—
    A look, a word of her winsome mouth,
        And a wild raspberry.

    A berry red, a guileless look,
        A still word,—strings of sand!   30
    And yet they made my wild, wild heart
        Fly down to her little hand.

    For standing artless as the air,
        And candid as the skies,
    She took the berries with her hand,   35
        And the love with her sweet eyes.

The fairest things have fleetest end,
    Their scent survives their close:
But the rose's scent is bitterness
    To him that loved the rose.   40

She looked a little wistfully,
    Then went her sunshine way:—
The sea's eye had a mist on it,
    And the leaves fell from the day.

She went her unremembering way,   45
    She Went and left in me
The pang of all the partings gone,
    And partings yet to be.

She left me marvelling why my soul
    Was sad that she was glad;   50
At all the sadness in the sweet,
    The sweetness in the sad.

Still, still I seemed to see her, still
    Look up with soft replies,
And take the berries with her hand,   55
    And the love with her lovely eyes.

Nothing begins, and nothing ends,
    That is not paid with moan;
For we are born in other's pain,
    And perish in our own.   60

Arthur I. (Ignatius) Conan Doyle (1859–1930)

469.   *The Frontier Line*

    What marks the frontier line?
        Thou man of India, say!
    Is it the Himalayas sheer,
    The rocks and valleys of Cashmere,
    Or Indus as she seeks the south   5
    From Attoch to the fivefold mouth?
        "Not that! Not that!"
        Then answer me, I pray!
    What marks the frontier line?

What marks the frontier line?
   Thou man of Burmah, speak!
Is it traced from Mandalay,
And down the marches of Cathay,
From Bhamo south to Kiang-mai,
And where the buried rubies lie?
   "Not that! Not that!"
   Then tell me what I seek:
What marks the frontier line?

What marks the frontier line?
   Thou Africander, say!
Is it shown by Zulu kraal,
By Drakensberg or winding Vaal,
Or where the Shiré waters seek
Their outlet east at Mozambique?
   "Not that! Not that!
   There is a surer way
To mark the frontier line."

What marks the frontier line?
   Thou man of Egypt, tell!
Is it traced on Luxor's sand,
Where Karnak's painted pillars stand,
Or where the river runs between
The Ethiop and Bishareen?
   "Not that! Not that!
   By neither stream nor well
We mark the frontier line.

"But be it east or west,
   One common sign we bear,
The tongue may change, the soil, the sky,
But where your British brothers lie,
The lonely cairn, the nameless grave,
Still fringe the flowing Saxon wave.
   'Tis that! 'Tis where
   They lie—the men who placed it there,
That marks the frontier line."

Ernest Rhys (1859–1946)

470. *At the Rhymers' Club*

I. THE TOAST

Set fools untó their folly!
  Our folly is pure wit,
As 'twere the Muse turned jolly:
For poets' melancholy,—
  We will not think of it.   5

As once Rare Ben and Herrick
  Set older Fleet Street mad,
With wit, not esoteric,
And laughter that was lyric,
  And roystering rhymes and glad   10

As they, we drink defiance
  To-night to all but Rhyme,
And most of all to Science,
And all such skins of lions
  That hide the ass of time.   15

To-night, to rhyme as they did
  Were well,—ah, were it ours,
Who find the Muse degraded,
And changed, I fear, and faded,
  Her laurel crown and flowers.   20

Ah, rhymers, for that sorrow
  The more o'ertakes delight,
The more this madness borrow:—
If care be king to-morrow,
  We toast Queen Rhyme to-night.   25

II. MARLOWE

With wine and blood and wit and deviltry,
He sped the heroic flame of English verse:
Bethink ye, rhymers, what your claim may be,
Who in smug suburbs put the Muse to nurse?

471.   *The Night Ride*

> To-night we rode beneath a moon
>   That made the moorland pale;
> And our horses' feet kept well the tune
>   And our pulses did not fail.
>
> The moon shone clear; the hoarfrost fell,   5
>   The world slept, as it seemed;
> Sleep held the night, but we rode well,
>   And as we rode we dreamed.
>
> We dreamed of ghostly horse and hound,
>   And flight at dead of night;—   10
> The more the fearful thoughts we found,
>   The more was our delight.
>
> And when we heard the white owl fly,
>   And hoot with mournful tone,
> We thought to see dead men go by,   15
>   And pressed our horses on.
>
> The merrier then was Silvia's song
>   Upon the homeward road,—
> Oh, whether the way be short or long
>   Is all in the rider's mood!   20
>
> And still our pulses kept the tale,
>   Our gallop kept the tune,
> As round and over hill and vale
>   We rode beneath the moon.

472.   *An Autobiography*

Wales England wed; so I was bred. 'Twas merry London gave me breath.
I dreamt of love, and fame: I strove. But Ireland taught me love was best:
And Irish eyes, and London cries, and streams of Wales, may tell the rest.
What more than these I asked of Life, I am content to have from Death.

Rosamund Marriott Watson (Graham R. Tomson) (1860–1911)

473.
Vespertilia

In the late autumn's dusky-golden prime,
When sickles gleam and rusts the idle plough,
The time of apples dropping from the bough,
And yellow leaves on sycamore and lime;
O'er grassy uplands far above the sea   5
Often at twilight would my footsteps fare,
And oft I met a stranger-woman there
   Who stayed and spake with me:
Hard by the ancient barrow smooth and green,
Whose rounded burg swells dark upon the sky,   10
Lording it high o'er dusky dell and dene,
   We wandered—she and I.

Ay, many a time as came the evening hour
And the red moon rose up behind the sheaves,
I found her straying by that barren bower,   15
Her fair face glimmering like a white wood-flower
That gleams through withered leaves.
Her mouth was redder than the pimpernel,
Her eyes seemed darker than the purple air
'Neath brows half hidden—I remember well—   20
'Mid mists of cloudy hair.

And all about her breast, around her head,
Was wound a wide veil shadowing cheek and chin,
Woven like the ancient grave-gear of the dead:
   A twisted clasp and pin   25
Confined her long blue mantle's heavy fold
Of splendid tissue dropping to decay,
   Faded like some rich raiment worn of old,
With rents and tatters gaping to the day.
Her sandals wrought about with threads of gold,   30
Scarce held together still, so worn were they,
Yet sewn with winking gems of green and blue,
And pale as pearls her naked feet shone through.

And all her talk was of some outland rare,
Where myrtles blossom by the blue sea's rim,
And life is ever good and sunny and fair;
"Long since," she sighed, "I sought this island grey—
Here, where the winds moan and the sun is dim,
When his beaked galleys cleft the ocean spray,
For love I followed him."

Once, as we stood, we heard the nightingale
Pipe from a thicket on the sheer hillside,
Breathless she hearkened, still and marble-pale,
Then turned to me with strange eyes open wide—
"Now I remember! ... Now I know!" said she,
"Love will be life ... ah, Love *is* Life!" she cried,
"And thou—thou lovest me?"

I took her chill hands gently in mine own,
"Dear, but no love is mine to give," I said,
"My heart is colder than the granite stone
That guards my true-love in her grassy bed;
My faith and troth are hers, and hers alone,
Are hers ... and she is dead."

Weeping, she drew her veil about her face,
And faint her accents were and dull with pain;
"Poor Vespertilia! gone her days of grace,
Now doth she plead for love—and plead in vain:
None praise her beauty now, or woo her smile!

. . . .

Ah, hadst thou loved me but a little while,
   I might have lived again."

Then slowly as a wave along the shore
She glided from me to yon sullen mound;
My frozen heart, relenting, smote me sore—
Too late—I searched the hollow slopes around,
Swiftly I followed her, but nothing found,
   Nor saw nor heard her more.

And now, alas, my true-love's memory,
Even as a dream of night-time half-forgot,
   Fades faint and far from me,
And all my thoughts are of the stranger still,
   Yea, though I loved her not:

I loved her not—and yet—I fain would see,
Upon the wind-swept hill,
Her dark veil fluttering in the autumn breeze;
Fain would I hear her changeful voice awhile, 75
Soft as the wind of spring-tide in the trees,
And watch her slow, sweet smile.

Ever the thought of her abides with me
Unceasing as the murmur of the sea;
When the round moon is low and night-birds flit, 80
When sink the stubble-fires with smouldering flame,
Over and o'er the sea-wind sighs her name,
   And the leaves whisper it.

"*Poor Vespertilia,*" sing the grasses sere,
"*Poor Vespertilia,*" moans the surf-beat shore; 85
Almost I feel her very presence near—
   Yet she comes nevermore.

474.   *A Ballad of the Were-Wolf*

The gudewife sits i' the chimney-neuk,
   An' looks on the louping flame;
The rain fa's chill, and the win' ca's shrill,
   Ere the auld gudeman comes hame.

"Oh, why is your cheek sae wan, gudewife? 5
   An' why do ye glower on me?
Sae dour ye luik i' the chimney-neuk,
   Wi' the red licht in your e'e!

"Yet this nicht should ye welcome me,
   This ae nicht mair than a', 10
For I hae scotched yon great grey wolf
   That took our bairnies twa.

"'Twas a sair, sair strife for my very life,
   As I warstled there my lane;
But I'll hae her heart or e'er we part, 15
   Gin ever we meet again.

"An' 'twas ae sharp stroke o' my bonny knife
    That gar'd her haud awa';
Fu' fast she went out-owre the bent
    Wi'outen her right fore-paw.   20

"Gae tak' the foot o' the drumlie brute,
    And hang it upo' the wa';
An' the next time that we meet, gudewife,
    The tane of us shall fa'."

He's flung his pouch on the gudewife's lap,   25
    I' the firelicht shinin' fair,
Yet naught they saw o' the grey wolf's paw,
    For a bluidy hand lay there.

O hooly, hooly rose she up,
    Wi' the red licht in her e'e,   30
Till she stude but a span frae the auld gudeman
    Whiles never a word spak' she.

But she stripped the claiths frae her lang richt arm,
    That were wrappit roun' and roun',
The first was white, an' the last was red;   35
    And the fresh bluid dreeped adown.

She stretchit him out her lang right arm,
    An' cauld as the deid stude he.
The flames louped bricht i' the gloamin' licht—
    There was nae hand there to see!   40

475.   *Of the Earth, Earthy*

Never for us those dreams aforetime shown
Of white-winged angels on a shining stair,
Or seas of sapphire round a jasper throne:
Give us the spangled dusk, the turbid street;
The dun, dim pavement trod by myriad feet,   5
Stained with the yellow lamplight here and there;
The chill blue skies beyond the spires of stone:

The world's invincible youth is all our own,
Here where we feel life's pulses burn and beat.

Here is the pride of Life, be it foul or fair,   10
This clash and swirl of streets in the twilight air;
Beauty and Grime, indifferent, side by side;
Surfeit and Thirst, Endeavour and Despair,
Content and Squalor, Lassitude and Care,
All in the golden lamplight glorified: 15
All quick, all real, hurrying near and wide.

Life and Life's worst and best be ours to share,
Charm of the motley! undefined and rare;
Melodious discord in the heart o' the tune,
Sweet with the hoarse note jarring everywhere!   20

Let us but live, and every field shall bear
Fruit for our joy; for Life is Life's best boon.

476.   *In the Rain*

Rain in the glimmering street—
Murmurous, rhythmical beat;
Shadows that flicker and fly;
Blue of wet road, of wet sky,
(Grey in the depths and the heights);   5
Orange of numberless lights,
Shapes fleeting on, going by.

Figures, fantastical, grim—
Figures, prosaical, tame,
Each with chameleon-stain,   10
Dun in the crepuscle dim,
Red in the nimbus of flame—
Glance through the veil of the rain.

Rain in the measureless street—
Vistas of orange and blue;   15
Music of echoing feet,
Pausing, and pacing anew.
Rain, and the clamour of wheels,
Splendour, and shadow, and sound;
Coloured confusion that reels   20
Lost in the twilight around.

. . . .

> When I lie hid from the light,
> Stark, with the turf overhead,
> Still, on a rainy Spring night,
> I shall come back from the dead.   25

477.   *Old Pauline*

So your boys are going to Paris? That's how I lost my own.
Lonely? Ah yes, but I know it, the old are always alone.
You remember my boys, Euphrasie? No? Was it before your day?
Each, when his turn came, kissed me, and cried; but they went away.
How I longed for them, always, vainly! and thought of them, early and late;   5
I would start and look round in the pasture if any one clicked the gate.
But a greater sorrow fell on me: my Marie, with eyes so blue,
Grew restless, poor bird! in the home-nest—she must seek her fortune too.
And, once the desire is on them, 'tis a fever, they cannot stay;
And Marie, my poor little Marie! well, I missed her one bright spring day.   10
'Twas *then* that my heart broke, 'Phrasie, for my children gay and tall,
For fair, vile, glittering Paris had taken them all.
Yet the good God is merciful always; I live, and I have no pain,
Only the old dumb longing for the children home again.
Still I watch the road to the city, up the glistening sun-set track,   15
But they never come back, Euphrasie—never come back!

478.   *The Moor Girl's Well*

> Where the still sunshine falls
>   On faded splendours of old days long done—
> The Moorish castle halls
>   Void and forsaken, save for wind and sun—
> Lies a square court-yard fenced with painted walls.   5
> There, where the yellow sunlight lies asleep,
>   Bound in a drowsy spell,
> Glimmers that silent water, clear and deep,
>   Our village maidens call the Moor Girl's Well.
>
> Fair are the village maidens—kind and fair—   10
>   And black-browed Manuela smiles on me,
>   Driving her white goats homeward leisurely
> Up from the pastures through the evening air,
>   And I fling back her jest,

Laughing, with all the will to woo her—yet
I pass—the words unspoke, mine eyelids wet.
   Why, my heart knoweth best.

Through the grey dusk of dawn
   I went one autumn morning, long ago,
     Forth, with my flock behind me trailing slow;
   And to that castle in the vale below—
I know not why—my vagrant steps were drawn.

And I beheld a woman, fair and young,
   Beside the well-spring in the court-yard bare,
   Dabbling her slim feet in the water there,
And singing softly in some outland tongue;
No veil about her golden beauty clung—
   No veil nor raiment rare,
   Save but her dusky hair.

Sweetly she smiled on me, and, lisping, spake,
   Even as a child that strives to say aright
Some unlearned language for its teacher's sake;
   Her long eyes pierced me with their diamond light.
   She told me of an old spell laid on her
That bound her in the semblance of a snake,
   Lonely and mute as in the sepulchre.

And he who would this bitter bondage break
   Must suffer her in serpent form to cling
Close to his breast, unshrinking, undismayed,
And let her cold, kiss on his lips be laid
   Thrice without faltering.

All this I promised her, for fervently
   I longed to free her from the evil spell—
Pity and love so swiftly wrought on me!
   (Scarce I beheld her but I loved her well.)
Then, as I spake, she vanished suddenly,
   And o'er the marble came
A great snake, brighter than a shifting flame;

With scales of emerald and of amethyst
   Her lithe coils dazzled me, and yet the same
Shone her sad eyes; but quickly, ere I wist,
She twined about me, clammy-chill and cold,
Staying my life-breath with her strangling fold;

The bright eyes neared mine own, the thin mouth hissed,
    And I, nigh swooning, shrank from her embrace.   55
  "Leave me," I gasped, and turned aside my face—
"Leave me, and loose me from thy loathly hold!"

The icy bands fell from me; numb with pain,
    Half blind, I sank beside the Moor Girl's Well,
Hearing a sough as of the summer rain,   60
A slow, sad voice from out the depths complain,
  "Redoubled tenfold is the cruel spell."

And sometimes when the yellow dawn is chill
    The memory grips my heart so that I rise,
And go with hurried footsteps down the hill   65
    Where the lone court-yard lies,
And kneeling gaze into those waters still
    Beneath the quiet skies:
"*Only come back and I shall do thy will!*"

I seek, and still the steely deep denies   70
The piercing sorrow of her diamond eyes;
I seek, but only see
Mine own gaze back at me.

479.   *Hic Jacet*

And is it possible?—and must it be—
At last, indifference 'twixt you and me?
We who have loved so well,
Must we indeed fall under that strange spell,
  The tyranny of the grave?   5

In sullen severance patient and resigned,
By each of each forgotten out of mind—
  Dear, is there none to save?
Must you whose heart makes answer to mine own,
Whose voice compels me with its every tone,   10
Must you forget my fealty to claim,
And I—to turn and tremble at your name,
  Sunk in dull slumber neath a lichened stone?
Shall not my pulses leap if you be near?
Shall these endure, the sun, the wind, the rain,   15
And naught of all our tenderness remain,
  Our joy—our hope—our fear? . . .

Sweet, 'tis the one thing certain—rail or weep,
Plead or defy, take counsel as we may,
It shall not profit us: this, only, pray 20
Of the blind powers that keep
The harvest of the years we sow and reap,
That naught shall sever nor estrange us—Nay,
Let us live out our great love's little day
Fair and undimmed, before we fall on sleep. 25

Amy Levy (1861–1889)

480.   *Magdalen*

All things I can endure, save one.
The bare, blank room where is no sun;
The parcelled hours; the pallet hard;
The dreary faces here within;
The outer women's cold regard; 5
The Pastor's iterated "sin";—
These things could I endure, and count
No overstrain'd, unjust amount;
No undue payment for such bliss—
Yea, all things bear, save only this: 10
That you, who knew what thing would be,
Have wrought this evil unto me.
It is so strange to think on still—
That you, that *you* should do me ill!
Not as one ignorant or blind, 15
But seeing clearly in your mind
How this must be which now has been,
Nothing aghast at what was seen.
Now that the tale is told and done,
It is so strange to think upon. 20

You were so tender with me, too!
One summer's night a cold blast blew,
Closer about my throat you drew
The half-slipt shawl of dusky blue.
And once my hand, on a summer's morn, 25
I stretched to pluck a rose; a thorn
Struck through the flesh and made it bleed
(A little drop of blood indeed!)

Pale grew your cheek; you stoopt and bound
Your handkerchief about the wound;
Your voice came with a broken sound;
With the deep breath your breast was riven;
I wonder, did God laugh in Heaven?

How strange, that you should work my woe!
How strange! I wonder, do you know
How gladly, gladly I had died
(And life was very sweet that tide)
To save you from the least, light ill?
How gladly I had borne your pain.
With one great pulse we seem'd to thrill,—
Nay, but we thrill'd with pulses twain.

Even if one had told me this,
"A poison lurks within your kiss,
Gall that shall turn to night his day":
Thereon I straight had turned away—
Ay, tho' my heart had crack'd with pain—
And never kiss'd your lips again.

At night, or when the daylight nears,
I hear the other women weep;
My own heart's anguish lies too deep
For the soft rain and pain of tears.
I think my heart has turn'd to stone.
A dull, dead weight that hurts my breast;
Here, on my pallet-bed alone,
I keep apart from all the rest.
Wide-eyed I lie upon my bed,
I often cannot sleep all night;
The future and the past are dead,
There is no thought can bring delight.
All night I lie and think and think;
If my heart were not made of stone,
But flesh and blood, it needs must shrink
Before such thoughts. Was ever known
A woman with a heart of stone?

The doctor says that I shall die.
It may be so, yet what care I?
Endless reposing from the strife,
Death do I trust no more than life.

For one thing is like one arrayed,
And there is neither false nor true;
But in a hideous masquerade
All things dance on, the ages through.
And good is evil, evil good;
Nothing is known or understood
Save only Pain. I have no faith
In God or Devil, Life or Death.

The doctor says that I shall die.
You, that I knew in days gone by,
I fain would see your face once more,
Con well its features o'er and o'er;
And touch your hand and feel your kiss,
Look in your eyes and tell you this:
That all is done, that I am free;
That you, through all eternity,
Have neither part nor lot in me.

481. *London Poets*

(In Memoriam)

They trod the streets and squares where now I tread,
With weary hearts, a little while ago;
When, thin and grey, the melancholy snow
Clung to the leafless branches overhead;
Or when the smoke-veiled sky grew stormy-red
In autumn; with a re-arisen woe
Wrestled, what time the passionate spring winds blow;
And paced scorched stones in summer:—they are dead.

The sorrow of their souls to them did seem
As real as mine to me, as permanent.
To-day, it is the shadow of a dream,
The half-forgotten breath of breezes spent.
So shall another soothe his woe supreme—
"No more he comes, who this way came and went."

482.   *To Death*

                    (From Lenau)

     If within my heart there's mould,
     If the flame of Poesy
     And the flame of Love grow cold,
     Slay my body utterly.

     Swiftly, pause not nor delay;   5
     Let not my life's field be spread
     With the ash of feelings dead,
     Let thy singer soar away.

483.   *Borderland*

     Am I waking, am I sleeping?
     As the first faint dawn comes creeping
     Thro' the pane, I am aware
     Of an unseen presence hovering,
     Round, above, in the dusky air: 5
     A downy bird, with an odorous wing,
     That fans my forehead, and sheds perfume,
     As sweet as love, as soft as death,
     Drowsy-slow through the summer-gloom.
     My heart in some dream-rapture saith,   10
     It is she. Half in a swoon,
     I spread my arms in slow delight.—
     O prolong, prolong the night,
     For the nights are short in June!

                              (1889)

484.   *The Birch-Tree at Loschwitz*

          At Loschwitz above the city
               The air is sunny and chill;
          The birch-trees and the pine trees
               Grow thick upon the hill.

  Lone and tall, with silver stem,
    A birch-tree stands apart;
  The passionate wind of spring-time
    Stirs in its leafy heart.

  I lean against the birch-tree,
    My arms around it twine;
  It pulses, and leaps, and quivers,
    Like a human heart to mine.

  One moment I stand, then sudden
    Let loose mine arms that cling:
  O God! the lonely hillside,
    The passionate wind of spring!

485.   *Captivity*

  The lion remembers the forest,
    The lion in chains;
  To the bird that is captive a vision
    Of woodland remains.

  One strains with his strength at the fetter,
    In impotent rage;
  One flutters in flights of a moment,
    And beats at the cage.

  If the lion were loosed from the fetter,
    To wander again;
  He would seek the wide silence and shadow
    Of his jungle in vain.

  He would rage in his fury, destroying;
    Let him rage, let him roam!
  Shall he traverse the pitiless mountain,
    Or swim through the foam?

  If they opened the cage and the casement,
    And the bird flew away;
  He would come back at evening, heartbroken,
    A captive for aye.

> Would come if his kindred had spared him,
>   Free birds from afar –
> There was wrought what is stronger than iron
>   In fetter and bar.
>
> I cannot remember my country,
>   The land whence I came;
> Whence they brought me and chained me and made me
>   Nor wild thing nor tame.
>
> This only I know of my country,
>   This only repeat: –
> It was free as the forest, and sweeter
>   Than woodland retreat.
>
> When the chain shall at last be broken,
>   The window set wide;
> And I step in the largeness and freedom
>   Of sunlight outside;
>
> Shall I wander in vain for my country?
>   Shall I seek and not find?
> Shall I cry for the bars that encage me,
>   The fetters that bind?

(1889)

486. *Run to Death (A True Incident of Pre-Revolutionary French History)*

> Now the lovely autumn morning breathes its freshness in earth's face,
> In the crowded castle courtyard the blithe horn proclaims the chase;
> And the ladies on the terrace smile adieux with rosy lips
> To the huntsmen disappearing down the cedar-shaded groves,
> Wafting delicate aromas from their scented finger tips,
> And the gallants wave in answer, with their gold-embroidered gloves.
> On they rode, past bush and bramble, on they rode, past elm and oak;
> And the hounds, widi anxious nostril, sniffed the heather-scented air,
> Till at last, within his stirrups, up Lord Gaston rose, and spoke—
> He, the boldest and the bravest of the wealthy nobles there:
> "Friends," quoth he, "the time hangs heavy, for it is not as we thought,
> And these woods, tho' fair and shady, will afford, I fear no sport.

Shall we hence, then, worthy kinsmen, and desert the hunter's track
For the chateau, where the wine cup and the dice cup tempt us back?"
"Ay," the nobles shout in chorus; "Ay," the powder'd lacquey cries;   15
Then they stop with eager movement, reining in quite suddenly;
Peering down with half contemptuous, half with wonder-opened eyes
At a "something" which is crawling, with slow step, from tree to tree.
Is't some shadow phantom ghastly? No, a woman and a child,
Swarthy woman, with the "gipsy" written clear upon her face;   20
Gazing round her with her wide eyes dark, and shadow-fringed, and wild,
With the cowed suspicious glances of a persecuted race.
Then they all, with unasked question, in each other's faces peer,
For a common thought has struck them, one their lips dare scarcely say,—
Till Lord Gaston cries, impatient, "Why regret the stately deer   25
When such sport as yonder offers? quick! unleash the dogs—away!"
Then they breath'd a shout of cheering, grey-haired man and stripling boy,
And the gipsy, roused to terror, stayed her step, and turned her head—
Saw the faces of those huntsmen, lit with keenest cruel joy—
Sent a cry of grief to Heaven, closer clasped her child, and fled!   30

    ★ ★ ★

O ye nobles of the palace! O ye gallant-hearted lords!
Who would stoop for Leila's kerchief, or for Clementina's gloves,
Who would rise up all indignant, with your shining sheathless swords,
At the breathing of dishonour to your languid lady loves!
O, I tell you, daring nobles, with your beauty-loving stare,   35
Who ne'er long the coy coquetting of the courtly dames withstood,
Tho' a woman be the lowest, and the basest, and least fair,
In your manliness forget not to respect her womanhood,
And thou, gipsy, that hast often the pursuer fled before,
That hast felt ere this the shadow of dark death upon thy brow,   40
That hast hid among the mountains, that hast roamed the forest o'er,
Bred to hiding, watching, fleeing, may thy speed avail thee now!

    ★ ★ ★

Still she flees, and ever fiercer tear the hungry hounds behind,
Still she flees, and ever faster follow there the huntsmen on,
Still she flees, her black hair streaming in a fury to the wind,   45
Still she flees, tho' all the glimmer of a happy hope is gone.
"Eh? what? baffled by a woman! Ah, *sapristi*! she can run!
Should she 'scape us, it would crown us with dishonour and disgrace;
It is time" (Lord Gaston shouted) "such a paltry chase were done!"
And the fleeter grew her footsteps, so the hotter grew the chase—   50
Ha! at last! the dogs are on her! will she struggle ere she dies?
See! she holds her child above her, all forgetful of *her* pain,

While a hundred thousand curses shoot out darkly from her eyes,
And a hundred thousand glances of the bitterest disdain.
Ha! the dogs are pressing closer! they have flung her to the ground; 55
Yet her proud lips never open with the dying sinner's cry—
Till at last, unto the Heavens, just two fearful shrieks resound,
While the soul is all forgotten in the body's agony!
Let them rest there, child and mother, in the shadow of the oak,
On the tender mother-bosom of that earth from which they came. 60
As they slow rode back those huntsmen neither laughed, nor sang, nor spoke,
Hap, there lurked unowned within them throbbings of a secret shame.
But before the flow'ry terrace, where the ladies smiling sat,
With their graceful nothings trifling all the weary time away,
Low Lord Gaston bowed, and raising high his richly 'broider'd hat, 65
"Fairest ladies, give us welcome! 'Twas a famous hunt to-day."

from *Moods and Thoughts*

487.   *The Old House*

    In through the porch and up the silent stair;
        Little is changed, I know so well the ways;—
    Here, the dead came to meet me; it was there
        The dream was dreamed in unforgotten days.

    But who is this that hurries on before, 5
        A flitting shade the brooding shades among?—
    She turned,—I saw her face,—O God, it wore
        The face I used to wear when I was young!

    I thought my spirit and my heart were tamed
        To deadness; dead the pangs that agonise. 10
    The old grief springs to choke me.—I am shamed
        Before that little ghost with eager eyes.

    O turn away, let her not see, not know!
        How should she bear it, how should understand?
    O hasten down the stairway, haste and go, 15
        And leave her dreaming in the silent land.

488.   *To Vernon Lee*

On Bellosguardo, when the year was young,
We wandered, seeking for the daffodil
And dark anemone, whose purples fill
The peasant's plot, between the corn-shoots sprung.

Over the grey, low wall the olive flung   5
Her deeper greyness; far off, hill on hill
Sloped to the sky, which, pearly-pale and still,
Above the large and luminous landscape hung.

A snowy blackthorn flowered beyond my reach;
You broke a branch and gave it to me there;   10
I found for you a scarlet blossom rare.

Thereby ran on of Art and Life our speech;
And of the gifts the gods had given to each—
Hope unto you, and unto me Despair.

489.   *Oh, is it Love?*

O is it Love or is it Fame,
    This thing for which I sigh?
Or has it then no earthly name
    For men to call it by?

I know not what can ease my pains,   5
    Nor what it is I wish;
The passion at my heart-strings strains
    Like a tiger in a leash.

490.   *Ballade of an Omnibus*

To see my love suffices me.
Ballades in Blue China

Some men to carriages aspire;
On some the costly hansoms wait;
Some seek a fly, on job or hire;
Some mount the trotting steed, elate.

> I envy not the rich and great,
> A wandering minstrel, poor and free,
> I am contented with my fate—
> An omnibus suffices me.
>
> In winter days of rain and mire
> I find within a corner strait;
> The 'busmen know me and my lyre
> From Brompton to the Bull-and-Gate.
> When summer comes, I mount in state
> The topmost summit, whence I see
> Crœsus look up, compassionate—
> An omnibus suffices me.
>
> I mark, untroubled by desire,
> Lucullus' phaeton and its freight.
> The scene whereof I cannot tire,
> The human tale of love and hate,
> The city pageant, early and late
> Unfolds itself, rolls by, to be
> A pleasure deep and delicate.
> An omnibus suffices me.
>
> Princess, your splendour you require,
> I, my simplicity; agree
> Neither to rate lower nor higher.
> An omnibus suffices me.

491.   *A Ballad of Religion and Marriage*

> Swept into limbo is the host
>   Of heavenly angels, row on row;
> The Father, Son, and Holy Ghost,
>   Pale and defeated, rise and go.
> The great Jehovah is laid low,
>   Vanished his burning bush and rod—
> Say, are we doomed to deeper woe?
>   Shall marriage go the way of God?
>
> Monogamous, still at our post,
>   Reluctantly we undergo
> Domestic round of boiled and roast,
>   Yet deem the whole proceeding slow.

Daily the secret murmurs grow;
    We are no more content to plod
Along the beaten paths—and so
    Marriage must go the way of God.

Soon, before all men, each shall toast
    The seven strings unto his bow,
Like beacon fires along the coast,
    The flames of love shall glance and glow.
Nor let nor hindrance man shall know,
    From natal bath to funeral sod;
Perennial shall his pleasures flow
    When marriage goes the way of God.

Grant, in a million years at most,
    Folk shall be neither pairs nor odd—
Alas! we sha'n't be there to boast
    "Marriage has gone the way of God!"

from *Two Translations of Jehudah Halevi from the German of Abraham Geiger*

492.   Jerusalem

Oh! city of the world, most chastely fair;
In the far west, behold I sigh for thee.
And in my yearning love I do bethink me,
Of bygone ages; of thy ruined fane,
Thy vanish'd splendour of a vanish'd day.
Oh! had I eagle's wings I'd fly to thee,
And with my falling tears make moist thine earth.
I long for thee; what though indeed thy kings
Have passed for ever; that where once uprose
Sweet balsam-trees the serpent makes his nest.
O that I might embrace thy dust, the sod
Were sweet as honey to my fond desire!

493.   *Epitaph*

                (On a commonplace person who died in bed)

            This is the end of him, here he lies:
            The dust in his throat, the worm in his eyes,
            The mould in his mouth, the turf on his breast;
            This is the end of him, this is best.
            He will never lie on his couch awake,   5
            Wide-eyed, tearless, till dim daybreak.
            Never again will he smile and smile
            When his heart is breaking all the while.
            He will never stretch out his hands in vain
            Groping and groping—never again.   10
            Never ask for bread, get a stone instead,
            Never pretend that the stone is bread.
            Never sway and sway 'twixt the false and true,
            Weighing and noting the long hours through.
            Never ache and ache with the chok'd-up sighs;   15
            This is the end of him, here he lies.

Mary E. (Elizabeth) Coleridge (1861–1907)

494.   *Winged Words*

            As darting swallows skim across a pool,
                Whose tranquil depths reflect a tranquil sky,
            So, o'er the depths of silence, dark and cool,
                Our winged words dart playfully,
                    And seldom break   5
                The quiet surface of the lake,
                    As they flit by.

495.   *The Other Side of a Mirror*

            I sat before my glass one day,
                And conjured up a vision bare,
            Unlike the aspects glad and gay,
                That erst were found reflected there –
            The vision of a woman, wild   5
                With more than womanly despair.

Her hair stood back on either side
   A face bereft of loveliness.
It had no envy now to hide
   What once no man on earth could guess. 10
It formed the thorny aureole
   Of hard unsanctified distress.

Her lips were open – not a sound
   Came through the parted lines of red.
Whate'er it was, the hideous wound 15
   In silence and in secret bled.
No sigh relieved her speechless woe,
   She had no voice to speak her dread.

And in her lurid eyes there shone
   The dying flame of life's desire, 20
Made mad because its hope was gone,
   And kindled at the leaping fire
Of jealousy, and fierce revenge,
   And strength that could not change nor tire.

Shade of a shadow in the glass, 25
   O set the crystal surface free!
Pass – as the fairer visions pass –
   Nor ever more return, to be
The ghost of a distracted hour,
   That heard me whisper, 'I am she!' 30

(1896)

496.   *Master and Guest*

There came a man across the moor,
   Fell and foul of face was he.
   He left the path by the cross-roads three,
And stood in the shadow of the door.

I asked him in to bed and board. 5
   I never hated any man so.
   He said he could not say me No.
He sat in the seat of my own dear lord.

'Now sit you by my side!' he said,
   'Else may I neither eat nor drink.
   You would not have me starve, I think.'
He ate the offerings of the dead.

'I'll light you to your bed,' quoth I.
   'My bed is yours – but light the way!'
I might not turn aside nor stay;
I showed him where we twain did lie.

The cock was trumpeting the morn.
   He said: 'Sweet love, a long farewell!
   You have kissed a citizen of Hell,
And a soul was doomed when you were born.

'Mourn, mourn no longer for your dear!
   Him may you never meet above.
   The gifts that Love hath given to Love,
Love gives away again to Fear.'

(1896)

497.   *Doubt*

Two forms of darkness are there. One is Night,
When I have been an animal, and feared
I knew not what, and lost my, soul, nor dared
Feel aught save hungry longing for the light.
And one is Blindness. Absolute and bright,
The Sun's rays smote me till they masked the Sun;
The Light itself was by the light undone;
The day was filled with terrors and affright.

Then did I weep, compassionate of those
Who see no friend in God – in Satan's host no foes.

(1896)

498.   *Marriage*

    No more alone sleeping, no more alone waking,
        Thy dreams divided, thy prayers in twain;
    Thy merry sisters to-night forsaking,
        Never shall we see thee, maiden, again.

    Never shall we see thee, thine eyes glancing,
        Flashing with laughter and wild in glee,
    Under the mistletoe kissing and dancing,
        Wantonly free.

    There shall come a matron walking sedately,
        Low-voiced, gentle, wise in reply.
    Tell me, O tell me, can I love her greatly?
        All for her sake must the maiden die!

                  (1899)

499.   *L'Oiseau Bleu*

    The lake lay blue below the hill.
        O'er it, as I looked, there flew
    Across the waters, cold and still,
        A bird whose wings were palest blue.

    The sky above was blue at last,
        The sky beneath me blue in blue.
    A moment, ere the bird had passed,
        It caught his image as he flew.

500.   *A Moment*

    The clouds had made a crimson crown
        Above the mountains high.
    The stormy sun was going down
        In a stormy sky.

Why did you let your eyes so rest on me,
    And hold your breath between?
In all the ages this can never be
    As if it had not been.

501.   Gone

About the little chambers of my heart
Friends have been coming—going—many a year.
    The doors stand open there.
Some, lightly stepping, enter; some depart.

Freely they come and freely go, at will.
The walls give back their laughter; all day long
    They fill the house with song.
One door alone is shut, one chamber still.

(1896)

502.   Eyes

Eyes, what are they? Coloured glass,
Where reflections come and pass.

Open windows—by them sit
Beauty, Learning, Love, and Wit.

Searching cross-examiners;
Comfort's holy ministers.

Starry silences of soul,
Music past the lips' control.

Fountains of unearthly light;
Prisons of the infinite.

(1896)

503.   'True to myself am I, and false to all'

> *'To thine own self be true;*
> *And it must follow, as the night the day,*
> *Thou canst not then be false to any man.'*

True to myself am I, and false to all.
   Fear, sorrow, love, constrain us till we die.
   But when the lips betray the spirit's cry,
The will, that should be sovereign, is a thrall.
Therefore let terror slay me, ere I call					5
   For aid of men. Let grief begrudge a sigh.
   'Are you afraid?' – 'unhappy?' 'No!' The lie
About the shrinking truth stands like a wall.
'And have you loved?' 'No, never!' All the while,
   The heart within my flesh is turned to stone.		10
Yea, none the less that I account it vile,
   The heart within my heart makes speechless moan,
   And when they see one face, one face alone,
The stern eyes of the soul are moved to smile.

                  (1896)

504.   *On a Bas–Relief of Pelops and Hippodameia*

> *Which was wrecked and lay many years under the sea.*

Thus did a nameless and immortal hand
   Make of rough stone, the thing least like to life,
   The husband and the wife
That the Most High, ere His creation, planned.
Hundreds of years they lay, unsunned, unscanned,				5
   Where the waves cut more smoothly than the knife,
   What time the winds tossed them about in strife,
And filled those lips and eyes with the soft sand.

Art, that from Nature stole the human form
   By slow device of brain, by simple strength,			10
Lent it to Nature's artless force to keep.
So with the human sculptor wrought the storm
   To round those lines of beauty, till at length
A perfect thing was rescued from the deep.

                  (1899)

Katharine Tynan (Hinkson) (1861–1931)

505. *Only in August*

Only in August I have not seen you.
    August comes with his wheat and poppies;
    Ruddy sunlight in corn and coppice:
Only in August I have not seen you.

Autumn beckons far-off like a greeting. 5
    I and Autumn have secrets of you,
    All the Winter was long to love you;
Wintry winds have a song of meeting.

Dear is Summer, but Spring is dearer.
    In the Spring there was heavenly weather; 10
    Love and sunshine and you together.
Dear is Summer, but Spring is dearer.

June is fled with her rose and pansies.
    More is gone than a drift of roses,
    More than the may that the May uncloses, 15
More than April—with songs and dances.

Only in August I have not seen you.
    Every month hath its share of graces,
    Flowers, and song, and beloved faces.
Only in August I have not seen you. 20

506. *To Inishkea*

I'll rise and go to Inishkea,
Where many a one will weep with me
The bravest boy that sailed the sea
    From Blacksod Bay to Killery.

I'll dress my boat in sails of black, 5
The widow's cloak I shall not lack,
I'll set my face and ne'er turn back
    Upon the way to Inishkea.

>   In Arran Island, cold as stone,
>   I wring my hands and weep my lone
>   Where never my true love's name was known:
>   It were not so in Inishkea.
>
>   The friends that knew him there will come
>   And kiss my cheek so cold and numb.
>   O comfort is not troublesome
>   To kindly friends in Inishkea!
>
>   'Tis there the children call your name,
>   The old men sigh, and sigh the same;
>   'Tis all your praise, and none your blame,
>   Your love will hear in Inishkea.
>
>   But you were dear to beast and bird,
>   The dogs once followed at your word,
>   Your feet once pressed the sand and sward—
>   My heart is sore for Inishkea.
>
>   I'll rise and go to Inishkea
>   O'er many a mile of tossing sea
>   That hides your darling face from me.
>   I'll live and die in Inishkea!

507. *Fra Angelico at Fiesole*

I

>   Home through the pleasant olive woods at even
>   He sees the patient milk-white oxen go;
>   Without his lattice doves wheel to and fro,
>   A great moon climbs the wan green fields of heaven.
>   An hour since, the sun-veil whereon are graven
>   Gold bells and pomegranates in scarlet show
>   Parted, and lo! the city's spires of snow
>   Flushed like an opal, and the streets gold paven!
>   Then the night's purple fell and hid the rest,
>   And this monk's eyes filled with the happy tears
>   That come to him beholding all things fair:
>   A bird's flight over wan skies to the nest;
>   The great sad eyes of beasts, the silk wheat ears,
>   Flowers, or the gold dust on a baby's hair.

II

In his small cell he hath high company, 15
The angels make it their abiding-place;
Their grave eternal eyes 'neath brows of grace
Watch him at work, their great wings silently
Wrap him around with peace; and it may be
That looking from his work a minute's space, 20
The sudden blue eyes of an angel's face
His happy startled eyes are raised to see.
Down through the shadowy corridor they glide,
Their wings auroral trailing soft and slow,
Each still face like a moon-lit lily in June; 25
They kiss with fair pale lips the canvas wide,
Whereon his colours like dropped jewels glow
Against a gold ground pale as the harvest moon.

508.   *The Children of Lir*

"And their stepmother, being jealous of their father's great love for them, cast upon the King's children, by sorcery, the shape of swans, and bade them go roaming, even till Patrick's mass-bell should sound in Erin,—but no farther in time than that did her power extend."
— *The Fate of the Children of Lir*

Out upon the sand-dunes thrive the coarse long grasses,
    Herons standing knee-deep in the brackish pool,
Overhead the sunset fire and flame amasses,
    And the moon to eastward rises pale and cool:
Rose and green around her, silver-grey and pearly, 5
    Chequered with the black rooks flying home to bed;
For, to wake at daybreak birds must couch them early,
    And the day's a long one since the dawn was red.

On the chilly lakelet, in that pleasant gloaming,
    See the sad swans sailing: they shall have no rest: 10
Never a voice to greet them save the bittern's booming
    Where the ghostly sallows sway against the West.
"Sister," saith the grey swan, "Sister, I am weary,"
    Turning to the white swan wet, despairing eyes;
"Oh," she saith, "my young one," "Oh," she saith, "my dearie," 15
Casts her wings about him with a storm of cries.

Woe for Lir's sweet children whom their vile stepmother
    Glamoured with her witch-spells for a thousand years;
Died their father raving—on his throne another—
    Blind before the end came from the burning tears.
She—the fiends possess her, torture her for ever.
    Gone is all the glory of the race of Lir;
Gone and long forgotten like a dream of fever:
    But the swans remember all the days that were.

Hugh, the black and white swan with the beauteous feathers,
    Fiachra, the black swan with the emerald breast,
Conn, the youngest, dearest, sheltered in all weathers,
    Him his snow-white sister loves the tenderest.
These her mother gave her as she lay a-dying,
    To her faithful keeping, faithful hath she been,
With her wings spread o'er them when the tempest's crying
    And her songs so hopeful when the sky's serene.

Other swans have nests made 'mid the reeds and rushes,
    Lined with downy feathers where the cygnets sleep
Dreaming, if a bird dreams, till the daylight blushes,
    Then they sail out swiftly on the current deep.
With the proud swan-father, tall, and strong, and stately,
    And the mild swan-mother, grave with household cares,
All well-born and comely, all rejoicing greatly:
    Full of honest pleasure is a life like theirs.

But alas! for my swans, with the human nature,
    Sick with human longings, starved for human ties,
With their hearts all human cramped in a bird's stature,
    And the human weeping in the bird's soft eyes,
Never shall my swans build nests in some green river,
    Never fly to Southward in the autumn grey,
Rear no tender children, love no mates for ever,
    Robbed alike of bird's joys and of man's are they.

Babbled Conn the youngest, "Sister, I remember
    At my father's palace how I went in silk,
Ate the juicy deer-flesh roasted from the ember,
    Drank from golden goblets my child's draught of milk.
Once I rode a-hunting, laughed to see the hurly,
    Shouted at the ball-play, on the lake did row,
You had for your beauty gauds that shone so rarely:"
    "Peace," saith Fionnuala, "that was long ago."

"Sister," saith Fiachra, "well do I remember
    How the flaming torches lit the banquet-hall,
And the fire leapt skyward in the mid-December,
    And amid the rushes slept our staghounds tall. 60
By our father's right hand you sat shyly gazing,
    Smiling half and sighing, with your eyes a-glow
As the bards sang loudly all your beauty praising:"
    "Peace," saith Fionnuala, "that was long ago."

"Sister," then saith Hugh, "most do I remember 65
    One I called my brother, you, earth's goodliest man,
Strong as forest oaks are where the wild vines clamber,
    First at feast or hunting, in the battle's van.
Angus, you were handsome, wise and true and tender,
    Loved by every comrade, feared by every foe: 70
Low, low, lies your beauty, all forgot your splendour:"
    "Peace," saith Fionnuala, "that was long ago."

Dews are in the clear air, and the roselight paling,
    Over sands and sedges shines the evening star,
And the moon's disk lonely high in heaven is sailing, 75
    Silvered all the spear-heads of the rushes are,—
Housèd warm are all things as the night grows colder,
    Water-fowl and sky-fowl dreamless in the nest;
But the swans go drifting, drooping wing and shoulder
    Cleaving the still waters where the fishes rest. 80

Mary Byron (M. Clarissa Gillington) (1861–1936)

509.   *The Tryst of the Night*

Out of the uttermost ridge of dusk, where the dark and the day are mingled,
The voice of the Night rose cold and calm—it called through the shadow-swept air;
Through all the valleys and lone hillsides, it pierced, it thrilled, it tingled—
It summoned me forth to the wild sea-shore, to meet with its mystery there.

Out of the deep ineffable blue, with palpitant swift repeating 5
Of gleam and glitter and opaline glow, that broke in ripples of light—
In burning glory it came and went,—I heard, I saw it beating,
Pulse by pulse, from star to star,—the passionate heart of the Night!

Out of the thud of the rustling sea—the panting, yearning, throbbing
Waves that stole on the startled shore, with coo and mutter of spray— 10
The wail of the Night came fitful-faint,—I heard her stifled sobbing:
The cold salt drops fell slowly, slowly, gray into gulfs of gray.

There through the darkness the great world reeled, and the great tides roared, assembling—
Murmuring hidden things that are past, and secret things that shall be;
There at the limits of life we met, and touched with a rapturous trembling— 15
One with each other, I and the Night, and the skies, and the stars, and sea.

Owen Seaman (1861–1936)

510. *Lilith Libifera*

    Exhumed from out the inner cirque of Hell
        By kind permission of the Evil One,
        Behold her devilish presentment, done
    By Master Aubrey's weird unearthly spell!
    This is the Lady known as Jezebel, 5
        Or Lilith, Eden's woman-scorpion,
        Libifera, that is, that takes the bun,
    Borgia, Vivien, Cussed Damosel.

    Hers are the bulging lips that fairly break
        The pumpkin's heart; and hers the eyes that shame 10
        The wanton ape that culls the cocoa-nuts.
    Even such the yellow-bellied toads that slake
        Nocturnally their amorous-ardent flame
        In the wan waste of weary water-butts.

May Kendall (1861–1943)

511. *Lay of the Trilobite*

    A mountain's giddy height I sought,
        Because I could not find
    Sufficient vague and mighty thought
        To fill my mighty mind;

And as I wandered ill at ease,
   There chanced upon my sight
A native of Silurian seas,
   An ancient Trilobite.

So calm, so peacefully he lay,
   I watched him even with tears:
I thought of Monads far away
   In the forgotten years.
How wonderful it seemed and right,
   The providential plan,
That he should be a Trilobite,
   And I should be a Man!

And then, quite natural and free
   Out of his rocky bed,
That Trilobite he spoke to me,
   And this is what he said:
'I don't know how the thing was done,
   Although I cannot doubt it;
But Huxley—he if anyone
   Can tell you all about it;

'How all your faiths are ghosts and dreams,
   How in the silent sea
Your ancestors were Monotremes—
   Whatever these may be;
How you evolved your shining lights
   Of wisdom and perfection
From Jelly-fish and Trilobites
   By Natural Selection.

'You've Kant to make your brains go round,
   Hegel you have to clear them,
You've Mr. Browning to confound,
   And Mr. Punch to cheer them!
The native of an alien land
   You call a man and brother,
And greet with hymn-book in one hand
   And pistol in the other!

'You've Politics to make you fight
   As if you were possessed:
You've cannon and you've dynamite
   To give the nations rest:

> The side that makes the loudest din 45
>   Is surest to be right,
> And oh, a pretty fix you're in!'
>   Remarked the Trilobite.

> 'But gentle, stupid, free from woe
>   I lived among my nation, 50
> I didn't care—I didn't know
>   That I was a Crustacean.
> I didn't grumble, didn't steal,
>   I *never* took to rhyme:
> Salt water was my frugal meal, 55
>   And carbonate of lime.'

> Reluctantly I turned away,
>   No other word he said;
> An ancient Trilobite, he lay
>   Within his rocky bed. 60
> I did not answer him, for that
>   Would have annoyed my pride:
> I merely bowed, and raised my hat,
>   But in my heart I cried:—

> 'I wish our brains were not so good, 65
>   I wish our skulls were thicker,
> I wish that Evolution could
>   Have stopped a little quicker;
> For oh, it was a happy plight,
>   Of liberty and ease, 70
> To be a simple Trilobite
>   In the Silurian seas!

512.   *A Pure Hypothesis*

(A Lover, in Four-dimensioned space, describes a Dream.)

> Ah, love, the teacher we decried,
>   That erudite professor grim,
> In mathematics drenched and dyed,
>   Too hastily we scouted him.
> He said: 'The bounds of Time and Space, 5
>   The categories we revere,
> May be in quite another case
>   In quite another sphere.'

He told us: 'Science can conceive
    A race whose feeble comprehension
Can't be persuaded to believe
    That there exists our Fourth Dimension,
Whom Time and Space for ever baulk;
    But of these beings incomplete,
Whether upon their heads they walk
    Or stand upon their feet—

We cannot tell, we do not know,
    Imagination stops confounded;
We can but say "It *may* be so,"
    To every theory propounded.'
Too glad were we in this our scheme
    Of things, his notions to embrace,—
But—I have dreamed an awful dream
    Of Three-dimensioned Space!

I dreamed—the horror seemed to stun
    My logical perception strong—
That everything beneath the sun
    Was so unutterably wrong.
I thought—what words can I command?—
    That nothing ever did come right.
No wonder you can't understand:
    I could not, till last night!

I would not, if I could, recall
    The horror of those novel heavens,
Where Present, Past, and Future all
    Appeared at sixes and at sevens,
Where Capital and Labor fought,
    And, in the nightmare of the mind,
No contradictories were thought
    As truthfully combined!

Nay, in that dream-distorted clime,
    These fatal wilds I wandered through,
The boundaries of Space and Time
    Had got most frightfully askew.
"What is 'askew'?" my love, you cry;
    I cannot answer, can't portray;
The sense of Everything awry
    No language can convey.

         I can't tell what my words denote,
            I know not what my phrases mean;
         Inexplicable terrors float
            Before this spirit once serene.
         Ah, what if on some lurid star
            There should exist a hapless race,
         Who live and love, who think and are,
            In Three-dimensioned Space!

513.   *Ballad of the Ichthyosaurus*

   (The Ichthyosaurus laments his imperfect advantages. He aspires after the Higher Life.)

            I abide in a goodly Museum,
            Frequented by sages profound:
            'Tis a kind of a strange mausoleum,
               Where the beasts that have vanished abound.
            There's a bird of the ages Triassic,
               With his antediluvian beak,
            And many a reptile Jurassic,
               And many a monster antique.

            Ere Man was developed, our brother,
               We swam and we ducked and we dived,
            And we dined, as a rule, on each other—
               What matter, the toughest survived.
            Our paddles were fins, and they bore us
               Through water: in air we could fly;
            But the brain of the Ichthyosaurus
               Was never a match for his eye.

            Geologists, active and eager,
               Its excellence hasten to own,
            And praise, with no eulogy meagre,
               The eye that is plated with bone.
            'See how, with unerring precision,
               His prey through the wave he could spy.
            Oh, wonderful organ of vision,
               Gigantic and beautiful Eye!'

            Then I listen in gloomy dejection,
               I gaze, and I wish I could weep;
            For what is mere visual perfection
               To Intellect subtle and deep?

A loftier goal is before us,
    For higher endowments we sigh.
But the brain of the Ichthyosaurus
    Was never a patch on his eye!

It owned no supreme constitution,
    Was shallow, and simple, and plain,
While mark but the fair convolution
    And size of the Aryan brain.
'Tis furnished for School Board inspections,
    And garnished for taking degrees,
And bulging in many directions,
    As every phrenologist sees.

Sometimes it explodes at high pressure
    Of some overwhelming demand,
But plied in unmerciful measure
    'Tis wonderful that it will stand!
In college, in cottage, in mansion,
    Bear witness, the girls and the boys,
How great are its powers of expansion,
    How very peculiar its joys!

Oh Brain that is bulgy with learning,
    Oh wisdom of women and men,
Oh Maids for a First that are yearning,
    Oh youths that are lectured by Wren!
You're acquainted with Pisces and Taurus,
    And all sorts of beasts in the sky,
But the brain of the Ichthyosaurus
    Was never so good as his eye!

Reconstructed by Darwin or Owen,
    We dwell in sweet Bloomsbury's halls,
But we couldn't have passed Little go in
    The Schools, we'd have floundered in Smalls!
Though so cleverly people restore us,
    We are bound to confess with a sigh
That the brain of the Ichthyosaurus
    Was *never* so good as his eye!

514. *Woman's Future*

Complacent they tell us, hard hearts and derisive,
    In vain is our ardour: in vain are our sighs:
Our intellects, bound by a limit decisive,
    To the level of Homer's may never arise.
We heed not the falsehood, the base innuendo,
    The laws of the universe, these are our friends.
Our talents shall rise in a mighty crescendo,
    We trust Evolution to make us amends!

But ah, when I ask you for food that is mental,
    My sisters, you offer me ices and tea!
You cherish the fleeting, the mere accidental,
    At cost of the True, the Intrinsic, the Free.
Your feelings, compressed in Society's mangle,
    Are vapid and frivolous, pallid and mean.
To slander you love; but you don't care to wrangle:
    You bow to Decorum, and cherish Routine.

Alas, is it woolwork you take for your mission,
    Or Art that your fingers so gaily attack?
Can patchwork atone for the mind's inanition?
    Can the soul, oh my sisters, be fed on a *plaque*?
Is this your vocation? My goal is another,
    And empty and vain is the end you pursue.
In antimacassars the world you may smother;
    But intellect marches o'er them and o'er you.

On Fashion's vagaries your energies strewing,
    Devoting your days to a rug or a screen,
Oh, rouse to a lifework—do something worth doing!
    Invent a new planet, a flying-machine.
Mere charms superficial, mere feminine graces,
    That fade or that flourish, no more you may prize;
But the knowledge of Newton will beam from your faces,
    The soul of a Spencer will shine in your eyes.

ENVOY.

Though jealous exclusion may tremble to own us,
    Oh, wait for the time when our brains shall expand!
When once we're enthroned, you shall never dethrone us—
    The poets, the sages, the seers of the land!

(1887)

515. *The Philanthropist and the Jelly-Fish*

    Her beauty, passive in despair,
        Through sand and seaweed shone,
    The fairest jelly-fish I e'er
        Had set mine eyes upon.

    It would have made a stone abuse 5
        The callousness of fate,
    This creature of prismatic hues,
        Stranded and desolate!

    Musing I said: 'My mind's unstrung,
        Joy, hope, are in their grave: 10
    Yet ere I perish all unsung
        One jelly-fish I'll save!'

    And yet I fancied I had dreamed
        Of somewhere having known
    Or met, a jelly-fish that seemed 15
        As utterly alone.

    But ah, if ever out to sea
        That jelly-fish I bore,
    Immediately awaited me
        A level hundred more! 20

    I knew that it would be in vain
        To try to float them all;
    And though my nature is humane,
        I *felt* that it would pall.

    'Yet this one jelly-fish,' I cried, 25
        'I'll rescue if I may.
    I'll wade out with her through the tide
        And leave her in the bay.'

    I paused, my feelings to control,
        To wipe away a tear— 30
    It seemed to me a murmur stole
        Out of the crystal sphere.

    She said: 'Your culture's incomplete,
        Though your intention's kind;
    The sand, the seaweed, and the heat 35
        I do not really mind.

'To wander through the briny deep
  I own I do not care;
I somehow seem to go to sleep
  Here, there, or anywhere.   40

'When wild waves tossed me to and fro,
  I never felt put out;
I never got depressed and low,
  Or paralysed by doubt.

''Twas not the ocean's soothing balm.   45
  Ah no, 'twas something more!
I'm just as peaceful and as calm
  Here shrivelling on the shore.

'It does not matter what may come,
  I'm dead to woe or bliss: 50
I haven't a Sensorium,
  And that is how it is.'

516.   *Church Echoes*

1. VICAR'S DAUGHTER.

Down in the depths of this fair church—
A man may find them if he search,
There lie six pews that are called Free,
And there the strange Bohemians be.
(Have mercy upon them, miserable offenders.)   5

We Philistines in cushioned pews
Have prayer-books more than we can use.
They have one prayer-book that they share.
They do not kneel: they sit and stare.
(Have mercy upon them, miserable offenders.)   10

Decorously we meet their view
As if they were an empty pew.
We are above them and beyond,
And reverently we respond.
(Have mercy upon them, miserable offenders.)   15

2. CHARITY CHILD.

The Vicar's daughters look so good,
We think that they are made of wood.
Like rests for hymn-books, there they stand,
With each a hymn-book in her hand.

Half through the sermon once we tried   20
To hold our eyelids open wide,
That we might know if they *could* keep
Awake, or sometimes went to sleep.

It was no use, we may be wrong.
The Vicar preached so very long;   25
And keep awake we never could—
We *think* that they are made of wood.

3. TRAMP.

Hardly includes us in its glance
The Vicar's glassy countenance:
The Verger with superior eyes   30
Surveys us in a still surprise.

But when the organ's notes begin
I heed not any Philistine:
To hear the music is my bliss;
And I'm at home where music is.   35

Through ranks of aliens to and fro
I see the true musician go.
So dim their eyes, they cannot trace
The light unknown upon his face.

Here week by week I come, and see   40
No hand stretched out to welcome me;
And I am in a friendless land—
But music takes me by the hand.

517.   *The Sandblast Girl and the Acid Man*

Of all the cities far and wide,
    The city that I most prefer,
Though hardly through the fog descried,
    Is Muggy Manchester.

Of all its buildings the most dear,
    I find a stained glass factory—
Because the sandblast girl works here,
    In the same room with me!

It made a most terrific din,
    Of yore, that sandblasting machine,
I cursed the room I laboured in,
    And all the dull routine,
And the *old* sandblast girl, who broke,
    Of coloured glass, so many a sheet,
In fruitless efforts to evoke
    Tracery clear and neat.

That sandblast girl, at last she left—
    They couldn't let her blunders pass.
But Maggie's hands are slim and deft,
    They never break the glass!
From ruby, orange, or from blue,
    The letters stand out clear as pearl.
The fellows say they never knew
    So smart a sandblast girl!

I raise my eyes: I see her stand,
    A sheet of glass her arms embrace;
Out spurts the narrow stream of sand
    On each uncovered space,
Till perfectly the work is done,
    And clear again grows Maggie's brow—
Till a fresh labour is begun,
    She's merely human, now!

And sometimes when her hands are free,
    While with my acid still I work,
She'll give a hasty glance at me,
    Embossing like a Turk.
Her pretty hair so soft and brown
    Is coiled about her shapely head,
And I look up and she looks down,
    And both of us go red!

She has a dress of navy blue,
    A turn-down collar, white and clean
As though no smoke it travelled through,
    And smuts had never seen.

I've noticed that white snowdrop bells
    Have a peculiar look of her!
And nothing but her pallor tells
    Of Muggy Manchester.

Just twenty shillings every week!
    And always somebody distressed
Wants helping; and you feel a sneak
    If you don't do your best.
Suppose that I began to hoard,
    And steeled my heart, my coffer hid,
I wonder if I could afford
    To — Would she, if I did?

She has a mother to support,
    And I've a sister. Trade's not brisk,
And for a working man, in short,
    Life is a fearful risk.
The Clarion I sometimes read,
    I muse upon in winter nights,
I wonder if they'll e'er succeed
    In putting things to rights!

I'm vastly better off than some!
    I think of how the many fare
Who perish slowly, crushed and dumb,
    For leisure, food and air.
'Tis hard, in Freedom's very van,
    To live and die a luckless churl.
'Tis hard to be an acid man,
    Without a sandblast girl!

518.   *Underground*

(The Porter Speaks.)

A quarter of an hour to wait,
    And quite sufficient too,
Since your remarks on Bishopsgate
    Impress the mind as true,
Unless you work here soon and late,
    Till 'tis like home to you.

You see, a chap stands what he must,
    He'll hang on anywhere;
He'll learn to live on smoke and dust,
    Though 'tisn't healthy fare.   10
We're used to breathing grime in, just
    Like you to breathing air.

And yet 'tis odd to think these trains,
    In half an hour, maybe,
Will be right out among green lanes,   15
    Where the air is pure and free.
Well, sir, there's Bishopsgate remains
    For us, and here are we!

Your train. First class, sir. That's your style!
    In future, I'll be bound,   20
You'll stick to hansoms, since you'd spile
    Here in the Underground.
I've got to wait a little while
    Before *my* train comes round.

519.   *The Ballad of the Flag Painter*

In a wideawake not worn for show
    He passes every day.
He's an artist, like myself, I know,
    But *he* is an R.A.

And a thousand pounds if *I* could make   5
    By painting some great lord,
I think a better wideawake
    I'd manage to afford!

Small difference between our tiles!
    Only my coat's in rags,   10
And it is canvas that *he* spiles,
    I merely spile the flags.

His reputation is immense—
    I never liked him less.
He's often flung a few odd pence   15
    To a comrade in distress.

And however green his hat may look,
    Of tin he must be flush—
They say he always has a duke
    Or duchess neath his brush!

His portraits in a gallery
    I've seen, but for my part,
Though painted very skilfully,
    I didn't call it *art!*

Devoid of beauty or of mirth,
    They only seemed to stare
As if they wondered who on earth
    The *other* portraits were.

No need of galleries for me,
    My works of art to hold!
Because the new ones, don't you see,
    I paint upon the old.

See how the silvery moonbeams fall
    On this forsaken pile
And ruined bridge—that's what I call
    The true poetic style!

Only—a shower will come some day,
    And spoil my pictures, when
I cannot see them washed away,
    Or paint them in again.

They'll run together, blue and pink,
    And sea and shore and sky,
There'll never be a soul to think
    Of keeping the things dry.

The flags, for me, will stay quite clean.
    But when I'm dead and gone,
His duchesses will smile serene
    Posterity upon.

And so he'll win—but I confess,
    I've very little doubt,
Some of his dukes and duchesses
    Had better be washed out!

from *Songs from Dreamland*

I. *A Warning to New Worlds*

You far-off star serene and cold,
    You've lived through cycles more than we:
In you the mystery is unrolled
    Right to the end, whate'er it be.
What light would on our darkness rise,
    Could we observe your bleak expanse,
Know why you left, all coldly wise,
    The shining stellar dance!

Ah, could some kindly messenger
    The lesson of your life rehearse,
He might remark, to Jupiter:—
    "Beware of changing bad for worse.
The ills of incandescence bear,
    Firmly a solid crust refuse.
Of protoplasm never dare
    The use or the abuse!"

What havoc saved among the stars
    That did not rush upon their fate!
Too late for Venus and for Mars,
    For *this* poor planet, all too late—
Star militant among the spheres,
    A star with many woes oppressed,
Who now the unknown watchword hears
    That passes to the rest.

Ere Being's germ the strong sun bears,
    Ours shall have fled, for good and all,
This luckless planet, from its cares
    Voices of fate already call,
And year by year to rest it wins.
    How many a millennium
Before the Sun *his* life begins,
    With all his woes to come!

Too late for even the youngest star,
    When nebulæ as it appears,
Without premeditation are
    Condensing into rising spheres,

> And *they* will follow the old plan,
>   Will name their system as they pass,
> The system that in gas began,
>   And that will end in gas.   40
>
> *They* are no politician's care,
>   No missionary travels through
> The gaseous vapours that prepare
>   New worlds, new woes, for races new.
> Philanthropists, ye do your best.   45
>   One world—how many worlds there be!
> Convert the masses; but arrest,
>   Arrest the nebulæ!

521.

II. *Ether Insatiable*

> Now Energy's bound to diminish—
>   The harder she struggles and moils,
> The faster she speeds to the finish,
>   The end of her infinite toils.
> A million of planets beneath her   5
>   Strong hands she may mould or efface—
> 'Tis all to the good of the ether,
>   That fills circumambient space!
> All's quietly caught up and muffled
>   By a strange and intangible foe,   10
> The ether serene and unruffled,
>   The ether we see not nor know.
> Life, radiance, in torrents dispelling,
>   The universe spins to its goal;
> And radiance and life find *one* dwelling—   15
>   This ether's the tomb of the whole.
> There is not a hushed malediction,
>   There is not a smile or a sigh,
> But aids in dispersing, by friction,
>   The cosmical heat in the sky;   20
> And whether a star falls, or whether
>   A heart breaks—for stars and for men
> Their labour is all for the ether,
>   That renders back nothing again.
> And we, howsoever we hated   25
>   And feared, or made love, or believed,

For all the opinions we stated,
    The woes and the wars we achieved,
We, too, shall lie idle together,
    In very uncritical case—
And no one will win—but the ether,
    That fills circumambient space!

522.   *The Conscientious Ghost*

                    (Psychical.)

'My duties,' he remarked with tears,
    'I've never sought to shun;
Yet hard it is that at my years
    They have again begun.

'No one believed in me, or cared
    If I my vigils kept;
My diligence the public spared,
    And undisturbed I slept.

'Yet now I never close my eyes
    But in my dreams I see
These *Psychical Societies*
    Descending upon me.

'They ask me whether I forgot
    To wander round the moat;
They wonder what I mean by not
    Steering my phantom boat.

'*They* would not think it such a joke
    To rattle fetters through
The weary night till morning broke,
    As Duty bids me do!

'Alas,' he groaned, 'on the blood-stained floors
    Again to fight and fall!
To shiver round the secret doors,
    The draughty banquet hall.

'I say it was a heartless thought—
    Wherever he may dwell
Who on us this disaster brought,
    I'd like to haunt him well.

'An ah!' he cried, with rapture grim,
    'One thing consoles me most:
We'll male it very warm for him
    When once he is a ghost!

'When every honest phantom sleeps
    He'll have to freeze in cells,
And wring his hands by mouldy keeps,
    And jangle rusty bells.'

He paused, his fetters to arrange,
    Adjust his winding-sheet;
He murmured, 'In this world of change
    One can't be too complete!'

He fixed me on a glance of woe,
    Then vanished into air;
I heard his clanking fetter go
    Right down the winding stair.

Yet sometimes when 'mid wind and rain
    I'm lying warm and dry,
I seem to hear him clank his chain
    Beneath the dismal sky.

A. (Arthur) C. (Christopher) Benson (1862–1925)

523. *Courage*

I have been brave in my way,
    Though men did not call me brave;
They deem that I creep away,
    If ever a pennon wave
Over the flashing fray.

Yet I have lain through the night
   Shuddering, open-eyed,
Straining my aching sight
   To see what leant at my side,
Angel or sullen sprite.

Then in the haggard day,—
   Cruel and cold it shone,—
Sighing in sad dismay,
   I bind my armour on;
I have been brave, I say.

524. *Self*

This is my chiefest torment, that behind
   The brave and subtle spirit, the swift brain,
   There sits and shivers, in a cell of pain,
A groping atom, melancholy, blind,
Which is myself;—though, when spring suns are kind,
   And rich leaves riot in the genial rain,
   I cheat him, dreaming: slip my rigorous chain,
Free as a skiff before the dancing wind.
Then he awakes: and vexed that I am glad,
   In dreary malice strains some nimble cord,
     Pricks his thin claw within some delicate nerve;
     And all at once I falter, start, and swerve
From my true course, to fall, unmanned and sad,
   Into gross darkness, tangible, abhorred.

Victor Plarr (1863–1929)

525. *Shadows*

A song of shadows: never glory was
   But it had some soft shadow that would lie
On wall, on quiet water, on smooth grass,
   Or in the vistas of the phantasy:

The shadow of the house upon the lawn,
   Upon the house the shadow of the tree,
And through the moon-steeped hours unto the dawn
   The shadow of thy beauty over me.

526.   *Epitaphium Citharistriæ*

Stand not uttering sedately
   Trite oblivious praise above her!
Rather say you saw her lately
   Lightly kissing her last lover:

Whisper not, 'There is a reason
   Why we bring her no white blossom:'
Since the snowy bloom's in season
   Strow it on her sleeping bosom:

Oh, for it would be a pity
   To o'erpraise her or to flout her:
She was wild, and sweet, and witty—
   Let's not say dull things about her.

527.   *Of Change of Opinions*

As you advance in years you long
   For what you scorned when but a boy:
Then 'twas the town, now the birds' song
   Is your obsession and your joy.

And, as you lie and die, maybe
   You will look back, unreconciled
To that dark hour, and clearly see
   Yourself a little wistful child.

Into the jaws of death you'll bring
   No virile triumph, wrought with pain;
But only to the monster fling
   The daydream and the daisy-chain,

    The lispéd word, the gentle touch,
        The wonder, and the mystic thought,
    For old gray Death upon his crutch   15
        To rake into his Bag of Nought.

528.   *Ad Cinerarium*

Who in this small urn reposes,
    Celt or Roman, man or woman,
Steel of steel, or rose of roses?

Whose the dust set rustling slightly,
    In its hiding-place abiding,   5
When this urn is lifted lightly?

Sure some mourner deemed immortal
    What thou holdest and enfoldest,
Little house without a portal!

When the artificers had slowly   10
    Formed thee, turned thee, sealed thee, burned thee,
Freighted with thy freightage holy,

Sure he thought there's no forgetting
    All the sweetness and completeness
Of his rising, of her setting,   15

And so bade them grave no token,
    Generation, age, or nation,
On thy round side still unbroken;—

Let them score no cypress verses,
    Funeral glories, prayers, or stories,   20
Mourner's tears, or mourner's curses,

Round thy brown rim time hath polished,—
    Left thee dumbly cold and comely
As some shrine of gods abolished.

Ah, 'twas well! It scarcely matters   25
    What is sleeping in the keeping
Of this house of human tatters,—

  Steel of steel, or rose of roses,
   Man or woman, Celt or Roman,
  If but soundly he reposes!   30

529.   *The Imperial Prayers*

Suggested by a passage in Mr Valentine Chirol's the 'Far Eastern Question'

Silenced the streets with sand of holy hue
Shrouded the curious houses with faint sheen
Of silk and broid'ry, which for months between
These awful feasts none but the moth dare view;
The Son of Heaven, the Unutterable Kwang Hsu,   5
Borne in his lofty-looming palanquin,
By slaves who, if they stumble, die unseen,
Flits like a ghost through midnight—what to do?

The West stands clamouring outside his door:
We plan division of his lands and fame,   10
Yet hold Heredity for proven Truth.
To pray to his great Fathers gone before,
—Might not Marc Brutus once have done the same?—
Goes that spoiled, wretched, and mysterious youth.

530.   *Twilight-Piece*

  The golden river-reach afar
   Kisses the golden skies of even,
  And there's the first faint lover's star
   Alight along the walls of heaven.

  The river murmurs to the boughs,   5
   The boughs make music each to each,
  And still an amorous west wind soughs
   And loiters down the lonesome reach.

  And here on the slim arch that spans
   The rippling stream, in dark outline,   10
  You see the poor old fisherman's
   Bowed form and patient rod and line.

A picture better than all art,
    Since none could catch that sunset stain,
Or set in the soft twilight's heart
    This small strange touch of human pain!

Stephen Phillips (1864–1915)

531.   *The Apparition*

I

My dead Love came to me, and said:
    "God gives me one hour's rest,
To spend upon the earth with thee:
    How shall we spend it best?"

"Why as of old," I said, and so
    We quarrelled as of old.
But when I turned to make my peace,
    That one short hour was told.

II

Nine nights she did not come to me:
    The heaven was filled with rain;
And as it fell, and fell, I said,
    "She will not come again."

Last night she came, not as before,
    But in a strange attire;
Weary she seemed, and very faint,
    As though she came from fire.

III

She is not happy! It was noon;
    The sun fell on my head:
And it was not an hour in which
    We think upon the dead.

She is not happy! I should know
    Her voice, much more her cry;
And close beside me a great rose
    Had just begun to die.

She is not happy! As I walked,
    Of her I was aware:
She cried out, like a creature hurt,
    Close by me in the air.

IV

Under the trembling summer stars,
    I turned from side to side;
When she came in and sat with me,
    As though she had not died.

And she was kind to me and sweet,
    She had her ancient way;
Remembered how I liked her hand
    Amid my hair to stray.

She had forgotten nothing, yet
    Older she seemed, and still:
All quietly she took my kiss,
    Even as a mother will.

She rose, and in the streak of dawn
    She turned as if to go:
But then again came back to me;
    My eyes implored her so!

She pushed the hair from off my brow,
    And looked into my eyes.
"I live in calm," she said, "and there
    Am learning to be wise."

"Why grievest thou? I pity thee
    Still turning on this bed."
"And art thou happy?" I exclaimed.
    "Alas!" she sighed, and fled.

V

I woke: she had been standing by,
    With wonder on her face.
She came toward me, very bright,   55
    As from a blessed place.

She touched me not, but smiling spoke,
    And softly as before.
"They gave me drink from some slow stream;
    I love thee now no more."   60

VI

The other night she hurried in,
    Her face was wild with fear:
"Old friend," she said, "I am pursued,
    May I take refuge here?"

532.   'O thou art put to many uses, sweet!'

O thou art put to many uses, sweet!
Thy blood will urge the rose, and surge in Spring;
But yet! ...

And all the blue of thee will go to the sky,
And all thy laughter to the rivers run;   5
But yet! ...

Thy tumbling hair will in the West be seen,
And all thy trembling bosom in the dawn;
But yet! ...

Thy briefness in the dewdrop shall be hung,   10
And all the frailness of thee on the foam;
But yet! ...

Thy soul shall be upon the moonlight spent,
Thy mystery spread upon the evening mere.
And yet! ...   15

533.	*Corona Corinnae*

BEING A CELEBRATION, IN SIX SONGS,
OF A MASQUE OF DANCING,
NAMED THE SEASONS.

I. TO HIS MUSE, BY WAY OF PROLOGUE.

Go! bid Love stay,
   And make a maddening rhyme
     Unto the dancing feet;
     That may perchance repeat,
   Within some other brain, another time,   5
This measure done, forgotten, put away!

Ah! if it might, might in an hastening year
   Re-woo its magic from the ravening past;
     Make suddenly the movement, the delight,
The gaiety, the freshness, re-appear: 10
   Although no longer than a thought it last!
          Ah, if it might!

II. OF THIS LAND OF LOVE'S.

This is Love's land, and here we find
   The birds and flowers, that are his own;
Nothing there is unlike his mind,   15
   Nothing, but he therein is shown:
For wings, and leaves, and blossoms, prove
Themselves the very heart of Love.

Here are the seasons, that Love's year,
   Nay, that each hour of Love, must know;   20
Though they the gaudy June do bear,
   They bring him wintry times also:
Still, still, methinks, he would not change;
Though, in their stead, 'twere his to range
Through the deep grass, by flowery roads,   25
Where gleam the white feet of the Gods.

III. THE MEASURE.

Between the pansies and the rye,
Flutters my purple butterfly;

Between her white brow and her chin,
Does Love his fairy wake begin: 30

By poppy-cups and drifts of heather,
Dances the sun and she together;

But o'er the scarlet of her mouth,
Whence those entreated words come forth,
Love hovers all the live-long day, 35
And cannot, through its spell, away;
But there, where he was born, must die,
Between the pansies and the rye.

IV. TO HERRICK.

In vain, at all to my content,
Have I my thoughts through nature sent 40
   To search, with keenest glance,
All things on high, around, below,
But for one figure, that would show
   Corinna in the dance.

Either my brain is dull, or we 45
With narrow bounds content must be;
   Contented, too, to find
The same sweet flowers, that used to win
The eyes of poets dead, within
   The meadows of the mind: 50

For only this worn image wrought,
In marble words, the eluding thought
   Justly; and one, I fear,
Familiar as the trees or sky:
"She dances like my heart, when I 55
   "Set eyes upon my dear."

Still might I say, as well I could,
When thinking of a summer wood;
   And, truly, one believes
It is the best yet hit upon: 60
"She dances like the dancing sun,
   "Among the dancing leaves."

But even this, expressing much,
Yet wants, I think, the human touch,
    Which all such styles demand;
For though it laughs upon the wing
Of verse, 'tis but a pretty thing,
    And lacks the master hand.

Ah! Herrick, now where are those rhymes,
Which we in former, thoughtless, times
    Had deemed omnipotent
To tell, as never yet was told
In song, all things, which Life of old
    Has unto Beauty lent?

Truly, to thee each joy, that stirs
That secret, wayward, heart of hers,
    Is clay upon the wheel:
These you can fashion as you list;
But not the turning of her wrist,
    The glancing of her heel.

V. "IF SHE BE MADE OF WHITE AND RED."

If she be made of white and red,
As all transcendent beauty shows;
If heaven be blue above her head,
And earth be golden, as she goes:
Nay, then thy deftest words restrain;
Tell not that beauty, it is vain.

If she be filled with love and scorn,
As all divinest natures are;
If 'twixt her lips such words are born,
As can but Heaven or Hell confer:
Bid Love be still, nor ever speak,
Lest he his own rejection seek.

VI. TO HIS MUSE IN INTERCESSION FOR LOVE.

Now all be hushed; all, all be wholly still;
For Love is far too glad for song or speech,
Love that hath stayed: now let him have his will;
The mouth, the eyes, the cheek, he did beseech.

Why should he sing? Is it not song enough,
That she, between those sighs that ever start
Suddenly from him, as from Boreas rough,
Should hear the measure from his beating heart?   100

Therefore constrain him, that he speak no word,
Till the consuming stillness do eclipse
All but delight: then shall no sound be heard,
Save only falling hair, and nestling lips.

534.   *Paradise Walk*

    She is living in Paradise Walk,
    With the dirt and the noise of the street;
    And heaven flies up, if she talk,
    With Paradise down at her feet.

    She laughs through a summer of curls;   5
    She moves in a garden of grace:
    Her glance is a treasure of pearls,
    How saved from the deeps of her face!

    And the magical reach of her thigh
    Is the measure, with which God began   10
    To build up the peace of the sky,
    And fashion the pleasures of man.

    With Paradise down at her feet,
    While heaven flies up if she talk;
    With the dirt and the noise of the street,   15
    She is living in Paradise Walk.

535.   '*Bella immagine d'un fior*'

    Lilia with the magic hair,
    Unto you an holy hour
    Love himself, constrained, hath granted;
    Lilia with the magic hair,
    Beautiful likeness of a flower.   5

Too happy, whom that time ordains,
By these high spells, to lie enchanted;
Red lips, white limbs with sapphire veins:
Lilia with the magic hair,
Beautiful likeness of a flower!   10

O Rare concent of all delight,
Put forth, and use, your utmost power;
Keep and entangle him to-night,
Lilia with the magic hair,
Beautiful likeness of a flower.   15

536.   *Cease, Cease Reproachful Eyes!*

Cease, cease reproachful eyes! I have not done
    Aught, that should bring me ever this unrest.
Tell me my fault! Have end! Search, one by one,
    All possible errors, which have Time possessed:
I swear you, naught upon me shall you prove;   5
Unless it be a fault in me to love.

Oh! were you here with me, that I might speak
    No matter what unheeded words, and vain;
I would persuade me, that the look I seek
    Was given: but for me there must remain,   10
Beneath the one, unalterable guise,
This torture. Nay! Cease, cease; relentless eyes!

W. (William) B. (Butler) Yeats (1865–1939)

from *Crossways* (1889)

537.   *Down by the Salley Gardens*

Down by the salley gardens my love and I did meet;
She passed the salley gardens with little snow-white feet.
She bid me take love easy, as the leaves grow on the tree;
But I, being young and foolish, with her would not agree.

In a field by the river my love and I did stand, 5
And on my leaning shoulder she laid her snow-white hand.
She bid me take life easy, as the grass grows on the weirs;
But I was young and foolish, and now am full of tears.

538. *The Ballad of Father O'Hart*

Good Father John O'Hart
In penal days rode out
To a shoneen who had free lands
And his own snipe and trout.

In trust took he John's lands; 5
Sleiveens were all his race;
And he gave them as dowers to his daughters,
And they married beyond their place.

But Father John went up,
And Father John went down; 10
And he wore small holes in his shoes,
And he wore large holes in his gown.

All loved him, only the shoneen,
Whom the devils have by the hair,
From the wives, and the cats, and the children, 15
To the birds in the white of the air.

The birds, for he opened their cages
As he went up and down;
And he said with a smile, 'Have peace now';
And he went his way with a frown. 20

But if when anyone died
Came keeners hoarser than rooks,
He bade them give over their keening;
For he was a man of books.

And these were the works of John, 25
When, weeping score by score,
People came into Colooney;
For he'd died at ninety-four.

There was no human keening;
The birds from Knocknarea
And the world round Knocknashee
Came keening in that day.

The young birds and old birds
Came flying, heavy and sad;
Keening in from Tiraragh,
Keening from Ballinafad;

Keening from Inishmurray,
Nor stayed for bite or sup;
This way were all reproved
Who dig old customs up.

from *The Rose* (1893)

539.   *The Lake Isle of Innisfree*

I will arise and go now, and go to Innisfree,
And a small cabin build there, of clay and wattles made:
Nine bean-rows will I have there, a hive for the honey-bee,
And live alone in the bee-loud glade.

And I shall have some peace there, for peace comes dropping slow,
Dropping from the veils of the morning to where the cricket sings;
There midnight's all a glimmer, and noon a purple glow,
And evening full of the linnet's wings.

I will arise and go now, for always night and day
I hear lake water lapping with low sounds by the shore;
While I stand on the roadway, or on the pavements grey,
I hear it in the deep heart's core.

540.   *The Sorrow of Love*

The brawling of a sparrow in the eaves,
The brilliant moon and all the milky sky,
And all that famous harmony of leaves,
Had blotted out man's image and his cry.

A girl arose that had red mournful lips   5
And seemed the greatness of the world in tears,
Doomed like Odysseus and the labouring ships
And proud as Priam murdered with his peers;

Arose, and on the instant clamorous eaves,
A climbing moon upon an empty sky,   10
And all that lamentation of the leaves,
Could but compose man's image and his cry.

541.   *A Dream of Death*

I dreamed that one had died in a strange place
Near no accustomed hand;
And they had nailed the boards above her face,
The peasants of that land,
Wondering to lay her in that solitude,   5
And raised above her mound
A cross they had made out of two bits of wood,
And planted cypress round;
And left her to the indifferent stars above
Until I carved these words: 10
She was more beautiful than thy first love,
But now lies under boards.

542.   *To Ireland in the Coming Times*

Know, that I would accounted be
True brother of a company
That sang, to sweeten Ireland's wrong,
Ballad and story, rann and song;
Nor be I any less of them,   5
Because the red-rose-bordered hem
Of her, whose history began
Before God made the angelic clan,
Trails all about the written page.
When Time began to rant and rage   10
The measure of her flying feet
Made Ireland's heart begin to beat;

And Time bade all his candles flare
To light a measure here and there;
And may the thoughts of Ireland brood   15
Upon a measured quietude.

Nor may I less be counted one
With Davis, Mangan, Ferguson,
Because, to him who ponders well,
My rhymes more than their rhyming tell   20
Of things discovered in the deep,
Where only body's laid asleep.
For the elemental creatures go
About my table to and fro,
That hurry from unmeasured mind   25
To rant and rage in flood and wind;
Yet he who treads in measured ways
May surely barter gaze for gaze.
Man ever journeys on with them
After the red-rose-bordered hem.   30
Ah, faeries, dancing under the moon,
A Druid land, a Druid tune!

While still I may, I write for you
The love I lived, the dream I knew.
From our birthday, until we die,   35
Is but the winking of an eye;
And we, our singing and our love,
What measurer Time has lit above,
And all benighted things that go
About my table to and fro,   40
Are passing on to where may be,
In truth's consuming ecstasy,
No place for love and dream at all;
For God goes by with white footfall.
I cast my heart into my rhymes,   45
That you, in the dim coming times,
May know how my heart went with them
After the red-rose-bordered hem.

from *The Wind Among the Reeds* (1899)

543. *The Lover Mourns for the Loss of Love*

Pale brows, still hands and dim hair,
I had a beautiful friend
And dreamed that the old despair
Would end in love in the end:
She looked in my heart one day   5
And saw your image was there;
She has gone weeping away.

544. *The Poet Pleads with the Elemental Powers*

The Powers whose name and shape no living creature knows
Have pulled the Immortal Rose;
And though the Seven Lights bowed in their dance and wept,
The Polar Dragon slept,
His heavy rings uncoiled from glimmering deep to deep: 5
When will he wake from sleep?

Great Powers of falling wave and wind and windy fire,
With your harmonious choir
Encircle her I love and sing her into peace,
That my old care may cease;   10
Unfold your flaming wings and cover out of sight
The nets of day and night.

Dim Powers of drowsy thought, let her no longer be
Like the pale cup of the sea,
When winds have gathered and sun and moon burned dim   15
Above its cloudy rim;
But let a gentle silence wrought with music flow
Whither her footsteps go.

545. *He Wishes for the Cloths of Heaven*

Had I the heavens' embroidered cloths,
Enwrought with golden and silver light,
The blue and the dim and the dark cloths
Of night and light and the half-light,

I would spread the cloths under your feet:
But I, being poor, have only my dreams;
I have spread my dreams under your feet;
Tread softly because you tread on my dreams.

Rudyard Kipling (1865–1936)

546. *Mandalay*

By the old Moulmein Pagoda, lookin' eastward at the sea,
There's a Burma girl a-settin', and I know she thinks o' me;
For the wind is in the palm-trees, and the temple-bells they say:
'Come you back, you British soldier; come you back to Mandalay!'
    Come you back to Mandalay,
    Where the old Flotilla lay:
    Can't you 'ear their paddles chunkin' from Rangoon to Mandalay?
    On the road to Mandalay,
    Where the flyin'-fishes play,
    An' the dawn comes up like thunder outer China 'crost the Bay!

'Er petticoat was yaller an' 'er little cap was green,
An' 'er name was Supi-yaw-lat–jes' the same as Theebaw's Queen,
An' I seed her first a-smokin' of a whackin' white cheroot,
An' a-wastin' Christian kisses on an 'eathen idol's foot:
    Bloomin' idol made o' mud–
    Wot they called the Great Gawd Budd–
    Plucky lot she cared for idols when I kissed 'er where she stud!
    On the road to Mandalay ...

When the mist was on the rice-fields an' the sun was droppin' slow,
She'd git 'er little banjo an' she'd sing '*Kulla-lo-lo!*'
With 'er arm upon my shoulder an' 'er cheek agin my cheek
We useter watch the steamers an' the *hathis* pilin' teak.
    Elephints a-pilin' teak
    In the sludgy, squdgy creek,
    Where the silence 'ung that 'eavy you was 'arf afraid to speak!
    On the road to Mandalay ...

But that's all shove be'ind me–long ago an' fur away,
An' there ain't no 'buses runnin' from the Bank to Mandalay;
An' I'm learnin' 'ere in London what the ten-year soldier tells:
'If you've 'eard the East a-callin', you won't never 'eed naught else.'

No! you won't 'eed nothin' else
But them spicy garlic smells,
An' the sunshine an' the palm-trees an' the tinkly temple-bells;
On the road to Mandalay ...

I am sick o' wastin' leather on these gritty pavin'-stones,   35
An' the blasted Henglish drizzle wakes the fever in my bones;
Tho' I walks with fifty 'ousemaids outer Chelsea to the Strand,
An' they talks a lot o' lovin', but wot do they understand?
    Beefy face an' grubby 'and–
    Law! wot do they understand?   40
    I've a neater, sweeter maiden in a cleaner, greener land!
    On the road to Mandalay ...

Ship me somewheres east of Suez, where the best is like the worst,
Where there aren't no Ten Commandments an' a man can raise a thirst;
For the temple-bells are callin', an' it's there that I would be–   45
By the old Moulmein Pagoda, looking lazy at the sea;
    On the road to Mandalay,
    Where the old Flotilla lay,
    With our sick beneath the awnings when we went to Mandalay!
    O the road to Mandalay,   50
    Where the flyin'-fishes play,
    An' the dawn comes up like thunder outer China 'crost the Bay!

547.   *Danny Deever*

'What are the bugles blowin' for?' said Files-on-Parade.
'To turn you out, to turn you out,' the Colour-Sergeant said.
'What makes you look so white, so white?' said Files-on-Parade.
'I'm dreadin' what I've got to watch,' the Colour-Sergeant said.
    For they're hangin' Danny Deever, you can hear the Dead March play,   5
    The regiment's in 'ollow square—they're hangin' him to-day;
    They've taken of his buttons off an' cut his stripes away,
    An' they're hangin' Danny Deever in the mornin'.

'What makes the rear-rank breathe so 'ard?' said Files-on-Parade.
'It's bitter cold, it's bitter cold,' the Colour-Sergeant said.   10
'What makes that front-rank man fall down?' said Files-on-Parade.
'A touch o' sun, a touch o' sun,' the Colour-Sergeant said.
    They are hangin' Danny Deever, they are marchin' of 'im round,
    They 'ave 'alted Danny Deever by 'is coffin on the ground;
    An' 'e'll swing in 'arf a minute for a sneakin' shootin' hound—   15
    O they're hangin' Danny Deever in the mornin'!

"Is cot was right-'and cot to mine,' said Files-on-Parade.
"E's sleepin' out an' far to-night,' the Colour-Sergeant said.
'I've drunk 'is beer a score o' times,' said Files-on-Parade.
"E's drinkin' bitter beer alone,' the Colour-Sergeant said. 20
   They are hangin' Danny Deever, you must mark 'im to 'is place,
   For 'e shot a comrade sleepin'—you must look 'im in the face;
   Nine 'undred of 'is county an' the Regiment's disgrace,
   While they're hangin' Danny Deever in the mornin'.

'What's that so black agin the sun?' said Files-on-Parade. 25
'It's Danny fightin' 'ard for life,' the Colour-Sergeant said.
'What's that that whimpers over'ead?' said Files-on-Parade.
'It's Danny's soul that's passin' now,' the Colour-Sergeant said.
   For they're done with Danny Deever, you can 'ear the quickstep play,
   The regiment's in column, an' they're marchin' us away; 30
   Ho! the young recruits are shakin', an' they'll want their beer to-day,
   After hangin' Danny Deever in the mornin'!

(1890)

Arthur Symons (1865–1945)

from *Amoris Victima*

548.   II. *Why?*

Why is it, since I know you now
   As light as any wanton is,
And, knowing, need not wonder how
   You work that wonder of your kiss,
Why is it, since I know you now, 5

Still, in some corner of my brain,
   There clings a lost, last, lingering
Doubt of my doubts of you again,
   A foolish, unforgetting thing,
Still, in some corner of my brain? 10

Is it because your lips are soft,
   And warm your hands, and strange your eyes,
That I believe again the oft
   Repeated, oft permitted lies,
Because your lips are warm and soft? 15

    For what you are I know you now,
        For what it means I know your kiss;
    Yet, knowing, need one wonder how,
        Beneath your kisses, how it is,
    Knowing you, I believe you now?   20

549.   XIII. 'And yet, there was a hunger in your eyes'

    And yet, there was a hunger in your eyes,
        Once, when you turned upon me suddenly;
    And suddenly you turned away from me,
    Once, when, evoking other memories,
    I said, "You hate me: answer: do you not   5
        Hate me?" and in your silence then I heard
        The ruined echo of another word,
    Love, Love, that wailed and would not be forgot.
    And once you laughed, that laugh I understand,
        Sadder than tears, a broken little laugh,   10
        As if a sob had shivered it in half.
    And once, when, pausing, I had laid my hand
    Upon your hand my hand could always thrill,
    The fingers stirred: ah! they remember still.

550.   *The Street-Singer*

    She sings a pious ballad wearily;
    Her shivering body creeps on painful feet
    Along the muddy runlets of the street;
    The damp is in her throat: she coughs to free
    The cracked and husky notes that tear her chest;   5
    From side to side she looks with eyes that grope
    Feverishly hungering in a hopeless hope,
    For pence that will not come; and pence mean rest,
    The rest that pain may steal at night from sleep,
    The rest that hunger gives when satisfied;   10
    Her fingers twitch to handle them; she sings
    Shriller; her eyes, too hot with tears to weep,
    Fasten upon a window, where, inside,
    A sweet voice mocks her with its carollings.

551.   *During Music*

    The music had the heat of blood,
    A passion that no words can reach;
    We sat together, and understood
    Our own heart's speech.

    We had no need of word or sign, 5
    The music spoke for us, and said
    All that her eyes could read in mine
    Or mine in hers had read.

552.   *Morbidezza*

    White girl, your flesh is lilies,
    Under a frozen moon,
    So still is
    The rapture of your swoon
    Of whiteness, snow or lilies. 5

    Virginal in revealment,
    Your bosom's wavering slope,
    Concealment,
    In fainting heliotrope,
    Of whitest white's revealment, 10

    Is like a bed of lilies,
    A jealous-guarded row,
    Whose will is
    Simply chaste dreams : but oh,
    The alluring scent of lilies! 15

553.   *The Absinthe-Drinker*

    Gently I wave the visible world away.
    Far off, I hear a roar, afar yet near,
    Far off and strange, a voice is in my ear,
    And is the voice my own? the words I say
    Fall strangely, like a dream, across the day; 5

And the dim sunshine is a dream. How clear,
New as the world to lovers' eyes, appear
The men and women passing on their way!

The world is very fair. The hours are all
Linked in a dance of mere forgetfulness.   10
I am at peace with God and man. O glide,
Sands of the hour-glass that I count not, fall
Serenely: scarce I feel your soft caress,
Rocked on this dreamy and indifferent tide.

554.   *La Mélinite: Moulin Rouge*

Olivier Metra's Waltz of Roses
Sheds in a rhythmic shower
The very petals of the flower;
And all its roses,
The rouge of petals in a shower.   5

Down the long hall the dance returning
Rounds the full circle, rounds
The perfect rose of lights and sounds,
The rose returning
Into the circle of its rounds.   10

Alone, apart, one dancer watches
Her mirrored, morbid grace;
Before the mirror, face to face,
Alone she watches
Her morbid, vague, ambiguous grace.   15

Before the mirror's dance of shadows
She dances in a dream,
And she and they together seem
A dance of shadows;
Alike the shadows of a dream.   20

The orange-rosy lamps are trembling
Between the robes that turn;
In ruddy flowers of flame that burn
The lights are trembling:
The shadows and the dancers turn.   25

    And, enigmatically smiling,
    In the mysterious night,
    She dances for her own delight,
    A shadow smiling
    Back to a shadow in the night.   30

555.   *Palm Sunday: Naples*

    Because it is the day of Palms,
    Carry a palm for me,
    Carry a palm in Santa Chiara,
    And I will watch the sea;
    There are no palms in Santa Chiara   5
    Today or any day for me.

    I sit and watch the little sail
    Lean sideways on the sea,
    The sea is blue from here to Sorrento,
    And the sea-wind comes to me,   10
    And I see the white clouds lift from Sorrento
    And the dark sail lean upon the sea.

    I have grown tired of all these things,
    And what is left for me?
    I have no place in Santa Chiara,   15
    There is no peace upon the sea;
    But carry a palm in Santa Chiara,
    Carry a palm for me.

from *Days and Nights*

556.   *Translations: Posthumous Coquetry*

    Let there be laid, when I am dead
    Ere 'neath the coffin-lid I lie,
    Upon my cheek a little red,
    A little black about the eye.

For I in my close bier would fain,
As on the night his vows were made,
Rose-red eternally remain,
With khol beneath my blue eye laid.

Wind me no shroud of linen down
My body to my feet, but fold
The white folds of my muslin gown
With thirteen flounces, as of old.

This shall go with me where I go:
I wore it when I won his heart;
His first look hallowed it, and so,
For him, I laid the gown apart.

No immortelles, no broidered grace
Of tears upon my cushion be;
Lay me on my own pillow's lace,
My hair across it, like a sea.

That pillow, those mad nights of old,
Has seen our slumbering brows unite,
And 'neath the gondola's black fold
Has counted kisses infinite.

Between my hands of ivory,
Together set for prayer and rest,
Place then the opal rosary
The holy Pope at Rome has blest.

I will lie down then on that bed
And sleep the sleep that shall not cease;
His mouth upon my mouth has said
Pater and *Ave* for my peace.

(1889)

557. *Maquillage*

The charm of rouge on fragile cheeks,
Pearl-powder, and, about the eyes,
The dark and lustrous eastern dyes;
A voice of violets that speaks
Of perfumed hours of day, and doubtful night
Of alcoves curtained close against the light.

Gracile and creamy white and rose,
Complexioned like the flower of dawn,
Her fleeting colours are as those
That, from an April sky withdrawn,   10
Fade in a fragrant mist of tears away
When weeping noon leads on the altered day.

(1891)

Dora Sigerson (later Shorter) (1866–1918)

558.   *Unknown Ideal*

Whose is the voice that will not let me rest?
I hear it speak.
Where is the shore will gratify my quest,
Show what I seek?
Not yours, weak Muse, to mimic that far voice,   5
With halting tongue;
No peace, sweet land, to bid my heart rejoice
Your groves among.

Whose is the loveliness I know is by,
Yet cannot place?   10
Is it perfection of the sea or sky,
Or human face?
Not yours, my pencil, to delineate
The splendid smile!
Blind in the sun, we struggle on with Fate   15
That glows the while.

Whose are the feet that pass me, echoing
On unknown ways?
Whose are the lips that only part to sing
Through all my days?   20
Not yours, fond youth, to fill mine eager eyes
That still adore
Beauty that tarries not, nor satisfies
For evermore.

559.   *With a Rose*

         In the heart of a rose
           Lies the heart of a maid;
           If you be not afraid
         You will wear it. Who knows?

         In the pink of its bloom,   5
           Lay your lips to her cheek;
           Since a rose cannot speak,
         And you gain the perfume.

         If the dews on the leaf
           Are the tears from her eyes;   10
           If she withers and dies,
         Why, you have the belief,

         That a rose cannot speak,
           Though the heart of a maid
           In its bosom must fade,   15
         And with fading must break.

               (1897)

560.   *A Vagrant Heart*

O to be a woman! to be left to pique and pine,
When the winds are out and calling to this vagrant heart of mine.
Whisht! it whistles at the windows, and how can I be still?
There! the last leaves of the beech-tree go dancing down the hill.
All the boats at anchor they are plunging to be free—   5
O to be a sailor, and away across the sea!
When the sky is black with thunder, and the sea is white with foam,
The grey-gulls whirl up shrieking and seek their rocky home,
Low his boat is lying leeward, how she runs upon the gale,
As she rises with the billows, nor shakes her dripping sail.   10
There is danger on the waters—there is joy where dangers be—
Alas! to be a woman and the nomad's heart in me.

Ochone! to be a woman, only sighing on the shore—
With a soul that finds a passion for each long breaker's roar,
With a heart that beats as restless as all the winds that blow—   15
Thrust a cloth between her fingers, and tell her she must sew;

Must join in empty chatter, and calculate with straws—
For the weighing of our neighbour—for the sake of social laws.
O chatter, chatter, chatter, when to speak is misery,
When silence lies around your heart—and night is on the sea.   20
So tired of little fashions that are root of all our strife,
Of all the petty passions that upset the calm of life.
The law of God upon the land shines steady for all time;
The laws confused that man has made, have reason not nor rhyme.

O bird that fights the heavens, and is blown beyond the shore,   25
Would you leave your flight and danger for a cage to fight no more?
No more the cold of winter, or the hunger of the snow,
Nor the winds that blow you backward from the path you wish to go?
Would you leave your world of passion for a home that knows no riot?
Would I change my vagrant longings for a heart more full of quiet?   30
No!—for all its dangers, there is joy in danger too:
On, bird, and fight your tempests, and this nomad heart with you!

The seas that shake and thunder will close our mouths one day,
The storms that shriek and whistle will blow our breaths away.
The dust that flies and whitens will mark not where we trod.   35
What matters then our judging? we are face to face with God.

(1898)

561.   *The Wind on the Hills*

Go not to the hills of Erin
When the night winds are about,
Put up your bar and shutter,
And so keep the danger out.

For the good-folk whirl within it,   5
And they pull you by the hand,
And they push you on the shoulder,
Till you move to their command.

And lo! you have forgotten
What you have known of tears,   10
And you will not remember
That the world goes full of years;

A year there is a lifetime,
And a second but a day,
And an older world will meet you   15
Each morn you come away.

Your wife grows old with weeping,
And your children one by one
Grow grey with nights of watching,
Before your dance is done.   20

And it will chance some morning
You will come home no more,
Your wife sees but a withered leaf
In the wind about the door.

And your children will inherit   25
The unrest of the wind,
They shall seek some face elusive,
And some land they never find.

When the wind is loud, they sighing
Go with hearts unsatisfied,   30
For some joy beyond remembrance,
For some memory denied.

And all your children's children,
They cannot sleep or rest,
When the wind is out in Erin   35
And the sun is in the West.

(1899)

John Gray (1866–1934)

562.   *Sensation*

I walk the alleys trampled through the wheat,
Through whole blue summer eves, on velvet grass.
Dreaming, I feel the dampness at my feet;
The breezes bathe my naked head and pass.

I do not think a single thought, nor say 5
A word, but in my soul the mists upcurl
Of infinite love. I will go far away
With nature, happily, as with a girl.

563.   *The Vines*

                    To André Chevrillon

"Have you seen the listening snake?"
Bramble clutches for his bride,
Lately she was by his side,
Woodbine, with her gummy hands.

In the ground the mottled snake 5
Listens for the dawn of day;
Listens, listening death away,
Till the day burst winter's bands.

Painted ivy is asleep,
Stretched upon the bank, all torn, 10
Sinewy though she be; love-lorn
Convolvuluses cease to creep.

Bramble clutches for his bride,
Woodbine, with her gummy hands
All his horny claws expands; 15
She has withered in his grasp.

"Till the day dawn, till the tide
Of the winter's afternoon."
"Who tells dawning?—"Listen, soon."
Half-born tendrils, grasping, gasp. 20

564.   'Lord, if thou are not present, where shall I'

Lord, if thou are not present, where shall I
Seek thee the absent? If thou art everywhere,
How is it that I do not see thee nigh?

Thou dwellest in a light remote and fair.
How can I reach that light, Lord? I beseech 5
Thee, teach my seeking, and thyself declare

Thyself the sought to me. Unless thou teach
Me, Lord, I cannot seek; nor can I find
Thee, if thou wilt not come within my reach.

Lord, let me seek, with sturdy heart and mind,   10
In passion of desire and longingly.
Let me desire thee, seeking thee; and find...

Loving thee, find thee; love thee, finding thee.

565.   *A Crucifix*

To Ernest Dowson

A gothic church. At one end of an aisle,
Against a wall where mystic sunbeams smile
Through painted windows, orange, blue, and gold,
The Christ's unutterable charm behold.
Upon the cross, adorned with gold and green,   5
Long fluted golden tongues of sombre sheen,
Like four flames joined in one, around the head
And by the outstretched arms, their glory spread.
The statue is of wood; of natural size;
Tinted; one almost sees before one's eyes   10
The last convulsion of the lingering breath.
"Behold the man!" Robust and frail. Beneath
That breast indeed might throb the Sacred Heart.
And from the lips, so holily dispart,
The dying murmur breaths "Forgive! Forgive!"   15
O wide-stretched arms! "I perish, let them live."
Under the torture of the thorny crown,
The loving pallor of the brow looks down
On human blindness, on the toiler's woes;
The while, to overturn Despair's repose,   20
And urge to Hope and Love, as Faith demands,
Bleed, bleed the feet, the broken side, the hands.
A poet, painter, Christian,—it was a friend
Of mine—his attributes most fitly blend—
Who saw this marvel, made an exquisite   25
Copy; and, knowing how I worshipped it,
Forgot it, in my room, by accident.
I write these verses in acknowledgment.

566.   *Spleen*

> The roses every one were red,
> And all the ivy leaves were black.
>
> Sweet, do not even stir your head,
> Or all of my despairs come back.
>
> The sky is too blue, too delicate: 5
> Too soft the air, too green the sea.
>
> I fear—how long had I to wait!—
> That you will tear yourself from me.
>
> The shining box-leaves weary me,
> The varnished holly's glistening,   10
>
> The stretch of infinite country;
> So, saving you, does everything.

567.   *Crocuses in Grass*

            To Charles Hazelwood Shannon

> Purple and white the crocus flowers,
>   And yellow, spread upon
>   The sober lawn; the hours
> Are not more idle in the sun.
>
> Perhaps one droops a prettier head,   5
>   And one would say: Sweet Queen,
>   Your lips are white and red,
> And round you lies the grass most green.
>
> And she, perhaps, for whom is fain
>   The other, will not heed;   10
>   Or, that he may complain,
> Babbles, for dalliaunce, with a weed.
>
> And he dissimulates despair,
>   And anger, and surprise;
>   The while white daisies stare   15
> —And stir not—with their yellow eyes.

568.   *Poem*

                    (To Arthur Edmonds)

   Geranium, houseleek, laid in oblong beds
   On the trim grass. The daisies' leprous stain
   Is fresh. Each night the daisies burst again,
   Though every day the gardener crops their heads.

   A wistful child, in foul unwholesome shreds,   5
   Recalls some legend of a daisy chain
   That makes a pretty necklace. She would fain
   Make one, and wear it, if she had some threads.

   Sun, leprous flowers, foul child. The asphalt burns.
   The garrulous sparrows perch on metal Burns.   10
   Sing! Sing! they say, and flutter with their wings.
   He does not sing, he only wonders why
   He is sitting there. The sparrows sing. And I
   Yield to the strait allure of simple things.

569.   *Battledore*

                         I

   No breath of wind, within, without;
   No stirring twig, no insect hum;
   The very beehives dumb;
   Till shrill and sharp, with shriek and shout,
   The laughing sisters come.   5

   Swarth, heavy-tressed runs Alison,
   Not corn than Blanche more debonair,
   They fill the voiceless air,
   Scarcely a scant scarf bound upon
   Their joyous, rebel hair.   10

   "Here, sister, here." "No, here i' the shade."
   "Look, sister, gather up your skirt;
   It trails upon the dirt."
   "Ah, malapert, now you have made
   My hand bleed; I am hurt."   15

"Sweet Alison, your hose is rent."
"Sweet Blanche, but look you, do you this:
Loosen your girdle, sis,
And draw your gown through." Indolent
Blanche laughs at her excess.   20

Their heart-shaped bats, bent, bound and strung
With ravelled bow-cord, light and stout
To drive the ball about,
Winged plaything from the soutar wrung
With supplicating pout.   25

Drum! Drum! How it spins! How straight it flies!
How blue 'tis! Bluer than the sky!
"Sister, you strike awry."
Hither and thither, hands and eyes,
And never feet more spry.   30

The chatelaine creeps forth a space,
Down the strait stair, with looks askance
For peeping eyes. "Constance!"
The girls cry out, "come, take a place."
Her eyes fixed, as in trance;   35

Thoughts flocking of Provençal fields,
Of her own youth, grown nigh and nigher,
Gathering her fine attire,
The weary Lady Constance yields
Unto a great desire.   40

Truth, she is little apt, although
She strive, and make a brave array
Of skill; the breathless day
Catches her throat for to and fro,
This way and that way. "Nay...."   45

One hand clasped on her face, and one
Against her waist, the frighted twain
Of girls, seeing her pain,
Shriek, cry: "Swift! Water!" Alison
Wrings at her hands in vain.   50

"A little sickness, child; 'til naught;
'Tis well. Dear Christ! if't be a wight,
Moris shall he be hight;
If't be a lass, Ysold. For aught
I joy, 't may be this night." 55

II

The sheltered garden sleeps among the tall
Black poplars which grow round it, next the wall.
The wall is very high, green grown on red.
All is within, white convent, chapel, all.

Slight supper past, the evening office said, 60
Gardening tools locked up, the poultry fed,
Little is done but lazy chaplets told,
Weeds plucked, and garden calvaries visited.

Some pace and stitch; some read in little, old,
Worn heavily bound missals, which they hold 65
With both red hands, where lawns are foiled with flowers,
Lily and Ladybell and Marygold.

This is the least unhushed of evening hours,
When blessed peace best wears its dearest dowers:
Quietly grouped are nuns and novices; 70
Two tiny ladies play with battledores.

Drunk with the blows, unsteady with the whizz
Of whirling flight, the shuttlecock seems, is

Alive and fluttering at each new shock.
Sisters are drawing close by twos and threes. 75

Asthmatic mother, as the shuttlecock
Flies straight at her, allows herself to knock
It onward with her leaf fan, muttering,
Half as excuse: 'Tis nearly nine o'clock.

What better warrant for a foolish thing: 80
With swift inventiveness the sisters bring
Whatever light thing strikes; old copybooks
Fulfil the purpose well. Such fluttering

Within the convent walls the sober rooks
Who live among the poplar branches—Sooks! —
Had seldom seen. Now all the place prevails
With cries and laughter to its furthest nooks.

The novices and nuns catch up their tails,
Better to bustle, darting till their veils
Float back and tangle in the merry fuss,
Till sombre weeds swell out like lusty sails....

Peace, croaks the mother, Peace, the angelus!

570.   *The Forge*

A long and narrow shop, magenta black
Mottled with rose; ten fires along one wall,
Faint day comes through the skylight overhead
Smoke-grimed to orange, when it comes at all.
The blast shut off for breakfast, fires are slack.

The buzzing neighbouring engine quieted,
You hear the mates talking from, berth to berth;
The silence is complete. The seldom noises
Reverberate as, quaintly, under earth
The graves repeat the sayings of the dead.

Contrasted with the metals, human voices
Sound hoarse and soft, as out of hollowed wood.
Their beverage made: of boiling water, stained
With tea and sugar, they prepare their food:
"Tiger," to envy, even where there choice is;

Here and now truly, not to be disdained.
Hear in what manner it is perfected;
How old word 'tis. The anvil polished bright
With leather skirt, two hearty chunks of bread,
Protecting ivory bacon, purple veined,

Are set thereon with caution; and the wight
Who owns the morsel, passes over it
A piece of red-hot iron till 'tis brown.
It cleans the tongue to hear it fizzle and spit,
If two hours' work vouchsafe no appetite.

This done, the smith has only to sit down
To eat his greasy "tiger," and drink off
His sweet, strong tea. This, being yet too hot,
Hangs in the rust-red water of the trough
To cool. The smith is sleeping, with a frown   30

Upon his shapeless features. This is not
The ballad wag they tell of: at his best
Maimed in his poor hands, wry, with crooked back,
Great-armed, bow-legged, and narrow in the chest.
It bends a man to make no matter what.   35

A rumour stirs, a hum, the blast comes back;
Shadows on wall and roof start forth and die.
Rattle of tongs, slosh, fume; unlovely night
Grown Chinese hell, to seeming, suddenly,
Where strange gods heap the fire and trim the rack.   40

Half shapes of light leap higher than man's height
Out from the blackness and as soon subside,
Flame-flesh-shapes sweat-swamped clinging cotton swathed
In violent action, following the guide
Of the smith's gesture bidding where to smite.   45

The smitten steel complains, all braised and scathed,
From thud to bark, from bark to metal scream;
Through ordeal of the fire and scaling trough,
To wake it from its long-embowelled dream,
To uses brought, flame-licked and torture-bathed.   50

This the arena wherein stubborn stuff
With man locks strength; where elements dispute
The mastery, where breath and fire bear blaze,

Where sullen water aids, to quell the brute
Earth into shape, to make it meek enough.   55

And this day is the type of many days.

571.   *The Barber*

I. I dreamed I was a barber; and there went
Beneath my hand, oh! manes extravagant.
Beneath my trembling fingers, many a mask
Of many a pleasant girl. It was my task
To gild their hair, carefully, strand by strand;   5
To paint their eyebrows with a timid hand;
To draw a bodkin, from a vase of kohl,
Through the closed lashes; pencils from a bowl
Of sepia to paint them underneath;
To blow upon their eyes with a soft breath.   10
They lay them back and watched the leaping bands.

II. The dream grew vague. I moulded with my hands
The mobile breasts, the valley; and the waist
I touched; and pigments reverently placed
Upon their thighs in sapient spots and stains,   15
Beryls and crysolites and diaphanes,
And gems whose hot harsh names are never said.
I was a masseur; and my fingers bled
With wonder as I touched their awful limbs.

III. Suddenly, in the marble trough, there seems   20
O, last of my pale mistresses, Sweetness!
A twylipped scarlet pansie. My caress
Tinges thy steelgray eyes to violet.
Adown thy body skips the pit-a-pat
Of treatment once heard in a hospital   25
For plagues that fascinate, but half appal.

IV. So, at the sound, the blood of me stood cold.
Thy chaste hair ripened into sullen gold.
The throat, the shoulders, swelled and were uncouth.
The breasts rose up and offered each a mouth.   30
And on the belly pallid blushes crept,
That maddened me, until I laughed and wept.

572.   *Mishka*

                To Henri Teixeira de Mattos

Mishka is poet among the beasts.
When roots are rotten, and rivers weep,
The bear is at play in the land of sleep.
Though his head be heavy between his fists.
The bear is poet among the beasts.   5

Wide and large are the monster's eyes,
Nought saying, save one word alone:
Mishka! Mishka, as turned to stone,
Hears no word else, nor in anywise
Can see aught save the monster's eyes.   10

Honey is under the monster's lips;
And Mishka follows into her lair,
Dragged in the net of her yellow hair,
Knowing all things when honey drips
On his tongue like rain, the song of the hips   15

Of the honey-child, and of each twin mound.
Mishka! there screamed a far bird-note,
Deep in the sky, when round his throat
The triple coil of her hair she wound.
And stroked his limbs with a humming sound.   20

Mishka is white like a hunter's son;
For he knows no more of the ancient south
When the honey-child's lips are on his mouth,
When all her kisses are joined in one,
And his body is bathed in grass and sun.   25

The shadows lie mauven beneath the trees,
And purple stains, where the finches pass,
Leap in the stalks of the deep, rank grass.
Flutter of wing, and the buzz of bees,
Deepen the silence, and sweeten ease.   30

The honey-child is an olive tree,
The voice of birds and the voice of flowers,
Each of them all and all the hours,
The honey-child is a wingèd bee,
Her touch is a perfume, a melody.   35

573.   *Summer Past*

                        To Oscar Wilde

There was the summer. There
    Warm hours of leaf-lipped song,
    And dripping amber sweat.

The great trees condescend to cast a pearl
Down to the myrtles; and the proud leaves curl   5
    In ecstasy.

Fruit of a quest, despair.
Smart of a sullen wrong.
Where may they hide them yet?
    One hour, yet one,   10
To find the mossgod lurking in his nest,
To see the naiads' floating hair, caressed
    By fragrant sun-

Beams. Softly lulled the eves
The song-tired birds to sleep,   15
That other things might tell
    Their secrecies.
The beetle humming neath the fallen leaves.
Deep in what hollow do the stern gods keep
Their bitter silence? By what listening well   20
    Where holy trees,

Song-set, unfurl eternally the sheen
    Of restless green?

Richard Le Gallienne (1866–1947)

574.   *The World is Wide*

The world is wide—around yon court,
    Where dirty little children play,
Another world of street on street
    Grows wide and wider every day.

And round the town for endless miles 5
    A great strange land of green is spread—
O wide the world, O weary-wide,
    But it is wider overhead.

For could you mount yon glittering stairs
    And on their topmost turret stand,— 10
Still endless shining courts and squares,
    And lanes of lamps on every hand.

And, might you tread those starry streets
    To where those long perspectives bend,
O you would cast you down and die— 15
    Street upon street, world without end.

575.   *A Ballad of London*

(To H. W. Massingham)

Ah, London! London! our delight,
Great flower that opens but at night,
Great City of the Midnight Sun,
Whose day begins when day is done.

Lamp after lamp against the sky 5
Opens a sudden beaming eye,
Leaping alight on either hand,
The iron lilies of the Strand.

Like dragonflies, the hansoms hover,
With jewelled eyes, to catch the lover; 10
The streets are full of lights and loves,
Soft gowns, and flutter of soiled doves.

The human moths about the light
Dash and cling close in dazed delight,
And burn and laugh, the world and wife, 15
For this is London, this is life!

Upon thy petals butterflies,
But at thy root, some say, there lies
A world of weeping trodden things,
Poor worms that have not eyes or wings. 20

From out corruption of their woe
Springs this bright flower that charms us so,
Men die and rot deep out of sight
To keep this jungle-flower bright.

Paris and London, World-Flowers twain   25
Wherewith the World-Tree blooms again,
Since Time hath gathered Babylon,
And withered Rome still withers on.

Sidon and Tyre were such as ye,
How bright they shone upon the Tree!   30
But Time hath gathered, both are gone,
And no man sails to Babylon.

Ah, London! London! our delight,
For thee, too, the eternal night,
And Circe Paris hath no charm   35
To stay Time's unrelenting arm.

Time and his moths shall eat up all.
Your chiming towers proud and tall
He shall most utterly abase,
And set a desert in their place.   40

(1895)

576.   *A Library in a Garden*

'A Library in a garden! The phrase seems to contain the whole felicity of man.'
—Mr. EDMUND GOSSE in *Gossip in a Library*

A world of books amid a world of green,
Sweet song without, sweet song again within
Flowers in the garden, in the folios too:
O happy Bookman, let me live with you!

Ernest Dowson (1867–1900)

577.   *Vitae Summa Brevis Spem Nos Vetat Incohare Longam*

        They are not long, the weeping and the laughter,
           Love and desire and hate:
        I think they have no portion in us after
           We pass the gate.

        They are not long, the days of wine and roses: 5
           Out of a misty dream
        Our path emerges for a while, then closes
           Within a dream.

578.   *Non Sum Qualis Eram Bonae Sub Regno Cynarae*

    Last night, ah, yesternight, betwixt her lips and mine
    There fell thy shadow, Cynara! thy breath was shed
    Upon my soul between the kisses and the wine;
    And I was desolate and sick of an old passion,
        Yea, I was desolate and bowed my head: 5
    I have been faithful to thee, Cynara! in my fashion.

    All night upon mine heart I felt her warm heart beat,
    Night-long within mine arms in love and sleep she lay;
    Surely the kisses of her bought red mouth were sweet;
    But I was desolate and sick of an old passion,   10
        When I awoke and found the dawn was gray:
    I have been faithful to thee, Cynara! in my fashion.

    I have forgot much, Cynara! gone with the wind,
    Flung roses, roses riotously with the throng,
    Dancing, to put thy pale, lost lilies out of mind;   15
    But I was desolate and sick of an old passion,
        Yea, all the time, because the dance was long:
    I have been faithful to thee, Cynara! in my fashion.

    I cried for madder music and for stronger wine,
    But when the feast is finished and the lamps expire,   20
    Then falls thy shadow, Cynara! the night is thine;
    And I am desolate and sick of an old passion,

       Yea hungry for the lips of my desire:
I have been faithful to thee, Cynara! in my fashion.

579.   *Flos Lunae*

           For Yvanhoé Rambosson

I would not alter thy cold eyes,
Nor trouble the calm fount of speech
With aught of passion or surprise.
The heart of thee I cannot reach:
I would not alter thy cold eyes!   5

I would not alter thy cold eyes;
Nor have thee smile, nor make thee weep:
Though all my life droops down and dies,
Desiring thee, desiring sleep,
I would not alter thy cold eyes.   10

I would not alter thy cold eyes;
I would not change thee if I might,
To whom my prayers for incense rise,
Daughter of dreams! my moon of night!
I would not alter thy cold eyes.   15

I would not alter thy cold eyes,
With trouble of the human heart:
Within their glance my spirit lies,
A frozen thing, alone, apart;
I would not alter thy cold eyes.   20

580.   *Spleen*

           For Arthur Symons

I was not sorrowful, I could not weep,
And all my memories were put to sleep.

I watched the river grow more white and strange,
All day till evening I watched it change.

All day till evening I watched the rain   5
Beat wearily upon the window pane.

I was not sorrowful, but only tired
Of everything that ever I desired.

Her lips, her eyes, all day became to me
The shadow of a shadow utterly. 10

All day mine hunger for her heart became
Oblivion, until the evening came,

And left me sorrowful, inclined to weep,
With all my memories that could not sleep.

581. 'You would have understood me, had you waited'

    You would have understood me, had you waited;
        I could have loved you, dear! as well as he:
    Had we not been impatient, dear! and fated
        Always to disagree.

    What is the use of speech? Silence were fitter: 5
        Lest we should still be wishing things unsaid.
    Though all the words we ever spake were bitter,
        Shall I reproach you dead?

    Nay, let this earth, your portion, likewise cover
        All the old anger, setting us apart: 10
    Always, in all, in truth was I your lover;
        Always, I held your heart.

    I have met other women who were tender,
        As you were cold, dear! with a grace as rare.
    Think you, I turned to them, or made surrender, 15
        I who had found you fair?

    Had we been patient, dear! ah, had you waited,
        I had fought death for you, better than he:
    But from the very first, dear! we were fated
        Always to disagree. 20

    Late, late, I come to you, now death discloses
        Love that in life was not to be our part:
    On your low lying mound between the roses,
        Sadly I cast my heart.

    I would not waken you: nay! this is fitter;
        Death and the darkness give you unto me;   25
    Here we who loved so, were so cold and bitter,
        Hardly can disagree.

582.   *Terre Promise*

                  For Herbert Percy Horne

Even now the fragrant darkness of her hair
Had brushed my cheek; and once, in passing by,
Her hand upon my hand lay tranquilly:
What things unspoken trembled in the air!

Always I know, how little severs me   5
From mine heart's country, that is yet so far;
And must I lean and long across a bar,
That half a word would shatter utterly?

Ah might it be, that just by touch of hand,
Or speaking silence, shall the barrier fall;   10
And she shall pass, with no vain words at all,
But droop into mine arms, and understand!

583.   *To William Theodore Peters on his Renaissance Cloak*

    The cherry-coloured velvet of your cloak
      Time hath not soiled: its fair embroideries
Gleam as when centuries ago they spoke
    To what bright gallant of Her Daintiness,
      Whose slender fingers, long since dust and dead,   5
    For love or courtesy embroidered
The cherry-coloured velvet of this cloak.

Ah! cunning flowers of silk and silver thread,
    That mock mortality! the broidering dame,
The page they decked, the kings. and courts are dead: 10
    Gone the age beautiful; Lorenzo's name,
    The Borgia's pride are but an empty sound;
    But lustrous still upon their velvet ground,
Time spares these flowers of silk and silver thread.

Gone is that age of pageant and of pride: 15
   Yet don your cloak, and haply it shall seem,
The curtain of old time is set aside;
   As through the sadder coloured throng you gleam;
   We see once more fair dame and gallant gay,
   The glamour and the grace of yesterday: 20
The elder, brighter age of pomp and pride.

584.   Nuns of the Perpetual Adoration

(For The Countess Sobieska von Platt)

Calm, sad, secure; behind high convent walls,
   These watch the sacred lamp, these watch and pray:
And it is one with them when evening falls,
   And one with them the cold return of day.

These heed not time; their nights and days they make 5
   Into a long, returning rosary,
Whereon their lives are threaded for Christ's sake:
   Meekness and vigilance and chastity.

A vowed patrol, in silent companies,
   Life-long they keep before the living Christ: 10
In the dim church, their prayers and penances
   Are fragrant incense to the Sacrificed.

Outside, the world is wild and passionate;
   Man's weary laughter and his sick despair
Entreat at their impenetrable gate: 15
   They heed no voices in their dream of prayer.

They saw the glory of the world displayed;
   They saw the bitter of it, and the sweet;
They knew the roses of the world should fade,
   And be trod under by the hurrying feet. 20

Therefore they rather put away desire,
   And crossed their hands and came to sanctuary;
And veiled their heads and put on coarse attire:
   Because their comeliness was vanity.

And there they rest; they have serene insight
    Of the illuminating dawn to be:
Mary's sweet Star dispels for them the night,
    The proper darkness of humanity.

Calm, sad, secure; with faces worn and mild:
    Surely their choice of vigil is the best?
Yea! for our roses fade, the world is wild;
    But there, beside the altar, there, is rest.

585.   *To One in Bedlam*

For Henry Davray

With delicate, mad hands, behind his sordid bars,
Surely he hath his posies, which they tear and twine;
Those scentless wisps of straw, that miserably line
His strait, caged universe, whereat the dull world stares,

Pedant and pitiful. O, how his rapt gaze wars
With their stupidity! Know they what dreams divine
Lift his long, laughing reveries like enchaunted wine,
And make his melancholy germane to the stars'?

O lamentable brother! if those pity thee,
Am I not fain of all thy lone eyes promise me;
Half a fool's kingdom, far from men who sow and reap,
All their days, vanity? Better than mortal flowers,
Thy moon-kissed roses seem: better than love or sleep,
The star-crowned solitude of thine oblivious hours!

Lionel Johnson (1867–1902)

586.   *A Decadent's Lyric*

Sometimes, in very joy of shame,
Our flesh becomes one living flame:
And she and I
Are no more separate, but the same.

Ardour and agony unite; 5
Desire, delirium, delight:
And I and she
Faint in the fierce and fevered night.

Her body music is: and ah,
The accords of lute and viola, 10
When she and I
Play on live limbs love's opera!

(1896)

587. *A Stranger*

To Will Rothenstein

Her face was like sad things: was like the lights
Of a great city, seen from far off fields,
Or seen from sea: sad things, as are the fires
Lit in a land of furnaces by night:
Sad things, as are the reaches of a stream 5
Flowing beneath a golden moon alone.
And her clear voice, full of remembrances,
Came like faint music down the distant air.
As though she had a spirit of dead joy
About her, looked the sorrow of her ways: 10
If light there be, the dark hills are to climb
First: and if calm, far over the long sea.
Fallen from all the world apart she seemed,
Into a silence and a memory.
What had the thin hands done, that now they strained 15
Together in such passion? And those eyes,
What saw they long ago, that now they dreamed
Along the busy streets, blind but to dreams?
Her white lips mocked the world, and all therein:
She had known more than this; she wanted not 20
This, who had known the past so great a thing.
Moving about our ways, herself she moved
In things done, years remembered, places gone.
Lonely, amid the living crowds, as dead,
She walked with wonderful and sad regard: 25
With us, her passing image: but herself
Far over the dark hills and the long sea.

(1889)

588.   *Love's Ways*

    You were not cruel always! Nay!
    When I said *Come!* one year ago:
    Could you have lingered by the way?
    Did not the very wind seem slow?

    Then, had you tarried, I had known 5
    Nor love's delight, nor lost love's pain:
    Then, always had I lived alone.
    Now, you need never come again.

                (1887)

589.   *The Dark Angel*

    Dark Angel, with thine aching lust
    To rid the world of penitence:
    Malicious Angel, who still dost
    My soul such subtile violence!

    Because of thee, no thought, no thing, 5
    Abides for me undesecrate:
    Dark Angel, ever on the wing,
    Who never reachest me too late!

    When music sounds, then changest thou
    Its silvery to a sultry fire: 10
    Nor will thine envious heart allow
    Delight untortured by desire.

    Through thee, the gracious Muses turn
    To Furies, O mine Enemy!
    And all the things of beauty burn 15
    With flames of evil ecstasy.

    Because of thee, the land of dreams
    Becomes a gathering place of fears:
    Until tormented slumber seems
    One vehemence of useless tears. 20

When sunlight glows upon the flowers,
Or ripples down the dancing sea:
Thou, with thy troop of passionate powers,
Beleaguerest, bewilderest, me.

Within the breath of autumn woods,
Within the winter silences:
Thy venomous spirit stirs and broods,
O Master of impieties!

The ardour of red flame is thine,
And thine the steely soul of ice:
Thou poisonest the fair design
Of nature, with unfair device.

Apples of ashes, golden bright;
Waters of bitterness, how sweet!
O banquet of a foul delight,
Prepared by thee, dark Paraclete!

Thou art the whisper in the gloom,
The hinting tone, the haunting laugh:
Thou art the adorner of my tomb,
The minstrel of mine epitaph.

I fight thee, in the Holy Name!
Yet, what thou dost, is what God saith:
Tempter! should I escape thy flame,
Thou wilt have helped my soul from Death:

The second Death, that never dies,
That cannot die, when time is dead:
Live Death, wherein the lost soul cries,
Eternally uncomforted.

Dark Angel, with thine aching lust!
Of two defeats, of two despairs:
Less dread, a change to drifting dust,
Than thine eternity of cares.

Do what thou wilt, thou shalt not so,
Dark Angel! triumph over me:
Lonely, unto the Lone I go;
Divine, to the Divinity.

(1893)

590.   *By the Statue of King Charles at Charing Cross*

To William Watson

Sombre and rich, the skies;
Great glooms, and starry plains.
Gently the night wind sighs;
Else a vast silence reigns.

The splendid silence clings
Around me: and around
The saddest of all kings
Crowned, and again discrowned.

Comely and calm, he rides
Hard by his own Whitehall:
Only the night wind glides:
No crowds, nor rebels, brawl.

Gone, too, his Court: and yet,
The stars his courtiers are:
Stars in their stations set;
And every wandering star.

Alone he rides, alone,
The fair and fatal king:
Dark night is all his own,
That strange and solemn thing.

Which are more full of fate:
The stars; or those sad eyes?
Which are more still and great:
Those brows; or the dark skies?

Although his whole heart yearn
In passionate tragedy:
Never was face so stern
With sweet austerity.

Vanquished in life, his death
By beauty made amends:
The passing of his breath
Won his defeated ends.

Brief life, and hapless? Nay:
Through death, life grew sublime.
Speak after sentence? Yea: 35
And to the end of time.

Armoured he rides, his head
Bare to the stars of doom:
He triumphs now, the dead,
Beholding London's gloom. 40

Our wearier spirit faints,
Vexed in the world's employ:
His soul was of the saints;
And art to him was joy.

King, tried in fires of woe! 45
Men hunger for thy grace:
And through the night I go,
Loving thy mournful face.

Yet, when the city sleeps;
When all the cries are still: 50
The stars and heavenly deeps
Work out a perfect will.

(1889)

591. *Lambeth Lyric*

Some seven score Bishops late at Lambeth sat,
Gray-whiskered and respectable debaters:
Each had on head a well-strung, curly hat;
    And each wore gaiters.

And when these prelates at their talk had been 5
Long time, they made yet longer proclamation,
Saying: "These creeds are childish! both Nicene,
    And Athanasian.

True, they were written by the Holy Ghost;
So, to re-write them were perhaps a pity. 10
Refer we their revision to a most
    Select Committee!

In ten years' time we wise Pan Anglicans
Once more around this Anglo Catholic table
Will meet, to prove God's word more weak than man's,   15
    His truth, less stable."

So saying homeward the good Fathers go;
Up Missisippi [*sic*] some and some up Niger.
For thine old mantle they have clearly no
    More use, Elijah!   20

Instead, an apostolic apron girds
Their loins, which ministerial fingers tie on:
And Babylon's song they sing, new tune and words,
    All over Zion.

The Creeds, the Scriptures, all the Faith of old,   25
They hack and hew to please each bumptious German,
Windy and vague, as mists and clouds that fold
    Tabor and Hermon.

Happy Establishment, in this thine hour!
Behold thy bishops to their sees retreating!   30
"Have at the Faith!" each cries: "good bye till our
    Next merry meeting!"

(1888)

George William Russell ('A.E.') (1867–1935)

592.   *Sacrifice*

    Those delicate wanderers,
    The wind, the star, the cloud,
    Ever before mine eyes,
    As to an altar bowed,
    Light and dew-laden airs   5
    Offer in sacrifice.

    The offerings arise:
    Hazes of rainbow light,
    Pure crystal, blue, and gold,
    Through dreamland take their flight;   10

And 'mid the sacrifice
God moveth as of old.

In miracles of fire
He symbols forth his days;
In gleams of crystal light
Reveals what pure pathways
Lead to the soul's desire,
The silence of the height.

593. *The Mid-World*

This is the red, red region
Your heart must journey through:
Your pains will here be legion
And joy be death for you.

Rejoice to-day: to-morrow
A turning tide shall flow
Through infinite tones of sorrow
To reach an equal woe.

You pass by love unheeding
To gain the goal you long –
But my heart, my heart is bleeding:
I cannot sing this song.

(Robert) Laurence Binyon (1869–1943)

from *London Visions*

594. I. *Whitechapel High Road*

Lusty life her river pours
Along a road of shining shores.
The moon of August beams
Mild as upon her harvest slopes; but here
From man's full breath'd abounding earth
Exiled she walks, as one of alien birth,
The pale neglected foster-mother of dreams.

For windows with resplendent stores
Along the pavement dazzle and outstare
The booths that front them; there,   10
To the throng which loiters by in laughing streams
Babble the criers, and 'mid eager sounds
The flaming torches toss to the wind their hair,
And ruddy in trembling waves the light
Flushes cheeks of wondering boys   15
Assembled, their lips parted and eyes bright,
As the medicine-seller his magic herb expounds,
Or some old man displays his painted toys.
Deaf with the vacant stillness of the tomb,
At intervals a road deserted gapes,   20
Where Night shrinks back into her proper gloom,
Frighted by boisterous flare
Of the flame, that now through a cluster of green grapes
Shines wanly, or on striped apple and smooth pear
Flits blushing; now on rug or carpet spread   25
In view of the merry buyers, the rude dyes
Re-crimsons, or an antic shadow throws
Over the chestnut brazier's glowing eyes;
And now the sleeping head
Of a gipsy child in his dim corner shows,   30
Huddled against a canvas wall, his bed
An ancient sack: nor torch nor hundred cries
Awake him from his sweet profound repose.
But thou, divine moon, with thine equal beam
Dispensing patience, stealest unawares   35
The thoughts of many that pass sorrowful on
Else undiverted, amid the crowd alone:
Embroiderest with beauties the worn theme
Of trouble; to a fancied harbour calm
Steerest the widow's ship of heavy cares;   40
And on light spirits of lovers, radiant grown,
Droppest an unimaginable balm.
Yet me to-night thy peace rejoices less
Than this warm human scene, that of rude earth
Pleasantly savours, nor dissembles mirth,   45
Nor grief, nor passion: sweet to me this press
Of life unnumbered, where if hard distress
Be tyrant, hunger is not fed
Nor misery pensioned with the ill-tasting bread
Of pity; but such help as earth ordains   50
Betwixt her creatures, bound in common pains,
Brother from brother without prayer obtains.

595.   *The Evening Takes Me From Your Side*

        The evening takes me from your side;
        The darkness creeps into my breast.
        Swift clouds across the dim heavens glide,
        And fill me with their vague unrest.

        I wander sad, and know not why: 5
        The lighted streets perplex my brain.
        I wish for wings, that I might fly
        From sound and glare, to you again.

Hubert Crackanthorpe (1870–1896)

from *Vignettes*

596.   *Rêverie*

I dreamed of an age grown strangely picturesque—of the rich enfeebled by monotonous ease; of the shivering poor clamouring nightly for justice; of a helpless democracy, vast revolt of the ill-informed; of priests striving to be rational; of sentimental moralists protecting iniquity; of middle-class princes; of sybaritic saints; of complacent and pompous politicians; of doctors hurrying the degeneration of the race; of artists discarding possibilities for limitations; of pressmen befooling a pretentious public; of critics refining upon the 'busman's methods; of inhabitants of Camberwell chattering of culture.

    And I dreamed of this great, dreamy London of ours; of her myriad fleeting moods; of the charm of her portentous provinciality; and I awoke all a-glad and hungering for life. . . .

597.   *In St. James's Park*

A sullen glow throbs overhead: golden will-o'-wisps are threading their shadowy groupings of gaunt-limbed trees; and the dull, distant rumour of feverish London waits on the still, night air. The lights of Hyde Park corner blaze like some monster, gilded constellation, shaming the dingy stars; and across the East there flares a sky-sign—a gaudy, crimson arabesque. . .

    And all the air hangs draped in the mysterious, sumptuous splendour of a murky London night. . . .

598.   *In the Strand*

The city disgorges.

All along the Strand, down the great, ebbing tide, the omnibuses, a congested press of gaudy craft, drift westwards, jostling and jamming their tall, loaded decks, with a clanking of chains, a rumble of lumbering wheels, a thudding of quick-loosed brakes, a humming of hammering hoofs....

The empty hansoms slink silently past; the street hawkers—a long row of dingy figures—line the pavement-edge; troops of frenzied newsboys dart yelling through the traffic; and here and there a sullen-faced woman struggles to stem the tide of men.

Somewhere, behind Pall Mall, unheeded the sun has set: the sky is powdered with crimson dust; one by one the shops gleam out, blazing their windows of burnished glass; the twilight throbs with a ceaseless shuffle of hurrying feet; and over all things hovers the spirit of London's grim unrest.

Hilaire Belloc (1870–1953)

599.   *The Poor of London*

    Almighty God, whose justice like a sun
    Shall coruscate along the floors of Heaven,
    Raising what's low, perfecting what's undone,
    Breaking the proud and making odd things even,
    The poor of Jesus Christ along the street   5
    In your rain sodden, in your snows unshod,
    They have nor hearth, nor sword, nor human meat,
    Nor even the bread of men: Almighty God.

    The poor of Jesus Christ whom no man hears
    Have waited on your vengeance much too long.   10
    Wipe out not tears but blood: our eyes bleed tears.
    Come smite our damnéd sophistries so strong
    That thy rude hammer battering this rude wrong
    Ring down the abyss of twice ten thousand years.

                                             *

    Lift up your hearts in Gumber, laugh the Weald   15
    And you my mother the Valley of Arun sing.
    Here am I homeward from my wandering,
    Here am I homeward and my heart is healed.
    You my companions whom the World has tired
    Come out to greet me. I have found a face   20

More beautiful than Gardens; more desired
Than boys in exile love their native place.

Lift up your hearts in Gumber, laugh the Weald
And you most ancient Valley of Arun sing.
Here am I homeward from my wandering, 25
Here am I homeward and my heart is healed.
If I was thirsty, I have heard a spring.
If I was dusty, I have found a field.

*

Whatever moisture nourishes the Rose,
The Rose of the World in laughter's garden-bed 30
Where Souls of men on faith secure are fed
And spirits immortal keep their pleasure-close.
Whatever moisture nourishes the Rose,
The burning Rose of the world, for me the same
To-day for me the spring without a name 35
Content or Grace or Laughter overflows.

This is that water from the Fount of Gold,
Water of Youth and washer out of cares,
Which Raymond of Saragossa sought of old
And finding in the mountain, unawares, 40
Returned to hear an ancient story told
To Bramimond, his love, beside the marble stairs.

600. *The Harbour*

I was like one that keeps the deck by night
    Bearing the tiller up against his breast;
I was like one whose soul is centred quite
    In holding course although so hardly prest,
And veers with veering shock now left now right, 5
    And strains his foothold still and still makes play
Of bending beams until the sacred light
    Shows him high lands and heralds up the day.

But now such busy work of battle past
I am like one whose barque at bar at last 10
Comes hardly heeling down the adventurous breeze;
And entering calmer seas,
I am like one that brings his merchandise
To Californian skies.

601. The Modern Traveller

I

The *Daily Menace*, I presume?
Forgive the litter in the room.
I can't explain to you
How out of place a man like me
Would be without the things you see –
The Shields and Assegais and odds
And ends of little savage gods.
Be seated; take a pew.
(Excuse the phrase. I'm rather rough,
And – pardon me! – but have you got
A pencil? I've another here:
The one that you have brought, I fear,
Will not be long enough.)
And so the Public want to hear
About the expedition
From which I recently returned:
Of how the Fetish Tree was burned;
Of how we struggled to the coast,
And lost our ammunition;
How we retreated, side by side;
And how, like Englishmen, we died.
Well, as you know, I hate to boast,
And, what is more, I can't abide
A popular position.
I told the Duke the other day
The way I felt about it.
He answered courteously –'Oh!'
An Editor (who had an air
Of what the Dutch call *savoir faire*)
Said, 'Mr Rooter, you are right,
And nobody can doubt it.'
The Duchess murmured, 'Very true.'
Her comments may be brief and few,
But very seldom trite.
Still, representing as you do
A public and a point of view,
I'll give you leave to jot
A few remarks – a very few –
But understand that this is not
A formal interview.
And first of all, I will begin
By talking of Commander Sin.

602.

The Marmozet

The species Man and Marmozet
Are intimately linked;

The Marmozet survives as yet,
But Men are all extinct.

603.

The Big Baboon

The Big Baboon is found upon
The plains of Cariboo:

He goes about with nothing on

(A shocking thing to do).

But if he dressed respectably

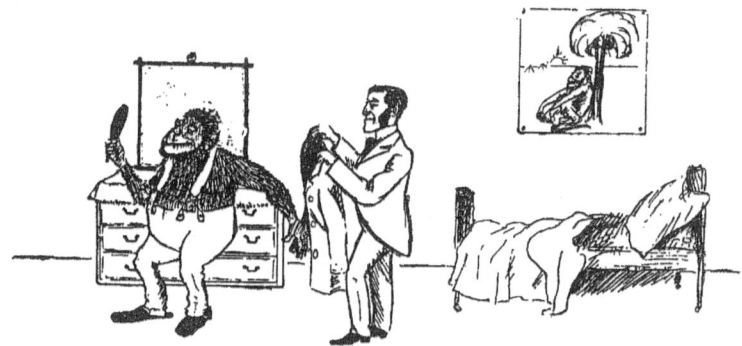

And let his whiskers grow,

How like this Big Baboon would be

To Mister So and So!

Nora Hopper (Mrs Chesson) (1871–1906)

604.   *Finvarragh*

(To William Butler Yeats)

I am the King of Faery:
 A thousand years ago
My elfin mother bore me
 Between the snow and snow.
My elfin mother bore me
 —Lightly, as fairies may—
To rule a doubtful country
 Between the dusk and day.

I am the King of Faery:
 And wise I am, and old,
And of my fairy wisdom
 A thousand hands take hold.
But those that seek my helping
 Are glad, for all their care.
My thousand years of wisdom
 Lie dark upon my hair.

I am the King of Faery:
 And none there is so gay
Among my gentle people
 That dance the dews away.
I am the King of Faery
 And none there is so sad,
Though Una is my lady
 And Aodh my serving-lad.

I am the King of Faery,
 And I, and all my kin,
May neither weep for sorrow,
 May neither serve nor sin.
But we shall fade as dewdrops
 That morning sun has dried:
So serve us who have served you,
 And set your kind doors wide.

(1896)

605.   *Two Women*

You are a snowdrop, sweet; but will
You look upon this daffodil
That in a careless hand has lain
So long, it cannot drink the rain
And be renewed, or by the sun   5
Find that unkindly grasp undone?

You are a snowdrop: put your white
By this spoiled gold, dear heart, to-night:
Touch leaves with this less happy flower
Undone by some too happy hour.   10
You might have been the daffodil
If I had kissed your prudence still.

                              (1900)

606.   *Marsh Marigolds*

Here in the water-meadows
    Marsh marigolds ablaze
Brighten the elder shadows
    Lost in an autumn haze.
Drunkards of sun and summer   5
    They keep their colours clear,
Flaming among the marshes
    At waning of the year.

Thicker than bee-swung clovers
    They crowd the meadow-space;   10
Each to the mist that hovers
    Lifts an undaunted face.
Time, that has stripped the sunflower,
    And driven the bees away,
Hath on these golden gipsies   15
    No power to dismay.

Marsh marigolds together
    Their ragged banners lift
Against the darkening weather,
    Long rains and frozen drift: 20

They take the lessening sunshine
   Home to their hearts to keep
Against the days of darkness,
   Against the time of sleep.

(1900)

Theodore Wratislaw (1871–1933)

607.   *The Music-Hall*

The curtain on the grouping dancers falls,
The heaven of colour has vanished from our eyes;
Stirred in our seats we wait with vague surmise
What haply comes that pleases or that palls.

Touched on the stand the thrice-struck baton calls,   5
Once more I watch the unfolding curtain rise,
I hear the exultant violins premise
The well-known tune that thrills me and enthralls.

Then trembling in my joy I see you flash
Before the footlights to the cymbals' clash,   10
With laughing lips, swift feet, and brilliant glance,

You, fair as heaven and as a rainbow bright,
You, queen of song and empress of the dance,
Flower of mine eyes, my love, my heart's delight!

from *Etching*

608.   III. *At the Empire*

The low and soft luxurious promenade,
Electric-light, pile-carpet, the device
Of gilded mirrors that repeat you thrice;
The crowd that lounges, strolls from yard to yard;

The calm and brilliant Circes who retard   5
Your passage with the skirts and rouge that spice
The changeless programme of insipid vice,
And stun you with a languid strange regard;

Ah! what are these, the perfume and the glow,
The ballet that coruscates down below,   10
The glittering songstress and the comic stars,

Ah! what are these, although we sit withdrawn
Above our sparkling tumblers and cigars,
To us so like to perish with a yawn?

609.   *Orchids*

Orange and purple, shot with white and mauve,
Such in a greenhouse wet with tropic heat
One sees these delicate flowers whose parents throve
In some Pacific island's hot retreat.

Their ardent colours that betray the rank   5
Fierce hotbed of corruption whence they rose
Please eyes that long for stranger sweets than prank
Wild meadow-blooms and what the garden shows.

Exotic flowers! How great is my delight
To watch your petals curiously wrought,   10
To lie among your splendours day and night
Lost in a subtle dream of subtler thought.

Bathed in your clamorous orchestra of hues,
The palette of your perfumes, let me sleep
While your mesmeric presences diffuse   15
Weird dreams: and then bizarre sweet rhymes shall creep

Forth from my brain and slowly form and make
Sweet poems as a weaving spider spins,
A shrine of loves that laugh and swoon and ache,
A temple of coloured sorrows and perfumed sins!   20

610.   Ἔρος δ' αὖτε . . .

        Crimson nor yellow roses, nor
        The savour of the mounting sea
        Are worth the perfume I adore
        That clings to thee.

        The languid-headed lilies tire,   5
        The changeless waters weary me.
        I ache with passionate desire
        Of thine and thee.

        There are but these things in the world—
        Thy mouth of fire,   10
        Thy breasts, thy hands, thy hair upcurled,
        And my desire!

611.   Odour

    So vague, so sweet a long regret!
    So sweet, so vague a dead perfume
    That lingers lest regret forget,
    A memory from an old-world tomb
    Where vainly sunshine gleams and vainly raindrops fret,   5
    And dying summer's wind-breath goes
    So lightly over petals of the fallen rose.

    Autumnal starlight, scents of hay
    Beneath the full September moon,
    And then, ah then! the sighing tune   10
    That fades and yet is fain to stay:
    Ah! weep for pleasures dead too soon,
    While like the love-song of an ancient day
    The distant music of the perfume dies away!

Aubrey Beardsley (1872–1898)

612. *The Three Musicians*

  Along the path that skirts the wood,
    The three musicians wend their way,
  Pleased with their thoughts, each other's mood,
    Franz Himmel's latest roundelay.
The morning's work, a new-found theme, their breakfast and the summer day. 5

  One's a soprano, lightly frocked
    In cool, white muslin that just shows
  Her brown silk stockings gaily clocked,
    Plump arms and elbows tipped with rose,
And frills of petticoats and things, and outlines as the warm wind blows. 10

  Beside her a slim, gracious boy
    Hastens to mend her tresses' fall,
  And dies her favour to enjoy,
    And dies for *réclame* and recall
At Paris and St Petersburg, Vienna and St James's Hall. 15

  The third's a Polish Pianist
    With big engagements everywhere,
  A light heart and an iron wrist,
    And shocks and shoals of yellow hair,
And fingers that can trill on sixths and fill beginners with despair. 20

  The three musicians stroll along
    And pluck the ears of ripened corn,
  Break into odds and ends of song,
    And mock the woods with Siegfried's horn,
And fill the air with Gluck, and fill the tweeded tourist's soul with scorn. 25

  The Polish genius lags behind,
    And, with some poppies in his hand,
  Picks out the strings and wood and wind
    Of an imaginary band,
Enchanted that for once his men obey his beat and understand. 30

The charming cantatrice reclines
    And rests a moment where she sees
Her château's roof that hotly shines
    Amid the dusky summer trees,
And fans herself, half shuts her eyes, and smoothes the frock about her knees.   35

The gracious boy is at her feet,
    And weighs his courage with his chance;
His fears soon melt in noonday heat.
    The tourist gives a furious glance,
Red as his guide-book grows, moves on, and offers up a prayer for France.   40

(wr. 1895; pub. 1896).

(Lady) Olive Eleanor Custance (Mrs Lord Alfred Douglas) (1874–1944)

613.   *Glamour of Gold*

The white hands of my lady's maid
Move deftly through the shining hair!
How my heart falters half afraid
Lest they should hurt a thing so fair
    As my sweet lady's head!   5
And how I wish that I stood there
    Twisting the strands instead!

Fortunate fingers those, that hold
The handles of the steel that fret
And dent each heavy tress of gold …   10
Till all the golden mass is set
    With waves bewildering,
Where fire and dusk together met
    Rival day's sunsetting!

Or so at least it seems to me   15
While gazing on my lady's face!
And when with leaping heart I see
Her soft shy breathing 'neath the lace
    That falls even to her feet …
The curves of her slim body trace—   20
    See her supremely sweet—

Ah! then love swoons too satisfied
Too passionate for words of praise
With but one prayer, to abide
Safely at her sweet side always! 25
    Even as that maiden there
That staid and silent still delays
    Winding the long gold hair! . . .

Cicely Fox Smith (1882–1954)

614.
The Colonists

We have heard a voice that calls us—
    A voice that bids us go—
A voice that bids us waken
    From the narrow world we know.
We go to do our duty, 5
    Unfearing toil and pain,
For the flag, the flag of England,
    The flag that rules the main!

There are fairer meads in England
    Than these, so parched and sere; 10
The wild birds' song in England
    Is sweeter far than here.
We may not dwell in England,
    For we have work to do
For the land, the land of England, 15
    The land we love so true!

Still, still the sons of England
    Pursue the onward track,
Tho' men who look not forward
    Strive hard to hold them back. 20
Still, still the word is "Onward!"
    With hearts that fear not blame,
On the way, the way of Britons,
    The way that leads to fame!

Evelyn Pyne (*fl.* 1875–1890)

615.   *A Witness*

    Wild and eerie was the night,
    And the snow fell thick and white,
    And across the moaning sea
    Sped the spirits wearily;
    And the north wind from the moor 5
    Railed and rattled at the door;
    And against the window-pane
    Smote the bitter hail and rain.

    Wild and eerie was the night,
    But the fire within burned bright, 10
    And my mother span apace,
    With the red light on her face;
    And my father, as he sat,
    Slowly stroked the purring cat,
    While she lay upon my knee;— 15
    For no fear or care had we.

    Wild and eerie was the night,
    Yet no cause had we for fright;
    And the moaning of the sea
    Seemed a cradle-song to me; 20
    And the loose wind-rattled pane,
    Smitten sharply by the rain,
    But a playmate singing low,
    Not the harbinger of woe.

    Wild and eerie was the night, 25
    Yet in Mary's blessed sight
    Darkest night is clear as day;
    And the sweet saints ever pray
    To the dear Lord on His throne,
    When the nights are dark and lone,— 30
    So our priest said constantly,
    And his word seemed truth to me.

Wild and eerie was the night,
Yet the faint and chequered light
Of the log-fire, cast athwart
Wheel and worker, subtly wrought
From the old forms that I knew
Visions strange, and weird, and new,
'Till I slept the young child's sleep
Dreamless, visionless, and deep.

★   ★   ★

Sudden woke I, with a start,
And a cold fear at my heart.
Through the clamour at the pane
Came a sound that was not rain,
Wind, or hail, or storm, or sea,
But a deadlier enemy!
With a crash, the fast-barred door
At my feet fell, on the floor!

Three men, through the open space,
Rushed into our dwelling-place;
Seized my father by the hair,
While my mother, in despair,
Strove to shield him with her breast.
God! how can I tell the rest?
Swift they dragged him from our sight,
Out into the fearful night!

Never, while I live, shall I
Lose the utter misery
Of my mother's maddened eyes!
Always to my ears will rise
Her despairing shriek, as they
Tore him from her arms away—
Bleeding, wounded, scarce alive;
How should one with three men strive?

Out into that awful night
Rushed they, from her tortured sight.
For an instant, with shrill groan,
Sank she fainting, cold as stone;
But full soon her face flushed red:
"Hear that sound, my child!" she said;
"'Tis your father's dying cry,
As they murder him hard-by!

"When he's dead (heed carefully
What I say; ah, woe is me!
Father's blood and mother's tears   75
Yield you strength beyond your years!)
Then will come my turn to die.
(Darling listen heedfully)
In yon cupboard must you hide;
By the small crack in its side   80

"Set your face, where you can see
All the bitter tragedy.
I will struggle as I may.
See, the fire is bright as day;"—
Here she flung logs fresh and dry,   85
And the fire blazed clear and high—
"In this light your eyes can scan
Face and form of every man."

Then she set me in my place,
With a smile on her wan face;   90
And she kissed me, held me near
Her poor heart, till I could hear
Its swift beats; and then she said,
"Help will come when I am dead;
And, my child, your voice must be   95
Raised to tell the truth for me.

"At each face, look well, my own;
Never think you are alone;
See, I lay upon your knee
Pussy for sweet company.   100
Very soon the sun will rise,"
(Oh, the anguish of her eyes!)
"Then, my darling, you will tell
What you saw. Watch well! watch well!"

As she kissed me, last of all,   105
Said she: "Let no whisper fall
From your lips, but silently
Heed whate'er you hear or see."
Hasty footsteps filled the place;
Muttered curses fell apace;   110
Back the murderers had sped.
God! and was my father dead?

Lurid flashed the new-fed fire,
Springing upwards, brighter, higher—
On her white face as she strove, 115
Strong in vengeance and in love,
'Gainst those red knives, dripping wet
With my father's life-blood yet.
Oh, my God! I know not well
How time sped! At last she fell! 120

Stricken through and through again,
With no feeling left but pain,
She had striven that each man
Well her child might note and scan:
Think you I forget those three? 125
Not till life forgetteth me!
Silent watched I till they fled,
Then I crept out to the dead,

And ye found me. Here I stand,
God's own book within my hand: 130
In His awful sight I swear
That the murderers stand there!

Sarah Robertson Matheson (*fl.* 1894)

616.　　　　　　*A Kiss of the King's Hand*

It wasna from a golden throne,
Or a bower with milk-white roses blown,
But mid the kelp on northern sand
That I got a kiss of the king's hand.

I durstna raise my een tae see 5
If he even cared to glance at me;
His princely brow with care was crossed
For his true men slain and kingdom lost.

Think not his hand was soft and white,
Or his fingers a' with jewels dight, 10
Or round his wrist were jewels grand
When I got a kiss of the king's hand.

But dearer far tae my twa een
Was the ragged sleeve of red and green
O'er that young weary hand that fain, 15
With the guid broadsword, had found its ain.

Farewell for ever, the distance gray
And the lapping ocean seemed to say—
For him a home in a foreign land,
And for me one kiss of the king's hand. 20

Jane Leck (*fl.* 1895)

617.
My Gourd

"Doest thou well to be angry for the gourd."

And Jonah's wrath was kindled for his gourd,
Rebellious words escaped his hasty lips:
"'Tis better for me far to die than live,
Since God had seen it fit to take from me
My only source of comfort and of joy." 5
I too had such a gourd, and I was glad
And tasted rest and peace a little space
Beneath its shade; then it, like Jonah's, died.
Lord, keep me from his sin; incline my heart
To praise Thee rather for the short-lived joy, 10
So undeserved, so sweet. Help me to trust
Thy wisdom and Thy love, and teach Thou me
By very sorrow for my cherished gourd,
To cling still closer to the living Vine.

618.
Disappointment

Fu' licht o' heart an' fleet o' step,
  Liltin' I roamed at morn;
Nicht saw me win forfochen hame,
  Wi' bleedin' hands an' torn;—
Ettlin' to pu' love's red, red rose, 5
  I only grasped the thorn.

619.	*Woman's Rights*

The cry of "woman's rights," though giving rise
Too oft to ridicule and scorn, yet seems
To bear in it the germ of future good;
For women as a rule think not too much,
But far too little, of their real rights.	5
What these rights are, when granted and by whom,
How lost and how recoverable, ought
To be impressed on ev'ry woman's heart.
But is it so? Nine out of ten will own
Their ignorance of what the phrase implies,	10
Except that someone says there's something wrong
Here, there, or somewhere, as our sex now stands.

Yet we have rights, by that same charter sealed,
That gave to man dominion o'er the earth.
Well pleased with all creation else, God said	15
"It is not good for man to be alone,"
And so he formed a woman, whom he called
A helpmeet for the man, since she alone,
Of all created beings, shared with him
A spirit quickened by the breath of God;—	20
A *help*meet, not a plaything but a help,—
No slave, a help*meet*, worthy of the man.

This, then, is our inalienable right,—
To supplement by ours the other sex,
To be most strong where it is weak, that so	25
By differing each may gain, as leaf and branch
Are needful both, to form a perfect tree.
It never was intended we should be
But men of smaller growth, and when we claim
Equality, forgetting that in us	30
Development must tend to other ends,
And anxious only that our weaker sort
Should match the stronger, and keep even pace,
We sacrifice our birthright, and outrage
The very essence of our womanhood.	35
Equality we do claim; woman's soul,
And heart, and mind, like man's, were gifts divine,

And therefore perfect, else she had not been
A fit companion for the God-made man.
No act of parliament could grant us rights
More precious than are those we overlook,
Or forfeit carelessly, or throw aside,
Pursuing shadows that elude our grasp:
The right to exercise a stronger faith
Where man wants fuller proof; the right to show
A quicker sympathy towards the weak—
Towards the erring, more of patient hope;
To cherish and keep pure that well of love,
The very centre of our moral life,
Twice sanctified since God made use of it
To typify His own. Did we but feel
The full significance of rights like these,
We would not seek for more, but humbly strive
To act more worthily of those we have.

Disuse alone can forfeit them; but that,
Like moss upon an ancient graven stone,
Obliterates through time the clearest signs,
And doubts arise if ever they were there.
Let us remove the moss, throw off our mask
Of carelessness, frivolity, or sin,
And clear as runes upon the stone will seem
The heavenly charter graven on our heart.

'Tis woman's right to influence for good,
So should her life be holy, true, and pure;
(The good within assures the good without)
For clear and swift as any stream may be,
Its waters rise no higher than their source.
Our life is best when likest some fair stream
That glides along unheard, and scarcely seen
Save by the fresher verdure and the flow'rs
That mark its windings, and attest its pow'r.
Our highest rights are sealed, our life is crowned,
When brother, husband, son, or friend, can say,
"O Lord, the woman whom Thou gavest me
Has proved indeed the helpmeet that Thou saidst,
Has helped me onwards, upwards, home to Thee."

Ada (Bartrick) Baker (*fl.* 1900)

620.   *House-Hunting*

Strangest of things are doors!—
Hearts'-doors,—that can shut so fast,
Bolt you and bar you out;
No single glimpse of their stores
(Though you press and push no doubt)   5
Can you get, let your patience last
Year in and year out!

Knock at the door, knock low,
Put a pleading in the sound;
Will an answer meet you so?   10
—Stifle that pulse's bound!
What you hear is no coming tread,
Only the-echo dead
Of the knock your hand gave. So
It will always be.—Yet no?   15
Still you are loth to go?
Knock louder, make urgent claim;
You've a need, let it sound as such.
Is your last, last hope too much?
Silent, and still the same   20
As through the years before,
Fronts you that barr'd, firm door.
Give it up—try no more!

Strangest of things hearts'-doors!
Standing, as some do, wide;   25
You may pass, look, step inside,
See—what? Smooth sanded floors;
A whitewash'd wall, square, bare,
Shows you its solid stare;
There's an empty, echoing sound   30
From your footsteps walking round.

All is so neat and trim—
Nay,—out with it!—cut-and-dried!
Would you like now, for a whim,
To take up your lodgment, bide   35

In a place so small of range,
So void of life and change?
Cover the walls, perhaps,
With sketches and jests in scraps?
Sing songs in a boisterous strain? 40
—Give up the thought. Too plain,
Here's a heart, though its doors stand wide,
Worth scarcely the look inside.

Strangest of things hearts'-doors!
Here's one you might pass some day. 45
Is the owner gone away?
There's a desolate look; sun pours,
And the summer breezes play
On its portal: all no use:
No latch relents, lets loose 50
An issuing form at last.
Folks look, then hurry past,
With, "Strange! Such a sunny day
In so dull a house to stay!"
But,—a secret in your ear: 55
No murderous tale, don't fear!
That heart is the House of a Tomb;
One liv'd there and died; so, dead,
Lies on in a sacred gloom.
Or a quiet waiting, say, 60
For a certain future day
When Death shall be Life instead.
—Pass any such close-seal'd door
With a softer step, be sure.

O strange indeed to my mind 65
Hearts'-doors! Here's another kind
With a secret lock and key
(Here's the true sort for me!)
Open or clos'd at will.
Long, if you like; but still, 70
If you have not the soul to guess
How by your hand's impress
You can touch the spring, make fly
Open the door's-leaves—why,
This is no house for you! 75
There's but one thing to do:
Give it up,—cease to try!

But *is* yours the soul to know
Just the right touch? If so,
Fancy possession's pride!   80
Mine all the wealth inside,
Mine every nook, recess,
Cranny and corner, quite:
Mine, too, no whit the less,
Terraces, gardens bright;   85
All that expanse, wide, clear,
Round in the house's rear.
Others say, "Out of sight."
I say, "My own, most dear;
Only myself comes here;   90
This is my chief delight."

Childhood, perhaps, believes
That tale of the Forty Thieves,
Marvellous, fancy's freak:
How Ali Baba heard   95
The terrible robbers speak
That one mysterious word,
That into his keeping gave
The wealth of the wondrous cave.
But this is *my* version, please!   100
Beautiful, strange, and true:—
Hearts'-Door unlock'd to *you*
Who show you've the soul to guess
How by your hand's impress
Just the right spring to touch!   105
Does it try your faith too much?

A thing that one scarcely sees?
—Too seldom, I grant you: *but*—
Palace, or cottage, hut,
Wigwam, or what you will,   110
Here's my one standpoint still.
I'll house in the Heart whose key
Belongs to just only me.
I believe in such things, you see!

621.   'Queen's Night'

                         June 22, 1897

    Flare, England! Lift thy banners of red flame
    To heav'n's high arches! Swift from hill to hill
    Flash on the shining watchword, spreading still:
    East, west, south, north,—let our Great Queen's great name
    Be greeted, every British heart acclaim   5
    Her sixty glorious years which now fulfil
    Their splendid circle, "on her People's will
    Broad based" and crown'd with the uttermost of fame.

    Flare, Ireland! And let many a Scottish height
    Break into flame along the summer night.   10
    Not suddenly to call stout hearts and bold
    To arms against the foe, as when of old
    We broke the pride of Spain; but all to show
    Our loyal love,—a Nation's heart aglow.

622.   *In Hospital*

So I'm shelved, you see, old fellow; and it seems a trifle rough,
    When you're longing to be at them with the rest;
But I don't lie here and mope; for the doctors say they hope
    I shall soon be fit and lively as the best.

And I had my glorious innings! Oh! we gave them piping hot   5
    Such a supper they're not likely to digest;
And d'ye think I cared a rap, though I'm only a poor chap,
    For the bullet that they landed in my chest?

Tell 'em all at home I'm waited on as if I was a lord,
    And the nurses are just angels—bar the wings: 10
When you're lying here so weak that you hardly care to speak,
    Oh! the comfort that a woman's tending brings.

                    Finished by the Nurse.

He was doing well, poor fellow! though the shot had touched his lung,
    And the doctors did their best to pull him through.
I was with him when he died. The two locks of hair inside,   15
    With his love, are for his mother, and for you.

Thomas Hardy (1840–1928)

623. *The Young Glass-Stainer*

'These Gothic windows, how they wear me out
With cusp and foil, and nothing straight or square,
Crude colours, leaden borders roundabout,
And fitting in Peter here, and Matthew there!

'What a vocation! Here do I draw now 5
The abnormal, loving the Hellenic norm;
Martha I paint, and dream of Hera's brow,
Mary, and think of Aphrodite's form.'

(1893)

624. *The Temporary the All*

(Sapphics)

Change and chancefulness in my flowering youthtime,
Set me sun by sun near to one unchosen;
Wrought us fellowlike, and despite divergence,
    Fused us in friendship.

'Cherish him can I while the true one forthcome - 5
Come the rich fulfiller of my prevision;
Life is roomy yet, and the odds unbounded.'
    So self-communed I.

'Thwart my wistful way did a damsel saunter,
Fair, albeit unformed to be all-eclipsing; 10
'Maiden meet,' held I, 'till arise my forefelt
    Wonder of women.'

Long a visioned hermitage deep desiring,
Tenements uncouth I was fain to house in:
'Let such lodging be for a breath-while,' thought I, 15
    'Soon a more seemly.

'Then high handiwork will I make my life-deed,
Truth and Light outshow; but the ripe time pending,
Intermissive aim at the thing sufficeth.'
    Thus I . . . But lo, me!   20

Mistress, friend, place, aims to be bettered straightway,
Bettered not has Fate or my hand's achievement;
Sole the showance those of my onward earth-track –
    Never transcended!

625.   *Nature's Questioning*

When I look forth at dawning, pool,
    Field, flock, and lonely tree,
    All seem to gaze at me
Like chastened children sitting silent in a school;

Their faces dulled, constrained, and worn,   5
    As though the master's ways
    Through the long teaching days
Had cowed them till their early zest was overborne.

Upon them stirs in lippings mere
    (As if once clear in call,   10
    But now scarce breathed at all) –
'We wonder, ever wonder, why we find us here!

'Has some Vast Imbecility,
    Mighty to build and blend,
    But impotent to tend,   15
Framed us in jest, and left us now to hazardry?

'Or come we of an Automaton
    Unconscious of our pains? . . .
    Or are we live remains
Of Godhead dying downwards, brain and eye now gone?   20

'Or is it that some high Plan betides,
    As yet not understood,
    Of Evil stormed by Good,
We the Forlorn Hope over which Achievement strides?'

Thus things around. No answerer I....
Meanwhile the winds, and rains,
And Earth's old glooms and pains
Are still the same, and Life and Death are neighbours nigh.

626.   *Unknowing*

When, soul in soul reflected,
We breathed an æthered air,
   When we neglected
   All things elsewhere,
And left the friendly friendless
To keep our love aglow,
   We deemed it endless...
   – We did not know!

When panting passion-goaded,
We planned to hie away,
   But, unforeboded,
   All the long day
The storm so pierced and pattered
That none could up and go,
   Our lives seemed shattered...
   – We did not know!

When I found you helpless lying,
And you waived my long misprise,
   And swore me, dying,
   In phantom-guise
To wing to me when grieving,
And touch away my woe,
   We kissed, believing...
   – We did not know!

But though, your powers outreckoning,
You tarry dead and dumb,
   Or scorn my beckoning,
   And will not come:

And I say, 'Why thus inanely
  Brood on her memory so!'
    I say it vainly —
  I feel and know!   30

627.   *Rome*

The Vatican: Sala delle Muse

(1887)

I sat in the Muses' Hall at the mid of the day,
And it seemed to grow still, and the people to pass away,
And the chiselled shapes to combine in a haze of sun,
Till beside a Carrara column there gleamed forth One.

She looked not this nor that of those beings divine,   5
But each and the whole — an essence of all the Nine;
With tentative foot she neared to my halting-place,
A pensive smile on her sweet, small, marvellous face.

'Regarded so long; we render thee sad?' said she.
'Not you,' sighed I, 'but my own inconstancy!   10
I worship each and each; in the morning one,
And then, alas! another at sink of sun.

'To-day my soul clasps Form; but where is my troth
Of yesternight with Tune: can one cleave to both?'
—'Be not perturbed,' said she. 'Though apart in fame,   15
As I and my sisters are one, those, too, are the same.'

—'But my love goes further - to Story, and Dance, and Hymn,
The lover of all in a sun-sweep is fool to whim —
Is swayed like a river-weed as the ripples run!'
—'Nay, wooer, thou sway'st not. These are but phases of one;   20

'And that one is I; and I am projected from thee,
One that out of thy brain and heart thou causest to be —
Extern to thee nothing. Grieve not, nor thyself becall,
Woo where thou wilt; and rejoice thou canst love at all!'

628. *A Wife in London*

(December 1899)

I

She sits in the tawny vapour
   That the Thames-side lanes have uprolled,
   Behind whose webby fold on fold
Like a waning taper
   The street-lamp glimmers cold.   5

A messenger's knock cracks smartly,
   Flashed news is in her hand
   Of meaning it dazes to understand
Though shaped so shortly:
   He —has fallen — in the far South Land. . . .   10

II

'Tis the morrow; the fog hangs thicker,
   The postman nears and goes:
   A letter is brought whose lines disclose
By the firelight flicker
   His hand, whom the worm now knows: 15

Fresh — firm — penned in highest feather —
   Page-full of his hoped return,
   And of home-planned jaunts by brake and burn
In the summer weather,
   And of new love that they would learn.   20

629. *The Slow Nature*

(An Incident of Froom Valley)

'Thy husband — poor, poor Heart! — is dead —
   Dead, out by Moreford Rise;
A bull escaped the barton-shed,
   Gored him, and there he lies!'

— 'Ha, ha — go away! 'Tis a tale, methink,   5
   Thou joker Kit!' laughed she.
'I've known thee many a year, Kit Twink,
   And ever hast thou fooled me!'

   – 'But, Mistress Damon – I can swear
      Thy goodman John is dead!   10
And soon th'lt hear their feet who bear
      His body to his bed.'

So unwontedly sad was the merry man's face –
      That face which had long deceived –
That she gazed and gazed; and then could trace   15
      The truth there; and she believed.

She laid a hand on the dresser-ledge,
      And scanned far Egdon-side;
And stood; and you heard the wind-swept sedge
      And the rippling Froom; till she cried: 20

'O my chamber's untidied, unmade my bed,
      Though the day has begun to wear!
"What a slovenly hussif!" it will be said,
      When they all go up my stair!'

She disappeared; and the joker stood   25
      Depressed by his neighbour's doom,
And amazed that a wife struck to widowhood
      Thought first of her unkempt room.

But a fortnight thence she could take no food,
      And she pined in a slow decay;   30
While Kit soon lost his mournful mood
      And laughed in his ancient way.

(1894)

630.   *An August Midnight*

I

A shaded lamp and a waving blind,
And the beat of a clock from a distant floor:
On this scene enter – winged, horned, and spined –
A longlegs, a moth, and a dumbledore;
While 'mid my page there idly stands   5
A sleepy fly, that rubs its hands. . . .

II

Thus meet we five, in this still place,
At this point of time, at this point in space.
— My guests besmear my new-penned line,
Or bang at the lamp and fall supine.   10
'God's humblest, they!' I muse. Yet why?
They know Earth-secrets that know not I.

(1899)

631.   *Her Immortality*

Upon a noon I pilgrimed through
    A pasture, mile by mile,
Unto the place where last I saw
    My dead Love's living smile.

And sorrowing I lay me down   5
    Upon the heated sod:
It seemed as if my body pressed
    The very ground she trod.

I lay, and thought; and in a trance
    She came and stood thereby –   10
The same, even to the marvellous ray
    That used to light her eye.

'You draw me, and I come to you,
    My faithful one,' she said,
In voice that had the moving tone   15
    It bore ere she was wed.

'Seven years have circled since I died:
    Few now remember me;
My husband clasps another bride:
    My children's love has she.   20

'My brethren, sisters, and my friends
    Care not to meet my sprite:
Who prized me most I did not know
    Till I passed down from sight.'

I said: 'My days are lonely here;
    I need thy smile alway:
I'll use this night my ball or blade,
    And join thee ere the day.'

A tremor stirred her tender lips,
    Which parted to dissuade:
'That cannot be, O friend,' she cried;
    'Think, I am but a Shade!

'A Shade but in its mindful ones
    Has immortality;
By living, me you keep alive,
    By dying you slay me.

'In you resides my single power
    Of sweet continuance here;
On your fidelity I count
    Through many a coming year.'

— I started through me at her plight,
    So suddenly confessed:
Dismissing late distaste for life,
    I craved its bleak unrest.

'I will not die, my One of all! —
    To lengthen out thy days
I'll guard me from minutest harms
    That may invest my ways!'

She smiled and went. Since then she comes
    Oft when her birth-moon climbs,
Or at the seasons' ingresses,
    Or anniversary times;

But grows my grief. When I surcease,
    Through whom alone lives she,
Her spirit ends its living lease,
    Never again to be!

632. *Thoughts of Phena*

At News of Her Death

Not a line of her writing have I,
    Not a thread of her hair,
No mark of her late time as dame in her dwelling, whereby
    I may picture her there;
  And in vain do I urge my unsight 5
    To conceive my lost prize
At her close, whom I knew when her dreams were upbrimming with light,
    And with laughter her eyes.

What scenes spread around her last days,
    Sad, shining, or dim? 10
Did her gifts and compassions enray and enarch her sweet ways
    With an aureate nimb?
Or did life-light decline from her years,
    And mischances control
Her full day-star; unease, or regret, or forebodings, or fears 15
    Disennoble her soul?

Thus I do but the phantom retain
    Of the maiden of yore
As my relic; yet haply the best of her – fined in my brain
    It may be the more 20
That no line of her writing have I,
    Nor a thread of her hair,
No mark of her late time as dame in her dwelling, whereby
    I may picture her there.

(1890)

633. *Friends Beyond*

William Dewy, Tranter Reuben, Farmer Ledlow late at plough,
    Robert's kin, and John's, and Ned's,
And the Squire, and Lady Susan, lie in Mellstock churchyard now!

'Gone,' I call them, gone for good, that group of local hearts and heads;
    Yet at mothy curfew-tide, 5
And at midnight when the noon-heat breathes it back from walls and leads,

They've a way of whispering to me — fellow-wight who yet abide —
    In the muted, measured note
Of a ripple under archways, or a lone cave's stillicide:

'We have triumphed: this achievement turns the bane to antidote,   10
    Unsuccesses to success,
Many thought-worn eves and morrows to a morrow free of thought.

'No more need we corn and clothing, feel of old terrestrial stress;
    Chill detraction stirs no sigh;
Fear of death has even bygone us: death gave all that we possess.'   15

W.D. — 'Ye mid burn the old bass-viol that I set such value by.'
Squire. — 'You may hold the manse in fee,
  You may wed my spouse, may let my children's memory of me die.'

Lady S. — 'You may have my rich brocades, my laces; take each household key;
    'Ransack coffer, desk, bureau;   20
  Quiz the few poor treasures hid there, con the letters kept by me.'

Far. — 'Ye mid zell my favourite heifer, ye mid let the charlock grow,
    Foul the grinterns, give up thrift.'
Far. Wife. — 'If ye break my best blue china, children, I shan't care or ho.'

All. — 'We've no wish to hear the tidings, how the people's fortunes shift;   25
    What your daily doings are;
Who are wedded, born, divided; if your lives beat slow or swift.

'Curious not the least are we if our intents you make or mar,
    If you quire to our old tune,
If the City stage still passes, if the weirs still roar afar.'   30

— Thus, with very gods' composure, freed those crosses late and soon
    Which, in life the Trine allow
(Why, none witteth), and ignoring all that haps beneath the moon,

William Dewy, Tranter Reuben, Farmer Ledlow late at plough,
    Robert's kin, and John's, and Ned's,   35
And the Squire, and Lady Susan, murmur mildly to me now.

634.   *Drummer Hodge*

I

They throw in Drummer Hodge, to rest
    Uncoffined – just as found:
His landmark is a kopje-crest
    That breaks the veldt around;
And foreign constellations west   5
    Each night above his mound.

II

Young Hodge the Drummer never knew –
    Fresh from his Wessex home –
The meaning of the broad Karoo,
    The Bush, the dusty loam,   10
And why uprose to nightly view
    Strange stars amid the gloam.

III

Yet portion of that unknown plain
    Will Hodge for ever be;
His homely Northern breast and brain   15
    Grow to some Southern tree,
And strange-eyed constellations reign
    His stars eternally.

635.   *Retrospect*

'I Have Lived with Shades'

I

I have lived with Shades so long,
And talked to them so oft,
Since forth from cot and croft
I went mankind among,
    That sometimes they   5
    In their dim style
    Will pause awhile
    To hear my say;

II

And take me by the hand,
And lead me through their rooms   10
In the To-be, where Dooms
Half-wove and shapeless stand:
    And show from there
    The dwindled dust
    And rot and rust   15
    Of things that were.

III

'Now turn,' they said to me
One day: 'Look whence we came,
And signify his name
Who gazes thence at thee.' –   20
    –'Nor name nor race
    Know I, or can,'
    I said, 'Of man
    So commonplace.

IV

'He moves me not at all;   25
I note no ray or jot
Of rareness in his lot,
Or star exceptional.
    Into the dim
    Dead throngs around   30
    He'll sink, nor sound
    Be left of him.'

V

'Yet,' said they, 'his frail speech
Hath accents pitched like thine –
Thy mould and his define   35
A likeness each to each –
    But go! Deep pain
    Alas, would be
    His name to thee,
    And told in vain!'   40

(1901)

636.   *De Profundis III*

'*Heu mihi, quia incolatus meus prolongatus est! Habitavi cum habitantibus Cedar; multum incola fuit anima mea.*'

Psalm cxix

There have been times when I well might have passed and the ending have come –
Points in my path when the dark might have stolen on me, artless, unrueing –
Ere I had learnt that the world was a welter of futile doing:
Such had been times when I well might have passed, and the ending have come!

Say, on the noon when the half-sunny hours told that April was nigh,   5
And I upgathered and cast forth the snow from the crocus-border,
Fashioned and furbished the soil into a summer-seeming order,
Glowing in gladsome faith that I quickened the year thereby.

Or on that loneliest of eves when afar and benighted we stood,
She who upheld me and I, in the midmost of Egdon together,   10
Confident I in her watching and ward through the blackening heather,
Deeming her matchless in might and with measureless scope endued.

Or on that winter-wild night when, reclined by the chimney-nook quoin,
Slowly a drowse overgat me, the smallest and feeblest of folk there,
Weak from my baptism of pain; when at times and anon I awoke there –   15
Heard of a world wheeling on, with no listing or longing to join.

Even then! While unweeting that vision could vex or that knowledge could numb,
That sweets to the mouth in the belly are bitter, and tart, and untoward,
Then, on some dim-coloured scene should my briefly raised curtain have lowered,
Then might the Voice that is law have said 'Cease!' and the ending have come. 20

(1901)

637.   *The Darkling Thrush*

      I leant upon a coppice gate
         When Frost was spectre-gray,
      And Winter's dregs made desolate
         The weakening eye of day.
      The tangled bine-stems scored the sky   5
         Like strings of broken lyres,

    And all mankind that haunted nigh
        Had sought their household fires.

The land's sharp features seemed to be
    The Century's corpse outleant,   10
His crypt the cloudy canopy,
    The wind his death-lament.
The ancient pulse of germ and birth
    Was shrunken hard and dry,
And every spirit upon earth   15
    Seemed fervourless as I.

At once a voice outburst among
    The bleak twigs overhead
In a full-hearted evensong
    Of joy illimited;   20
An aged thrush, frail, gaunt, and small,
    In blast-beruffled plume,
Had chosen thus to fling his soul
    Upon the growing gloom.

So little cause for carolings   25
    Of such ecstatic sound
Was written on terrestrial things
    Afar or nigh around,
That I could think there trembled through
    His happy good-night air   30
Some blessed Hope, whereof he knew
    And I was unaware.

                (1900)

638.   *V.R. 1819–1901: A Rêverie*

Moments the mightiest pass uncalendared,
    And when the Absolute
In backward Time outgave the deedful word
    Whereby all life is stirred:
'Let one be born and throned whose mould shall constitute   5
The norm of every royal-reckoned attribute,'
    No mortal knew or heard.

But in due days the purposed Life outshone –
    Serene, sagacious, free;
– Her waxing seasons bloomed with deeds well done,   10
    And the world's heart was won ...
Yet may the deed of hers most bright in eyes to be
Lie hid from ours – as in the All-One's thought lay she –
    Till ripening years have run.

(1901)

Sources and Notes

i.	John Addington Symonds. *New and Old* (1880).
ii.	Joseph Skipsey. *A Book of Lyrics* (1881).
iii.	Alice Meynell. *Poems* (1893).
iv.	Robert Louis Stevenson. *Songs of Travel* (1895).
v.	Louisa S. Guggenberger (formerly Bevington). *Key-notes* (1876).
vi.	Robert Bridges. *Shorter Poems* (1890).
vii.	Thomas Hardy. *Wessex Poems* (1898).
viii.	Rosamund Marriott Watson. *The Bird-Bride* (1889).
ix.	A. Mary F. Robinson. *Collected Poems* (1902).
x.	Mathilde Blind. *The Ascent of Man* (1889).
xi.	William Renton. *Oils and Watercolours* (1876).
xii.	Gerard Manley Hopkins. (1876); text, *Poems*, ed. Robert Bridges (1918).
1–2.	William Frederick Stevenson. *Qualte and Peedra* (1883).
3–6.	R. (Rowland) E. (Eyles) Egerton-Warburton. *Poems, Epigrams and Sonnets* (1877).
7.	Frederick Tennyson. *Poems of the Day and Year* (1895).
8–11.	Charles (Tennyson) Turner. **8–10.** *Sonnets, Lyrics and Translations* (1873). **11.** *Collected Sonnets* (1880).
12–42.	Alfred Lord Tennyson. **12.** *New York Ledger* (6 Jan. 1872). **13.** *Works* (1872–3). **14.** *Ode on the Opening of the Colonial and Indian Exhibition* (4 May 1886). **15.** *Macmillan's Magazine* (Apr. 1887). **16.** *Ballads and Other Poems* (1880). **17.** *Nineteenth Century* (Mar. 1887). **18–9, 22, 24.** *Tiresias and Other Poems* (1885). **20.** *Nineteenth Century: A Dramatic Monologue* (Nov. 1881). **21.** *Locksley Hall Sixty Years After* (1886). **23.** *Nineteenth Century* (Mar. 1883). **25, 27–34, 42.** *Demeter and Other Poems* (1889). **26.** *Macmillan's Magazine* (Nov. 1885). **35.** *The Death of Oenone* (1892). **36–41.** *Akbar's Dream, and Other Poems* (1892).
43.	Mary Cowden-Clarke (née Novello). *Honey from the Weed* (1881).
44–5.	Alfred Domett. *Flotsam and Jetsam* (1877).
46.	William Bell Scott. *A Poet's Harvest Home* (1882).
47–54.	Edward Lear. **47, 50.** *Nonsense Songs and Stories* (1888). **48–9.** *Laughable Lyrics* (1877). **51–4.** *More Nonsense* (1872).
55–70.	Robert Browning. **55–6.** *Pacchiarotto and How He Worked in Distemper* (1876). **57.** *Dramatic Idyls, Second Series* (1880). **58.** *Jocoseria* (1883). **59–65.** *Asolando* (1889). **66.** *Pall Mall Gazette* (4 Jan. 1888). **67.** *Athanaeum* (13 July 1889). **68.** *Why I am a Liberal, Being Definitions by the Best Minds of the Liberal Party* (1885). **69–70.** *Lippincott's Magazine*. XLV (1890), p. 686.
71.	Shirley Brooks. *Wit and Humour* (1875).
72.	George Eliot. *The Legend of Jubal, and Other Poems old and new* (Cabinet Edition, 1878).
73.	John Ruskin. *Poems* (1891).
74–7.	Jean Ingelow. **74.** *The Poetical Works of Jean Ingelow* (1898). **75.** *Poems* (1885). **76.** *Lyrical and Other Poems* (1886). **77.** *Poems* (1880).
78.	Frederick Locker-Lampson (formerly Locker). *London Lyrics* (1876).

79.	Matthew Arnold. *Fortnightly Review* (Jan. 1881).
80–1.	William Cory (formerly Johnson). *Ionica* (1891).
82–6.	Coventry Patmore. **82**. *Amelia, Tamerton Church Tower, Etc.* (1878). **83**. Excerpt from "The Angel in the House, Book II, Canto IX," *Poems* (1879). **84–6**. *Poems* (1879).
87.	Sydney Thompson Dobell. *Poetical Works* (1875).
88–91.	William Allingham. **88**. *Blackberries* (1884). **89**. *By the Way, Verses, Fragments and Notes* (1912). **90**. *Flower Pieces* (1888). **91**. *Thought and Word* (1890).
92–3.	(Sir) Francis Turner Palgrave. **92**. *Lyrical Poems* (1871). **93**. *Amenophis and Other Poems Sacred and Secular* (1892).
94–5.	George MacDonald. *Poetical Works* (1893).
96.	John Askham. *Sketches in Prose and Verse* (1893).
97–8.	Mortimer Collins. *Poetical Works (Selections)* (1886).
99–105.	Emily Pfeiffer. **99**. *Gerard's Monument and Other Poems* (1873). **100**. *Flowers of the Night* (1889). **101**. *Gerard's Monument and Other Poems (Second Edition)* (1878). **102–5**. *Poems* (1876).
106–111.	George Meredith. **106, 110**. *Ballads and Poems of Tragic Life* (1887). **107, 109**. *Poems and Lyrics of the Joy of Earth* (1883). **108**. *A Reading of the Earth* (1883). **111**. *Poems* (1892).
112–121.	Dante Gabriel Rossetti. **112–6**. *The House of Life: A Sonnet Sequence* (1898). **117–9**. *Ballads and Sonnets* (1881). **120–1**. *Works* (1886).
122–7.	Gerald Massey. *My Lyrical Life* (1889).
128–9.	Elizabeth ('Lizzie') Siddal (later Rossetti). *Ruskin: Rossetti: Pre-Raphaelitism*, ed. W. M. Rossetti (1889).
130–154.	Christina Rossetti. *The Complete Poems of Christina Rossetti* (1979).
155–162.	T. (Thomas) E. (Edward) Brown. *Collected Poems* (1900).
163.	Sebastian Evans. *In The Studio* (1875).
164.	James Clerk Maxwell. *Life of James Clerk Maxwell*, ed. Lewis Campbell (1884).
165.	C. (Charles) S. (Stuart) Calverley. *Fly-Leaves* (1872).
166–7.	Isa (Craig) Knox. *Songs of Consolation* (1874).
168.	(Edward) Robert Bulwer Lytton (Earl of Lytton, Owen Meredith). *After Paradise or Legends of Exile, with Other Poems*, ed. David Stott (1887).
169–172.	'Lewis Carroll' (Charles Lutwidge Dodgson). **169**. *Rhyme? And Reason?* (1883). **170–2**. *Through the Looking-Glass, and what Alice Found There* (1872). **171**. *The Hunting of the Snark: an Agony in Eight Fits* (1876).
173–4.	Joseph Skipsey. *Songs and Lyrics* (1892).
175.	Richard Watson Dixon. *Lyrical Poems* (1887).
176–177.	James Thomson. **176**. *National Reformer* (1874). **177**. *National Reformer* (17 Feb. 1867).
178–179.	Roden (Berkeley Wriothesley) Noel. *The Red Flag and Other Poems* (1872).
180–198.	William Morris. **180**. *Odyssey of Homer: done into English Verse* (1887). **181**. *Aeneids of Virgil: done into English Verse* (1876). **182**. *The Story of Sigurd the Volsung and the Fall of the Niblungs* (1898). **183**. *Atalanta's Race and Other Tales from the Earthly Paradise* (1888). **184–6**. *Chants for Socialists* (1885). **187–9, 191, 193–4, 196–8**. *Poems by the Way* (1891). **190, 195**. *Poems* (1908). **192**. *The Legend of the Briar Rose* (1890).

199–201.	John (Byrne) Leicester Warren, Lord de Tabley. *Poems, Dramatic and Lyrical* (1893).
202–3.	Sir Alfred Comyns Lyall. *Verses Written in India* (1882).
204–5.	Alfred Austin. **204**. *At the Gate of the Convent, and Other Poems* (1885). **205**. *Lyrical Poems* (1891).
206–8.	F. (Frances) Ridley Havergal. **206**. *Under the Surface.* (1874). **207–8**. *Poetical Works* (1884).
209–211.	Thomas Ashe. **209**. *Poems, Complete Edition* (1886). **210–1**. *Songs Now and Then* (1876).
212–213.	(Jane) Ellice Hopkins. *Autumn Swallows* (1883).
214.	W. (William) S. (Schwenk) Gilbert. *Patience; or, Bunthorn's Bridge!* (1881).
215.	H. (Henry) Cholmondeley Pennell. *From Grave to Gay* (1884).
216–224.	Algernon Charles Swinburne. **216–7**. *Poems and Ballads, Second Series* (1878). **218–9**. *The Heptalogia* (1880). **220**. *Poetical Works* (1884). **221**. *A Midsummer Holiday and Other Poems* (1884). **222–3**. *A Century of Roundels* (1883). **224**. *A Sequence of Sonnets on the Death of Robert Browning* (1890).
225–230.	(Julia) Augusta Webster. **225–8**. *A Book of Rhyme* (1881). **229**. *Selections from the Verse of Augusta Webster* (1893). **230**. *Mother and Daughter: An Uncompleted Sonnet Sequence* (1895).
231–2.	Sarah ('Sadie') Williams. *The Poets and the Poetry of the Century* (1892).
233.	Charlotte Elliot ('Florenz'). *Medusa and Other Poems* (1878).
234.	Walter Pater. *The Renaissance.* (1873, 1888).
235.	John Todhunter. *Forest Songs and Other Poems* (1881).
236–240.	John Addington Symonds. **236–7, 239–240**. *New and Old* (1880). **238**. *The Poets and the Poetry of the Century*, ed. A. H. Miles (1892).
241–4.	(William) Cosmo Monkhouse. **241–2, 244**. *Corn and Poppies* (1890). **243**. *Christ Upon the Hill: A Ballad* (1895).
245–9.	(Henry) Austin Dobson. **245**. *Old World Idylls and Other Verses* (1883). **246, 248–9**. *At the Sign of the Lyre* (1885). **247**. *Eighteenth Century Essays* (1882).
250–1.	Harriet Eleanor Hamilton King. **250**. *A Book of Dreams* (1883). **251**. *Ballads of the North* (1889).
252–9.	W. (Wilfrid) S. (Scawen) Blunt. **252–4, 257–9**. *The Poetry of Wilfrid Blunt* (1898). **255**. *The Love-Lyrics and Songs of Proteus* (1892). **256**. *Sonnets and Songs* (1875).
260–274.	Mathilde Blind. **260–1**. *Poetical Works* (1900). **262–4, 269**. *Dramas in Miniature* (1891). **265, 270–1**. *Songs and Sonnets* (1893). **266**. *The Prophecy of Saint Oran and Other Poems* (1881). **267–8, 272**. *Birds of Passage: Songs of the Orient and Occidnet* (1895). **273–4**. *The Ascent of Man* (1889).
275.	Robert Buchanan (T. Maitland). *Poetical Works* (1874).
276.	Rosa Mulholland (Lady Gilbert). *Vagrant Verses* (1886).
277–279.	Margaret Veley. **277, 279**. *A Marriage of Shadows and Other Poems* (1888). **278**. *Cornhill Magazine* 34 (1876).
280–2.	Edward Dowden. *Poems* (1876).
283–5.	Mary Montgomerie Lamb ('Violet Fane', Mrs. Sinclair). **283**. *Betwixt Two Seas: Poems and Ballads* (1900). **284**. *Under Cross and Crescent* (1896). **285**. *Collected Verses* (1880).
286.	Arthur O'Shaughnessy. *Music and Moonlights: Poems and Songs* (1874).

287–307. Gerard Manley Hopkins. **287–305.** *Poems*, ed. Robert Bridges (1918). **306.** *The Poets and the Poetry of the Century*, ed. A. H. Miles (1893) **307.** *Poems*, ed. Gardner and McKenzie (1970).

308–311. Andrew Lang. **308.** *Ballads in Blue China* (1880). **309.** *Ban and Arrière Ban: A Rally of Fugitive Rhymes* (1894). **310–1.** *Grass of Parnassus* (1888).

312–3. Caroline (née Fitzroy), Lady Lindsay. **312.** *The King's Last Vigil and Other Poems* (1894). **313.** *The Flower-Seller and Other Poems* (1896).

314. Samuel Waddington. *Sonnets and Other Verse* (1884).

315. Edward Carpenter. *Towards Democracy (Second Edition)* (1885).

316–7. Robert Bridges. **316.** *Poetical Works* (1898). **317.** *Poems: Third Series* (1880).

318. Lucy Knox. *Sonnets and Other Poems* (1872).

319–325. L. (Louisa) S. Bevington (Mrs. Guggenberger). **319–321, 323–4.** *Poems, Lyrics and Sonnets* (1882). **322.** *Liberty Lyrics* (1895). **325.** *Key-Notes* (1876).

326–332. Eugene Lee-Hamilton. **326, 331.** *Imaginary Sonnets* (1888). **327–330.** *Sonnets of the Wingless Hours* (1894). **332.** *Apollo and Marsyas and Other Poems* (1884).

333–7. Alexander Anderson ('Surfaceman'). **333.** *Ballads and Sonnets* (1879). **334.** *The Two Angels* (1875). **335–7.** *Songs of the Raid* (1878).

338–9. Emily H. (Henrietta) Hickey. **338.** *Michael Villiers, Idealist and Other Poems* (1891). **339.** *Verse-Tales, Lyrics and Translations* (1889).

340. William Canton. *A Lost Epic and Other Poems* (1887).

341–2. Alexander MacGregor Rose (Gordan). **341.** *Sir Wilfrid's Progress Through England and France in the Jubilee Year* (1887). **342.** *Hoch der Kaiser* (1900).

343–351. 'Michael Field' (Katherine Harris Bradley and Edith Emma Cooper). **343–4, 347–8.** *Underneath the Bough* (1893). **345–6.** *Sight and Song* (1892). **349–350.** *Underneath the Bough* (1898). **351.** *Long Ago* (1889).

352–3. James Logie Robertson. *Ochil Idyls* (1891).

354–360. Alice Meynell (née Thompson). **354–6.** *Poems* (1893). **357.** Privately printed pamphlet (1896). **358.** Privately printed pamphlet titled *Other Poems* (1896). **359.** *Saturday Review* (6 Jul. 1895). **360.** *Scots Observer* (31 May 1890).

361. George R. (Robert) Sims. *The Dagoner Ballads* (1879).

362. L. (Laura) Ormiston Chant *Verona and Other Poems* (1887).

363–8. W. (William) E. (Ernest) Henley. *A Book of Verses* (1888).

369. Henry Bellyse Baildon. *Morning Clouds: Being Divers Poems* (1877).

370–1. W. (William) H. (Hurrell) Mallock. **370.** *A Newdigate Prizeman* (1872). **371.** *Verses* (1893).

372. Edmund Gosse. *On Viol and Flute* (1890).

373–5. Philip Bourke Marston. **373–4.** *Collected Poems* (1892). **375.** *All in All: Poems and Sonnets* (1875).

376–384. Robert Louis (formerly Lewis) Balfour Stevenson. **376.** *Songs of Travel* (1895). **377, 381.** *Poems* (1916). **378.** *Works* (1898). **379.** *Underwoods* (1887). **380.** *Poetical Fragments* (1915). **382–4.** *A Child's Garden of Verses* (1885).

385. Elizabeth Rachel Chapman. *The New Purgatory, and Other Poems* (1887).

386. (The Revd. Canon) Hardwick Drummond Rawnsley. *Sonnets Round the Coast* (1887).

387. Francis William Bourdillon. *Ailes d'alouette* (1890).

388.	F. (Francis) B. (Burdett) Money-Coutts. *Chords* (1877).
389–391.	William Renton. *Oils and Watercolours* (1876).
392–3.	Herbert Edwin Clarke. *Songs in Exile* (1879).
394.	Annie Matheson. *The Religion of Humanity and Other Poems* (1890).
395–401.	Oscar (Fingal O'Flahertie Wills) Wilde. **395.** *Fortnightly Reviews* (1 Jul. 1894). **396.** *The Dramatic Review* (23 Jan. 1886). **397.** *The Centennial Magazine* (5 Feb. 1889). **398.** *The Lady's Pictorial Christmas Number* (1887). **399.** *Dramatic Review I* (11 April 1885). **400.** *Poems of Oscar Wilde* (1908). **401.** *Complete Works* (1898).
402–3.	Fiona Macleod (William Sharp). *Lyra Celtica* (1896).
404.	(Juliana Mary Louisa) May Probyn. *A Ballad of the Road* (1883).
405.	Margaret L. (Louisa) (Bradley) Woods. *Aïromancy and Other Poems* (1896).
406–7.	Eliza Keary. *Little Seal Skin and Other Poems* (1874).
408–417.	John Davidson. **408.** *Ballads and Songs* (1894). **409–411, 413.** *New Ballads* (1894). **412, 414–7.** *The Last Ballad and Other Poems* (1899).
418.	Jane Barlow. *Ghost-Bereft and other verses* (1901).
419–425.	A. Mary F. Robinson (Mme Darmesteter, Mme Duclaux). **419–420, 422–3, 425.** *Collected Poems* (1902). **421.** *Songs, Ballads, and a Garden Play* (1888). **424.** *Retrospect, and Other Poems* (1893).
426–434.	Constance (Caroline Woodhill) Naden. **426–430, 432–4.** *Poetical Works* (1894). **431.** *Songs and Sonnets of Springtime* (1881).
435–6.	Dollie (Caroline) (Mrs. Ernest) Radford (née Maitland). *A Light Load* (1891).
437–440.	Edith Nesbit (Mrs. Bland, Mrs. Tucker). **437, 439.** *Leaves of Life* (1889). **438.** *A Pomander of Verse* (1895). **440.** *Songs of Love and Empire* (1898).
441–2.	(Sir) William Watson. **441.** *Poems* (1936). **442.** *Epigrams of art, life, and nature* (1884).
443–451.	Elizabeth ('Bessie') Craigmyle. *Poems and Translations* (1886).
452–4.	J. (James) K. (Kenneth) Stephen. *Lapsus Calami* (1891).
455–461.	A. (Alfred) E. (Edward) Housman. **455.** *AEH: Some Poems, Some Letters, and a Personal Memoir by his Brother* (1937). **456.** *Last Poems* (1922). **457–461.** *A Shropshire Lad* (1896).
462–8.	Francis Thompson. **462, 465.** *Poems* (1893). **463–4, 466.** *New Poems* (1897). **467.** *Collected Poems*, ed. Wilfrid Maynell (1913). **468.** *Poems* (1897).
469.	Arthur I. (Ignatius) Conan Doyle. *Songs of Action* (1898).
470–3.	Ernest Rhys. **470.** *The Book of the Rhymers' Club*, ed. W. B. Yeats (1892). **471.** *Lyra Celtica* (1898). **472.** *Wales England Wed* (1940).
473–9.	Rosamund Marriott Watson (Graham R. Tomson). **473, 475, 479.** *Vespertilia* (1895). **474, 476, 478.** *A Summer Night, and Other Poems* (1891). **477.** *Tares* (1884).
480–493.	Amy Levy. **480, 482, 493.** *A Minor Poet and other Verse* (1884). **481, 483–5.** *A London Plane-Tree and Other Poems* (1889). **486.** *Xantippe and other verse* (1881). **487–490.** *A London Plane-Tree and other Poems* (1889). **491.** From a privately printed pamphlet (1915). **492.** *Jewish Portraits* ed. Lady Katie Magnus (1888).
494–504.	Mary E. (Elizabeth) Coleridge. **494–7, 499–503.** *Fancy's Following* (1896). **498, 504.** *The Garland* (1899).
505–508.	Katharine Tynan (Hinkson). **505–6, 508.** *Ballads and Lyrics* (1891). **507.** *Women's Voices*, ed. Elizabeth Sharpe (1887).

509.	Mary Byron (M. Clarissa Gillington). *Poems* (1892).
510.	Owen Seaman. *Punch* (3 Nov. 1894).
511–522.	May Kendall. **511–6, 522.** *Dreams to Sell* (1887). **517–521.** *Songs from Dreamland* (1894).
523–4.	A. (Arthur) C. (Christopher) Benson. *The Professor and other Poems* (1900).
525–530.	Victor Plarr. **525–6, 528, 530.** *In the Dorian Mood* (1896). **527, 529.** the Garland of New Poetry by Various Writers (1899).
531–2.	Stephen Phillips. **531.** *Christ in Hades and Other Poems* (1896). **532.** *Poems* (1897).
533–6.	Herbert Percy Horne. *Diverse Colores* (1891).
537–545.	W. (William) B. (Butler) Yeats. **537–8.** *Crossways* (1889). **539–542.** *The Rose* (1892). **543–5.** *The Wind Among the Reeds* (1899).
546–7.	Rudyard Kipling. *Barrack-Room Ballads* (1892).
548–557.	Arthur Symons. **548–9.** *Amoris Victima* (1897). **550.** *Days and Nights* (1889). **551–4, 557.** *Silhouettes* (1892). **555.** *Images of Good and Evil* (1899). **556.** *Collected Works* (1924).
558–561.	Dora Sigerson (later Shorter). **558.** *Lyra Celtica* (1896). **559.** *The Fairy Changeling and other Poems* (1897). **560.** *Collected Poems* (1907). **561.** *Ballads and Poems* (1899).
562–573.	John Gray. **562–3, 565–8, 571–3.** *Silverpoints* (1893). **564.** *Spiritual Poems* (1896). **569.** *The Dial* (1896). **570.** *The Savoy No. 2* (April 1896), p. 16–97.
574–6.	Richard Le Gallienne. **574, 576.** *English Poems* (1892). **575.** *Robert Louis Stevenson, An Elegy, and Other Poems mainly personal* (1895).
577–585.	Ernest Dowson. **577–582, 584–5.** *Verses* (1896). **583.** *Decorations in Verse and Prose* (1899).
586–591.	Lionel Johnson. **586.** *The Pageant* (1897). **587–588.** *Ireland, with Other Poems* (1897). **589–590.** *Poems* (1895). **591.** *Poems*, ed. Fletcher (1953).
592–3.	George William Russell ('A.E.'). **592.** *Homeward Songs by the Way* (1894). **593.** *The Earth Breath* (1897).
594–5.	(Robert) Laurence Binyon. **594.** *London Visions* (1896). **595.** *Poems* (1895).
596–8.	Hubert Crackanthorpe. *Vignettes* (1896).
599–603.	Hilaire Belloc. **599–600.** *Verses and Sonnets* (1896). **601.** *The Modern Traveller* (1898). **602–3.** *The Bad Child's Book of Beasts* (1896).
604–6.	Nora Hopper (Mrs. Chesson). **604.** *Under Quicken Boughs* (1896). **605–6.** *Songs of the Morning* (1900).
607–611.	Theodore Wratislaw. **607, 611.** *Caprices* (1893). **608–610.** *Orchids* (1896).
612.	Aubrey Beardsley. *The Savoy* (Jan. 1896).
613.	(Lady) Olive Eleanor Custance (Mrs. Lord Alfred Douglas). *Opals* (1897).
614.	Cicely Fox Smith. *Songs of Greater Britain and Other Poems* (1899).
615.	Evelyn Pyne. *The Poet in May* (1885).
616.	Sarah Robertson Matheson. *Celtic Monthly* (May 1894).
617–9.	Jane Leck. *Doon Lyrics* (1894).
620–2.	Ada (Bartrick) Baker. *A Palace of Dreams* (1901).
623–638.	Thomas Hardy. **623.** *Moments of a Vision and Miscellaneous Verses* (written Nov. 1893). **624–6, 629, 631–3.** *Wessex Poems* (1898). **627–8, 630, 635–8.** *Poems of the Past and the Present* (1901). **634.** *Literature* (25 Nov. 1899).

Explanatory Notes

53. Camera Obscura. Latin for 'dark chamber'. An optical device, based on a pin-hole camera, a precursor of Victorian photography but appreciated in principle much earlier by Aristotle and ancient China.
177. Waggawocky. A play on the title of Lewis Carroll's Jabberwocky, at p. 301.
185. Perdita. Latin for 'lost', as employed by Shakespeare in *The Winter's Tale*.
209. odalisque. Eastern, especially Turkish female slave or concubine.
228. Lucifer. Latin for 'morning star', so the title is allusive. The name of the angel fallen from heaven, frequently personified as Satan.
235. Astarte Syrica. Warrior goddess of fertility and beauty. Rossetti often wrote sonnets, such as this one, to accompany his paintings of the same name.
236. Proserpina. Daughter of Ceres by Jupiter, carried away by Pluto to become queen of the infernal regions. Called Persephone by the Greeks.
Gilead. In Hebrew, 'Hill of testimony'. A mountainous region east of the Jordan River, referred to in Genesis 31:21.
261. Opifex. Latin for 'manufacturer' or 'artisan', both essential concepts during this period.
262. Ibant Obscurae. 'The unknown (or dark) things are passing.'
273. Nabla. A symbol of an inverted triangle, derived from the Greek word for a Hebrew harp.
Tyndallic. Born in Ireland, John Tyndall 1820-1893 was a prominent Victorian scientist who took increasing interest in investigating atmospheric processes.
279. Poeta Fit, Non Nascitur. 'A poet is made, not born'.
307. To R. B. A cipher for Robert Browning. Compare the sequence of sonnets on the same subject by a different author at p. 422.
350. Aeneids of Virgil. Latin epic poem, written in dactylic hexameters, telling the story of the Trojan Aeneas's travels to Italy.
358. Atalanta. In Greek mythology, daughter of Iasius who set up a contest (a race) to win her hand in marriage.
424. Dulse (line 4 of *The Flowing Tide*.) Edible type of red seaweed.
427. Milch-kine. Food consisting of hay or oat, often used as consideration for marriage in rural English parishes from the middle ages to the nineteenth century. There is an additional figurative connotation of giving, or keeping, an object for regular profit, especially a person from whom money is easily obtained.
487. Piquet. A card game for two players, especially popular in nineteenth-century France.
503. Λέγεταί τι καινόν. 'What's news?'
518. Epithalamion. A wedding song. A popular form in the classical world, interest in which was revived long before the Victorians by Spenser. The word, derived from Greek, means 'the bridal chamber' (from 'thalamos', or nuptial chamber).
539. Lethe. One of the rivers of hell, which had the power of making dead souls forget whatever they had done, seen, or heard before; a common Victorian metaphor for oblivion.

540.	Procrustes. Famous robber of Attica, known in mythology for tying travelers to a bed. If their length exceeded that of the bed, he would cut off part of their limbs to make their length equal to that of the bed, but if they were shorter he stretched their bodies until they were of the same length.
541.	Ipsissimus. From the early twentieth century this denoted a magical order, of which the state of 'ipsissimus' was the highest order of attainment. This use appears to prefigure the concept.
563.	La Gioconda. The name of the portrait by Leonardo da Vinci of Lisa Gherardini, wife of Francesco del Giocondo, popularly known as the *Mona Lisa*. Pater revived Symbolist interest in both the painting and the artist. See also the poem at p. 540, 'On Leonardo's Head of Medusa'.
568.	Tiresias. Blind prophet of Thebes. After his death he was visited in the Underworld by Odysseus. Compare Tennyson's treatment of Tiresias. The Greek title is a fairly accurate paraphrase of the literal meaning, 'I am conscious of this as being my own thing'.
635.	Requiescat. 'May she rest'. A truncation of '*Requiescat in pace et in amore*' ('May she rest in peace and love'), a common inscription on Victorian gravestones.
707.	Memorat Memoria. 'Memory remembers'.
726.	Hic Jacet. 'Here lies.' Often used at the beginning of tomb inscriptions.
743.	Pelops. King of Pisa, the son of Tantalus and Dione. Hippodameia. Wife of Pelops.
749.	Lilith Libifera. Interest in Lilith, dark demoness of storm and wind, intensified towards the close of the century, exemplified in the painting by John Collier in 1892. 'Libifera' is a type of lichen. As a composite, the words denote the idea of Lilith as a species, possibly exhumed, from hell.
768.	Epitaphium Citharistriae. 'Epitaph of a devotee of Venus'.
769.	Ad Cinerarium. 'Poem on an Urn'. 'To an Urn' would seem logical but the poem appears not to be *to* the urn.
784.	Moulmein. (line 1 of *Mandalay*.) Refers most probably to the 'old' pagoda in Rangoon and thus looking eastwards to the sea, because if the pagoda was actually at Moulmein one would face westwards. Theebaw's Queen. (line 12.) A reference to the Kings of Burmah, who used to have four legitimate wives (with the duty of producing sons not daughters), who became Queens of the East, South, North and West. The *Times of India* reports the 'commotion' that ensued in November 1883 when King Theebaw's wife gave birth to yet another daughter, not a son. Cheroot. (line 13.) A cigar, or 'stogie', with square-cut ends, clipped during manufacture, traditional in India and Burma during the Empire. Smoking a cheroot was also supposed to aid resistance to malaria. Great Gawd Budd. (line 16.) The clay figure of the Buddha referred to in the poem.
788.	Morbidezza. There are two connotations. First, musically, to be played delicately; secondly, in the context of fine art, delicacy or softness in the representation of the flesh.

809.	Vitae Summa Brevis Spem Nos vetat Incohare Longam. 'The brief sum of life forbids (or denies) us the hope of enduring long'. Horace, *Odes* Book I. iv.
809.	Non Sum Qualis Eram Bonae Sub Regno Cynarae. From Horace, *Odes*, Book IV. i. Latin for 'I am not the man I was under the reign of Cynara'. Dowson went up to Oxford to read Greats, but by all accounts read very little and left without a degree. Scholars remain divided on how much of his decadent penchant for classical titles is amateur posturing. Nevertheless, despite the degree of attention given to French influences in this period, classical influences on Victorian poetry remain fundamental, not just to Dowson but to his epoch.
810.	Flos Lunae. 'Flowers of the moon.' Her eyes are like the cold moon, and thus are the flos-essence of it.
833.	Ἔρος δ' αὖ τε. 'And love, on the other hand …'
860.	De Profundis. 'Out of the deep'. The same title was used by Wilde in his famous letter from Reading prison. The quotation from Psalm 119 verses 5-6 is from St Jerome's Vulgate (Latin) edition of the Bible, which would be familiar to Hardy's readers, and translates as 'Woes is me, that my sojourning is prolonged! I have dwelt with the inhabitants of Cedar; my soul hath long been a sojourner.'
861	V.R. Victoria Regina (Latin for Queen), the Royal Cypher. After becoming an Empress, Victoria also used the initials V R I: Victoria Regina Imperatrix.

The editor and publisher are grateful for permission to include the following copyright material in this anthology:

Hilaire Belloc

The Poor of London and *The Harbour* from *Verses and Sonnets* (© 1896 The Estate of Hilaire Belloc) is reproduced by permission of PFD (www.pfd.co.uk) on behalf of The Estate of Hilaire Belloc. *The Modern Traveller* from *The Modern Traveller* (© 1898 The Estate of Hilaire Belloc) is reproduced by permission of PFD (www.pfd.co.uk) on behalf of The Estate of Hilaire Belloc. *The Marmozet* and *The Big Baboon* from *The Bad Child's Book of Beasts* (© 1896 The Estate of Hilaire Belloc) is reproduced by permission of PFD (www.pfd.co.uk) on behalf of The Estate of Hilaire Belloc.

John Gray

Battledore, The Forge from *The Poems of John Gray*, edited by Ian Fletcher (Greensboro: ELT Press, 1998). Reprinted by permission of Robert Langenfeld, University of North Carolina.

Arthur Symons

Palm Sunday: Naples from *Poetry and Prose* (Carcanet, 1974). Reprinted by permission of Carcanet Press.

During Music, Morbidezza, Maquillage and *The Absinthe Drinker* from *Silhouettes* (1896). Reprinted by permission of Arthur Symons Literary Estate.

Alfred Lord Tennyson

Mechanophilus, Poets and Critics, from *The Poems of Tennyson, Volume I*, edited by Christopher Ricks (Longman 1987); *England and America in 1782,* from *The Poems of Tennyson, Volume II*, edited by Christopher Ricks (Longman 1987); *Balin and Balan, Despair,*

Frater Ave atque Vale, Beautiful City, By an Evolutionist, Crossing the Bar, Far – Far – Away, God and the Universe, June Bracken and Heather, Locksley Hall Sixty Years After, Merlin and the Gleam, On One who affected an Effeminate Manner, Poets and their Bibliographies, Prefatory Sonnet to the 'Nineteenth Century', Rizpah, To E. FitzGerald, To the Queen, The Church–Warden and the Curate, with glossary, The Dawn, The Dead Prophet, The Making of Man, The Oak, The Silent Voices, To the Marquis of Dufferin and Ava, To Ulysses, Vastness from *The Poems of Tennyson, Volume III*, edited by Christopher Ricks (Longman 1987). Reprinted with accompanying notes by permission of Pearson Education Ltd.

Every effort has been made to contact or trace copyright holders. The publishers would be grateful to be notified of any editions that should be incorporated in the next edition of this volume.

Index of Titles

A Ballad of an Artist's Wife, 650
A Ballad of Boding, 246
A Ballad of Euthanasia, 646
A Ballad of London, 807
A Ballad of Past Meridian, 229
A Ballad of Religion and Marriage, 736
A Ballad of the Were-Wolf, 721
A Christmas Carol, 251
A Chrysalis, 213
'A city plum is not a plum', 253
A City Rhyme, 611
A Coast-Nightmare, 242
A Crucifix, 797
A Dead Astronomer, 707
A Decadent's Lyric, 814
A Disciple (The Inner Life), 496
A Dream of Burial in Mid Ocean, 439
A Dream of Death, 781
A Dream: July 22nd, 1881, 207
A Fantasy, 474
A Game of Piquet, 487
A Garden by the Sea, 381
A Garden Song (Here, in this sequestered close,), 456
A Garden Song (I scorn the doubts and cares that hurt), 578
'A girl', 566
A Golden Lot, 302
A Greek Reply, 240
A Japanese Fan, 489
A Kiss of the King's Hand, 840
A Library in a Garden, 808
A London Fête, 195
A Mid May Mystery, 457
A Midsummer Holiday, 420
A Moment, 741
A Mystery, 61
A Parodist's Apology, 697
A Pastoral of Parnassus, 671
A Peculiar Person, 239
A Planet of Descendance, 60
A Poet's Epitaph, 200

A Portrait, 564
A Pure Hypothesis, 751
A Sea Story, 556
A Sequence of Sonnets on the Death of Robert Browning, 422
A Sermon at Clevedon, 263
A Song for Women, 612
A Song of Derivations, 573
A Song of Faith Forsworn, 391
A Stranger, 815
A Town Garden, 494
A Trio of Triolets, 503
A Vagrant Heart, 793
A Vision of the Desert, 342
A Vision of Womanhood, 412
A Warning to New Worlds, 763
A Wife in London, 852
A Winter Landscape, 484
A Witness, 837
A Woman's Strength, 606
A Woman's 'Yes', 695
A Worker's Prayer, 406
Ad Cinerarium, 769
Advent, 251
Æolian Harp, 199
After a Parting, 578
After Nightfall, 59
Afternoon, 54
Age, 610
All for the Cause, 378
Alone in London, 585
Am I to Lose You?, 536
Among His Books, 687
An Ancient Chess King, 187
An Angel in the House, 240
An August Midnight, 853
An Autobiography, 718
An 'Immurata' Sister, 259
An Indian Flag, 405
An Invitation to the Sledge, 439
'And yet, there was a hunger in your eyes', 787

Index of Titles

Any Husband to Many a Wife, 210
Any Soul to Any Body, 452
Argument of a Dissenter, 62
Astarte Syrica, 235
At a Funeral, 464
At Christie's, 498
At Court, 340
At the Empire, 831
At the Gate of the Convent, 395
At the Rhymers' Club, 717
Atalanta's Race, 358
Aubade, 56
Autumn Tints, 483
Autumn Violets, 253
Bad Dreams I, 168
Bad Dreams II, 169
Bad Dreams III, 171
Bad Dreams IV, 172
Badminton, 395
Balin and Balan, 77
Ballad of the Ichthyosaurus, 753
Ballad of the Lords of Old Time, 416
Ballade of an Omnibus, 735
Ballade of Blue China, 524
'Balm in Gilead', 258
Battledore, 799
Beautiful City, 129
Beginning Work, 690
'Bella immagine d'un fior', 777
Block City, 604
Body and Soul, 142
Borderland, 730
Browning, 603
Builder of Ruins, 574
Burdens, 496
By an Evolutionist, 127
By the Statue of King Charles at Charing Cross, 818
Captivity, 731
Carmen Sæculare: A Jubilee Ode, 70
Catullian Hendecasyllabics, 690
Cease, Cease Reproachful Eyes!, 778
Chanclebury Ring, 462
Changes, 637
Christmas Thoughts, by a Modern Thinker, 593

Church Echoes, 757
Circe, 393
Clasped Hands, 694
Clive, 161
Cloud Groupings, 608
Conclusion of a Sonnet on 'Keely's Discovery', 177
Consecration Hymn, 407
Constancy, 567
Cor Mio, 244
Corona Corinnae, 774
Couplets, 209
Courage, 766
Cradle-Song at Twilight, 577
Crocuses in Grass, 798
Crossing the Bar, 141
Cyclamens, 563
Danny Deever, 785
Dartmoor, 267
Dawn on the Night-journey, 237
De Profundis III, 860
Dead Love, 241
Death-In-Love, 234
Despair, 88
Disappointment, 841
Discharged, 584
Letters on Life and the Morning A Parson's Letter to a young poet, 182
Doctor Emily, 639
Doubt, 740
Down by the Salley Gardens, 778
Drawing near the Light, 384
Dream of the Pine, 696
Drummer Hodge, 858
During Music, 788
'Earth has clear call of daily bells', 256
'Egoisme À Deux', 535
'Endure hardness', 257
England and America in 1782, 64
England Before the Storm, 232
Enter Patient, 581
Epitaph, 738
Epitaphium Citharistriæ, 768
Epithalamion, 518
Ἔρος δ'αὖτε..., 833

Eros, 530
Eros and the Bee, 63
Ether Insatiable, 764
Eutopia, 200
Every Man His Own Poet: or, The Inspired Singer's Recipe Book, 588
Expectation, 667
Eyes, 742
'Faite À Peindre', 415
Far - Far - Away, 128
Felix Randal, 521
Finvarragh, 829
Fireworks, 143
Flos Lunae, 810
Flower Fairies, 598
For the Briar Rose, 384
'Forever', 275
Fra Angelico at Fiesole, 745
Fragment, 600
Fragment on Death, 415
'Frater Ave atque Vale', 111
French Clocks, 1876, 61
Friends Beyond, 856
From the Suburbs, 683
Geist's Grave, 190
'Get Up!', 53
Glamour of Gold, 835
God and the Universe, 140
Gone, 742
Good-bye, 526
Green Leaves and Sere, 470
Grief's Aspects, 599
Harry Ploughman, 517
Haunted Streets, 473
He is Not a Poet, 461
He Wishes for the Cloths of Heaven, 783
Heaven and Earth, 693
Henry I to the Sea, 541
Her Dream, 554
Her Face, 441
Her Immortality, 854
Hero's Lamp, 235
Hic Jacet, 726
'High overhead', 262
Holiday at Hampton Court, 654

'Hollow-Sounding and Mysterious', 254
'Hope holds to Christ the mind's own mirror out', 514
Hope's Song, 579
House, 155
House-Hunting, 844
'How many seconds in a minute?', 253
'How pleasant to know Mr Lear!', 147
Hurrahing in Harvest, 516
'I Am the Way', 576
I Bended unto Me, 263
'I hear the incantation of the bells', 638
I Look Into My Glass, 56
'I planted a hand', 254
'I will not be a critic where I love.', 199
Ibant Obscuræ, 262
'If you're anxious for to shine in the high aesthetic line', 413
Imaginary Inscription (on a rock resembling colossal human features), 689
In a Manufacturing Town, 529
In After Days, 456
In an Artist's Studio, 242
II. In Guernsey, 421
In Hospital, 847
In St. James's Park, 823
In the Rain, 723
In the Room, 334
In the Strand, 824
In the Valley of the Elwy, 515
'In winter, when the fields are white', 282
Inapprehensiveness, 174
Insomnia, 649
Inspiration, 686
'Into my heart an air that kills', 702
Introduction to Imaginary Sonnets, 538
Invisible Sights, 146
Ipsissimus, 541
Irises, 563
'It nods and curtseys and recovers', 701
Jabberwocky, 301
Jerusalem, 737
June Bracken and Heather, 134

'Kaiser and Co. or, Hoch der Kaiser', 561
King Harald's Trance, 229
La Gioconda, 563
La Mélinite: Moulin Rouge, 789
Lambeth Lyric, 819
Lay of the Trilobite, 749
Les Ballons, 615
Lethe, 539
Letty's Globe, 64
Life and Impellance, 59
Life in Death, 410
Lilith Libifera, 749
Lines for the Jubilee Window, 175
Locksley Hall Sixty Years After, 93
L'Oiseau Bleu, 741
London, 643
London Poets, 729
London Snow, 531
'Lord, if thou are not present, where shall I', 796
Love and Language, 537
Love Fulfilled, 388
Love in Dreams, 440
Love Lies Bleeding, 245
Spring, 523
'Loveliest of trees, the cherry now', 701
Love's Blindness, 404
Love's Gleaning-Tide, 389
Love's Last Gift, 234
Love's Mirror, 676
Love's Resurrection, 695
Love's Ways, 816
Lucifer in Starlight, 228
Lullaby, 635
Lying in the Grass, 595
Magdalen, 727
Manchester by Night, 473
Mandalay, 784
'Many will love you; you were made for love', 471
Maquillage, 791
Marriage, 741
Marsh Marigolds, 830
Master and Guest, 739
Matinées I & II, 655

Mechanophilus, 136
Memorat Memoria, 707
Memorial Thresholds, 234
Merlin and the Gleam, 121
Mine and Thine (from a Flemish poem of the fourteenth century), 390
Mishka, 805
Modern Chivalry, 60
Monna Innominata No. 3, 260
Moon and Candle-light, 609
Moonlight and Gas, 679
Moonrise, 59
Morbidezza, 788
Mother and Daughter: An Uncompleted Sonnet-Sequence (I, IX, X, XI), 429
Motherhood, 485
Mourning Women, 484
Move Upward, 547
Music (Down the quiet eve,), 582
Music (Listless the silent ladies sit), 146
My Bookcase, 691
'My dreams are of a field afar', 702
My Gourd, 841
'My house, I say. But hark to the sunny doves', 603
My Shadow, 605
My Song, 189
Nature's Questioning, 849
Nephelidia, 417
No Death, 597
No End of No-Story, 202
Non Sum Qualis Eram Bonae Sub Regno Cynarae, 809
November: Across Country, 467
Nuns of the Perpetual Adoration, 813
Nuremberg Cemetery, 192
'O Englishwoman on the Pincian', 265
'O thou art put to many uses, sweet!', 773
October: Gambling at Monaco, 466
Ode, 501
Ode on the Opening of the Colonial and Indian Exhibition by the Queen, Written at the Request of the Prince of Wales, 68

Odour, 833
Of a Bird-Cage, 528
Of Change of Opinions, 768
Of the Earth, Earthy, 722
'Oh who is that young sinner with the handcuffs on his wrists?', 699
Oh, is it Love?, 735
Old Age, 642
Old Pauline, 724
On a Bas-Relief of Pelops and Hippodameia, 743
On Leonardo's Head of Medusa, 540
'On Life's long round by chance I found', 472
On One Who Affected an Effeminate Manner, 130
On the Hurry of this Time, 455
On the Sale by Auction of Keats' Love Letters, 614
On the Shortness of Time, 462
'On the way to Kew', 584
Only a Dream, 238
Only in August, 744
Opifex, 261
Orchids, 832
Pall-Bearing, 408
Palm Sunday: Naples, 790
Paradise Walk, 777
Passing and Glassing, 256
Past and Future, 212
'Peace to the odalisque, whose morning glory', 209
Perdita, 185
Père La Chaise, 201
Perhaps, 197
Personality (As one who goes between high garden walls,), 669
Personality (I know not what I am.—Oh dreadful thought!—), 437
Piper, Play!, 643
Poem, 799
Poems in Prose: The Artist, 614
Poems on Children: Daisy, 714
Poet and Botanist, 675
Poeta Fit, Non Nascitur, 279

Poets and Critics, 139
Poets and their Bibliographies, 111
Pomona, 383
Poverty, 486
Prayer of Women, 636
Prefatory Sonnet to the 'Nineteenth Century', 76
President Lincoln, 432
Proserpina (Afar away the light that brings cold cheer), 236
Proserpina (Lungi è la luce che in sù questo muro), 236
'Queen's Night', 847
Reading the Book, 544
Renewal, 567
Renouncement, 576
'Repeat that, repeat', 523
Requiescat, 635
Retrospect, 858
Rêverie, 823
Revolution, 536
Rispetti, 673
Rizpah, 72
Rome (The Vatican: Sala delle Muse), 851
Run to Death (A True Incident of Pre-Revolutionary French History), 732
Sacrifice, 820
Sappho's Cursing, 193
Scarabæus Sisyphus, 474
Sea-Pictures I, 557
Secret Parting, 233
Seeking God (The Inner Life), 497
Self, 767
Sensation, 795
Serenade, 645
The Enigma Solved, 272
Shadows, 767
Shop, 157
Six Studies in Exotic Forms of Verse: Triolet, 210
Snake-Charm, 436
'So live, so love, so use that fragile hour', 604
Society, 228
Solomon Redivivus, 673

Song (Love Me a Little), 463
Song of the Empire,
Song of the Night at Daybreak, 54
Sonnet: A Cry to Men, 532
Sonnet: 'God sent a poet to reform His earth', 668
Sonnet: Hope and Fear, 419
'Sooner or later: yet at last', 257
Sorrento Revisited, 279
Soul and Body, 528
Speculative, 168
Speech and Silence, 676
Spelt from Sibyl's Leaves, 521
Spleen (I was not sorrowful, I could not weep,), 810
Spleen (The roses every one were red,), 798
Stanza, 535
Steam-launches on the Thames, 698
'Stroke a flint, and there is nothing to admire', 254
'Struck out of dim fluctuant forces and shock of electrical vapour', 485
Style, 435
Suggestion for a Telegraphic Birthday Greeting, 177
Suicide, 583
Summer Past, 806
Symphony in Yellow, 615
Tapestry Trees, 382
Terre Promise, 812
'Thanatos, thy praise I sing', 565
The Absinthe-Drinker, 788
Tr. The Aeneids of Virgin (Books I and VI), 350
The Apparition, 771
The Ballad of Father O'Hart, 779
The Ballad of Prose and Rhyme, 453
The Ballad of Reading Gaol, 617
The Ballad of the Flag Painter, 761
The Barber, 804
The Big Baboon, 827
The Birch-Tree at Loschwitz, 730
The Bookworm, 672
The Box, 276
The Building of the City, 277

The Caged Skylark, 516
The Camel-Rider, 467
The Camera Obscura, 53
The Children of Lir, 746
The Christ upon the Hill: A Ballad, 445
The Church-Warden and the Curate, with glossary, 131
The Cities, 486
The City of Dreadful Night, 303
The Colonists, 836
The Conscientious Ghost, 765
The Dark Angel, 816
The Darkling Thrush, 860
The Darling, 302
The Dawn, 134
The Dead Prophet, 106
The Death of Moses, 178
The Discovery of America, 572
The Dong with a Luminous Nose, 150
The End of It. 713
The End of the Story, 696
'The evening darkens over', 55
The Evening Takes Me From Your Side, 823
The Flood of Is in Brittany, 427
The Flowering Orchard, 383
The Flowing Tide, 424
The Foreign Land, 195
The Forest, 383
The Forest Pool (Lean down and see your little face), 689
The Forest Pool (Lost amid gloom and solitude,), 471
The Forge, 802
The Fork of the Road, 610
The Frontier Line, 715
The Girl of All Periods: An Idyll, 194
The Harbour, 825
The Harlot's House, 616
The Haunted Homes of England, 525
The Higher Pantheism in a Nutshell, 418
The Hindu Ascetic, 394
The Hound of Heaven, 702
The Hunting of the Snark, 284
The Hydraulic Ram; or, the Influence of Sound on Mood, 63

Index of Titles 879

The Idea, 669
The Imperial Players, 770
The Inquest, 608
The Jet Worker, 607
The Jumblies, 152
The Lady and the Painter, 174
The Lady Doctor, 677
The Lady Poverty, 577
The Lake Isle of Innisfree, 780
The Land of Nod, 605
The Lantern out of Doors, 515
The Last Ballad, 656
The Last Chance, 526
The Last Rose, 666
'The laws of God, the laws of man', 700
The Life of a Leaf, 431
The Light-Keeper, 601
The Long White Seam, 188
The Lover Mourns for the Loss of Love, 783
The Lovers, 425
The Lust of the Eyes, 240
The Making of Man, 136
The March of the Workers, 379
The Marmozet, 827
The Message, 476
The Metropolitan Underground Railway, 690
The Mid-World, 821
The Modern Traveller, 826
The Moor Girl's Well, 724
'The morning drum-call on my eager ear', 54
The Muses, Eros, and Beauty, 63
The Music-Hall, 831
The Mystery of the Body, 302
The Nebular Theory, 676
The Night has a Thousand Eyes, 607
The Night Ride, 718
The Nuptials of Attila, 214
The Oak, 130
Tr. The Odyssey of Homer (Book I), 348
The Old House, 734
The Orchard-pit, 237
The Other Side of a Mirror, 738
The Pantheist's Song of Immortality, 681
The Philanthropist and the Jelly-Fish, 756

The Philosopher and the Philanthropist, 699
The Pilgrim Cranes, 391
The Poet and the Critics, 454
The Poet Pleads with the Elemental Powers, 783
The Poor of London, 824
The Positivists, 208
The Prospect of Evil Days, 62
The Pythoness, 433
The Quangle Wangle's Hat, 148
The Red Sunsets, 1883, 58
The Roots of the Mountains, 386
The San' Man, 545
The Sandblast Girl and the Acid Man, 758
The Scorched Fly, 196
'The shepherd's brow, fronting forked lightning, owns' 520
The Shortest and Sweetest of Songs, 207
The Silent Voices, 139
The Silver Jubilee, 513
The Singer Saith of his Song, 713
The Siren, 499
The Slow Nature, 852
The Sorrow of Love, 780
The Starlight Night, 514
The Story of Sigurd the Volsung, 356
The Street-Singer, 787
The Temporary the All, 848
The Three Musicians, 834
'The tropics vanish, and meseems that I', 600
The Tryst of the Night, 748
The Two Artists, 680
The Vines, 796
The Violet, 552
The Voice of Toil, 377
The White Winter – Hughie Snawed Up, 570
The Will, 438
The Wind on the Hills, 794
The World is Wide, 806
The Wreck of the Deutschland, 504
The Year, 197
The Young Glass-Stainer, 848
'Thee, God, I come from, to thee go', 522
'There was a Young Person of Ayr', 155

'There was an Old Man at a Station', 154
'There was an Old Man of Thames Ditton', 155
'There was an Old Person of Skye', 155
Thoughts of Phena, 856
Three, 532
Tiresias: but that I know by experience, 568
To a Moth that Drinketh of the Ripe October, 212
To Catullus, 421
To Death, 730
To E. FitzGerald, 84
To Edward FitzGerald, 176
To his Watch, 523
To Inishkea, 744
To Ireland in the Coming Times, 781
To my Muse, 668
To My Own Face, 527
To My Wheeled Bed, 540
To Nature, 210
To One in Bedlam, 814
To R. B., 524
To the Chief Musician upon Nabla: A Tyndallic Ode, 273
To the Dead Cardinal of Westminster, 708
To the Maids, Who Will Marry, 410
To the Marquis of Dufferin and Ava, 112
To the Queen, 66
To Two Bereaved, 410
To Ulysses, 118
To Vernon Lee, 735
To William Theodore Peters on his Renaissance Cloak, 812
Tom's Garland: on the Unemployed, 517
Touching 'Never', 255
Tour Abroad of Wilfrid the Great, 557
Translations: Posthumous Coquetry, 790
True Poets, 238
'True to myself am I, and false to all', 743
Trust Thou Thy Love, 181
Twilight (Grey the sky, and growing dimmer,), 537
Twilight (When I was young the twilight seemed too long.), 57
Twilight-Piece, 770

Two Songs, 682
Two Thoughts of Death, 243
Two Women, 830
Under Convoy, 685
Under the Oak, 444
Underground, 760
Unknowing, 850
Unknown Ideal, 792
Until the Day Break, 259
V.R. 1819–1901: A Rêverie, 861
Vastness, 115
Verses for Pictures, 385
Vespertilia, 719
Victoria, 497
Vitae Summa Brevis Spem Nos Vetat Incohare Longam, 809
Waggawocky, 177
Waiting, 582
'Wanting is – what?', 167
'We met as strangers on life's lonely way', 472
We Two, 425
'What shall I do for the land that bred me', 520
What the Sonnet Is, 539
Where Home Was, 426
Whitechapel High Road, 821
Why?, 786
'Why does she stare at you like that? The glow', 265
Why I Am a Liberal, 176
Winged Words, 738
With a Rose, 793
Womankind, 240
Woman's Future, 755
Woman's Rights, 842
Working-Girls in London, 459
Writing, 198
Yet a Little While (Heaven is not far, tho' far the sky), 245
Yet a Little While (I dreamed and did not seek: today I seek), 245
'Yonder see the morning blink', 701
'You would have understood me, had you waited', 811

Index of First Lines

A bee, within a rosebud lying, 63
A city plum is not a plum, 253
A cold wind stirs the blackthorn, 257
A couple old sat o'er the fire, 445
A crystal, flawless beauty on the brows, 564
A girl, 566
A gothic church. At one end of an aisle, 797
A greeting to thee, O most trusty friend!, 527
A jewelled kingdom set impregnable, 466
A long and narrow shop, magenta black, 802
A man who keeps a diary, pays, 198
A moth belated,—sun and zephyr-kist,—, 212
A mountain's giddy height I sought, 749
A pine-tree standeth lonely, 696
A planet of descendance rent, 60
A plot of ground—the merest scrap—, 494
A quarter of an hour to wait, 760
A shaded lamp and a waving blind, 853
A silent room—gray with a dusty blight, 687
A silver dream of waters to the East, 457
A song of shadows: never glory was, 767
A square, squat room (a cellar on promotion), 582
A sullen glow throbs overhead, 823
A tiny prison built by prisoned hands, 528
A woman is a foreign land, 195
A world of books amid a world of green, 808
About the little chambers of my heart, 742
Across and along, as the bay's breadth opens, and o'er us, 421
Afar away the light that brings cold cheer, 236
Against these turbid turquoise skies, 615
Ah, love, the teacher we decried, 751
Ah, yes! You must meet it, and brave it, 536
All night fell hammers, shock on shock, 195
All night, all day, in dizzy, downward flight, 484
All the mill-horses of Europe, 572
All my stars forsake me, 54
All the strong spells of Passion slowly breaking, 610
All things I can endure, save one, 727
All things that pass, 256
All veiled in black, with faces hid from sight, 484
All we can dream of loveliness within,—, 177
Almighty God, whose justice like a sun, 824
Along the path that skirts the wood, 834
Am I alone, 413
"Am I to lose you now?" The words were light, 536
Am I waking, am I sleeping?, 730
Ample the air above the western peaks, 59
They said 'Too late, too late, the work is done, 182
An omnibus across the bridge, 615
An utter moorland, high, and wide, and flat, 610
"And even our women," lastly grumbles Ben, 194
And is it possible?—and must it be—, 726
And Jonah's wrath was kindled for his gourd, 841
And Paris be it or Helen dying, 415
And that was at eve of the day; and lo now, Signy the white, 356
And we are lovers, lovers he and I, 425
And yet, there was a hunger in your eyes, 787

Are sorrows hard to bear,—the ruin, 496
As a dare-gale skylark scanted in a dúll cáge, 516
As darting swallows skim across a pool, 738
As I came round the harbour buoy, 188
As I walked restless and despondent through the gloomy city, 529
As I was carving images from clouds, 261
As one who goes between high garden walls, 669
As proper mode of quenching legal lust, 238
As the young phoenix, duteous to his sire, 567
As you advance in years you long, 768
At Loschwitz above the city, 730
At morning dawn I left my sheep, 671
At times our Britain cannot rest, 113
Athwart the sky a lowly sigh, 643
Ay, in heaven's name, let us move upward still, 547
Bancroft, the message-bearing wire, 177
Beautiful city, the centre and crater of European confusion, 129
Because it is the day of Palms, 790
Because our talk was of the cloud-control, 233
Because you never yet have loved me, dear, 255
Behold the city is building!—, 277
Beholding with a listless eye, 340
Beneath our eaves the moonbeams play, 609
Beneath the shadow of dawn's aerial cope, 419
Beneath this world of stars and flowers, 669
Beside the Convent Gate I stood, 395
Between two golden tufts of summer grass, 595
'Bind up her loose hair in the fillet, and wipe the cold dew from her cheek, 433
Blame not the times in which we live, 438

Blithe morning; sun and sea! Zone beyond zone, 557
Body to purifying flame, 200
Bring snow-white lilies, pallid heart-flushed roses, 681
Browning makes the verses, 603
By coasts where scalding deserts reek, 656
By her fault or by ill-fate, 585
By the old Moulmein Pagoda, lookin' eastward at the sea, 784
By woodman's edge I faint and fail, 383
Calm, sad, secure; behind high convent walls, 813
Carry me out, 584
Cease, cease reproachful eyes! I have not done, 778
Change the chancefulness in my flowering youthtime, 848
Climbing the hill a coil of snakes, 568
Close prisoner in his narrow dusty room, 607
Close within a downy cover, 431
Come, 207
Come forth, for dawn is breaking, 439
Come you living or dead to me, out of the silt of the Past, 707
Complacent they tell us, hard hearts and derisive, 755
Coral-coloured yew-berries, 483
Crests of foam where the milch-kine fed, 427
Crimson nor yellow roses, nor, 833
Dark Angel, with thine aching lust, 816
Dead! 107
Dear things! we would not have you learn too much—, 240
Der Kaiser auf der Vaterland, 561
Down by the Salley Gardens my love and I did meet, 778
Down in the depths of this fair church—, 757
Down the quiet eve, 582
Down through the deep deep grey-green seas, in sleep, 439
Draw not away thy hands, my love, 389

Earnest, earthless, equal, attuneable, vaulty, voluminous,..., 521
Earth grown old, yet still so green, 251
Earth has clear call of daily bells, 256
"Edith is fair," the painter said, 680
Eh? good daäy! good daäy! thaw it bean't not mooch of a daäy, 131
Electric clocks in Paris now on trial, 61
Eros, bound, in flowery bands, 63
Even now the fragrant darkness of her hair, 812
Exhumed from out the inner cirque of Hell, 749
Eyes, what are they? Coloured glass, 742
Fair are the bells of this bright-flowering weed, 675
Fair garden, where the man and woman dwelt, 212
Farewell has long been said; I have forgone thee, 578
Félix Rándal the fárrier, O is he déad then? my duty mall énded, 521
Fifty times the rose has flower'd and faded, 70
Fifty years' flight! Wherein should he rejoice, 175
Flare, England! Lift thy banners of red flame, 847
Flat as to an eagle's eye, 214
Fleet wheels had whirled for us, deep hedgerows threading, 667
Flower fairies—have you found them, 598
Fold your arms around me, Sweet, 554
Forever; 'tis a single word!, 275
Four years!—and didst thou stay above, 190
Fourteen small broidered berries on the hem, 539
From breakfast on through all the day, 605
From out the font of being, undefiled, 485
From side to side the sufferer tossed, 476
From the deph of the dreamy decline of the dawn through a, 417
Fu' licht o' heart an' fleet o' step, 841
Gently I wave the visible world away, 788
Geranium, houseleek, laid in oblong beds, 799
'Get up!' the caller calls, 'Get up!', 53
Go not to the hills of Erin, 794
Go on! Go on!, 263
Go! bid Love stay, 774
God sent a poet to reform His earth, 668
Good Father John O'Hart, 779
Great City of the Midnight Sun, 807
Grey the sky, and growing dimmer, 537
Grief does not come alike to all, I know, 599
Had I a painter's skill, 441
Had I the heavens' embroidered cloths, 783
Hands that I love have touched my key before, 690
Haply some Rajah first in the ages gone, 187
Hard as hurdle arms, with a broth of goldish flue, 517
Hardly a shot from the gate we stormed, 395
Hark, hearer, hear what I do; lend a thought now, make believe, 518
Hast thou longed through weary days, 388
"Have you seen the listening snake?", 796
He did not wear his scarlet coat, 617
He wakened quivering on a golden rack, 649
Hear a word, a word in season, for the day is drawing nigh, 378
Heartsease I found, where Love-lies-bleeding, 258
Heaven is not far, tho' far the sky, 245
Her beauty, passive in despair, 756
Her face was like sad things: was like the lights, 815
Her heart that loved me once is rottenness, 243
Her room, bare of all beauty, 639
Here as I sit by the Jumna bank, 394
Here begins the sea that ends not till the world's end. Where we stand, 420

Here in the water-meadows, 830
Here were a goodly place
 wherein to die;—, 690
Here, in this sequestered close, 456
High overhead, 262
Historic be the survey of our kind, 228
Historic, side-long, implicating eyes, 563
Home through the pleasant olive
 woods at even, 745
Hope holds to Christ the mind's
 own mirror out, 514
How many seconds in a minute?, 253
How many volumes do I miss!, 691
How pleasant to know Mr Lear!, 147
How shall I be a poet?, 279
How time flies! Have we been
 talking, 489
Hybrid of rack and of Procrustes'
 bed, 540
I abide in a goodly Museum, 753
I am Day; I bring again, 385
I am the ancient Apple-Queen, 383
I am the King of Faery, 829
I am the Roof-tree and the Keel, 382
I and Clive were friends – and why not?
 Friends! I think you laugh,
 my lad, 161
I awoke in the Midsummer not-to-call
 night, in the white and the walk
 of the morning, 59
I bended unto me a bough of May, 263
I care not for my Lady's soul, 240
I chanced upon a new book
 yesterday, 176
I come from fields of fractured ice, 273
I come from nothing; but from
 where, 573
I dream of you to wake: would
 that I might, 260
I dreamed and did not seek: today
 I seek, 245
I dreamed of an age grown strangely
 picturesque—, 823
I dreamed that one had died in a strange
 place, 781

I dreamt. There was a great crowd
 gazing, 143
I fled Him, down the nights and
 down the days, 702
'I go beyond the commandment.' So be it.
 Then mine be the blame, 185
I had a dream of Lethe,—of the brink, 539
I had a dream of Poverty by night, 486
I have a friend in ghostland—, 242
I have a little shadow that goes
 in and out with me, 605
I have been brave in my way, 766
I have lived with Shades so long, 858
I hear the incantation of the bells, 638
I heard him in the autumn winds, 410
I heard men saying, Leave hope and
 praying, 377
I know a little garden-close, 381
I know not what I am.—Oh dreadful
 thought!—, 437
I leant upon a coppice gate, 860
I live with love encompassed round, 676
I look into my glass, 56
I love her with the seasons,
 with the winds, 567
I loved her too, this woman
 who is dead, 464
I made a grave for Love
 two years ago, 695
I met her walking in the park, 695
I must not think of thee; and, tired yet
 strong, 576
I never to the church will give, 62
I planted a hand, 254
I remémber a house where
 all were good, 515
I remember, they sent, 408
I said "I will find God," and forth I went, 497
I sat before my glass one day, 738
I sat by night and read the Book, 544
I sat in the Muses' Hall at the mid
 of the day, 851
I saw in dreams a mighty
 multitude,—, 597
I scarcely know my worthless picture, 210

I scorn the doubts and cares that hurt, 578
I took my staff and wandered
    o'er the mountains, 486
I walk the alleys trampled
    through the wheat, 795
I wandered in the enchanted wood, 686
I was an Arab, 474
I was like one that keeps the
    deck by night, 825
I was not sorrowful, I could not
    weep, 810
I will arise and go now, and go to
    Innisfree, 780
I will not be a critic where I love, 199
I will not perturbate, 708
I would not alter thy cold eyes, 810
I would not, if I could, be called
    a poet, 461
I dreamed I was a barber;
    and there went, 804
If I could love without the
    thought of death, 462
If I've dared laugh at you,
    Robert Browning, 697
If those who wield the Rod forget, 454
If within my heart there's mould, 730
I'll rise and go to Inishkea, 744
Imperfect utterance is
    our saddest taint, 209
In a vase of gold, 563
In a wideawake not worn for show, 761
In after days when grasses high, 456
In hay-tide, through the
    day new-born, 386
In magic books she read at night, 646
In the bleak mid-winter, 251
In the coal-pit, or the factory, 302
In the hall grounds, by evening-glooms
    conceal'd, 63
In the heart of a rose, 793
In the hurry of life they pass us by, 694
In the late autumn's dusky-golden prime, 719
In the shake and rush of the engine, 549
In through the porch and up the
    silent stair, 734

In winter, when the fields are white, 282
Inside the skull the wakeful brain, 53
Into my heart an air that kills, 702
Into this dusky bower, 436
Is it all in vain?, 199
Is it ironical, a fool enigma, 267
Is it you, that preached in the chapel
    there looking over the sand?, 88
'Is not this the time of flowers, 459
It happened thus: my slab, though
    new, 172
It nods and curtseys and recovers, 701
It rushes home, our own express, 683
It wasna from a golden throne, 840
I've watched thee, Scarab! Yea,
    an hour in vain, 474
'Just the place for a Snark!' the
    Bellman cried, 284
Keep love for youth, and violets
    for the spring, 253
Kiss me, and say good-bye, 526
Know, that I would accounted be, 781
Last night I saw you in my sleep, 168
Last night returning from my
    twilight walk, 229
Last night, ah, yesternight, betwixt
    her lips and mine, 809
Late, my grandson! half the morning
    have I paced these sandy tracts, 94
Lean down and see your little face, 689
Lennavan-mo, 635
Let there be laid, when I am dead, 790
Life and the Universe show
    spontaneity, 208
Life flows down to death;
    we cannot bind, 259
Lilia with the magic hair, 777
Listless the silent ladies sit, 146
Live thy Life, 130
Lo I am he who led the song through
    slender reed to cry, 350
Lo silken my garden, and
    silken my sky, 383
Lo, happily walking in some clattering
    street—, 473

Lo, thus, as prostrate, 'In the dust
    I write, 303
Lo, when we wade the tangled wood, 384
Seest thou yon Sun in lustrous glory
    beaming, 272
Long ago, the Roman poet Catullus, 690
Look at the stars! look, look up
    at the skies!, 514
Lord, if thou are not present,
    where shall I, 796
Lord, speak to me, that I may speak, 406
Lost amid gloom and solitude, 471
Love hath his poppy-wreath, 440
Love me a little, love me as thou wilt, 463
Nothing is so beautiful as Spring —, 523
Love that is alone with love, 537
Love that is dead and buried,
    yesterday, 245
Love to his singer held a glistening
    leaf, 234
Loveliest of trees, the cherry now, 701
Lungi è la luce che in sù questo
    muro, 236
Lusty life her river pours, 821
'Made to be painted' – a Millais
    might give, 415
Man, but it's vexin'! There's the Law, 570
Many a hearth upon our dark globe sighs
    after many a vanished face, 116
Many will love you; you were made
    for love, 471
Master, they argued fast concerning
    Thee, 496
Methought I saw the morning
    bloom, 342
Misfortune is a darling, ever, 302
Mishka is poet among the beasts, 805
Moments the mightiest pass
    uncalendared, 861
Mortal my mate, bearing my
    rock-a-heart, 523
Moses, who spake with God as
    his friend, 178
My brother, my Valerius, dearest head, 421
My dead Love came to me, and said, 771

My dreams are of a field afar, 702
'My duties,' he remarked with tears, 765
My house, I say. But hark to the
    sunny doves, 603
My mother bore me 'neath the streaming
    moon, 673
My spirit stood and listened
    in its awe, 538
"My voice is sweeter than the lute, 499
Mystery: lo! betwixt the sun
    and moon, 235
Never for us those dreams
    aforetime shown, 722
Night went down; the twilight
    ceased, 655
No breath of wind, within, without, 799
No more alone sleeping, no more
    alone waking, 741
'No news in the *Times* to-day,' 503
Not a line of her writing have I, 856
Not labour kills us; no, nor joy, 608
November's here. Once more
    the pink we don, 467
Now do I know that love
    is blind, for I, 404
Now Energy's bound to diminish—, 764
Now first we stand and understand, 136
Now the furnaces are out, 643
Now the lovely autumn morning breathes
    its freshness in earth's face, 732
O Englishwoman on the Pincian, 265
O is it Love or is it Fame, 735
O loyal to the royal in thyself, 66
O Nature! thou whom I have
    thought to love, 210
O Sea, take all, since thou hast
    taken him, 541
O Spirit that broods upon the hills, 636
O thou art put to many uses, sweet!, 773
O thou, that sendest out the man, 65
O to be a woman! to be left
    to pique and pine, 793
O young Mariner, 122
O'er this huge town, rife with
    intestine wars, 473

Of all the cities far and wide, 758
Oh Bellosguardo, when the year was young, 735
Oh never weep for love that's dead, 241
"Oh, which is the last rose?", 666
Oh who is that young sinner with the handcuffs on his wrists?, 699
Oh! City of the world, most chastely fair, 737
Old Fitz, who from your suburb grange, 84
Old poets fostered under friendlier skies, 112
Olivier Metra's Waltz of Roses, 789
On a starred night Prince Lucifer uprose, 228
On life's long round by chance I found, 472
On the down line, and close beside the rail, 552
On the lizarded wall and the gold-orb'd tree, 279
On the way to Kew, 584
On top of the Crumpetty Tree, 148
One evening there came into his soul the desire to fashion an image of, 614
One face looks out from all his canvasses, 242
One, who is not, we see: but one, whom we see not, is, 418
Only a cottage border, 637
Only a moment in a dream of night, 207
Only in August I have not seen you, 744
Orange and purple, shot with white and mauve, 832
Others may need new life in Heaven –, 168
Out in the desert, half-submerged, a sphinx, 412
Out of the uttermost ridge of dusk, where the dark and the day are mingled, 748
Out upon the sand-dunes thrive the coarse long grasses, 746
Outside quaint Albert Durer's town, 192
Pale brows, still hands and dim hair, 783
Peace to the odalisque, whose morning glory, 209
Pellam the King, who held nad lost with Lot, 78
Piled deep below the screening apple-branch, 237
Purple and white the crocus flowers, 798
Purple headland over yonder, 54
Queen of so many nations that the sun, 497
Rain in the glimmering street—, 723
Red of the Dawn!, 135
Repeat that, repeat, 523
Row us out from Desenzano, to your Sirmione row!, 111
San' man frae the quarry hole, 545
Saw ye that spinster gaunt and grey, 677
Say to men, women starve, and will they heed?, 532
Say what you will, there is not in the world, 462
Scales of pearly cloud inlay, 654
Searching an infinite Where, 699
See, as you turn a page, 487
Set fools untó their folly!, 717
Shall I sonnet-sing you about myself?, 155
Shall we, to whom the stream by right belongs, 698
She brake the box, and on his head, 276
She did not love to love, but hated him, 713
She is living in Paradise Walk, 777
She sings a pious ballad wearily, 787
She sits in the tawny vapour, 852
SHE: Yet womanhood you reverence, 174
Silence. A while ago, 556
Silenced the streets with sand of holy hue, 770
Since all progress of mind consists for the most part, 435
Since here I dwelt the years are seven, 693
Smiling with a pliant grace, 302
'So far away so long – and now, 146
So I'm shelved, you see, old fellow: and it seems a trifle rough, 847

So live, so love, so use that fragile hour, 604
"So many are your foes, there arrows shroud, 240
So the old story ends, 696
So vague, so sweet a long regret!, 833
So we must part, my body, you and I, 452
So you boys are going to Paris? That's how I lost my own, 724
So, friend, your shop was all your house!, 157
Soft the windblow and sunshine, 444
Sombre and rich, the skies, 818
Some men to carriages aspire, 735
Some seven score Bishops late at Lambeth sat, 819
Sometimes a lantern moves along the night, 515
Sometimes, in very joy of shame, 814
Sooner or later: yet at last, 257
Stand not uttering sedately, 768
Staring corpselike at the ceiling, 583
Starry amorist, starward gone, 707
Still sometimes in my secret heart of hearts, 244
Strangest of things are doors!—, 844
Stroke a flint, and there is nothing to admire, 254
Struck out of dim fluctuant forces and shock of electrical vapour, 485
Such a wizened creature, 642
Summer énds now; now, bárbarous in béauty, the stóoks ríse, 516
Sunset and evening star, 141
"Sweet wife, this heavy-hearted age, 650
Swept into limbo is the host, 736
Sword in length a reaping-hook amain, 229
Take back your suit, 391
Take my life, and let it be, 407
Tell me, O Muse, of the Shifty, the man who wandered afar, 348
Ten heads and twenty hearts! So that this me, 197
Thanatos, thy praise I sing, 565

That lamp thou fill'st in Eros' name to-night, 235
The Big Baboon is found upon, 827
The boding sky was charactered with cloud, 58
The brawling of a sparrow in the eaves, 780
The brilliant kernel of the night, 601
The charm of rouge on fragile cheeks, 791
The cherry-coloured velvet of your cloak, 812
The child not yet is lulled to rest, 577
The city disgorges, 824
The clearest eyes in all the world they read, 422
The clouds had made a crimson crown, 741
The crocus, while the days are dark, 197
The cry of "woman's rights," though giving rise, 842
The curtain on the grouping dancers falls, 831
The *Daily Menace*, I presume?, 826
The day that is the night of days, 232
The evening darkens over, 55
The evening takes me from your side, 823
The vast Parnassus never knew thy face, 668
The fateful slumber floats and flows, 384
The field of death at Paris, 201
The fine delight that fathers thought; the strong, 524
The golden gates were opening, 405
The golden river-reach afar, 770
The guidewife sits I' the chimney-neuk, 721
The Haunted Homes of England, 525
The Lady Poverty was fair, 577
The lake lay blue below the hill, 741
The laws of God, the laws of man, 700
The lights are out in the street, and a cool wind swings, 56
The lion remembers the forest, 731
The livid and unutterable head, 540

The Lord let the house of a brute to the soul of a man, 127
The low and soft luxurious promenade, 831
The morning drum-call on my eager ear, 54
The morning mists still haunt the stony street, 581
The music had the heat of blood, 788
The night has a thousand eyes, 607
The pilgrim cranes are moving to their south, 391
The poet in theory worships the moon, 679
The Powers whose name and shape no living creature knows, 783
The road slopes on that leads us to the last, 425
The roses every one were red, 798
The roses on thy grave are now breast high, 142
The seafowl build in wrinkles of my face, 689
The shepherd's brow, fronting forked lightning, owns, 520
The slow green wave comes curling from the bay, 424
The species Man and Marmozet, 827
The sun was down, and twilight grey, 334
The sweetest song that a poet sings, 535
The touches of man's modern speech, 713
The tropics vanish, and meseems that I, 600
The white hands of my lady's maid, 835
The whole day long I sit and read, 672
The windows of the church are bright, 593
The world is wide—around yon court, 806
Thee, God, I come from, to thee go, 522
There are sleeping dreams and waking dreams, 246
There came a man across the moor, 739
There came an image in Life's retinue, 234
There have been times when I well might have passed and the ending have come –, 860
There is a garden where lilies, 200
There is a river, 202
There is no thing in all the world but love, 467
There on the top of the down, 134
There was a Young Person of Ayr, 155
There was an Old Man at a Station, 154
There was an Old Man of Thames Ditton, 155
There was an Old Person of Skye, 155
There was the summer. There, 806
There went most passionately to Life, Impellance, 59
There's a joy without canker or cark, 524
There's no replying, 254
These are the letters which Endymion wrote, 614
'These Gothic windows, how they wear me out, 848
They are not long, the weeping and the laughter, 809
They are terribly white, 563
"They killed him then? the cowards—be it so!, 432
They scowl and simper here in rows, 498
They throw in Drummer Hodge, to rest, 858
They trod the streets and squares where now I tread, 729
They went to sea in a Sieve, they did, 152
This is my chiefest torment, that behind, 767
This is the end of him, here he lies, 738
This is the genesis of Heaven and Earth, 676
This is the house of Circe, queen of charms—, 393
This is the red, red region, 821
This thing, that thing is the rage, 139
This was my dream: I saw a Forest, 171
Those clouds at even are swollen and pieced, 608

Those delicate wanderers, 820
Those that of late had fleeted far and fast, 76
Thou art the Way, 576
Thou mastering me, 504
Thou priest that art behind the screen, 541
Thou strainest through the mountain fern, 600
Though no high-hung bells or din, 513
Three tall poplars beside the pool, 470
Through thick Arcadian woods a hunter went, 358
Thus a young wife, alighting from the train, 61
Thus did a nameless and immortal hand, 743
'Thy husband – poor, poor Heart! – is dead –, 852
Till dawn the wind drove round me. It is past, 237
Time was, with sword and battle-axe, 60
'Tis not a time for triumph and delight, 62
To have attempted in former times a work of this description, would have, 588
Tom—gărlanded with squat and surly stĕel, 517
To-night I saw three maidens on the beach, 262
To-night we rode beneath a moon, 718
Too many the questions, too subtle, 685
Tread lightly, she is near, 635
True Poets conquer Glory— do not woo, 238
True to myself am I, and false to all, 743
Trust thou thy Love: if she be proud, is she not sweet?, 181
'Twas brillig, and the slithy toves, 301
'Twas Maytime, and the lawyer coves, 177
'Twas yesterday; 'twas long ago, 426
Two forms of darkness are there. One is Night, 740
Two words about the world we see, 390
Ulysses, much-experienced man, 119

Under the lamps the tide flows on, 611
Upon a noon I pilgrimed through, 854
Wailing, wailing, wailing the wind over land and sea–, 73
Wales England wed; so I was bred. 'Twas merry London gave me breath, 718
Wanting is – what?, 167
Warm from the wall she chose a peach, 210
We are standing on the threshold, sisters, 579
We are the music makers, 501
We build with strength the deep tower wall, 574
We caught the tread of dancing feet, 616
We have heard a voice that calls us—, 836
We met as strangers on life's lonely way, 472
We two stood simply friend-like side by side, 174
Welcome, welcome with one voice!, 68
W'en Queen Victoria calls her peup's, 557
What am I? Ah, you know it, 673
'What are the bugles blowin' for?' said Files-on-Parade, 785
What are you able to build with your blocks?, 604
What is this, the sound and rumour? What is this that all men hear, 379
What marks the frontier line?, 715
What more? Where is the third Calixt, 416
What of our time?, 532
What place so strange,—though unrevealèd snow, 234
What shall I do for the land that bred me, 520
What sight so lured him through the fields he knew, 128
When awful darkness and silence reign, 150
When gathering shells cast upwards by the waves, 213
When I look forth at dawning, pool, 849

When I was young the twilight seemed too long, 57
When Letty had scarce pass'd her third glad year, 64
When men were all asleep the snow came flying, 531
When some sweet voice flows forth in foreign speech, 676
When the dumb Hour, clothed in black, 139
When the great universe hung nebulous, 535
When the ways are heavy with mire and rut, 453
When will the day bring its pleasure?, 259
When, soul in soul reflected, 850
Where is one that, born of woman, altogether can escape, 136
Where the still sunshine falls, 724
Where the thistle lifts a purple crown, 714
Where wert thou, Soul, ere yet my body born, 528
While man and woman still are incomplete, 130
White girl, your flesh is lilies, 788
Who in this small urn reposes, 769
Who sins in hope; who, sinning, says, 196
Whose is the voice that will not let me rest?, 792
Why does she stare at you like that? The glow, 265
Why hast thou nothing in thy face?, 530
Why is it, since I know you now, 786
'Why?' Because all I haply can and do, 176
Wild and eerie was the night, 837
Will my tiny spark of being wholly vanish in your deeps and heights?, 140
William Dewy, Tranter Reuben, Farmer Ledlow late at plough, 856
Winds blow cold in the bright March weather, 682
With delicate, mad hands, behind his sordid bars, 814
With slower pen men used to write, 455
With stars, with trailing galaxies, 645
Within a dreary narrow room, 612
Within the streams, Pausanias saith, 526
Woman dead, lie there, 193
Yonder see the morning blink, 701
You are a snowdrop, sweet; but will, 830
You ask a Song, 189
You far-off star serene and cold, 763
You have your Angel in the House! but look, 240
You in the flesh and here –, 169
You merry maids, with yellow hair, or jet, 410
You must be sad; for though it is to Heaven, 410
You ought to be stronger than I, dear, 606
You perfect, pure, original, 239
You were not cruel always! Nay!, 816
You would have understood me, had you waited, 811
Young laughters, and my music! Aye till now, 429

Index of Poets

Allingham, William, 198
Anderson, Alexander ('Surfaceman'), 544
Arnold, Matthew, 190
Ashe, Thomas, 408
Askham, John, 207
Austin, Alfred, 395
Baildon, Henry Bellyse, 585
Baker, Ada (Bartrick), 844
Barlow, Jane, 667
Beardsley, Aubrey, 834
Belloc, Hilaire, 824
Benson, A. (Arthur) C. (Christopher), 766
Bevington, L. (Louisa) S.
    (Mrs Guggenberger), 532
Binyon, (Robert) Laurence, 821
Blind, Mathilde, 58
Blunt, W. (Wilfrid) S. (Scawen), 461
Bourdillon, Francis William, 607
Bridges, Robert, 55
Brooks, Shirley, 177
Brown, T. (Thomas) E. (Edward), 261
Browning, Robert, 155
Buchanan, Robert (T. Maitland), 486
Byron, Mary (M. Clarissa Gillington), 748
Calverley, C. (Charles) S. (Stuart), 275
Canton, William, 557
Carpenter, Edward, 529
Carroll, Lewis (Charles Lutwidge
    Dodgson), 279
Chant, L. (Laura) Ormiston, 579
Chapman, Elizabeth Rachel, 606
Clarke, Herbert Edwin, 610
Coleridge, Mary E. (Elizabeth), 738
Collins, Mortimer, 208
Cory, William (formerly Johnson), 192
Cowden-Clarke, Mary (née Novello), 142
Crackanthorpe, Hubert, 823
Craigmyle, Elizabeth ('Bessie'), 690
Custance, (Lady) Olive Eleanor
    (Mrs Lord Alfred Douglas), 835
Davidson, John, 643
Dixon, (Canon) Richard Watson, 302

Dobell, Sydney Thompson, 197
Dobson, (Henry) Austin, 453
Domett, Alfred, 143
Dowden, Edward, 496
Dowson, Ernest, 809
Doyle, Arthur I. (Ignatius) Conan, 715
Egerton-Warburton, R. (Rowland)
    E. (Eyles) 60
Eliot, George, 178
Elliot, Charlotte ('Florenz'), 433
Evans, Sebastian, 272
Field, Michael (Katherine Harris Bradley
    and Edith Emma Cooper), 563
Gilbert, W. (William) S. (Schwenk), 413
Gosse, Edmund, 595
Gray, John, 795
Hardy, Thomas, 56
Havergal, F. (Frances) Ridley, 405
Henley, W. (William) E. (Ernest), 581
Hickey, Emily H. (Henrietta), 554
Hopkins, (Jane) Ellice, 410
Hopkins, Gerard Manley, 59
Hopper, Nora (Mrs Chesson), 829
Horne, Herbert Percy, 774
Housman, A. (Alfred) E. (Edward), 699
Ingelow, Jean, 182
Johnson, Lionel, 814
Keary, Eliza, 639
Kendall, May, 749
King, Harriet Eleanor
    Baillie-Hamilton, 457
Kipling, Rudyard, 784
Knox, Isa (Craig), 276
Knox, Lucy, 532
Lamb, Mary Montgomerie
    ('Violet Fane', Mrs Sinclair), 497
Lang, Andrew, 524
Le Gallienne, Richard, 806
Lear, Edward, 147
Leck, Jane, 841
Lee-Hamilton, Eugene, 538
Levy, Amy, 727

Lindsay, Caroline Lady (née Fitzroy), 527
Locker-Lampson, Frederick
   (formerly Locker), 189
Lyall, Sir Alfred Comyns, 394
Lytton, (Edward) Robert Bulwer
   (Earl of Lytton, Owen Meredith), 279
MacDonald, George, 202
Macleod, Fiona (William Sharp), 635
Mallock, W. (William) H. (Hurrell), 588
Marston, Philip Bourke, 597
Massey, Gerald, 238
Matheson, Annie, 612
Matheson, Sarah Robertson, 840
Maxwell, James Clerk, 273
Meredith, George, 214
Meynell, Alice (née Thompson), 54
Money-Coutts, F. (Francis)
   B. (Burdett), 608
Monkhouse, (William) Cosmo, 441
Morris, William, 348
Mulholland, Rosa (Lady Gilbert), 486
Naden, Constance
   (Caroline Woodhill), 673
Nesbit, Edith (Mrs Bland,
   Mrs Tucker), 685
Noel, Roden
   (Berkeley Wriothesley), 340
O'Shaughnessy, Arthur, 501
Palgrave, (Sir) Francis Turner, 200
Pater, Walter, 435
Patmore, Coventry, 194
Cholmondeley-Pennell, H. (Henry), 415
Pfeiffer, Emily, 209
Phillips, Stephen, 771
Plarr, Victor, 767
Probyn, (Juliana Mary Louisa) May, 637
Pyne, Evelyn, 837
Radford, Dollie (Caroline) (Mrs Ernest)
   (née Maitland), 682
Rawnsley, (The Revd. Canon) Hardwicke
   Drummond, 607
Renton, William, 59
Rhys, Ernest, 717
Robertson, James Logie, 570

Robinson, A. Mary F. (Mme Darmesteter,
   Mme Duclaux), 57
Rose, Alexander MacGregor, 557
Rossetti, Christina, 242
Rossetti, Dante Gabriel, 233
Ruskin, John, 181
Russell, George William ('A.E.'), 820
Scott, William Bell, 146
Seaman, Owen, 749
Siddal, Elizabeth ('Lizzie')
   (later Rossetti), 240
Sigerson, Dora (later Shorter), 792
Sims, George R. (Robert), 578
Skipsey, Joseph, 53
Smith, Cicely Fox, 836
Stephen, J. (James) K. (Kenneth), 697
Stevenson, Robert Louis
   (formerly Lewis) Balfour, 600
Stevenson, William Frederick, 59
Swinburne, Algernon Charles, 415
Symonds, John Addington, 53
Symons, Arthur, 786
Tennyson, Alfred Lord, 64
Tennyson, Frederick, 62
Thompson, Francis, 702
Thomson, James, 303
Todhunter, John, 436
Turner, Charles (Tennyson), 63
Tynan, Katharine (Hinkson), 744
Veley, Margaret, 487
Waddington, Samuel, 528
Warren, John (Byrne) Leicester,
   Lord de Tabley, 391
Watson, (Sir) William, 689
Watson, Rosamund Marriott
   (Graham R. Tomson), 56
Webster, (Julia) Augusta, 424
Wilde, Oscar (Fingal O'Flahertie
   Wills), 614
Williams, Sarah ('Sadie'), 431
Woods, Margaret L. (Louisa)
   (Bradley), 638
Wratislaw, Theodore, 831
Yeats, W. (William) B. (Butler), 778

www.ingramcontent.com/pod-product-compliance
Lightning Source LLC
Chambersburg PA
CBHW032125010526
44111CB00033B/75